ST/ESA/STAT/SER.X/31

Department of Economic and Social Affairs
Statistics Division

NATIONAL ACCOUNTS STATISTICS: ANALYSIS OF MAIN AGGREGATES, 2001

UNITED NATIONS
NEW YORK, 2003

NOTE

Symbols of United Nations documents are composed of capital letters combined with figures. The first 14 editions of the *Yearbook* were issued without series symbols.

ST/ESA/STAT/SER.X/31

UNITED NATIONS PUBLICATION
Sales No. E.03.XVII.17

ISBN 92-1-161465-1

Inquiries should be directed to:
SALES SECTION
UNITED NATIONS
NEW YORK, NY 10017

CONTENTS

C. GROWTH RATES OF MAIN NATIONAL ACCOUNTING AGGREGATES AT CONSTANT PRICES OF 1990

D. IMPLICIT PRICE DEFLATORS OF GROSS DOMESTIC PRODUCT: INDIVIDUAL COUNTRIES OR AREAS (INDEX NUMBERS 1990=100)

I. Introduction

This is the thirty-third issue of the United Nations publication, *National Accounts Statistics: Analysis of Main Aggregates (AMA)*. It is presented as part of a series that also includes the annual principal publication containing detailed national accounts information, *National Accounts Statistics: Main Aggregates and Detailed Tables (MADT)*[i].

The last publication of AMA was prepared and published in 2002 by the Statistics Division of the Department of Economic and Social Affairs of the United Nations Secretariat with the assistance and cooperation of national statistical services. It is issued in accordance with the recommendation of the Statistical Commission at its first session[ii] that the Statistics Division of the United Nations should publish regularly the most recently available data on national accounts for as many countries and areas as possible.

The current publication presents, in the form of analytical tables, a summary of the principal national accounting aggregates based on official detailed national accounts data for more than 200 countries and areas of the world. The basic data was extracted from MADT and supplemented by estimates prepared by the Statistics Division of the United Nations when official data are not available.

SCOPE OF PUBLICATION

The present volume consists of two parts: *Introduction (I) and Analytical Tables (II).*

General information on the methods of data collection, estimation and derivation of analytical measures, the conversion factors used in converting national currency into United States dollars, conceptual references, country nomenclature, fiscal year references and regional groupings are included in the Introduction. Information on analytical measures is further elaborated in a separate section in part II, Analytical Tables, prior to the presentation of the tables.

The tables include analysis of data on gross domestic product (GDP) by different structural components. In general, data presented in the tables are based on GDP definitions as given in the 1993 System of National Accounts (SNA).

The types of analysis presented are classified into four major categories:

(a) Analysis of the level of total and per capita gross domestic product (Tables 1A and 1B);

(b) Analysis of economic structures expressed in terms of percentage shares of gross domestic product by type of expenditure and kind of economic activity (Tables 2 and 3);

(c) Analysis of economic development expressed in terms of the real growth of gross domestic product and its components by type of expenditure and kind of economic activity (Tables 4, 5 and 6); and,

(d) Analysis of price development expressed in terms of implicit price deflators of gross domestic product (Table 7).

The analytical presentations are based on a homogeneous data series that were made smooth and consistent from original individual country data series. The use of such homogeneous data series as the basis for the analyses presented in this volume serves to facilitate cross-table analysis concerning one or more countries and/or regions.

Users interested in making alternative analysis across countries may subscribe to the electronic output of the entire AMA data with the relevant specifications. All such requests should be addressed to the Director of the UN Statistics Division.

COLLECTION OF DATA

The present AMA database includes GDP estimates by type of expenditure and kind of economic activity expressed in current prices and constant prices of 1990 for some or all of the years 1970 to 2001 for total GDP. These

---

[i] United Nations publication, ST/ESA/STAT/SER.X.

[ii] Official Records of the Economic and Social Council, 1947, Supplement No. 6 (E/264), chap. VIII, para. 42.

were compiled from country replies to the regular national accounts questionnaire of the Statistics Division of the United Nations as well as from estimates prepared by its staff members so to adjust data inconsistencies and fill data gaps. The questionnaire is sent annually to the national statistical offices of all UN member states and areas of the world. Data submitted with the questionnaire are generally supplemented, for the purpose of the Analysis of Main Aggregates, by reliable information obtained from other national and international sources. The recipients of the questionnaire are requested to indicate where the scope and coverage of the country estimates differ, for conceptual or statistical reasons, from the definitions and classifications recommended in the 1993 SNA.

ESTIMATION OF DATA

The methodology employed to arrive at the basic data for computation of global and regional aggregates, growth rates and index numbers is as follows: official data of countries as reported in MADT are supplemented by estimates prepared by the Statistics Division of the United Nations, based on official and unofficial data and proxy economic indicators derived from national and international sources. For a majority of countries, both the official statistics and proxy indicators may be based on different series due to multiple data configurations and/or characteristics. Before merging these into one data file, all inconsistencies in series and coverages are smoothed out by linking the multiple series into one homogeneous set of data from which the analytical measures are derived.

The current price series are converted into a common unit of currency the United States dollars by applying the corresponding exchange rates. (For a more detailed explanation, reference is made to the general notes to Tables 1A and 1B)

The constant price series, principally based on officially reported data from member states and supplemented by estimates prepared by the Statistics Division of the United Nations, are presented in index numbers on country basis for each item and year and re-based to 1990. The indices are then applied to the corresponding 1990 current dollar values per country and item, which serve as weights, and extrapolated by individual growth rates in order to arrive at the regional and world totals for each year. (For a more detailed explanation in the calculation of growth rates and index numbers, reference is made to the general notes for Tables 4, 5, 6 and 7, respectively.)

In preparing estimates to supplement the official data, the sequence or priority of data sources sought is as follows: national publications, internet websites of national statistics offices, central banks or relevant government ministries, economic surveys and estimates prepared by the regional economic commissions of the United Nations, estimates and indicators available from other international organizations such as the International Monetary Fund (IMF), the World Bank and other international institutions, studies prepared by experts under the United Nations technical cooperation programmes, economic reports and studies by regional development banks. For countries that are members of regional affiliate organizations and specialized groups, such as the Organization of Petroleum Exporting Countries (OPEC), the Commonwealth of Independent States (CIS), etc., the information available from these organizations are given priority over non-United Nations sources.

DATA CONVERSION TO UNITED STATES DOLLARS

In converting estimates expressed in national currency units into United States dollars, the prevailing annual average of market exchange rates as reported by the IMF has been used. For countries that are non-members of the IMF, the conversion rate used is usually the annual average of United Nations operational rates of exchange.

It should be noted that the international comparability of data expressed in United States dollars between countries may not be entirely scientific because the exchange rates applied may, in practice, only be used for the conversion of a limited number of external transactions and may not be relevant for the much larger portion of GDP covering domestic transactions.

Alternative methods of making international comparisons have been developed in recent years. One is the Purchasing Power Parities (PPPs) which have been developed as part of the International Comparison Project (ICP); another one is the World Bank Atlas method of conversion based on the average of the exchange rates of the current year and the two immediately preceding years that have been adjusted for differences in inflation rates between individual countries and the average of G-5 countries (Germany, France, Japan, the United Kingdom, and the United States); and, the Statistics Division of the United Nations has developed the Price Adjusted Rates of Exchange (PARE)[iv] which, like the Atlas method, is designed to adjust exchange rates that do not adequately reflect relative movements of domestic and international inflation.

NOMENCLATURE

Designations for country or areas, which have changed in recent years, are as follows:

Hong Kong Special Administrative Region (SAR), China - Pursuant to a Joint Declaration signed on 19 December 1994, the United Kingdom re-stored Hong Kong to the People's Republic of China with effect from 1 July 1997; the People's Republic of China resumed the exercise of sovereignty over the territory with effect from that date.

The data for Hong Kong SAR is shown separately from that of the People's Republic of China.

Macao Special Administrative Region (SAR), China - Pursuant to a Joint Declaration signed on April 13, 1987, the Portugal re-stored Macao to the People's Republic of China with effect from 20 December 1999; the People's Republic of China resumed the exercise of sovereignty over the territory with effect from that date.

The data for Macao SAR is shown separately from that of the People's Republic of China.

Czech Republic, Slovakia - Data for Czech Republic and Slovakia are shown separately under the appropriate country name. For period prior to 1 January 1993, data for the former Czechoslovakia are shown under the country name Czechoslovakia (Former)

Yugoslavia (Former) – Following the adoption and the promulgation of the Constitutional Charter of Serbia and Montenegro by the Assembly of the Federal Republic of Yugoslavia on 4 February 2003, the name of the State of the Federal Republic of Yugoslavia was changed to Serbia and Montenegro. All data for former Yugoslavia prior to 1 January 1992 refer to the Socialist Federal Republic of Yugoslavia that was then composed of six republics. After that date, when available, data for the republics, Bosnia and Herzegovina, Croatia, Slovenia, The Former Yugoslav Republic of Macedonia, and Serbia and Montenegro are shown separately.

USSR (Former) - In 1991, the Union of Soviet Socialist Republics formally dissolved into fifteen independent republics (Armenia, Azerbaijan, Belarus, Georgia, Kazakhstan, Kyrgyzstan, Latvia, Lithuania, Republic of Moldova, Russian Federation, Tajikistan, Turkmenistan, Ukraine and Uzbekistan). When available, data are shown for the individual republics. All data for the former USSR are shown under the country name USSR (Former)

Ethiopia, Eritrea - Data for Ethiopia and Eritrea are shown separately under the appropriate country name. For the period prior to 1992, data for the former Ethiopia are shown under the country name Ethiopia (Former).

Germany – On October 1990, the Federal Republic of Germany and the German Democratic Republic united to form one sovereign State under the designation Germany. Official data from Germany for the period 1970—1990 is the combined data of the former Federal Republic of Germany and the former German Democratic Republic.

Yemen - In May 1990, Yemen and Democratic Yemen united to form a single State. Since that date they have been represented as one country with the name "Yemen".

Standard country or area designations and classification of geographical regions for statistical use are posted on the United Nations website. Interested users could refer to the following web-link for further details:

http://unstats.un.org/unsd/methods/m49/m49.htm

[iv] Reference could be made to the latest Report of the Committee on Contribution in the United Nations General Assembly Official Records.

COUNTRY COVERAGE AND GROUPINGS

There are two types of alternative country groupings or aggregations of country data applied in the tables: by geographical region and by grouping based on economic categories, i.e. developed, developing and transition economies. The tables on the level of GDP and growth rates by GDP components (Tables 1A, 1B and 4 through 6) include aggregations of country data by geographical region and economic categories while the tables on percentage distribution of GDP as well as implicit price deflators (Tables 2, 3 and 7), present country data only according to geographical regions. Where individual country data are presented, they are generally listed by region and, within the regions, in alphabetical order.

The designations "developed" and "developing" economies used in some tables are intended for statistical convenience and do not necessarily express a judgement about the stage reached by a particular country or area in the development process.

The geographical coverage for the world, regional and economic development groupings used in the analyses is as follows:

WORLD
Total of developed, developing and transition economies.

DEVELOPED ECONOMIES
North America, Europe, Japan, Australia and New Zealand

DEVELOPING ECONOMIES
Africa, Americas excluding Canada and the United States in Northern America, Caribbean, Central America, South America, Asia excluding Japan and Oceania excluding Australia and New Zealand.

TRANSITION ECONOMIES
Commonwealth of Independent Countries
Armenia, Azerbaijan, Belarus, Georgia, Kazakhstan, Kyrgyzstan, Republic of Moldova, Russian Federation, Tajikistan, Turkmenistan, Ukraine and Uzbekistan.

Other Europe
Albania, Bosnia and Herzegovina, Bulgaria, Croatia, Czech Republic, Estonia, Hungary, Latvia, Lithuania, Poland, Romania, Serbia and Montenegro, Slovakia, Slovenia, The Former Yugoslav Republic of Macedonia.

REGIONAL CLASSIFICATION[v]

AFRICA - comprised of Eastern Africa, Middle Africa, Northern Africa, Southern Africa and Western Africa.
Eastern Africa - Burundi, Comoros, Djibouti, Eritrea, Ethiopia, Kenya, Madagascar, Malawi, Mauritius, Mozambique, Reunion, Rwanda, Seychelles, Somalia, Uganda, United Republic of Tanzania, Zambia, Zimbabwe
Middle Africa - Angola, Cameroon, Central African Republic, Chad, Congo, Democratic Republic of the Congo, Equatorial Guinea, Gabon, Sao Tome and Principe
Northern Africa - Algeria, Egypt, Libyan Arab Jamahiriya, Morocco, Sudan, Tunisia
Southern Africa - Botswana, Lesotho, Namibia, South Africa, Swaziland
Western Africa - Benin, Burkina Faso, Cape Verde, Cote d'Ivoire, Gambia, Ghana, Guinea, Guinea-Bissau, Liberia, Mali, Mauritania, Niger, Nigeria, Senegal, Sierra Leone, Togo.

AMERICAS - comprised of Caribbean, Central America, South America and North America.
Caribbean - Anguilla, Antigua and Barbuda, Aruba, Bahamas, Barbados, British Virgin Islands, Cayman Islands, Cuba, Dominica, Dominican Republic, Grenada, Guadeloupe, Haiti, Jamaica, Martinique, Montserrat, Netherlands Antilles, Puerto Rico, Saint Kitts and Nevis, Saint Lucia, Saint Vincent and the Grenadines, Trinidad and Tobago.
Central America - Belize, Costa Rica, El Salvador, Guatemala, Honduras, Mexico, Nicaragua, Panama
South America - Argentina, Bolivia, Brazil, Chile, Colombia, Ecuador, French Guiana, Guyana, Paraguay, Peru, Suriname, Uruguay, Venezuela

---

[v] Not all countries or territories are included in the regional classification, as the Statistics Division of the United Nations may not have the access to reliable data sources or viable estimation methods to prepare data for all countries or areas.

North America - Bermuda, Canada, and United States of America.

ASIA - comprised of Eastern Asia, South-central Asia, South-eastern Asia and Western Asia.
Eastern Asia - China, Hong Kong Special Administrative Region of China, Macao Special Administrative Region of China, Democratic People's Republic of Korea, Japan, Mongolia, Republic of Korea.
South-central Asia - Afghanistan, Bangladesh, Bhutan, India, Iran (Islamic Republic of) Kazakhstan*, Kyrgyzstan*, Maldives, Nepal, Pakistan, Sri Lanka, Tajikistan*, Turkmenistan*, Uzbekistan*,
South-eastern Asia - Brunei Darussalam, Cambodia, Indonesia, Lao People's Democratic Republic, Malaysia, Myanmar, Philippines, Singapore, Thailand, Timor-Leste, Viet Nam.
Western Asia - Armenia*, Azerbaijan*, Bahrain, Cyprus, Georgia*, Iraq, Israel, Jordan, Kuwait, Lebanon, Oman, Qatar, Saudi Arabia, Syrian Arab Republic, Turkey, United Arab Emirates, Yemen.

EUROPE - comprised of Eastern Europe, Northern Europe, Southern Europe and Western Europe.
Eastern Europe - Belarus*, Bulgaria, Czech Republic, Hungary, Poland, Republic of Moldova*, Romania, Russian Federation*, Slovakia, Ukraine*,
Northern Europe –Denmark, Estonia*, Finland, Iceland, Ireland, Latvia*, Lithuania*, Norway, Sweden, United Kingdom of Great Britain and Northern Island.
Southern Europe - Albania, Andorra, Bosnia and Herzegovina, Croatia, Greece, Holy See, Italy, Malta, Portugal, San Marino, Serbia and Montenegro, Slovenia, Spain, The former Yugoslav Republic of Macedonia.
Western Europe - Austria, Belgium, France, Germany, Liechtenstein, Luxembourg, Monaco, Netherlands and Switzerland.

OCEANIA - comprised of Australia and New Zealand, Melanesia, Micronesia, and Polynesia.
Australia and New Zealand – Australia, New Zealand.
Melanesia - Fiji, New Caledonia, Papua New Guinea, Solomon Islands, Vanuatu
Micronesia –Kiribati, Marshall Islands, Micronesia (Federated States of), Nauru, Palau.
Polynesia –Cook Islands, French Polynesia, Samoa, Tonga, Tuvalu.

CONCEPTUAL REFERENCES

The concepts used in the statistical tables in the present volume are the same as those used in Main Aggregates and Detailed Tables. They generally conform to the recommendations in the revised System of National Accounts 1993.

INTERNATIONAL COMPARABILITY OF NATIONAL ACCOUNTS DATA

Every effort has been made to present the estimates of the various countries or areas in a form designed to facilitate international comparability. To this end, some important differences in concept, scope, coverage and classification have been described in respective footnotes for individual countries.

The data contained in the tables relate to the calendar year against which they are shown unless otherwise indicated as the following:

(a) Year beginning 1 July – Australia, Bangladesh, Cameroon, Egypt, Gambia, Pakistan, Puerto Rico, Saudi Arabia, Sierra Leone, Sudan and United Republic of Tanzania.

(b) Year beginning 1 April – Bermuda, India, Myanmar (except 1970-1974, which are ending 30 September), New Zealand and Nigeria.

(c) Year Beginning 21 March – Afghanistan and Iran (Islamic Republic of)

(d) Year ending 30 June – Botswana, Swaziland and Tonga.

(e) Year ending 7 July – Ethiopia

(f) Year ending 15 July – Nepal

(g) Year ending 30 September – Haiti

* Since 1990

EXPLANATION OF SYMBOLS

The following symbols have been employed:

Data not available	...
Category not applicable	..
Data in units	(u)
Data in thousands	(t)

Decimals and percentages in tables may not add up to totals due to rounding.

GENERAL DISCLAIMER

The designations employed and the presentation of material in this publication do not imply the expression of any opinion whatsoever on the part of the United Nations Secretariat concerning the legal status of any country, territory, or area or of its authorities, or concerning the delimitation of its frontiers or boundaries.

All data presented in this publication are prepared from the most recently available data by August 2003. In general, figures for the most recent years are to be regarded as provisional and subject to further revision. For more up-to-date information, interested users should login at: http://www.un.org/Depts/unsd/nataccts/.

II. Analytical Tables

A. Estimates of Main National Accounting Aggregates at Current Prices

Description of Analysis in Table 1A and Table 1B

A. Level of total and per capita gross domestic product.

Table 1A and Table 1B present estimates of total and per capita gross domestic product (GDP) expressed in current United States dollars. The tables are intended to facilitate international comparisons of levels of income generated in production. Countries within regions, country groupings into developed, developing and transition economies as well as global aggregations are shown in rows. The columns list total and per capita GDP in terms of United States dollars for the selected ten years 1970, 1980, 1990 and 1995 through 2001.

Official data and estimates of total and per capita GDP have been converted to United States dollars using prevailing exchange rates. As a rule, the exchange rates used for conversion of national currency data into US dollars are the average market exchange rates (MERs) as published by the International Monetary Fund in the *International Financial Statistics.* These are averages based on the market rates communicated to the IMF by the monetary authority of each member country or end-of-month quotations in the market of the country. MERs generally consist of three types of rates: a) market rates, determined largely by market forces; b) official rates, determined by government authorities; and c) principal rates, for countries maintaining multiple exchange rates arrangements. The preference is always market rates; only when a free market rate is not available is use made of other rates.

For non-members of the International Monetary Fund, the conversion rates used are the average of United Nations operational rates of exchange which were established for accounting purposes and which are applied in official transactions of the United Nations with those countries. These rates are based on official, commercial and/or tourist rates of exchange.

In a number of countries for some or all of the years, the use of MERs for conversion to US dollars may generate distortions in income levels due to a variety of reasons. For some, the use of official rates of exchange reflects government policies that fix conversion factors at unrealistic levels, thus resulting in estimates of GDP in US dollars that are not consonant with the true economic picture. Others suffer from inordinate growth in domestic inflation that movements in exchange rates cannot keep pace with.

The GDP estimates and exchange rate conversions have been prepared in response to numerous requests for statistics of this nature. However, it should be noted that there are practical constraints in the use of MERs for conversion purposes, particularly in the case of countries with multiple exchange rates, those coping with inordinate levels of inflation or experiencing misalignments caused by market distortions, the use of which may result in excessive fluctuations in the dollar income levels of a number of countries. Caution is therefore urged when making inter-country comparisons of incomes as expressed in US dollars over time. The comparability over time could be distorted due to excessive fluctuations in the exchange rates and domestic inflation movements. (In the present volume, price-adjusted rates of exchange, or PARE were applied for selected years in the cases of Afghanistan, Iraq, Liberia, Myanmar, Suriname and the Syrian Arab Republic, for conversion to US dollars due to large distortions in the dollar levels of per capita GDP with the use of MERs).

For inter-country comparisons over time, it would be more appropriate to use the growth rate information based on constant price data, presented in Table 4 of the present volume, which are more indicative of inter-country and intra- grouping comparisons of development trends of total GDP.

Table 1.A. Estimates of Gross Domestic Product in US Dollars at Current Prices by Major Area, Region and Country

Major area, region and country	(Millions of Dollars)									
	1970	1980	1990	1995	1996	1997	1998	1999	2000	2001
WORLD	**3 252 900**	**11 932 100**	**22 854 500**	**29 368 000**	**30 048 500**	**29 915 100**	**29 712 500**	**30 696 100**	**31 375 800**	**31 041 300**
DEVELOPED ECONOMIES	**2 186 600**	**7 997 800**	**16 961 200**	**22 748 700**	**22 805 000**	**22 382 900**	**22 677 900**	**23 791 000**	**23 988 500**	**23 666 900**
DEVELOPING ECONOMIES	**582 200**	**2 762 900**	**4 027 800**	**5 813 300**	**6 321 200**	**6 588 500**	**6 210 800**	**6 198 200**	**6 621 000**	**6 508 000**
TRANSITION ECONOMIES	**484 200**	**1 171 400**	**1 865 500**	**806 000**	**922 300**	**943 600**	**823 900**	**706 900**	**766 300**	**866 400**
AFRICA	**83 300**	**465 800**	**528 700**	**585 200**	**590 500**	**613 000**	**602 900**	**562 900**	**584 100**	**563 500**
Eastern Africa	*15 300*	*68 700*	*57 900*	*60 100*	*66 300*	*70 500*	*69 800*	*68 300*	*68 800*	*71 800*
Burundi	250	950	1 150	1 000	880	970	890	810	710	660
Comoros	20	140	250	210	210	190	200	200	180	200
Djibouti	70	340	460	510	500	490	500	540	550	570
Eritrea	...	...	...	570	630	650	680	650	610	680
Ethiopia	...	...	...	5 500	5 970	6 180	6 310	6 160	6 020	6 050
Ethiopia (Former)	1 780	4 110	8 130	...	...	...	...	...	...	...
Kenya	1 700	7 090	8 530	9 050	9 260	10 610	11 470	10 550	10 450	11 400
Madagascar	900	3 260	3 080	3 150	3 990	3 550	3 740	3 720	3 880	4 570
Malawi	320	1 240	1 750	1 400	2 310	2 590	1 750	1 790	1 740	1 960
Mauritius	190	1 150	2 590	4 040	4 410	4 180	4 150	4 270	4 550	4 530
Mozambique	2 770	4 320	2 650	2 250	2 840	3 380	3 870	3 980	3 680	3 440
Reunion	360	2 000	5 210	7 420	7 560	6 930	7 170	7 180	6 510	6 740
Rwanda	220	1 160	2 340	1 280	1 390	1 870	2 010	1 900	1 750	1 650
Seychelles	20	150	370	510	500	560	610	620	600	580
Somalia	340	2 750	990	1 120	1 260	1 480	1 930	2 010	1 840	1 000
Uganda	1 890	24 950	3 740	6 180	6 270	6 680	6 690	6 280	5 700	5 780
United Republic Of Tanzania	1 340	5 140	3 780	5 260	6 500	7 680	8 380	8 640	9 030	9 340
Zambia	1 660	4 640	4 080	3 470	3 310	3 960	3 380	3 520	3 500	3 650
Zimbabwe	1 510	5 350	8 770	7 130	8 550	8 500	6 050	5 490	7 440	8 970
Middle Africa	*7 400*	*37 500*	*45 200*	*29 400*	*31 800*	*33 500*	*32 200*	*31 100*	*35 000*	*33 700*
Angola	2 860	5 380	10 290	5 040	5 590	7 650	6 510	6 150	9 130	8 940
Cameroon	1 320	9 680	14 310	8 950	9 370	9 200	9 740	9 760	9 270	8 970
Central African Republic	150	710	1 300	1 070	1 000	930	980	990	910	910
Chad	410	920	1 540	1 440	1 590	1 540	1 700	1 490	1 300	1 480
Congo	260	1 710	2 800	2 120	2 540	2 320	1 950	2 220	3 000	2 760
Democratic Republic of the Congo	1 870	14 720	9 350	5 640	5 770	5 940	6 220	5 090	5 060	4 530
Equatorial Guinea	200	60	160	160	280	550	450	760	1 250	1 720
Gabon	340	4 280	5 430	4 960	5 630	5 340	4 670	4 610	5 020	4 330
Sao Tome and Principe	20	50	60	50	40	40	40	50	50	50
Northern Africa	*23 300*	*139 100*	*233 000*	*205 500*	*223 500*	*233 000*	*236 600*	*243 000*	*256 200*	*246 000*
Algeria	5 170	42 350	61 890	42 070	46 940	48 180	47 840	48 790	54 460	54 850
Egypt	6 830	24 500	71 060	67 630	78 400	84 810	90 790	100 170	103 310	96 070
Libyan Arab Jamahiriya	3 990	35 720	28 290	30 850	33 680	37 080	32 370	28 310	34 140	29 120
Morocco	3 960	18 820	25 820	32 990	36 640	33 410	35 820	35 250	33 320	33 880
Sudan	1 930	8 990	33 640	13 950	8 260	10 640	9 920	9 700	11 550	12 100
Tunisia	1 440	8 740	12 310	18 030	19 590	18 900	19 810	20 800	19 470	19 990
Southern Africa	*19 000*	*86 400*	*119 400*	*161 300*	*153 800*	*159 800*	*144 200*	*141 700*	*138 600*	*123 500*
Botswana	100	1 070	3 520	4 120	4 270	4 860	4 770	4 650	4 970	5 030
Lesotho	70	380	620	930	940	1 020	890	910	860	750
Namibia	510	2 020	2 340	3 500	3 490	3 640	3 400	3 390	3 460	3 160
South Africa	18 260	82 350	112 010	151 110	143 730	148 810	133 770	131 410	127 930	113 270
Swaziland	110	590	870	1 360	1 320	1 440	1 350	1 380	1 390	1 270
Western Africa	*18 200*	*134 100*	*73 300*	*128 800*	*115 100*	*116 200*	*120 100*	*78 700*	*85 500*	*88 500*
Benin	250	1 160	1 840	2 010	2 210	2 140	2 310	2 360	2 250	2 370
Burkina Faso	400	1 710	2 860	2 220	2 370	2 330	2 510	2 470	2 190	2 330
Cape Verde	60	140	310	490	500	510	540	590	560	560
Cote d'Ivoire	1 490	10 180	11 890	11 100	12 140	11 720	12 640	12 560	10 680	10 500
Gambia	50	240	330	370	390	390	420	430	430	410
Ghana	2 210	15 580	6 230	6 460	6 930	6 880	7 470	7 490	4 980	5 300
Guinea	720	1 940	2 820	3 730	3 960	3 890	3 780	3 630	3 160	3 090
Guinea-Bissau	90	240	230	240	270	280	210	230	220	240
Liberia	280	820	380	130	160	290	360	440	530	520
Mali	140	1 420	2 510	2 310	2 670	2 440	2 700	2 710	2 540	2 450
Mauritania	200	830	1 020	1 060	1 080	1 070	980	960	900	960
Niger	400	2 540	2 510	1 670	2 020	1 860	2 080	2 020	1 800	1 910
Nigeria	10 330	92 080	32 420	90 330	73 320	75 670	77 410	35 950	48 980	51 220
Senegal	870	2 990	5 700	4 480	4 650	4 380	4 650	4 750	4 370	4 610
Sierra Leone	410	1 100	630	940	950	830	660	700	640	750
Togo	260	1 130	1 570	1 310	1 450	1 500	1 420	1 410	1 240	1 280
AMERICAS	**1 317 100**	**3 970 700**	**7 483 900**	**9 692 200**	**10 279 100**	**10 969 100**	**11 417 000**	**11 710 400**	**12 421 900**	**12 611 700**
NORTHERN AMERICA	**1 111 000**	**3 038 400**	**6 327 000**	**7 922 600**	**8 358 200**	**8 887 000**	**9 330 200**	**9 865 900**	**10 472 100**	**10 717 800**
Bermuda	260	920	2 000	2 540	2 680	2 890	3 050	3 270	3 400	3 600
Canada	85 280	266 000	574 200	581 660	604 370	627 600	606 920	649 810	706 650	694 480
United States	1 025 500	2 771 500	5 750 800	7 338 400	7 751 100	8 256 500	8 720 200	9 212 800	9 762 100	10 019 700

Table 1.A. Estimates of Gross Domestic Product in US Dollars at Current Prices by Major Area, Region and Country

Major area, region and country	(Millions of Dollars) 1970	1980	1990	1995	1996	1997	1998	1999	2000	2001
LATIN AMERICA AND THE CARIBBEAN	**206 000**	**932 300**	**1 157 000**	**1 769 600**	**1 920 900**	**2 082 100**	**2 086 800**	**1 844 600**	**1 949 900**	**1 893 900**
Caribbean	*17 400*	*54 800*	*89 900*	*117 400*	*125 000*	*130 500*	*138 000*	*145 900*	*158 000*	*167 500*
Anguilla	...	10	50	70	80	90	90	100	110	110
Antigua and Barbuda	50	110	330	440	480	510	550	570	590	610
Aruba	380	640	1 080	1 320	1 380	1 530	1 670	1 720	1 860	1 890
Bahamas	500	1 440	3 050	3 070	3 090	3 120	3 140	3 160	3 190	3 210
Barbados	190	870	1 720	1 870	2 000	2 210	2 370	2 480	2 590	2 550
British Virgin Islands	20	40	240	380	440	510	590	660	690	780
Cayman Islands	20	130	710	1 020	1 080	1 170	1 240	1 280	1 360	1 440
Cuba	5 190	13 070	19 640	21 740	22 810	22 950	23 900	25 500	27 630	28 590
Dominica	30	60	170	220	240	250	260	270	270	260
Dominican Republic	1 780	7 960	9 140	15 420	16 910	15 060	15 850	17 360	19 600	21 330
Grenada	30	70	200	240	260	270	300	330	360	380
Guadeloupe	240	1 390	2 790	4 440	4 570	4 450	4 700	4 650	4 290	4 460
Haiti	330	1 380	2 610	2 460	2 860	3 210	3 630	4 040	3 640	3 620
Jamaica	1 520	2 920	4 620	5 690	6 400	7 290	7 480	7 530	7 710	7 780
Martinique	290	1 440	3 550	4 840	4 860	4 380	4 620	4 570	4 110	4 160
Montserrat	10	20	70	60	50	40	40	40	30	30
Netherlands Antilles	270	870	1 820	2 360	2 470	2 530	2 450	2 430	2 490	2 550
Puerto Rico	5 650	15 960	32 290	45 340	48 190	54 090	57 840	61 040	67 900	73 240
Saint Kitts and Nevis	20	50	160	230	250	270	290	300	330	340
Saint Lucia	40	110	420	550	570	580	630	680	710	730
Saint Vincent and the Grenadines	20	60	200	260	280	290	320	330	340	350
Trinidad and Tobago	820	6 240	5 070	5 330	5 760	5 740	6 040	6 810	8 170	9 100
Central America	*46 000*	*233 000*	*293 900*	*336 300*	*385 000*	*458 600*	*483 400*	*544 700*	*647 100*	*687 300*
Belize	50	190	410	590	600	620	630	690	760	770
Costa Rica	1 250	6 140	7 250	11 720	11 840	12 830	14 090	15 800	15 960	16 380
El Salvador	1 030	3 570	5 330	9 500	10 310	11 130	12 000	12 460	13 130	13 740
Guatemala	1 900	7 880	7 650	14 660	15 780	17 800	19 010	17 950	18 740	20 130
Honduras	690	2 570	3 050	3 960	4 080	4 720	5 260	5 420	5 900	6 360
Mexico	39 610	207 660	262 710	286 170	332 340	400 870	421 010	480 490	580 120	617 180
Nicaragua	510	1 440	2 150	1 840	1 920	1 970	2 070	2 210	2 430	2 560
Panama	1 000	3 540	5 310	7 910	8 150	8 660	9 340	9 640	10 020	10 190
South America	*142 600*	*644 500*	*773 200*	*1 315 900*	*1 410 900*	*1 493 000*	*1 465 400*	*1 154 000*	*1 144 800*	*1 039 100*
Argentina	31 030	206 840	141 350	258 100	272 240	293 010	299 100	283 660	206 790	197 670
Bolivia	1 010	5 020	4 870	6 720	7 400	7 930	8 500	8 290	8 360	7 970
Brazil	67 090	245 940	438 260	704 170	774 930	807 750	787 740	536 630	601 730	508 990
Chile	9 290	29 480	33 510	72 060	75 770	82 810	79 370	73 050	75 520	66 450
Colombia	8 550	39 590	47 740	92 500	97 150	106 670	98 510	86 300	83 210	82 420
Ecuador	1 760	12 350	11 250	20 200	21 270	23 640	23 260	16 670	15 930	21 020
French Guiana	50	290	1 200	1 680	1 670	1 500	1 520	1 490	1 320	1 310
Guyana	270	590	400	620	710	750	720	690	710	710
Paraguay	590	4 450	5 260	9 020	9 630	9 610	8 600	7 740	7 720	6 850
Peru	6 230	17 800	31 140	53 640	55 810	59 030	56 830	51 640	53 510	54 110
Suriname	280	890	1 220	520	760	850	1 020	880	890	840
Uruguay	2 300	9 640	8 370	19 300	20 520	21 700	22 370	13 800	13 600	13 140
Venezuela	14 130	71 580	48 600	77 390	73 060	77 720	77 850	73 110	75 480	77 580
ASIA	**497 600**	**2 431 900**	**5 597 500**	**8 785 200**	**8 544 600**	**8 250 300**	**7 503 000**	**8 292 000**	**8 883 600**	**8 262 300**
Eastern Asia	*320 900*	*1 522 100*	*3 948 100*	*6 913 500*	*6 497 900*	*6 180 000*	*5 659 800*	*6 332 900*	*6 798 200*	*6 225 300*
China	91 500	301 590	383 010	700 250	816 510	898 220	946 310	991 390	1 080 350	1 159 030
Democratic People's Rep. of Korea	2 860	8 670	16 800	5 240	10 590	10 320	10 270	10 280	10 610	11 020
Hong Kong SAR of China	3 860	28 930	75 930	141 710	156 570	173 670	165 250	160 630	165 360	163 990
Japan	206 810	1 075 220	3 053 140	5 303 790	4 706 300	4 323 060	3 946 210	4 469 580	4 763 830	4 175 590
Macao SAR of China	180	1 030	3 260	6 950	6 940	7 010	6 500	6 130	6 200	6 200
Mongolia	1 240	3 010	3 140	1 240	1 200	1 070	990	910	970	1 060
Republic of Korea	8 780	62 210	252 620	489 260	520 200	476 490	317 080	406 070	461 520	427 230
South Central Asia	*96 800*	*332 300*	*764 900*	*632 900*	*669 800*	*701 200*	*704 300*	*729 600*	*740 200*	*765 800*
Afghanistan	1 400	3 440	5 190	3 460	3 690	4 180	4 390	3 850	2 170	2 170
Bangladesh	10 330	19 750	31 830	41 290	43 240	45 610	46 840	48 300	48 630	48 630
Bhutan	50	140	280	310	330	390	400	440	480	510
India	60 990	183 320	324 250	366 360	386 140	419 280	421 950	448 180	464 600	482 760
Iran (Islamic Republic of)	9 960	91 300	188 560	101 810	109 670	102 720	101 480	103 310	99 250	108 010
Kazakhstan	...	...	71 880	16 640	21 040	22 170	22 140	16 870	18 290	22 150
Kyrgyzstan	...	...	12 850	1 490	1 830	1 770	1 640	1 250	1 370	1 530
Maldives	20	50	220	400	460	510	540	570	600	580
Nepal	970	1 950	3 520	4 220	4 390	4 840	4 560	5 010	5 320	5 450
Pakistan	10 700	28 230	47 240	67 320	67 620	65 440	65 380	64 070	63 680	60 180
Sri Lanka	2 400	4 160	7 990	13 010	14 050	15 210	15 800	15 700	16 280	15 630
Tajikistan	...	...	10 960	570	1 040	920	1 320	1 090	870	1 060
Turkmenistan	...	...	11 410	5 880	2 380	2 680	2 860	3 860	4 930	6 510
Uzbekistan	...	...	48 690	10 170	13 950	15 530	14 990	17 080	13 760	10 580
South-Eastern Asia	*38 100*	*191 500*	*357 300*	*672 600*	*746 400*	*710 300*	*493 500*	*569 600*	*606 200*	*582 400*
Brunei Darussalam	180	4 930	3 590	5 220	5 450	5 420	4 850	4 220	4 320	4 250
Cambodia	2 680	2 100	1 730	3 310	3 390	3 320	3 030	3 310	3 370	3 410
Indonesia	8 920	72 480	114 430	202 130	227 370	215 750	95 450	140 000	152 230	145 310

Table 1.A. Estimates of Gross Domestic Product in US Dollars at Current Prices by Major Area, Region and Country

Major area, region and country	(Millions of Dollars) 1970	1980	1990	1995	1996	1997	1998	1999	2000	2001
Lao People's Democratic Republic	300	850	870	1 760	1 870	1 750	1 290	1 450	1 730	1 750
Malaysia	3 460	24 490	44 020	88 830	100 850	100 170	72 180	79 150	90 040	88 050
Myanmar	2 840	5 850	18 880	25 070	26 680	28 190	29 590	31 280	32 990	34 570
Philippines	6 690	32 450	44 310	74 120	82 850	82 340	65 170	76 160	74 860	71 380
Singapore	1 900	11 720	37 450	83 090	90 950	94 480	82 230	82 640	92 740	85 650
Thailand	7 130	32 350	85 360	168 020	181 950	150 890	111 860	122 500	122 280	114 770
Timor-Leste	...	...	180	320	370	380	380	230	260	310
Vietnam	3 990	4 250	6 470	20 740	24 660	27 610	27 460	28 680	31 350	32 940
Western Asia	*41 800*	*386 000*	*527 200*	*566 100*	*630 500*	*658 700*	*645 400*	*660 000*	*739 000*	*688 900*
Armenia	...	...	15 110	1 290	1 600	1 640	1 890	1 850	1 910	2 120
Azerbaijan	...	...	22 010	2 420	3 180	3 960	4 450	4 580	5 270	5 660
Bahrain	250	3 290	4 290	5 850	6 100	6 350	6 180	6 620	7 970	8 330
Cyprus	550	2 150	5 580	8 860	8 920	8 500	9 060	9 240	8 820	9 120
Georgia	...	...	22 470	2 840	3 050	3 570	3 630	2 800	3 040	3 190
Iraq	3 520	43 650	39 450	10 390	10 610	13 270	15 260	16 480	18 290	21 030
Israel	6 010	23 500	57 240	95 110	104 070	107 900	107 500	107 920	119 440	116 870
Jordan	590	4 010	4 020	6 820	7 030	7 320	7 960	8 130	8 480	8 950
Kuwait	2 870	28 690	18 470	26 550	31 070	29 870	25 120	29 190	35 830	32 790
Lebanon	1 490	4 070	2 810	10 970	12 820	14 290	15 520	16 800	17 220	17 990
Oman	270	6 330	11 690	13 800	15 280	15 840	14 090	15 710	19 870	19 940
Qatar	300	7 840	7 360	8 140	9 060	11 300	10 260	12 390	17 760	17 130
Saudi Arabia	5 090	147 570	104 670	127 810	157 740	164 990	145 970	161 170	188 690	186 490
Syrian Arab Republic	1 790	13 060	14 340	21 180	23 270	24 430	26 090	25 160	25 320	26 180
Turkey	17 910	68 790	150 680	169 320	181 460	189 880	200 310	184 860	199 260	148 020
United Arab Emirates	660	29 630	33 780	42 280	47 400	48 750	45 900	49 780	53 310	57 040
Yemen	...	...	13 260	12 510	7 820	6 880	6 250	7 270	8 530	8 030
Yemen Arab Republic (Former)	280	2 780	...	...	...	...	...	...	...	...
Yemen Democratic (Former)	210	670	...	...	...	...	...	...	...	...
EUROPE	**1 303 800**	**4 867 800**	**8 879 000**	**9 856 000**	**10 136 000**	**9 584 000**	**9 749 000**	**9 654 100**	**9 033 000**	**9 170 600**
Eastern Europe	*468 300*	*1 099 300*	*1 507 100*	*678 400*	*792 200*	*804 100*	*681 400*	*565 400*	*633 900*	*727 600*
Belarus	...	...	65 020	10 540	14 500	14 100	15 220	12 160	10 420	12 350
Bulgaria	11 200	19 990	20 730	13 110	9 900	10 360	12 740	12 960	12 600	13 560
Czech Republic	...	32 120	34 890	52 040	57 730	53 000	56 970	55 030	51 420	57 190
Czechoslovakia (Former)	14 500	...	...	...	...	...	...	...	...	...
Hungary	6 200	24 740	36 110	44 670	45 160	45 720	47 050	48 040	46 680	51 830
Poland	19 380	52 830	58 980	127 050	143 850	144 040	159 280	155 050	163 900	183 030
Republic of Moldova	...	...	19 040	1 440	1 690	1 930	1 700	1 170	1 290	1 480
Romania	14 330	26 930	38 240	35 480	35 320	35 290	42 120	35 590	36 870	39 710
Russian Federation	...	...	967 270	337 890	419 010	428 460	282 430	193 620	259 720	309 950
Slovakia	...	14 280	16 120	19 150	20 510	21 080	22 000	20 200	19 740	20 460
Ukraine	...	...	250 750	37 010	44 560	50 150	41 880	31 580	31 260	38 010
USSR (Former)	402 710	928 350	...	...	...	...	...	...	...	...
Northern Europe	*204 200*	*878 000*	*1 726 600*	*1 928 600*	*2 027 800*	*2 131 300*	*2 240 500*	*2 297 300*	*2 249 900*	*2 234 700*
Denmark	16 290	68 450	133 360	180 240	182 950	169 030	172 430	173 120	158 450	159 230
Estonia	...	...	11 980	3 570	4 360	4 610	5 220	5 200	5 140	5 500
Finland	11 150	52 520	137 220	129 700	127 770	122 660	129 500	127 800	119 990	121 510
Iceland	520	3 360	6 230	6 840	7 140	7 230	8 000	8 390	8 370	7 600
Ireland	4 220	20 860	47 300	66 470	73 180	80 110	86 990	95 640	94 810	102 440
Latvia	...	...	18 750	4 420	5 100	5 630	6 090	6 650	7 170	7 580
Lithuania	...	...	20 140	6 030	7 890	9 590	10 750	10 660	11 290	11 990
Norway	12 750	63 650	116 110	147 980	159 220	157 120	150 050	158 100	166 910	169 780
Sweden	35 670	133 040	245 940	248 420	270 980	247 570	248 290	251 570	239 760	219 440
United Kingdom	123 640	536 130	989 560	1 134 940	1 189 180	1 327 800	1 423 240	1 460 160	1 437 990	1 429 670
Southern Europe	*181 500*	*822 500*	*1 863 800*	*1 983 500*	*2 149 100*	*2 028 700*	*2 092 000*	*2 099 400*	*1 919 200*	*1 965 800*
Albania	1 300	2 220	2 170	2 480	2 690	2 290	3 060	3 680	3 750	4 110
Andorra	20	200	680	1 000	1 100	1 060	1 160	1 240	1 210	1 310
Bosnia and Herzegovina	...	...	13 110	2 040	2 750	3 640	4 170	4 680	4 440	4 690
Croatia	...	...	24 780	18 810	19 870	20 290	21 630	19 910	18 430	19 530
Greece	11 280	48 820	84 070	117 560	124 360	121 340	121 960	125 840	113 420	117 160
Holy See	...	10	10	10	20	20	20	20	10	10
Italy	107 700	448 830	1 102 440	1 097 210	1 232 880	1 166 800	1 196 660	1 180 980	1 073 120	1 088 750
Malta	230	1 130	2 310	3 240	3 330	3 340	3 510	3 650	3 560	3 630
Portugal	7 360	29 860	71 470	107 240	112 080	106 370	112 390	115 090	106 450	110 050
San Marino	70	290	710	710	790	750	810	850	780	790
Serbia and Montenegro	...	...	30 200	25 770	16 060	19 310	15 550	17 840	11 280	10 630
Slovenia	...	...	17 380	18 740	18 880	18 210	19 590	20 070	18 120	18 810
Spain	38 960	221 220	509 970	584 190	609 850	561 550	588 020	602 150	561 380	583 120
TFYR Macedonia	...	...	4 480	4 400	4 410	3 700	3 500	3 430	3 200	3 230
Yugoslavia (Former)	14 550	69 960	...	...	...	...	...	...	...	...
Western Europe	*449 700*	*2 068 000*	*3 781 500*	*5 265 500*	*5 166 900*	*4 619 900*	*4 735 100*	*4 692 000*	*4 229 900*	*4 242 500*
Austria	14 920	79 470	161 690	235 160	231 420	205 750	211 900	210 050	190 750	189 580
Belgium	25 650	121 790	197 170	276 650	269 690	244 890	250 320	251 040	228 000	227 540
France	147 000	682 080	1 215 900	1 553 130	1 554 360	1 406 120	1 451 950	1 443 700	1 308 400	1 320 420
Germany	203 710	893 320	1 671 310	2 458 280	2 383 350	2 110 970	2 144 480	2 107 970	1 870 280	1 853 410
Liechtenstein	70	430	960	1 330	1 290	1 130	1 170	1 170	1 090	1 140
Luxembourg	1 260	5 220	11 080	18 080	18 150	17 470	18 900	20 100	19 640	19 760
Monaco	70	340	640	850	850	780	810	810	740	740

Table 1.A. Estimates of Gross Domestic Product in US Dollars at Current Prices by Major Area, Region and Country

Major area, region and country	(Millions of Dollars) 1970	1980	1990	1995	1996	1997	1998	1999	2000	2001
Netherlands	35 140	177 860	294 290	414 800	411 830	376 900	393 470	398 530	370 920	384 040
Switzerland	21 920	107 470	228 410	307 260	295 980	255 890	262 100	258 640	240 120	245 840
OCEANIA	**51 200**	**195 800**	**365 400**	**449 500**	**498 300**	**498 800**	**440 600**	**476 700**	**453 200**	**433 200**
Australia & New Zealand	*49 400*	*188 700*	*354 200*	*433 600*	*481 500*	*483 100*	*426 400*	*462 200*	*439 700*	*420 200*
Australia	42 870	165 830	310 590	372 730	414 670	416 530	371 850	405 580	388 040	368 760
New Zealand	6 550	22 850	43 620	60 820	66 840	66 610	54 570	56 660	51 690	51 390
Melanesia	*1 400*	*5 500*	*7 500*	*10 800*	*11 600*	*10 900*	*9 400*	*9 700*	*9 000*	*8 700*
Fiji	220	1 200	1 340	1 990	2 110	2 120	1 590	1 860	1 650	1 680
New Caledonia	380	1 180	2 530	3 630	3 610	3 180	3 430	3 820	3 350	3 460
Papua New Guinea	770	2 820	3 290	4 600	5 220	4 910	3 790	3 420	3 470	2 970
Solomon Islands	30	140	210	360	400	410	360	380	340	340
Vanuatu	30	110	150	230	240	240	230	230	230	220
Micronesia	*100*	*200*	*400*	*500*	*500*	*500*	*600*	*600*	*600*	*600*
Kiribati	10	30	30	50	50	50	50	50	50	40
Marshall Islands	10	20	70	110	100	90	100	100	100	100
Micronesia (Federated States of)	20	80	150	220	220	210	210	220	230	240
Nauru	10	40	50	40	40	40	30	30	30	30
Palau	10	20	80	130	140	150	190	180	200	240
Polynesia	*300*	*1 500*	*3 300*	*4 600*	*4 600*	*4 200*	*4 200*	*4 200*	*3 800*	*3 800*
Cook Islands	10	20	60	100	100	100	80	80	80	80
French Polynesia	210	1 260	2 930	4 110	4 120	3 700	3 750	3 700	3 300	3 290
Samoa	60	150	200	200	230	240	220	230	240	240
Tonga	10	50	110	160	170	160	150	150	150	130
Tuvalu	...	...	10	10	10	10	10	10	10	10

Table 1.B. Estimates of Per Capita Gross Domestic Product in US Dollars by Major Area, Region and Country

Major area, region and country	(Dollars) 1970	1980	1990	1995	1996	1997	1998	1999	2000	2001
WORLD	**880**	**2 690**	**4 350**	**5 180**	**5 230**	**5 130**	**5 030**	**5 130**	**5 170**	**5 050**
DEVELOPED ECONOMIES	**3 110**	**10 580**	**21 120**	**27 390**	**27 280**	**26 610**	**26 810**	**27 960**	**28 040**	**27 510**
DEVELOPING ECONOMIES	**220**	**840**	**1 000**	**1 310**	**1 400**	**1 440**	**1 340**	**1 310**	**1 380**	**1 340**
TRANSITION ECONOMIES	**1 370**	**3 040**	**4 530**	**1 950**	**2 230**	**2 290**	**2 000**	**1 720**	**1 870**	**2 110**
AFRICA	**230**	**990**	**850**	**830**	**810**	**830**	**790**	**720**	**730**	**690**
Eastern Africa	*140*	*480*	*300*	*270*	*290*	*300*	*290*	*280*	*270*	*280*
Burundi	70	230	205	166	145	160	146	131	113	103
Comoros	71	350	475	352	340	300	296	298	262	278
Djibouti	455	1 039	866	897	850	813	795	828	830	842
Eritrea	...	...	...	179	193	195	197	181	164	177
Ethiopia	...	...	...	96	101	102	101	96	92	90
Ethiopia (Former)	58	109	161	...	...	...	...	...	...	...
Kenya	149	433	362	330	330	369	390	352	342	367
Madagascar	129	361	258	229	281	242	248	240	243	278
Malawi	71	200	185	139	225	247	162	162	153	169
Mauritius	232	1 186	2 449	3 594	3 873	3 638	3 571	3 634	3 840	3 779
Mozambique	295	357	197	141	173	201	226	227	206	189
Reunion	787	3 949	8 627	11 177	11 191	10 075	10 253	10 102	9 014	9 188
Rwanda	57	226	345	250	258	317	306	263	226	205
Seychelles	379	2 311	5 200	6 778	6 640	7 354	7 868	7 983	7 603	7 335
Somalia	95	425	139	153	167	191	239	240	211	110
Uganda	200	2 002	215	305	300	311	302	275	243	239
United Republic Of Tanzania	97	273	145	170	205	236	251	253	259	263
Zambia	392	776	497	370	345	403	337	343	336	345
Zimbabwe	292	741	838	608	716	700	490	439	588	703
Middle Africa	*180*	*700*	*640*	*350*	*370*	*380*	*360*	*340*	*380*	*350*
Angola	513	764	1 102	464	501	668	555	511	737	700
Cameroon	199	1 105	1 227	667	681	652	673	660	613	582
Central African Republic	80	307	441	318	291	265	273	270	244	242
Chad	111	204	264	214	229	215	230	195	166	183
Congo	197	946	1 122	721	837	740	601	662	870	779
Democratic Republic of the Congo	91	527	250	127	127	129	133	107	104	91
Equatorial Guinea	669	257	461	408	676	1 310	1 037	1 707	2 746	3 680
Gabon	633	6 156	5 695	4 470	4 937	4 559	3 883	3 748	3 995	3 379
Sao Tome and Principe	290	497	497	347	334	318	288	323	311	312
Northern Africa	*270*	*1 250*	*1 630*	*1 300*	*1 390*	*1 420*	*1 420*	*1 430*	*1 480*	*1 390*
Algeria	376	2 260	2 474	1 509	1 654	1 670	1 633	1 639	1 801	1 784
Egypt	194	558	1 274	1 097	1 248	1 325	1 392	1 507	1 524	1 390
Libyan Arab Jamahiriya	2 010	11 739	6 570	6 493	6 954	7 508	6 428	5 512	6 518	5 453
Morocco	258	971	1 051	1 229	1 343	1 205	1 271	1 231	1 145	1 145
Sudan	133	464	1 350	497	287	362	330	315	367	376
Tunisia	281	1 352	1 501	2 015	2 158	2 056	2 129	2 210	2 045	2 077
Southern Africa	*740*	*2 620*	*2 840*	*3 450*	*3 230*	*3 300*	*2 930*	*2 840*	*2 750*	*2 420*
Botswana	130	1 081	2 600	2 854	2 689	2 987	2 868	2 743	2 881	2 872
Lesotho	71	297	394	554	553	592	508	515	483	419
Namibia	631	1 986	1 661	2 128	2 057	2 078	1 886	1 829	1 826	1 639
South Africa	806	2 826	3 040	3 692	3 450	3 515	3 114	3 020	2 907	2 550
Swaziland	246	990	1 028	1 453	1 378	1 460	1 340	1 341	1 330	1 204
Western Africa	*190*	*1 050*	*430*	*650*	*570*	*560*	*560*	*360*	*380*	*380*
Benin	93	336	397	367	393	371	390	389	362	371
Burkina Faso	73	250	320	215	223	213	223	213	184	190
Cape Verde	240	492	882	1 254	1 255	1 238	1 289	1 378	1 282	1 259
Cote d'Ivoire	271	1 207	951	773	827	782	828	808	675	652
Gambia	99	367	356	330	338	330	339	339	331	300
Ghana	257	1 411	408	369	386	375	398	391	254	265
Guinea	184	414	460	509	527	506	482	455	389	375
Guinea-Bissau	160	298	230	206	217	221	160	173	160	174
Liberia	200	438	180	63	71	121	139	160	179	169
Mali	25	202	277	223	251	223	240	235	214	200
Mauritania	162	515	503	460	457	441	394	375	340	353
Niger	97	454	328	185	216	192	207	195	167	171
Nigeria	215	1 431	377	906	714	716	713	322	427	435
Senegal	209	540	776	537	545	500	520	518	466	479
Sierra Leone	156	340	157	230	231	201	157	164	144	164
Togo	131	449	455	338	363	363	331	319	273	273
AMERICAS	**2 550**	**6 430**	**10 320**	**12 420**	**12 990**	**13 670**	**14 030**	**14 200**	**14 860**	**14 890**
NORTHERN AMERICA	**4 790**	**11 870**	**22 320**	**26 460**	**27 620**	**29 050**	**30 170**	**31 560**	**33 160**	**33 580**
Bermuda	4 462	13 545	26 901	32 951	34 465	36 904	38 743	41 247	42 533	44 753
Canada	3 927	10 850	20 729	19 816	20 379	20 956	20 076	21 302	22 966	22 385
United States	4 881	11 976	22 489	27 185	28 400	29 923	31 261	32 672	34 253	34 788

Table 1.B. Estimates of Per Capita Gross Domestic Product in US Dollars by Major Area, Region and Country

Major area, region and country	(Dollars) 1970	1980	1990	1995	1996	1997	1998	1999	2000	2001
LATIN AMERICA AND THE CARIBBEAN	**720**	**2 580**	**2 620**	**3 680**	**3 930**	**4 190**	**4 140**	**3 600**	**3 750**	**3 590**
Caribbean	*700*	*1 880*	*2 660*	*3 280*	*3 460*	*3 580*	*3 740*	*3 920*	*4 210*	*4 420*
Anguilla	425	1 236	6 058	7 315	7 568	8 320	8 691	9 493	9 613	9 643
Antigua and Barbuda	747	1 742	5 299	6 458	6 969	7 392	7 790	8 091	8 282	8 461
Aruba	6 764	10 698	16 399	16 746	16 853	18 041	18 950	19 017	19 922	19 762
Bahamas	2 952	6 843	11 934	10 836	10 743	10 671	10 615	10 566	10 520	10 476
Barbados	776	3 474	6 689	7 126	7 577	8 338	8 937	9 314	9 688	9 486
British Virgin Islands	1 583	3 703	13 956	20 752	23 541	26 933	30 789	33 891	34 849	38 530
Cayman Islands	1 778	7 669	27 464	32 914	33 515	35 288	35 952	35 990	36 912	37 891
Cuba	609	1 347	1 848	1 983	2 071	2 073	2 150	2 285	2 467	2 544
Dominica	393	795	2 322	2 919	3 119	3 210	3 374	3 459	3 465	3 367
Dominican Republic	403	1 398	1 295	2 006	2 164	1 894	1 960	2 112	2 347	2 514
Grenada	323	837	2 345	2 883	3 099	3 329	3 625	4 041	4 410	4 682
Guadeloupe	748	4 242	7 145	10 850	11 085	10 693	11 172	10 947	10 030	10 323
Haiti	73	254	378	328	377	417	466	511	455	447
Jamaica	816	1 368	1 951	2 303	2 565	2 899	2 950	2 945	2 988	2 990
Martinique	885	4 427	9 848	12 961	12 942	11 573	12 125	11 914	10 664	10 723
Montserrat	568	2 059	6 252	5 894	5 300	5 216	5 982	7 201	8 916	10 184
Netherlands Antilles	1 722	4 986	9 681	11 518	11 900	12 080	11 555	11 370	11 569	11 725
Puerto Rico	2 079	4 992	9 152	12 309	12 980	14 461	15 356	16 099	17 794	19 083
Saint Kitts and Nevis	358	1 084	3 893	5 301	5 639	6 343	6 684	7 168	7 821	8 187
Saint Lucia	395	1 003	3 166	3 955	4 042	4 057	4 370	4 730	4 863	4 994
Saint Vincent and the Grenadines	204	589	1 800	2 308	2 423	2 539	2 731	2 816	2 847	2 940
Trinidad and Tobago	847	5 765	4 171	4 227	4 543	4 504	4 725	5 302	6 340	7 031
Central America	*680*	*2 590*	*2 640*	*2 730*	*3 070*	*3 580*	*3 710*	*4 100*	*4 790*	*5 000*
Belize	376	1 354	2 183	2 748	2 757	2 744	2 740	2 932	3 152	3 123
Costa Rica	687	2 616	2 359	3 372	3 324	3 510	3 760	4 113	4 062	4 082
El Salvador	286	778	1 043	1 675	1 783	1 889	2 001	2 041	2 115	2 176
Guatemala	363	1 155	874	1 469	1 540	1 690	1 756	1 614	1 641	1 717
Honduras	267	719	626	703	704	791	859	862	914	960
Mexico	783	3 073	3 157	3 140	3 584	4 252	4 393	4 933	5 864	6 144
Nicaragua	242	495	563	415	422	420	430	448	480	492
Panama	666	1 818	2 204	2 961	2 991	3 114	3 294	3 331	3 396	3 391
South America	*740*	*2 660*	*2 610*	*4 090*	*4 310*	*4 490*	*4 340*	*3 370*	*3 300*	*2 950*
Argentina	1 295	7 363	4 346	7 423	7 728	8 210	8 273	7 747	5 578	5 267
Bolivia	240	937	730	898	967	1 014	1 064	1 017	1 005	940
Brazil	699	2 022	2 945	4 386	4 760	4 893	4 708	3 165	3 503	2 925
Chile	978	2 645	2 558	5 071	5 254	5 661	5 353	4 861	4 960	4 310
Colombia	379	1 392	1 365	2 400	2 474	2 668	2 421	2 084	1 975	1 924
Ecuador	295	1 551	1 096	1 771	1 831	1 999	1 934	1 364	1 283	1 666
French Guiana	1 076	4 225	10 299	12 091	11 656	10 086	9 854	9 341	8 011	7 737
Guyana	378	777	542	839	947	1 001	954	919	939	936
Paraguay	253	1 429	1 248	1 867	1 944	1 892	1 650	1 450	1 412	1 222
Peru	472	1 028	1 432	2 250	2 301	2 392	2 263	2 022	2 062	2 053
Suriname	758	2 507	3 039	1 268	1 840	2 046	2 429	2 095	2 085	1 965
Uruguay	818	3 307	2 694	5 996	6 327	6 644	6 796	4 160	4 070	3 905
Venezuela	1 318	4 743	2 492	3 536	3 267	3 402	3 338	3 072	3 109	3 134
ASIA	**240**	**940**	**1 770**	**2 560**	**2 460**	**2 340**	**2 100**	**2 290**	**2 420**	**2 220**
Eastern Asia	*330*	*1 290*	*2 920*	*4 870*	*4 530*	*4 270*	*3 880*	*4 310*	*4 590*	*4 170*
China	112	307	337	584	675	736	768	798	862	918
Democratic People's Rep. of Korea	199	504	842	245	490	474	468	465	476	492
Hong Kong SAR of China	978	5 743	13 311	22 821	24 700	26 820	24 989	23 821	24 106	23 499
Japan	1 982	9 205	24 714	42 271	37 406	34 269	31 203	35 258	37 500	32 809
Macao SAR of China	701	3 217	9 740	16 970	16 721	16 796	15 404	14 351	14 394	14 281
Mongolia	991	1 809	1 415	516	498	440	404	366	388	417
Republic of Korea	275	1 632	5 893	10 862	11 449	10 400	6 867	8 730	9 854	9 063
South Central Asia	*130*	*350*	*620*	*470*	*480*	*500*	*490*	*500*	*500*	*510*
Afghanistan	110	227	376	180	186	206	214	184	101	98
Bangladesh	156	232	291	335	342	353	355	358	352	345
Bhutan	44	106	168	171	180	208	203	222	234	241
India	110	266	383	393	407	434	429	448	457	467
Iran (Islamic Republic of)	346	2 321	3 325	1 632	1 733	1 602	1 564	1 573	1 494	1 606
Kazakhstan	...	...	4 276	1 005	1 284	1 369	1 385	1 068	1 170	1 426
Kyrgyzstan	...	...	2 925	327	396	377	344	258	278	306
Maldives	129	298	1 000	1 600	1 786	1 926	1 972	2 014	2 054	1 947
Nepal	80	131	189	202	205	220	203	218	226	226
Pakistan	173	350	426	538	527	496	483	461	446	411
Sri Lanka	195	286	475	732	783	840	864	851	876	834
Tajikistan	...	...	2 067	99	180	157	221	180	143	172
Turkmenistan	...	...	3 111	1 396	552	610	638	845	1 062	1 380
Uzbekistan	...	...	2 374	446	601	656	622	697	552	418
South-Eastern Asia	*130*	*540*	*810*	*1 400*	*1 520*	*1 430*	*980*	*1 110*	*1 160*	*1 100*
Brunei Darussalam	1 375	25 534	13 972	17 667	17 986	17 451	15 220	12 923	12 922	12 435
Cambodia	386	317	178	288	286	273	243	258	256	253

Table 1.B. Estimates of Per Capita Gross Domestic Product in US Dollars by Major Area, Region and Country

Major area, region and country	(Dollars)									
	1970	1980	1990	1995	1996	1997	1998	1999	2000	2001
Indonesia	74	483	628	1 025	1 136	1 063	464	671	720	678
Lao People's Democratic Republic	111	265	209	376	390	355	255	281	328	324
Malaysia	319	1 779	2 467	4 362	4 827	4 674	3 286	3 519	3 915	3 748
Myanmar	106	174	466	568	596	620	640	667	694	717
Philippines	183	675	725	1 084	1 186	1 154	895	1 026	989	925
Singapore	914	4 853	12 415	23 893	25 362	25 545	21 578	21 093	23 091	20 865
Thailand	197	698	1 569	2 905	3 112	2 554	1 874	2 031	2 007	1 865
Timor-Leste	...	...	244	375	448	487	502	319	374	438
Vietnam	93	80	98	285	333	368	361	372	401	416
Western Asia	*570*	*3 890*	*3 500*	*3 340*	*3 640*	*3 720*	*3 560*	*3 570*	*3 910*	*3 570*
Armenia	...	...	4 262	387	488	508	595	587	614	686
Azerbaijan	...	...	3 061	310	403	498	554	566	646	688
Bahrain	1 138	9 487	8 763	9 972	10 075	10 171	9 627	10 032	11 773	12 012
Cyprus	893	3 525	8 198	11 907	11 838	11 157	11 777	11 906	11 259	11 552
Georgia	...	...	4 115	531	571	672	683	529	579	611
Iraq	376	3 368	2 275	514	510	620	694	729	787	881
Israel	2 075	6 243	12 680	17 779	18 910	19 110	18 598	18 258	19 770	18 930
Jordan	366	1 803	1 235	1 604	1 587	1 595	1 679	1 663	1 684	1 726
Kuwait	3 860	20 867	8 619	15 660	17 957	16 332	12 759	13 791	15 947	13 935
Lebanon	603	1 526	1 037	3 481	3 970	4 333	4 620	4 913	4 951	5 087
Oman	364	5 327	6 332	6 165	6 601	6 634	5 726	6 202	7 615	7 421
Qatar	2 711	34 191	15 747	15 562	16 962	20 693	18 373	21 739	30 558	28 959
Saudi Arabia	887	15 365	6 323	6 738	8 077	8 191	7 019	7 507	8 520	8 169
Syrian Arab Republic	280	1 458	1 127	1 451	1 553	1 590	1 656	1 558	1 529	1 543
Turkey	495	1 491	2 616	2 685	2 830	2 913	3 025	2 749	2 918	2 136
United Arab Emirates	2 954	29 182	16 603	16 932	18 432	18 469	16 991	18 029	18 906	19 816
Yemen	...	...	1 110	827	497	422	371	418	474	431
Yemen Arab Republic (Former)	57	437	...	...	...	...	...	...	...	...
Yemen Democratic (Former)	138	359	...	...	...	...	...	...	...	...
EUROPE	**1 850**	**6 490**	**12 310**	**13 550**	**13 930**	**13 170**	**13 390**	**13 260**	**12 410**	**12 610**
Eastern Europe	*1 420*	*3 070*	*4 850*	*2 190*	*2 560*	*2 610*	*2 220*	*1 850*	*2 080*	*2 400*
Belarus	...	...	6 333	1 028	1 419	1 385	1 502	1 206	1 038	1 237
Bulgaria	1 319	2 256	2 377	1 559	1 187	1 251	1 549	1 587	1 556	1 688
Czech Republic	...	3 124	3 385	5 037	5 591	5 139	5 532	5 351	5 008	5 576
Czechoslovakia (Former)	1 012	...	...	...	...	...	...	...	...	...
Hungary	600	2 311	3 484	4 373	4 437	4 509	4 659	4 778	4 662	5 200
Poland	593	1 485	1 547	3 292	3 723	3 725	4 118	4 008	4 238	4 735
Republic of Moldova	...	...	4 363	332	391	447	395	273	301	346
Romania	708	1 213	1 648	1 564	1 562	1 564	1 869	1 581	1 640	1 770
Russian Federation	...	...	6 523	2 281	2 835	2 908	1 923	1 324	1 784	2 139
Slovakia	...	2 870	3 067	3 570	3 815	3 917	4 085	3 750	3 662	3 793
Ukraine	...	...	4 832	718	869	985	829	630	629	771
USSR (Former)	1 659	3 498	...	...	...	...	...	...	...	...
Northern Europe	*2 570*	*10 780*	*18 870*	*20 830*	*21 840*	*22 890*	*24 000*	*24 540*	*23 970*	*23 750*
Denmark	3 304	13 362	25 946	34 476	34 863	32 088	32 615	32 633	29 772	29 833
Estonia	...	...	7 561	2 467	3 060	3 280	3 751	3 767	3 760	4 065
Finland	2 420	10 988	27 519	25 392	24 924	23 857	25 124	24 739	23 177	23 424
Iceland	2 563	14 719	24 432	25 568	26 405	26 453	28 934	30 005	29 659	26 686
Ireland	1 428	6 134	13 458	18 418	20 083	21 745	23 335	25 345	24 824	26 503
Latvia	...	...	6 911	1 768	2 071	2 312	2 524	2 778	3 022	3 224
Lithuania	...	...	5 385	1 691	2 230	2 718	3 054	3 036	3 224	3 441
Norway	3 289	15 578	27 374	33 946	36 327	35 659	33 879	35 519	37 317	37 783
Sweden	4 436	16 008	28 735	28 143	30 620	27 947	28 027	28 406	27 072	24 766
United Kingdom	2 255	9 655	17 434	19 670	20 540	22 855	24 414	24 962	24 502	24 281
Southern Europe	*1 400*	*5 850*	*13 040*	*13 810*	*14 930*	*14 050*	*14 430*	*14 440*	*13 160*	*13 460*
Albania	607	831	660	778	851	731	980	1 181	1 205	1 317
Andorra	1 127	6 068	12 982	15 647	16 892	16 209	17 743	18 943	18 236	19 397
Bosnia and Herzegovina	...	...	3 042	597	802	1 032	1 132	1 218	1 117	1 152
Croatia	...	...	5 117	4 225	4 499	4 602	4 891	4 486	4 145	4 394
Greece	1 283	5 063	8 275	11 246	11 795	11 400	11 350	11 615	10 403	10 702
Holy See	2 001	7 953	19 437	19 148	21 483	20 307	20 810	20 528	18 651	18 928
Italy	2 001	7 953	19 437	19 148	21 483	20 307	20 810	20 528	18 651	18 928
Malta	752	3 501	6 420	8 588	8 757	8 713	9 103	9 426	9 136	9 274
Portugal	848	3 058	7 220	10 814	11 284	10 687	11 268	11 514	10 629	10 968
San Marino	3 615	13 490	30 687	28 280	31 298	29 194	30 917	32 282	28 982	29 078
Serbia and Montenegro	...	...	2 973	2 443	1 519	1 824	1 470	1 688	1 068	1 008
Slovenia	...	...	9 063	9 419	9 460	9 117	9 816	10 075	9 109	9 463
Spain	1 153	5 893	12 975	14 628	15 211	13 947	14 541	14 829	13 775	14 266
TFYR Macedonia	...	...	2 346	2 279	2 235	1 862	1 752	1 706	1 626	1 586
Yugoslavia (Former)	668	2 902	...	...	...	...	...	...	...	...
Western Europe	*2 710*	*12 130*	*21 480*	*29 090*	*28 440*	*25 350*	*25 920*	*25 630*	*23 050*	*23 060*
Austria	1 998	10 527	20 920	29 224	28 647	25 420	26 163	25 932	23 545	23 388
Belgium	2 656	12 353	19 782	27 292	26 533	24 038	24 520	24 541	22 242	22 150
France	2 895	12 659	21 431	26 714	26 625	23 993	24 683	24 449	22 066	22 168
Germany	2 606	11 411	21 041	30 103	29 097	25 722	26 102	25 638	22 730	22 507
Liechtenstein	3 543	17 007	33 422	43 164	41 416	35 725	36 556	36 067	33 384	34 449
Luxembourg	3 727	14 341	29 346	44 638	44 137	41 871	44 662	46 842	45 117	44 783

Table 1.B. Estimates of Per Capita Gross Domestic Product in US Dollars by Major Area, Region and Country

Major area, region and country	(Dollars)									
	1970	1980	1990	1995	1996	1997	1998	1999	2000	2001
Monaco	2 892	12 649	21 435	26 715	26 623	23 989	24 677	24 446	22 019	22 015
Netherlands	2 695	12 570	19 683	26 832	26 480	24 096	25 017	25 203	23 332	24 029
Switzerland	3 543	17 007	33 423	43 165	41 416	35 725	36 556	36 063	33 478	34 274
OCEANIA	**2 650**	**8 640**	**13 820**	**15 690**	**17 130**	**16 900**	**14 720**	**15 710**	**14 740**	**13 910**
Australia & New Zealand	*3 220*	*10 670*	*17 490*	*20 000*	*21 940*	*21 760*	*18 990*	*20 360*	*19 170*	*18 140*
Australia	3 420	11 382	18 391	20 625	22 662	22 491	19 846	21 404	20 260	19 056
New Zealand	2 322	7 342	12 980	16 874	18 328	18 077	14 674	15 104	13 662	13 470
Melanesia	*420*	*1 250*	*1 370*	*1 740*	*1 820*	*1 660*	*1 410*	*1 420*	*1 290*	*1 210*
Fiji	424	1 898	1 848	2 592	2 719	2 693	1 995	2 312	2 031	2 046
New Caledonia	3 592	8 285	14 786	18 792	18 254	15 719	16 589	18 100	15 560	15 750
Papua New Guinea	302	871	799	978	1 081	992	747	656	650	545
Solomon Islands	199	627	653	975	1 044	1 026	872	897	774	760
Vanuatu	404	968	1 008	1 323	1 350	1 308	1 229	1 180	1 148	1 085
Micronesia	*470*	*1 010*	*1 610*	*2 060*	*2 060*	*2 030*	*2 120*	*2 120*	*2 220*	*2 340*
Kiribati	293	482	396	592	631	613	565	626	539	468
Marshall Islands	345	763	1 546	2 202	2 004	1 878	1 914	1 921	1 910	1 938
Micronesia (Federated States of)	390	1 059	1 572	2 009	2 020	1 958	1 952	2 029	2 138	2 215
Nauru	2 008	4 798	5 428	3 772	3 716	3 290	2 773	2 837	2 698	2 500
Palau	1 041	1 585	5 444	7 493	7 872	8 469	10 161	9 357	10 609	12 051
Polynesia	*790*	*3 490*	*6 890*	*9 020*	*9 030*	*8 140*	*8 040*	*7 890*	*7 040*	*6 940*
Cook Islands	571	1 318	3 487	5 366	5 420	5 082	4 212	4 469	4 254	4 388
French Polynesia	1 917	8 341	14 995	19 150	18 877	16 668	16 617	16 129	14 131	13 891
Samoa	414	997	1 255	1 210	1 351	1 451	1 316	1 353	1 363	1 402
Tonga	124	549	1 158	1 573	1 708	1 652	1 470	1 481	1 473	1 284
Tuvalu	185	607	1 079	1 234	1 376	1 414	1 394	1 469	1 409	1 342

B. Percentage Distribution of Main National Accounting Aggregates at Current Prices: Individual Countries or Areas

Description of Analysis in Tables 2 and 3

A. Economic structure expressed in terms of percentage shares of gross domestic product.

The tables included in this section of the publication disaggregate GDP at current market prices into component parts and express these as percentage shares that outline the different economic structures existing in countries. The years of coverage vary: for countries that have officially reported complete data, percentage shares are listed for the years 1970, 1975, 1980, 1985, 1990, and 1995 through 2001; while, for those countries with very limited data and for which estimates have been made by the Statistics Division of United Nations in order to supplement the official data, percentage shares are only shown for selected years.

GDP estimates according to type of expenditure are shown in Table 2 and by kind of economic activity in Table 3. Differences in the concepts and coverage in classifications used are indicated in the footnotes. Both tables are designed to provide an overview of the structure of the economic system expressed in current prices.

GDP estimates of the countries are expressed in millions of the national currency as indicated in the first column of both tables. For tabulation purposes, the values of the GDP estimates of some countries prior to a high inflation period might be qualified with unit (u) or thousand (t) to reflect the measurement in a single unit or thousand of units of national currency.

Table 2 features the distribution of GDP based on expenditure components. It shows what portion of income is spent by the household sector or by the government on consumption, what is spent on investment, and what revenues are obtained from exports after deducting the expenditures on imports.

It is noted that in some instances the shares for changes in inventories should be used with caution as countries may also include such items in statistical errors. This problem is apparent in the inordinately high shares of changes in inventories as a percentage of GDP for many consecutive years.

Table 3 presents the shares of the components of GDP by kind of economic activity: agriculture; total industrial activity consisting of mining, manufacturing and utilities; manufacturing (as a separate activity); construction; wholesale and retail trade, restaurants and hotels; transport, storage and communication; and other activities which include financial and community services, producers of government services and other producers.

As in the preceding table, the distributive shares of GDP are presented, this time originating from each Industry component based on the classification by tabulation category of the International Standard Industrial Classification of all Economic Activities[iii]. This table reflects the economic structure of production in the country. For example, it identifies the value-added shares from different sources of production, e.g., oil, gas and other minerals. It also illustrates that many developing countries heavily depend on income mainly originating in agriculture, while relatively more developed countries generate a much larger portion of income in the industrial and services sectors.

Note that the breakdown in shares of GDP at current market prices by type of expenditure in Table 2 might not add-up to 100 percent due to statistical discrepancies. The breakdown by kind of economic activity in Table 3 might not add-up to 100 percent due to one or a combination of the following treatments: (i) taxes on production and imports, (ii) Financial Intermediation Services Indirectly Measured (FISIM), and (iii) statistical discrepancies.

[iii] Statistical Papers, Series M, No. 4, Rev. 3 (United Nations publication, Sales No. E.90.XVII.11)

Table 2. Gross Domestic Product by Type of Expenditure: Individual Countries or Areas

Major area, region and country	Year	Gross Domestic Product (at current prices) Million	Household final consumption expenditure 1	General government final consumption expenditure 2	Gross fixed capital formation 3	Changes in inventories 4	Exports of goods and services 5	Imports of goods and services 6
			Percentage Distribution					
AFRICA								
Algeria	1970	25509	59	13	31	3	22	27
(Dinars)	1975	61574	51	13	39	6	34	43
	1980	162507	43	14	34	5	34	30
	1985	291597	48	16	32	1	24	20
	1990	554388	57	16	26	3	23	25
	1995	2004995	56	17	27	5	27	31
	1996	2570028	52	16	25	0	30	23
	1997	2780168	51	17	23	0	30	21
	1998	2810124	55	18	26	1	23	23
	1999	3248198	51	17	24	2	28	23
	2000	4098817	42	14	21	2	42	20
	2001	4235620	44	15	23	5	37	23
Angola	1970	82 (u)	67	15	13	...	28	23
(Readjusted Kwanzas)	1975	80 (u)	52	21	8	...	48	29
	1980	161 (u)	48	21	9	...	52	30
	1985	205 (u)	47	31	17	1	33	29
	1990	308 (u)	29	45	11	1	39	24
	1995	14	50	34	18	7	69	78
	2000	91666	30	18	23	...	93	68
	2001	197111	32	24	23	...	79	69
Benin	1970	69711	78	13	15	...	28	35
(CFA Francs)	1975	113112	85	12	20	...	27	49
	1980	245613	90	9	20	...	24	46
	1985	469778	80	13	13	2	33	41
	1990	502300	80	13	13	1	20	28
	1995	1002900	79	10	19	5	27	39
	2000	1605400	81	9	19	1	22	31
	2001	1738400	78	8	19	1	30	36
Botswana [1]	1970	70	64	18	32	3	23	55
(Pula)	1975	263	53	17	24	13	41	56
	1980	832	46	19	31	4	49	59
	1985	2146	36	22	21	0	61	48
	1990	6552	30	24	33	6	56	50
	1995	12262	33	29	26	0	50	39
	1996	14204	31	28	26	-2	52	37
	1997	17740	28	27	24	2	66	38
	1998	20163	29	27	26	4	57	44
	1999	21524	31	31	29	8	47	46
	2000	25363	29	30	27	-8	60	39
	2001	29353	28	32	23	-7	56	33
Burkina Faso	1970	109936	93	8	8	2	9	20
(CFA Francs)	1975	168467	82	17	21	4	13	38
	1980	360929	85	17	24	2	16	45
	1985	622711	85	15	20	6	10	31
	1990	778376	80	15	22	1	11	29
	1995	1106300	81	17	25	-0	14	30
	2000	1560700	77	15	28	-0	11	30
	2001	1706900	75	15	27	...	11	28
Burundi	1970	21476	87	10	4	1	11	11
(Francs)	1975	32671	91	12	9	-2	8	19
	1980	85607	82	9	13	1	9	20
	1985	141347	77	8	14	-1	10	18
	1990	196656	83	11	15	-1	8	25
	1995	249865	84	13	9	0	13	25
	2000	511789	85	14	7	2	8	18
	2001	548656	85	17	8	2	9	20
Cameroon	1970	365638	81	14	15	2	22	37
(CFA Francs)	1975	747890	82	13	17	0	19	33
	1980	2044294	76	10	23	2	18	33
	1985	4672835	70	13	23	0	18	27

Table 2. Gross Domestic Product by Type of Expenditure: Individual Countries or Areas

Major area, region and country	Year	Gross Domestic Product (at current prices) Million	Household final consumption expenditure 1	General government final consumption expenditure 2	Gross fixed capital formation 3	Changes in inventories 4	Exports of goods and services 5	Imports of goods and services 6
			Percentage Distribution					
	1990	3896040	77	11	15	-0	18	21
	1995	4465080	68	12	13	-0	24	18
	1996	4793080	68	12	13	-0	25	17
	1997	5370580	70	12	13	0	24	19
	1998	5744000	71	12	14	-0	24	20
	1999	6008400	64	9	17	...	22	17
	2000	6602500	61	9	15	...	27	15
	2001	6577194	65	9	16	...	25	16
Cape Verde	1970	1844	83	13	43	-0	9	49
(Escudos)	1975	3009	119	18	43	-4	6	87
	1980	5715	93	15	39	3	17	67
	1985	12625	88	24	47	-2	23	79
	1990	21573	89	19	41	3	17	69
	1995	37705	86	23	39	2	17	66
	1996	41476	110	20	16	1	19	62
	1997	47158	103	20	18	1	22	63
	1998	52867	100	18	23	1	19	60
	1999	60400	107	20	22	1	19	66
	2000	64700	95	25	32	0	18	70
	2001	69000	105	19	29	1	18	70
Central African Republic	1970	41341	72	20	18	...	32	42
(CFA Francs)	1975	86470	88	17	14	...	21	40
	1980	149718	94	15	7	0	25	41
	1985	337755	79	15	12	3	22	32
	1990	353000	88	14	11	...	17	30
	1995	531738	84	13	13	...	14	24
	2000	646020	92	4	10	...	13	16
	2001	669923	96	3	8	...	12	15
Chad	1970	114202	85	11	10	1	23	30
(CFA Francs)	1975	187481	90	9	17	1	17	34
	1980	193869	86	10	16	1	22	35
	1985	412267	92	17	12	-1	16	36
	1990	419083	96	21	11	-1	18	46
	2000	928000	91	18	16	2	18	45
	2001	1088000	87	17	39	2	17	62
Comoros	1970	5424	83	18	24	1	18	42
(Comoro Francs)	1975	12832	99	17	22	1	11	46
	1980	28628	75	28	23	6	11	43
	1985	51700	73	28	28	4	17	50
	1990	68074	80	26	12	8	12	37
	1995	80343	80	21	18	3	17	39
	2000	98694	82	18	...	16	21	38
	2001	110780	83	19	...	17	20	40
Congo	1970	72453	62	21	26	4	30	42
(CFA Francs)	1975	146458	58	24	25	3	38	48
	1980	360397	41	18	33	3	56	51
	1985	970850	41	16	29	2	57	45
	1990	762000	51	19	17	-1	49	34
	1995	1056200	47	17	13	0	48	26
	2000	2134500	20	12	31	0	91	54
	2001	2021900	26	11	38	0	86	61
Cote d'Ivoire	1970	414862	59	16	20	2	37	34
(CFA Francs)	1975	834545	62	17	22	0	38	39
	1980	2149886	65	17	24	2	36	44
	1985	3134800	59	14	12	1	47	32
	1990	3238000	69	21	8	-2	29	25
	1995	5543000	64	17	12	2	37	32
	1996	6209810	65	16	14	-3	41	33
	1997	6841856	63	15	14	-0	43	35
	1998	7457508	65	14	14	1	41	35

Table 2. Gross Domestic Product by Type of Expenditure: Individual Countries or Areas

Major area, region and country	Year	Gross Domestic Product (at current prices) Million		Household final consumption expenditure 1	General government final consumption expenditure 2	Gross fixed capital formation 3	Changes in inventories 4	Exports of goods and services 5	Imports of goods and services 6
				Percentage Distribution					
	1999	7734000		63	15	15	-1	40	31
	2000	7605000		67	16	12	-1	40	34
	2001	7697909		65	15	14	-1	40	33
Democratic Republic of the Congo (Zaires)	1970	0.003	(u)	44	28	22	4	44	43
	1975	0.006	(u)	63	24	29	3	27	46
	1980	0.14	(u)	61	16	20	5	36	37
	1985	1.2	(u)	48	12	22	8	72	61
	1990	22.4	(u)	55	18	22	...	59	55
	1995	396		80	5	9	...	60	54
	2000	334926		93	5	3	...	...	9
	2001	1556120		98	4	4	0	0	13
Djibouti (Djibouti Francs)	1970	15300		65	21	14	...	53	54
	1975	30100		66	24	16	...	46	54
	1980	60313		64	34	13	1	39	51
	1985	62303		70	44	24	...	51	89
	1990	81203		67	34	27	-0	81	109
	1995	90572		63	35	19	-0	39	56
	1996	88233		65	34	19	-1	40	57
	1997	87289		59	35	21	0	42	58
	1998	88461		67	29	23	0	43	63
	1999	95275		79	26	9	...	47	61
	2000	98267		80	25	13	...	45	63
	2001	101932		80	25	10	...	45	60
Egypt [2] (Egyptian Pounds)	1970	2971		68	24	11	2	13	18
	1975	5247		59	26	24	9	18	36
	1980	17149		65	17	30	1	31	43
	1985	40820		73	17	32	2	20	32
	1990	110143		76	10	22	-1	28	36
	1995	229400		77	10	16	1	21	27
	1996	265900		77	11	18	-0	19	25
	1997	287400		78	11	20	0	16	26
	1998	307600		76	12	19	1	15	23
	1999	340100		77	11	18	1	16	23
	2000	358700		76	11	17	1	17	22
	2001	381700		77	12	16	0	18	23
Equatorial Guinea (CFA Francs)	1970	13780		71	35	19	...	32	58
	1975	12306		71	35	19	...	32	57
	1980	11908		70	30	10	...	31	60
	1985	38067		80	16	12	-5	27	31
	1990	44349		80	40	17	...	32	70
	1995	81600		56	16	76	...	55	104
	2000	891900		19	7	38	...	95	58
	2001	1263873		14	4	39	...	102	60
Eritrea (Nafka)	1992	1226		92	33	5	...	20	57
	1995	3533		92	47	19	...	30	88
	2000	4998		82	50	38	...	16	86
	2001	5755		87	50	39	...	13	89
Ethiopia (Birr)	1992	20792		87	10	9	...	5	11
	1995	33885		82	11	16	...	14	24
	2000	49459		79	23	13	-1	16	31
	2001	51180		81	18	17	-1	15	31
Gabon (CFA Francs)	1970	93100		40	19	28	2	48	37
	1975	402441		24	12	56	7	60	48
	1980	904500		26	13	28	...	65	32
	1985	1645800		30	19	37	...	57	43
	1990	1477400		50	13	21	0	46	31
	1995	2475200		42	14	22	1	59	37
	2000	3576883		36	9	21	...	66	33
	2001	3176703		39	11	23	...	62	35

Table 2. Gross Domestic Product by Type of Expenditure: Individual Countries or Areas

Major area, region and country	Year	Gross Domestic Product (at current prices) Million	Household final consumption expenditure 1	General government final consumption expenditure 2	Gross fixed capital formation 3	Changes in inventories 4	Exports of goods and services 5	Imports of goods and services 6
			Percentage Distribution					
Gambia [3]	1970	97	69	17	35	...	32	44
(Dalasis)	1975	278	71	13	30	...	28	52
	1980	412	84	21	47	...	23	71
	1985	1073	73	15	16	...	44	47
	1990	2627	82	14	18	...	43	58
	1995	3508	88	11	20	...	45	64
	2000	5551	83	13	17	...	48	61
	2001	6357	84	13	18	...	47	61
Ghana [4]	1970	2259	74	13	12	2	23	24
(Cedis)	1975	5283	73	13	12	1	19	18
	1980	42854	84	11	6	-0	8	9
	1985	343048	83	9	10	0	10	12
	1990	2031700	85	11	12	0	15	24
	1995	7752600	76	12	21	-1	24	33
	1996	11339200	76	12	21	1	25	35
	1997	14113400	80	10	23	1	24	38
	1998	17296000	78	10	22	1	27	38
	1999	20002100	79	10	23	1	24	37
	2000	27153000	83	16	24	...	50	71
	2001	38014000	81	13	24	...	37	54
Guinea	1970	17742	73	11	16	...	29	29
(French Francs)	1975	25991	73	11	16	...	29	29
	1980	36837	73	11	16	...	29	29
	1985	61031	73	11	16	...	29	29
	1990	1860450	70	12	18	...	31	31
	1995	3696760	78	7	21	...	19	25
	2000	5511780	74	8	18	1	27	28
	2001	6031710	73	8	18	1	27	28
Guinea-Bissau	1970	41	77	20	30	...	4	30
(CFA Francs)	1975	65	82	23	15	...	5	26
	1980	123	73	28	28	...	13	42
	1985	608	95	18	35	...	10	58
	1990	7848	87	10	30	...	10	37
	1995	68045	95	6	8	14	12	35
	2000	159900	95	14	18	...	32	58
	2001	179600	93	12	17	...	28	51
Kenya	1970	606	61	16	19	5	28	29
(Kenyan Pounds)	1975	1194	68	18	20	-2	30	35
	1980	2629	61	20	24	6	29	40
	1985	5042	58	17	18	8	25	26
	1990	9777	62	19	21	4	26	31
	1995	23264	69	15	21	0	33	39
	1996	26436	68	16	20	1	33	37
	1997	31168	73	16	18	1	28	35
	1998	34606	74	16	16	1	25	33
	1999	37107	73	17	15	1	26	31
	2000	39799	77	17	15	1	27	36
	2001	44764	78	17	14	1	26	35
Lesotho	1970	52	119	8	9	-0	11	45
(Loti)	1975	110	164	15	19	-1	14	105
	1980	296	138	24	32	1	23	124
	1985	568	160	23	39	-1	14	141
	1990	1600	132	14	53	-0	17	122
	1995	3384	111	18	61	-1	21	120
	1996	4054	111	16	58	0	24	118
	1997	4720	105	17	55	-1	27	112
	1998	4921	102	21	49	-2	27	107
	1999	5565	91	21	48	1	24	95
	2000	5986	91	20	44	-2	30	92
	2001	6478	93	18	43	-3	39	100

Table 2. Gross Domestic Product by Type of Expenditure: Individual Countries or Areas

Major area, region and country	Year	Gross Domestic Product (at current prices) Million	Household final consumption expenditure 1	General government final consumption expenditure 2	Gross fixed capital formation 3	Changes in inventories 4	Exports of goods and services 5	Imports of goods and services 6
			Percentage Distribution					
Liberia [5]	1970	277	47	13	22	-2	77	59
(Liberian Dollars)	1975	544	42	12	26	9	66	61
	1980	818	47	20	21	5	67	67
	1985	942	67	13	12	1	45	31
	1990	384	70	13	10	0	34	28
	1995	135	70	13	10	0	36	29
	2000	526	71	12	7	1	29	25
	2001	523	72	12	6	1	28	24
Libyan Arab Jamahiriya	1970	1426	33	18	17	0	61	28
(Lybian Dinars)	1975	3780	32	28	28	3	54	44
	1980	10575	27	22	23	1	62	35
	1985	8277	38	32	20	0	37	27
	1990	8010	33	26	21	...	50	30
	1995	10679	56	21	12	0	28	22
	2000	17395	46	21	13	0	36	15
	2001	17379	43	20	12	0	34	15
Madagascar [6]	1970	249400	67	18	16	...	23	24
(Malagasy Francs)	1975	395200	76	15	13	...	19	23
	1980	689800	76	17	23	1	14	31
	1985	1553400	78	13	14	...	14	20
	1990	4601600	86	8	17	...	16	27
	1995	13458000	90	7	11	...	24	31
	2000	26242000	83	9	15	...	31	38
	2001	30100000	83	9	15	...	28	35
Malawi [7]	1970	267	71	15	23	3	23	35
(Kwacha)	1975	530	69	14	25	9	29	46
	1980	1005	72	19	22	...	25	39
	1985	1929	74	18	13	...	24	30
	1990	4782	92	16	17	...	25	36
	1995	21376	75	19	15	3	34	45
	1996	35359	84	13	10	3	24	33
	1997	42634	88	12	10	2	22	35
	1998	54308	80	12	11	2	33	38
	1999	79060	88	12	12	2	28	43
	2000	103799	85	12	12	1	26	36
	2001	141730	83	13	11	1	22	31
Mali	1970	70300	71	11	13	4	10	19
(CFA Francs)	1975	129500	77	10	17	2	17	27
	1980	300600	82	10	16	1	18	30
	1985	520200	84	20	19	-2	19	39
	1990	683300	79	15	20	2	17	34
	1995	1152970	78	14	23	...	21	36
	2000	1811189	77	14	21	...	26	38
	2001	1798300	80	15	20	...	31	42
Mauritania	1970	11330	53	16	21	2	42	34
(Ouguiyas)	1975	20595	57	25	34	10	39	64
	1980	38070	74	24	20	6	30	56
	1985	52665	67	22	29	4	59	81
	1990	82350	68	19	18	0	58	60
	1995	137340	60	17	14	0	59	59
	2000	215010	74	20	13	3	42	52
	2001	245677	73	20	13	3	43	52
Mauritius	1970	1067	69	16	14	...	50	48
(Rupees)	1975	3416	55	13	33	...	66	65
	1980	8805	75	15	23	-2	51	61
	1985	16825	66	12	18	5	53	55
	1990	38462	65	13	31	-1	67	74
	1995	70283	64	13	24	2	59	61
	1996	79086	63	13	26	-1	64	64
	1997	88099	62	13	27	3	62	66
	1998	99564	63	13	23	2	66	67

Table 2. Gross Domestic Product by Type of Expenditure: Individual Countries or Areas

Major area, region and country	Year	Gross Domestic Product (at current prices) Million	Household final consumption expenditure 1	General government final consumption expenditure 2	Gross fixed capital formation 3	Changes in inventories 4	Exports of goods and services 5	Imports of goods and services 6
			Percentage Distribution					
	1999	107444	64	13	28	-1	64	68
	2000	119529	62	13	23	2	62	62
	2001	131835	61	13	22	-1	69	63
Morocco	1970	20020	73	12	15	4	18	21
(Dirhams)	1975	36410	68	16	25	1	23	33
	1980	74090	67	18	22	2	18	27
	1985	129510	65	16	23	4	25	33
	1990	212850	65	15	24	1	25	30
	1995	281702	75	11	21	-1	28	34
	1996	319340	67	17	19	0	22	26
	1997	318342	65	18	21	0	23	27
	1998	344005	64	18	22	0	23	27
	1999	345593	62	19	24	-1	24	29
	2000	354068	64	19	24	-0	26	33
	2001	382897	61	19	22	1	28	31
Mozambique	1970	79532	95	11	8	2	5	24
(Meticais)	1975	112329	95	11	8	2	5	24
	1980	142600	90	10	9	2	7	23
	1985	268746	95	9	4	-0	2	8
	1990	2515606	102	12	20	-0	6	38
	1995	20678102	99	10	27	4	13	52
	1996	32718600	93	8	20	2	12	36
	1997	39819429	89	9	21	-0	11	31
	1998	46911782	82	10	18	6	10	28
	1999	51913228	78	12	20	17	10	38
	2000	56917388	78	14	51	-17	13	39
	2001	71134761	73	15	22	4	22	35
Namibia [8]	1970	362	51	11	17	...	66	45
(Namibia Dollars)	1975	696	60	13	33	...	72	79
	1980	1574	45	19	29	2	75	76
	1985	2735	50	32	16	-4	62	60
	1990	6054	47	31	21	13	52	68
	1995	12706	53	30	22	-0	49	56
	1996	15011	54	30	24	-0	51	59
	1997	16754	57	30	20	1	48	58
	1998	18790	56	30	23	3	46	58
	1999	20681	56	30	23	0	46	57
	2000	23995	56	28	19	1	45	51
	2001	27231	58	28	22	2	44	54
Niger	1970	111000	85	12	7	3	15	22
(CFA Francs)	1975	180300	77	13	20	3	19	33
	1980	536208	71	10	25	6	24	37
	1985	647100	79	15	14	1	21	30
	1990	682300	74	17	12	1	17	21
	1995	834600	78	16	12	3	20	28
	2000	1280400	82	12	12	1	16	23
	2001	1399100	84	12	12	2	15	24
Nigeria	1970	7381	67	11	18	-1	13	10
(Naira)	1975	22722	62	12	20	-0	24	18
	1980	50346	58	12	20	-1	30	20
	1985	72355	75	10	8	-1	17	9
	1990	260637	60	4	12	0	43	19
	1995	1977737	76	7	16	0	44	44
	2000	4981000	38	17	19	...	44	34
	2001	5697000	46	16	24	...	41	50
Reunion	1970	2013	71	33	28	-2	14	45
(French Francs)	1975	4540	75	34	21	3	6	39
	1980	8449	84	33	21	2	7	47
	1985	17054	85	33	22	-3	6	45
	1990	28374	80	28	29	-0	4	41

Table 2. Gross Domestic Product by Type of Expenditure: Individual Countries or Areas

Major area, region and country	Year	Gross Domestic Product (at current prices) Million	Household final consumption expenditure 1	General government final consumption expenditure 2	Gross fixed capital formation 3	Changes in inventories 4	Exports of goods and services 5	Imports of goods and services 6
			Percentage Distribution					
	1995	37037	80	28	28	...	4	39
	2000	46379	80	28	28	...	3	39
	2001	49439	80	28	28	...	3	39
Rwanda (Francs)	1970	21560	82	14	8	-0	12	15
	1975	52770	78	17	13	1	9	18
	1980	107990	83	12	12	4	14	26
	1985	173700	81	11	16	2	11	20
	1990	192900	83	17	12	-1	8	19
	1995	336489	101	9	14	...	6	29
	2000	681455	90	9	18	...	6	23
	2001	732276	90	10	17	...	9	26
Sao Tome and Principe (Dobras)	1970	614	64	33	23	...	43	59
	1975	881	78	24	25	...	34	62
	1980	1629	84	34	31	...	25	75
	1985	2319	76	47	34	...	30	86
	1990	8250	80	38	36	...	23	72
	1995	64613	80	28	41	...	24	73
	2000	369500	75	28	43	...	35	82
	2001	422000	71	27	50	...	35	83
Senegal (CFA Francs)	1970	241668	78	13	10	-1	24	26
	1975	409054	76	14	11	-1	33	34
	1980	631400	83	20	13	-2	28	42
	1985	1158200	85	17	11	-2	30	41
	1990	1551500	76	15	13	1	25	30
	1995	2234000	79	12	15	2	32	40
	1996	2380000	79	12	16	2	31	40
	1997	2554300	77	12	16	2	29	36
	1998	2746000	76	12	18	2	30	37
	1999	2925000	74	13	20	1	30	38
	2000	3114000	73	14	17	6	30	40
	2001	3379700	75	16	18	-0	29	38
Seychelles [9] (Rupees)	1970	110	81	14	42	-3	56	90
	1975	292	65	22	37	2	65	90
	1980	942	55	29	37	2	50	72
	1985	1205	58	35	23	...	48	64
	1990	1967	52	28	23	2	62	67
	1995	2420	49	28	30	0	53	60
	1996	2500	48	29	33	-1	64	74
	1997	2830	50	30	28	4	-11	...
	1998	3201	50	31	34	1	-16	...
	1999	3330	45	28	41	2	-16	...
	2000	3424	39	27	36	0	-3	...
	2001	3419	59	27	36	...	78	91
Sierra Leone [10] (Leones)	1970	346	77	9	13	2	31	32
	1975	573	83	11	13	2	27	37
	1980	1156	91	8	15	1	23	38
	1985	4785	84	7	9	1	10	11
	1990	96133	80	8	9	0	26	24
	1995	710389	76	9	6	-0	29	19
	2000	1330300	91	17	8	...	17	33
	2001	1485507	91	14	9	...	18	28
Somalia [11] (Shillings)	1970	2436	97	8	7	2	8	19
	1975	4765	97	16	11	3	10	35
	1980	17341	89	14	10	-1	5	17
	1985	87290	90	11	9	3	4	17
	1990	1738800	71	10	23	1	1	6
	1995	6424840	72	8	21	0	0	2
	2000	17618100	72	9	20	0	0	2
	2001	16798653	72	9	20	0	0	2

Table 2. Gross Domestic Product by Type of Expenditure: Individual Countries or Areas

Major area, region and country	Year	Gross Domestic Product (at current prices) Million	Household final consumption expenditure 1	General government final consumption expenditure 2	Gross fixed capital formation 3	Changes in inventories 4	Exports of goods and services 5	Imports of goods and services 6
			Percentage Distribution					
South Africa..	1970	13045	64	13	24	4	21	24
(Rand)	1975	27868	60	14	29	3	27	29
	1980	64141	53	14	26	5	35	27
	1985	128773	56	18	23	-3	31	22
	1990	289816	63	20	19	-2	25	19
	1995	548100	63	18	16	2	23	22
	1996	617954	62	19	16	1	25	23
	1997	685730	63	19	17	0	25	23
	1998	739504	63	19	17	-0	26	25
	1999	802840	63	18	15	0	26	23
	2000	887795	63	18	15	1	29	26
	2001	975196	62	18	15	1	31	27
Sudan...	1970	67	69	21	10	2	16	18
(Sudanese Pounds)	1975	168	82	14	14	3	11	25
	1980	449	76	13	20	6	10	25
	1985	1703	76	13	20	6	10	25
	1990	15139	76	13	20	6	10	25
	1995	810318	73	7	11	9	7	17
	1996	1033070	82	7	12	10	8	19
	1997	1676940	86	5	12	6	10	19
	1998	1991610	87	6	12	6	10	20
	1999	2448880	89	6	17	...	8	15
	2000	2969450	82	5	17	...	16	16
	2001	3130000	86	5	18	...	13	16
Swaziland [12]..	1970	78	65	14	22	3	70	74
(Lilangeni)	1975	216	63	17	19	-1	70	67
	1980	460	96	19	25	5	66	109
	1985	813	103	23	24	2	54	99
	1990	2253	79	18	19	1	73	89
	1995	4949	79	19	19	1	75	93
	1996	5686	84	21	20	1	72	98
	1997	6613	72	25	20	1	76	93
	1998	7449	73	24	22	...	79	99
	1999	8408	74	22	19	...	73	88
	2000	9639	75	20	20	...	64	79
	2001	10971	77	18	18	...	70	83
Togo..	1970	73171	77	10	13	2	30	31
(CFA Francs)	1975	128302	75	15	23	6	28	46
	1980	238872	66	15	29	7	38	55
	1985	338200	66	14	23	5	42	51
	1990	427600	70	13	22	0	23	28
	1995	652500	86	12	15	2	36	51
	2000	885800	81	11	20	...	35	49
	2001	938000	82	11	20	...	34	46
Tunisia...	1970	756	66	17	21	1	22	26
(Dinars)	1975	1741	62	15	26	2	31	36
	1980	3541	62	14	28	1	41	46
	1985	7018	59	17	28	2	32	38
	1990	10816	64	16	24	3	44	51
	1995	17052	63	16	24	1	45	49
	1996	19066	61	16	23	2	42	44
	1997	20898	60	16	25	2	44	46
	1998	22561	61	16	25	2	43	46
	1999	24672	60	16	25	1	43	45
	2000	26685	61	16	26	1	44	48
	2001	28759	61	16	26	2	48	52
Uganda..	1970	135	73	10	12	1	22	19
(New Shillings)	1975	321	81	14	7	1	8	10
	1980	1851	83	14	2	1	3	6
	1985	27578	84	12	8	...	11	13
	1990	1602094	91	8	14	...	7	20
	1995	5991763	87	10	17	-0	11	24
	1996	6555380	90	9	17	-0	14	28

Table 2. Gross Domestic Product by Type of Expenditure: Individual Countries or Areas

Major area, region and country	Year	Gross Domestic Product (at current prices) Million	Household final consumption expenditure 1	General government final consumption expenditure 2	Gross fixed capital formation 3	Changes in inventories 4	Exports of goods and services 5	Imports of goods and services 6
			Percentage Distribution					
	1997	7230521	92	10	17	-0	11	26
	1998	8298977	91	9	17	...	10	28
	1999	9132410	91	9	20	...	10	29
	2000	9371358	81	14	20	0	10	25
	2001	10145469	79	15	20	0	11	26
United Republic Of Tanzania (Shillings)	1970	9568	68	13	23	3	23	27
	1975	19829	72	16	21	3	17	30
	1980	42118	77	13	20	3	13	26
	1985	112000	76	15	17	2	7	17
	1990	736338	73	10	38	4	14	39
	1995	3020500	84	15	20	0	24	41
	1996	3767640	83	12	16	0	20	32
	1997	4703460	84	9	15	0	16	26
	1998	5571640	88	8	16	0	13	28
	1999	6432910	88	7	15	0	14	26
	2000	7225690	84	7	18	0	15	23
	2001	8186480	85	6	17	0	16	25
Zambia (Kwacha)	1970	1185	17	41	25	...	58	40
	1975	1837	24	69	24	...	31	48
	1980	3656	21	64	18	...	35	38
	1985	9351	18	66	16	...	29	29
	1990	123487	14	55	31	...	34	34
	1995	2998202	22	29	44	...	34	30
	2000	10900735	26	23	54	...	25	28
	2001	13170001	27	24	49	...	27	27
Zimbabwe (Zimbabwe Dollars)	1970	1079	66	12	16	3	25	25
	1975	1998	60	13	23	4	30	31
	1980	3441	63	20	15	3	30	33
	1985	9097	61	20	14	4	22	22
	1990	21494	63	19	18	-1	23	23
	1995	61759	64	18	25	-5	38	41
	1996	85551	63	17	18	1	36	36
	1997	102982	71	16	18	1	37	44
	1998	143364	63	17	21	0	43	45
	1999	210409	69	15	15	1	46	47
	2000	330345	61	24	14	2	30	31
	2001	493800	65	20	14	2	38	39
NORTHERN AMERICA								
Bermuda (Bermudian Dollars)	1970	259	66	9	12	-0	51	41
	1975	480	68	10	12	-0	52	42
	1980	919	67	10	18	-0	52	45
	1985	1433	64	12	20	-0	47	41
	1990	1997	68	12	17	-0	48	44
	1995	2544	63	12	14	-0	45	36
	1996	2680	62	12	15	-0	47	37
	1997	2889	61	12	16	0	48	38
	1998	3053	60	11	19	1	47	39
	1999	3272	61	11	19	1	47	39
	2000	3397	60	11	19	1	47	39
	2001	3599	60	11	21	1	47	40
Canada (Canadian Dollars)	1970	89112	55	21	22	0	23	20
	1975	171435	53	22	24	1	23	24
	1980	311015	52	22	23	-0	28	26
	1985	470029	53	22	20	1	28	26
	1990	669967	55	23	22	-0	26	26
	1995	798300	55	22	18	1	38	35
	1996	824041	56	21	18	0	39	35
	1997	868979	56	20	20	1	40	38
	1998	900350	56	20	20	1	42	40
	1999	965440	55	19	20	1	44	40
	2000	1049450	54	19	20	1	46	41
	2001	1075580	55	19	20	-1	44	39

Table 2. Gross Domestic Product by Type of Expenditure: Individual Countries or Areas

Major area, region and country	Year	Gross Domestic Product (at current prices) Million	Household final consumption expenditure 1	General government final consumption expenditure 2	Gross fixed capital formation 3	Changes in inventories 4	Exports of goods and services 5	Imports of goods and services 6
			Percentage Distribution					
United States [13]	1970	1025500	63	18	18	0	6	5
(Dollars)	1975	1617800	64	18	18	-0	9	8
	1980	2771500	64	17	20	-0	10	11
	1985	4174900	65	18	20	1	7	10
	1990	5750800	67	17	17	0	10	11
	1995	7338400	68	15	18	0	11	12
	1996	7751100	68	15	18	0	11	12
	1997	8256500	67	15	19	1	12	13
	1998	8720200	67	14	19	1	11	13
	1999	9212800	68	14	20	1	11	13
	2000	9762100	68	15	20	1	11	15
	2001	10019700	70	15	19	-1	10	14
LATIN AMERICA and the CARIBBEAN								
Anguilla	1970	6	50	15	43	...	65	73
(EC Dollars)	1975	12	50	15	43	...	65	73
	1980	24	50	15	43	...	65	73
	1985	52	46	15	44	...	69	72
	1990	147	52	13	41	...	76	80
	1995	202	77	18	29	...	76	100
	1996	214	80	18	29	...	74	102
	1997	240	74	18	25	...	76	94
	1998	255	70	14	35	...	88	107
	1999	283	86	15	44	...	68	114
	2000	292	87	20	43	...	64	115
	2001	298	72	22	31	...	67	91
Antigua and Barbuda	1970	98	58	18	21	...	66	62
(EC Dollars)	1975	152	58	18	21	...	66	62
	1980	297	69	19	31	...	67	87
	1985	541	70	18	28	-1	74	94
	1990	902	42	19	37	-3	83	83
	1995	1176	43	22	41	-3	74	83
	2000	1603	30	23	53	-4	61	67
	2001	1651	25	26	54	-4	57	62
Argentina	1970	1.2 (u)	65	10	...	25	7	8
(Pesos)	1975	19.2 (u)	58	13	...	30	6	7
	1980	3800 (u)	63	13	...	26	5	8
	1985	5	65	11	...	18	12	6
	1990	68922	68	12	...	14	10	5
	1995	258032	69	13	...	18	10	10
	1996	272150	69	13	...	18	10	11
	1997	292859	69	12	...	19	11	13
	1998	298948	69	12	...	20	10	13
	1999	283522	70	14	...	18	10	12
	2000	284204	69	14	...	16	11	12
	2001	268697	69	14	...	14	11	10
Aruba	1970	685	31	4	45	-10	78	44
(Aruban Florin)	1975	888	34	5	41	-7	79	50
	1980	1151	38	7	37	-5	79	55
	1985	1492	42	10	34	-3	80	62
	1990	1934	46	13	31	-1	80	69
	1995	2364	50	20	28	3	85	86
	1996	2470	53	20	26	2	87	89
	1997	2742	50	24	28	2	83	86
	1998	2981	50	22	29	3	80	84
	1999	3087	52	22	27	2	81	84
	2000	3326	50	20	24	1	75	70
	2001	3381	53	23	20	1	72	69
Bahamas	1970	502	61	9	0	3	32	1
(Bahamian Dollars)	1975	723	60	9	2	4	39	10
	1980	1438	75	13	15	0	62	57
	1985	2171	51	13	10	8	50	26
	1990	3047	67	14	21	0	56	53

Table 2. Gross Domestic Product by Type of Expenditure: Individual Countries or Areas

Major area, region and country	Year	Gross Domestic Product (at current prices) Million	Household final consumption expenditure 1	General government final consumption expenditure 2	Gross fixed capital formation 3	Changes in inventories 4	Exports of goods and services 5	Imports of goods and services 6
			Percentage Distribution					
	1995	3069	68	16	23	0	55	59
	1996	3093	67	16	23	0	54	60
	1997	3116	67	17	23	1	54	61
	1998	3140	67	17	23	1	53	62
	1999	3164	67	17	23	1	53	63
	2000	3189	67	18	23	1	52	64
	2001	3213	66	18	23	1	52	65
Barbados (Barbados Dollars)	1970	370	81	20	25	...	49	75
	1975	812	74	17	19	1	50	60
	1980	1730	62	15	23	2	70	72
	1985	2410	58	19	15	0	68	60
	1990	3440	64	20	19	-0	49	52
	1995	3742	62	20	15	1	58	55
	1996	3995	59	21	16	-1	60	55
	1997	4413	63	21	18	0	55	57
	1998	4747	63	21	18	0	53	55
	1999	4965	65	21	19	1	51	57
	2000	5183	67	21	18	0	50	56
	2001	5093	65	22	16	-0	51	54
Belize (Belize Dollars)	1970	77	68	14	24	3	70	78
	1975	189	66	11	28	4	51	57
	1980	389	77	15	23	1	35	46
	1985	418	56	21	17	4	60	60
	1990	811	60	14	26	0	60	61
	1995	1173	65	16	23	-1	51	54
	1996	1207	63	16	22	0	51	53
	1997	1231	66	17	22	2	54	61
	1998	1258	67	17	21	3	53	62
	1999	1377	65	17	26	3	51	63
	2000	1514	68	15	31	3	49	67
	2001	1533	67	14	29	4	54	67
Bolivia (Bolivianos)	1970	12 (t)	75	8	17	-0	25	25
	1975	48 (t)	73	10	19	4	25	33
	1980	123 (t)	67	13	15	1	26	20
	1985	2867	63	8	12	5	29	17
	1990	15443	77	12	13	-0	23	24
	1995	32235	76	14	16	-0	23	27
	1996	37537	75	13	16	0	23	27
	1997	41044	75	14	19	1	21	29
	1998	46822	75	14	23	0	20	33
	1999	48156	77	15	19	-0	17	27
	2000	51667	77	14	18	-0	18	27
	2001	52652	78	15	14	-1	18	24
Brazil (Reais)	1970	0.1 (u)	61	9	24	2	6	6
	1975	0.6 (u)	61	8	29	3	7	10
	1980	4.7 (u)	50	21	29	3	4	6
	1985	448 (u)	70	11	18	-0	13	8
	1990	11	58	17	23	-0	8	6
	1995	646192	60	20	21	2	8	9
	1996	778887	63	18	19	2	7	9
	1997	870743	63	18	20	2	8	10
	1998	914188	62	19	20	1	7	10
	1999	973846	62	19	19	1	10	12
	2000	1101255	61	19	19	2	11	12
	2001	1200060	61	19	19	2	13	14
British Virgin Islands [14] (US Dollars)	1970	16	69	8	48	13	21	60
	1975	21	70	8	26	14	40	58
	1980	44	53	10	28	11	62	63
	1985	72	53	14	28	2	89	86
	1990	240	49	14	25	1	95	84
	1995	385	49	14	25	1	95	84
	2000	691	42	11	26	...	108	83
	2001	777	41	11	25	...	105	80

Table 2. Gross Domestic Product by Type of Expenditure: Individual Countries or Areas

Major area, region and country	Year	Gross Domestic Product (at current prices) Million	Household final consumption expenditure 1	General government final consumption expenditure 2	Gross fixed capital formation 3	Changes in inventories 4	Exports of goods and services 5	Imports of goods and services 6
			Percentage Distribution					
Cayman Islands (Dollars)	1970	16	72	12	24	-0	52	64
	1975	45	70	13	23	1	57	65
	1980	110	68	15	25	-1	68	76
	1985	264	63	16	20	0	70	70
	1990	590	61	14	21	-0	63	58
	1995	849	63	14	22	-0	60	59
	2000	1131	65	15	23	-0	63	61
	2001	1198	65	15	23	-0	63	62
Chile (Pesos)	1970	105	67	16	18	-1	15	14
	1975	37891	69	19	21	-7	25	27
	1980	1149700	68	15	19	2	22	27
	1985	2930460	65	14	18	-0	27	24
	1990	10216526	60	10	25	1	33	29
	1995	28593362	61	11	25	1	29	27
	1996	31237289	63	11	26	1	27	29
	1997	34722636	63	11	27	1	27	29
	1998	36534873	64	11	26	1	26	30
	1999	37164386	64	12	21	0	29	27
	2000	40436215	64	12	21	1	32	30
	2001	42191778	65	13	21	-1	35	33
Colombia [15] (Pesos)	1970	157666	70	10	22	2	12	16
	1975	480111	71	10	19	2	15	15
	1980	1871842	68	11	21	2	15	16
	1985	5886995	68	12	22	1	12	13
	1990	23979488	64	11	20	2	19	16
	1995	84439109	66	15	22	3	15	21
	1996	100711389	65	18	22	1	15	21
	1997	121707501	65	20	20	1	15	21
	1998	140483322	66	20	19	1	15	21
	1999	151565005	64	22	13	-0	18	18
	2000	173729806	64	22	13	1	20	20
	2001	189525312	65	22	12	2	19	21
Costa Rica (Colones)	1970	8291	87	10	18	-3	24	33
	1975	21352	86	12	20	-4	26	36
	1980	52610	80	15	22	-3	23	35
	1985	251474	73	13	17	1	27	31
	1990	664322	75	15	20	-1	30	39
	1995	2105687	71	14	19	-1	38	40
	1996	2459957	74	13	17	-1	39	43
	1997	2984020	73	13	18	0	41	45
	1998	3625330	69	13	20	0	47	50
	1999	4512763	65	13	18	-1	52	46
	2000	4917764	67	13	18	-1	48	46
	2001	5387526	68	14	18	2	42	45
Cuba (Cuban Pesos)	1970	5192	54	32	13	2	15	20
	1975	9742	45	27	18	8	27	28
	1980	13075	53	32	19	5	33	38
	1985	19145	52	31	25	3	34	45
	1990	19645	54	31	25	0	30	41
	1995	21737	71	24	8	-1	13	16
	1996	22815	71	24	10	-3	16	18
	1997	22952	72	24	10	-2	16	19
	1998	23901	72	24	10	-2	15	18
	1999	25504	71	23	10	-2	16	19
	2000	27635	69	23	11	-1	16	18
	2001	28589	41	31	12	-1	39	21
Dominica (EC Dollars)	1970	55	84	25	27	...	37	73
	1975	73	73	23	24	...	43	63
	1980	160	92	27	46	4	22	93
	1985	266	72	22	28	...	37	60
	1990	452	64	20	40	1	50	75
	1995	592	64	21	32	...	51	67
	1996	638	61	20	29	...	52	62

Table 2. Gross Domestic Product by Type of Expenditure: Individual Countries or Areas

Major area, region and country	Year	Gross Domestic Product (at current prices) Million	Household final consumption expenditure 1	General government final consumption expenditure 2	Gross fixed capital formation 3	Changes in inventories 4	Exports of goods and services 5	Imports of goods and services 6
			Percentage Distribution					
	1997	662	55	22	31	...	56	64
	1998	701	55	22	27	...	58	62
	1999	723	61	22	28	...	58	68
	2000	728	63	23	28	...	55	68
	2001	711	65	23	25	...	51	64
Dominican Republic [16] (Pesos)	1970	1784	77	9	15	4	28	39
	1975	4323	66	5	21	3	45	44
	1980	7964	77	6	22	4	32	46
	1985	16782	76	6	18	2	48	55
	1990	77911	77	3	19	2	42	47
	1995	209646	76	4	16	3	33	37
	1996	232993	78	4	17	3	17	25
	1997	214864	80	6	23	-1	19	32
	1998	241977	79	7	27	-1	18	35
	1999	278347	77	7	28	-1	18	33
	2000	321783	79	7	28	-2	18	35
	2001	361569	80	5	25	0	18	34
Ecuador (Sucres)	1970	1762	73	17	16	2	13	19
	1975	4536	62	21	22	4	25	34
	1980	12351	56	21	23	3	24	27
	1985	16797	62	17	15	2	26	22
	1990	11248	67	13	18	-1	31	29
	1995	20196	68	13	19	3	26	28
	1996	21268	66	12	18	2	26	24
	1997	23636	66	12	18	4	26	26
	1998	23255	69	12	20	5	21	28
	1999	16674	66	13	17	-2	32	25
	2000	15934	64	10	20	-0	37	31
	2001	21024	69	10	22	4	27	31
El Salvador (Colones)	1970	2571	75	11	12	1	25	25
	1975	4478	73	11	23	-1	33	38
	1980	8917	72	14	14	-0	34	33
	1985	14331	81	15	12	-1	22	30
	1990	36487	89	10	14	0	19	31
	1995	83129	87	9	19	1	22	38
	1996	90261	88	9	16	-1	21	34
	1997	97428	87	9	16	-1	26	38
	1998	105074	85	10	17	1	25	37
	1999	109066	86	10	16	0	25	37
	2000	114967	88	10	17	-0	27	42
	2001	120215	88	10	17	-1	29	43
French Guiana (French Francs)	1970	287	81	53	28	1	3	64
	1975	575	79	51	23	-1	2	55
	1980	1219	87	53	40	1	8	90
	1985	3173	68	42	38	0	54	102
	1990	6526	64	35	48	-0	67	114
	1995	8362	59	37	34	2	63	95
	2000	9372	59	37	32	2	62	91
	2001	9589	59	37	31	2	62	91
Grenada (EC Dollars)	1970	60	76	18	2	3	84	89
	1975	107	83	20	7	6	68	89
	1980	202	85	21	26	4	53	89
	1985	311	77	22	31	-2	48	76
	1990	541	65	20	39	3	44	72
	1995	649	57	16	35	0	34	47
	1996	693	64	16	39	-0	33	56
	1997	740	66	16	40	-1	33	61
	1998	801	65	16	41	-1	38	65
	1999	888	54	15	41	-1	47	60
	2000	964	57	14	44	-2	46	65
	2001	1020	59	13	49	-5	43	64

Table 2. Gross Domestic Product by Type of Expenditure: Individual Countries or Areas

Major area, region and country	Year	Gross Domestic Product (at current prices) Million	Household final consumption expenditure 1	General government final consumption expenditure 2	Gross fixed capital formation 3	Changes in inventories 4	Exports of goods and services 5	Imports of goods and services 6
			Percentage Distribution					
Guadeloupe	1970	1330	91	27	20	1	16	54
(French Francs)	1975	2826	87	28	19	-0	13	47
	1980	5860	87	32	25	1	8	53
	1985	9802	95	35	22	0	7	59
	1990	15200	93	31	34	1	5	63
	1995	22157	88	30	31	1	5	56
	2000	30578	92	32	33	1	5	59
	2001	32693	93	32	33	1	5	59
Guatemala [17]	1970	1904	78	8	13	0	19	18
(Quetzalas)	1975	3646	79	7	16	0	22	24
	1980	7879	79	8	16	-1	22	25
	1985	11180	83	7	11	1	18	20
	1990	34317	84	7	13	1	20	24
	1995	85157	86	6	15	1	19	25
	1996	95479	87	5	13	-1	18	23
	1997	107943	87	5	15	-1	18	24
	1998	121548	87	6	16	-0	18	26
	1999	132588	86	7	17	-1	19	27
	2000	145486	85	8	15	1	20	29
	2001	158201	86	8	15	0	18	28
Guyana [18]	1970	536	60	17	21	2	56	57
(Dollars Guyana)	1975	1188	47	20	29	4	75	74
	1980	1508	53	29	27	3	69	81
	1985	1964	54	36	21	...	53	63
	1990	15665	61	14	42	...	68	92
	1995	88271	46	16	45	...	122	130
	1996	99038	45	18	44	...	120	126
	1997	106678	45	20	44	...	116	125
	1998	108002	49	21	42	-0	113	125
	1999	123665	44	24	35	2	116	121
	2000	130013	50	28	32	6	113	129
	2001	133544	60	18	38	...	113	130
Haiti	1970	1656	85	10	10	...	16	21
(Gourdes)	1975	3407	84	9	16	...	23	32
	1980	6919	88	11	18	...	31	48
	1985	10047	83	11	17	...	27	38
	1990	13068	82	7	14	...	18	22
	1995	37135	96	7	13	...	10	31
	1996	44952	93	6	14	...	12	29
	1997	53447	93	7	12	...	11	26
	1998	60898	93	6	12	...	13	28
	1999	68421	93	6	13	...	13	27
	2000	77149	96	6	12	...	13	31
	2001	88502	100	6	11	...	13	31
Honduras	1970	1382	73	12	19	2	29	35
(Lempiras)	1975	2248	78	12	21	-2	30	40
	1980	5132	69	13	25	0	37	44
	1985	7279	74	13	17	0	25	30
	1990	12537	67	13	20	3	37	40
	1995	37507	64	9	24	8	44	48
	1996	47763	64	10	24	7	47	52
	1997	61322	65	9	26	7	46	52
	1998	70438	67	10	28	3	46	54
	1999	77095	69	11	30	5	41	56
	2000	87523	70	12	27	5	42	56
	2001	98379	69	12	27	6	41	55
Jamaica	1970	1270	61	12	31	0	33	37
(Jamaican Dollars)	1975	2833	66	18	23	2	35	45
	1980	5200	66	20	14	1	51	53
	1985	12204	69	16	23	2	58	68
	1990	33202	62	14	27	0	52	56
	1995	200027	67	12	31	0	55	67
	1996	237382	66	14	32	0	48	60

Table 2. Gross Domestic Product by Type of Expenditure: Individual Countries or Areas

Major area, region and country	Year	Gross Domestic Product (at current prices) Million	Household final consumption expenditure 1	General government final consumption expenditure 2	Gross fixed capital formation 3	Changes in inventories 4	Exports of goods and services 5	Imports of goods and services 6
			Percentage Distribution					
	1997	258026	66	16	32	0	43	57
	1998	273429	65	18	28	0	44	55
	1999	294076	63	17	28	0	45	54
	2000	329171	64	17	29	0	45	55
	2001	358036	64	17	29	0	45	56
Martinique (French Francs)	1970	1600	87	31	24	-1	10	51
	1975	3358	81	34	18	-1	12	44
	1980	6102	90	37	21	3	9	59
	1985	12484	87	34	17	-0	12	49
	1990	19320	84	30	27	2	8	50
	1995	24148	84	29	25	1	7	46
	2000	29282	85	29	25	1	8	49
	2001	30501	85	29	25	1	8	50
Mexico [19] (New Pesos)	1970	495	74	7	20	5	8	11
	1975	1226	70	9	21	4	7	11
	1980	4766	63	10	24	6	13	16
	1985	50530	63	9	18	5	18	13
	1990	738898	70	8	18	5	19	20
	1995	1837020	67	10	16	4	30	28
	1996	2525580	65	10	18	5	32	30
	1997	3174280	64	10	20	6	30	30
	1998	3846350	67	10	21	3	31	33
	1999	4593690	66	11	21	2	31	32
	2000	5485370	67	11	21	2	31	33
	2001	5765920	69	12	20	1	28	30
Montserrat (EC Dollars)	1970	13	107	23	36	4	33	102
	1975	25	107	23	36	4	33	102
	1980	66	109	18	33	8	24	92
	1985	100	86	20	33	2	33	73
	1990	181	62	18	72	2	29	81
	1995	162	62	23	33	2	61	81
	1996	131	24	41	38	2	109	114
	1997	110	49	52	50	0	56	107
	1998	101	63	56	66	0	38	124
	1999	95	43	57	64	0	60	125
	2000	94	77	47	47	-3	44	117
	2001	94	77	48	40	...	39	109
Netherlands Antilles [20] (Guilders)	1970	517	75	26	16	3	100	119
	1975	824	75	26	16	3	100	119
	1980	1558	72	27	16	3	93	111
	1985	1966	70	32	15	1	67	84
	1990	3253	26	26	24	2	78	90
	1995	4224	67	27	21	-0	72	87
	2000	4458	60	18	17	0	64	64
	2001	4557	61	17	16	0	61	62
Nicaragua (Gold Cordobas)	1970	1 (u)	75	10	17	2	27	30
	1975	2 (u)	80	9	23	-1	28	38
	1980	4 (u)	85	19	14	2	23	43
	1985	22 (u)	49	36	21	2	15	23
	1990	303	68	32	21	-1	25	45
	1995	13855	87	16	25	0	32	60
	1996	16204	92	17	27	1	31	67
	1997	18601	96	17	31	1	37	82
	1998	21881	93	17	33	0	37	81
	1999	26130	95	19	43	0	35	92
	2000	30858	92	19	35	-0	36	82
	2001	34242	92	20	33	0	32	78
Panama (Balboas)	1970	1003	63	15	26	4	82	93
	1975	1820	59	19	30	4	103	121
	1980	3545	58	19	25	6	97	104
	1985	5006	66	21	17	-0	68	72
	1990	5313	57	18	9	8	87	79

Table 2. Gross Domestic Product by Type of Expenditure: Individual Countries or Areas

Major area, region and country	Year	Gross Domestic Product (at current prices) Million	Household final consumption expenditure 1	General government final consumption expenditure 2	Gross fixed capital formation 3	Changes in inventories 4	Exports of goods and services 5	Imports of goods and services 6
			Percentage Distribution					
	1995	7906	52	15	26	4	101	98
	1996	8151	53	16	25	5	93	92
	1997	8658	54	16	27	5	98	100
	1998	9345	57	16	28	4	90	95
	1999	9637	55	16	30	3	77	81
	2000	10019	57	16	26	2	79	81
	2001	10195	56	16	26	2	80	81
Paraguay [21]	1970	74921	77	9	15	0	15	16
(Guaranies)	1975	190439	75	6	21	3	13	19
	1980	560459	71	6	27	2	14	20
	1985	1393890	76	6	21	1	22	26
	1990	6474434	77	6	22	1	33	39
	1995	17699000	85	7	23	1	35	51
	1996	19804807	85	8	23	1	29	45
	1997	20934352	85	8	23	1	27	43
	1998	23436984	86	8	22	1	28	45
	1999	24144290	82	9	22	1	23	37
	2000	26920974	83	10	21	1	20	34
	2001	28118844	88	9	19	1	22	38
Peru	1970	241 (u)	72	13	13	...	21	18
(New Soles)	1975	573 (u)	75	13	20	...	13	24
	1980	5143 (u)	62	12	22	...	26	25
	1985	170530 (u)	64	12	20	...	24	17
	1990	5851	72	9	19	-1	14	13
	1995	120859	71	10	24	1	13	18
	1996	136929	72	10	22	0	13	18
	1997	157274	71	10	24	0	14	19
	1998	166513	71	11	24	0	13	19
	1999	174719	70	11	22	-0	15	17
	2000	186757	71	11	20	-0	16	18
	2001	189769	70	11	20	...	17	18
Puerto Rico	1970	5647	73	16	28	2	41	63
(US Dollars)	1975	8969	81	18	20	2	47	70
	1980	15956	73	15	14	1	68	73
	1985	21969	70	14	11	-0	67	63
	1990	32287	62	14	16	0	78	71
	1995	45341	59	14	17	1	64	57
	1996	48187	60	14	18	1	64	59
	1997	54086	57	13	17	0	67	56
	1998	57841	56	13	20	1	70	62
	1999	61045	57	12	19	1	73	63
	2000	67897	53	11	17	1	78	63
	2001	73244	52	11	17	1	82	66
Saint Kitts and Nevis	1970	34	98	22	15	6	34	73
(EC Dollars)	1975	74	77	16	10	2	63	69
	1980	129	72	20	38	...	67	97
	1985	211	71	23	28	2	55	79
	1990	430	58	18	55	...	52	85
	1995	623	57	20	46	...	51	75
	1996	663	61	20	46	...	52	79
	1997	742	54	19	44	...	53	71
	1998	775	53	19	43	...	52	67
	1999	823	68	21	36	...	47	72
	2000	891	59	21	49	...	46	75
	2001	928	49	20	57	...	45	71
Saint Lucia	1970	79	95	19	26	5	41	82
(EC Dollars)	1975	129	95	19	26	5	41	82
	1980	305	80	14	44	9	70	115
	1985	441	61	17	18	...	45	53
	1990	1123	70	15	25	...	68	78
	1995	1496	59	17	25	...	69	70
	1996	1543	64	17	25	...	62	68
	1997	1562	65	18	27	...	62	72

Table 2. Gross Domestic Product by Type of Expenditure: Individual Countries or Areas

Major area, region and country	Year	Gross Domestic Product (at current prices) Million	Household final consumption expenditure 1	General government final consumption expenditure 2	Gross fixed capital formation 3	Changes in inventories 4	Exports of goods and services 5	Imports of goods and services 6
			Percentage Distribution					
	1998	1695	66	18	25	...	61	69
	1999	1848	70	16	26	...	55	67
	2000	1913	70	16	25	1	55	65
	2001	1980	69	16	26	1	55	66
Saint Vincent and the Grenadines.................	1970	37	83	23	32	...	53	91
(EC Dollars)	1975	71	83	23	32	...	53	91
	1980	160	88	23	39	...	56	107
	1985	305	58	20	25	3	73	79
	1990	535	68	21	30	1	66	77
	1995	712	64	20	30	...	52	66
	1996	752	65	20	28	...	53	67
	1997	793	80	19	30	...	50	78
	1998	858	79	18	32	...	50	78
	1999	890	70	19	32	...	53	74
	2000	905	62	19	27	...	53	61
	2001	940	65	20	30	...	51	65
Suriname..	1970	532	52	25	18	...	54	49
(Guilders)	1975	931	53	21	27	5	62	68
	1980	1590	58	21	22	5	69	74
	1985	1746	55	34	18	-3	37	40
	1990	3170	54	24	18	2	27	27
	1995	229510	16	20	44	8	100	88
	1996	303970	59	15	29	6	66	74
	1997	340220	60	18	24	6	57	65
	1998	407130	71	19	23	...	42	56
	1999	758905	47	16	26	10	77	76
	2000	1172225	47	16	26	10	77	76
	2001	1834219	47	16	26	10	77	76
Trinidad and Tobago.....................................	1970	1644	62	13	21	5	46	49
(Trinidad and Tobago Dollars)	1975	5300	44	12	20	7	57	42
	1980	14966	47	12	28	3	55	46
	1985	18071	56	23	20	-1	35	34
	1990	21539	55	16	14	0	49	34
	1995	31697	49	16	19	2	54	39
	1996	34587	50	16	23	1	51	41
	1997	35871	58	15	29	1	54	57
	1998	38065	58	14	31	2	48	54
	1999	42889	59	15	21	0	50	44
	2000	51485	54	12	20	0	59	45
	2001	56700	54	13	22	0	53	43
Uruguay [22]..	1970	1	69	16	14	2	13	14
(Pesos)	1975	8	71	14	17	3	17	21
	1980	87	70	13	21	4	16	22
	1985	479	69	14	10	2	27	21
	1990	9784	69	14	11	0	26	20
	1995	122521	73	12	14	2	19	19
	1996	163546	72	13	14	1	20	20
	1997	204926	72	12	14	1	21	21
	1998	234267	72	13	15	1	20	21
	1999	237143	73	13	14	1	18	19
	2000	243027	75	13	13	1	19	21
	2001	247211	74	14	13	1	18	20
Venezuela [23]...	1970	62884	53	11	25	11	21	17
(Bolivares)	1975	142749	48	11	29	7	30	23
	1980	307262	54	12	28	1	31	23
	1985	464741	61	10	17	1	25	16
	1990	2279261	61	8	14	-4	39	20
	1995	13685686	68	7	16	2	27	22
	1996	29437682	62	5	16	1	37	21
	1997	43343669	64	6	19	2	28	22
	1998	52482466	70	8	19	3	20	21

Table 2. Gross Domestic Product by Type of Expenditure: Individual Countries or Areas

Major area, region and country	Year	Gross Domestic Product (at current prices) Million	Household final consumption expenditure 1	General government final consumption expenditure 2	Gross fixed capital formation 3	Changes in inventories 4	Exports of goods and services 5	Imports of goods and services 6
			Percentage Distribution					
	1999	62577039	67	8	16	2	22	16
	2000	82450674	62	7	14	3	28	16
	2001	91324773	65	9	16	3	22	17
ASIA								
Armenia [24]	1990	50	49	17	44	3	35	46
(Drams)	1995	522256	106	11	16	2	24	62
	1996	661209	100	11	18	2	23	56
	1997	804336	103	11	16	3	20	58
	1998	955385	100	11	16	3	19	53
	1999	987444	96	12	16	2	21	50
	2000	1031338	97	12	18	0	23	51
	2001	1175487	94	11	17	2	26	46
Azerbaijan [25]	1990	1466	52	18	20	6	44	39
(Azerbaijan Manats)	1995	10669000	84	13	16	8	32	53
	1996	13663200	87	12	29	-0	25	56
	1997	15791400	73	13	37	-3	29	53
	1998	17203100	79	15	36	-2	23	55
	1999	18875400	74	16	29	-2	28	42
	2000	23590500	63	15	23	-2	40	38
	2001	26341900	60	12	21	-0	43	38
Bahrain [26]	1970	119	64	11	30	-4	95	100
(Dinars)	1975	410	63	12	18	1	103	103
	1980	1241	51	11	22	16	92	102
	1985	1472	48	29	22	5	77	81
	1990	1614	56	24	18	-1	92	90
	1995	2199	53	21	17	-3	82	70
	1996	2294	54	20	12	2	88	76
	1997	2387	54	19	12	5	79	70
	1998	2325	57	21	14	7	65	64
	1999	2489	55	21	14	-5	77	62
	2000	2996	47	18	14	-3	88	64
	2001	3131	46	17	13	...	87	63
Bangladesh [27]	1970	75214	83	1	10	0	7	...
(Taka)	1975	145481	90	4	14	0	4	13
	1980	305196	84	4	23	1	6	15
	1985	614824	85	4	17	0	6	13
	1990	1100331	83	4	15	2	7	12
	1995	1663240	81	4	20	...	11	19
	1996	1807013	80	4	21	...	12	18
	1997	2001766	78	5	22	...	13	18
	1998	2196972	78	5	22	...	13	19
	1999	2370856	78	5	23	...	14	19
	2000	2535464	77	5	23	...	15	22
	2001	2714142	78	4	23	...	17	23
Bhutan	1970	346	75	25	43	-3	16	56
(Ngultrum)	1975	870	75	25	43	-3	16	56
	1980	1095	68	25	30	1	13	37
	1985	2392	63	23	42	3	15	47
	1990	4983	52	16	37	-1	28	32
	1995	10064	34	24	45	2	37	42
	1996	11808	44	21	43	2	34	43
	1997	14314	50	26	39	-4	33	43
	1998	16337	57	20	38	0	32	47
	1999	19123	53	22	42	1	30	48
	2000	21698	52	20	44	0	30	46
	2001	24126	52	20	44	0	30	46
Brunei Darussalam [28]	1970	546	7	17	3	0	90	17
(Brunei Darussalam Dollars)	1975	2770	11	17	5	0	90	23
	1980	10554	7	8	3	0	93	12
	1985	7752	11	9	10	-0	88	19
	1990	6509	11	12	10	-0	106	39

Table 2. Gross Domestic Product by Type of Expenditure: Individual Countries or Areas

Major area, region and country	Year	Gross Domestic Product (at current prices) Million	Household final consumption expenditure 1	General government final consumption expenditure 2	Gross fixed capital formation 3	Changes in inventories 4	Exports of goods and services 5	Imports of goods and services 6
			Percentage Distribution					
	1995	7394	11	11	9	-0	90	26
	1996	7685	11	11	9	-0	100	31
	1997	8051	11	11	9	-0	100	31
	1998	8111	11	11	9	-0	100	31
	1999	7145	11	12	11	-2	100	37
	2000	7441	11	12	11	-2	99	35
	2001	7619	11	10	11	-2	101	37
Cambodia	1970	10708	93	7	12	-0	2	10
(Riels)	1975	8830	93	7	12	-0	2	10
	1980	8395	93	7	12	-0	2	10
	1985	16965	93	7	12	-0	2	10
	1990	723653	95	7	9	-0	2	8
	1995	8110680	89	5	13	0	33	44
	1996	8885580	88	6	12	2	27	40
	1997	9778060	87	6	13	1	34	42
	1998	11363640	88	5	12	-1	37	45
	1999	12587090	86	5	14	1	38	46
	2000	12931530	82	6	15	-2	49	51
	2001	13364930	80	6	16	2	51	53
China [29]	1970	225270	65	8	23	6	3	3
(Yuan Renminbi)	1975	299730	62	8	24	7	5	5
	1980	451780	51	15	29	6	6	7
	1985	872944	53	14	30	9	10	14
	1990	1831950	50	12	26	9	18	12
	1995	5847810	46	11	35	6	21	19
	1996	6788460	47	12	34	5	21	19
	1997	7446260	47	12	34	4	23	19
	1998	7834520	47	12	36	3	22	18
	1999	8206750	48	13	36	1	22	19
	2000	8944220	49	13	36	-0	26	23
	2001	9593330	50	14	37	-0	26	24
Cyprus [30]	1970	229	80	10	24	3	38	47
(Pounds)	1975	260	86	18	20	5	35	56
	1980	760	66	14	34	4	45	63
	1985	1481	63	14	27	3	49	59
	1990	2556	59	17	25	2	52	57
	1995	4007	64	16	19	3	47	50
	1996	4161	65	18	20	2	47	53
	1997	4371	66	19	19	1	47	52
	1998	4694	67	19	19	2	44	51
	1999	5019	66	17	18	1	45	48
	2000	5487	69	16	18	1	46	52
	2001	5865	69	17	17	1	47	52
Georgia	1990	1	61	17	24	7	40	46
(Laris)	1995	3694	76	8	19	5	14	29
	1996	3846	102	8	10	1	13	33
	1997	4638	97	10	10	1	15	41
	1998	5041	86	11	11	1	16	37
	1999	5666	83	10	18	1	19	38
	2000	6016	88	8	17	1	23	40
	2001	6617	83	9	17	1	23	39
Hong Kong SAR of China	1970	23369	62	7	20	1	93	85
(Hong Kong Dollars)	1975	50012	61	7	22	1	83	78
	1980	143976	57	6	33	3	88	89
	1985	275832	58	7	21	1	107	98
	1990	591507	53	7	26	1	132	123
	1995	1096263	57	9	31	4	146	150
	1996	1210925	56	9	31	1	140	140
	1997	1344546	56	8	34	1	130	133
	1998	1279850	56	9	30	-1	127	125
	1999	1246134	55	10	26	-1	131	125
	2000	1288338	53	9	27	1	147	142
	2001	1278995	54	10	27	-0	141	136

Table 2. Gross Domestic Product by Type of Expenditure: Individual Countries or Areas

Major area, region and country	Year	Gross Domestic Product (at current prices) Million	Household final consumption expenditure 1	General government final consumption expenditure 2	Gross fixed capital formation 3	Changes in inventories 4	Exports of goods and services 5	Imports of goods and services 6
			Percentage Distribution					
India [31]	1970	457435	82	9	15	3	4	4
(Rupees)	1975	834698	79	10	17	4	6	7
	1980	1441446	78	10	19	2	6	9
	1985	2779213	73	11	21	4	5	8
	1990	5675511	67	12	23	2	7	9
	1995	11880120	64	11	24	2	11	12
	1996	13682080	66	11	23	-1	11	12
	1997	15225470	64	11	22	1	11	12
	1998	17409350	65	12	22	-0	11	13
	1999	19296410	65	13	22	2	12	14
	2000	20879880	64	13	22	1	14	15
	2001	22779949	64	13	22	2	13	14
Indonesia	1970	3238000	80	9	14	...	13	16
(Rupiahs)	1975	12643000	69	10	20	...	23	22
	1980	45446000	61	10	21	...	30	22
	1985	96997000	59	11	23	5	22	20
	1990	210866000	57	9	28	2	25	24
	1995	454513000	61	8	28	3	26	28
	1996	532567000	62	8	30	1	26	26
	1997	627695000	61	7	28	3	28	28
	1998	955754000	67	6	25	-9	53	43
	1999	1099732000	73	7	20	-9	36	27
	2000	1282018000	67	7	21	-6	42	32
	2001	1490974000	66	7	21	-4	41	33
Iran (Islamic Republic of) [32]	1970	754383	43	18	36	-3	20	30
(Rials)	1975	3282929	34	24	42	-13	43	49
	1980	6447256	43	22	33	3	13	24
	1985	15335563	49	16	26	-1	8	12
	1990	35623226	55	12	23	11	15	27
	1995	175703100	50	14	22	4	23	14
	1996	240616600	47	14	28	5	22	15
	1997	285509100	49	14	30	3	18	16
	1998	325332000	55	15	30	-1	14	16
	1999	430990500	51	14	31	-2	22	15
	2000	568799400	46	14	30	1	23	17
	2001	665656300	45	15	31	3	20	18
Iraq	1970	1257	46	22	15	1	35	19
(Dinars)	1975	4090	35	21	26	9	51	41
	1980	15948	23	15	24	7	63	31
	1985	15494	52	29	28	-4	24	29
	1990	23297	50	26	27	-4	18	18
	1995	1940994	75	22	5	-2	2	2
	1996	2379254	78	23	2	-1	5	7
	1997	3269914	76	19	7	-1	10	12
	1998	4570100	75	18	8	-0	12	13
	1999	6809790	75	17	9	-0	13	14
	2000	7398604	74	16	11	-0	15	15
	2001	8878324	74	15	12	-0	16	17
Israel	1970	2	48	39	28	0	22	39
(New Shekels)	1975	9	45	45	30	0	25	45
	1980	120	46	38	23	-0	38	47
	1985	31593	50	33	19	0	38	43
	1990	115397	54	28	20	0	31	35
	1995	286397	55	28	24	1	29	37
	1996	332167	54	28	24	1	28	36
	1997	372190	53	28	23	1	29	34
	1998	408522	53	27	21	0	30	33
	1999	446760	53	27	21	2	34	38
	2000	487013	52	26	19	1	39	39
	2001	491499	54	28	18	2	34	37
Japan	1970	74450690	48	10	36	4	11	9
(Yen)	1975	150563261	53	14	33	0	13	13
	1980	243796700	54	13	32	1	13	14

Table 2. Gross Domestic Product by Type of Expenditure: Individual Countries or Areas

Major area, region and country	Year	Gross Domestic Product (at current prices) Million	Household final consumption expenditure 1	General government final consumption expenditure 2	Gross fixed capital formation 3	Changes in inventories 4	Exports of goods and services 5	Imports of goods and services 6
			Percentage Distribution					
	1985	326815700	54	14	28	1	14	11
	1990	442072300	52	13	32	1	10	9
	1995	498872300	54	15	28	0	9	8
	1996	511946800	54	15	28	1	10	9
	1997	523051100	54	15	28	1	11	10
	1998	516579200	55	16	27	0	11	9
	1999	509115900	55	16	26	-0	10	8
	2000	513376800	54	17	26	-0	11	9
	2001	507455500	55	17	26	-0	10	10
Jordan [33] (Dinars)	1970	212	76	36	13	-1	8	36
	1975	390	83	37	25	2	30	77
	1980	1196	74	27	36	4	39	80
	1985	2020	89	26	19	1	39	74
	1990	2668	74	25	26	6	62	93
	1995	4773	64	23	29	3	51	72
	1996	4982	69	24	29	1	52	77
	1997	5193	70	25	26	-0	49	71
	1998	5646	72	24	21	1	45	64
	1999	5765	74	25	19	...	45	64
	2000	6012	76	24	20	...	47	66
	2001	6343	77	24	19	...	47	67
Kazakhstan (Tenge)	1990	96	63	12	39	8	8	30
	1995	1014190	70	14	23	0	39	44
	1996	1415750	66	13	17	-1	35	36
	1997	1672142	70	12	16	-1	35	37
	1998	1733264	73	11	16	0	30	35
	1999	2016456	72	12	16	2	42	40
	2000	2599902	61	12	17	1	57	48
	2001	3250593	57	13	24	3	46	48
Kuwait (Dinars)	1970	1026	39	14	12	-0	60	24
	1975	3485	22	11	12	1	81	26
	1980	7755	30	11	13	1	78	33
	1985	6450	48	22	20	-1	54	43
	1990	5328	59	39	16	0	45	58
	1995	7925	41	33	14	1	54	43
	1996	9303	44	28	14	1	53	40
	1997	9060	46	27	14	0	54	40
	1998	7656	57	31	19	0	45	53
	1999	8886	51	28	15	0	47	41
	2000	10991	42	23	8	...	59	32
	2001	10057	48	26	9	...	55	37
Kyrgyzstan (Som)	1990	43	68	25	22	2	29	50
	1995	16145	73	20	20	-2	29	42
	1996	23399	80	19	22	3	31	57
	1997	30686	67	17	12	9	38	46
	1998	34181	87	18	13	3	36	58
	1999	48744	74	19	16	2	42	57
	2000	65358	63	20	18	2	42	48
	2001	73883	62	17	17	1	37	37
Lao People's Democratic Republic (Kips)	1970	36	90	8	7	...	3	8
	1975	194	90	8	7	...	3	8
	1980	8484	90	8	7	...	4	8
	1985	84406	90	9	7	...	4	10
	1990	612681	93	12	17	...	18	40
	1995	1419090	80	8	26	...	23	37
	2000	13671292	81	6	25	...	37	48
	2001	15669988	78	6	25	...	37	48
Lebanon (Lebanese Pounds)	1970	4866	86	11	19	-1	24	39
	1975	7500	87	6	18	...	19	30
	1980	14000	92	25	54	-38	39	72
	1985	29988	120	59	36	...	15	130
	1990	1954275	90	46	39	...	16	91

Table 2. Gross Domestic Product by Type of Expenditure: Individual Countries or Areas

Major area, region and country	Year	Gross Domestic Product (at current prices) Million	Household final consumption expenditure 1	General government final consumption expenditure 2	Gross fixed capital formation 3	Changes in inventories 4	Exports of goods and services 5	Imports of goods and services 6
			Percentage Distribution					
	1995	17779000	108	10	36	...	11	65
	2000	25959168	104	10	21	...	7	42
	2001	27127330	103	10	21	...	7	42
Macao SAR of China	1970	1060	80	3	21	0	111	104
(Dollars)	1975	2361	65	4	22	0	110	96
	1980	5250	53	5	22	1	109	89
	1985	10950	45	6	22	3	105	80
	1990	26175	37	9	25	1	97	67
	1995	55333	33	8	29	0	74	46
	1996	55294	36	9	21	1	76	44
	1997	55894	37	10	21	0	76	45
	1998	51902	39	12	19	-0	77	47
	1999	49021	40	14	18	0	80	53
	2000	49742	40	12	12	0	94	59
	2001	49802	40	12	10	0	98	62
Malaysia	1970	10588	60	16	16	3	41	36
(Ringgit)	1975	22332	59	18	25	-2	46	45
	1980	53308	51	17	31	-1	58	55
	1985	77470	52	15	30	-2	55	50
	1990	119081	52	14	33	-1	74	72
	1995	222473	48	12	44	0	94	98
	1996	253732	46	11	42	-1	92	90
	1997	281795	45	11	43	-0	93	92
	1998	283243	42	10	27	-0	116	94
	1999	300764	42	11	22	0	121	96
	2000	342157	42	11	26	1	125	105
	2001	334589	45	13	25	-1	116	98
Maldives	1970	74	36	18	32	...	92	77
(Rufiyaa)	1975	152	36	18	32	...	92	77
	1980	356	36	18	32	...	92	77
	1985	596	36	18	32	...	92	77
	1990	2060	36	18	32	...	92	77
	1995	4714	37	17	31	...	92	77
	2000	7035	34	24	22	...	94	75
	2001	7146	34	25	23	...	93	76
Mongolia	1970	4980	54	24	60	4	29	62
(Tughriks)	1975	6530	54	24	60	4	29	62
	1980	8723	54	24	60	4	29	62
	1985	12102	54	25	62	5	31	68
	1990	13514	63	27	41	0	19	40
	1995	554249	63	13	27	5	48	49
	1996	659698	65	14	27	2	40	47
	1997	846344	60	13	25	2	58	52
	1998	833727	66	17	34	2	54	67
	1999	925346	68	17	35	2	59	72
	2000	1044580	70	17	31	4	64	81
	2001	1158210	70	18	29	...	72	92
Myanmar [34]	1970	13504	42	50	11	3	4	12
(Kyats)	1975	23477	42	49	7	3	5	6
	1980	38609	38	44	19	3	8	12
	1985	55989	41	48	15	0	5	9
	1990	151941	76	12	15	-1	2	4
	1995	604729	75	12	14	1	1	2
	1996	791980	76	12	15	-3	1	1
	1997	1109554	76	12	14	-1	1	1
	1998	1559996	77	13	12	-1	1	1
	1999	1615142	77	11	13	-1	0	1
	2000	1878745	80	12	11	-3	0	1
	2001	2264960	81	11	9	-2	0	1

Table 2. Gross Domestic Product by Type of Expenditure: Individual Countries or Areas

Major area, region and country	Year	Gross Domestic Product (at current prices) Million	Household final consumption expenditure 1	General government final consumption expenditure 2	Gross fixed capital formation 3	Changes in inventories 4	Exports of goods and services 5	Imports of goods and services 6
			Percentage Distribution					
Nepal (Rupees)	1970	9816	86	9	5	1	5	7
	1975	16571	81	8	13	1	9	13
	1980	23351	81	7	16	3	11	19
	1985	46587	77	9	20	2	12	20
	1990	103416	83	9	16	2	11	21
	1995	219175	75	9	22	3	24	35
	1996	248913	76	9	23	5	22	36
	1997	280513	76	9	22	4	26	38
	1998	300845	77	9	22	3	23	34
	1999	342036	77	9	19	1	23	30
	2000	378033	76	9	19	4	24	33
	2001	408218	76	10	19	4	23	32
Oman [35] (Rials)	1970	113	31	8	12	-1	67	19
	1975	767	23	21	29	2	65	42
	1980	2185	42	14	20	-0	59	36
	1985	3591	41	22	25	-0	48	36
	1990	4493	41	27	12	...	47	28
	1995	5307	49	28	15	...	44	36
	1996	5874	48	25	14	-0	50	36
	1997	6090	48	23	18	...	50	39
	1998	5416	58	26	24	0	42	49
	1999	6041	50	24	15	0	49	37
	2000	7639	39	21	12	0	59	31
	2001	7668	41	24	13	...	57	35
Pakistan (Rupees)	1970	50938	76	10	15	2	8	10
	1975	130741	76	11	20	-0	11	18
	1980	278196	81	10	17	2	13	22
	1985	514532	76	13	17	2	12	20
	1990	1020600	68	14	17	2	17	18
	1995	2120173	73	13	17	2	17	21
	1996	2428312	75	12	16	2	16	21
	1997	2677656	72	11	15	3	16	18
	1998	2938379	76	10	14	2	15	17
	1999	3147167	74	11	14	2	16	18
	2000	3416252	75	10	14	2	18	19
	2001	3726611	75	11	12	2	18	18
Philippines (Pesos)	1970	39505	66	9	18	3	22	21
	1975	107953	62	11	25	6	21	27
	1980	243749	63	9	27	2	24	28
	1985	571883	74	8	16	-2	24	22
	1990	1077237	71	10	23	1	28	33
	1995	1905951	74	11	22	0	36	44
	1996	2171922	73	12	23	1	41	49
	1997	2426743	73	13	24	0	49	59
	1998	2665060	74	13	21	-1	52	59
	1999	2976904	73	13	19	-0	51	51
	2000	3308318	71	13	19	-0	56	50
	2001	3639980	70	13	17	0	48	47
Qatar (Riyals)	1970	1437	23	21	23	1	63	30
	1975	9707	23	21	23	1	63	30
	1980	28663	16	20	17	0	74	26
	1985	22398	25	35	18	0	51	30
	1990	26792	28	33	17	1	53	32
	1995	29622	32	32	30	5	44	43
	1996	32976	27	33	35	1	44	40
	1997	41124	23	30	35	1	40	36
	1998	37330	25	32	31	1	51	40
	1999	45111	21	26	18	1	60	26
	2000	64646	15	19	19	1	67	22
	2001	62341	16	21	23	1	66	26

Table 2. Gross Domestic Product by Type of Expenditure: Individual Countries or Areas

Major area, region and country	Year	Gross Domestic Product (at current prices) Million	Household final consumption expenditure 1	General government final consumption expenditure 2	Gross fixed capital formation 3	Changes in inventories 4	Exports of goods and services 5	Imports of goods and services 6
			Percentage Distribution					
Republic of Korea [36]	1970	2725190	74	9	26	-0	14	24
(Wons)	1975	10228100	68	11	27	2	27	36
	1980	37788500	63	12	32	-0	33	41
	1985	81312300	56	10	29	1	33	32
	1990	178797000	51	10	37	0	29	30
	1995	377350000	54	10	37	0	30	32
	1996	418479000	55	10	37	1	30	34
	1997	453276000	55	10	35	-1	35	36
	1998	444367000	54	11	30	-9	50	36
	1999	482744000	55	10	28	-1	42	35
	2000	521959000	56	10	28	-0	45	42
	2001	551558000	58	10	27	-0	42	40
Saudi Arabia [37]	1970	22921	28	17	13	-1	66	23
(Riyals)	1975	164526	15	18	20	0	73	26
	1980	490942	22	17	21	-0	71	30
	1985	313941	51	36	24	-3	36	44
	1990	391993	40	32	19	2	47	39
	1995	478652	40	26	20	1	44	31
	1996	590749	44	25	17	1	40	27
	1997	617902	42	26	18	1	39	26
	1998	546648	46	28	21	2	30	27
	1999	603589	42	26	20	2	35	23
	2000	706657	37	26	17	1	44	25
	2001	698403	37	27	18	1	42	24
Singapore [38]	1970	5805	68	12	33	6	-20	...
(Singapore Dollars)	1975	13443	60	11	36	4	-11	...
	1980	25091	51	10	41	6	-9	...
	1985	38924	45	14	42	0	-2	...
	1990	67879	45	10	32	4	9	...
	1995	117768	41	9	34	1	16	...
	1996	128244	41	10	38	-1	14	...
	1997	140279	40	9	39	-0	14	...
	1998	137618	39	10	37	-4	19	...
	1999	140070	41	10	34	-2	19	...
	2000	159888	40	11	29	2	18	...
	2001	153455	42	12	29	-5	22	...
Sri Lanka [39]	1970	14259	71	12	17	3	24	27
(Rupees)	1975	27227	80	10	13	2	27	34
	1980	68809	78	10	33	1	31	53
	1985	158852	74	12	24	0	27	39
	1990	320098	74	13	20	1	30	38
	1995	666956	70	15	26	0	36	45
	1996	776739	68	14	26	1	35	43
	1997	897218	67	14	26	0	36	43
	1998	1018330	66	14	26	0	36	42
	1999	1108845	68	14	26	1	35	43
	2000	1253622	70	14	25	1	39	50
	2001	1397453	69	13	21	2	39	46
Syrian Arab Republic	1970	6848	73	17	13	1	17	21
(Syrian Pounds)	1975	20711	63	21	25	4	21	34
	1980	51270	66	23	28	...	18	35
	1985	83225	66	24	24	...	12	25
	1990	268328	69	14	17	...	28	28
	1995	570975	66	13	27	...	31	38
	1996	690857	71	12	24	...	32	38
	1997	745569	69	11	21	...	32	34
	1998	790444	69	11	21	...	31	31
	1999	819092	70	11	19	...	32	32
	2000	903944	63	12	17	...	36	29
	2001	947808	61	15	18	...	38	31

Table 2. Gross Domestic Product by Type of Expenditure: Individual Countries or Areas

Major area, region and country	Year	Gross Domestic Product (at current prices) Million	Household final consumption expenditure 1	General government final consumption expenditure 2	Gross fixed capital formation 3	Changes in inventories 4	Exports of goods and services 5	Imports of goods and services 6
			Percentage Distribution					
Tajikistan	1990	7	63	7	7	5	57	40
(Tajik Roubles)	1995	70	59	11	21	7	112	121
	1996	308	57	9	13	9	73	63
	1997	518	58	11	18	2	82	85
	1998	1025	67	8	13	2	50	57
	1999	1345	69	9	17	2	68	66
	2000	1807	68	8	20	...	91	96
	2001	2512	71	9	22	...	76	86
Thailand	1970	148274	69	11	26	2	15	19
(Baht)	1975	305149	68	10	25	4	18	23
	1980	662482	65	12	28	1	24	30
	1985	1056496	62	14	27	1	23	26
	1990	2184000	57	9	40	1	34	42
	1995	4186212	53	10	41	1	42	49
	1996	4611041	54	10	41	1	39	46
	1997	4732610	55	10	34	-0	48	47
	1998	4626447	54	11	22	-2	59	43
	1999	4632132	56	12	21	-0	58	46
	2000	4904725	56	11	22	1	67	58
	2001	5099642	57	12	23	1	66	60
Timor-Leste	1997	384	...	...	...	53	13	46
(Rupiah)	1998	375	...	...	...	47	15	44
	1999	228	...	...	...	28	20	43
	2000	263	...	...	...	38	10	61
	2001	312	...	...	...	43	12	66
Turkey	1970	206000	66	8	18	1	4	6
(Liras)	1975	674000	65	9	20	3	5	11
	1980	5231000	74	7	16	1	5	12
	1985	35095000	65	7	22	0	16	19
	1990	393060000	61	9	23	1	13	18
	1995	7762460000	63	9	24	2	20	24
	1996	14772100000	60	9	25	-1	22	28
	1997	28835900000	60	9	26	-1	25	30
	1998	52224900000	61	10	25	-0	24	28
	1999	77415300000	63	11	22	1	23	27
	2000	1.24583E+11	63	11	22	2	24	32
	2001	1.81409E+11	63	11	18	-1	33	31
Turkmenistan	1990	7600	49	23	38	2	58	70
(Manats)	1995	652044	60	8	23	10	142	145
	1996	7751754	49	7	41	9	106	107
	1997	11108783	68	13	41	8	51	82
	1998	13994739	54	15	64	12	39	85
	1999	20056000	39	10	56	10	47	70
	2000	25648000	45	12	58	11	42	74
	2001	33863000	44	11	59	11	47	75
United Arab Emirates	1970	3160	13	12	20	4	85	34
(Dirhams)	1975	39460	16	8	31	...	75	29
	1980	109833	17	11	27	1	78	34
	1985	99416	28	20	25	0	58	31
	1990	124008	39	16	19	1	65	41
	1995	155210	49	17	29	...	67	63
	2000	195779	51	17	27	...	68	62
	2001	209483	51	17	27	...	66	60
Uzbekistan [40]	1990	32	60	25	31	1	29	48
(Sums)	1995	302787	50	22	33	-9	32	29
	1996	559072	54	22	37	-14	34	35
	1997	976830	60	20	34	-15	30	30
	1998	1416157	59	21	30	-9	-1	...
	1999	2128660	61	21	27	-10	0	...
	2000	3255600	61	19	24	-4	-0	...
	2001	4868400	61	18	26	-6	-0	...

Table 2. Gross Domestic Product by Type of Expenditure: Individual Countries or Areas

Major area, region and country	Year	Gross Domestic Product (at current prices) Million	Household final consumption expenditure 1	General government final consumption expenditure 2	Gross fixed capital formation 3	Changes in inventories 4	Exports of goods and services 5	Imports of goods and services 6
			Percentage Distribution					
Vietnam [41] (Dong)	1970	3989	90	7	12	2	-21	...
	1975	4071	90	7	12	2	-21	...
	1980	14031	90	7	11	2	-21	...
	1985	123000	91	6	12	2	-14	...
	1990	41955000	90	8	13	1	-9	...
	1995	228892000	74	8	25	2	-9	...
	1996	272036000	74	8	26	2	-11	...
	1997	313623000	72	8	27	2	-8	...
	1998	361017000	71	8	27	2	-7	...
	1999	399942000	69	7	26	2	-3	...
	2000	444139000	67	6	27	2	-2	...
	2001	485109000	65	6	28	2	-2	...
Yemen (Rials)	1990	129960	72	17	12	3	14	20
	1995	511058	84	14	21	1	22	42
	1996	736385	66	13	21	2	39	41
	1997	888808	64	13	22	3	36	38
	1998	849321	68	15	32	1	28	43
	1999	1132619	68	14	23	1	36	43
	2000	1379812	58	14	18	1	50	41
	2001	1354509	59	15	20	...	48	43
EUROPE								
Albania (Leks)	1970	6480	56	9	33	1	23	23
	1975	11462	56	9	33	1	23	23
	1980	15533	56	9	33	1	23	23
	1985	16857	59	9	33	0	16	18
	1990	16813	39	44	35	-10	15	23
	1995	229793	47	53	18	...	12	34
	1996	280998	52	57	16	...	14	41
	1997	341716	51	57	16	...	10	36
	1998	460631	51	56	16	...	9	32
	1999	506205	48	54	17	0	12	35
	2000	539210	49	55	19	0	14	38
	2001	590237	94	11	20	-0	15	39
Austria (Euros)	1970	28184	52	15	25	4	30	29
	1975	49196	54	18	26	-1	31	31
	1980	74723	53	18	25	2	36	38
	1985	100772	55	20	22	1	40	40
	1990	133603	54	19	24	1	40	38
	1995	172287	54	20	23	1	37	38
	1996	178045	55	20	23	0	38	39
	1997	182486	56	20	24	0	42	43
	1998	190628	55	20	24	0	43	44
	1999	197154	55	20	23	1	45	46
	2000	207037	55	19	24	0	50	51
	2001	211857	56	19	23	-0	52	52
Belarus [42] (Belarussian Roubles)	1990	4	45	24	22	5	46	44
	1995	121403	56	21	25	0	50	54
	1996	191839	57	21	21	2	46	50
	1997	366830	55	20	25	2	60	66
	1998	702161	55	20	26	1	59	64
	1999	3026064	57	20	26	-3	59	62
	2000	9133800	55	19	25	0	69	72
	2001	17173200	56	22	23	1	67	70
Belgium (Euros)	1970	31788	51	18	25	2	52	49
	1975	57501	53	21	25	-0	53	53
	1980	88287	55	23	23	1	58	61
	1985	121935	57	23	18	-0	72	71
	1990	163341	54	20	22	-0	71	69
	1995	202174	53	21	20	0	69	65
	1996	206989	53	22	20	-0	71	67
	1997	217173	53	21	20	-0	75	70
	1998	225244	53	21	21	-0	75	71

Table 2. Gross Domestic Product by Type of Expenditure: Individual Countries or Areas

Major area, region and country	Year	Gross Domestic Product (at current prices) Million	Household final consumption expenditure 1	General government final consumption expenditure 2	Gross fixed capital formation 3	Changes in inventories 4	Exports of goods and services 5	Imports of goods and services 6
			Percentage Distribution					
	1999	235632	52	21	21	-0	76	71
	2000	247469	53	21	21	0	86	82
	2001	254282	53	22	21	-0	85	82
Bosnia and Herzegovina (Convertible Marka)	1990	1	69	20	19	1	48	56
	1995	2861	67	25	16	3	43	55
	1996	4125	51	23	16	4	34	45
	1997	6311	63	29	20	5	43	56
	1998	7336	62	28	20	5	42	55
	1999	8604	61	28	20	5	41	54
	2000	9433	61	28	20	5	41	54
	2001	10247	59	27	19	4	40	53
Bulgaria [43] (Leva)	1970	13	58	4	37	...	33	39
	1975	18	59	6	39	...	33	48
	1980	26	62	6	28	...	33	35
	1985	33	61	8	26	...	33	35
	1990	45	67	7	21	...	33	37
	1995	880	70	15	15	0	45	46
	1996	1761	74	12	14	-5	55	50
	1997	17433	73	13	11	-1	58	54
	1998	22421	67	15	13	4	47	47
	1999	23790	71	17	15	3	45	50
	2000	26753	69	18	16	3	56	61
	2001	29618	69	18	18	3	56	63
Croatia (Kuna)	1990	280	66	24	13	...	78	81
	1995	98382	64	28	16	2	39	49
	1996	107981	61	25	20	1	40	50
	1997	123811	62	24	24	3	41	57
	1998	137604	59	25	23	1	40	49
	1999	141579	58	27	23	-0	41	49
	2000	152519	59	25	22	-2	47	52
	2001	162909	60	22	23	-1	49	55
Czech Republic [44] (Koruny)	1980	458393	45	20	23	7	54	49
	1985	522853	45	23	25	-0	53	45
	1990	626189	49	23	25	-0	45	43
	1995	1381050	50	20	32	2	54	58
	1996	1566970	51	20	32	2	53	59
	1997	1679920	53	20	31	2	57	62
	1998	1839090	52	19	29	1	59	60
	1999	1902290	53	20	28	0	61	62
	2000	1984830	53	20	28	1	70	73
	2001	2175240	52	20	28	2	71	73
Denmark (Kroner)	1970	122143	55	21	25	1	27	30
	1975	223381	53	25	22	-0	29	30
	1980	385808	53	27	20	-0	32	33
	1985	634018	51	26	21	1	36	36
	1990	825311	48	26	20	0	36	31
	1995	1009760	50	26	19	1	35	31
	1996	1060890	49	26	19	0	36	31
	1997	1116320	49	25	20	1	36	33
	1998	1155410	50	26	21	1	36	34
	1999	1207750	49	26	20	-0	38	33
	2000	1280780	47	25	21	0	44	38
	2001	1325270	46	26	20	0	45	39
Estonia [45] (Krooni)	1990	798	64	13	24	6	42	50
	1995	40897	58	26	26	1	72	80
	1996	52423	60	25	27	1	67	79
	1997	64045	59	23	28	3	78	90
	1998	73538	58	23	30	-0	80	90
	1999	76327	58	23	25	-0	77	82
	2000	87236	56	21	25	2	94	98
	2001	96571	56	20	26	2	91	94

Table 2. Gross Domestic Product by Type of Expenditure: Individual Countries or Areas

Major area, region and country	Year	Gross Domestic Product (at current prices) Million	Household final consumption expenditure 1	General government final consumption expenditure 2	Gross fixed capital formation 3	Changes in inventories 4	Exports of goods and services 5	Imports of goods and services 6
			Percentage Distribution					
Finland (Euros)	1970	7874	52	15	28	4	24	26
	1975	17897	51	18	34	2	23	29
	1980	32948	50	19	28	4	32	33
	1985	57032	50	20	27	-0	29	28
	1990	88244	48	22	30	0	23	24
	1995	95251	49	23	17	1	37	29
	1996	98709	50	23	18	-0	37	30
	1997	107103	48	22	19	0	39	31
	1998	116395	47	22	19	1	39	30
	1999	119961	48	22	20	-0	38	29
	2000	130234	47	21	20	1	43	34
	2001	135791	48	21	20	0	40	32
France [46] (Euros)	1970	124467	55	17	25	3	15	15
	1975	230245	55	20	25	-1	18	18
	1980	439384	55	22	24	1	20	23
	1985	727369	57	24	20	-0	23	24
	1990	1009350	55	22	23	1	21	22
	1995	1181850	55	24	19	0	23	21
	1996	1212180	55	24	18	-0	23	21
	1997	1251160	54	24	18	-0	26	23
	1998	1305850	54	23	18	1	26	23
	1999	1355100	54	23	19	0	26	24
	2000	1420140	54	23	20	1	29	27
	2001	1475580	54	23	20	0	28	26
Germany (Euros)	1970	381209	56	17	28	2	16	18
	1975	580477	59	22	23	-0	19	21
	1980	830212	59	22	25	1	20	25
	1985	1034570	58	21	22	-0	25	27
	1990	1380690	55	20	23	0	25	25
	1995	1801300	55	20	22	0	24	24
	1996	1833700	56	20	22	-0	25	24
	1997	1871600	56	19	21	0	28	27
	1998	1929400	56	19	21	0	29	28
	1999	1978600	57	19	22	0	30	29
	2000	2030000	57	19	22	0	34	33
	2001	2071200	58	19	20	-0	35	33
Greece (Euros)	1970	993	65	11	26	5	10	17
	1975	2305	62	13	24	7	17	23
	1980	6106	65	13	29	-3	24	28
	1985	16646	64	17	22	4	20	27
	1990	39111	71	15	23	0	18	28
	1995	79927	73	15	19	0	18	25
	1996	87851	73	15	19	0	18	26
	1997	97235	72	15	20	0	20	27
	1998	105773	71	15	21	0	20	28
	1999	112881	70	15	22	-0	20	28
	2000	121628	69	16	23	-0	24	32
	2001	130927	68	15	23	0	23	29
Hungary (Forints)	1970	372184	48	19	36	-3	29	29
	1975	538863	48	19	40	-3	39	43
	1980	804910	49	20	34	-4	37	36
	1985	1153910	50	21	27	-2	40	35
	1990	2282420	48	22	22	3	30	26
	1995	5614040	53	24	20	2	44	44
	1996	6893940	51	22	21	4	48	48
	1997	8540670	49	22	22	4	55	54
	1998	10087400	50	22	24	5	63	64
	1999	11393500	51	22	24	5	65	68
	2000	13172300	51	21	24	7	75	79
	2001	14849600	52	21	24	4	74	76

Table 2. Gross Domestic Product by Type of Expenditure: Individual Countries or Areas

Major area, region and country	Year	Gross Domestic Product (at current prices) Million	Household final consumption expenditure 1	General government final consumption expenditure 2	Gross fixed capital formation 3	Changes in inventories 4	Exports of goods and services 5	Imports of goods and services 6
			Percentage Distribution					
Iceland	1970	460	58	13	25	0	44	43
(Kroner)	1975	2148	55	17	33	3	33	41
	1980	16112	55	17	26	2	35	35
	1985	120373	61	18	22	-2	41	41
	1990	362817	58	20	20	-0	34	33
	1995	442256	56	22	16	1	36	33
	1996	474586	57	22	19	0	37	37
	1997	512679	55	22	20	0	37	37
	1998	567572	55	23	24	0	36	41
	1999	606558	57	23	22	0	35	40
	2000	658247	57	24	24	0	35	42
	2001	740747	53	24	22	-0	41	41
Ireland	1970	2231	69	16	22	2	34	43
(Euros)	1975	5222	64	20	22	0	40	47
	1980	12891	66	21	28	-1	46	60
	1985	24500	59	20	18	1	56	56
	1990	36312	56	16	19	2	57	52
	1995	52641	51	16	17	1	76	65
	1996	58080	51	16	19	1	78	66
	1997	67098	48	15	21	1	80	67
	1998	77568	47	14	22	2	86	75
	1999	89770	46	14	24	1	88	74
	2000	102910	45	14	24	1	98	84
	2001	114479	45	15	23	0	98	83
Italy	1970	34765	57	16	25	1	16	16
(Euros)	1975	71985	58	17	26	-1	20	20
	1980	198524	58	17	25	2	22	25
	1985	420324	58	19	22	2	22	23
	1990	682153	57	20	21	1	20	20
	1995	923052	58	18	18	1	27	23
	1996	982443	58	18	18	0	26	21
	1997	1026290	58	18	18	0	26	22
	1998	1073020	59	18	18	1	26	23
	1999	1108500	60	18	19	0	26	23
	2000	1164770	60	18	20	0	28	27
	2001	1216690	60	18	20	-0	28	27
Latvia [47]	1990	62	53	8	23	17	48	49
(Lats)	1995	2329	63	22	15	2	47	50
	1996	2807	68	22	18	0	51	59
	1997	3270	66	19	19	4	51	60
	1998	3592	64	21	27	0	51	65
	1999	3890	63	21	25	2	44	54
	2000	4348	62	20	26	1	46	54
	2001	4759	62	19	27	3	45	56
Lithuania [48]	1990	134	57	19	28	5	52	61
(Litas)	1995	24103	67	20	23	2	53	65
	1996	31569	66	19	23	1	53	63
	1997	38340	65	19	24	2	55	65
	1998	42990	63	24	24	0	47	59
	1999	42655	65	22	22	1	40	50
	2000	45148	64	21	19	2	45	52
	2001	47958	63	20	19	3	50	56
Luxembourg	1970	1567	50	12	21	2	94	81
(Euros)	1975	2469	58	18	25	-5	98	94
	1980	3784	59	20	25	-2	93	95
	1985	5842	59	19	16	2	114	110
	1990	9180	51	18	23	2	104	100
	1995	13214	47	18	22	0	109	97
	1996	13927	47	19	21	1	111	100
	1997	15490	44	18	22	1	119	106
	1998	17006	43	17	23	1	127	112

Table 2. Gross Domestic Product by Type of Expenditure: Individual Countries or Areas

Major area, region and country	Year	Gross Domestic Product (at current prices) Million	Household final consumption expenditure 1	General government final consumption expenditure 2	Gross fixed capital formation 3	Changes in inventories 4	Exports of goods and services 5	Imports of goods and services 6
			Percentage Distribution					
	1999	18870	40	17	24	1	136	119
	2000	21313	38	16	21	0	152	130
	2001	22082	40	17	22	0	152	133
Malta [49]	1970	95	78	19	29	3	50	80
(Maltese Lira)	1975	166	72	18	23	1	83	96
	1980	392	65	16	22	2	91	96
	1985	476	70	18	26	2	73	88
	1990	735	63	18	32	2	85	99
	1995	1146	61	21	32	0	94	107
	1996	1201	64	22	29	-0	87	101
	1997	1288	62	20	25	0	85	94
	1998	1362	62	20	24	-1	88	93
	1999	1456	63	19	23	1	91	96
	2000	1558	64	19	26	2	103	114
	2001	1632	64	20	23	-3	87	92
Netherlands	1970	57725	49	24	28	2	43	46
(Euros)	1975	104780	49	27	23	-1	48	46
	1980	160463	51	28	23	0	51	53
	1985	199847	50	25	21	-0	61	57
	1990	243174	49	23	22	1	54	51
	1995	302233	49	24	20	1	57	52
	1996	315059	49	23	21	0	58	52
	1997	333725	49	23	21	0	61	55
	1998	354194	49	23	22	1	61	56
	1999	374070	50	23	23	0	60	56
	2000	402599	49	23	23	-0	67	62
	2001	429172	49	23	22	-0	65	60
Norway	1970	91100	49	16	27	6	37	37
(Kroner)	1975	169896	47	19	34	3	36	42
	1980	314363	44	19	27	1	43	37
	1985	547286	45	18	25	2	43	35
	1990	726799	47	21	21	2	40	34
	1995	937445	47	22	20	3	38	32
	1996	1026920	46	21	20	1	41	32
	1997	1111350	45	20	22	2	41	33
	1998	1132130	47	22	25	2	38	36
	1999	1233040	45	21	22	2	39	32
	2000	1469080	41	19	19	2	47	29
	2001	1526600	41	20	18	2	46	29
Poland	1970	78	77	20	15	-4	42	55
(Zlotych)	1975	138	70	19	24	-5	40	53
	1980	234	65	18	27	-5	31	38
	1985	965	59	19	23	0	20	21
	1990	56027	48	19	21	5	29	22
	1995	308104	60	17	19	1	25	23
	1996	387827	62	16	21	1	24	26
	1997	472350	63	16	23	1	25	30
	1998	553560	63	15	25	1	28	33
	1999	615115	63	16	25	1	26	32
	2000	712322	63	18	24	1	28	35
	2001	749311	64	18	21	0	28	32
Portugal	1970	1056	63	13	24	4	22	27
(Euros)	1975	2240	74	14	27	-8	18	28
	1980	7458	65	13	30	4	24	36
	1985	20923	65	14	23	-1	33	35
	1990	50817	62	16	26	1	33	39
	1995	80827	62	19	23	1	30	36
	1996	86230	62	19	23	1	30	36
	1997	93014	61	19	26	1	30	38
	1998	100963	61	19	27	1	31	40
	1999	108030	61	20	27	1	30	40
	2000	115546	60	21	28	1	32	43
	2001	122978	59	21	27	1	31	41

Table 2. Gross Domestic Product by Type of Expenditure: Individual Countries or Areas

Major area, region and country	Year	Gross Domestic Product (at current prices) Million	Household final consumption expenditure 1	General government final consumption expenditure 2	Gross fixed capital formation 3	Changes in inventories 4	Exports of goods and services 5	Imports of goods and services 6
			Percentage Distribution					
Republic of Moldova	1990	13	61	10	23	7	49	51
(Lei)	1995	6480	56	26	16	9	60	68
	1996	7798	67	26	20	4	55	74
	1997	8917	67	29	20	4	53	74
	1998	9122	75	25	22	4	45	72
	1999	12322	74	15	18	4	52	65
	2000	16020	88	15	15	9	50	77
	2001	19019	90	14	14	7	50	74
Romania [50]	1970	227348	52	21	24	5	22	26
(Lei)	1975	384219	48	22	28	7	22	33
	1980	484684	52	13	35	5	22	22
	1985	623460	51	12	30	3	29	20
	1990	857851	65	13	20	10	17	26
	1995	72135548	67	14	21	3	28	33
	1996	108919636	69	13	23	3	28	37
	1997	252925736	74	12	21	-1	29	36
	1998	373798214	75	15	18	-0	23	31
	1999	545730127	73	14	18	-2	28	33
	2000	800308100	69	16	19	1	33	39
	2001	1154126400	70	15	19	3	34	42
Russian Federation	1990	644200	47	21	29	1	18	18
(Roubles)	1995	1540493	49	19	21	5	28	24
	1996	2145656	49	20	21	3	25	21
	1997	2478594	51	22	19	4	24	21
	1998	2741051	55	19	17	-1	31	24
	1999	4766834	53	15	14	0	44	26
	2000	7305742	46	15	16	3	44	24
	2001	9040690	50	14	18	4	37	24
San Marino	1970	22	57	16	25	2	16	16
(Italian Lire)	1975	46	58	17	26	-1	20	20
	1980	128	58	17	25	3	22	25
	1985	271	58	19	22	2	22	23
	1990	439	57	20	21	1	20	20
	1995	595	58	18	18	1	27	23
	2000	842	43	13	43	5	219	233
	2001	879	43	13	43	4	218	227
Serbia and Montenegro [51]	1990	34174	65	21	13	4	11	14
(New Dinars)	1995	43984	67	21	12	5	7	11
	1996	79396	72	22	12	5	16	27
	1997	109352	67	26	12	6	18	27
	1998	148370	72	28	12	2	23	33
	1999	191099	67	26	11	4	20	29
	2000	381661	68	27	11	3	21	30
	2001	699600	68	26	11	3	21	30
Slovakia	1980	203804	49	21	30	6	30	36
(Koruny)	1985	241506	49	21	28	3	31	32
	1990	289380	53	23	30	3	25	34
	1995	568923	50	21	25	1	57	56
	1996	628588	52	23	32	3	53	64
	1997	708617	52	22	34	1	56	66
	1998	775002	53	22	36	-2	59	70
	1999	835721	55	20	30	-2	61	65
	2000	908801	55	20	29	-3	72	74
	2001	989297	56	20	31	1	74	82
Slovenia [52]	1990	196762	52	17	19	-2	91	79
(Tolars)	1995	2221459	57	20	21	2	55	57
	1996	2555369	56	20	22	1	56	57
	1997	2907277	55	20	23	1	57	58
	1998	3253751	55	20	25	1	57	58
	1999	3648401	55	20	27	1	53	57
	2000	4035518	54	21	27	1	59	63
	2001	4566191	53	21	25	1	60	60

Table 2. Gross Domestic Product by Type of Expenditure: Individual Countries or Areas

Major area, region and country	Year	Gross Domestic Product (at current prices) Million	Household final consumption expenditure 1	General government final consumption expenditure 2	Gross fixed capital formation 3	Changes in inventories 4	Exports of goods and services 5	Imports of goods and services 6
			Percentage Distribution					
Spain (Euros)	1970	16392	62	10	27	1	13	14
	1975	37638	63	11	27	2	13	17
	1980	95334	64	14	23	1	15	17
	1985	175624	62	16	21	0	22	20
	1990	312424	60	17	26	1	16	20
	1995	437787	59	18	22	0	23	23
	1996	464251	59	18	22	0	24	23
	1997	494140	59	18	22	0	27	26
	1998	527975	59	17	23	0	27	27
	1999	565199	59	17	24	0	28	29
	2000	609319	58	18	25	0	30	32
	2001	651641	58	17	25	0	30	32
Sweden (Kroner)	1970	184554	49	23	24	4	23	23
	1975	322315	48	26	22	4	27	27
	1980	562684	47	31	21	2	28	30
	1985	921782	47	29	21	1	34	32
	1990	1455670	46	29	24	1	29	28
	1995	1772020	48	27	16	1	39	33
	1996	1817150	48	28	16	0	38	31
	1997	1890190	48	27	16	0	41	34
	1998	1973850	48	28	16	1	42	36
	1999	2078550	48	27	17	0	43	36
	2000	2196760	47	27	18	1	46	40
	2001	2266620	47	27	18	0	45	39
Switzerland (Swiss Francs)	1970	95863	55	10	29	5	31	33
	1975	148190	58	12	25	-1	30	27
	1980	180095	60	12	25	4	35	38
	1985	237206	59	13	24	1	38	37
	1990	317304	55	14	27	1	36	36
	1995	363329	58	14	21	0	35	31
	1996	365833	58	15	20	0	36	32
	1997	371372	59	14	20	1	40	35
	1998	379989	59	14	20	1	40	36
	1999	388518	59	14	20	-1	42	37
	2000	405530	58	14	21	0	46	41
	2001	414881	58	14	20	1	45	41
TFYR Macedonia (Denars)	1990	507	66	19	18	1	26	36
	1995	169521	70	19	17	4	33	43
	1996	176444	72	18	17	3	28	39
	1997	184982	73	20	17	4	38	51
	1998	190827	74	21	18	5	42	57
	1999	195284	74	22	18	3	45	56
	2000	216845	80	22	20	...	55	69
	2001	219537	76	24	20	...	50	60
Ukraine (Hryvnias)	1990	2	55	16	23	5	28	29
	1995	54516	50	21	23	3	47	50
	1996	81519	53	22	21	2	46	48
	1997	93365	54	24	20	2	41	44
	1998	102593	57	22	20	1	42	44
	1999	130442	55	20	19	-2	54	49
	2000	170070	54	19	20	0	62	57
	2001	204190	55	20	20	2	55	54
United Kingdom (Pounds Sterling)	1970	51515	59	18	19	1	22	21
	1975	105773	59	22	21	-1	25	27
	1980	230695	58	22	19	-1	27	25
	1985	354952	58	21	18	0	29	28
	1990	557300	61	20	21	-0	24	27
	1995	719176	62	20	16	1	28	29
	1996	762214	62	19	16	0	29	30
	1997	811067	62	18	17	1	29	29
	1998	859384	62	18	18	1	27	28

Table 2. Gross Domestic Product by Type of Expenditure: Individual Countries or Areas

Major area, region and country	Year	Gross Domestic Product (at current prices) Million	Household final consumption expenditure 1	General government final consumption expenditure 2	Gross fixed capital formation 3	Changes in inventories 4	Exports of goods and services 5	Imports of goods and services 6
			Percentage Distribution					
	1999	902459	63	18	17	1	26	28
	2000	950415	64	19	17	1	28	30
	2001	993124	64	19	17	0	27	29
OCEANIA								
Australia (Australian Dollars)	1970	38277	56	14	29	2	13	14
	1975	79386	57	19	25	0	14	14
	1980	145643	58	19	27	0	16	18
	1985	248131	58	20	26	0	16	19
	1990	397881	59	19	23	-0	17	17
	1995	502828	60	18	22	-0	20	20
	1996	529886	59	18	22	-0	20	20
	1997	561229	60	18	23	0	20	21
	1998	591917	60	18	23	1	19	21
	1999	628621	60	18	24	0	20	22
	2000	669307	60	18	21	-0	23	23
	2001	712980	60	18	22	0	21	22
Cook Islands [53] (New Zealand Dollars)	1970	11	80	32	26	...	32	71
	1975	14	108	32	26	...	30	96
	1980	24	120	32	26	...	22	100
	1985	56	119	32	26	...	11	89
	1990	107	115	32	26	...	8	81
	1995	155	85	32	26	...	4	48
	2000	172	86	32	26	...	4	48
	2001	191	86	32	26	...	4	48
Fiji (Fiji Dollars)	1970	192	65	14	18	4	48	52
	1975	562	68	12	18	2	43	44
	1980	984	58	16	25	6	48	52
	1985	1316	64	19	18	1	44	45
	1990	1980	73	17	17	2	62	67
	1995	2799	63	16	13	1	55	58
	2000	3518	62	18	10	1	60	64
	2001	3831	62	17	11	1	59	61
French Polynesia [54] (French Francs)	1970	21468	81	47	23	...	13	63
	1975	45020	67	42	30	...	11	50
	1980	96832	61	50	24	...	7	43
	1985	220772	63	42	36	...	9	39
	1990	290064	62	40	20	...	9	32
	1995	373136	63	42	17	...	9	28
	2000	426800	63	42	17	...	9	28
	2001	438732	63	42	17	...	9	28
Kiribati (Australian Dollars)	1970	13	45	22	8	...	59	33
	1975	42	45	22	8	...	59	33
	1980	25	45	22	8	...	59	33
	1985	30	45	22	8	...	59	33
	1990	36	45	22	8	...	59	33
	1995	62	45	22	8	...	59	33
	2000	78	45	22	8	...	59	33
	2001	77	45	22	8	...	59	33
Marshall Islands (US Dollars)	1970	7	57	28	11	...	44	39
	1975	15	37	18	5	...	68	28
	1980	23	94	59	33	...	23	110
	1985	38	97	53	56	...	20	126
	1990	69	98	50	88	...	11	147
	1995	105	91	54	56	...	13	114
	2000	98	90	54	56	...	12	112
	2001	100	90	54	56	...	12	113
Micronesia (Federated States of) (U.S. Dollars)	1970	24	45	22	8	...	59	33
	1975	56	45	22	8	...	59	33
	1980	77	45	22	8	...	59	33
	1985	102	45	22	8	...	59	33

Table 2. Gross Domestic Product by Type of Expenditure: Individual Countries or Areas

Major area, region and country	Year	Gross Domestic Product (at current prices) Million	Household final consumption expenditure 1	General government final consumption expenditure 2	Gross fixed capital formation 3	Changes in inventories 4	Exports of goods and services 5	Imports of goods and services 6
			Percentage Distribution					
	1990	151	45	22	8	...	59	33
	1995	215	45	22	8	...	59	33
	2000	229	45	22	8	...	59	33
	2001	238	45	22	8	...	59	33
Nauru (US Dollars)	1970	12	45	22	8	...	59	33
	1975	19	45	22	8	...	59	33
	1980	32	45	22	8	...	59	33
	1985	52	45	22	8	...	59	33
	1990	66	45	22	8	...	59	33
	1995	55	45	22	8	...	59	33
	2000	57	45	22	8	...	59	33
	2001	60	45	22	8	...	59	33
New Caledonia [55] (CFP Francs)	1970	38204	57	28	11	...	44	39
	1975	63643	37	18	5	...	68	28
	1980	90847	94	59	33	0	23	110
	1985	139650	97	53	58	-2	20	126
	1990	250427	98	50	93	-5	11	147
	1995	329296	89	49	69	-5	12	114
	2000	433607	89	50	67	-4	12	113
	2001	461108	89	50	66	-4	12	112
New Zealand (New Zealand Dollars)	1970	5846	61	16	23	2	22	25
	1975	11334	60	18	29	-1	23	30
	1980	23464	58	21	20	0	30	31
	1985	46212	58	19	27	-0	30	33
	1990	73113	60	19	20	-0	27	27
	1995	92679	58	18	21	1	29	29
	1996	97239	59	17	21	1	28	28
	1997	100739	59	18	20	1	28	28
	1998	101959	60	18	19	0	30	30
	1999	107068	60	19	20	1	31	32
	2000	113778	59	18	19	1	36	34
	2001	122241	57	18	19	2	36	33
Palau (Australian Dollars)	1970	12	45	22	8	...	59	33
	1975	39	45	22	8	...	59	33
	1980	19	45	22	8	...	59	33
	1985	41	45	22	8	...	59	33
	1990	83	45	22	8	...	59	33
	1995	128	45	22	8	...	59	33
	2000	204	45	22	8	...	59	33
	2001	237	45	22	8	...	59	33
Papua New Guinea (Kina)	1970	689	56	30	37	5	18	49
	1975	1185	50	36	13	4	37	38
	1980	1894	55	25	19	3	43	46
	1985	2451	59	25	17	3	45	49
	1990	3138	52	26	23	1	43	45
	1995	5888	42	17	20	3	62	43
	2000	9650	74	18	13	2	49	53
	2001	10078	76	19	13	1	50	56
Samoa (Tala)	1970	43	94	18	39	...	22	73
	1975	85	94	18	39	...	22	73
	1980	142	87	18	33	...	25	63
	1985	271	87	18	31	...	28	64
	1990	465	81	19	34	...	31	65
	1995	496	83	22	40	...	27	76
	2000	775	106	29	52	...	24	113
	2001	852	106	29	52	-2	24	113
Solomon Islands (Solomon Islands Dollars)	1970	29	81	19	19	-5	25	40
	1975	50	90	19	19	5	24	58
	1980	119	99	21	19	3	51	93
	1985	237	64	28	21	5	51	70

Table 2. Gross Domestic Product by Type of Expenditure: Individual Countries or Areas

Major area, region and country	Year	Gross Domestic Product (at current prices) Million	Household final consumption expenditure 1	General government final consumption expenditure 2	Gross fixed capital formation 3	Changes in inventories 4	Exports of goods and services 5	Imports of goods and services 6
			Percentage Distribution					
	1990	526	57	31	17	3	47	57
	1995	1242	49	33	18	2	58	59
	2000	1721	49	32	18	1	59	59
	2001	1766	49	32	18	1	59	59
Tonga [56]	1970	10	88	17	21	...	38	64
(Pa 'anga)	1975	25	89	17	23	5	43	72
	1980	47	93	15	29	1	30	68
	1985	86	100	16	23	3	30	72
	1990	147	94	19	18	0	34	65
	1995	199	107	20	22	-0	20	69
	1996	209	112	20	21	1	22	72
	1997	208	100	22	17	2	21	62
	1998	219	108	22	18	1	17	66
	1999	237	96	23	21	1	13	53
	2000	261	90	21	21	1	15	51
	2001	277	97	22	20	1	15	56
Tuvalu	1970	1	57	28	11	...	44	39
(Australian dollars)	1975	2	37	18	5	...	68	28
	1980	4	94	59	33	...	23	110
	1985	5	100	55	58	...	21	126
	1990	12	103	53	93	...	12	147
	1995	16	91	54	56	...	13	114
	2000	25	91	54	56	...	13	114
	2001	27	91	54	56	...	13	114
Vanuatu	1970	3508	55	34	29	...	48	68
(Vatu)	1975	5084	55	34	29	...	48	68
	1980	7746	55	34	29	...	48	68
	1985	12870	55	35	22	5	50	70
	1990	17638	64	29	41	3	47	78
	1995	25550	50	27	32	2	47	57
	1996	26711	52	29	27	1	48	57
	1997	27565	53	28	26	1	50	57
	1998	29289	53	28	26	2	51	55
	1999	29206	55	29	30	2	50	65
	2000	31108	53	28	28	2	49	58
	2001	31831	53	28	28	2	49	58

Notes for Table 2

1/ (a) Exports of goods and services
1972-1986
Exports of goods only.

(b) Imports of goods and services
1972-1986
Includes imports of goods plus net imports of services.

2/ Gross domestic product
1970-1979
Estimates relate to calendar year.

3/ (a) Gross fixed capital formation
1970-1972, 1974-1988
Estimates refer to central government capital formation only.

(b) Exports of goods and services
1970-1993
Includes net travel and tourism income.

(c) Imports of goods and services
1970-1993
Includes net freight and insurance.

4/ (a) Changes in inventories
1970-1996
Cocoa is valued at cost to the Ghana Cocoa Marketing Board. Stocks of other export commodities, including minerals, are valued at export prices.

(b) Gross domestic product
1970-1979, 1986-1990
Gross domestic product at purchaser's prices.

5/ Changes in inventories
1970-1989
Includes only increase in iron ore stocks. Beginning 1981, it includes increase in iron ore and rubber stocks.

6/ Household final consumption expenditure
1970-1985, 1987-1992
Obtained as a residual.

7/ Household final consumption expenditure
1970-1996
Includes Changes in inventories.

8/ Household final consumption expenditure
1980-1989
Obtained as a residual.

9/ Exports of goods and services
1994-1999
Exports less imports.

10/ (a) Exports of goods and services
1970-1990
Includes an upward adjustments for the estimated value of diamond smuggled out of the country.

(b) Imports of goods and services
1989-1990
Discrepancy between components and total.

11/ (a) Household final consumption expenditure
1970-1987
Obtained as a residual.

(b) General government final consumption expenditure
Gross fixed capital formation
1970-1987
The value of Technical Assistance from abroad is included in Gross fixed capital formation rather than Government final consumption expenditure.

(c) Changes in inventories
1970-1987
Includes livestock only.

(d) Exports of goods and services
1970-1987
Exports of goods only.

(e) Imports of goods and services
1970-1987
Refers to imports of goods and non-factor services.

12/ (a) Household final consumption expenditure
1970-1979
Item shows significant increases from 1975 due to the sharp increases in salary. Estimates also include errors and omissions.

(b) Exports of goods and services
1970-2000
Estimates are on calendar year basis.

(c) Imports of goods and services
1970-2000
Estimates are on calendar year basis.

13/ Household final consumption expenditure
1980-2001
Includes Final consumption expenditure of NPISH's.

14/ Changes in inventories
1970-1989
Includes also unrecorded increases in stocks.

15/ Household final consumption expenditure
1980-1992
Excludes direct purchases abroad by resident households; includes direct purchases in the domestic market by non-resident households.

16/ (a) Changes in inventories
1970-1991
Includes only increase of stocks of mining, manufacturing, peanuts, raw tobacco and beans.

(b) Exports of goods and services
1984-2001
Beginning 1984, estimates were converted from dollars to pesos by using the annual average exchange rates fixed by the Central Bank.

(c) Imports of goods and services
1970-1979
Beginning 1984, estimates were converted from dollars to pesos by using the annual average exchange rates fixed by the Central Bank.

17/ Exports of goods and services
1976
Does not include 51.2 million quetzales for insurance service charges.

18/ Gross domestic product
2000
Discrepancy between components and total.

19/ Household final consumption expenditure
1987-1992
Includes NPISHs final consumption expenditure.

20/ Exports of goods and services
Imports of goods and services
1979-1985
Exports and imports of merchandise are recorded on the basis of the crossing of frontiers. No data are available on the basis of changes in the ownership of the goods. Imports and exports are recorded on a cash basis and the imports and exports of oil refineries are not included in the estimates.

21/ (a) Gross fixed capital formation
1980-1995
Includes communications equipment.

(b) Changes in inventories
1980-1995
Includes livestock only.

22/ (a) Changes in inventories
1970-1986
This item refers to increase in stocks of wool and livestock in the private sector, and to stocks held by the public sector.

23/ Exports of goods and services
Imports of goods and services
1990-2001
Estimates valued at market exchange rate.

24/ Changes in inventories
1990-2001
Includes Acquisitions less disposals of valuables.

25/ Changes in inventories
1990-2001
Includes Acquisitions less disposals of valuables.

26/ Changes in inventories
1987-1992
Includes net errors and omissions.

27/ Exports of goods and services
Imports of goods and services
1972-1979
Refers to imports of goods and non-factor services.

28/ Changes in inventories
1974-1979
Land improvement is not included in Other construction and land improvement, etc..

29/ Exports of goods and services
1984-1991
Exports less imports.

30/ Gross domestic product
2000-2001
Provisional data.

31/ (a) Household final consumption expenditure
1980-1993
Refers to expenditure in the domestic market only.

(b) Gross fixed capital formation
1970-1993
Figures are based on type of assets, not on industry of use.

32/ Gross domestic product
1982, 1989-1992
Discrepancy between components and total.

33/ General government final consumption expenditure
Gross fixed capital formation
1970-1979, 1987-1998
Government final consumption expenditure includes pension payments less employees' pension contributions.
Some non-capital development expenditure of the central government is included in fixed capital formation.

34/ Gross domestic product
1970-1974
Estimates refer to year ending 30 September.

35/ (a) Household final consumption expenditure
1970-1974, 1976-1979
Includes Changes in inventories.

(b) Gross domestic product
2001
Provisional data.

36/ Changes in inventories
1970-2001
Includes Acquisitions less disposal of valuables.

37/ Gross domestic product
2000-2001
Provisional data.

38/ Exports of goods and services
1970-2001
Exports less imports.

39/ Changes in inventories
1970-1975
Includes a statistical discrepancy.

40/ Exports of goods and services
1988-1989, 1998-2001
Exports less imports.

41/ Exports of goods and services
1988-2000
Exports less imports.

42/ Changes in inventories
1990-2001
Includes Acquisitions less disposals of valuables.

43/ Changes in inventories
1991-2001
Includes Acquisitions less disposal of valuables.

44/ (a) General government final consumption expenditure
1987-1990
Includes consumption expenditure of the private non-profit institutions serving

(b) Changes in inventories
1985-1990
Includes Acquisitions less disposals of valuables.

(c) Exports of goods and services
1987-1990
Exports less imports.

45/ Changes in inventories
1990-2001
Includes Acquisitions less disposals of valuables.

46/ Gross domestic product
2001
Discrepancy between components and total.

47/ (a) Household final consumption expenditure
1996, 2000-2001
Includes NPISHs final consumption expenditure.

(b) Changes in inventories
1990-2001
Includes Acquisitions less disposals of valuables.

48/ Changes in inventories
1990-2001
Includes Acquisitions less disposal of valuables.

49/ (a) Changes in inventories
1970-2001
Includes a statistical discrepancy.

(b) Gross domestic product
2000-2001
Provisional data.

50/ Changes in inventories
1980-2001
Includes Acquisitions less disposal of valuables.

51/ Changes in inventories
1994-2000
Includes Acquisitions less disposals of valuables.

52/ Changes in inventories
1990-1994, 1997-2000
Includes Acquisitions less disposals of valuables.

Current price estimates established by the Executive Council.

53/ (a) Exports of goods and services
1970-2001
Valued f.o.b.

(b) Imports of goods and services
1970-2001
Valued c.i.f. instead of f.o.b.

54/ Gross domestic product
1992
Discrepancy between components and total.

55/ Household final consumption expenditure
General government final consumption expenditure
1970-1992

Education and health are included in Government final consumption expenditure rather than in Household final consumption expenditure.

56/ Household final consumption expenditure
1994-2001

Includes NPISHs final consumption expenditure.

Table 3. Gross Domestic Product by Kind of Economic Activity: Individual Countries or Areas

Major area, region and country	Year	Gross Domestic Product (at current prices) Million	Agriculture hunting forestry and fishing A-B	Mining Manufacturing and Utilities C-E	Of which: Manufacturing D	Construction F	Wholesale, retail trade, restaurants and hotels G-H	Transport storage and communication I	Other Activities J-P
			Percentage Distribution						
AFRICA									
Algeria	1970	25509	10	28	13	9	18	5	21
(Dinars)	1975	61574	8	36	9	11	10	5	18
	1980	162507	8	45	10	10	12	5	17
	1985	291597	8	37	11	13	14	5	14
	1990	554388	11	35	11	10	13	5	20
	1995	2004995	10	36	8	10	15	5	19
	1996	2570028	11	39	7	8	14	6	19
	1997	2780168	9	39	7	9	14	7	17
	1998	2810124	11	33	8	9	15	7	19
	1999	3248198	10	37	7	8	14	7	18
	2000	4098817	8	48	6	7	12	7	15
	2001	4235620	8	48	6	7	12	7	15
Angola	1970	82 (u)	13	21	13	5	12	6	34
(Readjusted Kwanzas)	1975	80 (u)	12	47	11	2	12	3	33
	1980	161 (u)	14	31	5	3	7	3	26
	1985	205 (u)	13	38	10	5	13	5	25
	1990	308 (u)	18	38	5	3	11	3	27
	1995	14	7	63	4	3	18	0	12
	2000	91666	6	69	3	3	14	...	7
	2001	197111	8	61	4	4	16	...	9
Benin [1]	1970	69711	39	9	...	2	14	6	32
(CFA Francs)	1975	113112	32	10	9	3	19	8	33
	1980	245613	37	6	5	3	20	8	25
	1985	469778	32	6	3	3	16	8	20
	1990	502300	40	5	5	6	18	9	22
	1995	1002900	40	5	5	7	17	7	19
	2000	1605400	37	10	9	4	18	8	16
	2001	1738400	36	10	9	4	18	8	16
Botswana	1970	70	32	18	6	10	15	3	19
(Pula)	1975	263	31	18	7	9	8	3	23
	1980	832	13	37	4	7	8	2	23
	1985	2146	6	48	5	5	7	3	24
	1990	6552	5	52	5	7	7	3	23
	1995	12262	4	41	5	6	10	4	31
	1996	14204	4	41	5	6	10	4	31
	1997	17740	3	46	5	6	10	3	28
	1998	20163	3	45	5	6	10	3	28
	1999	21524	3	38	5	6	11	4	33
	2000	25303	3	40	5	6	11	4	31
	2001	29353	2	42	5	5	11	4	30
Burkina Faso	1970	109936	40	13	13	4	14	7	16
(CFA Francs)	1975	168467	45	14	13	3	9	5	19
	1980	360929	40	12	11	3	13	8	20
	1985	622711	47	13	11	1	10	7	20
	1990	778376	43	17	15	5	2	4	18
	1995	1106300	42	14	13	2	5	5	25
	2000	1560700	36	14	12	4	18	5	27
	2001	1706900	39	14	11	4	18	5	26
Burundi	1970	21476	63	7	6	2	7	1	12
(Francs)	1975	32671	60	7	7	3	9	1	12
	1980	85607	56	8	8	4	8	2	14
	1985	141347	55	13	12	4	11	2	13
	1990	196656	51	17	16	3	5	3	18
	1995	249865	49	11	11	5	5	3	18
	2000	511789	46	10	9	6	6	4	23
	2001	548656	44	11	10	6	6	4	24
Cameroon	1970	365638	21	17	15	4	21	4	26
(CFA Francs)	1975	747890	24	15	14	5	16	5	25
	1980	2044294	19	23	13	7	13	3	25
	1985	4672835	15	27	16	8	16	3	26
	1990	3896040	18	27	19	5	15	4	29

Table 3. Gross Domestic Product by Kind of Economic Activity: Individual Countries or Areas

Major area, region and country	Year	Gross Domestic Product (at current prices) Million	Agriculture hunting forestry and fishing A-B	Mining Manufacturing and Utilities C-E	Of which: Manufacturing D	Construction F	Wholesale, retail trade, restaurants and hotels G-H	Transport storage and communication I	Other Activities J-P
			Percentage Distribution						
	1995	4465080	23	26	20	2	19	4	20
	2000	6602500	22	26	20	2	19	5	19
	2001	6577194	23	27	21	2	20	6	21
Cape Verde	1970	1844	19	5	4	13	34	7	16
(Escudos)	1975	3009	18	6	5	10	32	9	20
	1980	5715	19	5	5	12	30	9	19
	1985	12625	13	7	6	11	28	15	21
	1990	21573	14	8	7	12	21	15	23
	1995	37705	14	8	7	9	17	17	27
	1996	41476	14	8	7	9	17	17	27
	1997	47158	14	7	6	9	18	18	28
	1998	52867	14	7	6	8	19	18	28
	1999	60400	14	7	6	9	18	18	28
	2000	64700	13	7	6	9	18	18	28
	2001	69000	14	7	6	9	18	18	28
Central African Republic [2]	1970	41341	34	14	8	2	26	5	18
(CFA Francs)	1975	86470	37	13	9	2	23	4	21
	1980	149718	39	12	8	2	22	4	18
	1985	337755	42	11	7	3	22	4	18
	1990	353000	43	11	7	3	23	5	16
	1995	531738	43	10	7	3	23	5	15
	2000	646020	55	15	10	5	14	3	9
	2001	669923	55	15	10	5	13	3	8
Chad [3]	1970	114202	46	14	13	2	26	3	8
(CFA Francs)	1975	187481	41	13	11	3	28	2	12
	1980	193869	64	10	9	1	16	4	12
	1985	412267	52	13	12	2	22	4	13
	1990	419083	39	18	17	2	21	4	18
	1995	720000	35	14	13	2	22	3	17
	2000	928000	38	12	11	2	21	3	18
	2001	1088000	37	14	13	2	22	3	17
Comoros	1970	5424	41	5	5	13	20	3	14
(Comoro Francs)	1975	12832	38	6	6	12	23	4	14
	1980	28628	45	4	4	8	16	4	22
	1985	51700	41	5	4	10	18	4	22
	1990	68074	41	5	4	3	25	4	23
	1995	80343	43	6	5	7	25	5	23
	2000	98694	41	6	5	6	22	4	21
	2001	110780	38	5	5	6	24	4	22
Congo	1970	72453	22	16	13	6	12	11	25
(CFA Francs)	1975	146458	15	29	10	4	12	9	24
	1980	360397	12	42	8	5	10	9	20
	1985	970850	7	48	6	6	11	7	18
	1990	762000	14	39	8	1	13	9	22
	1995	1056200	15	35	9	1	10	11	28
	2000	2134500	6	74	18	2	7	5	13
	2001	2021900	6	65	16	2	7	5	14
Cote d'Ivoire [4]	1970	414862	27	15	13	7	20	8	18
(CFA Francs)	1975	834545	29	15	13	7	18	9	18
	1980	2149886	29	13	11	7	18	7	21
	1985	3134800	27	16	12	6	18	7	24
	1990	3238000	30	22	20	2	17	7	22
	1995	5543000	24	19	17	2	19	5	13
	1996	6209810	25	19	17	2	18	5	12
	1997	6841856	23	24	22	2	18	5	11
	1998	7457508	24	23	20	2	19	6	10
	1999	7734000	22	24	21	3	21	5	11
	2000	7605000	24	23	22	3	18	5	13
	2001	7697909	23	23	21	3	19	5	11
Democratic Republic of the Congo [5]	1970	0.003 (u)	17	31	8	5	11	8	23
(Zaires)	1975	0.006 (u)	20	21	10	6	17	4	28
	1980	0.14 (u)	31	27	3	4	15	2	20
	1985	1.2 (u)	27	32	2	5	17	1	17

Table 3. Gross Domestic Product by Kind of Economic Activity: Individual Countries or Areas

Major area, region and country	Year	Gross Domestic Product (at current prices) Million	Agriculture hunting forestry and fishing A-B	Mining Manufacturing and Utilities C-E	Of which: Manufacturing D	Construction F	Wholesale, retail trade, restaurants and hotels G-H	Transport storage and communication I	Other Activities J-P
			Percentage Distribution						
	1990	22 (u)	31	25	1	6	18	1	19
	1995	396	52	14	6	3	18	3	8
	2000	334926	55	13	5	2	20	3	9
	2001	1556120	56	14	4	4	15	3	6
Djibouti [6]	1970	15300	3	15	11	11	31	9	21
(Djibouti Francs)	1975	30100	2	17	14	12	25	9	25
	1980	60313	3	10	7	5	17	8	34
	1985	62303	3	13	4	5	15	17	35
	1990	81203	3	9	3	10	16	15	34
	1995	90572	3	9	2	5	13	19	38
	1996	88233	3	8	2	5	14	19	38
	1997	87289	3	8	2	5	14	20	36
	1998	88461	3	7	2	6	14	23	35
	1999	95275	3	7	3	6	14	25	33
	2000	98267	3	8	3	6	14	24	33
	2001	101932	3	8	3	6	14	25	33
Egypt [7]	1970	2971	23	20	17	2	11	4	28
(Egyptian Pounds)	1975	5247	28	21	17	5	14	5	24
	1980	17149	20	30	13	4	13	9	22
	1985	40820	19	24	16	6	22	9	21
	1990	110143	16	27	16	5	20	10	16
	1995	229400	14	29	17	4	20	11	20
	1996	265900	16	24	16	5	17	9	23
	1997	287400	16	24	17	5	17	8	23
	1998	307600	16	24	18	5	16	8	23
	1999	340100	16	26	18	4	16	8	22
	2000	358700	15	26	18	4	16	8	23
	2001	381700	15	27	18	4	15	9	23
Equatorial Guinea	1970	13780	73	1	1	5	4	1	12
(CFA Francs)	1975	12306	60	4	1	8	5	1	18
	1980	11908	60	3	1	7	7	2	19
	1985	38067	57	4	2	3	8	3	18
	1990	44349	52	5	1	4	7	2	27
	1995	81600	42	4	1	6	11	2	28
	2000	891900	42	4	1	6	11	2	28
	2001	1263873	42	4	1	6	11	2	28
Eritrea	1992	1226	14	14	13	5	28	15	23
(Nafka)	1995	3533	11	16	14	7	26	13	27
	2000	4998	16	16	14	12	22	10	25
	2001	5755	16	16	14	12	21	10	25
Ethiopia	1992	20792	61	6	5	2	7	4	16
(Birr)	1995	33885	61	6	5	2	7	4	17
	2000	49459	52	8	7	3	9	5	23
	2001	51180	52	8	7	3	9	5	23
Gabon [8]	1970	93100	17	39	4	6	13	5	19
(CFA Francs)	1975	462441	9	47	5	17	7	4	12
	1980	904500	7	51	5	7	7	4	19
	1985	1645800	6	53	5	6	7	5	18
	1990	1477400	8	44	6	4	12	6	25
	1995	2475200	9	47	5	4	13	6	21
	2000	3576883	6	50	4	3	14	6	21
	2001	3176703	8	47	4	3	14	6	22
Gambia	1970	97	50	3	2	2	26	4	14
(Dalasis)	1975	278	38	6	5	5	23	6	24
	1980	412	28	7	7	8	24	8	27
	1985	1073	26	6	6	4	34	10	22
	1000	2627	23	7	0	5	40	11	17
	1995	3508	26	7	5	6	25	16	22
	2000	5551	38	7	5	6	15	11	28
	2001	6357	38	7	5	6	19	13	17

Table 3. Gross Domestic Product by Kind of Economic Activity: Individual Countries or Areas

Major area, region and country	Year	Gross Domestic Product (at current prices) Million	Agriculture hunting forestry and fishing A-B	Mining Manufacturing and Utilities C-E	Of which: Manufacturing D	Construction F	Wholesale, retail trade, restaurants and hotels G-H	Transport storage and communication I	Other Activities J-P
			Percentage Distribution						
Ghana [9]	1970	2259	47	14	11	4	12	4	17
(Cedis)	1975	5283	48	17	14	4	12	4	15
	1980	42854	58	9	8	2	17	3	11
	1985	343048	45	14	12	3	25	5	8
	1990	2031700	45	15	9	6	3	2	14
	1995	7752600	39	17	9	8	6	4	17
	1996	11339200	39	16	9	8	6	4	16
	1997	14113400	36	16	9	8	6	4	16
	1998	17296000	36	16	8	8	6	4	16
	1999	20002100	36	17	8	8	7	4	18
	2000	27153000	35	17	9	8	7	5	18
	2001	38014000	35	17	9	8	7	5	18
Guinea	1970	17742	20	21	4	9	27	6	13
(French Francs)	1975	25991	20	21	4	9	27	6	13
	1980	36837	20	21	4	9	27	6	13
	1985	61031	20	21	4	9	27	6	13
	1990	1860450	20	21	4	9	27	6	13
	1995	3696760	20	21	4	9	27	6	13
	2000	5511780	20	21	4	9	26	6	12
	2001	6031710	19	22	4	10	26	6	12
Guinea-Bissau	1970	41	59	11	11	2	15	2	10
(CFA Francs)	1975	65	51	14	14	3	19	3	11
	1980	123	46	17	17	5	18	3	11
	1985	608	44	16	16	6	19	3	12
	1990	7848	45	8	7	10	26	4	8
	1995	68045	43	8	7	8	24	4	8
	2000	159900	59	10	9	2	16	4	10
	2001	179600	56	10	9	2	17	4	10
Kenya [10]	1970	606	33	12	10	6	10	5	27
(Kenyan Pounds)	1975	1194	30	13	11	5	10	5	27
	1980	2629	28	13	11	6	9	5	27
	1985	5042	29	12	10	5	10	6	29
	1990	9777	25	12	10	5	10	6	31
	1995	23264	26	10	8	4	14	7	28
	1996	26436	25	10	9	4	15	7	27
	1997	31168	24	10	9	3	18	7	28
	1998	34606	23	10	9	3	19	6	28
	1999	37107	20	12	11	4	19	6	28
	2000	39799	17	12	11	4	20	6	26
	2001	44764	16	12	11	4	22	6	26
Lesotho [11]	1970	52	32	7	5	2	15	3	45
(Loti)	1975	110	28	7	7	4	14	5	40
	1980	296	23	13	6	7	8	3	42
	1985	568	20	11	10	9	9	3	45
	1990	1600	19	13	11	14	8	4	33
	1995	3384	15	16	14	18	9	3	27
	1996	4054	16	18	14	17	9	3	26
	1997	4720	15	21	14	17	10	3	26
	1998	4921	16	20	16	14	9	3	28
	1999	5565	16	21	15	17	9	3	28
	2000	5986	17	21	15	16	10	3	28
	2001	6478	17	21	16	16	10	3	27
Liberia	1970	277	42	18	8	4	7	11	22
(Liberian Dollars)	1975	544	42	18	8	4	7	11	20
	1980	818	42	18	8	4	7	11	20
	1985	942	43	18	9	4	7	11	19
	1990	384	54	13	11	3	7	10	14
	1995	135	82	4	3	2	3	5	7
	2000	526	75	6	5	1	4	5	9
	2001	523	74	7	7	1	4	4	8
Libyan Arab Jamahiriya	1970	1426	2	59	2	7	3	3	19
(Lybian Dinars)	1975	3780	2	55	2	12	6	5	18
	1980	10575	2	65	2	9	5	3	14
	1985	8277	3	46	4	11	7	5	25

Table 3. Gross Domestic Product by Kind of Economic Activity: Individual Countries or Areas

Major area, region and country	Year	Gross Domestic Product (at current prices) Million	Agriculture hunting forestry and fishing A-B	Mining Manufacturing and Utilities C-E	Of which: Manufacturing D	Construction F	Wholesale, retail trade, restaurants and hotels G-H	Transport storage and communication I	Other Activities J-P
			Percentage Distribution						
	1990	8010	7	36	8	12	8	7	30
	1995	10679	9	42	7	4	12	8	25
	2000	17395	8	47	6	6	10	7	22
	2001	17379	9	44	6	7	10	7	23
Madagascar	1970	249400	30	18	17	5	16	13	18
(Malagasy Francs)	1975	395200	41	18	16	5	13	10	14
	1980	689800	36	18	16	5	14	11	16
	1985	1553400	42	16	15	5	14	11	13
	1990	4601600	32	14	12	1	10	17	25
	1995	13458000	33	13	10	1	11	17	24
	2000	26242000	26	13	11	1	11	17	22
	2001	30100000	25	12	10	2	14	21	27
Malawi [12]	1970	267	39	14	12	4	13	6	22
(Kwacha)	1975	530	37	15	13	4	14	7	20
	1980	1005	33	17	16	6	9	4	20
	1985	1929	28	15	14	2	10	4	21
	1990	4782	33	20	19	2	15	4	25
	1995	21376	33	20	19	2	15	4	25
	2000	103799	33	20	19	2	15	4	25
	2001	141730	33	20	19	2	15	4	25
Mali [13]	1970	76300	69	7	4	4	9	2	9
(CFA Francs)	1975	129500	59	8	5	5	13	3	12
	1980	300600	61	7	4	4	14	3	11
	1985	520200	38	14	7	4	13	5	20
	1990	683300	46	13	8	4	14	5	14
	1995	1152970	50	11	8	4	14	5	11
	2000	1811189	41	15	11	6	17	6	14
	2001	1798300	44	19	14	8	16	6	14
Mauritania	1970	11330	27	28	2	5	6	5	22
(Ouguiyas)	1975	20595	25	22	1	5	11	5	25
	1980	38070	32	15	2	5	9	7	26
	1985	52665	20	20	9	6	13	6	23
	1990	82350	27	18	6	5	12	10	20
	1995	137340	24	28	10	7	13	7	24
	2000	215010	24	26	11	7	12	9	24
	2001	245677	24	25	11	6	12	8	24
Mauritius [14]	1970	1067	21	16	14	4	9	10	35
(Rupees)	1975	3416	27	19	17	8	8	8	33
	1980	8805	11	21	19	6	13	10	31
	1985	16825	14	25	22	4	12	9	28
	1990	38462	11	25	23	6	15	9	25
	1995	70283	9	23	20	6	15	10	29
	1996	79086	9	23	21	6	16	9	29
	1997	88099	8	22	21	5	16	10	29
	1998	99564	8	22	21	5	16	10	29
	1999	107444	5	22	21	5	17	11	31
	2000	119529	6	22	21	5	16	11	32
	2001	131835	6	23	20	5	16	12	32
Morocco [15]	1970	20020	20	23	16	4	20	4	25
(Dirhams)	1975	36410	18	29	17	7	17	4	24
	1980	74090	18	25	17	6	14	5	25
	1985	129510	17	28	19	6	14	6	25
	1990	212850	18	27	18	5	13	6	26
	1995	281702	15	29	18	4	13	6	29
	1996	319340	19	27	17	4	24	6	17
	1997	318342	15	28	18	5	24	6	18
	1998	344005	17	27	17	4	24	6	18
	1999	345593	15	27	17	5	24	6	19
	2000	354068	14	27	18	5	25	7	19
	2001	382897	16	26	17	5	24	7	20
Mozambique	1970	79532	67	17	13	6	5	6	3
(Meticais)	1975	112329	67	18	13	6	4	6	2
	1980	142600	67	19	13	6	4	6	2

Table 3. Gross Domestic Product by Kind of Economic Activity: Individual Countries or Areas

Major area, region and country	Year	Gross Domestic Product (at current prices) Million	Agriculture hunting forestry and fishing A-B	Mining Manufacturing and Utilities C-E	Of which: Manufacturing D	Construction F	Wholesale, retail trade, restaurants and hotels G-H	Transport storage and communication I	Other Activities J-P
			Percentage Distribution						
	1985	268746	67	16	13	5	3	6	2
	1990	2515606	64	17	14	8	3	6	2
	1995	20678102	34	8	7	6	23	9	19
	2000	56917388	24	15	12	9	23	9	19
	2001	71134761	24	16	14	9	22	10	19
Namibia [16]......................	1970	362	14	36	5	6	14	8	17
(Namibia Dollars)	1975	696	17	33	5	5	16	6	18
	1980	1574	14	46	4	5	8	5	21
	1985	2735	12	38	5	3	8	5	33
	1990	6054	11	32	12	2	7	5	33
	1995	12706	11	22	11	3	10	7	37
	1996	15011	11	21	9	3	10	6	39
	1997	16754	10	22	10	3	11	6	39
	1998	18790	10	23	11	3	11	6	38
	1999	20681	10	22	10	2	11	6	38
	2000	23995	10	23	10	2	13	6	37
	2001	27231	9	25	10	3	13	5	36
Niger......................	1970	111000	50	14	7	3	10	4	17
(CFA Francs)	1975	180300	49	14	8	3	10	4	18
	1980	536208	43	14	4	6	12	4	15
	1985	647100	37	18	7	4	16	4	19
	1990	682300	42	16	9	5	14	4	22
	1995	834600	43	16	6	2	17	5	18
	2000	1280400	34	16	7	2	19	5	17
	2001	1399100	37	16	7	2	18	5	17
Nigeria [17]......................	1970	7381	47	15	8	6	15	4	16
(Naira)	1975	22722	32	29	10	6	12	4	19
	1980	50346	27	37	9	5	13	5	12
	1985	72355	37	28	10	2	13	5	14
	1990	260637	32	40	6	2	14	2	10
	1995	1977737	32	46	6	1	14	2	5
	2000	4981000	35	15	5	2	7	2	25
	2001	5697000	34	14	5	2	9	2	23
Reunion......................	1970	2013	6	10	...	8	18	3	50
(French Francs)	1975	4540	6	9	...	6	19	3	52
	1980	8449	6	11	...	5	17	4	54
	1985	17054	4	12	...	5	16	5	54
	1990	28374	4	13	...	6	20	4	50
	1995	37037	4	14	...	7	20	5	51
	2000	46379	4	14	...	7	20	5	51
	2001	49439	4	14	...	7	20	5	51
Rwanda [18]......................	1970	21560	52	15	13	3	10	1	12
(Francs)	1975	52770	49	15	12	4	14	1	14
	1980	107990	46	17	15	4	15	2	12
	1985	173700	42	15	14	9	12	5	15
	1990	192900	48	19	18	7	11	5	19
	1995	336489	44	11	10	5	14	4	22
	2000	681455	41	11	10	9	10	7	22
	2001	732276	41	11	10	9	10	7	21
Sao Tome and Principe......................	1970	614	30	9	7	8	5	6	39
(Dobras)	1975	881	25	11	9	7	7	9	39
	1980	1629	26	10	7	8	6	7	44
	1985	2319	23	11	9	6	10	10	39
	1990	8250	28	9	5	7	11	5	40
	1995	64613	26	10	4	10	9	2	42
	2000	369500	20	5	3	12	20	3	39
	2001	422000	20	6	3	12	20	3	39
Senegal......................	1970	241668	24	0	...	2	54	...	13
(CFA Francs)	1975	409054	30	0	...	2	42	...	12
	1980	631400	19	13	11	3	23	10	33
	1985	1158200	19	15	13	3	25	10	29

Table 3. Gross Domestic Product by Kind of Economic Activity: Individual Countries or Areas

Major area, region and country	Year	Gross Domestic Product (at current prices) Million	Agriculture hunting forestry and fishing A-B	Mining Manufacturing and Utilities C-E	Of which: Manufacturing D	Construction F	Wholesale, retail trade, restaurants and hotels G-H	Transport storage and communication I	Other Activities J-P
			Percentage Distribution						
	1990	1551500	20	16	13	3	24	10	27
	1995	2234000	20	16	13	3	26	10	24
	1996	2380000	21	16	13	4	26	10	24
	1997	2554300	20	16	12	4	26	11	23
	1998	2746000	18	16	12	4	27	11	23
	1999	2925000	19	15	12	4	27	11	23
	2000	3114000	19	15	12	4	26	12	22
	2001	3379700	20	16	13	4	26	12	22
Seychelles [19]	1970	110	13	2	1	12	28	7	31
(Rupees)	1975	292	12	5	5	11	24	9	31
	1980	942	7	8	7	8	25	14	30
	1985	1205	6	12	10	6	25	14	29
	1990	1967	5	11	10	5	27	12	25
	1995	2420	4	15	13	8	9	30	27
	1996	2500	4	16	13	8	10	27	28
	1997	2830	3	17	14	8	10	29	27
	1998	3201	3	18	15	8	9	30	27
	1999	3330	3	17	15	10	8	31	26
	2000	3424	3	16	14	10	9	32	26
	2001	3419	3	16	14	9	9	32	27
Sierra Leone	1970	346	28	26	9	4	12	10	17
(Leones)	1975	573	34	21	8	3	13	10	17
	1980	1156	32	19	7	4	13	14	17
	1985	4785	43	11	5	3	16	11	15
	1990	96133	37	14	7	2	25	11	11
	1995	710389	38	7	3	2	27	9	9
	2000	1330300	47	23	9	6	14	5	4
	2001	1485507	49	24	10	7	12	4	4
Somalia	1970	2436	53	7	6	5	9	6	12
(Shillings)	1975	4765	53	5	3	5	10	8	13
	1980	17341	64	5	4	3	9	4	10
	1985	87290	64	5	5	2	10	6	9
	1990	1738800	70	2	2	4	9	7	9
	1995	6424840	62	3	3	4	11	10	13
	2000	17618100	63	4	3	5	10	9	12
	2001	16798653	63	4	3	5	10	9	11
South Africa	1970	13045	7	31	21	4	14	10	28
(Rand)	1975	27868	7	34	21	5	13	10	26
	1980	64141	6	42	20	3	11	9	23
	1985	128773	5	37	20	3	10	9	29
	1990	289816	4	33	21	3	13	7	30
	1995	548100	4	29	19	3	13	8	35
	1996	617954	4	28	18	3	13	8	36
	1997	685730	4	27	18	3	13	8	37
	1998	739504	3	26	17	3	12	9	38
	1999	802840	3	26	17	3	12	9	39
	2000	887795	3	26	17	3	12	9	38
	2001	975196	3	26	17	3	12	9	39
Sudan [20]	1970	67	39	11	9	3	15	7	20
(Sudanese Pounds)	1975	168	39	11	9	4	16	6	19
	1980	449	33	10	9	5	15	11	21
	1985	1703	34	11	8	4	18	10	17
	1990	15139	29	12	9	5	20	11	19
	1995	810318	26	11	9	4	17	10	15
	1996	1033070	29	13	10	4	19	11	17
	1997	1676940	29	13	10	4	19	11	17
	1998	1991610	30	14	10	4	19	11	17
	1999	2448880	41	12	9	4	19	11	17
	2000	2969450	35	13	10	4	17	10	15
	2001	3130000	38	13	10	4	18	11	16
Swaziland	1970	78	21	24	12	2	12	6	26
(Lilangeni)	1975	216	20	21	15	3	10	5	29
	1980	460	18	22	17	4	8	5	22
	1985	813	16	18	13	3	10	6	28
	1990	2253	11	33	29	2	8	5	23

Table 3. Gross Domestic Product by Kind of Economic Activity: Individual Countries or Areas

Major area, region and country	Year	Gross Domestic Product (at current prices) Million	Agriculture hunting forestry and fishing A-B	Mining Manufacturing and Utilities C-E	Of which: Manufacturing D	Construction F	Wholesale, retail trade, restaurants and hotels G-H	Transport storage and communication I	Other Activities J-P
			Percentage Distribution						
	1995	4949	12	32	29	4	7	4	21
	1996	5686	14	30	28	4	7	4	21
	1997	6613	13	30	28	4	7	4	20
	1998	7449	13	30	28	4	7	4	19
	1999	8408	12	28	26	4	7	3	18
	2000	9639	11	26	25	5	6	4	17
	2001	10971	10	26	25	4	6	4	16
Togo..	1970	73171	25	21	9	3	20	7	17
(CFA Francs)	1975	128302	25	19	7	6	17	7	18
	1980	238872	27	18	7	5	19	6	24
	1985	338200	29	16	6	3	20	6	26
	1990	427600	29	20	7	4	22	6	24
	1995	652500	26	21	7	3	21	5	23
	2000	885800	38	19	6	3	16	4	20
	2001	938000	39	18	6	3	16	4	19
Tunisia [21]..	1970	756	17	16	8	5	20	6	23
(Dinars)	1975	1741	18	20	9	6	20	5	19
	1980	3541	14	25	12	6	18	5	19
	1985	7018	16	30	17	6	11	6	25
	1990	10816	16	26	17	4	14	7	25
	1995	17052	11	25	19	5	15	7	27
	1996	19066	14	24	18	4	15	7	26
	1997	20898	13	24	18	4	15	8	26
	1998	22561	13	24	18	5	15	8	26
	1999	24672	13	24	18	5	15	8	25
	2000	26685	12	24	18	5	15	8	26
	2001	28759	12	24	19	5	15	8	26
Uganda..	1970	135	43	5	4	3	30	2	21
(New Shillings)	1975	321	60	4	3	2	18	1	20
	1980	1851	59	2	1	1	17	1	20
	1985	27578	53	5	4	3	13	2	16
	1990	1602094	51	6	5	5	13	4	15
	1995	5991763	44	8	6	6	12	4	18
	1996	6555380	40	9	7	7	13	4	19
	1997	7230521	38	10	8	7	13	4	19
	1998	8298977	40	10	8	7	12	4	18
	1999	9132410	39	10	8	7	13	5	18
	2000	9371358	34	11	9	8	12	5	23
	2001	10145469	31	12	9	8	12	5	24
United Republic Of Tanzania [22].................	1970	9568	34	14	10	5	13	8	19
(Shillings)	1975	19829	34	13	11	5	13	8	20
	1980	42118	39	12	10	4	11	7	18
	1985	112000	46	8	7	2	13	6	15
	1990	736338	50	10	8	5	14	5	10
	1995	3020500	44	10	7	4	14	5	20
	1996	3767640	44	10	7	4	13	5	20
	1997	4703460	43	9	6	4	12	5	22
	1998	5571640	41	10	7	5	11	4	23
	1999	6432910	42	10	7	5	12	5	23
	2000	7225690	42	10	7	5	11	5	22
	2001	8186480	40	9	7	5	11	4	22
Zambia...	1970	1185	7	41	10	8	9	9	23
(Kwacha)	1975	1837	9	33	14	8	11	9	26
	1980	3656	8	33	13	5	15	8	28
	1985	9351	9	45	19	4	9	6	21
	1990	123487	17	38	29	3	11	5	12
	1995	2998202	16	27	10	4	16	6	24
	2000	10900735	21	25	10	5	19	6	23
	2001	13170001	22	30	12	5	19	6	24
Zimbabwe [23]...	1970	1079	14	29	19	5	14	8	25
(Zimbabwe Dollars)	1975	1998	16	31	22	5	13	7	25
	1980	3441	13	34	23	3	13	6	28
	1985	9097	21	23	18	2	16	5	26
	1990	21494	15	27	20	3	15	6	27
	1995	61759	13	24	19	2	19	6	26

Table 3. Gross Domestic Product by Kind of Economic Activity: Individual Countries or Areas

Major area, region and country	Year	Gross Domestic Product (at current prices) Million	Agriculture hunting forestry and fishing A-B	Mining Manufacturing and Utilities C-E	Of which: Manufacturing D	Construction F	Wholesale, retail trade, restaurants and hotels G-H	Transport storage and communication I	Other Activities J-P
			Percentage Distribution						
	1996	85551	19	21	17	2	18	5	25
	1997	102982	17	20	16	2	17	5	28
	1998	143364	19	18	14	3	16	5	27
	1999	210409	17	19	15	2	17	5	28
	2000	330345	17	18	13	2	16	8	28
	2001	493800	20	19	14	3	18	10	32
NORTHERN AMERICA									
Bermuda..	1970	259	1	9	3	7	21	7	59
(Bermudian Dollars)	1975	480	1	7	3	7	21	7	53
	1980	919	1	6	3	7	22	7	50
	1985	1433	1	6	3	8	20	6	56
	1990	1997	1	6	3	7	19	7	57
	1995	2544	1	5	3	5	18	7	62
	1996	2680	1	5	2	6	18	7	61
	1997	2889	1	5	2	6	18	7	63
	1998	3053	1	5	3	4	19	7	64
	1999	3272	1	5	2	6	17	7	64
	2000	3397	1	5	3	6	17	7	64
	2001	3599	1	5	3	7	16	7	64
Canada..	1970	89112	4	25	19	7	13	8	32
(Canadian Dollars)	1975	171435	4	25	18	8	13	7	33
	1980	311015	4	28	17	7	12	7	34
	1985	478829	3	28	17	6	13	8	38
	1990	669967	3	23	16	6	14	7	42
	1995	798300	3	24	17	5	13	7	43
	1996	824041	3	24	17	5	13	7	43
	1997	868979	2	24	17	5	13	7	43
	1998	900350	2	23	17	5	13	7	43
	1999	965440	2	24	18	5	13	7	43
	2000	1049450	2	25	18	5	13	7	42
	2001	1075580	2	25	18	5	13	7	42
United States..	1970	1025500	3	29	24	5	19	7	39
(Dollars)	1975	1617800	3	27	22	5	19	7	40
	1980	2771500	2	28	21	5	18	7	41
	1985	4174900	2	26	19	4	18	7	43
	1990	5750800	2	23	18	4	17	6	47
	1995	7338400	2	22	18	4	18	7	48
	1996	7751100	2	21	17	4	18	7	48
	1997	8250500	2	21	17	4	18	7	49
	1998	8720200	1	20	16	4	18	7	50
	1999	9212800	1	19	16	5	18	7	50
	2000	9762100	1	19	16	5	18	7	51
	2001	10019700	1	18	14	5	18	7	52
LATIN AMERICA and the CARIBBEAN									
Anguilla..	1970	6	5	4	1	15	30	13	25
(EC Dollars)	1975	12	5	4	1	15	30	13	25
	1980	24	5	4	1	15	30	13	25
	1985	52	5	3	1	14	32	13	25
	1990	147	5	3	1	17	33	10	25
	1995	202	3	3	1	11	35	12	25
	1996	214	3	4	1	12	32	12	28
	1997	240	3	4	1	12	33	13	26
	1998	255	3	5	1	12	33	13	25
	1999	283	2	5	1	14	31	12	26
	2000	292	2	5	1	12	29	13	29
	2001	298	2	5	1	10	31	13	31
Antigua and Barbuda.................................	1970	98	9	12	8	6	16	13	37
(EC Dollars)	1975	152	9	10	7	6	17	13	35
	1980	297	6	8	5	8	22	14	32
	1985	541	4	8	4	7	23	15	35
	1990	902	4	10	3	12	23	15	37
	1995	1176	4	9	2	10	22	15	38
	2000	1603	4	8	2	13	21	15	38
	2001	1651	4	9	2	14	20	15	38

Table 3. Gross Domestic Product by Kind of Economic Activity: Individual Countries or Areas

Major area, region and country	Year	Gross Domestic Product (at current prices) Million	Agriculture hunting forestry and fishing A-B	Mining Manufacturing and Utilities C-E	Of which: Manufacturing D	Construction F	Wholesale, retail trade, restaurants and hotels G-H	Transport storage and communication I	Other Activities J-P
			Percentage Distribution						
Argentina (Pesos)	1970	1.2 (u)	7	40	35	6	15	7	17
	1975	19.2 (u)	5	42	38	9	14	5	18
	1980	3800 (u)	5	34	29	8	16	5	32
	1985	5	8	34	30	6	16	5	32
	1990	68922	8	32	27	4	16	5	36
	1995	258032	5	20	16	5	16	7	39
	1996	272150	6	20	16	5	16	8	37
	1997	292859	5	20	16	5	17	8	36
	1998	298948	5	19	16	5	17	8	36
	1999	283522	4	19	15	5	16	8	39
	2000	284204	5	19	15	5	15	8	39
	2001	268697	5	19	14	4	15	9	42
Aruba [24] (Aruban Florin)	1970	685	1	5	1	9	28	6	43
	1975	888	1	6	1	9	28	7	42
	1980	1151	1	6	1	8	28	7	42
	1985	1492	1	7	1	8	28	8	42
	1990	1934	1	8	1	7	27	8	42
	1995	2364	1	9	3	6	25	9	48
	1996	2470	0	8	3	7	25	8	49
	1997	2742	0	9	2	8	23	8	48
	1998	2981	0	9	3	8	24	8	47
	1999	3087	0	10	3	6	23	8	49
	2000	3326	0	9	3	6	24	9	49
	2001	3381	0	10	3	6	25	9	52
Bahamas [25] (Bahamian Dollars)	1970	502	2	11	10	4	29	10	45
	1975	723	2	9	8	4	29	10	43
	1980	1438	2	6	5	4	29	10	33
	1985	2171	2	5	3	4	29	10	31
	1990	3047	2	5	3	4	31	10	30
	1995	3069	3	7	3	2	23	10	40
	1996	3093	3	8	3	2	22	9	43
	1997	3116	4	8	3	2	20	9	45
	1998	3140	4	9	3	2	19	9	48
	1999	3164	5	11	3	2	20	10	56
	2000	3189	5	12	3	2	19	10	63
	2001	3213	6	14	3	1	20	11	72
Barbados (Barbados Dollars)	1970	370	11	9	8	7	19	6	37
	1975	812	12	10	9	6	24	6	29
	1980	1730	9	13	11	7	29	5	26
	1985	2410	6	14	10	5	28	8	30
	1990	3440	5	10	7	6	27	7	32
	1995	3742	5	9	6	4	26	9	32
	1996	3995	6	9	5	4	26	9	32
	1997	4413	4	8	5	5	24	8	32
	1998	4747	3	8	5	5	25	8	33
	1999	4965	4	8	5	5	24	9	33
	2000	5183	4	9	5	5	24	9	33
	2001	5093	4	8	5	5	22	9	35
Belize (Belize Dollars)	1970	77	14	10	9	5	16	7	42
	1975	189	28	13	12	6	14	6	30
	1980	389	24	22	21	5	15	4	26
	1985	418	18	17	15	5	13	8	38
	1990	811	18	16	13	7	16	9	28
	1995	1173	17	15	12	5	15	9	31
	1996	1207	18	15	11	5	15	9	32
	1997	1231	17	15	12	5	16	9	32
	1998	1258	16	14	11	5	16	9	32
	1999	1377	16	14	11	5	17	9	30
	2000	1514	15	15	11	6	19	9	30
	2001	1533	16	15	11	6	18	9	30
Bolivia (Bolivianos)	1970	12 (t)	20	26	13	5	12	6	25
	1975	48 (t)	21	26	12	5	13	6	25
	1980	123 (t)	18	31	15	4	11	6	29
	1985	2867	29	25	12	4	11	11	22
	1990	15443	15	29	17	3	12	9	25
	1995	32235	15	26	17	3	11	10	25

Table 3. Gross Domestic Product by Kind of Economic Activity: Individual Countries or Areas

Major area, region and country	Year	Gross Domestic Product (at current prices)	Agriculture hunting forestry and fishing A-B	Mining Manufacturing and Utilities C-E	Of which: Manufacturing D	Construction F	Wholesale, retail trade, restaurants and hotels G-H	Transport storage and communication I	Other Activities J-P
		Million	Percentage Distribution						
	1996	37537	14	25	16	3	11	10	26
	1997	41644	15	24	15	3	11	11	27
	1998	46822	13	22	14	4	11	12	29
	1999	48156	13	22	14	3	11	12	32
	2000	51667	13	23	14	3	11	11	31
	2001	52652	14	23	13	2	11	12	31
Brazil [26] (Reais)	1970	0.1 (u)	10	28	26	6	16	3	28
	1975	0.6 (u)	8	29	26	7	15	4	25
	1980	4.7 (u)	5	32	30	7	9	7	28
	1985	448 (u)	7	38	33	6	10	5	40
	1990	11	7	31	27	7	9	5	53
	1995	646192	8	24	21	8	8	4	41
	1996	778887	7	22	19	8	7	4	44
	1997	870743	7	23	19	9	7	5	44
	1998	914188	7	22	19	9	6	5	45
	1999	973846	7	23	18	8	6	5	43
	2000	1101255	7	25	20	8	7	5	41
	2001	1200060	7	26	20	8	7	5	41
British Virgin Islands (US Dollars)	1970	16	5	5	3	16	16	11	30
	1975	21	7	5	3	8	25	11	37
	1980	44	5	4	3	5	32	10	37
	1985	72	4	6	3	7	27	10	42
	1990	240	3	7	3	6	26	12	38
	1995	385	2	6	4	8	29	12	45
	2000	691	1	6	4	8	28	11	47
	2001	777	1	6	4	8	28	11	47
Cayman Islands [27] (Dollars)	1970	16	4	7	2	12	32	4	40
	1975	45	2	6	2	12	28	5	41
	1980	110	1	6	2	13	26	9	48
	1985	264	0	5	2	9	20	12	48
	1990	590	0	5	2	9	24	11	49
	1995	849	0	5	2	9	22	10	46
	2000	1131	0	5	2	9	22	10	46
	2001	1198	0	5	2	9	22	10	46
Chile (Pesos)	1970	105	6	30	17	8	14	5	32
	1975	37891	5	28	13	9	14	6	39
	1980	1149700	6	26	14	8	14	5	43
	1985	2930460	6	29	14	7	12	5	39
	1990	10216526	7	31	17	7	12	6	30
	1995	28593362	6	29	18	9	11	6	32
	1996	31237289	5	27	18	9	11	6	34
	1997	34722636	5	26	17	10	11	6	35
	1998	36534873	6	24	17	9	11	7	36
	1999	37164386	6	26	17	8	11	7	37
	2000	40436215	6	28	17	7	11	7	36
	2001	42191778	6	27	16	8	11	7	34
Colombia (Pesos)	1970	157666	27	20	18	4	10	7	33
	1975	480111	26	22	20	3	11	6	32
	1980	1871842	21	23	20	5	11	6	33
	1985	5886995	18	24	19	7	11	6	31
	1990	23979488	18	27	17	5	11	7	29
	1995	84439109	14	22	15	7	12	7	35
	1996	100711389	13	22	14	7	12	7	38
	1997	121707501	13	21	14	6	11	7	40
	1998	140483322	13	21	14	6	12	7	40
	1999	151565005	13	23	14	4	11	7	40
	2000	173729806	12	24	15	4	11	7	38
	2001	189525312	12	24	15	3	11	8	38
Costa Rica (Colones)	1970	8291	16	20	19	6	19	6	26
	1975	21352	15	23	22	7	17	7	25
	1980	52610	13	21	20	8	18	6	25
	1985	251474	13	26	23	5	18	7	23
	1990	664322	11	23	20	4	18	7	29
	1995	2105687	13	23	20	4	18	8	29
	1996	2459957	12	23	20	3	18	8	29

Table 3. Gross Domestic Product by Kind of Economic Activity: Individual Countries or Areas

Major area, region and country	Year	Gross Domestic Product (at current prices) Million	Agriculture hunting forestry and fishing A-B	Mining Manufacturing and Utilities C-E	Of which: Manufacturing D	Construction F	Wholesale, retail trade, restaurants and hotels G-H	Transport storage and communication I	Other Activities J-P
			Percentage Distribution						
	1997	2984020	12	23	20	3	18	8	29
	1998	3625330	12	24	21	4	19	8	29
	1999	4512763	10	29	27	3	17	7	29
	2000	4917764	9	26	23	4	18	8	31
	2001	5387526	8	23	20	4	18	8	34
Cuba..	1970	5192	8	43	40	7	33	7	7
(Cuban Pesos)	1975	9742	8	40	37	6	30	7	9
	1980	13075	7	33	30	6	31	7	17
	1985	19145	10	29	27	7	27	7	21
	1990	19645	11	27	24	7	25	6	24
	1995	21737	6	41	38	4	23	4	21
	1996	22815	7	40	37	5	21	4	21
	1997	22952	7	40	37	5	21	4	21
	1998	23901	6	41	37	5	21	4	21
	1999	25504	6	42	39	5	20	4	20
	2000	27635	7	41	37	6	21	5	20
	2001	28589	7	33	28	4	22	6	29
Dominica..	1970	55	32	7	4	5	10	6	30
(EC Dollars)	1975	73	26	7	4	7	12	6	32
	1980	160	28	7	4	12	9	7	32
	1985	266	23	8	5	6	9	11	30
	1990	452	21	9	6	6	11	13	28
	1995	592	16	11	6	8	10	15	33
	1996	638	17	11	6	8	10	15	32
	1997	662	16	11	6	7	10	15	31
	1998	701	16	12	7	7	10	15	32
	1999	723	16	12	7	7	10	15	32
	2000	728	15	13	7	7	10	14	33
	2001	711	15	12	7	7	10	14	35
Dominican Republic [28]................................	1970	1784	17	31	27	4	20	9	16
(Pesos)	1975	4323	15	34	31	6	21	7	17
	1980	7964	14	26	23	6	20	7	20
	1985	16782	12	30	26	5	21	10	18
	1990	77911	12	22	20	7	18	8	26
	1995	209646	9	21	18	7	16	8	31
	1996	232993	9	22	19	7	20	9	32
	1997	214864	11	22	19	8	23	12	24
	1998	241977	10	22	19	9	24	12	23
	1999	278347	10	21	19	10	24	13	22
	2000	321783	10	22	19	10	24	13	21
	2001	361569	10	21	18	9	24	14	22
Ecuador [29]...	1970	1762	36	17	10	2	11	6	36
(Sucres)	1975	4536	27	24	8	3	12	5	33
	1980	12351	18	26	9	4	11	7	36
	1985	16797	20	29	10	2	12	8	27
	1990	11248	20	24	10	2	16	8	21
	1995	20196	17	21	11	3	15	9	29
	1996	21268	16	22	11	4	15	9	30
	1997	23636	16	20	11	4	15	8	31
	1998	23255	14	17	12	5	16	10	31
	1999	16674	12	23	10	5	15	11	26
	2000	15934	11	28	5	7	17	11	19
	2001	21024	9	22	8	7	16	16	23
El Salvador [30]...	1970	2571	28	21	19	3	23	5	21
(Colones)	1975	4478	23	20	19	5	26	4	22
	1980	8917	28	17	15	3	23	4	25
	1985	14331	18	19	16	3	27	4	28
	1990	36487	17	23	22	3	18	7	31
	1995	83129	13	23	21	4	20	7	27
	1996	90261	13	23	21	4	20	8	28
	1997	97428	13	23	21	4	20	8	29
	1998	105074	12	24	21	4	19	8	30
	1999	109066	10	25	23	4	19	8	30
	2000	114967	10	25	23	4	19	8	30
	2001	120215	9	25	23	5	20	8	30

Table 3. Gross Domestic Product by Kind of Economic Activity: Individual Countries or Areas

Major area, region and country	Year	Gross Domestic Product (at current prices) Million	Agriculture hunting forestry and fishing A-B	Mining Manufacturing and Utilities C-E	Of which: Manufacturing D	Construction F	Wholesale, retail trade, restaurants and hotels G-H	Transport storage and communication I	Other Activities J-P
			Percentage Distribution						
French Guiana (French Francs)	1970	287	6	6	...	8	11	5	62
	1975	575	6	6	...	8	11	5	62
	1980	1219	6	3	...	8	13	5	65
	1985	3173	6	4	...	11	13	12	54
	1990	6526	10	8	...	13	13	8	47
	1995	8362	7	10	...	11	11	10	53
	2000	9372	7	10	...	11	11	9	54
	2001	9589	7	10	...	11	11	9	54
Grenada (EC Dollars)	1970	60	24	5	3	7	17	11	30
	1975	107	24	5	3	7	17	11	30
	1980	202	20	5	3	6	17	11	27
	1985	311	14	6	4	6	16	10	30
	1990	541	13	7	4	8	15	11	27
	1995	649	9	8	4	8	19	13	24
	1996	693	8	8	4	8	19	13	24
	1997	740	7	8	4	8	18	13	25
	1998	801	7	8	5	9	18	14	24
	1999	888	7	8	5	9	19	13	24
	2000	964	7	9	5	10	18	13	24
	2001	1020	7	8	5	8	17	13	26
Guadeloupe (French Francs)	1970	1330	11	7	...	4	17	3	54
	1975	2826	13	8	...	5	18	3	50
	1980	5860	7	6	...	4	17	4	57
	1985	9802	10	4	...	5	17	6	56
	1990	15200	7	6	...	7	18	6	55
	1995	22157	7	8	...	7	17	7	55
	2000	30578	7	8	...	7	18	7	57
	2001	32693	7	8	...	7	18	7	58
Guatemala (Quetzalas)	1970	1904	27	17	16	2	29	5	20
	1975	3646	28	17	15	2	28	6	19
	1980	7879	25	19	17	3	27	7	19
	1985	11180	26	18	16	2	25	7	22
	1990	34317	26	18	15	2	24	8	22
	1995	85157	24	18	14	2	25	9	23
	1996	95479	24	18	14	2	25	9	23
	1997	107943	24	18	14	2	25	9	23
	1998	121548	23	18	14	2	25	9	23
	1999	132588	23	18	13	2	24	9	23
	2000	145486	23	18	13	2	25	10	23
	2001	158201	22	18	13	1	24	10	24
Guyana [31] (Dollars Guyana)	1970	536	17	28	11	7	10	5	20
	1975	1188	29	25	14	6	8	4	20
	1980	1508	21	25	11	6	8	5	24
	1985	1964	26	11	8	6	7	7	27
	1990	15665	38	13	5	4	6	7	20
	1995	88271	41	18	3	4	4	4	14
	1996	99038	38	19	3	4	4	5	15
	1997	106678	36	18	3	4	4	5	17
	1998	108002	34	16	3	5	4	6	19
	1999	123665	35	16	3	4	3	6	21
	2000	130013	30	16	3	4	4	6	23
	2001	133544	29	16	3	4	4	7	23
Haiti (Gourdes)	1970	1656	44	15	13	3	16	2	18
	1975	3407	41	16	14	5	17	2	23
	1980	6919	34	19	17	5	18	2	28
	1985	10047	34	17	16	6	17	2	33
	1990	13068	35	16	15	6	17	2	34
	1995	37135	33	8	7	9	13	2	35
	1996	44952	33	8	7	10	13	2	35
	1997	53447	34	0	7	11	13	2	35
	1998	60898	34	8	7	12	13	2	35
	1999	68421	29	8	7	12	13	2	29
	2000	77149	35	10	8	16	17	3	16
	2001	88502	35	9	9	16	17	3	16

Table 3. Gross Domestic Product by Kind of Economic Activity: Individual Countries or Areas

Major area, region and country	Year	Gross Domestic Product (at current prices) Million	Agriculture hunting forestry and fishing A-B	Mining Manufacturing and Utilities C-E	Of which: Manufacturing D	Construction F	Wholesale, retail trade, restaurants and hotels G-H	Transport storage and communication I	Other Activities J-P
			Percentage Distribution						
Honduras (Lempiras)	1970	1382	28	16	13	5	13	6	24
	1975	2248	25	18	14	5	14	6	24
	1980	5132	21	17	13	5	14	6	26
	1985	7279	19	16	13	5	12	6	31
	1990	12537	20	19	15	5	10	6	30
	1995	37507	19	22	16	5	10	4	27
	1996	47763	19	23	16	4	10	4	26
	1997	61322	20	22	16	4	10	4	27
	1998	70438	16	22	16	4	10	4	28
	1999	77095	14	23	17	5	11	4	29
	2000	87523	13	23	17	5	11	5	30
	2001	98379	12	23	18	5	11	5	32
Jamaica (Jamaican Dollars)	1970	1270	7	28	15	12	19	5	32
	1975	2833	8	26	17	9	20	6	36
	1980	5200	9	31	16	5	19	5	34
	1985	12204	6	27	19	8	22	8	31
	1990	33202	7	30	19	11	19	8	32
	1995	200027	9	24	15	11	21	8	28
	1996	237382	8	22	14	10	21	8	31
	1997	258026	8	21	14	10	21	9	30
	1998	273429	8	20	13	10	21	10	31
	1999	294076	7	21	13	9	20	10	33
	2000	329171	6	21	13	9	20	10	32
	2001	358036	6	21	13	10	20	11	31
Martinique (French Francs)	1970	1600	10	8	...	4	16	3	51
	1975	3358	10	9	...	5	18	3	51
	1980	6102	6	7	...	4	17	4	60
	1985	12484	8	8	...	4	17	5	55
	1990	19320	6	10	...	5	18	6	53
	1995	24148	5	10	...	5	18	6	53
	2000	29282	5	10	...	5	19	6	53
	2001	30501	5	10	...	5	19	6	53
Mexico [32] (New Pesos)	1970	495	11	21	18	5	26	5	29
	1975	1226	10	20	18	5	26	6	27
	1980	4766	8	22	18	6	24	7	26
	1985	50530	8	24	19	4	24	8	25
	1990	738898	7	22	19	4	23	8	28
	1995	1837020	5	22	19	4	19	9	37
	1996	2525580	6	22	20	4	20	9	33
	1997	3174280	5	22	19	4	19	10	32
	1998	3846350	5	22	19	4	18	10	33
	1999	4593690	4	22	19	5	18	10	34
	2000	5485370	4	21	18	5	19	10	33
	2001	5765920	4	20	18	4	19	10	34
Montserrat (EC Dollars)	1970	13	4	10	7	10	18	8	44
	1975	25	4	10	7	10	18	8	44
	1980	66	4	9	5	8	16	6	48
	1985	100	4	10	5	7	16	10	45
	1990	181	2	4	2	30	10	10	35
	1995	162	5	6	3	6	13	14	48
	1996	131	4	8	5	7	12	15	45
	1997	110	1	6	3	14	7	12	50
	1998	101	1	3	1	21	5	13	49
	1999	95	1	4	1	19	6	12	48
	2000	94	1	6	1	13	5	12	53
	2001	94	1	7	1	12	5	11	58
Netherlands Antilles [33] (Guilders)	1970	517	1	10	8	9	21	20	46
	1975	824	1	10	8	9	21	20	45
	1980	1558	1	10	9	10	21	20	42
	1985	1966	1	10	7	8	23	11	51
	1990	3253	1	10	7	7	28	11	50
	1995	4224	1	11	7	7	25	13	49
	2000	4458	1	10	6	7	24	11	52
	2001	4557	1	10	6	7	24	11	52

Table 3. Gross Domestic Product by Kind of Economic Activity: Individual Countries or Areas

Major area, region and country	Year	Gross Domestic Product (at current prices) Million	Agriculture hunting forestry and fishing A-B	Mining Manufacturing and Utilities C-E	Of which: Manufacturing D	Construction F	Wholesale, retail trade, restaurants and hotels G-H	Transport storage and communication I	Other Activities J-P
			Percentage Distribution						
Nicaragua [34]	1970	1 (u)	21	23	20	3	21	5	28
(Gold Cordobas)	1975	2 (u)	21	24	22	5	22	5	25
	1980	4 (u)	21	28	26	3	19	6	25
	1985	22 (u)	21	30	28	5	17	4	23
	1990	303	30	19	18	3	26	4	20
	1995	13855	33	19	17	3	23	4	18
	1996	16204	33	18	16	4	23	4	18
	1997	18601	33	18	16	4	23	3	18
	1998	21881	32	18	16	4	24	4	18
	1999	26130	32	17	15	6	23	3	19
	2000	30858	33	16	14	6	22	3	19
	2001	34242	33	16	14	6	22	3	19
Panama	1970	1003	13	17	15	6	21	8	38
(Balboas)	1975	1820	11	17	15	7	23	10	42
	1980	3545	9	15	11	6	23	15	42
	1985	5006	9	17	13	4	17	17	49
	1990	5313	9	14	9	1	17	16	43
	1995	7906	8	13	9	5	21	14	40
	1996	8151	8	13	9	4	20	14	41
	1997	8658	7	13	9	4	21	14	42
	1998	9345	7	12	8	5	20	15	43
	1999	9637	7	12	8	5	18	16	44
	2000	10019	7	12	7	5	18	17	44
	2001	10195	8	13	7	4	18	16	42
Paraguay [35]	1970	74921	32	18	17	3	24	4	19
(Guaranies)	1975	190439	37	17	16	4	23	4	15
	1980	560459	29	19	16	6	26	4	15
	1985	1393890	29	19	16	6	26	4	16
	1990	6474434	28	20	17	5	29	4	14
	1995	17699000	25	20	16	6	29	4	16
	1996	19804807	25	20	15	6	28	4	16
	1997	20934352	25	20	15	6	28	4	17
	1998	23436984	24	21	15	6	27	4	18
	1999	24144290	25	20	14	6	24	4	20
	2000	26920974	25	20	14	6	23	5	21
	2001	28118844	24	21	14	5	24	5	21
Peru	1970	241 (u)	9	22	17	3	19	6	28
(New Soles)	1975	573 (u)	7	22	17	4	22	7	28
	1980	5143 (u)	6	24	16	4	20	7	29
	1985	170530 (u)	7	22	15	3	19	7	33
	1990	5851	8	22	15	4	19	8	30
	1995	120859	8	21	15	6	18	7	29
	1996	136929	8	21	15	6	18	7	29
	1997	157274	8	21	15	7	19	8	29
	1998	166513	8	20	14	7	18	8	29
	1999	174719	8	22	14	6	18	8	30
	2000	186757	8	22	15	6	18	8	29
	2001	189769	8	24	16	5	18	9	31
Puerto Rico [36]	1970	5647	3	27	24	8	19	5	33
(US Dollars)	1975	8969	3	37	33	4	19	6	35
	1980	15956	2	39	36	3	16	5	31
	1985	21969	2	42	39	1	16	6	32
	1990	32287	1	42	39	2	16	5	34
	1995	45341	1	44	41	2	15	5	34
	1996	48187	1	43	40	3	15	5	35
	1997	54086	1	45	43	3	15	5	33
	1998	57841	1	43	40	3	15	5	33
	1999	61045	1	41	38	3	15	5	35
	2000	67897	1	42	40	3	14	5	35
	2001	73244	1	41	39	3	14	5	35
Saint Kitts and Nevis	1970	34	16	12	11	9	10	9	30
(EC Dollars)	1975	74	16	12	11	8	9	9	31
	1980	129	13	14	13	9	14	8	30
	1985	211	8	11	10	7	18	10	35
	1990	430	5	12	11	12	18	13	28
	1995	623	5	11	9	10	19	13	32

Table 3. Gross Domestic Product by Kind of Economic Activity: Individual Countries or Areas

Major area, region and country	Year	Gross Domestic Product (at current prices) Million	Agriculture hunting forestry and fishing A-B	Mining Manufacturing and Utilities C-E	Of which: Manufacturing D	Construction F	Wholesale, retail trade, restaurants and hotels G-H	Transport storage and communication I	Other Activities J-P
			Percentage Distribution						
	1996	663	4	11	9	10	20	13	32
	1997	742	5	11	9	9	20	13	32
	1998	775	3	10	8	10	21	12	33
	1999	823	3	11	9	11	20	12	34
	2000	891	2	11	9	14	17	12	36
	2001	928	2	10	8	15	17	11	35
Saint Lucia [37]	1970	79	16	10	7	10	19	7	38
(EC Dollars)	1975	129	16	10	7	10	19	7	38
	1980	305	12	13	9	12	25	12	31
	1985	441	15	13	8	7	23	10	38
	1990	1123	12	10	7	5	22	14	26
	1995	1496	8	10	6	7	22	16	30
	1996	1543	7	9	6	6	23	16	30
	1997	1562	7	9	5	6	24	16	31
	1998	1695	7	9	5	7	23	16	30
	1999	1848	8	9	5	7	23	15	28
	2000	1913	8	8	4	7	23	15	28
	2001	1980	6	8	4	6	19	16	28
Saint Vincent and the Grenadines.............	1970	37	17	12	9	11	14	17	29
(EC Dollars)	1975	71	17	12	9	11	14	17	29
	1980	160	12	12	9	12	13	15	26
	1985	305	16	13	10	6	11	15	25
	1990	535	18	12	7	8	12	17	23
	1995	712	12	12	7	10	15	17	24
	1996	752	11	12	7	9	15	18	25
	1997	793	8	12	7	11	15	18	25
	1998	858	9	11	6	12	16	17	24
	1999	890	9	10	5	11	16	18	25
	2000	905	9	11	5	10	17	17	26
	2001	940	9	11	5	10	17	16	26
Suriname..	1970	532	7	44	19	3	17	5	23
(Guilders)	1975	931	6	29	16	4	15	5	23
	1980	1590	8	27	16	6	17	4	27
	1985	1746	8	21	12	6	15	7	38
	1990	3170	10	21	12	6	18	6	37
	1995	229510	19	35	16	4	18	8	18
	1996	303970	17	26	11	4	13	8	21
	1997	340220	13	27	10	3	14	7	26
	1998	407130	9	19	9	4	14	5	48
	1999	758905	8	18	8	3	14	6	42
	2000	1172225	10	20	8	3	14	8	40
	2001	1834219	9	24	5	3	10	7	37
Trinidad and Tobago [38]...............................	1970	1644	5	34	24	7	19	14	21
(Trinidad and Tobago Dollars)	1975	5300	3	51	15	8	14	7	19
	1980	14966	2	49	9	13	10	10	21
	1985	18071	3	32	9	12	14	9	33
	1990	21539	3	36	13	9	15	8	26
	1995	31697	2	31	15	9	17	8	27
	1996	34587	2	31	16	9	16	8	26
	1997	35871	2	31	16	10	18	9	29
	1998	38065	1	29	17	12	18	10	31
	1999	42889	2	34	22	11	18	10	30
	2000	51485	1	32	19	10	18	9	26
	2001	56700	1	34	21	10	18	9	26
Uruguay [39]..	1970	1	17	25	23	5	11	7	38
(Pesos)	1975	8	15	29	26	6	13	6	34
	1980	87	14	29	27	6	13	5	35
	1985	479	14	33	29	3	13	6	40
	1990	9784	11	29	26	3	13	7	43
	1995	122521	9	24	20	5	15	7	43
	2000	243027	6	21	17	6	13	9	49
	2001	247211	6	21	16	5	13	9	51
Venezuela [40]...	1970	62884	5	33	18	8	15	5	27
(Bolivares)	1975	142749	4	39	18	11	13	4	25
	1980	307262	4	38	18	12	11	5	27

Table 3. Gross Domestic Product by Kind of Economic Activity: Individual Countries or Areas

Major area, region and country	Year	Gross Domestic Product (at current prices) Million	Agriculture hunting forestry and fishing A-B	Mining Manufacturing and Utilities C-E	Of which: Manufacturing D	Construction F	Wholesale, retail trade, restaurants and hotels G-H	Transport storage and communication I	Other Activities J-P
			Percentage Distribution						
	1985	464741	6	37	22	6	16	5	27
	1990	2279261	5	46	21	5	18	5	23
	1995	13685686	5	34	17	5	18	8	29
	1996	29437682	4	42	18	5	15	7	23
	1997	43343669	4	34	16	6	15	9	27
	1998	52482466	5	26	14	7	17	9	33
	1999	62577039	5	28	13	5	16	9	34
	2000	82450674	4	34	13	5	14	8	32
	2001	91324773	4	28	12	6	15	9	35
ASIA									
Afghanistan (Afghanis)	1970	62833	65	20	...	2	8	3	2
	1975	109677	62	21	...	3	8	4	1
	1980	151642	62	21	...	4	7	4	1
	1985	191084	58	24	...	5	8	3	1
	1990	560976	52	26	...	7	9	4	2
	1995	2883410	64	14	...	6	11	2	2
	1996	8602604	64	14	...	6	11	2	2
	1997	12526398	64	14	...	6	11	2	2
	1998	13182818	64	14	...	6	11	2	2
	1999	11553672	64	14	...	6	11	2	2
	2000	6506380	64	14	...	6	11	2	2
	2001	6506380	64	14	...	6	11	2	2
Armenia [41] (Drams)	1990	50	16	32	32	18	4	7	16
	1995	522256	41	25	25	7	10	4	14
	1996	661209	35	24	24	7	10	6	15
	1997	804336	29	23	23	8	9	8	17
	1998	955385	31	21	21	8	9	7	17
	1999	987444	27	22	22	8	9	8	19
	2000	1031338	23	23	23	10	9	7	19
	2001	1175487	25	21	21	11	10	7	18
Azerbaijan [42] (Azerbaijan Manats)	1990	1466	27	25	25	8	2	8	22
	1995	10669000	25	29	29	4	5	17	14
	1996	13663200	25	27	27	9	5	10	15
	1997	15791400	20	26	26	12	6	10	19
	1998	17203100	18	23	23	13	6	12	25
	1999	18875400	18	28	6	11	7	11	21
	2000	23590500	16	36	5	7	7	12	17
	2001	26341900	16	36	5	6	7	12	17
Bahrain (Dinars)	1970	110	1	39	10	10	16	6	31
	1975	410	1	43	12	6	14	5	28
	1980	1241	1	46	12	7	13	6	35
	1985	1472	1	36	7	9	10	9	55
	1990	1614	1	34	12	6	11	7	51
	1995	2199	1	34	18	5	13	7	49
	1996	2294	1	34	15	4	13	7	51
	1997	2387	1	35	15	4	11	7	52
	1998	2325	1	28	13	4	12	8	57
	1999	2489	1	32	12	4	11	8	54
	2000	2996	1	41	11	4	10	7	49
	2001	3131	1	38	10	3	9	6	43
Bangladesh (Taka)	1970	75214	37	17	17	6	12	8	17
	1975	145481	41	14	14	4	13	7	16
	1980	305196	34	16	16	6	13	10	18
	1985	614824	33	14	14	6	13	9	20
	1990	1100331	30	15	13	6	12	9	24
	1995	1663240	25	17	15	7	13	9	26
	1996	1807013	25	17	15	7	13	9	26
	1997	2001766	24	18	16	7	13	8	26
	1998	2196972	25	17	15	7	13	8	26
	1999	2370856	25	17	15	7	13	8	26
	2000	2535464	23	17	15	8	13	9	26
	2001	2714142	23	18	15	8	14	9	26

Table 3. Gross Domestic Product by Kind of Economic Activity: Individual Countries or Areas

Major area, region and country	Year	Gross Domestic Product (at current prices) Million	Agriculture hunting forestry and fishing A-B	Mining Manufacturing and Utilities C-E	Of which: Manufacturing D	Construction F	Wholesale, retail trade, restaurants and hotels G-H	Transport storage and communication I	Other Activities J-P
			Percentage Distribution						
Bhutan (Ngultrum)	1970	346	53	5	4	11	11	4	16
	1975	870	53	5	4	11	11	4	16
	1980	1095	57	4	3	8	11	4	17
	1985	2392	52	6	5	12	8	4	17
	1990	4983	42	17	8	8	6	7	18
	1995	10064	39	23	11	9	7	7	12
	1996	11808	38	23	12	9	8	7	12
	1997	14314	38	25	11	10	7	7	15
	1998	16337	37	23	10	10	7	8	15
	1999	19123	35	23	9	11	7	9	15
	2000	21698	36	21	8	13	7	9	15
	2001	24126	36	22	9	11	7	9	15
Brunei Darussalam (Brunei Darussalam Dollars)	1970	546	1	89	9	1	2	1	6
	1975	2770	1	88	12	2	3	1	7
	1980	10554	1	83	12	2	9	1	6
	1985	7752	1	70	10	2	11	2	16
	1990	6509	2	51	9	4	13	4	28
	1995	7394	3	38	...	5	11	5	40
	1996	7685	3	37	...	6	12	5	40
	1997	8051	3	36	...	6	12	5	41
	1998	8111	3	34	...	7	13	5	42
	1999	7145	3	36	...	6	12	5	40
	2000	7441	3	36	...	6	12	5	41
	2001	7619	3	36	...	6	12	5	41
Cambodia (Riels)	1970	10708	40	6	2	4	21	6	19
	1975	8830	40	6	2	4	21	6	19
	1980	8395	40	6	2	4	21	6	19
	1985	16965	40	6	2	4	21	6	19
	1990	723653	51	10	7	2	14	7	18
	1995	8110680	49	8	7	5	15	6	14
	1996	8885580	46	9	8	5	15	6	14
	1997	9778060	46	11	10	4	15	6	14
	1998	11363640	46	12	12	4	14	6	14
	1999	12587090	43	12	12	5	14	6	14
	2000	12931530	38	16	15	5	14	7	15
	2001	13364930	37	16	16	6	14	7	14
China (Yuan Renminbi)	1970	225270	35	37	...	4	6	4	12
	1975	299730	32	41	...	4	5	5	11
	1980	451780	30	44	...	4	6	5	12
	1985	872944	29	40	...	5	10	5	15
	1990	1831950	27	37	...	5	8	6	18
	1995	5847810	21	42	...	7	8	5	17
	1996	6788460	20	43	...	7	8	5	17
	1997	7446260	19	43	...	7	8	6	17
	1998	7834520	19	43	...	7	8	5	17
	1999	8206750	18	43	...	7	8	5	18
	2000	8944220	16	44	...	7	8	5	18
	2001	9593330	17	43	...	7	8	5	18
Cyprus (Pounds)	1970	229	16	19	12	7	13	8	32
	1975	260	15	19	15	7	13	6	34
	1980	760	10	20	18	13	15	8	30
	1985	1481	7	18	16	10	19	9	32
	1990	2556	7	16	14	9	21	9	33
	1995	4007	5	14	12	8	21	8	37
	1996	4161	5	14	12	8	21	8	39
	1997	4371	4	14	11	8	21	8	40
	1998	4694	4	13	11	8	21	9	41
	1999	5019	4	13	10	7	21	9	42
	2000	5487	4	12	10	7	22	9	42
	2001	5865	4	12	10	7	22	10	42
Georgia [43] (Laris)	1990	1	30	24	24	9	6	7	19
	1995	3694	42	10	10	2	26	8	6
	1996	3846	33	20	20	3	7	12	22
	1997	4638	29	18	18	4	10	11	23
	1998	5041	27	17	17	5	13	10	24

Table 3. Gross Domestic Product by Kind of Economic Activity: Individual Countries or Areas

Major area, region and country	Year	Gross Domestic Product (at current prices) Million	Agriculture hunting forestry and fishing A-B	Mining Manufacturing and Utilities C-E	Of which: Manufacturing D	Construction F	Wholesale, retail trade, restaurants and hotels G-H	Transport storage and communication I	Other Activities J-P
			Percentage Distribution						
	1999	5666	25	18	18	4	14	12	23
	2000	6016	20	17	17	4	15	14	24
	2001	6617	21	17	17	4	16	14	24
Hong Kong SAR of China [44]	1970	23369	2	33	31	4	20	8	33
(Hong Kong Dollars)	1975	50012	1	29	27	6	21	7	36
	1980	143976	1	24	22	6	20	7	42
	1985	275832	0	23	20	5	21	8	40
	1990	591507	0	19	17	5	24	9	43
	1995	1096263	0	10	8	5	25	10	52
	1996	1210925	0	9	7	5	26	9	53
	1997	1344546	0	9	6	5	24	9	54
	1998	1279850	0	9	6	6	24	9	55
	1999	1246134	0	8	5	5	24	9	55
	2000	1288338	0	9	6	5	25	10	54
	2001	1278995	0	8	5	5	25	10	68
India	1970	457435	42	15	13	4	8	3	21
(Rupees)	1975	834698	37	16	14	4	10	4	21
	1980	1441446	35	18	15	4	10	4	20
	1985	2779213	30	19	15	5	11	5	20
	1990	5675511	28	20	15	5	11	5	20
	1995	11880120	26	21	16	5	12	6	21
	1996	13682080	27	20	16	5	13	6	21
	1997	15225470	25	20	15	5	13	6	22
	1998	17409350	25	19	14	5	13	6	23
	1999	19296410	24	18	14	5	13	6	24
	2000	20879880	23	19	14	6	13	7	25
	2001	22779949	23	18	14	5	19	...	25
Indonesia [45]	1970	3238000	49	15	9	3	17	3	14
(Rupiahs)	1975	12643000	32	29	9	5	17	4	14
	1980	45446000	25	38	12	6	14	4	13
	1985	96997000	23	30	16	5	16	6	19
	1990	210866000	19	34	21	6	17	6	18
	1995	454513000	17	34	24	8	17	7	18
	1996	532567000	17	36	26	8	16	7	17
	1997	627695000	16	37	27	7	16	6	18
	1998	955754000	18	39	25	6	15	5	16
	1999	1099732000	20	37	26	6	16	5	16
	2000	1282018000	17	41	26	6	15	5	16
	2001	1490974000	16	41	26	6	16	5	16
Iran (Islamic Republic of) [46]	1970	754383	15	29	11	5	10	5	31
(Rials)	1975	3282929	8	47	8	7	8	6	20
	1980	6447256	13	22	8	11	8	9	42
	1985	15335563	15	18	7	10	14	8	35
	1990	35623226	17	22	10	5	17	8	28
	1995	175703100	19	31	12	4	15	7	25
	1996	240616600	15	31	13	5	15	7	26
	1997	285509100	15	29	13	4	15	8	29
	1998	325332000	17	23	13	4	16	8	31
	1999	430990500	15	29	13	4	15	7	30
	2000	568799400	13	32	13	3	14	8	28
	2001	665656300	13	30	14	4	14	9	30
Iraq [47]	1970	1257	15	40	9	3	8	6	23
(Dinars)	1975	4090	8	57	7	9	5	5	17
	1980	15948	5	65	4	8	5	4	13
	1985	15494	14	33	10	9	12	5	27
	1990	23297	20	24	9	7	15	9	30
	1995	1940994	65	4	5	1	10	27	12
	1996	2379254	46	3	3	1	27	22	14
	1997	3269914	36	3	3	1	22	29	16
	1998	4570100	37	3	3	1	22	27	16
	1999	6809790	32	4	4	1	19	26	14
	2000	7398604	31	5	5	1	19	29	19
	2001	8878324	28	4	3	1	20	27	20
Israel	1970	2	6	21	...	9	10	10	37
(New Shekels)	1975	9	6	18	...	9	10	8	37
	1980	120	5	16	...	7	11	8	38

Table 3. Gross Domestic Product by Kind of Economic Activity: Individual Countries or Areas

Major area, region and country	Year	Gross Domestic Product (at current prices) Million	Agriculture hunting forestry and fishing A-B	Mining Manufacturing and Utilities C-E	Of which: Manufacturing D	Construction F	Wholesale, retail trade, restaurants and hotels G-H	Transport storage and communication I	Other Activities J-P
			Percentage Distribution						
	1985	31593	4	18	...	3	11	8	39
	1990	115397	3	20	18	5	9	9	44
	1995	286397	2	17	15	7	9	8	47
	1996	332167	2	17	15	7	9	7	49
	1997	372190	2	17	15	7	9	7	48
	1998	408522	2	17	16	6	9	7	49
	1999	446760	2	17	16	5	9	7	49
	2000	487013	1	17	16	5	9	7	50
	2001	491499	1	16	15	4	9	7	51
Japan (Yen)	1970	74450690	6	38	35	8	14	7	25
	1975	150563261	5	32	30	10	13	6	29
	1980	243796700	4	32	29	9	12	6	36
	1985	326815700	3	32	29	8	13	6	39
	1990	442072300	2	29	27	10	13	7	47
	1995	498872300	2	26	23	8	15	7	52
	1996	511946800	2	26	23	8	15	7	53
	1997	523051100	2	26	23	8	15	7	53
	1998	516579200	2	25	22	8	15	7	56
	1999	509115900	1	25	22	8	14	6	57
	2000	513376800	1	25	22	7	14	6	58
	2001	507455500	1	24	21	7	14	6	60
Jordan (Dinars)	1970	212	6	13	10	5	17	9	43
	1975	390	6	15	10	7	16	9	42
	1980	1196	5	15	10	12	15	10	35
	1985	2020	5	17	12	7	15	14	36
	1990	2668	7	25	16	4	8	14	36
	1995	4773	4	18	13	6	10	12	37
	1996	4982	3	17	11	5	10	13	38
	1997	5193	3	18	12	4	11	13	39
	1998	5646	3	18	13	3	11	13	39
	1999	5765	2	18	13	3	10	13	39
	2000	6012	2	18	13	3	10	13	40
	2001	6343	3	18	13	3	10	13	40
Kazakhstan [48] (Tenge)	1990	96	34	23	23	12	8	9	14
	1995	1014190	12	32	32	6	17	11	17
	1996	1415750	12	31	31	4	17	11	20
	1997	1672142	11	31	31	4	16	12	21
	1998	1733264	9	24	12	5	16	14	27
	1999	2016456	10	28	14	5	14	12	26
	2000	2599902	8	33	17	5	13	11	24
	2001	3250593	9	31	16	5	12	11	26
Kuwait [49] (Dinars)	1970	1026	0	65	4	3	8	3	20
	1975	3485	0	77	6	2	6	2	12
	1980	7755	0	70	6	4	8	2	15
	1985	6450	1	53	6	4	9	4	30
	1990	5328	1	50	12	2	8	4	37
	1995	7925	0	50	11	3	8	5	35
	1996	9303	0	56	12	3	7	4	31
	1997	9060	0	54	13	3	7	4	34
	1998	7656	0	43	12	3	9	6	43
	1999	8886	0	48	11	3	8	5	39
	2000	10991	0	57	7	2	6	5	44
	2001	10057	0	51	7	2	7	5	38
Kyrgyzstan [50] (Som)	1990	43	33	29	29	8	4	6	18
	1995	16145	41	13	13	6	11	5	19
	1996	23399	46	12	12	6	10	5	15
	1997	30686	41	17	17	5	10	4	16
	1998	34181	36	17	17	4	13	4	18
	1999	48744	35	22	22	3	13	5	15
	2000	65358	34	24	24	4	12	4	16
	2001	73883	35	23	23	4	12	4	15
Lao People's Democratic Republic (Kips)	1970	36	55	15	10	2	13	8	7
	1975	194	55	15	10	2	13	8	7
	1980	8484	55	15	10	2	13	8	7
	1985	84406	54	16	10	2	13	9	6

Table 3. Gross Domestic Product by Kind of Economic Activity: Individual Countries or Areas

Major area, region and country	Year	Gross Domestic Product (at current prices) Million	Agriculture hunting forestry and fishing A-B	Mining Manufacturing and Utilities C-E	Of which: Manufacturing D	Construction F	Wholesale, retail trade, restaurants and hotels G-H	Transport storage and communication I	Other Activities J-P
			Percentage Distribution						
	1990	612681	61	11	10	3	7	5	12
	1995	1419090	54	15	14	3	8	5	12
	2000	13671292	52	20	17	2	9	6	9
	2001	15669988	51	21	18	2	10	6	9
Lebanon (Lebanese Pounds)	1970	4866	8	26	12	4	28	7	27
	1975	7500	10	17	15	3	34	6	31
	1980	14000	9	17	12	3	29	4	38
	1985	29988	9	18	13	3	28	4	40
	1990	1954275	9	18	13	3	28	4	38
	1995	17779000	13	24	18	9	30	3	28
	2000	25959168	11	17	9	4	23	2	43
	2001	27127330	10	17	8	4	23	2	43
Macao SAR of China (Dollars)	1970	1060	...	12	10	6	10	4	70
	1975	2361	...	12	9	6	10	3	69
	1980	5250	...	11	9	6	10	3	67
	1985	10950	...	12	10	7	10	4	71
	1990	26175	...	10	8	6	9	3	64
	1995	55333	...	9	7	5	9	3	63
	1996	55294	...	9	7	4	11	4	61
	1997	55894	...	9	7	4	9	6	62
	1998	51902	...	10	8	3	8	6	63
	1999	49021	...	11	8	3	8	6	61
	2000	49742	...	11	8	2	9	7	62
	2001	49802	...	11	8	3	9	6	62
Malaysia (Ringgit)	1970	10588	29	24	15	4	12	5	23
	1975	22332	29	31	18	4	12	5	23
	1980	53308	21	38	21	6	10	5	20
	1985	77470	19	33	21	3	13	6	26
	1990	119081	15	38	24	4	14	6	25
	1995	222473	13	35	26	6	15	7	26
	1996	253732	12	37	28	7	15	7	26
	1997	281795	11	38	28	7	15	7	27
	1998	283243	13	39	29	5	15	7	27
	1999	300764	11	42	31	5	15	7	26
	2000	342157	9	47	33	4	14	7	24
	2001	334589	9	45	31	4	14	7	26
Maldives (Rufiyaa)	1970	74	41	7	5	1	12	18	18
	1975	152	41	7	5	1	12	18	18
	1980	356	28	10	7	4	12	21	22
	1985	590	21	12	0	3	20	6	31
	1990	2060	17	12	9	3	20	11	31
	1995	4714	11	10	8	3	38	11	27
	2000	7035	8	12	8	3	36	15	27
	2001	7146	9	12	8	3	37	16	24
Mongolia [51] (Tughriks)	1970	4980	16	25	11	3	20	18	13
	1975	6530	16	25	11	3	20	18	13
	1980	8723	16	25	11	3	20	18	13
	1985	12102	15	25	11	3	20	18	13
	1990	13514	16	28	12	3	18	17	12
	1995	554249	38	26	12	2	11	6	12
	1996	659698	43	17	5	3	11	7	16
	1997	846344	35	22	5	2	15	8	14
	1998	833727	37	17	5	2	14	10	17
	1999	925346	37	18	6	2	21	9	13
	2000	1044580	28	20	6	2	23	11	15
	2001	1158210	24	22	7	2	25	13	15
Myanmar [52] (Kyats)	1970	13504	41	11	10	2	26	5	13
	1975	23477	47	10	0	1	20	3	10
	1980	38609	47	11	10	2	26	4	11
	1985	55989	48	11	10	2	24	4	11
	1990	151941	57	9	8	2	23	3	7
	1995	604729	60	8	7	2	23	3	4
	1996	791980	60	8	7	2	23	3	3
	1997	1109554	59	8	7	2	23	4	3
	1998	1559996	59	8	7	2	24	4	3

Table 3. Gross Domestic Product by Kind of Economic Activity: Individual Countries or Areas

Major area, region and country	Year	Gross Domestic Product (at current prices) Million	Agriculture hunting forestry and fishing A-B	Mining Manufacturing and Utilities C-E	Of which: Manufacturing D	Construction F	Wholesale, retail trade, restaurants and hotels G-H	Transport storage and communication I	Other Activities J-P
			Percentage Distribution						
	1999	1615142	60	7	7	2	24	4	2
	2000	1878745	57	9	8	2	24	5	3
	2001	2264960	57	9	8	2	24	5	3
Nepal [53] (Rupees)	1970	9816	69	4	4	7	3	3	13
	1975	16571	69	4	4	4	3	4	12
	1980	23351	58	4	4	7	4	7	14
	1985	46587	49	6	5	8	10	6	17
	1990	103416	49	7	6	9	10	6	17
	1995	219175	39	11	9	11	11	6	18
	1996	248913	39	11	9	10	11	6	18
	1997	280513	39	11	9	10	11	7	18
	1998	300845	37	11	9	10	11	8	19
	1999	342036	39	11	9	10	11	7	19
	2000	378033	38	11	9	10	11	8	19
	2001	408218	36	11	9	10	11	8	20
Oman (Rials)	1970	113	16	55	0	4	7	2	15
	1975	767	3	55	0	9	9	3	19
	1980	2185	3	62	1	5	8	3	20
	1985	3591	2	53	2	6	11	4	24
	1990	4493	3	52	3	2	11	5	29
	1995	5307	3	44	5	3	14	6	32
	1996	5874	3	47	4	2	13	6	30
	1997	6090	3	45	4	3	14	7	30
	1998	5416	3	37	5	4	16	8	34
	1999	6041	3	45	4	2	14	7	31
	2000	7639	2	55	5	2	11	6	26
	2001	7668	2	52	8	2	12	6	27
Pakistan [54] (Rupees)	1970	50938	34	16	14	4	13	7	18
	1975	130741	31	14	13	5	13	8	21
	1980	278196	27	16	13	4	13	9	19
	1985	514532	25	17	15	4	14	8	22
	1990	1020600	23	19	16	4	15	8	21
	1995	2120173	23	19	15	3	15	9	22
	1996	2428312	24	18	15	3	15	9	22
	1997	2677656	25	19	15	3	14	9	22
	1998	2938379	25	19	14	3	14	9	22
	1999	3147167	25	18	14	3	14	10	23
	2000	3416252	23	18	15	3	14	10	23
	2001	3726611	22	18	14	3	14	11	25
Philippines (Pesos)	1970	39505	30	28	25	4	11	3	24
	1975	107953	30	28	26	7	11	4	20
	1980	243749	25	30	26	9	13	5	18
	1985	571883	25	30	25	5	16	6	19
	1990	1077237	22	28	25	6	16	5	23
	1995	1905951	22	26	23	6	15	5	26
	1996	2171922	21	26	23	6	15	5	27
	1997	2426743	19	26	22	6	15	5	29
	1998	2665060	17	26	22	6	15	5	31
	1999	2976904	17	25	22	5	16	5	31
	2000	3308318	16	26	23	5	16	6	30
	2001	3639980	15	27	23	5	16	7	30
Qatar (Riyals)	1970	1437	1	67	3	9	6	2	17
	1975	9707	1	72	3	8	4	2	15
	1980	28663	1	71	3	5	5	1	19
	1985	22398	1	52	8	6	5	2	36
	1990	26792	1	52	13	4	6	3	36
	1995	29622	1	47	8	7	8	4	36
	1996	32976	1	48	8	7	8	4	36
	1997	41124	1	52	8	7	7	4	32
	1998	37330	1	44	8	7	8	5	37
	1999	45111	1	54	6	5	7	4	31
	2000	64646	0	60	5	3	5	3	22
	2001	62341	0	71	6	3	6	4	23

Table 3. Gross Domestic Product by Kind of Economic Activity: Individual Countries or Areas

Major area, region and country	Year	Gross Domestic Product (at current prices) Million	Agriculture hunting forestry and fishing A-B	Mining Manufacturing and Utilities C-E	Of which: Manufacturing D	Construction F	Wholesale, retail trade, restaurants and hotels G-H	Transport storage and communication I	Other Activities J-P
			Percentage Distribution						
Republic of Korea	1970	2725190	27	24	21	5	17	7	19
(Wons)	1975	10228100	25	29	26	5	18	6	17
	1980	37788500	15	32	28	8	13	8	23
	1985	81312300	13	33	29	8	14	7	24
	1990	178797000	9	32	29	11	13	7	28
	1995	377350000	6	32	29	11	13	7	32
	1996	418479000	6	31	29	12	12	7	33
	1997	453276000	5	31	29	12	11	7	34
	1998	444367000	5	34	31	10	10	7	35
	1999	482744000	5	34	31	9	11	7	35
	2000	521959000	5	34	31	8	12	7	34
	2001	551558000	4	34	30	8	12	7	35
Saudi Arabia	1970	22921	4	65	9	4	5	6	14
(Riyals)	1975	164526	1	72	5	10	4	2	11
	1980	490942	1	70	4	10	4	3	11
	1985	313941	4	37	8	12	10	8	30
	1990	391993	6	44	8	9	7	6	27
	1995	478652	7	44	9	9	7	6	27
	1996	590749	5	45	10	7	6	4	33
	1997	617902	5	43	10	6	6	4	34
	1998	546648	6	35	11	7	8	5	38
	1999	603589	6	40	10	7	8	5	35
	2000	706657	5	47	10	6	7	4	31
	2001	698403	5	45	10	6	7	4	32
Singapore	1970	5805	2	23	20	7	27	11	30
(Singapore Dollars)	1975	13443	2	26	24	8	25	11	30
	1980	25091	1	32	29	6	22	14	29
	1985	38924	1	26	24	11	17	13	39
	1990	67879	0	31	29	5	19	13	37
	1995	117768	0	26	25	7	20	12	40
	1996	128244	0	25	24	8	19	12	40
	1997	140279	0	25	23	9	18	11	42
	1998	137618	0	25	23	9	17	11	42
	1999	140070	0	26	24	8	18	12	42
	2000	159888	0	28	27	6	19	11	40
	2001	153455	0	25	23	6	19	11	44
Sri Lanka [55]	1970	14259	36	15	14	6	14	9	14
(Rupees)	1975	27227	28	25	24	4	15	9	10
	1980	68809	26	20	17	9	14	10	11
	1985	158852	24	18	16	7	15	11	12
	1990	320008	23	20	17	7	15	10	13
	1995	666956	19	20	17	7	18	10	15
	1996	776739	18	20	17	7	18	10	15
	1997	897218	18	21	18	6	18	11	15
	1998	1018330	17	20	18	6	19	11	16
	1999	1108845	17	20	17	7	18	11	15
	2000	1253622	16	21	18	6	20	11	15
	2001	1397453	16	21	18	6	19	11	15
Syrian Arab Republic	1970	6848	20	23	19	3	20	11	23
(Syrian Pounds)	1975	20711	18	20	7	5	22	12	23
	1980	51270	20	16	4	7	25	7	25
	1985	83225	21	15	8	7	22	10	25
	1990	268328	28	20	5	4	23	10	15
	1995	570975	28	14	6	4	26	12	16
	1996	690857	28	22	8	4	22	11	14
	1997	745569	26	25	7	4	20	12	14
	1998	790444	29	23	8	4	19	11	14
	1999	819092	24	27	6	3	19	13	14
	2000	903944	25	30	2	3	15	13	14
	2001	947808	26	27	6	3	16	13	16
Tajikistan [56]	1990	7	30	34	34	11	8	7	19
(Tajik Roubles)	1995	70	39	36	36	2	6	2	20
	1996	308	39	28	28	3	15	2	8
	1997	518	32	25	25	3	21	3	9
	1998	1025	25	24	24	4	23	4	16

Table 3. Gross Domestic Product by Kind of Economic Activity: Individual Countries or Areas

Major area, region and country	Year	Gross Domestic Product (at current prices) Million	Agriculture hunting forestry and fishing A-B	Mining Manufacturing and Utilities C-E	Of which: Manufacturing D	Construction F	Wholesale, retail trade, restaurants and hotels G-H	Transport storage and communication I	Other Activities J-P
			Percentage Distribution						
	1999	1345	17	22	22	3	14	2	34
	2000	1807	19	23	23	3	22	4	29
	2001	2512	19	22	22	3	19	3	34
Thailand (Baht)	1970	148274	26	19	16	4	24	6	21
	1975	305149	27	21	19	3	25	5	20
	1980	662482	23	24	22	4	23	5	20
	1985	1056496	16	27	22	5	24	7	21
	1990	2184000	12	25	22	6	19	7	17
	1995	4186212	11	27	24	7	11	7	25
	1996	4611041	11	27	23	7	11	7	25
	1997	4732610	11	28	24	5	12	8	25
	1998	4626447	12	29	25	4	13	8	24
	1999	4632132	11	31	26	3	13	8	24
	2000	4904725	10	32	28	3	13	8	24
	2001	5099642	9	34	29	3	14	8	25
Timor-Leste (Rupiah)	1998	375	41	6	3	2	18	7	19
	1999	228	43	7	3	3	17	6	18
	2000	263	26	8	3	3	23	8	24
	2001	312	25	8	3	2	25	8	25
Turkey (Liras)	1970	206000	37	17	15	6	12	8	18
	1975	674000	34	18	16	5	14	9	18
	1980	5231000	26	19	17	6	16	11	22
	1985	35095000	20	22	18	6	19	13	17
	1990	393060000	17	26	22	6	19	12	19
	1995	7762460000	16	26	23	5	20	13	19
	1996	14772100000	17	25	21	6	20	13	20
	1997	28835900000	15	25	22	6	21	14	21
	1998	52224900000	18	23	20	6	20	14	23
	1999	77415300000	16	23	20	6	20	13	26
	2000	1.24583E+11	15	23	20	5	21	14	23
	2001	1.81409E+11	14	25	22	5	22	15	23
Turkmenistan [57] (Manats)	1990	7600	11	76	76	5	2	4	6
	1995	652044	16	56	56	6	4	5	9
	1996	7751754	13	57	57	10	3	6	7
	1997	11108783	20	35	35	11	4	10	15
	1998	13994739	25	30	30	13	4	8	17
	1999	20056000	25	31	31	12	4	7	21
	2000	25648000	23	35	35	7	4	7	25
	2001	33863000	25	37	37	6	4	5	24
United Arab Emirates (Dirhams)	1970	3160	1	72	2	5	7	6	9
	1975	39460	1	69	1	11	8	3	10
	1980	109833	1	69	4	9	8	3	12
	1985	99416	1	57	9	9	9	4	23
	1990	124008	2	55	7	8	9	5	23
	1995	155210	3	49	9	8	8	6	27
	2000	195779	3	49	10	8	7	6	27
	2001	209483	3	51	11	7	7	6	25
Uzbekistan [58] (Sums)	1990	32	33	23	23	11	4	6	25
	1995	302787	28	18	18	7	8	7	21
	1996	559072	22	19	19	8	9	7	22
	1997	976830	28	16	16	7	10	7	20
	1998	1416157	27	15	15	8	8	7	21
	1999	2128660	29	14	14	7	9	7	21
	2000	3255600	30	14	14	6	9	8	19
	2001	4868400	23	15	15	9	10	7	24
Vietnam (Dong)	1970	3989	43	20	16	3	11	2	20
	1975	4071	43	20	16	3	11	2	20
	1980	14031	43	20	16	3	11	2	20
	1985	123000	44	21	17	3	10	2	20
	1990	41955000	39	19	12	4	17	3	18
	1995	228892000	27	22	15	7	20	4	20
	1996	272036000	28	23	15	7	19	4	19
	1997	313623000	26	26	16	7	19	4	19
	1998	361017000	26	27	17	6	19	4	19

Table 3. Gross Domestic Product by Kind of Economic Activity: Individual Countries or Areas

Major area, region and country	Year	Gross Domestic Product (at current prices) Million	Agriculture hunting forestry and fishing A-B	Mining Manufacturing and Utilities C-E	Of which: Manufacturing D	Construction F	Wholesale, retail trade, restaurants and hotels G-H	Transport storage and communication I	Other Activities J-P
			Percentage Distribution						
	1999	399942000	25	29	18	5	18	4	18
	2000	444139000	24	31	19	6	18	4	17
	2001	485109000	25	30	18	5	18	4	18
Yemen	1990	129960	25	22	8	3	9	14	25
(Rials)	1995	511058	19	29	14	4	12	13	24
	1996	736385	16	38	11	4	10	11	19
	1997	888808	16	39	10	5	10	12	18
	1998	849321	19	28	10	5	11	14	22
	1999	1132619	16	38	8	5	9	12	21
	2000	1379812	15	42	7	4	9	10	19
	2001	1354509	16	41	8	4	9	10	20
EUROPE									
Albania [59]	1970	6480	38	40	...	7	8	3	...
(Leks)	1975	11462	38	40	...	7	8	3	...
	1980	15533	38	40	...	7	8	3	...
	1985	16857	39	40	...	7	8	3	...
	1990	16813	40	37	...	7	13	3	...
	1995	229793	55	12	...	10	20	4	...
	1996	280998	53	13	...	11	20	3	...
	1997	341716	56	12	...	11	18	3	...
	1998	460631	54	12	...	13	18	3	...
	1999	506205	53	12	...	14	19	3	...
	2000	539210	51	12	...	15	19	3	...
	2001	590237	49	12	...	16	20	4	...
Andorra	1970	9	11	22	21	10	14	8	28
(Spanish pesetas)	1975	27	9	22	20	10	14	8	30
	1980	87	7	20	18	9	16	8	33
	1985	200	6	21	18	7	18	9	35
	1990	419	5	21	18	9	18	8	35
	1995	751	4	21	18	7	18	8	38
	1996	836	5	21	18	7	18	8	38
	1997	932	4	21	18	7	18	8	37
	1998	1042	4	21	18	7	18	8	37
	1999	1166	4	20	17	7	18	8	37
	2000	1311	3	19	17	8	18	8	37
	2001	1462	3	19	17	8	19	8	37
Austria	1970	28184	7	34	30	8	16	7	25
(Euros)	1975	49196	5	29	26	9	15	6	27
	1080	74723	5	26	22	8	17	7	30
	1985	100772	4	25	21	6	16	7	35
	1990	133603	3	24	21	6	17	7	36
	1995	172287	2	22	19	7	16	7	40
	1996	178045	2	21	18	8	16	7	41
	1997	182486	2	22	19	8	16	7	40
	1998	190628	2	22	19	8	16	7	40
	1999	197154	2	22	19	8	16	7	40
	2000	207037	2	22	19	7	16	6	40
	2001	211857	2	22	20	7	16	7	41
Belarus [60]	1990	4	23	40	40	8	3	6	17
(Belarussian Roubles)	1995	121403	16	31	31	5	8	12	22
	1996	191839	15	31	31	5	7	11	21
	1997	366830	13	32	32	6	7	11	20
	1998	702161	12	31	31	6	9	10	20
	1999	3026064	13	30	30	6	10	11	19
	2000	9133800	12	29	29	6	10	11	20
	2001	17173200	10	28	28	6	10	12	23
Bolgium	1970	31788	4	32	31	7	11	6	30
(Euros)	1975	57501	3	28	26	7	12	6	32
	1980	88287	3	24	21	7	11	6	40
	1985	121935	3	24	21	5	11	6	46
	1990	163341	2	24	21	5	13	6	43
	1995	202174	2	22	19	5	13	7	47
	1996	206989	2	21	18	5	13	6	47
	1997	217173	2	21	18	5	12	6	47

Table 3. Gross Domestic Product by Kind of Economic Activity: Individual Countries or Areas

Major area, region and country	Year	Gross Domestic Product (at current prices) Million	Agriculture hunting forestry and fishing A-B	Mining Manufacturing and Utilities C-E	Of which: Manufacturing D	Construction F	Wholesale, retail trade, restaurants and hotels G-H	Transport storage and communication I	Other Activities J-P
			Percentage Distribution						
	1998	225244	1	21	18	4	12	6	48
	1999	235632	1	20	18	5	12	6	48
	2000	247469	1	20	18	5	12	6	48
	2001	254282	1	19	17	5	12	6	48
Bosnia and Herzegovina............................	1990	1	25	22	21	3	23	6	12
(Convertible Marka)	1995	2861	25	22	21	3	23	6	12
	1996	4125	17	18	18	4	19	5	20
	1997	6311	19	24	23	6	23	7	27
	1998	7336	12	24	24	6	20	9	30
	1999	8604	10	24	24	5	18	10	28
	2000	9433	11	24	23	6	19	9	29
	2001	10247	10	24	23	5	18	9	28
Bulgaria...	1970	13	20	42	34	5	4	3	24
(Leva)	1975	18	19	44	36	5	3	4	20
	1980	26	14	40	33	5	5	4	27
	1985	33	12	47	38	6	4	3	30
	1990	45	18	39	31	5	5	4	26
	1995	880	13	26	21	5	10	6	36
	1996	1761	14	25	20	4	11	7	33
	1997	17433	23	23	17	2	9	8	24
	1998	22421	17	23	17	4	8	8	29
	1999	23790	15	21	15	4	9	9	32
	2000	26753	12	22	16	4	9	10	31
	2001	29618	12	21	16	4	9	11	30
Croatia [61]..	1990	280	10	26	...	5	16	8	27
(Kuna)	1995	98382	9	23	19	5	12	8	27
	1996	107981	8	22	18	6	13	7	28
	1997	123811	8	22	18	6	13	7	28
	1998	137604	8	21	18	6	13	7	30
	1999	141579	8	21	17	4	11	7	33
	2000	152519	7	21	18	4	11	8	32
	2001	162909	7	21	...	4	12	9	31
Czech Republic [62]....................................	1980	458393	8	39	28	10	8	6	13
(Koruny)	1985	522853	7	37	26	10	10	5	13
	1990	626189	8	34	25	10	12	4	27
	1995	1381050	4	31	24	8	14	8	28
	1996	1566970	4	34	26	7	12	7	28
	1997	1679920	4	32	26	7	14	8	28
	1998	1839090	4	30	25	7	15	8	30
	1999	1902290	4	29	24	7	15	7	30
	2000	1984830	4	30	25	7	15	8	29
	2001	2175240	4	30	25	6	16	8	28
Denmark..	1970	122143	5	20	18	8	17	7	33
(Kroner)	1975	223381	5	19	18	7	16	6	39
	1980	385808	5	18	17	6	13	6	41
	1985	634018	5	19	17	4	14	6	40
	1990	825311	4	18	16	5	13	7	44
	1995	1009760	3	18	15	4	13	7	44
	1996	1060890	3	18	15	4	13	7	43
	1997	1116320	3	18	15	4	13	7	43
	1998	1155410	2	18	15	4	13	7	44
	1999	1207750	2	18	14	4	13	7	44
	2000	1280780	2	19	15	4	13	8	43
	2001	1325270	2	19	15	4	13	8	44
Estonia...	1990	798	14	41	37	7	8	6	36
(Krooni)	1995	40897	8	22	17	6	14	10	30
	1996	52423	7	21	16	6	15	10	29
	1997	64045	7	20	16	6	14	11	30
	1998	73538	6	20	16	6	15	13	30
	1999	76327	6	19	15	5	14	14	32
	2000	87236	5	20	16	5	14	15	30
	2001	96571	5	20	16	5	14	15	30

Table 3. Gross Domestic Product by Kind of Economic Activity: Individual Countries or Areas

Major area, region and country	Year	Gross Domestic Product (at current prices) Million	Agriculture hunting forestry and fishing A-B	Mining Manufacturing and Utilities C-E	Of which: Manufacturing D	Construction F	Wholesale, retail trade, restaurants and hotels G-H	Transport storage and communication I	Other Activities J-P
			Percentage Distribution						
Finland (Euros)	1970	7874	9	27	23	9	12	7	27
	1975	17897	9	27	24	10	12	7	28
	1980	32948	8	29	25	7	12	8	29
	1985	57032	7	26	23	6	12	8	32
	1990	88244	6	23	20	7	12	8	35
	1995	95251	4	26	23	4	10	9	38
	1996	98709	4	24	22	4	11	9	38
	1997	107103	4	24	22	4	11	9	37
	1998	116395	3	25	23	5	11	9	36
	1999	119961	3	24	22	5	11	9	37
	2000	130234	3	25	23	5	10	9	37
	2001	135791	3	24	22	5	10	9	38
France (Euros)	1970	124467	7	28	26	7	11	6	33
	1975	230245	5	27	25	7	12	6	36
	1980	439384	4	26	23	6	11	6	39
	1985	727369	4	24	21	5	11	7	42
	1990	1009350	3	21	19	5	13	6	45
	1995	1181850	3	20	17	5	12	6	47
	1996	1212180	3	19	17	5	12	6	48
	1997	1251160	3	19	17	4	12	6	48
	1998	1305850	3	19	17	4	12	6	48
	1999	1355100	3	19	17	4	12	6	49
	2000	1420140	3	18	16	4	12	6	49
	2001	1475580	2	18	16	4	12	6	49
Germany (Euros)	1970	381209	3	36	33	8	12	6	27
	1975	580477	3	33	30	7	12	6	35
	1980	830212	2	31	28	7	11	6	36
	1985	1034570	2	31	28	6	11	5	40
	1990	1380690	2	29	27	6	11	5	41
	1995	1801300	1	24	21	6	11	5	46
	1996	1833700	1	23	21	6	11	5	47
	1997	1871600	1	23	21	6	11	5	47
	1998	1929400	1	24	21	5	11	5	47
	1999	1978600	1	23	21	5	11	5	48
	2000	2030000	1	23	21	5	12	5	47
	2001	2071200	1	23	21	4	12	6	48
Greece (Euros)	1970	993	14	22	19	10	19	8	36
	1975	2305	14	22	20	8	22	8	33
	1980	6106	13	21	19	9	19	7	32
	1985	16646	12	21	17	7	20	7	32
	1990	39111	10	18	15	7	18	7	35
	1995	79927	9	15	12	6	19	6	38
	1996	87851	8	15	12	6	20	6	38
	1997	97235	8	13	11	6	20	6	38
	1998	105773	7	13	11	6	19	6	39
	1999	112881	7	13	10	7	19	6	39
	2000	121628	7	13	10	7	19	7	38
	2001	130927	6	13	10	7	20	7	38
Hungary [63] (Forints)	1970	372184	15	31	24	7	8	7	18
	1975	538863	15	31	24	7	8	7	18
	1980	804910	15	31	24	7	8	7	19
	1985	1153910	14	32	24	6	8	7	20
	1990	2282420	11	25	19	5	12	6	18
	1995	5614040	6	23	20	4	12	8	35
	1996	6893940	6	23	20	4	12	8	35
	1997	8540670	5	25	21	4	12	9	34
	1998	10087400	5	25	21	4	12	9	34
	1999	11393500	4	24	21	4	11	9	35
	2000	13172300	4	24	21	5	11	7	36
	2001	14849600	4	23	20	4	12	7	38
Iceland (Kroner)	1970	460	12	18	16	12	14	7	29
	1975	2148	9	18	14	10	9	10	29
	1980	16112	10	20	16	8	9	7	29
	1985	120373	10	21	16	7	10	7	31
	1990	362817	10	18	14	7	13	7	33
	1995	442256	10	18	14	6	12	8	34

Table 3. Gross Domestic Product by Kind of Economic Activity: Individual Countries or Areas

Major area, region and country	Year	Gross Domestic Product (at current prices) Million	Agriculture hunting forestry and fishing A-B	Mining Manufacturing and Utilities C-E	Of which: Manufacturing D	Construction F	Wholesale, retail trade, restaurants and hotels G-H	Transport storage and communication I	Other Activities J-P
			Percentage Distribution						
	1996	474586	10	18	14	6	12	8	34
	1997	512679	9	17	14	7	12	7	36
	1998	567572	9	16	13	7	13	7	35
	1999	606558	8	14	11	7	13	7	38
	2000	658247	7	18	15	8	15	9	35
	2001	740747	6	19	15	8	14	9	35
Ireland (Euros)	1970	2231	16	24	23	8	13	6	22
	1975	5222	17	24	23	8	12	6	23
	1980	12891	12	27	25	10	12	5	29
	1985	24500	10	27	25	6	13	5	30
	1990	36312	8	27	25	5	14	5	31
	1995	52641	7	29	27	5	11	5	33
	1996	58080	6	29	26	5	12	5	33
	1997	67098	5	30	27	5	12	5	33
	1998	77568	4	31	29	5	11	5	33
	1999	89770	4	32	30	6	11	5	32
	2000	102910	3	31	30	7	11	5	32
	2001	114479	3	31	30	7	11	5	33
Italy (Euros)	1970	34765	8	29	27	9	14	6	28
	1975	71985	7	30	28	9	15	6	32
	1980	198524	6	31	29	7	16	7	31
	1985	420324	4	27	25	6	17	7	35
	1990	682153	3	25	22	6	16	7	39
	1995	923052	3	23	21	5	16	7	40
	1996	982443	3	23	20	5	16	7	41
	1997	1026290	3	22	20	5	16	7	41
	1998	1073020	3	22	20	4	16	7	41
	1999	1108500	3	22	19	4	15	7	41
	2000	1164770	3	22	19	4	15	7	42
	2001	1216690	3	21	19	5	16	7	42
Latvia (Lats)	1990	62	21	35	33	9	7	10	14
	1995	2329	9	25	20	4	11	14	24
	1996	2807	8	23	18	4	14	15	23
	1997	3270	5	24	19	4	15	15	24
	1998	3592	4	20	15	6	16	14	26
	1999	3890	4	17	13	6	17	13	30
	2000	4348	4	16	13	6	17	14	31
	2001	4759	4	17	13	5	18	14	31
Lithuania [64] (Litas)	1990	134	27	21	21	10	9	8	27
	1995	24103	11	24	20	7	18	9	24
	1996	31569	11	24	20	7	17	9	25
	1997	38340	10	22	18	7	16	9	25
	1998	42990	9	21	17	8	16	9	27
	1999	42655	7	20	16	7	15	10	29
	2000	45148	7	23	19	6	15	11	28
	2001	47958	6	25	20	6	15	11	27
Luxembourg (Euros)	1970	1567	4	40	37	5	12	5	18
	1975	2469	3	28	25	7	16	5	39
	1980	3784	2	26	24	7	16	6	33
	1985	5842	3	27	25	5	17	6	68
	1990	9180	2	22	20	7	16	7	44
	1995	13214	1	16	14	7	14	9	56
	1996	13927	1	15	13	6	14	10	58
	1997	15490	1	14	13	6	14	10	56
	1998	17006	1	14	12	6	13	10	56
	1999	18870	1	13	11	6	12	9	56
	2000	21313	1	12	11	6	12	9	52
	2001	22082	1	12	11	6	12	10	55
Malta [65] (Maltese Lira)	1970	95	6	30	19	...	14	3	33
	1975	166	6	37	28	...	13	4	32
	1980	392	3	37	29	...	13	6	29
	1985	476	4	36	27	...	14	5	32
	1990	735	3	34	24	...	13	5	33
	1995	1146	2	29	21	...	12	6	37
	1996	1201	3	29	21	...	11	6	40
	1997	1288	3	28	20	...	10	5	40

Table 3. Gross Domestic Product by Kind of Economic Activity: Individual Countries or Areas

Major area, region and country	Year	Gross Domestic Product (at current prices) Million	Agriculture hunting forestry and fishing A-B	Mining Manufacturing and Utilities C-E	Of which: Manufacturing D	Construction F	Wholesale, retail trade, restaurants and hotels G-H	Transport storage and communication I	Other Activities J-P
			Percentage Distribution						
	1998	1362	2	29	20	...	10	6	41
	1999	1456	2	29	20	...	10	6	40
	2000	1558	2	29	22	...	10	6	39
	2001	1632	2	27	20	...	9	6	40
Netherlands (Euros)	1970	57725	6	29	25	8	14	7	31
	1975	104780	4	27	21	7	13	6	37
	1980	160463	3	25	18	7	13	6	41
	1985	199847	4	26	17	5	13	6	40
	1990	243174	4	22	18	6	15	7	41
	1995	302233	3	21	17	5	14	7	43
	1996	315059	3	21	16	5	14	7	44
	1997	333725	3	20	16	5	14	7	44
	1998	354194	3	19	15	5	14	7	44
	1999	374070	3	18	15	5	14	7	45
	2000	402599	2	19	15	5	14	7	45
	2001	429172	2	18	14	5	14	6	45
Norway (Kroner)	1970	91100	5	22	19	6	15	14	27
	1975	169896	4	24	19	6	15	10	30
	1980	314363	4	31	14	5	12	9	30
	1985	547286	3	33	12	4	12	8	30
	1990	726799	3	27	12	4	12	10	36
	1995	937445	2	26	12	4	11	9	36
	1996	1026920	2	28	11	4	11	9	34
	1997	1111350	2	29	11	4	11	9	34
	1998	1132130	2	24	9	4	11	9	36
	1999	1233040	2	26	10	4	10	9	36
	2000	1469080	2	34	13	3	9	8	33
	2001	1526600	1	31	12	4	10	8	34
Poland (Zlotych)	1970	78	9	45	32	11	12	7	27
	1975	138	9	45	32	12	7	8	27
	1980	234	9	43	32	9	11	7	26
	1985	965	9	43	32	11	12	6	26
	1990	56027	9	42	32	10	13	5	25
	1995	308104	6	28	21	6	18	6	23
	1996	387827	6	26	20	6	19	6	24
	1997	472350	5	26	20	7	19	6	25
	1998	553560	4	24	19	8	19	6	27
	1999	615115	3	24	18	8	19	6	27
	2000	712322	3	22	17	7	19	6	30
	2001	749311	3	21	16	6	19	0	31
Portugal (Euros)	1970	1056	25	32	30	4	12	6	20
	1975	2240	22	32	31	5	12	7	20
	1980	7458	16	22	19	6	20	6	28
	1985	20923	12	23	19	5	20	8	30
	1990	50817	8	22	19	6	17	6	34
	1995	80827	5	21	18	6	16	6	38
	1996	86230	5	21	18	6	16	6	38
	1997	93014	4	21	18	7	16	6	39
	1998	100963	4	20	17	7	16	6	39
	1999	108030	3	19	16	7	15	6	39
	2000	115546	3	19	16	7	15	6	40
	2001	122978	3	19	16	7	15	6	40
Republic of Moldova (Lei)	1990	13	35	29	...	7	5	7	14
	1995	6480	29	25	23	4	9	5	19
	1996	7798	27	23	21	4	10	6	23
	1997	8917	26	20	18	5	9	6	23
	1998	9122	26	17	14	3	11	7	25
	1999	12322	25	17	13	3	16	8	25
	2000	16020	25	16	14	3	13	10	23
	2001	19019	22	19	16	3	13	10	23
Romania [66] (Lei)	1970	227348	19	42	38	10	4	6	13
	1975	384219	17	47	42	8	7	6	13
	1980	484684	14	50	44	7	6	7	13
	1985	623460	15	46	41	7	6	6	13
	1990	857851	22	41	37	5	6	6	15
	1995	72135548	20	33	26	7	10	8	18

Table 3. Gross Domestic Product by Kind of Economic Activity: Individual Countries or Areas

Major area, region and country	Year	Gross Domestic Product (at current prices) Million	Agriculture hunting forestry and fishing A-B	Mining Manufacturing and Utilities C-E	Of which: Manufacturing D	Construction F	Wholesale, retail trade, restaurants and hotels G-H	Transport storage and communication I	Other Activities J-P
			Percentage Distribution						
	1996	108919636	19	33	29	6	12	9	16
	1997	252925736	18	31	26	5	11	9	18
	1998	373798214	14	26	21	5	13	10	21
	1999	545730127	13	25	19	5	14	10	23
	2000	800308100	11	25	20	5	14	10	24
	2001	1154126400	13	26	20	5	14	10	23
Russian Federation [67] (Roubles)	1990	644200	15	37	37	9	5	9	18
	1995	1540493	7	28	28	8	18	11	21
	1996	2145656	7	28	28	8	17	11	21
	1997	2478594	6	27	27	7	16	11	24
	1998	2741051	5	28	28	6	18	10	24
	1999	4766834	7	28	28	6	21	9	20
	2000	7305742	6	29	29	6	21	8	19
	2001	9040690	6	26	26	7	20	9	19
San Marino (Italian Lire)	1970	22	8	29	27	9	14	6	28
	1975	46	7	30	28	9	15	6	32
	1980	128	6	31	29	7	16	7	31
	1985	271	4	27	25	6	17	7	35
	1990	439	3	25	22	6	16	7	39
	1995	595	3	23	21	5	16	7	40
	2000	842	3	22	19	4	15	7	42
	2001	879	3	21	19	5	16	7	42
Serbia and Montenegro (New Dinars)	1990	34174	18	31	28	6	13	6	25
	1995	43984	16	27	23	5	10	6	22
	1996	79396	15	25	19	4	8	6	20
	1997	109352	18	31	22	5	8	8	24
	1998	148370	17	32	23	5	9	9	23
	1999	191099	19	28	20	4	10	9	23
	2000	381661	20	27	21	4	11	7	26
	2001	699600	19	27	21	4	10	8	25
Slovakia (Koruny)	1980	203804	10	45	28	14	3	8	21
	1985	241506	7	43	27	15	3	9	21
	1990	289380	8	39	25	13	4	6	21
	1995	568923	6	31	25	5	13	10	29
	1996	628588	5	29	24	7	12	10	29
	1997	708617	5	25	21	7	14	10	31
	1998	775002	5	25	21	6	15	10	31
	1999	835721	4	26	22	5	15	10	31
	2000	908801	4	25	21	5	15	10	32
	2001	989297	4	24	21	5	15	11	32
Slovenia (Tolars)	1990	196762	5	33	30	4	12	8	28
	1995	2221459	4	28	25	4	13	7	31
	1996	2555369	4	28	24	5	13	7	31
	1997	2907277	4	28	24	5	13	7	32
	1998	3253751	4	28	24	5	13	7	31
	1999	3648401	3	27	24	5	13	7	32
	2000	4035518	3	28	24	5	13	7	33
	2001	4566191	3	27	24	5	13	7	33
Spain (Euros)	1970	16392	10	30	26	9	14	6	26
	1975	37638	9	31	26	9	15	6	28
	1980	95334	7	29	24	8	17	7	31
	1985	175624	6	27	23	6	17	7	41
	1990	312424	5	24	20	8	17	7	43
	1995	437787	4	21	18	7	18	8	38
	1996	464251	5	21	18	7	18	8	38
	1997	494140	4	21	18	7	18	8	37
	1998	527975	4	21	18	7	18	8	37
	1999	565199	4	20	17	7	18	8	37
	2000	609319	3	19	17	8	18	8	37
	2001	651641	3	19	16	8	18	8	38
Sweden (Kroner)	1970	184554	5	26	23	7	10	9	32
	1975	322315	5	27	25	6	11	8	32
	1980	562684	4	23	20	6	11	9	35
	1985	921782	4	23	20	5	11	7	37
	1990	1455670	3	21	18	6	11	8	41

Table 3. Gross Domestic Product by Kind of Economic Activity: Individual Countries or Areas

Major area, region and country	Year	Gross Domestic Product (at current prices) Million	Agriculture hunting forestry and fishing A-B	Mining Manufacturing and Utilities C-E	Of which: Manufacturing D	Construction F	Wholesale, retail trade, restaurants and hotels G-H	Transport storage and communication I	Other Activities J-P
			Percentage Distribution						
	1995	1772020	2	23	20	4	11	7	42
	1996	1817150	2	22	19	4	11	7	43
	1997	1890190	2	23	20	4	11	8	43
	1998	1973850	2	23	20	4	11	8	43
	1999	2078550	2	22	20	4	11	8	43
	2000	2196760	2	22	20	4	11	7	44
	2001	2266620	2	22	19	4	11	7	44
Switzerland (Swiss Francs)	1970	95863	4	30	28	5	16	7	42
	1975	148190	4	30	28	5	16	7	42
	1980	180095	4	30	28	6	16	7	39
	1985	237206	3	27	25	7	18	6	38
	1990	317304	3	26	24	8	19	6	40
	1995	363329	3	25	23	8	17	6	44
	1996	365833	3	25	23	8	17	6	44
	1997	371372	3	25	23	8	17	6	44
	1998	379989	3	25	23	8	17	6	44
	1999	388518	3	25	23	8	17	6	44
	2000	405530	3	25	23	8	17	6	43
	2001	414881	3	24	22	8	16	6	42
TFYR Macedonia [68] (Denars)	1990	507	8	36	34	7	8	6	25
	1995	169521	11	24	22	5	13	6	28
	1996	176444	11	24	22	5	13	6	28
	1997	184982	11	26	23	5	13	6	27
	1998	190827	10	26	24	6	13	6	27
	1999	195284	10	25	23	6	13	7	26
	2000	216845	8	26	23	6	16	8	25
	2001	219537	9	25	23	6	15	7	26
Ukraine [69] (Hryvnias)	1990	2	25	36	36	8	4	7	16
	1995	54516	14	33	33	7	5	12	21
	1996	81519	12	29	29	6	6	13	24
	1997	93365	13	27	27	5	8	13	23
	1998	102593	12	27	27	5	7	12	22
	1999	130442	12	29	29	4	7	12	20
	2000	170070	14	28	28	4	9	12	19
	2001	204190	13	31	31	4	9	11	18
United Kingdom (Pounds Sterling)	1970	51515	3	34	30	6	13	8	31
	1975	105773	3	31	26	7	13	8	36
	1980	230695	2	33	24	6	12	7	36
	1985	354952	2	31	22	5	12	6	38
	1990	557300	2	25	21	6	13	7	40
	1995	719176	2	24	19	5	13	7	42
	1996	762214	2	24	19	5	13	7	42
	1997	811067	1	23	19	5	13	7	42
	1998	859384	1	22	18	5	14	7	44
	1999	902459	1	21	17	5	14	7	44
	2000	950415	1	20	16	5	14	7	45
	2001	993124	1	20	15	5	14	7	46
OCEANIA									
Australia (Australian Dollars)	1970	38277	6	26	20	7	11	7	29
	1975	79386	6	25	18	8	11	7	35
	1980	145643	6	26	17	7	10	7	37
	1985	248131	5	25	15	6	12	8	36
	1990	397881	4	21	13	6	13	8	41
	1995	502828	3	20	13	6	13	8	42
	1996	529886	3	19	12	6	13	8	42
	1997	561229	3	19	12	6	13	8	43
	1998	591917	3	18	12	6	13	8	44
	1999	628621	3	18	11	6	13	8	44
	2000	669307	3	18	11	5	12	8	45
	2001	712980	3	18	11	6	12	7	44
Cook Islands (New Zealand Dollars)	1970	11	16	6	...	3	30	7	42
	1975	14	16	6	...	3	30	7	42
	1980	24	18	5	...	4	29	8	36
	1985	56	15	5	...	3	27	10	41
	1990	107	21	6	...	2	24	9	41

Table 3. Gross Domestic Product by Kind of Economic Activity: Individual Countries or Areas

Major area, region and country	Year	Gross Domestic Product (at current prices) Million	Agriculture hunting forestry and fishing A-B	Mining Manufacturing and Utilities C-E	Of which: Manufacturing D	Construction F	Wholesale, retail trade, restaurants and hotels G-H	Transport storage and communication I	Other Activities J-P
			Percentage Distribution						
	1995	155	18	5	...	2	26	12	40
	2000	172	17	5	...	3	31	17	31
	2001	191	18	5	...	3	30	14	34
Fiji (Fiji Dollars)	1970	192	24	15	12	6	17	5	24
	1975	562	21	12	10	7	16	8	30
	1980	984	20	12	11	7	16	8	30
	1985	1316	16	13	8	5	16	9	34
	1990	1980	20	12	11	4	20	13	28
	1995	2799	19	12	11	4	20	14	25
	2000	3518	16	12	11	4	23	16	22
	2001	3831	15	12	11	4	24	17	21
French Polynesia [70] (French Francs)	1970	21468	7	8	6	6	24	8	47
	1975	45020	5	7	6	10	25	5	48
	1980	96832	5	8	7	10	23	6	48
	1985	226772	4	9	9	12	24	6	46
	1990	290064	5	9	7	6	23	7	48
	1995	373136	4	9	7	6	23	7	47
	2000	426800	4	9	7	6	23	7	47
	2001	438732	4	9	7	6	23	7	47
Kiribati (Australian Dollars)	1970	13	34	3	1	4	15	14	30
	1975	42	34	3	1	4	15	14	30
	1980	25	34	3	1	4	15	14	30
	1985	30	35	3	1	4	14	12	31
	1990	36	19	4	1	4	20	16	37
	1995	62	21	3	1	2	16	15	43
	2000	78	18	2	1	3	16	13	48
	2001	77	18	2	1	3	16	13	48
Marshall Islands (US Dollars)	1970	7	13	1	1	11	23	1	50
	1975	15	13	1	1	11	23	1	50
	1980	23	13	1	1	11	23	1	50
	1985	38	13	1	1	11	23	1	50
	1990	69	13	1	1	11	23	1	50
	1995	105	15	5	3	10	17	6	47
	1996	97	14	4	2	7	18	9	47
	1997	92	14	5	2	7	18	10	47
	1998	95	14	4	2	10	18	7	48
	1999	97	14	4	2	9	18	7	48
	2000	98	14	4	2	11	18	5	48
	2001	100	14	4	2	10	18	6	48
Micronesia (Federated States of) (U.S. Dollars)	1970	24	34	3	1	4	15	14	30
	1975	56	34	3	1	4	15	14	30
	1980	77	34	3	1	4	15	14	30
	1985	102	35	3	1	4	14	12	31
	1990	151	19	4	1	4	20	16	37
	1995	215	21	3	1	2	16	15	43
	2000	229	18	2	1	3	16	13	48
	2001	238	18	2	1	3	16	13	48
Nauru (US Dollars)	1970	12	34	3	1	4	15	14	30
	1975	19	34	3	1	4	15	14	30
	1980	32	34	3	1	4	15	14	30
	1985	52	35	3	1	4	14	12	31
	1990	66	19	4	1	4	20	16	37
	1995	55	21	3	1	2	16	15	43
	2000	57	18	2	1	3	16	13	48
	2001	60	18	2	1	3	16	13	48
New Caledonia [71] (CFP Francs)	1970	38204	27	13	0	4	17	17	23
	1975	63643	27	13	0	4	17	17	23
	1980	90847	27	13	0	4	17	17	23
	1985	139650	31	15	1	4	12	11	27
	1990	250427	16	20	1	3	17	14	31
	1995	329296	18	18	1	2	13	13	36
	2000	433607	17	18	1	2	12	12	38
	2001	461108	17	18	1	2	12	12	38

Table 3. Gross Domestic Product by Kind of Economic Activity: Individual Countries or Areas

Major area, region and country	Year	Gross Domestic Product (at current prices) Million	Agriculture hunting forestry and fishing A-B	Mining Manufacturing and Utilities C-E	Of which: Manufacturing D	Construction F	Wholesale, retail trade, restaurants and hotels G-H	Transport storage and communication I	Other Activities J-P
			Percentage Distribution						
New Zealand (New Zealand Dollars)	1970	5846	10	27	24	6	21	8	29
	1975	11334	10	24	22	8	21	7	33
	1980	23464	10	26	22	5	19	8	32
	1985	46212	8	26	22	5	19	7	37
	1990	73113	6	22	17	4	16	8	41
	1995	92679	7	21	17	4	15	8	40
	1996	97239	7	20	17	4	14	8	42
	1997	100739	7	20	16	4	14	8	42
	1998	101959	6	19	16	4	15	7	44
	1999	107068	7	19	16	4	16	9	41
	2000	113778	7	19	16	4	16	10	41
	2001	122241	7	18	15	4	16	10	41
Palau (Australian Dollars)	1970	12	4	3	1	8	32	8	44
	1975	39	4	3	1	8	32	8	44
	1980	19	4	3	1	8	32	8	44
	1985	41	4	3	1	8	32	8	44
	1990	83	4	3	1	8	32	8	44
	1995	128	6	2	1	8	33	9	42
	2000	204	4	5	1	8	31	9	42
	2001	237	4	5	1	8	30	9	42
Papua New Guinea [72] (Kina)	1970	689	35	7	6	23	9	7	16
	1975	1185	30	22	9	8	9	6	13
	1980	1894	33	25	10	5	10	5	15
	1985	2451	33	23	11	4	10	5	16
	1990	3138	29	26	9	5	9	6	22
	1995	5888	29	34	8	3	9	5	21
	2000	9650	27	37	8	4	9	4	19
	2001	10078	28	37	9	3	9	4	18
Samoa [73] (Tala)	1970	43	17	23	20	7	14	10	29
	1975	85	17	23	20	7	14	10	29
	1980	142	17	23	20	7	14	10	29
	1985	271	17	23	20	7	14	10	29
	1990	465	17	23	20	7	14	10	29
	1995	496	19	22	19	8	15	10	27
	2000	775	16	18	15	7	20	13	26
	2001	852	14	19	16	7	21	14	26
Solomon Islands (Solomon Islands Dollars)	1970	29	59	5	3	2	8	2	26
	1975	50	58	5	3	3	8	2	28
	1980	119	50	4	3	3	9	3	30
	1985	237	45	5	3	4	9	5	37
	1990	520	37	4	3	3	7	4	29
	1995	1242	40	4	3	3	8	4	32
	2000	1721	43	5	3	4	8	5	34
	2001	1766	39	4	3	3	7	4	31
Tonga [74] (Pa 'anga)	1970	10	50	4	3	5	8	3	17
	1975	25	42	6	4	3	11	3	20
	1980	47	33	7	6	5	15	7	20
	1985	86	32	6	5	7	12	6	22
	1990	147	30	7	5	5	12	8	25
	1995	199	25	6	4	6	13	7	25
	1996	209	25	6	4	6	12	7	26
	1997	208	24	6	4	5	12	7	28
	1998	219	26	6	4	5	12	7	28
	1999	237	26	6	5	5	11	7	28
	2000	261	23	6	5	5	12	7	27
	2001	277	22	6	4	6	11	7	28
Tuvalu (Australian dollars)	1970	1	8	2	1	9	27	-9	63
	1975	2	8	2	1	9	27	-9	63
	1980	1	8	2	1	9	27	-9	63
	1985	5	9	4	2	10	11	1	64
	1990	12	24	5	3	8	18	1	36
	1995	16	23	8	4	5	14	6	37
	2000	25	19	9	3	10	15	7	35
	2001	27	19	9	3	10	15	7	35

Table 3. Gross Domestic Product by Kind of Economic Activity: Individual Countries or Areas

Major area, region and country	Year	Gross Domestic Product (at current prices) Million	Agriculture hunting forestry and fishing A-B	Mining Manufacturing and Utilities C-E	Of which: Manufacturing D	Construction F	Wholesale, retail trade, restaurants and hotels G-H	Transport storage and communication I	Other Activities J-P
			Percentage Distribution						
Vanuatu.......... (Vatu)	1970	3508	25	6	4	4	30	8	28
	1975	5084	25	6	4	4	30	8	28
	1980	7746	25	6	4	4	30	8	28
	1985	12870	28	6	4	3	26	9	28
	1990	17638	21	7	5	5	27	11	29
	1995	25550	17	7	5	5	34	12	27
	1996	26711	17	7	5	3	34	11	28
	1997	27565	16	7	5	3	34	12	29
	1998	29289	17	7	5	3	34	11	28
	1999	29206	16	7	5	3	34	12	28
	2000	31108	15	7	5	4	33	12	29
	2001	31831	13	7	5	4	34	12	29

Notes for Table 3

1/ Wholesale and retail trade, restaurants and hotels
Other activities
For 1970-1989
Restaurants and hotels are included in "Other activities".

2/ (a) Wholesale and retail trade, restaurants and hotels
Other activities
For 1970-1985
Restaurants and hotels are included in "Other activities".

(b) Gross domestic product
For 1970-1988
For the first series, Gross domestic production. This differs from domestic product, primarily in the exclusion of the product originating in general government agencies and in public establishments of administrative nature.

3/ Mining, manufacturing and utilities
For 1992-2001
Excludes gas.

4/ Wholesale and retail trade, restaurants and hotels
For 1970-1979
Includes the profit or loss of the Marketing Board.

5/ Wholesale and retail trade, restaurants and hotels
For 1970-1977
Restaurants and hotels are included in "Other activities".

6/ (a) Agriculture, hunting, forestry, fishing
For 1990-1998
Does not include hunting.

(b) Mining, manufacturing and utilities
For 1990-1998
Does not include gas.

7/ (a) Mining, manufacturing and utilities
For 1970-1991
Refers to oil and its products.

(b) Manufacturing
For 1996-2001
Includes non-petroleum mining activities.

(c) Wholesale and retail trade, restaurants and hotels
For 1986-1991
Includes finance and insurance.

(d) Other activities
1996-2001
Includes utilities.

(e) Gross domestic product
For 1970-1979
For years 1972-1979 estimates relate to calendar year.

8/ Manufacturing
For 1972-1989
Includes repair services.

9/ Gross domestic product
For 1970-1979
Gross domestic product at purchaser's prices.

10/ Wholesale and retail trade, restaurants and hotels
Other activities
For 1970-1991
Restaurants and hotels are included in "Other activities".

11/ (a) Manufacturing
For 1970-1992
Includes handicrafts.

(b) Gross domestic product
For 1970-1980
First series, estimates refer to year beginning 1 April.

12/ Agriculture, hunting, forestry, fishing
For 1970-1979
Includes all non-monetary output.

13/ Manufacturing
For 1981-1992
Includes handicrafts.

14/ Other activities
For 1970-1979
FISIM is netted out of Financial intermediation, real estate, renting and business activities.

15/ (a) Mining, manufacturing and utilities
For 1970-2001
Does not include gas.

(b) Wholesale and retail trade, restaurants and hotels
For 1996-2001
Includes Financial intermediation; real estate, renting and business actvities.

16/ Other activities
For 1980-1991
FISIM is netted out of Financial intermediation, real estate, renting and business activities.

17/ Wholesale and retail trade, restaurants and hotels
For 1970-1994
Includes import duties.

18/ Other activities
For 1970-1979
FISIM is netted out of Financial intermediation, real estate, renting and business activities.

19/ (a) Manufacturing
For 1980-2000
Includes mining and handicrafts.

(b) Gross domestic product
For 1996-2000
Breakdown with respect to Transport, storage and communications and Financial intermediation; real estate, renting and business activities revised starting 1996. In previous years, import duties were included in Transport and Financial intermediation did not include Real estate, renting and business activities.

20/ Wholesale and retail trade, restaurants and hotels
For 1991-1994, 1996-1997
Includes Transport, storage and communications; Financial intermediation, real estate, renting and business activities; and Education, health and social work; other community, social and personal services, and Private households with employed persons.

21/ (a) Mining, manufacturing and utilities
For 1970-2001
Does not include gas.

(b) Wholesale and retail trade, restaurants and hotels
For 1970-1979
Restaurants and hotels are included in "Other activities".

(c) Other activities
For 1980-2001
Includes Hotels and restaurants and Business activities.

22/ Manufacturing
For 1970-1994
Includes handicrafts.

23/ Mining, manufacturing and utilities
For 1970-1998
Does not include gas.

24/ (a) Agriculture, hunting, forestry, fishing
For 1994-2000
Includes Mining and quarrying.

(b) Manufacturing
For 1994-2000
Excludes oil refining.

25/ (a) Agriculture, hunting, forestry, fishing
For 1989-1995
Does not include Hunting and Forestry.

(b) Mining, manufacturing and utilities
For 1989-1995
Does not include gas.

26/ (a) Wholesale and retail trade, restaurants and hotels
For 1992-2001
Does not include repair of motor vehicles, motorcycles and personal and household goods, hotels and restaurants.

(b) Other activities
For 1992-2001
Includes Hotels and restaurants.

27/ Other activities
For 1972-1991
Excludes banks and insurance companies registered in Cayman Islands but with no physical presence in the . Islands.

28/ (a) Manufacturing
For 1970-1991
Includes handicrafts.

(b) Wholesale and retail trade, restaurants and hotels
For 1970-1979
Restaurants and hotels are included in "Other activities".

29/ (a) Mining, manufacturing and utilities
For 1970-2001
Does not include petroleum refining.

(b) Manufacturing
For 1970-1979
Does not include petroleum refining.

30/ Other activities
For 1980-2001
Includes Hotels and restaurants and beginning 1990, includes rents of owner-occupied dwellings.

31/ (a) Manufacturing
For 1980-2001
Includes Electricity, gas and water supply.

(b) Construction
For 1970-2001
Includes engineering and sewage services.

(c) Wholesale and retail trade, restaurants and hotels
Other activities
For 1970-1990
Restaurants and hotels are included in "Other activities".

32/ Manufacturing
1970-2000
Basic petroleum manufacturing is included in "Mining, manufacturing and utilities".

33/ Agriculture, hunting, forestry, fishing
For 1980-1997
Includes Mining and quarrying.

34/ (a) Manufacturing
For 1970-1978
For 1972, item "Manufacturing" excludes damages by earthquake amounting to 21.7 million cordobas at current prices, and 17.9 million cordobas at constant prices.

(b) Wholesale and retail trade, restaurants and hotels
For 1970-1978
Restaurants and hotels are included in "Other activities".

35/ (a) Wholesale and retail trade, restaurants and hotels
For 1980-1995
Includes Financal intermediation, except insurance and pension funding.

(b) Other activities
For 1980-1995
Includes Hotels and restaurants and business activities.

36/ Construction
For 1970-2000
Refers to contract construction only.

37/ Gross domestic product
For 1975-1987
At factor cost.

38/ (a) Other activities
For 1980-2000
Includes hotels and guest houses.

(b) Gross domestic product
For 1992-2000
Discrepancy between components and total.

39/ Mining, manufacturing and utilities
For 1970-1986
Electricity, gas and water supply includes sewage services.

40/ (a) Agriculture, hunting, forestry, fishing
For 1989-2001
Includes agricultural products and improvements and other non-agricultural products.

(b) Manufacturing
For 1970-2001
Includes petroleum refining.

41/ Manufacturing
For 1990-2001
Includes Mining and quarrying, and Electricity, gas and water supply.

42/ Manufacturing
For 1990-1998
Includes Mining and quarrying, and Electricity, gas and water supply.

43/ Manufacturing
For 1990-2001
Includes Mining and quarrying, and Electricity, gas and water supply.

44/ (a) Agriculture, hunting, forestry, fishing
For 1980-2001
Refers to Agriculture and fishing only.

(b) Wholesale and retail trade, restaurants and hotels
For 1980-2001
Refers to Wholesale, retail and import/export trades, restaurants and hotels only.

45/ (a) Other activities
For 1977-2001
Includes Ownership of dwellings.

(b) Other activities
For 1980-2001
Includes Hotels and restaurants and Business activities.

46/ (a) Mining, manufacturing and utilities
For 1970-1979, 1987-1992
Includes oil production.

(b) Gross domestic product
For 1992-2001
Discrepancy between total and components since FISIM is subtracted twice.

47/ (a) Agriculture, hunting, forestry, fishing
Manufacturing
For 1970-2000
Agricultural services and related activities such as cotton ginning and pressing are included in Manufacturing.

(b) Wholesale and retail trade, restaurants and hotels
For 1970-2000
Includes distribution of petroleum products.

48/ Manufacturing
For 1990-1997
Includes Mining and quarrying, and Electricity, gas and water supply.

49/ Mining, manufacturing and utilities
For 1970-2001
Beginning 1980, the cost of fuel (natural gas, crude petroleum and gas-oil) consumed in the production of electricity and water has been taken into account as intermediate consumption in estimating the value added of Electricity, gas and water supply.

50/ Manufacturing
For 1990-2001
Includes Mining and quarrying, and Electricity, gas and water supply.

51/ Gross domestic product
For 1995-1998
Discrepancy between components and total since GDP figures have not been revised.

52/ (a) Wholesale and retail trade, restaurants and hotels
Other activities
For 1970-1979
Restaurants and hotels are included in "Other activities".

(b) Other activities
For 1980-1998
Includes Gas and water, Restaurant and hotels.

(c) Gross domestic product
For 1970-1974
Estimates refer to year ending 30 September.

53/ Manufacturing
For 1970-1999
Includes cottage industries.

54/ Wholesale and retail trade, restaurants and hotels
For 1970-1979
Restaurants and hotels are included in "Other activities".

55/ (a) Agriculture, hunting, forestry, fishing
For 1970-1975
Estimates on processing of tea and rubber are included in the agricultural sector.

(b) Manufacturing
For 1970-1975
Estimates on processing of tea and rubber are included in the agricultural sector.

56/ Manufacturing
For 1990-2000
Includes Mining and quarrying, and Electricity, gas and water supply.

57/ Manufacturing
For 1992-2001
Includes Mining and quarrying, and Electricity, gas and water supply.

58/ Manufacturing
For 1990-2000
Includes Mining and quarrying, and Electricity, gas and water supply.

59/ Wholesale and retail trade, restaurants and hotels
For 1990-2000
Includes "Other activities"

60/ Manufacturing
For 1990-2001
Includes Mining and quarrying, and Electricity, gas and water supply.

61/ Mining, manufacturing and utilities
For 1990-1994
Excludes electricity and gas.

62/ Gross domestic product
For 1980-1990
Data derived from Material Product Balances (MPS) data.

63/ (a) Agriculture, hunting, forestry, fishing
For 1988-1991
Includes veterinary services and operation of irrigation systems (part of Electricity, gas and water).

(b) Manufacturing
For 1988-1991
Includes Gas.

(c) Mining, manufacturing and utilities
For 1980-1988
Excludes gas and operation of irrigation systems.

(d) Other activities
For 1988-1991
Gross output of finance, insurance and owner-occupied housing are estimated at cost level.

64/ Manufacturing
For 1990-1994
Includes Mining and quarrying, and Electricity, gas and water supply.

65/ (a) Mining, manufacturing and utilities
For 1970-2001
Construction included in "Mining, manufacturing and utilities".

(b) Mining, manufacturing and utilities
For 1970-2001
Electricity, gas and water supply refers to all government enterprises.

(c) Wholesale and retail trade, restaurants and hotels
Other activities
For 1970-1997
Restaurants and hotels are included in "Other activities".

66/ Other activities
For 1980-1988
Excludes personal services.

67/ Manufacturing
For 1990-2001
Includes Mining and quarrying, and Electricity, gas and water supply.

68/ Manufacturing
For 1990-2000
Includes Mining and quarrying.

69/ Manufacturing
For 1989-2000
Includes Mining and quarrying, and Electricity, gas and water supply.

70/ Mining, manufacturing and utilities
Manufacturing
For 1970-1993
Includes manufacturing of energy-generating products.

71/ Wholesale and retail trade, restaurants and hotels
Other activities
For 1970-1996
Restaurants and hotels are included in "Other activities".

72/ Other activities
1970-1999
Includes Hotels and restaurants, and Private households with employed persons.

73/ Mining, manufacturing and utilities
For 1972-2000
Item "Mining and quarrying" includes forestry and fishing.

74/ Other activities
For 1994-2001
Includes ownership of dwellings.

C. Growth Rates of Main National Accounting Aggregates at Constant Prices of 1990

Description of Analysis in Tables 4, 5 and 6

A. Economic development expressed in rates of growth in real terms of gross domestic product and its components.

Tables 4 to 6 reflect trends in economic development expressed as rates of real growth of GDP and its components for the world, developed, developing and transition economies, as well as for individual countries or areas during the period 1970-2001, with 1990 as the base year.

The figures shown in these tables are computed as geometric mean of annual rates of growth expressed in percentages for the years and periods of years indicated. The growth rates for the individual countries are based on the estimates of gross domestic product (GDP) at constant 1990 prices and their components by type of expenditure and by kind of economic activity. Table 4 presents growth rates of total GDP, while Tables 5 and 6 show growth rates of its principal components by expenditure and by kind of economic activity, respectively.

The growth rates presented in the tables, however, may not be fully consistent between countries and regions. Their comparability could be affected by the wide variety of base years that are used by countries in the compilation of GDP at constant prices.

The first column of the three tables lists individual countries and their aggregation into world, regions and level of economic development totals. The next column in each table highlights the base year weights in 1990 of GDP, representing for individual countries' and sub-regions' weights of their GDP as a percentage of the region and those for the regions and economic development groupings, as a percentage of the world. In Tables 5 and 6, an additional third column presents, respectively, the shares of each expenditure and industry components as a percentage of GDP in 1990. The next three columns of the tables contain the growth rates of GDP during the average periods 1970-1979, 1980-1989 and 1990-1999. The remaining columns show the annual rates of growth over the preceding year starting from 1996 through 2001.

Table 5 includes the rates of growth of each expenditure component of GDP as follows: (a) household final consumption expenditure;(b) general government final consumption expenditure; (c) gross fixed capital formation; (d) exports of goods and services; and (e) imports of goods and services.

In deriving the growth rates of the individual expenditure categories by regions and for the three economic groups of the developed, developing and transition economies, expenditures expressed in US dollars for the base year 1990 were used as weights. Global and regional growth rates for each of the expenditure categories were calculated by adding the expenditures of individual countries in US dollars that were derived by extrapolating the 1990 current price figures by the corresponding growth at constant prices. The expenditure totals of countries expressed in 1990 US dollars were first aggregated according to the economic development region that each belongs and then added up to arrive at the global level.

The country indicators utilized in the calculation were derived principally from official estimates, in national currency, of gross domestic product by type of expenditure at constant prices. For some countries, the indicator series were obtained by linking together separate series covering the full period.

Table 6 lists the average rates of growth of each economic activity component of GDP: (a) agriculture, (b) mining, manufacturing and utilities, (c) manufacturing, (d) construction, (e) wholesale and retail trade, restaurants and hotels , (f) transport, storage and communication and (g) other activities.

The calculation of the regional and world growth rates of the separate economic activity categories in table 6 was done in a similar manner as was described above in table 5 for the expenditure components. Value-added data at constant prices for each economic activity group were first compiled from appropriate series of indicators for all countries concerned and combined to form regional totals after conversion to 1990 United States dollars. These were then combined into separate totals for developed, developing and transition economies.

The country indicators utilized in the calculation were derived from estimates of gross domestic product at constant prices. The basic data were generally absolute figures of product expressed in national currency units; in a limited number of cases, indices computed by the countries themselves were used directly. For some countries, the indicators' series were obtained by linking together separate series covering the full period.

Various methods were utilized to obtain indicators for countries where constant price estimates of gross domestic product by kind of economic activity were not available. For example, the national indices of the quantum of production were employed for agriculture, total industrial activity (mining, manufacturing and utilities), manufacturing and, in some cases, for construction. Where such national indices were not available for agriculture, indices compiled by the Food and Agricultural Organization of the United Nations were utilized, In the absence of an official series for total industrial activity or manufacturing, use was made of indicators for those components which were officially provided and utilized in compiling the world index of industrial production of the Statistics Division of the United Nations Secretariat. In the remaining cases, estimates from unofficial sources were utilized or estimated from indicator series prepared by the Statistics Division, generally by deflating related series at current prices with suitable price indices.

The country and regional weights used in the derivation of growth rates of expenditure and activity components of GDP are based on 1990 values expressed in US dollars of that year. In making the conversion and subsequent aggregation to calculate the growth rates, the same exchange rate for 1990 were used for the derivation of growth rates for total GDP (Table 4) as were used in the derivation of the growth rates of its expenditure and activity components shown in Tables 5 and 6.

Table 4. Annual Average Rate of Growth of Gross Domestic Product by Major Area, Region and Country

Major area, region and country	Base year weights as percentage of total for world or region in 1990	Average rates of growth			Annual rate of change (percentage)					
		1970-1979	1980-1989	1990-1999	1996	1997	1998	1999	2000	2001
WORLD	**100.0**	**4.0**	**2.9**	**2.4**	**3.2**	**3.6**	**2.5**	**3.1**	**4.0**	**1.5**
DEVELOPED ECONOMIES	**74.2**	**3.6**	**2.8**	**2.3**	**2.7**	**3.2**	**2.8**	**2.9**	**3.5**	**1.0**
DEVELOPING ECONOMIES	**17.6**	**5.7**	**3.4**	**4.7**	**5.8**	**5.3**	**2.1**	**3.6**	**5.4**	**2.7**
TRANSITION ECONOMIES	**8.2**	**5.4**	**3.0**	**-4.5**	**-1.2**	**2.1**	**-1.0**	**3.6**	**7.2**	**5.4**
AFRICA	**2.3**	**4.3**	**2.7**	**2.4**	**4.9**	**3.4**	**3.8**	**3.3**	**3.2**	**3.7**
Eastern Africa	*10.9*	*3.1*	*2.9*	*3.0*	*6.0*	*4.3*	*3.3*	*3.3*	*2.1*	*3.5*
Burundi	0.2	3.2	3.8	-1.2	-8.6	0.3	4.6	-1.0	-0.9	3.2
Comoros	0.0	4.4	3.3	-0.1	1.7	-1.1	-1.1	1.9	-1.1	2.0
Djibouti	0.1	1.6	1.8	1.6	-5.1	4.6	-0.2	2.2	0.7	1.9
Eritrea	...	...	...	4.1	6.8	7.9	3.9	0.8	-8.2	4.0
Ethiopia	...	...	...	5.8	10.6	5.2	-0.5	6.3	5.4	7.9
Ethiopia (Former)	1.5	2.3	2.3	-2.0	...	...	...	...	...	...
Kenya	1.6	5.2	4.4	2.1	4.1	2.1	1.6	1.3	-0.2	1.1
Madagascar	0.6	1.0	0.5	1.6	2.1	3.7	3.9	4.7	4.8	6.0
Malawi	0.3	7.4	3.2	4.0	-2.5	6.7	1.5	3.1	3.3	-1.5
Mauritius	0.5	8.2	4.3	5.1	5.6	5.8	6.0	2.9	9.2	5.5
Mozambique	0.5	3.9	-0.3	4.6	6.8	11.1	12.6	7.5	1.5	13.0
Reunion	1.0	6.0	4.2	3.0	2.9	3.1	3.0	3.0	3.0	2.4
Rwanda	0.4	5.0	3.0	0.0	14.9	14.3	9.2	6.5	6.3	6.6
Seychelles	0.1	6.7	2.6	4.7	4.9	11.7	7.4	2.0	1.4	1.0
Somalia	0.2	3.3	1.4	-3.3	3.9	-2.7	2.5	2.1	3.0	3.0
Uganda	0.7	0.0	2.9	6.7	5.6	5.3	7.2	5.0	8.0	6.4
United Republic of Tanzania	0.7	3.7	2.3	4.2	4.2	3.3	5.0	5.3	2.5	5.9
Zambia	0.8	0.8	1.6	-0.4	6.6	3.3	-1.9	2.2	3.6	5.2
Zimbabwe	1.7	1.9	4.7	2.8	10.4	2.7	2.9	-0.7	-7.8	-7.3
Middle Africa	*8.6*	*1.7*	*2.8*	*-0.1*	*5.0*	*4.2*	*3.9*	*0.3*	*3.4*	*4.8*
Angola	1.9	0.2	2.7	0.4	11.4	7.7	5.5	2.7	3.6	5.2
Cameroon	2.7	4.8	4.1	0.4	5.0	5.1	5.0	4.2	5.3	4.6
Central African Republic	0.2	1.9	0.9	1.1	-3.2	5.7	4.8	3.6	1.8	0.0
Chad	0.3	-1.7	5.0	3.0	1.7	6.0	5.3	-0.1	-0.4	8.7
Congo	0.5	4.6	6.2	0.5	4.3	-0.5	3.8	-3.2	8.1	2.9
Democratic Republic of the Congo	1.8	0.2	1.8	-6.2	-0.9	-5.8	-1.6	-10.4	-4.3	-4.4
Equatorial Guinea	0.0	2.2	2.8	21.7	45.3	71.2	22.0	41.4	16.9	53.4
Gabon	1.0	1.1	0.4	2.4	4.0	4.5	2.1	-6.2	2.0	2.5
Sao Tome and Principe	0.0	7.0	-1.4	1.2	1.5	1.0	2.5	2.5	3.0	4.0
Northern Africa	*44.1*	*6.0*	*3.0*	*2.8*	*5.0*	*3.1*	*5.1*	*4.2*	*3.5*	*4.3*
Algeria	11.7	6.4	2.8	1.3	3.0	1.9	4.7	3.6	1.7	4.3
Egypt	13.4	5.8	5.7	3.7	5.1	4.0	6.1	5.4	3.5	3.2
Libyan Arab Jamahiriya	5.4	8.1	-1.8	-0.4	3.9	1.3	0.4	0.1	3.2	3.3
Morocco	4.9	5.4	3.9	2.5	12.2	-2.2	7.7	-0.1	1.0	6.5
Sudan	6.4	3.6	2.9	4.9	3.0	6.7	5.0	6.9	6.9	5.3
Tunisia	2.3	7.3	3.6	5.0	7.2	5.4	4.8	6.1	4.7	4.9
Southern Africa	*22.6*	*3.1*	*2.4*	*1.6*	*4.4*	*2.8*	*1.1*	*2.2*	*3.5*	*2.5*
Botswana	0.7	16.3	12.0	5.1	5.5	5.6	8.1	4.1	8.1	9.2
Lesotho	0.1	8.6	3.6	3.9	10.0	8.1	-4.6	0.2	1.5	3.4
Namibia	0.4	2.2	1.7	4.2	3.2	4.5	3.3	4.3	3.9	0.6
South Africa	21.2	3.0	2.2	1.4	4.3	2.6	0.8	2.1	3.4	2.2
Swaziland	0.2	9.6	6.8	3.8	3.9	3.8	3.2	3.5	2.1	1.8
Western Africa	*13.9*	*4.1*	*1.9*	*3.3*	*4.9*	*4.2*	*3.8*	*3.3*	*2.8*	*3.5*
Benin	0.3	1.8	3.9	4.3	5.0	4.0	4.0	5.0	5.8	5.0
Burkina Faso	0.5	4.5	3.4	4.8	6.5	5.7	5.5	6.4	2.4	5.8
Cape Verde	0.1	0.3	5.7	5.2	4.0	5.4	7.4	8.6	6.8	3.0
Cote d'Ivoire	2.2	7.3	2.3	2.6	6.7	5.7	5.1	1.9	-2.7	-0.9
Gambia	0.1	4.7	3.9	3.8	5.3	0.8	9.9	6.4	5.6	5.7
Ghana	1.2	0.7	1.9	4.3	4.6	4.2	4.7	4.4	3.7	4.2
Guinea	0.5	2.8	2.5	4.1	4.6	4.8	4.5	3.7	5.0	3.0
Guinea-Bissau	0.0	3.0	2.9	0.8	5.0	6.3	-28.0	7.6	7.5	7.8
Liberia	0.1	3.1	-4.6	-6.8	12.1	101.5	29.7	22.9	20.3	5.3
Mali	0.5	3.6	2.2	4.7	10.1	6.8	5.9	6.8	3.7	1.4
Mauritania	0.2	2.9	1.5	3.8	2.7	5.0	3.7	4.1	5.0	4.6
Niger	0.5	4.6	0.7	2.0	3.9	2.4	9.9	-1.6	-0.3	5.9
Nigeria	6.1	4.6	1.8	3.4	3.9	3.2	2.3	2.8	3.8	4.2

Table 4. Annual Average Rate of Growth of Gross Domestic Product by Major Area, Region and Country

Major area, region and country	Base year weights as percentage of total for world or region in 1990	Average rates of growth			Annual rate of change (percentage)					
		1970-1979	1980-1989	1990-1999	1996	1997	1998	1999	2000	2001
Senegal	1.1	2.3	2.4	3.2	5.2	5.4	5.7	5.0	5.6	5.6
Sierra Leone	0.1	2.0	1.4	-4.6	6.1	-17.6	-0.8	-8.1	3.8	5.4
Togo	0.3	3.4	0.7	1.5	4.0	4.3	-2.2	2.9	-1.9	2.8
AMERICAS	**32.7**	**4.1**	**2.8**	**2.9**	**3.5**	**4.6**	**4.0**	**3.7**	**3.9**	**0.4**
NORTHERN AMERICA	**27.7**	**3.7**	**3.0**	**3.0**	**3.4**	**4.5**	**4.3**	**4.3**	**3.8**	**0.4**
Bermuda	0.0	3.7	1.1	1.9	2.9	3.3	3.4	3.6	2.0	-0.5
Canada	7.7	4.6	2.9	2.4	1.6	4.2	4.1	5.5	4.6	1.5
United States	76.8	3.7	3.0	3.0	3.6	4.5	4.3	4.1	3.8	0.3
LATIN AMERICA AND THE CARIBBEAN	**5.1**	**5.8**	**1.9**	**2.8**	**3.8**	**5.2**	**2.4**	**0.5**	**4.0**	**0.5**
Caribbean	*1.2*	*4.3*	*3.1*	*2.3*	*5.0*	*4.7*	*4.5*	*4.1*	*5.4*	*3.4*
Anguilla	0.0	3.8	7.0	4.7	3.5	9.2	5.2	8.7	-0.1	1.6
Antigua and Barbuda	0.0	1.0	6.5	3.3	-7.6	5.6	4.9	4.9	0.8	2.3
Aruba	0.0	9.1	9.8	6.0	6.0	6.0	6.0	6.0	6.0	6.0
Bahamas	0.0	2.7	3.8	0.2	4.2	3.3	3.0	5.3	4.5	4.1
Barbados	0.0	4.0	1.7	0.5	2.5	2.8	4.2	2.9	3.0	-2.6
British Virgin Islands	0.0	3.2	6.7	7.9	9.6	9.7	11.4	9.1	10.1	10.1
Cayman Islands	0.0	9.4	9.4	1.8	0.2	0.5	1.5	1.5	1.2	1.2
Cuba	0.3	5.4	3.9	-2.2	7.8	2.5	1.2	6.2	5.6	3.0
Dominica	0.0	-1.6	5.3	2.4	3.5	2.5	3.2	0.6	0.1	-4.3
Dominican Republic	0.1	7.0	3.7	5.1	8.3	8.2	7.4	8.0	7.3	3.2
Grenada	0.0	1.7	1.9	3.6	3.0	4.1	7.3	7.4	6.5	3.5
Guadeloupe	0.0	5.7	2.0	1.8	4.3	9.2	4.1	0.6	4.6	4.6
Haiti	0.0	4.5	0.7	-1.1	2.4	1.8	2.9	1.9	0.2	-1.7
Jamaica	0.1	-0.2	1.3	0.8	-1.1	-1.7	-0.3	-0.4	0.7	1.7
Martinique	0.0	4.2	4.9	1.3	1.6	1.6	4.1	0.6	2.1	2.1
Montserrat	0.0	3.8	4.6	-7.9	-21.4	-20.0	-10.1	-12.6	-2.7	-7.8
Netherlands Antilles	0.0	2.9	0.6	1.3	1.3	-0.6	-2.1	-1.9	-2.3	0.0
Puerto Rico	0.4	4.0	3.6	4.1	4.9	5.5	5.4	2.4	5.6	4.4
Saint Kitts and Nevis	0.0	3.2	5.8	5.9	6.6	6.7	1.2	3.5	3.4	2.2
Saint Lucia	0.0	5.3	6.3	2.3	2.9	-0.8	4.6	3.5	0.7	0.5
Saint Vincent and the Grenadines	0.0	3.0	5.7	3.6	1.1	3.0	5.8	4.1	1.5	0.2
Trinidad and Tobago	0.1	4.7	-1.6	3.8	5.2	6.9	7.7	10.6	11.3	2.6
Central America	*3.9*	*6.2*	*2.0*	*3.4*	*4.8*	*6.5*	*5.0*	*3.7*	*6.2*	*0.0*
Belize	0.0	3.6	4.6	4.6	1.6	3.2	1.5	6.5	10.4	5.0
Costa Rica	0.1	6.2	2.1	5.4	0.9	5.6	8.4	8.2	1.8	1.1
El Salvador	0.1	4.6	-1.2	4.7	1.7	4.2	3.8	3.4	2.2	1.8
Guatemala	0.1	5.9	0.9	4.0	3.0	4.3	4.8	3.8	3.6	2.3
Honduras	0.0	5.9	2.5	2.7	3.6	5.0	2.9	-1.9	5.0	3.0
Mexico	3.5	6.4	2.1	3.3	5.2	6.8	5.0	3.6	6.6	-0.3
Nicaragua	0.0	0.0	-0.9	2.8	4.8	5.1	4.1	7.4	5.5	3.1
Panama	0.1	4.5	3.1	5.0	2.8	4.5	4.4	3.2	2.5	0.9
South America	*10.3*	*5.8*	*1.8*	*2.7*	*3.3*	*4.8*	*1.2*	*-1.1*	*3.0*	*0.4*
Argentina	1.9	2.7	-0.8	4.2	5.5	8.1	3.9	-3.4	-0.8	-4.4
Bolivia	0.1	4.5	-0.4	4.0	4.4	5.0	5.0	0.4	2.4	1.2
Brazil	5.9	8.4	2.9	1.8	2.7	3.3	0.2	0.8	4.5	1.5
Chile	0.4	2.0	3.3	6.3	7.4	6.6	3.2	-1.0	4.4	2.8
Colombia	0.6	5.7	3.4	2.8	2.1	3.4	0.6	-4.2	2.7	1.4
Ecuador	0.2	9.4	2.3	2.2	2.4	4.1	2.1	-6.3	2.8	5.1
French Guiana	0.0	10.8	9.1	4.2	1.6	1.6	1.6	1.6	1.6	1.6
Guyana	0.0	1.7	-2.3	4.7	7.0	6.2	-1.7	3.8	-1.3	1.9
Paraguay	0.1	8.5	3.9	2.3	1.3	2.6	-0.4	0.5	-0.4	2.7
Peru	0.4	3.7	-0.2	3.1	2.5	6.7	-0.5	0.9	3.1	0.1
Suriname	0.0	3.9	0.4	0.2	2.1	6.6	2.6	-1.3	-1.0	4.9
Uruguay	0.1	2.7	1.0	3.3	5.6	4.9	4.2	-2.4	-1.4	-3.3
Venezuela	0.6	4.8	-0.2	2.3	-0.2	6.4	0.2	-6.1	3.2	2.8
ASIA	**24.5**	**5.2**	**4.2**	**3.8**	**5.1**	**3.8**	**0.3**	**2.6**	**4.8**	**2.2**
Eastern Asia	*70.5*	*5.0*	*4.7*	*3.3*	*4.7*	*3.4*	*0.1*	*2.5*	*4.6*	*1.8*
China	6.8	5.2	9.4	9.7	9.6	8.8	7.8	7.1	7.9	7.3
Democratic People's Rep. of Korea	0.3	11.9	8.1	-3.2	-3.6	-6.3	-1.1	6.2	1.3	3.7

Table 4. Annual Average Rate of Growth of Gross Domestic Product by Major Area, Region and Country

Major area, region and country	Base year weights as percentage of total for world or region in 1990	Average rates of growth			Annual rate of change (percentage)					
		1970-1979	1980-1989	1990-1999	1996	1997	1998	1999	2000	2001
Hong Kong SAR of China	1.4	8.8	7.2	3.8	4.3	5.1	-5.0	3.4	10.2	0.6
Japan	54.5	4.6	3.9	1.7	3.4	1.8	-1.1	0.1	2.8	0.4
Macao SAR of China	0.1	7.7	7.4	2.8	-0.4	-0.3	-4.6	-3.0	4.6	2.1
Mongolia	0.1	5.7	6.3	-0.5	2.4	4.0	3.5	2.5	1.1	1.1
Republic of Korea	4.5	8.5	7.5	6.1	6.8	5.0	-6.7	10.9	9.3	3.1
South Central Asia	*13.7*	*3.5*	*3.6*	*6.3*	*5.9*	*4.5*	*4.7*	*5.0*	*4.5*	*5.6*
Afghanistan	0.1	5.1	-1.6	-2.5	6.6	13.3	5.2	-12.4	-43.7	0.0
Bangladesh	0.6	0.5	3.8	4.7	5.4	5.2	4.9	5.9	5.3	4.8
Bhutan	0.0	6.4	8.4	6.1	5.2	7.6	6.4	7.4	5.7	5.9
India	5.8	2.6	5.9	5.6	7.4	4.5	6.0	7.1	3.9	5.4
Iran (Islamic Republic of)	3.4	4.7	0.2	4.8	6.7	5.4	3.8	1.7	5.2	5.0
Kazakhstan	1.3	...	...	-5.0	0.5	1.7	-1.9	2.7	9.8	13.5
Kyrgyzstan	0.2	...	...	-5.0	7.1	9.9	2.1	3.7	5.4	5.3
Maldives	0.0	11.5	11.7	7.4	8.8	11.2	-2.2	7.4	4.6	2.1
Nepal	0.1	2.6	4.0	4.7	5.3	5.0	2.3	4.1	6.5	4.9
Pakistan	0.8	5.1	6.2	3.9	1.0	2.6	3.7	4.3	2.7	4.4
Sri Lanka	0.1	4.2	4.2	5.3	3.8	6.4	4.7	4.3	6.0	-1.4
Tajikistan	0.2	...	...	-11.6	-16.7	1.7	5.3	3.7	8.3	10.2
Turkmenistan	0.2	...	...	-3.5	6.7	-11.4	5.0	16.0	17.6	20.5
Uzbekistan	0.9	...	...	-0.6	1.7	5.2	4.4	4.4	3.8	4.5
South-Eastern Asia	*6.4*	*6.7*	*5.3*	*5.3*	*7.3*	*4.1*	*-7.5*	*3.8*	*6.0*	*2.0*
Brunei Darussalam	0.1	10.1	-2.6	2.2	3.6	4.1	1.0	2.6	2.8	1.5
Cambodia	0.0	-7.3	-1.1	5.1	4.6	4.3	2.1	6.9	7.7	6.3
Indonesia	2.0	7.8	6.4	4.6	7.8	4.7	-13.1	0.8	4.9	3.3
Lao People's Democratic Republic	0.0	0.1	4.9	6.4	6.9	6.9	4.0	7.3	5.8	5.7
Malaysia	0.8	9.7	5.7	7.1	10.0	7.3	-7.4	6.1	8.3	0.4
Myanmar	0.3	3.9	1.7	5.5	6.4	5.7	5.0	5.7	5.5	4.8
Philippines	0.8	6.0	1.9	2.8	5.8	5.2	-0.6	3.4	4.4	3.2
Singapore	0.7	8.9	7.4	7.5	7.7	8.5	-0.1	6.9	10.3	-2.0
Thailand	1.5	7.0	7.2	5.1	5.9	-1.4	-10.5	4.4	4.6	1.8
Timor-Leste	0.0	...	...	7.8	10.8	4.1	-2.1	0.8	4.8	15.0
Vietnam	0.1	-0.1	4.5	7.4	9.3	8.2	5.8	4.8	6.8	6.8
Western Asia	*9.4*	*7.4*	*0.5*	*3.6*	*4.8*	*5.4*	*3.1*	*-0.8*	*5.6*	*-0.4*
Armenia	0.3	...	...	-4.8	5.9	3.3	7.3	3.3	5.9	9.6
Azerbaijan	0.4	...	...	-6.8	1.3	5.8	10.0	7.4	11.1	9.9
Bahrain	0.1	12.8	-0.3	4.9	4.1	3.1	4.8	4.3	5.3	3.5
Cyprus	0.1	3.4	6.1	4.4	1.9	2.5	4.9	4.6	5.1	4.0
Georgia	0.4	...	...	-10.5	11.2	10.6	2.9	3.0	1.9	4.7
Iraq	0.7	11.8	-1.0	-8.4	2.1	25.0	15.0	8.0	11.0	15.0
Israel	1.0	5.6	3.1	5.3	5.0	3.1	2.9	2.8	8.0	-0.9
Jordan	0.1	6.3	3.7	4.4	2.1	3.1	2.9	1.5	2.7	3.5
Kuwait	0.3	-0.1	-1.8	1.2	-2.7	1.2	3.2	-4.9	-10.1	-1.1
Lebanon	0.1	-1.2	-6.7	6.6	4.0	3.5	3.0	4.0	2.0	3.0
Oman	0.2	4.8	8.1	4.9	2.9	6.2	2.7	-0.2	5.5	9.3
Qatar	0.1	4.2	2.5	5.5	4.8	24.0	8.4	3.2	10.0	6.2
Saudi Arabia	1.9	10.2	-4.1	2.8	1.4	2.6	2.8	-0.8	4.9	1.2
Syrian Arab Republic	0.3	9.7	1.6	6.3	9.8	5.0	6.8	-3.6	0.6	3.4
Turkey	2.7	4.8	4.0	3.8	7.0	7.5	3.1	-4.7	7.4	-7.4
United Arab Emirates	0.6	35.6	1.0	3.5	10.4	1.9	-7.0	2.5	5.4	5.0
Yemen	0.2	...	...	4.1	5.9	8.1	4.9	3.7	5.1	4.6
Yemen Arab Republic (Former)	...	8.9	6.4	...	...	...	...	...	...	...
Yemen Democratic (Former)	...	1.9	4.2	...	...	...	...	...	...	...
EUROPE	**38.8**	**3.5**	**2.4**	**0.9**	**1.3**	**2.5**	**2.4**	**2.8**	**3.8**	**2.0**
Eastern Europe	*17.0*	*5.3*	*3.1*	*-6.2*	*-2.6*	*1.2*	*-2.4*	*3.9*	*7.3*	*5.0*
Belarus	0.7	...	...	-2.0	2.8	11.4	8.4	3.4	5.8	4.7
Bulgaria	0.2	7.1	3.6	-3.4	-9.4	-5.6	4.0	2.3	5.4	4.0
Czech Republic	0.4	...	1.7	-0.3	4.3	-0.8	-1.0	0.5	3.3	3.1
Czechoslovakia (Former)	...	4.7	...	...	...			...	...	...
Hungary	0.4	5.3	1.5	-0.1	1.3	4.6	4.9	4.2	5.2	3.8
Poland	0.7	6.7	0.3	2.0	6.0	6.8	4.8	4.1	4.0	1.0
Republic of Moldova	0.2	...	...	-11.4	-5.9	1.6	-6.5	-3.4	2.1	6.1
Romania	0.4	10.0	1.5	-1.2	3.9	-6.1	-4.8	-1.2	1.8	5.3
Russian Federation	10.9	...	...	-5.4	-3.4	0.9	-4.9	5.4	9.0	5.0
Slovakia	0.2	...	1.0	0.4	5.8	5.6	4.0	1.3	2.2	3.3
Ukraine	2.8	...	...	-9.5	-10.0	-3.0	-1.9	-0.2	5.9	9.2

Table 4. Annual Average Rate of Growth of Gross Domestic Product by Major Area, Region and Country

Major area, region and country	Base year weights as percentage of total for world or region in 1990	Average rates of growth			Annual rate of change (percentage)					
		1970-1979	1980-1989	1990-1999	1996	1997	1998	1999	2000	2001
USSR (Former)	...	5.2	3.2	...	...	...	...	...	...	...
Northern Europe	*19.4*	*2.6*	*2.4*	*2.4*	*2.9*	*4.0*	*3.4*	*3.1*	*3.7*	*2.0*
Denmark	1.5	2.2	1.4	2.1	2.5	3.0	2.5	2.6	2.9	1.4
Estonia	0.1	...	...	-2.3	4.0	10.4	5.0	-0.7	6.9	5.4
Finland	1.5	3.5	3.6	1.5	3.9	6.4	4.9	3.4	5.5	0.6
Iceland	0.1	6.4	3.2	2.2	5.1	4.6	5.5	3.9	5.5	2.9
Ireland	0.5	4.9	3.1	7.1	8.1	10.9	8.8	11.1	10.0	5.7
Latvia	0.2	...	...	-5.5	3.7	8.4	4.8	2.8	6.8	7.7
Lithuania	0.2	...	...	-4.5	4.7	7.3	5.1	-3.9	3.8	5.9
Norway	1.3	4.8	2.9	3.6	5.3	5.2	2.6	2.1	2.8	1.9
Sweden	2.8	2.0	2.2	1.6	1.3	2.4	3.6	4.6	4.4	1.1
United Kingdom	11.1	2.4	2.4	2.1	2.6	3.4	2.9	2.4	3.1	2.1
Southern Europe	*21.0*	*3.8*	*2.4*	*2.1*	*2.0*	*3.0*	*2.9*	*2.5*	*3.5*	*2.2*
Albania	0.0	6.2	2.9	-0.5	9.1	-7.0	8.0	7.3	7.8	5.5
Andorra	0.0	9.3	6.9	7.6	7.5	9.0	9.1	8.8	8.7	7.3
Bosnia and Herzegovina	0.1	...	...	7.1	50.0	27.8	23.1	17.0	10.7	7.4
Croatia	0.3	...	...	-2.0	5.9	6.8	2.5	-0.9	2.9	3.8
Greece	0.9	5.0	0.8	1.9	2.4	3.6	3.4	3.6	4.2	4.1
Holy See	0.0	4.5	2.8	1.6	1.1	2.2	1.8	1.7	3.0	1.8
Italy	12.4	3.6	2.4	1.5	1.1	2.0	1.8	1.6	2.9	1.8
Malta	0.0	10.8	4.0	5.0	3.8	4.8	3.5	3.9	4.8	3.9
Portugal	0.8	4.8	3.3	2.8	3.5	4.0	4.6	3.8	3.7	1.6
San Marino	0.0	3.6	2.4	2.8	1.1	2.0	7.5	9.0	2.9	1.8
Serbia and Montenegro	0.3	...	...	-8.8	5.9	7.4	2.5	-21.9	6.4	-5.5
Slovenia	0.2	...	...	1.5	3.5	4.6	3.8	5.2	4.6	3.0
Spain	5.7	3.8	2.8	2.6	2.4	4.0	4.3	4.2	4.2	2.7
TFYR Macedonia	0.1	...	...	-1.7	1.2	1.4	2.9	2.7	5.1	-4.0
Yugoslavia (Former)	...	6.2	1.1	...	...	...	...	...	...	...
Western Europe	*42.6*	*3.0*	*2.1*	*2.1*	*1.1*	*1.9*	*2.7*	*2.7*	*3.3*	*1.2*
Austria	1.8	3.8	2.1	2.5	2.0	1.6	3.9	2.7	3.5	0.7
Belgium	2.2	3.2	2.1	2.1	1.2	3.6	2.0	3.2	3.7	0.8
France	13.7	3.5	2.4	1.7	1.1	1.9	3.4	3.2	3.8	2.1
Germany	18.8	2.9	1.9	2.2	0.8	1.4	2.0	2.0	2.9	0.6
Liechtenstein	0.0	2.4	2.9	1.6	1.2	2.8	3.6	2.8	4.1	2.3
Luxembourg	0.1	2.8	4.5	5.2	3.3	8.3	6.9	8.7	8.9	1.2
Monaco	0.0	4.1	3.1	2.4	1.8	2.6	4.1	3.9	4.4	2.5
Netherlands	3.3	3.1	2.0	3.0	3.0	3.8	4.3	4.0	3.3	1.3
Switzerland	2.6	0.9	2.1	0.9	0.3	1.7	2.4	1.5	3.2	0.9
OCEANIA	**1.6**	**2.8**	**3.2**	**3.3**	**3.7**	**3.9**	**4.6**	**4.0**	**1.8**	**3.8**
Australia & New Zealand	*96.9*	*2.8*	*3.2*	*3.3*	*3.8*	*4.1*	*4.7*	*4.1*	*1.9*	*3.9*
Australia	85.0	3.0	3.4	3.4	3.8	4.5	5.3	4.0	1.8	3.9
New Zealand	11.9	1.9	2.0	2.6	3.5	1.5	0.4	5.0	2.7	3.5
Melanesia	*2.1*	*2.5*	*2.4*	*3.1*	*4.6*	*-1.6*	*1.6*	*1.2*	*-0.8*	*-0.9*
Fiji	0.4	5.7	1.7	3.0	3.1	-0.9	1.4	9.7	-2.8	2.6
New Caledonia	0.7	1.7	4.4	1.0	0.5	2.0	-3.2	0.9	2.1	-0.8
Papua New Guinea	0.9	1.6	1.4	4.4	7.7	-3.9	4.4	-0.8	-1.2	-1.9
Solomon Islands	0.1	8.1	1.5	4.5	3.5	-2.3	1.1	-1.3	-14.0	-5.0
Vanuatu	0.0	7.7	2.8	3.6	2.5	1.5	2.2	-2.5	3.7	-0.5
Micronesia	*0.1*	*4.5*	*0.7*	*1.5*	*-1.6*	*-1.2*	*0.7*	*1.6*	*-0.5*	*0.8*
Kiribati	0.0	2.9	-4.9	4.2	3.0	5.7	5.0	6.2	0.2	1.8
Marshall Islands	0.0	6.6	6.1	-0.9	-15.9	-9.4	1.1	0.1	-0.9	1.7
Micronesia (Federated States of)	0.0	6.6	4.5	1.6	-1.8	-5.1	-2.1	0.9	2.1	1.5
Nauru	0.0	6.8	4.9	-5.4	-7.3	-7.3	-1.9	-1.9	-1.0	-0.8
Palau	0.0	2.9	-5.5	4.7	10.9	10.4	3.9	2.8	-3.9	-0.7
Polynesia	*0.9*	*4.8*	*5.0*	*2.9*	*1.8*	*1.0*	*1.1*	*2.7*	*3.1*	*2.4*
Cook Islands	0.0	-3.4	2.0	2.2	-0.2	-2.8	-4.2	5.8	9.8	3.0
French Polynesia	0.8	5.6	5.6	3.1	1.6	1.1	1.1	2.7	2.7	2.1
Samoa	0.1	3.1	0.4	0.5	7.3	1.2	2.4	2.6	6.9	6.5
Tonga	0.0	2.6	5.1	2.1	-0.4	0.1	2.4	3.1	6.7	3.0
Tuvalu	0.0	6.6	-1.5	6.1	10.3	3.5	14.9	3.0	3.0	3.0

Table 5.A. Average Rates of Growth of Gross Domestic Product by Expenditure - Household Final Consumption Expenditure

Major area, region and country	Base year weights as percentage of total for world or region in 1990	Base year share as percentage of total GDP in 1990	Average rates of growth			Annual rate of change (percentage)					
			1970-1979	1980-1989	1990-1999	1996	1997	1998	1999	2000	2001
WORLD	**100.0**	**58.4**	**4.2**	**3.0**	**2.3**	**3.0**	**3.1**	**2.7**	**3.4**	**3.8**	**2.6**
DEVELOPED ECONOMIES	**74.8**	**58.8**	**3.8**	**2.8**	**2.4**	**2.6**	**2.6**	**3.3**	**3.6**	**3.3**	**2.2**
DEVELOPING ECONOMIES	**18.0**	**59.5**	**5.3**	**3.5**	**4.5**	**5.7**	**4.4**	**1.6**	**3.6**	**5.1**	**2.8**
TRANSITION ECONOMIES	**7.2**	**51.6**	**5.7**	**3.2**	**-2.6**	**-1.3**	**4.7**	**-0.4**	**-1.0**	**6.4**	**6.2**
AFRICA	**2.5**	**64.2**	**4.4**	**3.3**	**3.2**	**6.5**	**4.4**	**2.5**	**2.5**	**3.0**	**3.8**
Eastern Africa	*11.9*	*70.1*	*3.6*	*2.8*	*3.3*	*6.0*	*5.2*	*1.4*	*4.8*	*4.9*	*4.1*
Burundi	0.3	83.0	2.9	3.4	-2.8	-13.3	-2.0	3.5	3.8	-2.3	3.9
Comoros	0.1	79.7	-0.1	3.4	0.8	1.5	-1.2	-1.7	1.8	-5.7	4.9
Djibouti	0.1	67.2	2.6	-0.1	2.6	-12.5	8.4	12.6	51.9	2.0	1.5
Eritrea	...	...	...	...	4.2	0.0	6.3	12.1	1.8	-18.3	10.4
Ethiopia	...	...	...	...	4.3	10.0	-1.3	-1.2	19.9	5.6	11.5
Ethiopia (Former)	1.7	72.9	2.7	1.0	3.3	...	...	...	...	...	...
Kenya	1.6	62.2	4.6	3.9	1.8	2.8	7.4	-0.6	-7.0	6.4	-4.3
Madagascar	0.8	86.0	0.4	0.5	1.8	3.3	4.2	3.8	-3.3	4.2	8.9
Malawi	0.5	91.6	8.5	2.8	3.5	1.9	8.6	1.5	3.1	3.3	-1.5
Mauritius	0.5	64.6	7.4	4.8	4.9	4.9	4.8	6.1	3.9	3.5	2.8
Mozambique	0.8	101.8	3.9	1.2	2.4	-0.2	8.3	5.9	4.6	-1.8	2.3
Reunion	1.2	79.9	7.9	5.6	2.6	2.6	2.8	2.9	2.8	2.8	2.8
Rwanda	0.6	82.9	5.0	3.3	-2.5	6.6	21.2	5.1	2.1	1.3	9.2
Seychelles	0.1	52.0	7.5	4.9	6.0	13.0	9.9	11.0	-3.7	-13.9	-6.3
Somalia	0.2	71.0	2.6	0.4	-3.1	5.1	-2.0	2.4	1.5	3.1	2.9
Uganda	1.0	91.5	1.2	4.2	6.6	8.0	6.0	3.2	3.0	15.6	5.1
United Republic Of Tanzania	0.8	72.7	2.8	1.6	3.9	1.0	1.5	7.7	7.7	3.9	5.0
Zambia	0.2	14.1	3.1	3.7	0.0	6.6	4.6	-2.0	7.2	3.7	1.1
Zimbabwe	1.6	62.5	3.9	3.3	1.0	19.4	14.1	-6.2	0.7	4.4	-1.4
Middle Africa	*7.7*	*57.5*	*2.5*	*2.6*	*-1.1*	*4.0*	*5.0*	*1.3*	*-7.9*	*-5.1*	*5.5*
Angola	0.9	28.6	0.2	0.8	-5.7	15.8	7.0	-4.5	-32.6	-26.6	14.1
Cameroon	3.2	76.7	6.3	3.2	-0.7	3.5	8.1	5.0	-12.5	1.6	5.5
Central African Republic	0.3	88.1	3.7	1.3	1.2	-2.9	5.0	4.9	6.0	5.1	4.8
Chad	0.4	96.3	-1.9	5.9	3.2	2.0	-2.8	8.4	11.3	-1.6	2.6
Congo	0.4	50.9	4.3	5.9	-3.9	5.7	0.5	-0.9	-37.5	-17.7	18.9
Democratic Republic of the Congo	1.5	55.1	-0.2	0.7	-4.2	-1.0	-3.8	0.4	-10.5	-4.3	-4.4
Equatorial Guinea	0.0	80.3	1.2	3.2	10.8	27.8	58.5	57.5	-40.7	-9.2	13.2
Gabon	0.8	49.7	1.6	4.2	1.7	4.4	5.2	-20.0	53.2	-17.5	10.1
Sao Tome and Principe	0.0	79.9	8.5	0.0	1.1	1.5	8.7	3.0	-2.7	-0.4	-1.0
Northern Africa	*43.8*	*63.8*	*6.2*	*3.6*	*4.2*	*7.2*	*2.6*	*4.6*	*3.5*	*0.3*	*3.9*
Algeria	10.3	50.0	0.5	3.5	0.5	2.0	1.1	2.1	2.9	1.8	4.1
Egypt	16.0	76.3	5.2	4.0	5.3	12.7	3.7	5.2	5.0	3.9	3.5
Libyan Arab Jamahiriya	2.7	32.6	...	...	0.3	-0.5	6.4	7.6	-0.7	-21.5	-2.5
Morocco	4.9	64.6	3.4	3.6	1.6	11.7	-3.0	5.6	0.2	3.6	3.3
Sudan	7.6	76.3	6.5	2.9	4.6	2.9	5.5	3.9	2.9	26.0	5.4
Tunisia	2.3	63.6	7.8	4.5	4.4	4.4	4.5	5.6	5.8	5.5	5.8
Southern Africa	*21.8*	*62.0*	*3.5*	*3.4*	*2.2*	*4.6*	*3.3*	*1.4*	*1.6*	*3.1*	*2.7*
Botswana	0.3	30.0	10.5	4.0	6.1	-0.4	2.9	7.9	6.1	4.1	2.8
Lesotho	0.2	131.6	9.6	4.0	-0.4	9.4	0.3	-8.2	-13.8	-12.8	0.3
Namibia	0.3	47.2	2.3	3.8	2.3	10.7	7.6	2.4	1.0	2.0	-1.8
South Africa	20.7	62.8	3.3	3.4	2.2	4.5	3.3	1.4	1.4	3.3	2.8
Swaziland	0.2	79.2	10.3	7.1	4.5	4.2	4.8	3.1	32.9	6.5	7.8
Western Africa	*14.8*	*68.4*	*3.5*	*3.2*	*3.7*	*8.5*	*9.9*	*-0.5*	*2.9*	*-5.3*	*4.1*
Benin	0.4	80.4	4.2	3.6	3.4	5.9	4.8	4.8	2.3	2.9	0.5
Burkina Faso	0.7	79.7	2.9	3.2	3.3	2.5	4.8	6.2	9.2	4.3	6.7
Cape Verde	0.1	88.9	-2.1	5.1	8.0	34.5	-2.3	4.6	16.1	-6.6	15.5
Cote d'Ivoire	2.4	69.0	6.9	0.7	1.4	7.2	2.1	5.6	2.5	-0.9	2.4
Gambia	0.1	82.1	5.0	-2.2	4.2	2.9	15.4	7.9	-22.5	6.8	8.7
Ghana	1.6	85.5	-3.8	57.9	3.5	0.4	11.7	3.4	4.9	15.0	1.1
Guinea	0.6	70.3	2.8	2.7	4.1	4.8	-2.0	5.5	6.2	2.9	4.7
Guinea-Bissau	0.1	86.9	1.6	3.1	1.3	3.4	-10.1	-21.6	13.9	3.5	3.3
Liberia	0.1	69.8	3.7	-3.5	-4.8	12.1	96.7	29.7	23.0	25.9	6.1
Mali	0.6	79.0	4.9	2.7	4.5	10.3	-3.7	-1.0	21.5	6.2	-1.8
Mauritania	0.2	67.9	6.4	0.2	2.8	2.9	5.0	4.2	-1.1	-14.2	24.7
Niger	0.5	74.1	4.3	-0.3	3.0	3.2	-0.3	12.0	-4.0	6.9	1.5
Nigeria	5.7	59.6	1.9	2.9	5.4	13.1	18.1	-6.6	1.5	-18.0	5.0

Table 5.A. Average Rates of Growth of Gross Domestic Product by Expenditure - Household Final Consumption Expenditure

Major area, region and country	Base year weights as percentage of total for world or region in 1990	Base year share as percentage of total GDP in 1990	Average rates of growth			Annual rate of change (percentage)					
			1970-1979	1980-1989	1990-1999	1996	1997	1998	1999	2000	2001
Senegal	1.3	76.4	3.2	2.0	2.0	5.9	1.1	3.7	3.3	3.7	8.3
Sierra Leone	0.1	80.1	1.7	1.2	-4.6	-4.1	-5.9	0.1	-11.6	14.8	4.3
Togo	0.3	69.8	1.2	3.8	1.2	7.9	12.2	7.2	-8.0	-0.6	3.2
AMERICAS	**36.7**	**65.3**	**4.1**	**2.9**	**3.2**	**3.1**	**3.8**	**4.0**	**4.5**	**4.6**	**2.2**
NORTHERN AMERICA	**31.1**	**65.6**	**3.8**	**3.2**	**3.0**	**3.1**	**3.6**	**4.6**	**4.9**	**4.3**	**2.5**
Bermuda	0.0	68.3	3.5	3.0	1.5	0.7	3.8	2.8	5.0	5.7	2.5
Canada	6.5	55.1	4.8	2.8	2.1	2.6	4.7	2.7	3.9	3.8	2.6
United States [1]	78.4	66.6	3.7	3.2	3.1	3.2	3.6	4.8	4.9	4.3	2.5
LATIN AMERICA AND THE CARIBBEAN	**5.5**	**63.9**	**5.6**	**1.5**	**3.9**	**2.7**	**4.8**	**1.1**	**2.7**	**6.3**	**1.0**
Caribbean	*1.2*	*62.7*	*4.1*	*2.3*	*2.3*	*4.5*	*4.4*	*4.8*	*3.5*	*4.5*	*3.0*
Anguilla	0.0	51.6	3.8	6.3	11.2	7.4	0.6	0.0	33.1	0.3	-15.9
Antigua and Barbuda	0.0	41.7	-4.3	9.1	0.4	-1.5	-3.3	-5.6	-6.0	-12.4	-14.5
Aruba	0.0	45.5	11.4	11.9	7.6	7.6	7.5	7.5	7.5	7.4	7.4
Bahamas	0.0	66.5	2.3	5.0	-1.7	-3.3	-3.3	8.4	2.4	1.2	0.4
Barbados	0.0	63.6	2.5	0.4	0.9	-1.7	9.9	3.9	7.0	5.9	-6.6
British Virgin Islands	0.0	49.0	0.9	4.7	6.5	5.2	0.6	5.8	8.2	14.4	6.3
Cayman Islands	0.0	61.1	8.3	9.2	0.9	0.2	0.5	1.5	0.7	0.7	0.7
Cuba	0.2	53.9	5.2	2.3	-3.1	3.9	0.6	1.8	4.1	4.6	2.1
Dominica	0.0	64.1	-0.4	2.5	0.7	-0.9	-7.8	2.5	11.8	4.0	-1.3
Dominican Republic	0.1	76.6	5.6	3.7	4.6	8.3	7.5	7.6	4.7	11.1	5.1
Grenada	0.0	64.9	5.0	1.3	1.6	16.7	9.5	4.7	-11.5	14.7	-3.8
Guadeloupe	0.1	92.8	5.3	2.3	2.1	4.3	9.2	4.1	5.9	5.9	5.9
Haiti	0.0	82.5	3.2	1.2	2.5	-2.4	2.3	4.4	1.6	15.9	-1.6
Jamaica	0.1	62.3	0.2	1.9	0.3	-2.6	-2.8	-1.8	-2.7	1.4	2.3
Martinique	0.1	83.6	4.4	4.3	1.5	1.6	1.6	4.1	2.5	2.5	2.5
Montserrat	0.0	61.6	4.0	-0.7	-11.5	-69.2	60.5	16.2	-39.8	72.3	-7.3
Netherlands Antilles	0.0	25.6	2.3	-1.3	1.4	-4.9	-5.6	-4.2	-1.0	-3.4	2.0
Puerto Rico	0.4	61.5	3.3	3.0	4.2	5.8	4.4	5.4	2.7	1.5	3.2
Saint Kitts and Nevis	0.0	57.9	-0.7	3.0	8.6	15.6	-5.8	-1.2	33.0	-10.8	-14.1
Saint Lucia	0.0	69.8	5.2	4.6	1.6	-5.9	30.7	5.7	11.6	6.9	-1.1
Saint Vincent and the Grenadines	0.0	68.4	3.5	3.8	3.2	2.5	26.5	4.6	-7.8	-10.5	5.3
Trinidad and Tobago	0.1	54.7	8.0	-4.0	3.7	13.0	17.1	8.8	10.8	7.2	4.8
Central America	*4.2*	*70.1*	*5.7*	*1.8*	*3.2*	*2.4*	*6.3*	*5.4*	*4.4*	*7.5*	*3.2*
Belize	0.0	60.4	8.3	-1.4	3.6	-3.0	-1.9	5.9	-7.4	12.4	-1.5
Costa Rica	0.1	74.9	5.0	1.2	4.7	2.4	5.1	5.4	2.2	1.0	1.3
El Salvador	0.1	88.9	4.2	-1.3	4.9	1.5	3.0	2.4	3.7	3.8	0.9
Guatemala	0.1	83.6	5.4	1.3	5.2	2.8	4.0	4.2	15.8	2.7	3.4
Honduras	0.0	66.8	5.0	3.1	2.6	5.2	3.1	4.5	-1.0	3.8	0.7
Mexico [2]	3.7	69.6	5.9	1.9	3.0	2.2	6.5	5.4	4.3	8.3	3.4
Nicaragua	0.0	67.6	-0.1	-0.3	4.6	7.5	8.4	6.0	3.3	-2.2	1.6
Panama	0.1	57.0	4.1	3.3	3.5	9.1	14.0	9.8	-4.0	3.6	0.4
South America	*9.8*	*61.7*	*5.8*	*1.3*	*4.4*	*2.7*	*4.3*	*-0.7*	*2.1*	*6.1*	*0.0*
Argentina	2.0	67.8	2.4	-0.4	4.8	5.5	9.0	3.5	-2.0	-0.7	-5.7
Bolivia	0.1	76.9	3.4	0.9	3.6	3.3	5.4	5.3	2.8	2.4	1.5
Brazil	5.2	58.5	8.9	1.7	4.9	1.7	2.4	-3.4	6.1	9.9	1.3
Chile	0.4	60.1	0.8	2.9	7.1	9.7	6.6	4.7	-1.0	3.5	1.4
Colombia [3]	0.6	63.8	5.7	2.8	1.9	1.1	2.4	-0.8	-5.4	3.5	0.6
Ecuador	0.2	67.0	7.2	2.6	1.8	1.4	4.2	4.5	-7.0	3.8	5.4
French Guiana	0.0	64.4	12.8	7.3	1.8	1.6	0.9	0.4	1.0	1.0	1.0
Guyana	0.0	60.9	0.2	-2.1	2.0	-2.1	7.1	3.5	2.4	0.0	20.1
Paraguay	0.1	77.2	6.4	4.1	4.3	-3.4	8.6	-0.8	-4.5	-1.0	9.1
Peru	0.5	71.7	2.0	0.3	3.0	3.1	4.3	-0.8	-0.4	3.9	0.2
Suriname	0.0	53.8	4.7	-3.0	2.1	271.6	9.0	21.8	-35.2	-1.0	4.9
Uruguay [4]	0.1	69.1	1.0	1.4	4.7	8.5	5.5	7.0	-1.6	-1.6	-2.3
Venezuela	0.6	60.9	9.6	1.8	1.1	-4.6	5.2	-0.2	-4.3	3.8	4.7
ASIA	**22.7**	**54.2**	**5.3**	**4.0**	**3.8**	**4.8**	**2.7**	**0.8**	**2.3**	**3.2**	**2.8**
Eastern Asia	*67.9*	*52.1*	*5.4*	*4.1*	*3.2*	*4.0*	*2.1*	*-0.1*	*2.2*	*2.8*	*2.7*
China	6.3	49.7	5.0	8.7	8.4	10.3	4.7	6.6	6.7	6.3	7.3
Democratic People's Rep. of Korea	0.4	72.7	11.9	8.9	-1.4	-3.6	-6.3	-1.1	6.2	0.3	4.3
Hong Kong SAR of China	1.3	52.7	9.5	7.2	4.2	3.0	7.3	-7.9	0.7	6.5	1.2

Table 5.A. Average Rates of Growth of Gross Domestic Product by Expenditure - Household Final Consumption Expenditure

Major area, region and country	Base year weights as percentage of total for world or region in 1990	Base year share as percentage of total GDP in 1990	Average rates of growth			Annual rate of change (percentage)					
			1970-1979	1980-1989	1990-1999	1996	1997	1998	1999	2000	2001
Japan	52.6	52.2	5.2	3.2	1.9	2.4	0.9	-0.4	0.0	1.2	1.7
Macao SAR of China	0.0	36.7	6.2	6.7	4.0	3.6	0.9	-1.5	0.1	1.9	2.5
Mongolia	0.1	63.3	5.7	6.3	-0.5	2.4	4.0	3.5	2.5	1.1	1.1
Republic of Korea	4.3	51.3	6.8	6.8	5.5	7.1	3.5	-11.9	11.2	8.1	4.8
South Central Asia	*16.0*	*63.9*	*3.6*	*3.9*	*5.9*	*5.5*	*3.7*	*5.9*	*3.7*	*3.4*	*4.3*
Bangladesh	0.9	83.3	-0.5	3.8	2.4	4.7	1.1	1.3	4.1	4.7	5.4
Bhutan	0.0	52.4	6.4	5.4	5.3	35.3	22.5	21.8	-0.9	4.9	5.9
India [5]	7.2	67.2	2.8	5.1	4.8	7.8	3.0	6.5	5.6	2.4	4.2
Iran (Islamic Republic of)	3.4	55.1	6.0	1.3	5.4	3.7	4.3	6.7	1.2	5.0	4.4
Kazakhstan	1.5	63.4	...	...	-6.9	-4.0	4.5	0.0	-0.2	0.6	7.0
Kyrgyzstan	0.3	68.0	...	...	-6.5	6.4	-8.8	18.5	0.0	-5.2	2.2
Maldives	0.0	35.7	11.5	11.7	6.9	3.7	7.0	3.4	2.9	3.0	-0.4
Nepal	0.1	82.7	2.2	3.9	4.6	7.9	5.4	4.2	0.4	4.7	4.3
Pakistan	1.1	68.3	6.0	4.5	4.4	4.2	1.6	7.5	0.4	2.1	3.3
Sri Lanka	0.2	74.3	5.2	5.4	5.4	2.7	4.6	9.6	0.8	4.0	-0.2
Tajikistan	0.2	63.0	...	...	-10.7	-19.1	3.6	22.2	5.5	6.7	9.2
Turkmenistan	0.2	49.3	...	...	-4.3	-13.7	23.0	-15.6	-2.4	28.7	15.3
Uzbekistan	1.0	59.8	...	...	-0.4	10.6	15.9	2.1	8.8	6.7	3.1
South-Eastern Asia	*6.9*	*58.1*	*6.0*	*5.6*	*5.5*	*7.1*	*4.0*	*-5.6*	*4.1*	*5.4*	*3.9*
Brunei Darussalam	0.0	11.4	14.8	-2.0	1.6	-1.4	3.0	2.0	2.5	2.3	2.4
Cambodia	0.1	94.5	-7.3	-1.1	3.1	2.2	-0.8	2.3	3.8	2.4	1.9
Indonesia	2.1	56.8	8.0	6.1	7.7	9.7	7.1	-5.7	4.2	3.6	5.4
Lao People's Democratic Republic	0.0	92.8	0.1	6.1	2.7	9.1	8.8	-10.7	7.3	-1.7	2.8
Malaysia	0.8	51.8	9.0	5.0	5.5	6.9	4.3	-10.2	2.9	12.5	2.8
Myanmar	0.5	76.0	3.1	8.2	2.7	1.0	1.3	0.9	5.0	4.6	4.9
Philippines	1.0	71.2	4.7	2.9	3.7	4.6	5.0	3.4	2.6	3.5	3.6
Singapore	0.6	45.3	7.2	5.9	5.8	8.1	5.5	-3.8	6.4	9.9	0.5
Thailand	1.6	56.5	6.3	5.5	4.6	5.8	-1.4	-11.5	4.3	4.9	3.4
Vietnam	0.2	89.6	...	3.7	4.8	9.1	5.9	4.5	2.5	4.0	4.5
Western Asia	*9.2*	*52.9*	*6.9*	*3.2*	*3.9*	*7.8*	*4.8*	*4.7*	*-1.1*	*4.6*	*-1.0*
Armenia	0.2	48.6	...	...	-1.7	4.0	7.6	5.4	1.3	8.3	6.3
Azerbaijan	0.4	52.3	...	...	-2.0	11.2	13.4	15.1	12.8	12.1	9.9
Bahrain	0.1	56.0	7.7	0.9	3.1	1.3	-0.9	-0.2	6.8	2.8	1.1
Cyprus	0.1	59.1	4.1	6.0	5.2	3.5	4.0	8.4	3.1	8.7	5.0
Georgia	0.5	61.1	...	...	-7.4	49.9	5.3	-9.5	0.0	8.2	-1.3
Iraq	0.7	50.5	5.0	6.4	-5.2	6.4	21.6	14.1	7.2	10.2	14.8
Israel	1.0	54.4	7.2	5.0	6.3	5.0	3.4	4.3	2.7	7.3	2.5
Jordan	0.1	74.1	6.4	1.6	5.1	11.3	3.9	6.2	4.3	5.5	5.5
Kuwait	0.4	58.6	10.2	3.8	-1.0	20.2	0.8	5.3	0.2	37.9	1.8
Lebanon	0.1	90.0	-1.2	-6.1	7.9	4.2	3.1	-0.2	4.0	1.7	2.3
Oman	0.2	41.4	9.4	2.2	6.9	7.6	4.3	9.1	-3.6	0.0	-1.5
Qatar	0.1	27.8	13.1	2.0	-0.6	11.8	0.9	-1.3	-1.4	1.7	6.3
Saudi Arabia	1.4	39.8	9.6	1.5	1.6	10.2	-1.2	11.8	-9.9	-8.3	1.5
Syrian Arab Republic	0.3	68.7	9.8	2.6	2.7	6.1	1.0	5.9	-4.5	-2.9	-0.8
Turkey	3.0	61.2	5.0	2.4	4.1	8.5	8.4	0.6	-2.6	6.2	-9.0
United Arab Emirates	0.4	38.6	36.3	8.7	6.0	10.1	0.5	3.5	5.9	1.8	2.5
Yemen	0.3	72.1	...	...	3.0	-17.1	5.9	10.6	3.9	-10.7	5.5
Yemen Arab Republic (Former)	...	...	9.1	3.9	...	...	...	...	...	...	...
Yemen Democratic (Former)	...	...	4.2	2.2	...	...	...	...	...	...	...
EUROPE	**36.5**	**54.8**	**3.9**	**2.5**	**0.5**	**1.4**	**2.4**	**2.6**	**2.9**	**3.4**	**2.6**
Eastern Europe	*15.3*	*49.5*	*5.7*	*3.2*	*-7.1*	*-3.1*	*3.8*	*-1.4*	*-2.0*	*6.5*	*8.0*
Belarus	0.6	44.6	...	...	-0.8	6.3	11.7	14.7	9.8	8.2	18.7
Bulgaria	0.3	66.8	7.1	3.2	-2.8	-2.7	-10.9	2.4	9.7	4.3	5.0
Czech Republic	0.4	48.9	...	1.7	1.4	7.9	2.4	-1.8	1.9	2.3	3.8
Czechoslovakia (Former)	...	...	5.2	...	...	...	...	...	...	...	...
Hungary [6]	0.4	47.8	3.8	0.8	-0.5	-3.9	1.9	4.6	5.6	5.5	5.7
Poland	0.6	48.0	6.1	0.1	2.7	8.9	7.1	4.9	5.4	2.5	2.0
Republic of Moldova	0.2	61.2	...	...	-9.5	13.4	2.0	4.4	-4.9	20.6	8.6
Romania	0.5	65.0	8.9	3.6	1.2	9.1	-4.8	4.5	-6.2	-1.8	3.6
Russian Federation	9.4	47.3	...	...	-2.0	-4.7	4.8	-4.3	-4.1	8.3	8.4
Slovakia	0.2	52.7	...	2.5	-0.1	9.1	6.0	5.8	2.9	-1.8	4.0
Ukraine	2.8	55.1	...	...	-7.5	-9.5	-0.1	2.0	-1.7	2.5	9.4
USSR (Former)	...	...	5.7	3.4	...	...	...	...	...	...	...
Northern Europe	*19.7*	*55.4*	2.6	2.8	*2.4*	*3.9*	*3.8*	*3.6*	*4.3*	*4.5*	*3.2*
Denmark	1.3	48.3	1.6	0.7	2.0	2.5	2.9	2.3	0.7	-2.0	0.3
Estonia	0.2	64.4	...	...	-4.9	8.0	8.9	5.4	-0.8	8.0	3.4

Table 5.A. Average Rates of Growth of Gross Domestic Product by Expenditure - Household Final Consumption Expenditure

Major area, region and country	Base year weights as percentage of total for world or region in 1990	Base year share as percentage of total GDP in 1990	Average rates of growth			Annual rate of change (percentage)					
			1970-1979	1980-1989	1990-1999	1996	1997	1998	1999	2000	2001
Finland	1.4	47.9	3.1	3.8	0.9	3.5	3.5	4.3	3.4	3.3	1.6
Iceland	0.1	58.1	6.5	3.0	2.6	5.7	3.3	10.4	7.4	4.0	-3.2
Ireland	0.5	56.4	4.5	1.8	4.8	6.7	7.5	8.2	9.8	9.2	5.1
Latvia [7]	0.2	52.7	...	...	-8.1	10.0	4.9	1.1	3.8	7.4	7.1
Lithuania	0.2	56.8	...	...	-1.4	10.6	9.1	4.1	2.0	4.4	2.4
Norway	1.1	46.5	3.9	1.8	3.1	6.9	3.4	2.8	3.3	4.0	2.6
Sweden	2.3	46.1	1.9	1.6	1.0	1.6	2.7	3.0	4.1	4.2	0.1
United Kingdom	12.3	60.6	2.5	3.3	2.3	3.9	3.9	3.7	4.6	5.1	4.1
Southern Europe	*22.6*	*58.9*	*4.0*	*2.7*	*2.2*	*2.0*	*3.4*	*3.8*	*3.2*	*3.2*	*1.0*
Albania	0.0	38.7	6.2	3.4	3.7	12.2	-7.4	8.0	7.1	4.5	4.2
Andorra	0.0	59.7	9.7	6.4	7.3	7.2	8.1	9.3	9.5	8.6	7.3
Bosnia and Herzegovina	0.2	69.3	...	...	6.5	37.1	30.0	20.0	27.1	10.7	7.4
Croatia	0.3	66.3	...	...	-2.1	0.3	13.0	-0.6	-2.7	4.5	4.2
Greece	1.2	71.2	5.8	1.9	2.3	2.4	2.7	3.5	2.9	2.6	2.8
Holy See	0.0	57.1	4.6	3.5	1.7	1.2	3.4	3.2	2.5	2.8	1.1
Italy	12.9	57.1	3.7	3.1	1.6	1.2	3.2	3.2	2.4	2.7	1.1
Malta	0.0	62.7	5.6	4.3	4.3	7.3	1.5	2.6	6.2	5.9	3.8
Portugal	0.9	61.5	4.3	2.6	3.4	3.0	3.4	5.1	5.2	2.5	1.2
San Marino	0.0	57.1	3.5	2.7	-0.2	0.4	-15.5	3.7	2.5	2.1	1.3
Serbia and Montenegro	0.4	64.6	...	...	-8.4	14.2	-3.0	7.8	-23.8	7.7	-6.1
Slovenia	0.2	52.2	...	...	2.7	2.1	2.8	3.3	6.1	0.8	-70.9
Spain	6.3	59.7	4.1	2.3	2.3	2.2	3.2	4.4	4.7	3.9	2.5
TFYR Macedonia	0.1	66.2	...	...	0.9	3.0	3.3	3.6	3.6	7.7	-8.5
Yugoslavia (Former)	...	...	6.1	0.2	...	...	...	...	...	...	...
Western Europe	*42.4*	*54.6*	*3.6*	*1.8*	*1.9*	*1.3*	*0.8*	*2.6*	*3.4*	*2.2*	*1.8*
Austria	1.8	53.7	4.2	2.4	2.6	3.2	2.1	2.7	2.4	3.4	1.5
Belgium	2.2	54.2	4.2	1.6	2.0	1.1	2.1	3.1	2.0	3.3	1.0
France	13.7	54.9	3.7	2.0	1.4	1.3	0.1	3.4	3.2	2.7	2.6
Germany	19.0	55.4	3.6	1.7	2.1	0.9	0.5	1.7	3.6	1.4	1.5
Liechtenstein	0.0	55.0	3.4	2.4	1.7	1.7	2.5	3.5	3.5	3.1	3.4
Luxembourg	0.1	50.9	4.2	2.8	3.1	4.3	3.8	6.6	2.3	4.6	4.4
Monaco	0.0	54.9	4.3	2.7	2.1	2.0	0.8	4.1	3.9	3.2	3.2
Netherlands	3.0	49.0	3.8	1.0	2.8	4.0	3.0	4.9	4.8	3.3	1.2
Switzerland	2.6	55.0	1.9	1.7	1.0	0.8	1.4	2.3	2.2	1.9	1.7
OCEANIA	**1.6**	**59.2**	**3.3**	**3.1**	**3.1**	**3.1**	**4.5**	**4.4**	**4.1**	**2.8**	**3.6**
Australia & New Zealand	*96.4*	*58.9*	*3.3*	*3.1*	*3.1*	*3.1*	*4.4*	*4.5*	*4.1*	*2.8*	*3.7*
Australia	84.3	58.7	3.7	3.3	3.2	2.9	4.8	4.8	4.1	3.0	3.8
New Zealand	12.1	59.9	1.5	1.7	2.4	4.2	2.0	2.4	3.7	1.6	2.9
Melanesia	*2.5*	*71.3*	*2.8*	*4.6*	*2.3*	*6.8*	*7.3*	*0.0*	*4.7*	*1.9*	*-0.2*
Fiji	0.5	72.9	7.5	2.0	2.5	1.5	-1.1	9.3	-4.6	3.6	2.8
New Caledonia	1.1	97.6	1.0	11.0	0.1	1.4	3.9	-9.2	4.7	2.0	-0.8
Papua New Guinea	0.8	51.6	1.8	0.9	4.7	16.7	15.5	5.7	8.6	2.1	-0.5
Solomon Islands	0.1	57.4	9.5	-0.1	-0.3	2.5	-2.8	1.7	-1.5	-14.0	-4.9
Vanuatu	0.0	63.9	7.7	3.8	2.5	4.9	1.8	2.6	1.1	-0.3	-0.5
Micronesia	*0.1*	*54.1*	*4.5*	*2.4*	*0.8*	*-3.7*	*-2.5*	*0.8*	*1.4*	*-0.5*	*0.9*
Kiribati	0.0	44.6	2.9	-4.9	4.2	3.0	5.7	5.0	6.2	0.2	1.8
Marshall Islands	0.0	97.6	5.8	13.3	-2.0	-15.9	-10.3	1.6	0.0	-1.0	1.7
Micronesia (Federated States of)	0.0	44.6	6.6	4.5	1.6	-1.8	-5.1	-2.1	0.9	2.1	1.5
Nauru	0.0	44.6	6.8	4.9	-5.4	-7.3	-7.3	-1.9	-1.9	-1.0	-0.8
Palau	0.0	44.6	2.9	-5.5	4.7	10.9	10.4	3.9	2.8	-3.9	-0.7
Polynesia	*1.0*	*65.3*	*2.4*	*4.6*	*3.3*	*2.0*	*0.7*	*1.6*	*2.7*	*4.2*	*3.0*
Cook Islands	0.0	114.8	1.3	1.2	-0.6	-4.8	6.8	-7.6	5.8	9.8	3.0
French Polynesia	0.8	61.9	2.1	5.6	3.8	1.6	1.1	1.1	2.7	2.7	2.1
Samoa	0.1	81.4	3.6	-1.0	1.2	7.0	1.6	4.7	11.5	23.1	6.5
Tonga	0.0	93.6	3.7	5.3	1.7	4.2	-10.2	10.5	-8.5	-0.3	11.8
Tuvalu	0.0	102.9	5.8	5.2	5.0	10.3	3.5	14.9	3.0	3.0	3.0

Notes for Table 5.A - Household final consumption expenditure

1/ 2000
Includes NPISH's final consumption expenditure.

2/ 1970-2000
Includes NPISH's final consumption expenditure.

3/ 1970-1992
Includes NPISH's final consumption expenditure.

4/ 1989-2001
Includes NPISH's final consumption expenditure.

5/ 1970-1979
Refers to expenditure in the domestic market only.

6/ 1988-1991
Includes total final consumption expenditure of households purchased in the domestic market at market prices. Consumption from own-account production is evaluated at basic prices. The wage-like part of the business travel cost (i.e. per diem) is treated as household consumption expenditure.

7/ 1977-2001
Includes NPISH's final consumption expenditure.

Table 5.B. Average Rates of Growth of Gross Domestic Product by Expenditure - General Government Final Consumption Expenditure

Major area, region and country	Base year weights as percentage of total for world or region in 1990	Base year share as percentage of total GDP in 1990	Average rates of growth 1970-1979	1980-1989	1990-1999	Annual rate of change (percentage) 1996	1997	1998	1999	2000	2001
WORLD	**100.0**	**17.4**	**3.6**	**2.7**	**2.2**	**1.9**	**1.6**	**1.6**	**3.0**	**2.9**	**3.0**
DEVELOPED ECONOMIES	**76.8**	**18.0**	**3.0**	**2.6**	**1.5**	**1.4**	**1.1**	**1.7**	**2.7**	**2.7**	**2.8**
DEVELOPING ECONOMIES	**14.1**	**13.9**	**6.6**	**3.2**	**3.5**	**5.0**	**5.2**	**4.5**	**1.5**	**4.1**	**3.5**
TRANSITION ECONOMIES	**9.1**	**19.3**	**8.5**	**3.5**	**-2.8**	**0.3**	**-0.7**	**-7.4**	**10.4**	**2.1**	**4.7**
AFRICA	**2.2**	**16.6**	**6.0**	**1.2**	**2.1**	**4.5**	**2.2**	**5.2**	**-0.6**	**1.7**	**3.1**
Eastern Africa	*13.0*	*19.6*	*5.9*	*2.4*	*3.1*	*-0.6*	*1.0*	*9.9*	*1.4*	*18.0*	*-3.5*
Burundi	0.1	10.7	3.9	4.1	2.7	3.8	4.3	6.7	-6.9	-8.7	-5.1
Comoros	0.1	25.7	4.4	3.3	-3.5	2.7	0.3	-2.8	-22.9	-9.3	7.0
Djibouti	0.2	33.6	2.9	3.2	-1.0	-5.3	3.5	-14.8	-8.0	-3.6	-1.0
Eritrea	...	...	...	...	10.7	2.8	-21.9	56.2	4.1	-8.8	4.4
Ethiopia	...	...	...	...	14.6	9.9	13.1	30.6	6.7	38.5	-18.1
Ethiopia (Former)	1.8	19.2	6.7	1.8	6.8	...	...	...	...	...	...
Kenya	1.8	18.7	9.2	1.8	7.9	2.7	4.2	3.4	4.3	4.3	4.3
Madagascar	0.3	8.0	2.3	-2.7	2.0	3.4	3.4	3.0	8.7	3.2	9.5
Malawi	0.3	16.2	7.5	5.2	4.1	-2.0	7.6	1.5	3.1	3.3	-1.5
Mauritius	0.4	12.7	10.6	3.1	4.7	6.7	3.8	3.5	5.6	6.5	4.5
Mozambique	0.4	11.9	3.9	1.0	3.6	-6.6	22.4	20.9	10.0	11.0	17.9
Reunion	1.7	28.2	6.2	4.9	2.9	2.9	2.8	3.0	2.9	2.9	2.9
Rwanda	0.5	17.2	5.0	4.0	-3.5	30.4	-3.4	4.9	7.1	-9.5	15.9
Seychelles	0.1	27.7	8.3	1.9	2.6	-2.5	-9.0	7.6	3.1	-3.7	8.4
Somalia	0.1	10.3	4.0	-3.3	-5.0	0.8	-4.2	2.0	-10.7	4.2	2.4
Uganda	0.3	8.0	3.0	-0.9	6.2	2.1	10.3	2.6	1.3	20.8	7.3
United Republic Of Tanzania	0.4	9.8	3.6	2.3	2.2	7.4	1.9	-1.0	-1.0	3.0	6.0
Zambia	2.5	54.7	4.0	0.2	-5.4	-16.2	-2.9	13.6	-12.0	5.2	18.7
Zimbabwe	1.9	19.4	12.0	7.4	-1.8	-11.6	-20.4	6.0	-6.1	79.7	-24.7
Middle Africa	*11.1*	*21.6*	*0.1*	*2.2*	*-0.3*	*-10.7*	*7.3*	*1.6*	*-3.7*	*-2.1*	*22.2*
Angola	5.3	44.8	0.2	2.3	1.1	-23.7	11.0	-10.4	31.4	1.5	35.2
Cameroon	1.9	11.4	1.3	4.1	-1.3	3.6	8.4	5.3	-18.8	6.3	3.2
Central African Republic	0.2	13.6	-1.7	0.3	-10.8	-3.4	4.3	4.8	-69.8	-10.3	-13.6
Chad	0.4	21.3	-3.9	9.5	3.7	-10.2	-2.8	8.4	11.3	-1.6	2.6
Congo	0.6	18.6	6.8	5.3	-5.2	6.3	2.4	0.8	-51.7	-29.5	30.2
Democratic Republic of the Congo	1.9	17.9	-1.8	-2.6	-6.4	-4.4	-0.6	3.3	-10.4	-4.3	-4.4
Equatorial Guinea	0.0	15.3	9.4	-2.5	18.2	47.5	72.1	22.9	-60.6	-23.8	-3.9
Gabon	0.8	13.4	2.0	5.6	-1.5	9.4	7.2	14.7	-49.7	-22.9	14.3
Sao Tome and Principe	0.0	38.2	15.3	9.7	3.5	1.3	0.8	2.3	18.4	5.3	-37.2
Northern Africa	*39.8*	*15.0*	*8.6*	*0.9*	*2.8*	*10.1*	*1.8*	*7.7*	*-3.2*	*-5.4*	*3.0*
Algeria	11.5	16.2	9.0	5.4	3.1	2.8	2.6	2.6	2.5	2.8	4.8
Egypt	8.1	10.0	3.5	4.2	3.9	21.3	3.0	2.6	2.8	4.9	5.0
Libyan Arab Jamahiriya	8.4	26.0	11.2	-2.4	1.2	10.5	0.6	11.7	-12.6	-2.2	-2.5
Morocco	4.6	15.5	9.7	3.4	2.5	12.2	-2.5	6.5	0.2	2.1	11.9
Sudan	4.9	12.8	3.3	1.1	5.7	8.4	4.4	15.5	3.5	-54.7	5.4
Tunisia	2.3	16.4	6.8	5.5	3.9	3.2	6.2	3.9	3.8	5.0	4.8
Southern Africa	*27.2*	*20.0*	*5.2*	*4.3*	*1.0*	*3.8*	*2.5*	*-1.1*	*0.0*	*0.8*	*2.1*
Botswana	1.0	23.8	13.5	15.4	7.1	4.5	8.1	7.8	5.6	8.2	13.7
Lesotho	0.1	14.0	16.1	5.3	5.3	-1.3	6.0	18.0	-3.7	0.8	-3.6
Namibia	0.8	30.8	2.2	4.3	4.4	2.6	3.8	3.0	2.0	-0.3	0.9
South Africa	25.1	19.7	5.1	4.1	0.5	3.8	2.1	-1.9	-0.7	0.5	1.4
Swaziland	0.2	18.4	13.9	2.5	7.4	2.3	3.6	2.4	37.1	-5.8	-3.7
Western Africa	*9.0*	*10.7*	*4.3*	*-4.6*	*2.0*	*-2.8*	*0.8*	*3.8*	*15.9*	*27.0*	*1.3*
Benin	0.3	13.2	2.4	-0.3	4.4	4.6	4.7	4.8	-24.5	1.8	2.7
Burkina Faso	0.5	15.4	10.2	4.4	2.7	1.9	2.9	4.9	4.9	0.3	4.9
Cape Verde	0.1	18.9	0.8	8.7	4.8	-5.8	4.6	-2.6	16.6	30.8	-18.6
Cote d'Ivoire	2.8	20.7	9.1	-1.6	-0.8	6.1	2.6	-1.6	8.5	-2.0	1.6
Gambia	0.1	14.5	3.6	7.1	2.2	5.4	17.2	8.0	-35.6	14.1	5.2
Ghana	0.8	10.9	1.0	-18.2	4.3	0.9	-12.0	11.4	-0.1	57.8	-14.9
Guinea	0.4	11.9	2.8	0.2	2.0	1.8	12.8	-6.6	10.8	12.5	8.2
Guinea-Bissau	0.0	10.3	0.3	2.0	1.0	-1.2	-12.8	-8.0	45.0	27.6	-6.2
Liberia	0.1	13.0	6.4	-8.3	-7.0	12.1	81.4	29.4	22.7	25.4	5.8
Mali	0.4	15.2	3.9	4.5	4.2	9.7	-6.7	-4.4	79.2	-0.6	1.3
Mauritania	0.2	18.8	10.4	-2.8	2.7	1.8	3.8	2.5	6.2	19.7	-3.4
Niger	0.5	17.2	1.4	3.1	0.9	-17.2	25.3	4.9	13.4	-23.6	12.8
Nigeria	1.6	4.4	6.1	-3.7	5.9	-21.7	-5.5	11.6	47.7	86.2	0.6

Table 5.B. Average Rates of Growth of Gross Domestic Product by Expenditure - General Government Final Consumption Expenditure

Major area, region and country	Base year weights as percentage of total for world or region in 1990	Base year share as percentage of total GDP in 1990	Average rates of growth			Annual rate of change (percentage)					
			1970-1979	1980-1989	1990-1999	1996	1997	1998	1999	2000	2001
Senegal	1.0	14.7	4.9	3.1	1.2	0.6	6.9	4.9	9.9	14.9	21.6
Sierra Leone	0.1	7.8	0.6	-0.7	-2.1	4.2	-1.4	1.1	3.8	56.9	-13.2
Togo	0.2	12.6	10.6	-3.0	0.3	3.2	-4.3	11.0	9.0	-5.1	5.6
AMERICAS	**31.8**	**16.9**	**1.9**	**3.0**	**0.8**	**1.1**	**1.7**	**1.8**	**2.3**	**2.4**	**3.4**
NORTHERN AMERICA	**27.9**	**17.5**	**1.5**	**2.8**	**0.9**	**0.5**	**1.0**	**1.7**	**3.0**	**2.9**	**3.8**
Bermuda	0.0	12.5	3.9	2.7	2.3	3.4	1.3	11.8	5.0	5.7	2.5
Canada	10.3	22.5	3.8	2.4	0.8	-1.2	-1.0	3.2	1.9	2.3	3.3
United States	77.6	17.0	1.2	2.9	0.9	0.7	1.3	1.5	3.1	2.9	3.9
LATIN AMERICA AND THE CARIBBEAN	**3.9**	**13.3**	**6.0**	**3.8**	**0.6**	**5.9**	**6.0**	**2.6**	**-2.2**	**-0.8**	**0.4**
Caribbean	*1.3*	*18.2*	*5.2*	*2.7*	*1.0*	*4.7*	*2.0*	*3.2*	*-0.1*	*2.9*	*2.2*
Anguilla	0.0	13.4	3.8	6.0	5.9	3.7	13.9	-20.2	17.0	34.8	8.4
Antigua and Barbuda	0.0	19.0	1.1	7.3	4.8	-8.6	1.3	11.7	7.7	0.1	17.5
Aruba	0.0	13.3	16.2	16.8	12.3	12.2	12.2	12.1	12.1	12.1	12.0
Bahamas	0.0	13.6	4.2	6.7	2.4	1.1	1.1	13.3	7.0	5.7	4.9
Barbados	0.0	20.2	1.1	3.1	1.9	8.3	1.7	2.5	2.9	4.3	3.2
British Virgin Islands	0.0	14.3	5.6	11.0	4.5	0.3	2.9	8.4	0.5	14.4	6.3
Cayman Islands	0.0	13.9	11.6	9.2	1.5	0.2	0.5	1.5	0.7	0.7	0.7
Cuba	0.5	31.0	5.2	1.6	-1.1	4.0	0.6	1.8	2.7	2.8	3.3
Dominica	0.0	20.3	1.8	0.2	3.1	0.5	9.7	4.1	1.6	2.6	-4.3
Dominican Republic	0.0	2.6	2.1	5.2	6.8	8.8	0.8	6.1	6.4	9.5	-17.5
Grenada	0.0	20.5	6.2	1.1	2.2	3.2	6.9	2.2	0.1	3.9	-12.9
Guadeloupe	0.1	30.8	7.3	2.3	1.9	4.3	9.2	4.1	5.9	5.9	5.9
Haiti	0.0	6.8	1.6	-5.2	5.6	-2.4	2.3	4.4	1.6	1.0	14.4
Jamaica	0.1	14.0	5.4	-1.9	3.1	15.1	12.4	8.2	-2.6	-2.1	2.1
Martinique	0.1	29.7	5.7	3.3	1.2	1.6	1.6	4.1	2.5	2.5	2.5
Montserrat	0.0	17.7	4.4	2.4	2.7	40.9	2.4	-2.6	-11.0	-19.8	-6.1
Netherlands Antilles	0.0	25.7	2.3	0.7	0.1	0.6	-8.5	-9.0	-6.7	-17.5	-8.8
Puerto Rico	0.4	14.4	5.2	4.8	1.8	5.2	1.9	4.3	-5.7	4.6	0.9
Saint Kitts and Nevis	0.0	18.0	2.7	4.1	8.0	4.2	3.3	0.3	15.1	2.6	-3.8
Saint Lucia	0.0	15.2	3.6	7.7	4.5	28.2	7.0	3.1	-11.3	-15.0	-0.9
Saint Vincent and the Grenadines	0.0	20.9	3.3	3.4	3.4	1.1	-3.6	2.4	6.8	5.2	1.9
Trinidad and Tobago	0.1	16.2	9.9	1.8	0.6	2.6	-0.2	-4.6	3.1	-3.3	5.7
Central America	*2.1*	*8.9*	*8.3*	*3.1*	*2.2*	*-0.3*	*3.1*	*3.2*	*3.4*	*2.4*	*-0.6*
Belize	0.0	14.4	6.6	3.7	5.5	-1.2	5.6	5.4	8.2	-1.8	-8.3
Costa Rica	0.1	15.0	7.4	0.6	1.8	-0.6	4.6	2.2	1.8	1.4	3.5
El Salvador	0.0	9.9	6.8	2.0	2.5	2.8	2.8	2.5	0.4	1.0	1.1
Guatemala	0.0	6.8	5.2	3.6	1.8	0.0	5.6	32.6	-31.8	15.4	12.5
Honduras	0.0	12.9	5.5	4.3	-0.3	5.3	-1.0	15.4	9.8	8.3	6.0
Mexico	1.7	8.4	8.7	3.3	2.4	-0.7	2.9	2.3	4.7	2.0	-1.4
Nicaragua	0.1	32.5	7.1	3.0	-1.9	6.4	-0.3	0.1	11.3	2.0	9.5
Panama	0.1	18.1	6.5	2.0	2.0	3.4	7.0	4.3	-2.0	5.5	0.5
South America	*8.8*	*14.4*	*5.6*	*4.1*	*0.2*	*7.8*	*7.4*	*2.3*	*-3.9*	*-2.1*	*0.4*
Argentina	1.3	12.0	3.8	-0.7	4.4	2.2	3.2	3.4	2.6	0.6	-2.1
Bolivia	0.0	11.8	8.7	-2.4	3.2	2.6	3.3	3.8	3.2	0.7	3.2
Brazil	5.9	16.9	6.6	6.3	-2.6	9.8	8.0	2.1	-9.3	-5.4	0.3
Chile	0.3	10.4	4.0	-0.6	3.7	4.2	5.8	2.2	2.5	2.8	2.7
Colombia	0.4	11.4	6.5	5.1	9.9	23.9	15.8	2.1	3.6	-0.5	3.8
Ecuador	0.1	13.0	12.3	-0.3	-0.8	-5.2	4.7	-2.2	-5.5	4.7	0.5
French Guiana	0.0	35.0	11.7	6.1	2.7	1.6	2.0	1.8	1.8	1.8	1.8
Guyana	0.0	13.6	7.9	1.3	7.8	11.3	12.8	1.7	8.6	-11.0	-32.9
Paraguay	0.0	6.2	4.3	5.6	6.7	9.4	2.3	0.7	3.7	14.1	-12.5
Peru	0.2	8.9	3.4	0.5	3.2	4.4	7.6	2.5	3.5	5.1	0.2
Suriname	0.0	24.4	2.6	3.6	-5.7	-24.3	28.4	8.8	-14.3	-1.0	4.9
Uruguay	0.1	13.0	3.9	1.5	2.2	3.0	2.9	2.9	1.8	-0.3	-4.2
Venezuela	0.3	8.4	4.8	2.1	1.1	-7.6	4.2	1.4	3.0	5.0	6.4
ASIA	**19.1**	**13.6**	**6.1**	**3.7**	**3.8**	**3.5**	**3.0**	**3.4**	**3.9**	**5.6**	**3.7**
Eastern Asia	*67.9*	*13.1*	*5.6*	*4.3*	*3.8*	*4.2*	*2.2*	*2.9*	*4.2*	*5.4*	*3.2*
China	6.2	12.3	10.2	8.5	10.0	9.5	8.1	8.4	8.4	12.0	7.3
Democratic People's Rep. of Korea	0.2	10.2	11.9	7.9	2.6	-3.6	-6.3	-1.1	6.2	0.3	4.3
Hong Kong SAR of China	0.7	7.3	7.9	6.6	4.5	3.8	2.5	0.3	3.0	2.2	6.0

Table 5.B. Average Rates of Growth of Gross Domestic Product by Expenditure - General Government Final Consumption Expenditure

Major area, region and country	Base year weights as percentage of total for world or region in 1990	Base year share as percentage of total GDP in 1990	Average rates of growth 1970-1979	1980-1989	1990-1999	Annual rate of change (percentage) 1996	1997	1998	1999	2000	2001
Japan	53.5	13.3	5.3	3.7	2.9	2.9	1.0	2.1	4.4	4.7	2.6
Macao SAR of China	0.0	8.8	11.7	13.8	7.3	4.5	4.1	2.5	15.5	-9.8	1.6
Mongolia	0.1	26.6	5.7	6.3	-0.5	2.4	4.0	3.5	2.5	1.1	1.1
Republic of Korea	3.5	10.5	5.4	5.2	3.8	8.2	1.5	-0.4	1.3	0.1	1.3
South Central Asia	*12.9*	*12.9*	*5.4*	*1.2*	*6.8*	*1.1*	*7.0*	*7.1*	*6.6*	*4.5*	*7.3*
Bangladesh	0.2	4.4	19.2	3.9	4.3	3.3	13.2	0.6	0.9	4.5	4.5
Bhutan	0.0	15.7	6.4	6.2	7.2	-6.5	29.5	-15.5	18.4	-3.5	5.9
India	5.0	11.8	4.3	7.3	6.1	4.5	11.1	12.9	12.0	6.5	9.9
Iran (Islamic Republic of)	3.0	11.9	5.9	-5.8	5.3	1.9	5.7	5.6	-1.8	1.9	-1.3
Kazakhstan	1.2	12.4	...	...	-6.5	-14.2	-9.7	-14.4	7.3	14.6	18.8
Kyrgyzstan	0.4	25.0	...	...	-9.6	7.0	-4.8	4.3	4.0	5.9	-1.2
Maldives	0.0	17.8	11.5	11.7	9.7	8.8	23.7	9.8	13.1	14.1	7.7
Nepal	0.0	8.6	3.0	5.9	3.4	6.6	1.2	2.9	1.4	9.1	15.1
Pakistan	0.9	14.3	5.9	10.1	0.7	-8.4	6.8	-6.9	7.5	-5.3	18.2
Sri Lanka	0.1	13.1	3.5	4.2	5.4	8.4	7.1	5.3	3.9	5.3	-1.7
Tajikistan	0.1	6.8	...	...	-9.3	-31.3	20.6	-22.9	14.5	2.6	11.5
Turkmenistan	0.3	23.0	...	...	-10.7	-10.0	66.1	16.7	-10.6	35.1	12.7
Uzbekistan	1.6	25.4	...	...	-2.9	1.0	-2.5	4.6	4.9	-0.9	7.0
South-Eastern Asia	*4.7*	*10.0*	*6.8*	*2.4*	*4.4*	*7.0*	*2.1*	*-3.2*	*6.2*	*5.8*	*7.0*
Brunei Darussalam	0.1	11.7	-6.8	6.5	5.0	-0.3	3.0	2.0	13.5	-2.6	-9.8
Cambodia	0.0	6.9	-7.3	-1.1	4.7	18.5	-4.2	-12.6	5.6	15.5	13.1
Indonesia	1.3	8.8	11.9	5.7	0.6	2.7	0.1	-15.4	0.7	6.5	8.2
Lao People's Democratic Republic	0.0	11.6	0.1	9.6	-2.5	1.8	-2.1	-26.4	7.3	-9.5	-1.1
Malaysia	0.8	13.8	9.7	5.9	5.7	0.7	5.7	-8.9	17.1	3.0	17.6
Myanmar	0.3	12.4	2.8	-10.3	5.4	8.8	5.1	6.5	6.9	6.8	6.5
Philippines	0.6	10.1	7.3	1.0	3.5	4.1	4.6	-1.9	6.7	6.1	0.3
Singapore	0.5	10.0	7.0	6.6	8.3	19.3	7.1	8.0	6.1	14.0	6.6
Thailand	1.1	9.4	9.6	4.5	5.4	12.1	-2.8	3.9	3.2	2.6	1.9
Vietnam	0.1	7.5	-0.3	6.2	6.6	7.4	4.0	3.2	-5.0	0.9	3.3
Western Asia	*14.4*	*20.8*	*9.0*	*3.3*	*1.0*	*0.1*	*4.7*	*5.7*	*-1.5*	*7.8*	*1.7*
Armenia	0.3	16.8	...	...	-1.1	-2.2	-2.1	-2.2	1.3	2.8	0.0
Azerbaijan	0.5	17.6	...	...	-4.5	1.0	3.1	0.7	-0.8	2.2	4.9
Bahrain	0.1	23.8	11.6	4.9	3.8	5.7	2.6	4.3	5.2	3.1	2.3
Cyprus	0.1	17.3	5.6	7.3	4.6	11.7	4.9	7.3	-7.7	-2.6	10.1
Georgia	0.5	16.8	...	...	-15.3	7.9	42.6	13.8	-4.4	-16.6	15.7
Iraq	1.4	26.4	6.7	6.0	-12.9	3.5	6.6	5.8	3.3	4.2	6.9
Israel	2.1	28.2	3.4	1.2	3.2	5.3	1.9	2.1	3.0	1.3	3.3
Jordan	0.1	24.9	4.3	1.2	3.7	6.0	7.8	-1.4	3.0	0.8	2.2
Kuwait	0.9	38.6	9.5	4.5	0.3	-19.1	-2.5	-1.0	-0.4	39.2	-1.2
Lebanon	0.2	45.5	6.1	2.1	-9.2	8.6	4.2	-3.5	5.5	3.0	3.4
Oman	0.4	26.6	6.5	9.5	3.3	-3.1	1.0	-0.4	3.3	8.6	15.1
Qatar	0.3	32.9	14.7	4.7	1.4	7.0	5.7	-1.6	-1.7	11.0	-23.5
Saudi Arabia	4.4	31.8	12.6	1.9	-0.9	-3.2	9.6	11.5	-10.8	6.8	5.1
Syrian Arab Republic	0.3	14.3	13.8	-1.3	1.5	0.2	1.2	2.0	-1.6	19.1	8.6
Turkey	1.7	8.6	7.2	5.8	5.1	8.6	4.1	7.8	6.5	7.1	-8.6
United Arab Emirates	0.7	16.3	32.1	5.9	2.7	5.6	1.6	1.0	5.2	5.4	8.1
Yemen	0.3	17.0	...	...	-2.1	-3.2	7.4	17.0	-2.4	7.2	4.8
Yemen Arab Republic (Former)	...	...	10.9	10.0	...	...	...	...	...	...	...
Yemen Democratic (Former)	...	...	2.6	8.9	...	...	...	...	...	...	...
EUROPE	**45.1**	**20.2**	**3.8**	**2.2**	**2.4**	**1.5**	**0.8**	**0.3**	**3.1**	**1.9**	**2.4**
Eastern Europe	*16.5*	*19.7*	*8.7*	*4.9*	*8.6*	*0.0*	*-1.7*	*-10.0*	*12.9*	*1.8*	*1.5*
Belarus	0.9	23.8	...	...	-2.9	-0.7	7.5	7.3	6.1	6.1	4.0
Bulgaria	0.1	7.2	7.1	5.3	-7.3	-27.1	-3.0	11.1	5.0	11.6	2.4
Czech Republic [1]	0.4	22.9	...	2.8	-2.4	3.6	-4.4	-4.4	2.3	-1.0	5.3
Czechoslovakia (Former)	...	...	6.5	...	...	...	...	...	...	...	...
Hungary [2]	0.4	21.7	5.3	1.8	-0.5	-2.0	3.0	1.6	1.5	1.9	4.3
Poland	0.6	18.7	7.0	0.4	2.9	2.2	3.2	1.5	1.0	1.0	0.5
Republic of Moldova	0.1	10.4	...	...	-7.5	-5.6	12.7	-19.8	-40.1	-2.3	1.5
Romania	0.3	13.3	10.5	-4.8	0.6	7.1	-10.3	-2.3	5.9	13.4	1.7
Russian Federation	11.2	20.8	...	...	-3.1	0.8	-2.4	-15.4	23.1	1.4	-0.7
Slovakia	0.2	23.0	...	2.1	-0.7	17.4	-4.5	11.5	-7.7	1.3	5.1
Ukraine	2.3	16.2	...	...	-3.4	-5.7	-2.8	-3.5	-7.7	1.0	10.2
USSR (Former)	...	...	10.0	6.3	...	...	...	...	...	...	...
Northern Europe	*20.7*	*21.4*	*3.2*	*1.3*	*1.7*	*1.6*	*0.5*	*2.5*	*2.5*	*1.3*	*2.3*
Denmark	1.9	25.6	3.9	1.2	2.0	3.4	0.8	3.1	2.0	1.1	2.1
Estonia	0.1	13.2	...	...	0.5	-1.0	1.8	4.5	3.8	0.1	0.3

Table 5.B. Average Rates of Growth of Gross Domestic Product by Expenditure - General Government Final Consumption Expenditure

Major area, region and country	Base year weights as percentage of total for world or region in 1990	Base year share as percentage of total GDP in 1990	Average rates of growth			Annual rate of change (percentage)					
			1970-1979	1980-1989	1990-1999	1996	1997	1998	1999	2000	2001
Finland	1.6	21.5	5.2	3.2	1.1	2.9	3.3	2.1	1.4	0.4	1.2
Iceland	0.1	20.1	7.5	4.9	2.6	1.2	2.5	3.4	4.6	3.8	2.9
Ireland	0.4	16.4	6.2	0.2	4.1	3.5	5.1	6.5	6.7	7.6	10.5
Latvia	0.1	8.5	...	...	1.2	1.8	0.3	6.1	0.0	-1.9	-4.4
Lithuania	0.2	19.2	...	...	-5.3	0.1	1.5	22.9	-17.5	-0.7	0.4
Norway	1.4	21.2	5.0	2.8	3.4	3.1	2.5	3.3	3.2	1.3	2.7
Sweden	3.9	28.5	3.3	1.7	0.9	0.7	-1.0	3.4	1.7	-1.1	0.9
United Kingdom	10.9	19.8	2.5	0.8	1.4	1.2	0.1	1.5	3.1	2.1	2.5
Southern Europe	*19.7*	*18.9*	*4.3*	*3.2*	*1.7*	*1.6*	*1.7*	*1.9*	*2.1*	*2.9*	*4.2*
Albania	0.1	44.2	6.2	2.4	1.7	2.0	-6.1	9.4	20.3	-3.8	2.7
Andorra	0.0	16.7	11.3	8.9	8.3	6.2	7.8	8.4	8.9	8.7	7.7
Bosnia and Herzegovina	0.1	19.7	...	...	9.9	67.1	30.0	20.0	4.9	10.7	7.4
Croatia	0.3	23.6	...	...	0.1	-2.9	3.1	3.9	2.9	-2.4	-4.2
Greece	0.7	15.1	6.9	1.3	1.0	0.9	3.0	1.7	1.6	2.0	-0.9
Holy See	0.0	20.2	4.5	3.2	0.5	1.0	0.4	0.3	1.4	1.8	2.3
Italy	12.4	20.2	3.6	2.9	0.4	1.0	0.2	0.2	1.3	1.7	2.2
Malta	0.0	17.6	6.2	4.9	4.8	8.3	-1.2	-3.6	-1.0	5.1	1.9
Portugal	0.6	16.2	8.4	5.3	3.3	3.4	2.2	4.1	5.6	4.0	2.8
San Marino	0.0	20.2	4.5	3.9	-1.7	2.3	-19.7	0.7	1.4	8.8	3.2
Serbia and Montenegro	0.4	21.2	...	...	-6.7	12.2	21.4	10.9	-24.9	8.5	-6.4
Slovenia	0.2	17.4	...	...	2.9	3.4	4.3	5.8	4.6	3.1	189.6
Spain	4.7	16.7	5.6	4.7	3.3	1.3	2.9	3.7	4.2	5.0	3.1
TFYR Macedonia	0.0	19.0	...	...	-0.7	0.2	-2.4	4.1	4.5	1.9	4.0
Yugoslavia (Former)	...	...	6.8	-0.9	...	...	...	...	...	...	...
Western Europe	*43.2*	*20.5*	*3.6*	*2.0*	*1.9*	*1.8*	*1.1*	*1.3*	*1.5*	*1.9*	*1.9*
Austria	1.7	18.9	3.5	1.6	2.3	1.2	-1.5	2.8	3.1	0.0	-0.5
Belgium	2.2	20.3	4.3	1.2	1.4	2.4	0.2	1.0	3.6	2.3	2.2
France	15.1	22.3	3.5	2.7	2.0	2.3	2.1	-0.1	1.5	2.8	3.0
Germany	18.4	19.7	3.9	1.5	1.9	1.8	0.3	1.9	1.0	1.2	0.8
Liechtenstein	0.0	13.9	3.7	3.6	2.1	2.6	0.9	2.4	1.6	0.7	1.1
Luxembourg	0.1	18.3	3.0	4.0	4.2	5.6	3.0	1.3	7.1	5.1	6.5
Monaco	0.0	22.3	4.0	3.5	2.7	3.0	2.8	0.5	2.2	3.3	3.1
Netherlands	3.9	23.5	3.0	2.1	2.1	-0.4	3.2	3.6	2.5	1.9	3.1
Switzerland	1.8	13.9	2.2	2.8	1.5	1.7	-0.2	1.2	1.2	1.4	3.0
OCEANIA	**1.8**	**19.3**	**4.1**	**3.3**	**2.8**	**1.8**	**4.1**	**3.1**	**4.6**	**1.7**	**3.2**
Australia & New Zealand	*94.5*	*18.8*	*4.2*	*3.2*	*2.9*	*1.4*	*4.4*	*3.3*	*4.9*	*1.6*	*3.4*
Australia	82.7	18.8	4.4	3.5	2.9	1.4	3.8	4.0	4.6	2.2	3.3
New Zealand	11.9	19.2	3.5	1.6	2.4	1.4	8.8	-2.2	7.3	-2.1	3.8
Melanesia	*3.5*	*32.9*	*1.0*	*4.1*	*1.3*	*12.1*	*0.1*	*0.8*	*-1.4*	*2.2*	*-0.3*
Fiji	0.3	17.5	9.1	2.3	2.5	3.4	2.8	10.0	0.6	4.9	-2.1
New Caledonia	1.8	50.2	2.9	9.8	0.7	2.8	3.6	-10.1	5.0	2.2	-0.7
Papua New Guinea	1.2	26.2	-1.0	-0.7	1.6	32.0	-4.4	9.5	-9.6	3.1	1.0
Solomon Islands	0.1	31.1	7.3	8.4	3.7	2.1	-6.1	4.2	-1.9	-14.4	-4.5
Vanuatu	0.1	28.7	7.7	2.1	2.6	8.8	-4.6	3.3	1.1	1.1	-0.5
Micronesia	*0.1*	*27.3*	*4.7*	*2.4*	*1.1*	*-4.3*	*-2.8*	*0.9*	*1.4*	*-0.5*	*0.9*
Kiribati	0.0	22.3	2.9	-4.9	4.2	3.0	5.7	5.0	6.2	0.2	1.8
Marshall Islands	0.0	50.2	7.8	12.1	-0.7	-15.9	-10.3	1.6	0.0	-1.0	1.7
Micronesia (Federated States of)	0.0	22.3	6.6	4.5	1.6	-1.8	-5.1	-2.1	0.9	2.1	1.5
Nauru	0.0	22.3	6.8	4.9	-5.4	-7.3	-7.3	-1.9	-1.9	-1.0	-0.8
Palau	0.0	22.3	2.9	-5.5	4.7	10.9	10.4	3.9	2.8	-3.9	-0.7
Polynesia	*1.8*	*38.2*	*5.7*	*3.6*	*3.4*	*1.8*	*1.2*	*1.1*	*3.1*	*3.4*	*2.4*
Cook Islands	0.0	32.0	-3.4	2.0	2.2	-0.2	-2.8	-4.2	5.8	9.8	3.0
French Polynesia	1.7	40.4	6.2	3.7	3.3	1.6	1.1	1.1	2.7	2.7	2.1
Samoa	0.1	18.8	3.3	-0.4	4.2	7.0	1.6	4.7	11.5	23.1	6.5
Tonga	0.0	19.1	1.0	6.7	4.8	3.2	7.7	0.3	7.6	-0.4	6.2
Tuvalu	0.0	52.8	7.8	4.1	6.3	10.3	3.5	14.9	3.0	3.0	3.0

Notes for Table 5.B - General government final consumption expenditure

1/ 1987-1990

Includes final consumption expenditure of the private non-profit institutions serving households.

2/ 1988-1991

Includes health, social and cultural expenditure of enterprises and final consumption expenditure of non-profit institutions.

Table 5.C. Average Rates of Growth of Gross Domestic Product by Expenditure - Gross Fixed Capital Formation

Major area, region and country	Base year weights as percentage of total for world or region in 1990	Base year share as percentage of total GDP in 1990	Average rates of growth			Annual rate of change (percentage)					
			1970-1979	1980-1989	1990-1999	1996	1997	1998	1999	2000	2001
WORLD	**100.0**	**23.1**	**3.8**	**2.8**	**3.1**	**5.6**	**5.2**	**3.8**	**3.7**	**5.2**	**0.0**
DEVELOPED ECONOMIES	**73.4**	**22.6**	**3.0**	**3.0**	**2.8**	**5.3**	**5.2**	**5.3**	**4.9**	**4.3**	**-1.0**
DEVELOPING ECONOMIES	**17.1**	**23.5**	**7.9**	**2.2**	**5.6**	**7.7**	**5.3**	**-0.9**	**0.8**	**7.8**	**2.5**
TRANSITION ECONOMIES	**9.5**	**26.5**	**3.6**	**1.6**	**-9.4**	**-1.9**	**5.8**	**4.8**	**-2.9**	**6.4**	**7.0**
AFRICA	**1.7**	**20.0**	**5.2**	**-0.3**	**3.7**	**8.8**	**6.0**	**4.4**	**8.9**	**8.1**	**3.8**
Eastern Africa	*13.6*	*21.1*	*-3.9*	*0.9*	*4.2*	*2.1*	*5.9*	*1.0*	*5.3*	*6.0*	*-1.5*
Burundi	0.2	15.1	17.0	4.6	-0.6	1.5	-0.6	2.6	-10.2	-24.4	-17.3
Comoros	0.0	12.2	2.6	-1.1	1.7	2.8	0.6	-6.0	64.0	-13.4	9.7
Djibouti	0.1	27.2	-1.4	1.5	-6.6	-9.6	26.0	9.0	-79.1	45.6	-17.6
Eritrea	...	...	...	...	38.3	62.3	51.1	-20.7	25.9	-10.8	5.5
Ethiopia	...	...	...	...	18.4	28.9	5.9	-5.7	14.1	-30.8	41.5
Ethiopia (Former)	1.1	12.5	-0.8	8.2	-19.1	...	...	...	...	...	...
Kenya	2.0	20.7	3.1	-0.4	1.8	1.3	2.0	-0.1	-4.8	-2.3	1.8
Madagascar	0.6	17.0	-3.8	0.5	1.8	4.6	2.7	2.2	50.4	5.8	8.1
Malawi	0.3	17.1	4.2	-2.8	1.0	-5.9	40.4	1.5	3.1	3.3	-1.5
Mauritius	0.9	30.9	9.6	4.4	6.4	15.0	10.8	-5.9	21.6	-7.9	1.4
Mozambique	0.6	19.7	3.9	2.8	6.6	-3.0	16.3	0.0	15.9	156.7	-53.4
Reunion	1.7	29.1	1.5	5.3	2.6	2.5	2.5	2.4	2.4	2.4	2.4
Rwanda	0.3	12.4	5.0	1.4	2.9	29.6	17.6	12.6	18.9	7.3	6.1
Seychelles	0.1	23.0	1.6	6.7	6.0	-1.8	16.8	8.7	16.9	-11.5	10.7
Somalia	0.3	23.0	7.2	4.3	-4.6	0.4	-4.0	3.0	5.5	2.1	3.5
Uganda	0.6	14.2	-7.4	14.5	8.1	-3.0	6.4	11.2	2.9	0.1	6.0
United Republic Of Tanzania	1.6	38.3	4.3	3.5	7.7	4.2	3.3	5.0	5.3	4.0	6.0
Zambia	1.4	30.7	-11.0	-8.9	-2.8	4.5	5.0	-2.5	-5.4	20.0	14.8
Zimbabwe	1.8	18.2	-1.5	3.5	1.9	-30.1	-2.8	7.7	-4.2	-4.4	-3.7
Middle Africa	*8.2*	*16.4*	*2.2*	*-0.1*	*9.5*	*9.9*	*8.7*	*13.3*	*112.5*	*-1.1*	*10.4*
Angola	1.3	11.0	0.1	-3.3	25.8	5.4	22.0	9.6	451.8	3.6	5.2
Cameroon	2.4	15.3	4.7	4.6	1.1	2.8	2.2	4.7	42.8	-7.9	11.0
Central African Republic	0.2	11.1	-7.5	-0.7	1.2	-0.9	6.7	6.7	-19.5	-16.5	-12.6
Chad	0.2	11.3	...	5.7	3.7	8.5	7.9	0.0	13.5	11.0	173.6
Congo	0.5	16.5	5.5	-0.7	-3.7	7.3	-1.4	-3.4	-20.1	-6.3	10.7
Democratic Republic of the Congo	2.3	22.3	6.2	-0.6	-8.2	-4.2	-3.8	1.6	-10.4	-4.3	-4.4
Equatorial Guinea	0.0	17.4	-1.1	2.6	37.2	116.2	-1.0	70.1	-15.6	-19.8	61.1
Gabon	1.3	21.4	0.2	-3.5	3.3	17.7	15.9	22.6	-15.5	-13.0	7.0
Sao Tome and Principe	0.0	36.2	-0.4	-1.0	5.8	7.4	-1.2	-4.3	27.9	6.6	-21.7
Northern Africa	*41.7*	*22.9*	*10.9*	*0.3*	*3.3*	*10.3*	*7.1*	*3.4*	*5.7*	*13.3*	*3.2*
Egypt	17.6	22.4	11.1	1.4	2.8	5.8	16.4	1.8	-2.1	-2.2	0.6
Libyan Arab Jamahiriya	6.5	20.8	14.3	-3.8	-4.5	20.0	-10.4	-7.5	-0.8	24.6	-2.5
Morocco	6.9	24.0	15.9	7.1	3.4	10.7	-2.7	7.5	0.2	2.5	6.1
Sudan	7.4	19.7	5.2	-0.4	8.5	16.6	9.6	7.7	26.2	40.6	5.4
Tunisia	3.3	24.4	10.8	-1.5	5.5	2.2	8.6	5.8	8.5	7.1	6.0
Southern Africa	*26.2*	*19.8*	*3.8*	*0.4*	*0.8*	*9.0*	*5.2*	*5.7*	*-14.7*	*10.9*	*1.7*
Botswana	1.3	32.8	17.0	10.8	5.1	6.5	5.9	16.9	18.0	1.5	-8.2
Lesotho	0.4	53.1	22.7	6.5	3.8	4.9	3.6	-11.3	-7.1	6.9	-3.0
Namibia	0.6	21.3	10.5	-5.1	8.9	17.4	-11.1	24.8	6.6	8.5	-19.2
South Africa	23.8	19.1	3.5	0.2	0.2	9.0	5.7	5.0	-17.3	11.8	3.3
Swaziland	0.2	18.6	6.5	5.4	2.6	3.5	5.7	6.7	0.9	10.6	-3.7
Western Africa	*10.3*	*12.6*	*8.4*	*-5.1*	*6.4*	*11.1*	*1.8*	*4.4*	*18.8*	*-2.9*	*9.7*
Benin	0.3	13.4	1.8	5.4	0.7	4.2	3.1	2.9	6.2	3.1	6.7
Burkina Faso	0.7	21.7	10.0	5.9	6.9	28.5	3.0	15.0	-9.5	-9.4	1.6
Cape Verde	0.1	40.7	-0.2	5.9	0.0	-58.1	23.6	34.1	2.5	58.4	-7.8
Cote d'Ivoire	1.0	7.7	12.5	-8.9	5.7	23.5	2.9	6.4	8.2	-49.1	-11.5
Gambia	0.1	17.9	20.1	1.8	4.2	2.8	23.4	8.0	-37.0	5.7	9.2
Ghana	0.8	12.2	-3.3	-1.0	15.7	42.4	14.8	-6.2	14.2	-55.1	2.8
Guinea	0.5	17.5	2.8	6.8	0.7	2.8	-18.2	4.3	14.1	10.0	3.5
Guinea-Bissau	0.1	29.9	-3.0	5.3	-4.4	0.8	4.6	-62.9	63.8	3.5	3.3
Liberia	0.0	10.5	8.0	-17.2	-7.8	12.1	68.8	18.3	12.2	9.8	-3.9
Mali	0.6	20.0	7.1	3.9	4.5	8.8	6.5	4.2	35.5	7.4	-9.6
Mauritania	0.2	18.3	2.0	0.4	2.8	1.3	-8.8	0.3	24.2	18.0	-4.4
Niger	0.3	11.7	21.1	-1.8	0.4	38.3	16.2	15.0	-9.9	2.4	18.2
Nigeria	4.2	11.8	10.4	-9.1	6.4	-6.8	-7.5	5.1	42.1	39.7	18.5

Table 5.C. Average Rates of Growth of Gross Domestic Product by Expenditure - Gross Fixed Capital Formation

Major area, region and country	Base year weights as percentage of total for world or region in 1990	Base year share as percentage of total GDP in 1990	Average rates of growth			Annual rate of change (percentage)					
			1970-1979	1980-1989	1990-1999	1996	1997	1998	1999	2000	2001
Senegal	0.8	12.9	2.6	3.5	7.1	14.0	4.4	19.4	20.6	-2.7	10.4
Sierra Leone	0.1	9.1	2.0	2.2	-5.0	-3.3	-0.7	1.3	7.6	-12.3	17.0
Togo	0.4	22.2	17.5	-3.6	-1.5	20.9	-0.4	-2.1	-5.1	5.9	0.0
AMERICAS	**25.5**	**18.1**	**5.4**	**2.2**	**4.9**	**7.5**	**10.0**	**9.0**	**6.2**	**5.7**	**-2.1**
NORTHERN AMERICA	**21.5**	**17.8**	**4.9**	**2.7**	**5.2**	**8.2**	**10.0**	**9.7**	**7.9**	**5.6**	**-2.5**
Bermuda	0.0	16.6	6.2	4.1	1.7	20.3	0.0	13.7	5.0	5.7	2.5
Canada	9.3	21.6	5.7	4.9	1.9	4.4	15.2	2.4	7.8	6.5	1.7
United States	75.1	17.4	4.8	2.5	5.6	8.6	9.5	10.4	7.9	5.5	-2.9
LATIN AMERICA AND THE CARIBBEAN	**3.9**	**20.4**	**7.7**	**-0.3**	**3.0**	**3.6**	**10.3**	**5.3**	**-4.1**	**6.6**	**0.3**
Caribbean	*1.3*	*20.4*	*0.6*	*5.2*	*3.0*	*11.6*	*8.2*	*15.2*	*3.9*	*0.7*	*4.4*
Anguilla	0.0	40.8	3.8	7.0	4.8	4.2	-5.9	48.1	34.7	-0.7	-27.9
Antigua and Barbuda	0.0	37.2	7.3	9.5	4.1	-0.6	4.2	15.3	10.1	6.0	5.4
Aruba	0.0	31.4	7.2	7.9	4.1	4.1	4.1	4.1	4.1	4.1	4.1
Barbados	0.0	18.9	2.7	0.1	0.5	10.3	16.2	6.3	6.5	-0.9	-11.4
British Virgin Islands	0.0	25.5	-3.8	5.9	8.3	4.2	14.2	16.4	2.1	14.4	6.3
Cayman Islands	0.0	21.4	9.3	8.6	1.2	0.2	0.5	1.5	0.7	0.7	0.7
Cuba	0.4	24.5	5.0	13.8	-8.9	37.1	4.0	5.7	7.1	2.0	1.1
Dominica	0.0	39.7	-1.7	9.3	-1.0	-5.4	11.6	-10.3	2.3	-0.2	-12.6
Dominican Republic	0.1	19.1	11.5	3.6	7.9	16.4	19.1	28.8	16.4	2.5	-0.9
Grenada	0.0	38.9	37.9	5.2	5.0	15.2	8.4	9.2	9.6	15.2	-3.3
Guadeloupe	0.1	33.9	5.9	5.9	3.1	4.3	9.2	4.1	5.9	5.9	5.9
Haiti	0.0	14.3	13.0	-0.2	-0.2	-1.6	-1.5	7.4	4.0	18.3	-15.2
Jamaica	0.1	27.3	-6.5	6.2	1.0	0.6	-1.9	-10.8	-0.1	2.4	3.8
Martinique	0.1	26.7	1.3	7.6	2.2	1.6	1.6	4.1	2.5	2.5	2.5
Montserrat	0.0	71.7	5.6	8.4	-7.1	-11.0	5.2	20.5	-15.3	-29.0	-21.7
Netherlands Antilles	0.0	23.6	4.3	4.0	-2.1	19.4	-19.8	-8.6	-5.7	-10.2	-3.8
Puerto Rico	0.4	15.5	-4.6	4.4	7.4	12.1	3.8	26.5	1.6	-0.8	8.4
Saint Kitts and Nevis	0.0	55.4	13.7	11.5	0.8	5.6	2.6	-1.3	-14.2	43.8	17.7
Saint Lucia	0.0	24.6	5.5	5.2	0.8	8.8	-35.3	2.7	9.7	5.5	6.8
Saint Vincent and the Grenadines	0.0	29.7	3.6	3.0	5.8	-5.1	7.8	13.2	6.7	-14.7	8.5
Trinidad and Tobago	0.1	13.8	4.7	-8.0	6.8	11.1	71.6	-0.8	-12.2	-10.8	13.0
Central America	*3.9*	*17.6*	*7.4*	*-1.0*	*6.2*	*13.1*	*19.9*	*10.9*	*8.8*	*9.2*	*-5.1*
Belize	0.0	26.0	7.1	4.2	4.0	-6.9	0.1	0.1	37.4	28.5	-6.1
Costa Rica	0.1	20.2	10.6	-0.3	6.5	-7.8	15.3	25.5	-4.1	-0.9	1.5
El Salvador	0.1	13.7	9.5	-2.2	5.7	-12.8	8.1	9.6	-0.8	5.2	-0.8
Guatemala	0.1	13.0	7.8	-2.6	10.0	-2.0	19.9	11.9	43.8	-6.0	0.1
Honduras	0.0	20.2	7.2	0.1	7.4	6.2	15.8	10.3	6.3	-4.6	3.0
Mexico	3.5	17.9	7.6	-1.0	5.7	16.4	21.0	10.3	7.7	11.4	-5.9
Nicaragua	0.0	21.0	-9.5	14.3	6.2	9.6	18.3	11.8	40.1	-8.3	-2.1
Panama	0.0	8.5	1.5	-9.5	24.5	-2.8	5.2	15.8	21.7	-7.7	0.2
South America	*10.3*	*21.7*	*8.5*	*-0.6*	*1.8*	*0.1*	*7.4*	*2.1*	*-10.2*	*6.1*	*2.5*
Bolivia	0.0	12.6	6.8	-4.0	9.7	11.7	26.8	29.2	-15.3	-8.1	-21.0
Brazil	7.6	22.9	9.4	-0.4	1.2	-0.2	6.2	3.6	-5.6	8.2	2.0
Chile	0.6	24.5	-1.0	6.1	7.0	8.9	10.5	1.9	-18.4	8.5	2.0
Colombia	0.7	20.4	4.3	3.2	-1.2	-1.4	-2.0	-6.3	-34.6	-0.8	9.8
Ecuador	0.1	17.6	10.4	-2.6	-1.3	-4.3	2.7	3.9	-27.7	12.1	12.1
French Guiana	0.0	47.8	13.4	15.7	-0.7	1.6	-2.5	0.8	0.0	0.0	0.0
Guyana	0.0	42.3	-0.2	-3.9	0.4	-0.4	6.9	-6.8	-12.5	-9.5	18.6
Paraguay [1]	0.1	22.0	17.3	2.1	1.2	-0.4	-1.4	-5.0	-4.3	-0.8	-19.3
Peru	0.4	19.0	5.8	-2.4	6.7	-2.9	15.3	-1.4	-11.1	-5.0	0.0
Suriname	0.0	18.4	6.0	-2.3	5.0	-32.3	-12.1	-0.8	12.2	-1.0	4.9
Uruguay	0.1	10.8	8.4	-5.9	7.5	10.5	9.5	8.7	-9.0	-13.1	-9.0
Venezuela	0.5	14.1	10.1	-7.1	1.9	-6.3	23.9	-2.5	-16.4	1.1	13.6
ASIA	**31.5**	**29.4**	**5.6**	**4.3**	**3.7**	**7.5**	**2.7**	**-3.2**	**-0.2**	**5.6**	**1.5**
Eastern Asia	*75.3*	*31.3*	*4.8*	*5.0*	*3.0*	*7.1*	*2.1*	*-1.9*	*0.8*	*5.0*	*0.0*
China	6.0	25.8	7.6	8.2	13.5	10.6	6.0	14.2	6.7	8.3	7.3
Democratic People's Rep. of Korea	0.2	24.4	11.9	7.4	-10.6	-3.6	-6.3	-1.1	6.2	0.3	4.3
Hong Kong SAR of China	1.2	26.5	11.9	5.2	5.1	10.9	12.6	-7.3	-16.6	11.0	2.9
Japan	59.8	32.2	3.9	4.4	0.6	6.4	0.9	-3.9	-0.9	2.7	-0.9

Table 5.C. Average Rates of Growth of Gross Domestic Product by Expenditure - Gross Fixed Capital Formation

Major area, region and country	Base year weights as percentage of total for world or region in 1990	Base year share as percentage of total GDP in 1990	Average rates of growth 1970-1979	1980-1989	1990-1999	Annual rate of change (percentage) 1996	1997	1998	1999	2000	2001
Macao SAR of China	0.0	24.5	7.9	9.0	2.1	-22.1	1.9	-12.4	-6.8	-28.4	-7.8
Mongolia	0.1	40.8	5.7	6.3	-0.5	2.4	4.0	3.5	2.5	1.1	1.1
Republic of Korea	5.7	37.3	15.9	8.2	4.8	7.3	-2.2	-21.2	3.7	11.4	-1.8
South Central Asia	*11.2*	*24.3*	*4.6*	*1.7*	*7.8*	*5.6*	*3.3*	*5.5*	*7.0*	*6.1*	*16.6*
Bangladesh	0.3	14.5	6.0	2.1	8.2	11.1	12.1	9.9	7.3	5.8	6.5
Bhutan	0.0	36.7	6.4	6.5	7.9	1.8	-4.0	4.8	20.3	8.3	5.9
India [2]	4.5	23.0	4.0	7.0	6.9	1.5	2.1	8.7	8.6	4.7	22.7
Iran (Islamic Republic of)	2.7	23.3	4.8	-3.9	5.7	26.3	8.8	4.5	7.1	8.1	9.9
Kazakhstan	1.7	39.0	...	...	-7.1	-23.9	3.3	-7.2	0.5	16.1	25.3
Kyrgyzstan	0.2	22.0	...	...	-8.8	-13.0	-29.6	-1.6	28.1	26.9	-1.9
Maldives	0.0	31.6	11.5	11.7	10.0	14.6	27.2	1.6	9.9	-19.3	6.7
Nepal	0.0	16.4	14.4	6.4	5.1	10.1	-3.3	-4.7	-2.7	8.2	3.5
Pakistan	0.5	17.4	4.9	5.2	1.8	-4.0	-3.7	-4.5	5.0	0.9	-3.1
Sri Lanka	0.1	20.5	7.1	0.9	6.0	5.4	5.8	11.0	1.5	7.3	-17.3
Tajikistan	0.0	6.8	...	...	-2.0	-48.1	35.2	-20.0	32.8	25.3	14.2
Turkmenistan	0.3	37.9	...	...	2.5	90.4	-12.1	63.9	18.0	16.6	21.0
Uzbekistan	0.9	30.7	...	...	-1.9	13.4	-3.4	-8.1	-4.5	-4.6	9.1
South-Eastern Asia	*6.6*	*30.2*	*10.2*	*6.4*	*4.0*	*12.0*	*0.4*	*-30.2*	*-7.5*	*11.1*	*1.3*
Brunei Darussalam	0.0	9.9	16.5	5.1	1.5	-2.3	3.0	2.0	2.6	2.8	1.5
Cambodia	0.0	9.3	-7.3	-1.1	9.0	-7.5	23.7	1.2	15.4	7.6	-0.6
Indonesia	2.0	28.3	14.6	8.7	2.5	14.5	8.6	-33.0	-18.2	13.8	7.5
Lao People's Democratic Republic	0.0	16.9	0.1	14.7	10.9	19.3	1.4	-5.8	7.3	0.7	4.0
Malaysia	0.9	33.0	15.2	6.6	6.2	8.2	9.2	-43.0	-6.5	25.7	-2.8
Myanmar	0.2	14.7	7.4	-2.2	14.8	22.8	7.7	10.1	9.2	6.8	4.6
Philippines	0.6	23.1	11.0	0.4	3.4	12.0	11.5	-11.2	-2.3	3.1	-2.2
Singapore	0.7	31.8	9.7	6.4	8.7	23.1	9.7	-6.1	-4.0	6.3	-4.6
Thailand	2.1	40.4	6.7	8.5	-0.3	7.0	-20.5	-44.3	-3.2	5.5	0.8
Vietnam	0.1	13.1	0.0	3.0	19.5	14.0	10.2	12.4	1.6	10.9	10.8
Western Asia	*6.9*	*21.4*	*12.6*	*-0.9*	*4.2*	*8.7*	*10.9*	*6.8*	*-13.5*	*5.3*	*-9.3*
Armenia	0.4	44.3	...	...	-20.9	10.3	2.1	12.0	0.6	16.2	4.0
Azerbaijan	0.3	20.3	...	...	8.3	111.4	67.0	45.0	-48.9	2.6	20.6
Bahrain	0.0	18.2	19.0	0.3	1.7	-24.6	0.4	14.9	11.4	18.6	3.4
Cyprus	0.1	24.6	3.1	3.8	0.3	7.4	-4.5	8.0	-1.4	4.6	1.4
Georgia	0.3	23.7	...	...	-13.1	-44.6	16.3	13.1	67.3	-4.7	7.6
Iraq	0.6	26.7	17.9	1.3	-18.6	-64.5	371.5	43.2	17.5	29.6	27.9
Israel	0.7	19.5	3.8	0.0	9.0	9.0	-0.9	-3.7	0.1	1.7	-6.1
Jordan	0.1	26.0	17.3	-0.3	2.4	1.3	-9.3	-15.5	-6.1	3.6	2.3
Kuwait	0.2	15.6	13.8	-3.8	3.9	24.2	-7.3	14.9	-7.0	-7.8	1.9
Lebanon	0.1	39.0	10.0	-7.9	-0.2	-13.6	-6.2	-7.2	-5.2	-3.9	4.3
Oman	0.1	12.3	10.6	-1.0	4.2	-2.4	31.9	22.2	-28.4	2.6	8.0
Qatar	0.1	17.0	12.3	-1.0	7.9	35.0	29.5	-18.0	-29.4	54.5	-13.3
Saudi Arabia	1.2	19.1	18.8	-6.5	2.8	-9.7	4.2	20.2	-6.0	-6.6	5.1
Syrian Arab Republic	0.1	16.5	15.2	-2.7	6.0	-0.3	-5.0	3.2	-2.6	-2.3	8.0
Turkey	2.1	22.9	4.5	6.6	4.3	14.1	14.8	-3.9	-15.7	16.9	-31.7
United Arab Emirates	0.4	19.4	44.0	-3.6	5.2	2.0	2.5	-2.2	1.0	1.6	1.4
Yemen	0.1	12.4	...	...	5.2	9.3	8.6	53.4	-23.0	-18.2	7.5
Yemen Arab Republic (Former)	...	...	21.6	-4.3	...	...	...	...	...	...	...
Yemen Democratic (Former)	...	...	4.4	-15.2	...	...	...	...	...	...	...
EUROPE	**39.8**	**23.4**	**1.9**	**2.3**	**1.1**	**1.6**	**3.5**	**6.3**	**4.6**	**4.7**	**0.1**
Eastern Europe	*19.2*	*26.5*	*3.4*	*2.1*	*-6.8*	*-6.5*	*2.3*	*1.4*	*0.8*	*6.7*	*3.1*
Belarus	0.7	21.9	...	...	-5.6	-3.1	21.7	10.1	-4.0	2.3	-2.3
Bulgaria	0.2	21.3	7.1	4.3	-7.0	-21.2	-20.9	35.2	20.8	15.4	19.9
Czech Republic	0.4	25.3	...	1.8	1.3	8.2	-2.9	0.7	-1.0	5.3	5.5
Czechoslovakia (Former)	...	...	4.7		...	...	...	...	...	...	...
Hungary	0.4	22.1	5.8	-0.9	2.2	6.7	9.2	13.3	5.9	7.7	3.5
Poland	0.6	21.0	10.0	-3.2	7.3	19.7	21.7	14.2	6.5	3.0	-9.8
Republic of Moldova	0.2	23.0	...	...	-13.6	16.5	2.4	3.6	-19.2	-14.5	-7.0
Romania	0.4	19.8	13.8	0.6	-6.4	11.6	7.4	-19.7	-17.5	5.9	10.8
Russian Federation	13.4	28.7	...	...	-17.3	-17.2	-7.1	-6.6	2.3	9.1	7.3
Slovakia	0.2	30.1	...	0.5	0.4	30.9	14.3	11.0	-18.5	1.2	9.6
Ukraine	2.7	22.8	...	...	-18.6	-22.7	2.1	2.6	0.1	12.4	6.2
USSR (Former)	...	...	2.3	2.5	...	...	...	...	...	...	...
Northern Europe	*18.1*	*21.8*	*1.4*	*3.4*	*1.8*	*5.9*	*8.1*	*11.8*	*1.4*	*3.0*	*1.0*
Denmark	1.3	19.9	0.7	0.8	3.2	3.9	10.9	10.0	1.4	8.6	2.1
Estonia	0.1	23.8	...	...	0.4	11.4	17.5	11.3	-14.6	2.0	17.2
Finland	2.0	29.8	1.1	5.0	-2.5	7.5	13.1	8.2	1.8	4.0	3.8

Table 5.C. Average Rates of Growth of Gross Domestic Product by Expenditure - Gross Fixed Capital Formation

Major area, region and country	Base year weights as percentage of total for world or region in 1990	Base year share as percentage of total GDP in 1990	Average rates of growth			Annual rate of change (percentage)					
			1970-1979	1980-1989	1990-1999	1996	1997	1998	1999	2000	2001
Iceland	0.1	19.9	6.4	1.8	4.0	25.7	10.0	32.9	-3.8	14.7	-6.9
Ireland	0.4	18.7	7.1	-0.9	8.8	16.8	18.1	14.8	14.0	7.0	-0.4
Latvia	0.2	23.1	...	...	-7.7	22.3	20.7	44.0	-4.0	20.0	17.0
Lithuania	0.3	27.6	...	...	-3.6	17.6	22.0	9.9	-6.3	-3.9	8.7
Norway	1.2	21.5	4.8	0.3	3.1	10.3	15.5	13.1	-5.6	-3.6	-4.2
Sweden	2.8	23.5	0.2	4.2	-0.2	4.5	-0.3	7.8	8.2	6.6	0.8
United Kingdom	9.8	20.5	1.1	4.1	2.0	4.7	6.9	12.8	0.6	1.9	1.0
Southern Europe	*20.3*	*22.6*	*2.1*	*2.1*	*2.4*	*4.0*	*4.4*	*6.8*	*6.7*	*6.0*	*2.8*
Albania	0.0	34.6	6.2	3.1	-6.4	-13.4	-3.1	9.2	19.4	13.7	10.3
Andorra	0.0	25.9	7.1	8.9	7.8	7.1	9.9	14.8	13.7	10.4	7.0
Bosnia and Herzegovina	0.1	18.6	...	...	7.3	78.6	30.0	20.0	13.4	10.7	7.4
Croatia	0.2	13.4	...	...	5.5	37.6	23.3	2.5	-3.9	-3.8	9.7
Greece	0.9	23.1	4.9	-3.0	3.3	8.4	6.8	10.6	6.2	8.0	5.9
Holy See	0.0	21.5	2.5	2.2	1.4	3.6	2.2	4.0	5.7	6.6	2.4
Italy	11.4	21.5	1.6	1.8	1.3	3.6	2.1	4.0	5.7	6.5	2.4
Malta	0.0	31.7	1.4	6.0	4.5	-3.4	-3.7	-3.9	4.0	17.5	-2.5
Portugal	0.9	26.2	3.2	3.0	5.5	5.7	13.9	11.5	6.4	4.4	0.0
San Marino	0.0	21.5	3.3	0.9	9.8	1.1	113.5	3.5	22.1	6.6	1.7
Serbia and Montenegro	0.2	12.7	...	...	-9.9	5.7	5.2	-2.1	-20.1	5.2	-5.0
Slovenia	0.2	18.8	...	...	7.0	8.9	11.6	11.3	19.1	0.2	-1.9
Spain	6.4	25.9	1.7	4.7	2.9	2.1	5.0	10.0	8.7	5.7	3.2
TFYR Macedonia	0.0	18.4	...	...	-3.5	6.5	-4.3	-2.6	-1.4	15.7	-8.0
Yugoslavia (Former)	...	...	8.6	-7.3	...	...	...	...	...	...	...
Western Europe	*42.3*	*23.2*	*1.5*	*2.0*	*1.9*	*0.1*	*1.4*	*4.4*	*5.5*	*4.5*	*-2.1*
Austria	1.8	23.7	3.9	1.6	2.8	2.2	2.0	3.9	2.1	5.9	-2.2
Belgium	2.1	22.5	1.9	2.6	2.1	0.9	7.2	3.0	4.3	4.1	0.5
France	13.2	22.6	2.6	3.2	1.2	0.0	-0.1	7.0	8.3	7.7	2.3
Germany	18.8	23.4	1.2	1.0	2.3	-0.8	0.6	3.0	4.1	2.5	-5.3
Liechtenstein	0.0	27.1	1.5	4.9	1.4	-1.5	2.6	5.8	4.9	7.0	-0.3
Luxembourg	0.1	23.5	1.5	4.8	6.1	3.8	12.7	11.8	14.8	-3.8	4.8
Monaco	0.0	22.6	3.1	3.9	1.9	0.7	0.6	7.7	9.0	8.4	2.9
Netherlands	3.2	22.5	0.3	1.8	3.1	6.3	6.6	4.2	7.8	3.5	-0.8
Switzerland	3.0	27.1	0.0	4.1	0.6	-2.4	1.5	4.5	2.7	5.8	-5.2
OCEANIA	**1.6**	**22.8**	**1.9**	**4.5**	**4.0**	**7.0**	**8.0**	**5.6**	**8.4**	**-6.8**	**8.8**
Australia & New Zealand	*94.9*	*22.3*	*2.0*	*4.4*	*4.1*	*7.5*	*8.4*	*5.8*	*8.7*	*-7.0*	*9.1*
Australia	84.6	22.7	2.2	4.4	4.2	7.8	9.5	6.9	8.7	-7.7	9.6
New Zealand	10.3	19.7	0.6	4.5	3.0	5.7	-0.9	-4.1	8.6	-0.6	4.7
Melanesia	*4.1*	*45.6*	*-3.8*	*8.5*	*0.4*	*-6.8*	*-2.5*	*-0.3*	*-2.0*	*-0.9*	*-0.2*
Fiji	0.3	16.6	7.3	-3.4	2.6	-17.5	1.0	26.1	9.8	-24.0	15.2
New Caledonia	2.8	93.1	5.0	20.5	1.9	-5.4	2.2	-0.9	0.9	1.8	-1.4
Papua New Guinea	0.9	22.9	-8.2	2.6	-4.5	-7.9	-14.7	-5.2	-16.2	0.3	0.2
Solomon Islands	0.0	17.4	8.1	5.3	0.1	6.3	-0.1	-1.1	-0.6	-13.8	-5.4
Vanuatu	0.1	41.1	7.7	3.6	3.2	-14.4	-4.1	2.7	12.9	-2.7	-0.5
Micronesia	*0.1*	*22.5*	*5.0*	*7.5*	*-0.2*	*-8.7*	*-6.0*	*1.3*	*0.9*	*-0.8*	*1.2*
Kiribati	0.0	8.1	2.9	-4.9	4.2	3.0	5.7	5.0	6.2	0.2	1.8
Marshall Islands	0.1	88.4	10.0	22.4	-1.8	-15.9	-11.2	2.0	0.0	-1.1	1.8
Micronesia (Federated States of)	0.0	8.1	6.6	4.5	1.6	-1.8	-5.1	-2.1	0.9	2.1	1.5
Nauru	0.0	8.1	6.8	4.9	-5.4	-7.3	-7.3	-1.9	-1.9	-1.0	-0.8
Palau	0.0	8.1	2.9	-5.5	4.7	10.9	10.4	3.9	2.8	-3.9	-0.7
Polynesia	*0.8*	*21.1*	*6.4*	*3.0*	*0.7*	*2.0*	*0.3*	*1.7*	*4.2*	*5.6*	*2.7*
Cook Islands	0.0	26.2	-3.4	2.0	2.2	-0.2	-2.8	-4.2	5.8	9.8	3.0
French Polynesia	0.7	20.0	7.2	4.3	-0.1	1.6	1.1	1.1	2.7	2.7	2.1
Samoa	0.1	34.4	5.1	-5.1	6.0	7.0	1.6	4.7	11.5	23.1	6.5
Tonga	0.0	18.0	6.1	1.7	2.4	-4.9	-19.1	9.4	16.2	6.9	-0.7
Tuvalu	0.0	93.1	10.0	13.7	5.3	10.3	3.5	14.9	3.0	3.0	3.0

Notes for Table 5.C - Gross fixed capital formation

1/ 1988-1996
Includes communications equipment.

2/ 1970-1979
Data based on type of assets.

Table 5.D. Average Rates of Growth of Gross Domestic Product by Expenditure - Exports of Goods and Services

Major area, region and country	Base year weights as percentage of total for world or region in 1990	Base year share as percentage of total GDP in 1990	Average rates of growth			Annual rate of change (percentage)					
			1970-1979	1980-1989	1990-1999	1996	1997	1998	1999	2000	2001
WORLD	**100.0**	**19.7**	**6.6**	**4.5**	**19.4**	**2.1**	**3.9**	**3.1**	**9.4**	**10.9**	**2.1**
DEVELOPED ECONOMIES	**67.1**	**17.8**	**6.2**	**4.6**	**6.0**	**5.9**	**10.4**	**4.8**	**5.0**	**11.2**	**-0.3**
DEVELOPING ECONOMIES	**22.3**	**25.0**	**7.7**	**3.9**	**7.7**	**4.0**	**8.8**	**4.4**	**8.1**	**16.6**	**0.4**
TRANSITION ECONOMIES	**10.5**	**25.5**	**7.2**	**4.0**	**47.2**	**0.7**	**1.2**	**2.4**	**11.1**	**10.1**	**3.1**
AFRICA	**3.3**	**27.7**	**5.1**	**2.0**	**3.2**	**6.5**	**3.5**	**3.6**	**6.1**	**12.0**	**-0.6**
Eastern Africa	*7.5*	*19.0*	*2.7*	*2.0*	*6.6*	*10.1*	*5.1*	*-0.3*	*15.3*	*0.1*	*6.0*
Burundi	0.1	8.0	3.7	2.1	2.9	4.5	4.7	7.3	-3.9	6.8	3.8
Comoros	0.0	11.7	-0.7	1.1	2.6	1.8	-1.2	10.8	1.7	8.7	-2.2
Djibouti	0.3	81.4	-0.5	-0.2	-2.4	-2.4	9.5	2.5	10.0	-3.8	2.4
Eritrea	...	...	...	...	-5.6	13.3	5.7	-46.6	-36.0	42.4	-14.5
Ethiopia	...	...	...	...	30.4	4.8	50.9	-9.4	87.0	-15.8	3.3
Ethiopia (Former)	0.4	7.7	3.1	-0.6	-22.5	...	...	...	...	...	...
Kenya	1.5	26.2	1.9	3.3	3.2	4.7	-13.5	-4.5	12.2	8.9	6.9
Madagascar	0.3	15.9	-1.2	1.4	7.4	4.0	4.0	5.6	15.6	31.5	-2.4
Malawi	0.3	25.3	5.6	0.7	5.7	16.5	-5.8	1.5	3.1	3.3	-1.5
Mauritius	1.2	66.8	4.2	8.1	5.6	10.4	3.5	8.3	1.5	4.1	17.2
Mozambique	0.1	6.1	3.9	-10.4	13.5	28.4	8.6	10.5	-1.5	33.2	50.1
Reunion	0.1	3.7	-0.4	-9.3	0.8	2.3	2.0	1.4	1.7	1.6	1.6
Rwanda	0.1	7.7	5.0	3.6	-1.9	30.0	22.9	-10.4	13.2	-29.1	33.2
Seychelles	0.2	62.5	9.1	6.8	5.2	10.2	9.3	2.9	2.2	33.0	-9.9
Somalia	0.0	0.9	-2.0	-7.9	-10.3	17.0	-2.0	2.0	-73.8	-1.1	5.1
Uganda	0.2	7.0	-17.2	11.7	10.2	54.9	-13.2	-1.6	7.6	-1.3	16.3
United Republic Of Tanzania	0.4	14.4	3.7	1.1	7.6	10.1	-0.6	2.5	5.3	6.0	7.0
Zambia	1.0	34.3	1.6	-2.3	1.5	14.8	8.5	-10.6	-2.5	-3.7	8.5
Zimbabwe	1.4	22.9	130.0	7.5	6.3	6.3	6.3	6.3	6.3	-7.8	-7.3
Middle Africa	*11.3*	*36.6*	*3.6*	*3.5*	*4.8*	*6.1*	*3.2*	*5.6*	*27.3*	*15.3*	*-3.6*
Angola	2.7	39.0	0.2	8.0	5.6	12.8	0.0	13.4	4.5	8.3	-10.3
Cameroon	1.8	17.9	2.4	2.1	11.9	4.0	6.3	6.6	151.6	31.8	-6.6
Central African Republic	0.2	17.3	4.3	4.4	-7.6	-6.5	0.4	1.6	-33.8	19.0	-7.9
Chad	0.2	18.2	-2.6	4.7	2.8	-11.3	24.2	13.0	-19.6	8.9	-7.7
Congo	0.9	48.6	9.5	6.9	2.6	6.2	0.5	-1.0	42.8	17.1	-1.1
Democratic Republic of the Congo	3.8	59.4	3.2	4.5	-3.0	-3.0	-3.9	0.0	-10.3	-4.3	-4.4
Equatorial Guinea	0.0	32.2	7.6	1.0	35.5	104.2	122.5	23.1	30.4	18.2	65.4
Gabon	1.7	46.0	7.4	-2.4	4.5	8.4	3.6	-2.7	4.4	11.0	-5.2
Sao Tome and Principe	0.0	22.9	8.7	0.2	9.1	0.0	20.6	2.0	37.0	0.0	0.0
Northern Africa	*43.4*	*27.3*	*8.4*	*1.4*	*1.9*	*2.0*	*0.9*	*3.2*	*5.5*	*17.1*	*-3.9*
Algeria	9.9	23.4	2.5	2.4	2.8	7.1	6.3	1.6	6.0	7.4	-0.8
Egypt	13.6	28.1	5.1	5.8	3.3	-3.4	-3.6	9.1	3.8	3.3	-7.8
Libyan Arab Jamahiriya	9.7	50.4	24.4	-5.2	-8.1	1.6	-4.8	-27.4	28.7	53.8	-2.5
Morocco	4.3	24.6	5.0	4.1	4.3	13.3	-2.7	8.7	0.2	3.7	7.2
Sudan	2.3	9.8	-0.4	2.4	4.2	1.8	5.5	3.8	4.8	144.9	-23.0
Tunisia	3.7	43.6	10.8	4.8	4.5	-0.8	10.1	4.4	4.7	5.3	12.2
Southern Africa	*21.6*	*26.5*	*1.4*	*2.0*	*4.0*	*8.6*	*5.6*	*2.5*	*0.8*	*9.2*	*2.7*
Botswana [1]	1.3	55.8	32.8	14.2	0.8	9.2	12.6	6.0	-19.6	39.8	0.0
Lesotho	0.1	16.7	13.3	3.7	8.6	23.3	22.1	-12.5	15.1	25.1	32.6
Namibia	0.8	52.1	4.7	2.6	4.5	2.8	-2.7	-0.3	8.7	-1.4	1.8
South Africa	18.9	24.7	0.9	1.3	4.2	8.9	5.5	2.5	1.4	8.3	2.4
Swaziland	0.4	73.4	8.8	7.7	5.1	4.9	3.3	3.0	17.5	-8.6	16.6
Western Africa	*16.2*	*32.4*	*6.2*	*2.7*	*2.0*	*13.6*	*5.8*	*7.4*	*-3.9*	*8.6*	*1.6*
Benin	0.3	20.4	6.1	-3.8	6.5	6.0	3.6	3.0	14.7	-1.8	47.1
Burkina Faso	0.2	11.2	8.4	-0.8	5.2	-5.1	5.7	43.4	2.6	-7.7	7.4
Cape Verde	0.0	17.1	-8.9	7.6	4.6	15.6	25.5	-6.0	3.7	0.9	3.9
Cote d'Ivoire	2.3	28.8	8.7	3.2	5.7	30.9	9.0	2.3	9.5	-2.0	3.3
Gambia	0.1	43.2	-0.3	4.9	5.3	9.1	20.5	21.6	-60.2	13.3	5.6
Ghana	0.7	15.4	-4.6	0.6	9.5	23.4	-0.4	16.0	-4.5	115.7	-23.0
Guinea	0.6	30.9	2.8	-1.3	5.8	3.2	10.3	14.0	12.8	18.7	9.1
Guinea-Bissau	0.0	9.9	9.1	15.3	6.3	0.4	21.1	-51.9	114.5	26.1	-5.7
Liberia	0.1	34.2	0.6	-7.9	-10.5	-23.0	163.8	23.6	17.2	20.1	1.2
Mali	0.3	17.3	-0.8	6.5	9.2	10.0	54.0	12.7	-10.4	6.5	17.2
Mauritania	0.4	57.6	1.6	7.2	3.4	4.9	4.2	3.6	3.9	0.5	-1.0
Niger	0.3	16.8	10.5	2.3	1.6	2.2	-0.6	19.7	-10.7	-5.1	2.5
Nigeria	9.6	43.2	11.1	3.9	-1.6	13.1	-0.5	5.4	-12.4	-6.0	5.5

Table 5.D. Average Rates of Growth of Gross Domestic Product by Expenditure - Exports of Goods and Services

Major area, region and country	Base year weights as percentage of total for world or region in 1990	Base year share as percentage of total GDP in 1990	Average rates of growth			Annual rate of change (percentage)					
			1970-1979	1980-1989	1990-1999	1996	1997	1998	1999	2000	2001
Senegal	1.0	25.4	1.5	2.1	5.4	-2.9	23.6	10.5	7.2	2.9	7.4
Sierra Leone	0.1	26.3	3.3	0.4	-4.2	-3.9	-12.5	0.3	-5.6	-41.0	10.6
Togo	0.2	23.2	2.9	1.9	1.7	3.0	7.5	-0.3	22.8	8.0	-1.0
AMERICAS	**20.3**	**12.3**	**6.2**	**5.4**	**7.2**	**8.0**	**10.7**	**4.2**	**5.4**	**9.8**	**-3.5**
NORTHERN AMERICA	**15.7**	**11.2**	**6.3**	**5.5**	**7.1**	**7.6**	**11.4**	**3.6**	**4.9**	**9.3**	**-5.0**
Bermuda	0.1	47.5	3.5	1.2	1.7	4.6	5.2	0.8	5.0	5.7	2.5
Canada	16.3	26.0	5.1	4.9	7.9	5.7	8.3	9.1	10.1	8.0	-3.8
United States	60.7	9.7	6.7	5.7	6.9	8.2	12.2	2.1	3.4	9.7	-5.4
LATIN AMERICA AND THE CARIBBEAN	**4.7**	**18.2**	**5.9**	**4.9**	**7.2**	**9.4**	**8.4**	**6.5**	**7.0**	**11.3**	**1.3**
Caribbean	*5.2*	*52.6*	*5.3*	*4.4*	*2.4*	*2.1*	*7.7*	*2.5*	*7.1*	*14.2*	*6.2*
Anguilla	0.0	75.6	3.8	9.8	2.4	1.8	11.4	21.7	-15.3	-6.1	6.5
Antigua and Barbuda	0.0	82.7	3.5	5.2	2.3	-15.5	7.5	2.6	0.9	-6.0	-4.2
Aruba	0.1	80.1	9.2	10.0	6.1	6.1	6.1	6.1	6.1	6.1	6.1
Bahamas	0.2	55.7	7.6	3.9	1.3	-0.8	-0.8	11.3	5.2	3.9	3.2
Barbados	0.1	49.1	7.5	-0.9	0.7	4.9	-4.7	0.2	-0.7	0.1	-0.5
British Virgin Islands	0.0	94.5	15.8	11.9	8.8	14.9	14.0	11.2	10.9	14.4	6.3
Cayman Islands	0.0	62.6	11.8	8.8	1.4	0.2	0.5	1.5	0.7	0.7	0.7
Cuba	0.6	30.2	6.4	7.2	0.8	24.6	2.7	-8.2	22.8	0.6	3.5
Dominica	0.0	50.1	-4.6	9.4	5.9	4.7	11.4	7.6	-0.3	-5.5	-10.4
Dominican Republic	0.4	42.2	11.3	1.3	6.6	7.1	9.0	6.1	7.4	17.5	8.6
Grenada	0.0	44.4	0.2	-2.1	8.8	3.7	5.4	20.1	35.4	3.8	-28.8
Guadeloupe	0.0	4.9	0.5	-3.8	1.5	4.3	9.2	4.1	5.9	5.9	5.9
Haiti	0.1	18.1	8.9	0.1	4.5	37.0	5.8	21.8	3.5	6.3	-4.9
Jamaica	0.3	51.7	4.0	1.1	0.3	-14.5	-12.4	3.6	0.2	1.4	1.4
Martinique	0.0	8.4	4.0	2.2	1.0	1.6	1.6	4.1	2.5	2.5	2.5
Montserrat	0.0	28.6	2.5	4.9	-1.4	40.7	-59.1	-39.4	39.6	-28.5	-19.0
Netherlands Antilles	0.2	77.7	2.3	-2.3	0.8	-1.4	0.6	-3.6	-5.1	-6.2	-3.5
Puerto Rico	2.7	78.0	5.1	5.8	2.0	-0.4	12.1	3.5	6.3	17.3	8.9
Saint Kitts and Nevis	0.0	52.2	9.9	5.1	4.1	7.0	10.7	-1.1	-6.1	-0.6	1.0
Saint Lucia	0.0	68.5	5.4	6.7	-2.0	-0.8	-13.3	3.2	-6.0	29.8	0.9
Saint Vincent and the Grenadines	0.0	65.8	3.0	7.8	1.4	4.6	-4.0	5.3	11.3	1.9	-4.4
Trinidad and Tobago	0.3	49.1	1.1	1.9	4.0	-8.5	13.9	-0.7	3.6	45.0	-0.4
Central America	*6.5*	*20.4*	*7.7*	*6.3*	*11.4*	*15.8*	*11.0*	*11.6*	*11.4*	*15.3*	*-4.7*
Belize	0.0	60.3	-3.4	13.3	4.2	1.2	19.7	-0.5	13.5	5.5	11.3
Costa Rica	0.2	29.9	7.2	5.2	11.7	6.2	8.6	26.7	21.3	-0.3	-9.2
El Salvador	0.1	18.6	7.5	-6.5	14.7	8.7	30.2	6.2	7.1	17.2	11.0
Guatemala	0.2	19.7	6.7	-2.2	6.3	8.6	10.2	8.5	1.2	10.7	-6.4
Honduras	0.1	37.2	5.8	0.2	0.6	8.1	1.3	1.6	-11.2	8.0	0.1
Mexico	5.3	18.6	8.6	7.9	12.3	18.2	10.7	12.1	12.4	16.4	-5.1
Nicaragua	0.1	24.9	5.1	-3.5	1.4	7.2	20.8	9.2	9.3	11.6	5.2
Panama	0.5	86.8	4.4	5.1	2.6	-9.4	12.7	-2.4	-8.5	6.5	1.9
South America	*11.2*	*13.3*	*5.4*	*4.3*	*6.1*	*7.1*	*6.6*	*3.6*	*3.1*	*6.6*	*5.8*
Argentina	1.6	10.3	5.9	2.9	8.0	7.6	12.2	10.6	-1.3	2.7	2.7
Bolivia	0.1	22.8	3.7	1.1	4.2	4.1	-2.1	6.5	-12.8	14.5	4.8
Brazil	3.8	7.9	8.6	9.8	4.7	6.1	1.8	0.2	12.0	11.0	10.1
Chile	1.2	33.1	9.8	6.7	9.5	11.8	11.2	5.2	6.6	7.5	9.7
Colombia	1.0	18.6	6.4	4.9	6.6	9.6	3.2	7.4	5.9	2.9	4.3
Ecuador	0.4	31.4	15.9	3.9	6.9	2.4	7.8	-5.1	7.8	-1.0	-1.3
French Guiana	0.1	67.3	2.7	24.4	4.7	1.6	1.2	3.6	2.1	2.1	2.1
Guyana	0.0	68.1	-2.7	-1.7	7.6	12.1	3.2	-4.5	6.1	-3.1	0.0
Paraguay	0.2	33.2	13.6	4.2	1.9	-5.6	-11.8	-7.2	-27.0	-15.1	-0.4
Peru	0.5	14.5	4.5	-1.3	5.7	8.9	13.1	5.6	7.6	7.9	9.3
Suriname	0.0	27.4	4.8	-3.9	7.6	-33.1	-6.6	-24.4	78.8	-1.0	4.9
Uruguay	0.2	26.2	7.6	3.8	5.7	10.5	13.7	0.0	-7.3	6.4	-8.8
Venezuela	2.1	39.5	1.8	-0.6	5.1	7.8	9.4	4.2	-10.8	5.5	-0.9
ASIA	**22.7**	**18.3**	**9.3**	**4.8**	**7.6**	**3.0**	**9.8**	**2.1**	**7.2**	**17.1**	**-0.6**
Eastern Asia	*62.4*	*16.2*	*10.8*	*8.9*	*7.3*	*2.2*	*12.5*	*1.9*	*7.5*	*17.9*	*-2.2*
China	6.6	17.7	73.8	15.1	10.3	-28.2	22.9	7.2	13.9	32.0	7.3
Democratic People's Rep. of Korea	0.2	9.8	16.6	10.6	-3.3	-3.6	-6.3	-1.1	6.2	0.3	4.3
Hong Kong SAR of China	9.8	131.6	8.2	13.5	8.4	5.9	5.0	-3.9	4.0	16.5	-1.8

Table 5.D. Average Rates of Growth of Gross Domestic Product by Expenditure - Exports of Goods and Services

Major area, region and country	Base year weights as percentage of total for world or region in 1990	Base year share as percentage of total GDP in 1990	Average rates of growth 1970-1979	1980-1989	1990-1999	Annual rate of change (percentage) 1996	1997	1998	1999	2000	2001
Japan	31.0	10.4	8.6	6.2	3.9	6.5	11.3	-2.3	1.5	12.4	-6.1
Macao SAR of China	0.3	96.9	8.2	7.9	2.4	-0.6	-1.7	-2.5	1.1	18.9	7.3
Mongolia	0.1	18.9	5.7	6.3	-0.5	2.4	4.0	3.5	2.5	1.1	1.1
Republic of Korea	7.2	29.1	21.8	11.3	14.0	11.2	21.4	14.1	15.8	20.5	0.7
South Central Asia	*9.8*	*13.2*	*4.0*	*0.9*	*10.7*	*0.4*	*-5.1*	*6.0*	*16.0*	*12.9*	*7.7*
Bangladesh	0.2	6.7	-3.1	9.6	11.3	16.5	12.3	6.0	4.8	22.8	16.8
Bhutan	0.0	28.3	6.4	15.2	6.5	-3.9	6.4	0.6	1.8	5.3	5.9
India	2.3	7.2	2.6	5.5	11.7	6.3	-2.3	13.9	18.0	23.4	6.0
Iran (Islamic Republic of)	2.7	14.8	5.3	-3.5	6.9	0.1	-4.1	15.1	22.1	-0.9	3.0
Kazakhstan	0.5	7.8	...	...	-4.6	2.0	1.2	-11.9	3.0	28.7	-1.1
Kyrgyzstan	0.4	29.2	...	...	-9.3	6.7	21.1	-8.7	-10.4	10.5	-3.2
Maldives	0.0	91.6	11.5	11.7	8.9	14.2	9.6	7.2	7.6	7.7	0.0
Nepal	0.0	10.5	13.1	3.4	12.6	-3.2	24.3	-10.1	2.8	11.1	0.6
Pakistan	0.8	16.9	1.6	7.7	4.5	-6.5	-5.7	-2.9	16.0	11.8	5.4
Sri Lanka	0.2	30.3	0.6	5.4	8.3	3.9	11.6	0.1	5.8	17.1	-8.0
Tajikistan	0.6	57.4	...	...	-9.9	-45.6	13.8	-36.0	41.7	43.5	-11.2
Turkmenistan	0.6	57.5	...	...	-4.0	-20.8	-57.0	-19.9	62.4	0.8	30.5
Uzbekistan	1.4	28.8	...	...	-3.7	10.2	-8.2	-12.5	-9.2	-5.6	51.6
South-Eastern Asia	*10.8*	*30.8*	*9.4*	*6.7*	*9.1*	*4.4*	*7.8*	*4.4*	*-0.2*	*17.7*	*-2.5*
Brunei Darussalam	0.4	105.6	10.8	-1.3	1.4	10.9	3.0	2.0	2.5	2.3	2.4
Cambodia	0.0	1.9	-7.3	-1.1	16.5	-11.0	33.9	12.2	15.0	36.5	14.6
Indonesia	2.8	25.3	9.1	1.7	4.4	7.6	7.8	11.2	-31.8	26.5	1.9
Lao People's Democratic Republic	0.0	18.3	0.2	23.9	14.1	4.5	13.9	59.1	7.3	33.2	20.2
Malaysia	3.2	74.5	11.0	9.4	12.5	9.2	5.5	0.5	13.2	16.1	-7.5
Myanmar	0.0	1.9	5.2	2.9	10.9	10.2	21.2	17.3	23.9	12.0	8.6
Philippines	1.2	27.5	6.7	6.8	5.9	15.4	17.2	-21.0	3.6	17.7	-5.2
Singapore	0.3	8.8	-6.1	37.5	13.1	-17.5	7.2	59.3	19.3	2.7	31.8
Thailand	2.8	34.1	9.7	13.2	10.3	-5.5	7.2	8.2	9.0	17.6	-4.2
Vietnam [2]	-0.1	-9.2	-0.1	0.6	0.8	12.9	-12.0	15.6	-35.9	-14.1	-8.2
Western Asia	*17.0*	*32.9*	*9.2*	*-3.5*	*6.1*	*7.3*	*8.6*	*-1.7*	*8.4*	*15.8*	*4.7*
Armenia	0.5	35.0	...	...	-18.4	7.2	-6.5	-1.6	13.7	19.0	22.9
Azerbaijan	0.9	43.9	...	...	7.4	1.1	45.0	13.9	50.0	15.4	34.1
Bahrain	0.4	91.9	10.2	-0.2	4.2	4.0	0.7	1.5	1.7	8.0	3.0
Cyprus	0.3	51.5	7.5	9.6	2.0	4.1	0.8	-2.4	6.3	9.1	4.1
Georgia	0.9	40.0	...	...	-17.6	6.7	26.5	10.1	19.7	23.5	4.4
Iraq	0.7	18.5	19.0	-10.9	-12.5	205.2	143.1	26.7	25.6	20.2	26.0
Israel	1.7	30.8	9.2	4.9	7.8	5.1	8.4	6.9	12.0	25.3	-11.7
Jordan	0.2	61.9	24.1	8.5	1.9	4.2	-3.6	-6.0	2.9	6.1	4.3
Kuwait	0.8	44.8	-0.9	-4.1	1.3	1.4	0.0	0.3	-8.1	-30.4	-4.8
Lebanon	0.0	16.3	-9.5	-10.7	5.7	3.4	-33.9	-1.2	-0.7	5.9	7.5
Oman	0.5	47.2	2.8	10.7	6.0	9.1	8.7	1.1	1.3	9.8	20.4
Qatar	0.4	53.5	3.8	-2.8	8.8	-1.5	27.2	39.1	12.1	6.0	33.8
Saudi Arabia	4.8	46.8	10.3	-9.2	1.7	-6.7	0.4	-22.1	15.8	31.4	-2.8
Syrian Arab Republic	0.4	28.3	2.2	4.9	10.7	13.5	15.1	0.5	9.6	0.5	13.1
Turkey	2.0	13.3	4.6	15.2	9.1	22.0	19.1	12.0	-7.0	19.2	7.4
United Arab Emirates	2.2	65.4	33.7	-1.4	7.1	13.1	4.1	-10.1	9.7	6.0	4.2
Yemen	0.2	13.9	...	...	13.1	86.7	0.3	-19.2	36.4	46.2	2.0
Yemen Arab Republic (Former)	...	...	30.3	15.5	...	...	...	...	...	...	...
Yemen Democratic (Former)	...	...	2.4	-5.3	...	...	...	...	...	...	...
EUROPE	**52.2**	**26.5**	**5.9**	**4.1**	**25.7**	**1.4**	**2.7**	**3.1**	**10.1**	**10.4**	**2.9**
Eastern Europe	*14.6*	*22.9*	*7.6*	*6.2*	*73.0*	*0.7*	*1.2*	*2.4*	*11.2*	*10.1*	*3.0*
Belarus	1.3	46.0	...	...	-7.2	7.8	33.9	-8.3	7.0	12.7	10.5
Bulgaria	0.3	33.1	7.1	3.6	2.4	11.8	12.8	-4.7	-5.0	16.6	8.5
Czech Republic [3]	0.7	45.2	...	15.9	6.8	8.2	9.2	10.0	6.1	17.0	11.9
Hungary [4]	0.5	30.3	9.1	3.8	6.9	8.4	26.4	16.7	12.4	21.0	8.8
Poland	0.7	28.6	5.7	1.3	9.3	12.1	12.4	14.4	-2.6	23.1	10.2
Republic of Moldova	0.4	48.7	...	...	-10.7	-13.4	-2.3	-20.9	12.3	-3.2	6.1
Romania	0.3	16.7	10.0	0.8	0.7	3.6	15.6	-14.1	-17.0	37.6	6.8
Russian Federation	7.5	18.2	...	...	64.1	0.6	1.1	2.3	11.3	10.0	2.9
Slovakia	0.2	25.5	...	-0.9	10.8	-1.3	19.0	13.2	5.2	13.8	6.5
Ukraine	2.9	27.5	...	...	-7.9	16.9	-5.4	1.2	-2.2	21.5	3.5
Northern Europe	*20.7*	*28.3*	*5.1*	*3.7*	*6.8*	*7.7*	*10.2*	*5.8*	*6.6*	*12.0*	*1.7*
Denmark	2.0	35.8	4.5	5.0	4.4	4.3	4.1	4.3	12.3	13.0	3.0
Estonia	0.2	42.0	...	...	6.4	2.2	30.3	12.6	-0.6	30.8	-2.1
Finland	1.3	22.5	5.7	3.1	7.6	5.7	13.7	9.2	6.5	19.3	-2.3
Iceland	0.1	34.4	6.2	2.8	2.7	9.8	5.8	2.0	4.0	5.0	7.9

Table 5.D. Average Rates of Growth of Gross Domestic Product by Expenditure - Exports of Goods and Services

Major area, region and country	Base year weights as percentage of total for world or region in 1990	Base year share as percentage of total GDP in 1990	Average rates of growth			Annual rate of change (percentage)					
			1970-1979	1980-1989	1990-1999	1996	1997	1998	1999	2000	2001
Ireland	1.1	57.0	7.5	8.3	13.8	12.2	17.4	21.0	15.2	20.6	6.7
Latvia	0.4	47.7	...	...	-2.8	20.2	13.1	4.9	-6.4	12.0	6.9
Lithuania [5]	0.4	52.1	...	...	-3.8	19.3	18.7	0.7	-16.1	12.9	20.8
Norway	2.0	40.4	6.0	4.9	5.7	10.2	7.7	0.6	2.8	4.0	4.1
Sweden	3.0	29.0	4.3	4.0	6.8	3.7	13.8	8.6	7.4	11.3	-0.8
United Kingdom	10.1	24.0	5.0	2.9	5.7	8.2	8.3	3.0	5.3	10.1	0.9
Southern Europe	*16.5*	*20.8*	*7.9*	*3.7*	*7.0*	*4.3*	*10.1*	*5.6*	*3.1*	*11.3*	*1.8*
Albania	0.0	14.9	6.2	2.9	-0.5	2.0	-6.1	9.4	12.1	2.0	3.3
Andorra	0.0	16.3	13.3	9.3	14.8	15.8	20.8	13.2	12.4	14.5	8.0
Bosnia and Herzegovina	0.3	48.0	...	...	5.5	43.4	30.0	20.0	21.0	10.7	7.4
Croatia	0.8	77.7	...	...	-7.3	9.8	7.6	3.9	0.7	12.0	8.6
Greece	0.6	18.1	14.5	2.8	5.3	3.5	20.0	5.3	8.0	19.7	-1.6
Holy See	0.0	19.7	8.9	3.2	5.6	0.6	6.5	3.5	0.3	11.8	0.8
Italy	9.2	19.7	7.9	2.8	5.5	0.6	6.4	3.4	0.3	11.7	0.8
Malta	0.1	85.3	13.0	2.9	6.1	-6.6	4.1	7.9	8.4	6.0	2.5
Portugal	1.0	32.9	4.5	7.1	5.3	7.1	7.1	9.1	2.9	8.0	1.4
San Marino	0.0	19.7	8.4	0.3	29.4	-3.5	825.4	-7.3	6.4	14.2	1.5
Serbia and Montenegro	0.1	11.3	...	...	-2.8	140.1	20.5	29.6	-30.1	12.6	-8.1
Slovenia	0.7	90.8	...	...	-1.5	3.6	11.6	6.7	1.7	12.7	6.2
Spain	3.5	16.3	7.6	5.1	9.5	10.4	15.3	8.2	7.7	10.1	3.4
TFYR Macedonia	0.0	25.8	...	...	2.2	-12.9	29.3	8.5	6.9	21.5	-12.0
Yugoslavia (Former)	...	...	4.8	6.2	...	...	...	...	...	...	...
Western Europe	*48.2*	*30.0*	*5.7*	*4.3*	*5.6*	*4.2*	*10.3*	*7.2*	*5.4*	*12.3*	*3.0*
Austria	2.7	39.6	7.0	4.5	5.5	5.2	12.4	8.1	8.5	13.4	7.4
Belgium	5.9	70.8	5.3	4.1	4.4	2.9	6.1	5.9	5.0	8.2	1.1
France	11.0	21.2	7.4	4.1	5.9	3.5	11.8	8.3	4.3	12.6	1.6
Germany	17.8	25.1	5.0	4.6	6.1	5.1	11.2	7.0	5.6	13.7	5.0
Liechtenstein	0.0	36.3	5.6	4.4	3.7	3.4	9.8	6.2	7.1	12.7	0.4
Luxembourg	0.5	104.1	3.6	5.4	8.2	5.8	14.8	14.1	14.4	16.7	3.4
Monaco	0.0	21.2	8.0	4.9	6.6	4.2	12.6	9.0	5.0	13.4	1.2
Netherlands	6.7	54.0	5.5	4.1	6.3	4.6	8.8	7.4	5.1	10.9	1.7
Switzerland	3.5	36.3	4.1	3.6	2.9	2.5	8.6	5.0	5.8	11.4	-1.0
OCEANIA	**1.5**	**18.3**	**4.4**	**4.4**	**7.2**	**9.0**	**3.1**	**2.2**	**8.9**	**6.8**	**-1.4**
Australia & New Zealand	*95.1*	*17.9*	*4.3*	*4.7*	*7.4*	*9.5*	*3.7*	*2.2*	*9.0*	*7.1*	*-1.3*
Australia	77.5	16.7	4.4	5.0	7.7	10.5	3.7	2.0	9.3	7.3	-1.9
New Zealand	17.6	27.0	3.8	3.6	5.7	4.7	3.8	2.9	7.3	6.2	2.0
Melanesia	*4.0*	*35.9*	*7.5*	*0.1*	*3.5*	*-0.8*	*-10.6*	*3.0*	*5.6*	*0.2*	*-5.3*
Fiji	1.2	62.3	4.9	3.4	4.2	12.5	-4.2	2.4	13.5	-3.0	1.0
New Caledonia	0.4	11.0	5.5	-7.7	-2.8	4.1	6.3	-9.1	3.4	1.6	-0.2
Papua New Guinea	2.1	43.0	10.9	3.0	4.5	-6.1	-16.4	5.6	3.7	2.4	-8.9
Solomon Islands	0.1	47.0	17.7	3.4	3.6	6.4	-2.9	0.6	-0.8	-14.1	-5.0
Vanuatu	0.1	47.1	7.7	1.5	5.4	2.8	4.5	5.0	-5.3	2.9	-0.5
Micronesia	*0.3*	*50.1*	*4.8*	*-0.6*	*1.6*	*0.7*	*-0.1*	*0.6*	*1.8*	*-0.4*	*0.7*
Kiribati	0.0	58.7	2.9	-4.9	4.2	3.0	5.7	5.0	6.2	0.2	1.8
Marshall Islands	0.0	11.0	10.5	-5.8	-4.7	-15.9	-10.3	1.6	0.0	-1.0	1.7
Micronesia (Federated States of)	0.1	58.7	6.6	4.5	1.6	-1.8	-5.1	-2.1	0.9	2.1	1.5
Nauru	0.0	58.7	6.8	4.9	-5.4	-7.3	-7.3	-1.9	-1.9	-1.0	-0.8
Palau	0.1	58.7	2.9	-5.5	4.7	10.9	10.4	3.9	2.8	-3.9	-0.7
Polynesia	*0.6*	*11.5*	*-0.3*	*5.5*	*2.3*	*2.5*	*0.8*	*0.5*	*0.9*	*3.2*	*2.6*
Cook Islands	0.0	7.6	-6.6	-13.0	-0.5	-31.5	-6.4	20.8	5.8	9.8	3.0
French Polynesia	0.4	9.4	-1.1	7.7	3.8	1.6	1.1	1.1	2.7	2.7	2.1
Samoa	0.1	30.6	4.5	3.1	-1.4	7.0	1.6	4.7	-0.2	-1.7	6.5
Tonga	0.1	33.9	-1.6	4.7	-4.7	8.6	-4.7	-17.7	-22.5	28.9	0.3
Tuvalu	0.0	11.6	10.5	-12.6	2.0	10.3	3.5	14.9	3.0	3.0	3.0

Notes for Table 5.D - Exports of goods and services

1/ 1987-1975
Exports of goods only.

2/ 1988-2000
Exports less imports.

3/ 1988-1990
Exports less imports.

4/ 1988-1991
Does not include direct purchases in the domestic market by non-resident households.

5/ 1980-1990
Exports less imports.

Table 5.E. Average Rates of Growth of Gross Domestic Product by Expenditure - Imports of Goods and Services

Major area, region and country	Base year weights as percentage of total for world or region in 1990	Base year share as percentage of total GDP in 1990	Average rates of growth			Annual rate of change (percentage)					
			1970-1979	1980-1989	1990-1999	1996	1997	1998	1999	2000	2001
WORLD	**100.0**	**20.2**	**6.0**	**4.2**	**6.6**	**5.9**	**9.5**	**6.1**	**6.3**	**12.3**	**0.0**
DEVELOPED ECONOMIES	**70.1**	**18.3**	**5.3**	**4.6**	**6.2**	**6.1**	**9.9**	**8.6**	**7.9**	**11.2**	**-0.1**
DEVELOPING ECONOMIES	**22.3**	**24.8**	**7.9**	**3.1**	**7.1**	**4.2**	**8.4**	**-0.6**	**3.1**	**15.0**	**-1.4**
TRANSITION ECONOMIES	**7.6**	**27.2**	**7.2**	**1.2**	**-1.3**	**13.8**	**11.7**	**7.8**	**-1.9**	**15.7**	**11.1**
AFRICA	**3.3**	**27.8**	**6.1**	**-1.0**	**3.6**	**5.7**	**6.2**	**3.2**	**2.5**	**9.1**	**2.9**
Eastern Africa	*11.8*	*30.1*	*1.2*	*2.3*	*5.4*	*0.7*	*12.9*	*-2.3*	*9.0*	*5.3*	*2.6*
Burundi	0.2	25.3	8.7	-0.3	3.9	3.4	1.1	4.4	2.7	3.6	3.1
Comoros	0.1	37.3	-3.9	1.4	0.5	2.5	0.3	2.3	-10.6	-11.3	8.3
Djibouti	0.3	109.3	0.4	-0.2	-3.2	-13.4	26.5	9.0	-10.3	3.6	-3.5
Eritrea	...	...	...	...	11.6	11.9	4.8	1.9	6.0	-14.2	7.6
Ethiopia	...	...	...	...	20.2	21.1	1.8	11.7	123.9	25.3	9.6
Ethiopia (Former)	0.7	12.2	7.1	1.7	-13.9	...	...	...	...	...	...
Kenya	1.8	31.4	0.7	0.3	5.2	1.8	2.6	-4.4	-6.1	18.1	-1.2
Madagascar	0.6	26.9	-1.8	-1.2	8.2	3.5	3.8	5.4	20.3	23.5	0.4
Malawi	0.4	36.2	4.1	-1.0	3.7	15.9	8.5	1.5	3.1	3.3	-1.5
Mauritius	1.3	74.3	7.5	6.7	5.5	11.2	9.9	7.5	4.5	-1.9	7.0
Mozambique	0.7	38.3	3.9	0.7	5.3	-14.4	0.4	8.4	40.4	-9.0	-14.9
Reunion	1.4	40.7	6.0	7.2	1.2	2.0	1.7	2.0	1.8	1.9	1.9
Rwanda	0.3	19.2	5.0	4.3	-6.3	1.2	36.4	-8.0	-0.1	-26.4	30.2
Seychelles	0.2	66.7	7.6	9.8	5.9	13.1	1.5	7.7	3.0	-1.9	-5.1
Somalia	0.0	5.7	2.8	-6.7	-14.9	1.7	0.0	1.5	-57.1	3.0	3.0
Uganda	0.5	20.1	-15.9	25.1	8.6	9.4	-3.2	13.0	0.5	2.4	10.9
United Republic Of Tanzania	1.0	38.9	3.2	2.3	6.3	2.5	-1.7	6.7	7.8	1.0	7.5
Zambia	0.9	33.8	-6.7	-3.2	-0.6	-10.5	25.4	-11.9	-8.6	5.8	12.4
Zimbabwe	1.4	22.8	-9.4	4.9	9.3	-15.0	71.9	-23.3	-3.9	-7.8	-7.3
Middle Africa	*9.8*	*32.0*	*5.1*	*-0.7*	*5.3*	*12.4*	*7.4*	*13.1*	*24.8*	*-12.6*	*14.9*
Angola	1.7	23.7	-0.3	0.1	8.0	12.1	6.0	12.0	40.2	-27.5	7.6
Cameroon	2.1	21.1	5.9	-3.1	10.6	3.0	4.8	4.9	146.5	-7.9	11.0
Central African Republic	0.3	30.1	0.7	3.5	-8.7	-3.8	1.5	3.9	-59.3	12.4	-8.1
Chad [1]	0.5	45.9	-1.6	7.6	3.0	4.1	8.2	1.0	4.6	10.0	50.7
Congo	0.6	33.9	8.2	1.9	-5.6	6.5	-0.6	-2.8	-39.7	-16.3	17.8
Democratic Republic of the Congo	3.5	54.7	7.8	-0.5	-3.4	-3.4	-2.8	3.6	-10.5	-4.3	-4.4
Equatorial Guinea	0.1	69.6	16.3	-3.1	37.5	123.7	31.7	71.6	-31.9	-18.4	58.0
Gabon	1.1	30.9	7.4	-1.4	2.0	23.5	15.0	-7.5	15.3	-13.4	7.3
Sao Tome and Principe	0.0	72.5	1.8	6.1	6.2	4.5	3.7	2.4	25.7	1.4	-25.1
Northern Africa	*48.8*	*30.8*	*0.2*	*1.5*	*1.5*	*3.5*	*3.4*	*3.2*	*-1.1*	*16.6*	*0.8*
Algeria	10.6	25.1	10.6	0.2	-2.7	-13.3	2.4	6.5	1.7	7.0	8.8
Egypt	17.5	36.2	5.5	-0.9	2.2	5.4	8.0	2.9	-3.4	-1.1	-6.0
Libyan Arab Jamahiriya	5.7	29.8	23.7	-5.6	-2.8	10.8	-7.3	-4.0	-17.5	-7.2	-2.5
Morocco	5.2	29.9	8.2	3.1	2.4	11.0	-4.1	6.4	0.2	11.0	5.1
Sudan	5.6	24.5	8.0	-5.5	6.4	12.9	2.5	1.7	6.5	75.9	-0.6
Tunisia	4.2	50.6	11.5	2.1	3.6	-3.4	8.8	5.7	3.0	8.9	13.6
Southern Africa	*17.5*	*21.6*	*0.2*	*2.5*	*4.7*	*8.4*	*5.6*	*2.4*	*-5.5*	*4.6*	*0.6*
Botswana [2]	1.2	49.7	18.4	9.2	4.4	1.0	16.2	23.0	5.5	-7.8	-9.8
Lesotho	0.5	121.9	17.2	3.4	1.0	7.7	1.1	-11.3	-11.1	-6.1	7.1
Namibia	1.1	67.7	4.1	7.4	4.5	15.7	3.4	7.7	0.1	-12.4	4.8
South Africa	14.2	18.6	-0.6	1.8	4.8	8.4	5.4	1.5	-7.5	7.2	0.4
Swaziland	0.5	88.9	8.4	7.2	5.6	4.2	4.8	3.1	46.9	-5.8	11.5
Western Africa	*12.0*	*24.2*	*7.9*	*-5.1*	*5.9*	*9.9*	*9.2*	*3.7*	*5.3*	*14.3*	*5.3*
Benin	0.4	28.2	9.1	-1.8	3.5	7.2	5.8	5.3	3.7	-5.1	23.3
Burkina Faso	0.6	28.8	10.5	-0.8	3.9	6.5	-1.0	32.1	-6.2	-9.9	3.5
Cape Verde	0.1	68.6	-6.0	6.5	6.0	-3.7	6.7	2.7	18.7	14.0	3.3
Cote d'Ivoire	2.0	24.6	10.9	-1.4	5.7	25.1	8.6	5.6	-0.1	-17.0	-3.8
Gambia	0.1	57.7	5.8	-4.3	5.3	5.5	26.8	18.3	-67.6	9.5	7.3
Ghana	1.0	24.0	-5.0	1.2	7.6	12.0	11.7	4.1	1.0	101.6	-21.3
Guinea	0.6	30.6	2.8	2.0	2.6	-2.7	-0.6	11.2	8.3	18.6	5.6
Guinea-Bissau	0.1	37.0	1.2	7.6	0.3	-5.4	-14.9	-37.4	49.0	34.1	-8.2
Liberia	0.1	27.8	4.4	-14.1	-5.7	-31.1	221.2	23.8	17.5	14.9	0.6
Mali	0.6	33.7	5.2	4.0	7.8	9.8	8.3	-0.8	63.9	8.5	5.8
Mauritania	0.4	60.1	12.0	2.1	1.3	3.5	6.5	5.5	-8.8	-6.3	21.2
Niger	0.4	20.9	10.3	-0.6	2.8	-0.2	5.3	20.9	-15.4	6.4	4.4
Nigeria	4.2	19.1	11.2	-10.8	8.7	7.6	11.4	-3.3	14.9	16.0	18.9

Table 5.E. Average Rates of Growth of Gross Domestic Product by Expenditure - Imports of Goods and Services

Major area, region and country	Base year weights as percentage of total for world or region in 1990	Base year share as percentage of total GDP in 1990	Average rates of growth 1970-1979	1980-1989	1990-1999	Annual rate of change (percentage) 1996	1997	1998	1999	2000	2001
Senegal	1.2	30.3	4.1	1.7	1.4	4.1	-1.6	13.9	-4.9	-3.3	2.4
Sierra Leone	0.1	23.8	2.0	-1.0	-4.9	-6.1	-5.4	-4.0	-2.5	39.0	-12.8
Togo	0.3	27.8	9.9	2.7	-2.3	19.5	16.7	2.1	2.9	12.2	-2.7
AMERICAS	**21.9**	**12.9**	**5.7**	**4.7**	**8.2**	**8.2**	**14.4**	**10.4**	**7.7**	**12.5**	**-2.6**
NORTHERN AMERICA	**17.6**	**12.3**	**5.5**	**5.9**	**8.0**	**8.0**	**13.8**	**10.6**	**10.4**	**12.4**	**-3.3**
Bermuda	0.1	43.7	3.9	4.2	1.4	7.4	2.2	7.3	5.0	5.7	2.5
Canada	15.4	26.0	7.3	6.3	6.2	5.1	14.3	5.1	7.8	8.2	-5.8
United States	64.9	10.9	5.1	5.8	8.3	8.6	13.7	11.8	10.9	13.2	-2.9
LATIN AMERICA AND THE CARIBBEAN	**4.3**	**16.4**	**6.4**	**1.1**	**9.0**	**8.9**	**16.5**	**9.9**	**-1.6**	**13.0**	**0.0**
Caribbean	*5.2*	*56.2*	*4.1*	*3.1*	*2.1*	*5.1*	*6.9*	*7.7*	*3.5*	*7.5*	*5.3*
Anguilla	0.0	79.7	3.8	9.1	7.3	5.4	0.8	20.2	15.1	0.9	-19.2
Antigua and Barbuda	0.0	82.6	2.5	8.4	1.8	-8.7	0.4	4.2	-0.4	-8.0	-4.4
Aruba	0.1	69.2	11.5	12.3	8.3	8.3	8.3	8.3	8.3	8.3	8.3
Bahamas	0.2	53.0	41.6	13.6	2.3	0.5	0.5	12.7	6.5	5.3	4.5
Barbados	0.1	51.7	4.2	-2.4	1.7	2.6	7.0	0.3	6.0	2.1	-7.2
British Virgin Islands	0.0	84.2	3.7	9.6	7.6	11.1	8.0	5.8	9.5	14.4	6.3
Cayman Islands	0.0	58.5	10.6	8.6	0.2	0.2	0.5	1.5	0.7	0.7	0.7
Cuba	0.8	40.9	4.3	2.1	-4.8	24.3	10.5	-5.8	16.0	-8.0	2.9
Dominica	0.0	75.3	0.8	3.1	1.6	-5.0	6.4	0.2	10.7	-0.5	-9.8
Dominican Republic	0.4	47.2	8.1	0.9	6.6	11.3	12.9	18.2	7.0	14.7	7.0
Grenada	0.0	71.8	10.8	-0.1	5.3	23.5	13.0	13.4	2.3	14.5	-30.0
Guadeloupe	0.2	63.5	4.7	3.5	2.0	4.3	9.2	4.1	5.9	5.9	5.9
Haiti	0.1	21.7	12.3	-1.0	10.5	3.1	4.0	13.9	2.2	29.3	-4.6
Jamaica	0.3	55.8	3.0	2.7	0.4	-10.3	-8.0	-2.6	-2.4	1.9	3.2
Martinique	0.2	50.3	4.4	3.8	1.5	1.6	1.6	4.1	2.5	2.5	2.5
Montserrat	0.0	81.4	4.3	1.3	-3.3	10.9	-25.4	4.3	-11.4	-8.8	-14.5
Netherlands Antilles	0.2	89.7	2.3	-2.5	-0.5	-0.5	-11.1	-8.6	-5.7	-10.2	-3.8
Puerto Rico	2.4	71.4	1.8	4.9	2.6	4.4	5.7	10.7	2.6	8.1	7.1
Saint Kitts and Nevis	0.0	85.0	4.8	5.9	4.2	12.1	-3.7	-4.0	11.3	7.2	-3.1
Saint Lucia	0.0	78.1	5.4	4.4	-2.2	2.4	-5.7	3.1	-0.4	29.6	1.1
Saint Vincent and the Grenadines	0.0	76.8	3.8	3.8	2.4	2.3	20.2	6.2	-1.8	-15.5	5.6
Trinidad and Tobago	0.2	33.5	14.0	-3.1	2.5	1.9	59.2	-1.8	-14.6	21.2	8.6
Central America	*6.7*	*22.0*	*7.7*	*2.1*	*12.3*	*17.8*	*21.6*	*16.0*	*13.6*	*18.8*	*-2.4*
Belize	0.0	61.3	4.0	5.9	3.4	-5.3	15.5	5.2	12.3	15.8	0.5
Costa Rica	0.3	39.0	7.3	2.4	9.3	2.7	14.7	25.2	0.4	-2.6	0.0
El Salvador	0.2	31.2	8.3	-4.3	10.0	-6.1	16.8	9.2	2.7	14.5	3.6
Guatemala	0.2	23.7	5.7	-3.3	14.4	-6.9	19.5	19.8	68.0	10.6	-2.0
Honduras	0.1	39.9	5.2	-0.3	3.5	2.4	-1.4	7.5	4.3	3.7	1.0
Mexico	5.3	19.7	8.8	2.7	13.3	22.9	22.7	16.6	14.1	21.5	-2.9
Nicaragua	0.1	45.1	-0.4	7.7	4.7	13.6	24.5	9.4	14.0	-8.8	1.9
Panama	0.4	78.7	3.3	1.6	5.2	-4.1	17.2	4.5	-8.3	1.4	1.2
South America	*7.7*	*9.7*	*7.0*	*-0.8*	*9.7*	*4.8*	*16.2*	*6.4*	*-14.5*	*9.2*	*0.8*
Argentina	0.7	4.6	6.7	-4.1	17.8	17.5	26.9	8.4	-11.3	-0.2	-13.9
Bolivia	0.1	23.9	3.9	-0.4	6.2	7.9	13.5	22.3	-17.1	2.6	-7.4
Brazil	2.8	6.1	9.6	-1.1	9.6	5.9	13.9	8.9	-14.8	13.8	1.2
Chile	1.0	29.4	3.5	2.9	10.3	11.8	13.2	6.7	-9.3	12.6	-1.3
Colombia	0.8	16.0	5.3	2.2	8.0	2.3	6.2	-3.9	-24.7	8.6	10.7
Ecuador	0.3	28.6	10.4	-0.8	1.0	-10.2	15.4	7.0	-29.5	15.8	17.2
French Guiana	0.1	114.3	15.9	12.0	-2.0	1.6	-5.1	-2.4	-2.0	-2.0	-2.0
Guyana	0.0	92.3	-1.7	-2.5	5.7	9.7	5.5	-2.5	2.2	3.1	0.7
Paraguay	0.2	39.5	13.1	3.5	8.5	-9.7	-0.2	-7.0	-27.1	-6.7	-1.6
Peru	0.4	13.0	1.5	-2.7	9.5	0.1	12.2	2.3	-15.2	3.6	12.9
Suriname	0.0	26.6	6.0	-6.8	10.9	-13.3	-6.6	-12.2	35.4	-1.0	4.9
Uruguay	0.2	20.1	4.9	-0.3	10.0	12.0	13.2	7.3	-5.8	-0.4	-6.5
Venezuela	1.0	20.2	8.0	-2.3	6.4	-11.2	33.9	9.4	-14.6	15.4	11.0
ASIA	**23.0**	**18.4**	**9.1**	**4.9**	**6.6**	**5.1**	**5.0**	**-4.9**	**4.3**	**15.1**	**-0.9**
Eastern Asia	*56.6*	*14.6*	*9.5*	*7.0*	*6.5*	*5.3*	*5.1*	*-6.8*	*8.4*	*15.2*	*-1.9*
China	4.6	12.2	76.0	12.3	7.8	-27.7	11.1	3.1	22.3	24.8	7.3
Democratic People's Rep. of Korea	0.3	17.2	17.6	14.3	-1.9	-3.6	-6.3	-1.1	6.2	0.3	4.3
Hong Kong SAR of China	9.2	123.2	10.0	13.4	9.0	4.4	6.8	-6.3	-0.2	16.8	-1.7

Table 5.E. Average Rates of Growth of Gross Domestic Product by Expenditure - Imports of Goods and Services

Major area, region and country	Base year weights as percentage of total for world or region in 1990	Base year share as percentage of total GDP in 1990	Average rates of growth			Annual rate of change (percentage)					
			1970-1979	1980-1989	1990-1999	1996	1997	1998	1999	2000	2001
Japan	28.2	9.4	7.0	4.1	3.3	13.2	1.2	-6.8	3.0	9.5	0.1
Macao SAR of China	0.2	67.4	9.1	9.3	3.3	-7.9	-1.1	-1.0	11.1	7.9	8.8
Mongolia	0.1	39.9	5.7	6.3	-0.5	2.4	4.0	3.5	2.5	1.1	1.1
Republic of Korea	7.5	30.3	17.3	9.0	10.3	14.2	3.2	-22.1	28.8	20.0	-3.0
South Central Asia	*15.7*	*21.1*	*3.4*	*0.8*	*7.9*	*0.2*	*1.6*	*7.9*	*1.6*	*8.4*	*8.7*
Bangladesh	0.4	12.3	0.0	5.4	6.5	-1.7	0.2	5.0	7.4	23.5	13.4
Bhutan	0.0	32.3	6.4	4.6	8.4	9.6	6.2	16.9	9.4	1.7	5.9
India	2.7	8.6	2.6	6.0	12.8	-2.5	13.2	20.8	7.0	6.5	3.5
Iran (Islamic Republic of)	5.1	27.4	2.6	-2.4	-1.4	17.2	-6.7	-0.1	-7.3	6.7	18.8
Kazakhstan	2.1	30.5	...	...	-14.0	-17.1	7.5	-7.2	0.6	26.1	2.5
Kyrgyzstan	0.6	49.5	...	...	-13.8	6.9	-20.2	1.5	-4.9	0.4	-13.8
Maldives	0.0	76.8	11.5	11.7	9.8	10.6	20.5	2.3	16.2	-5.2	1.9
Nepal	0.1	21.1	10.3	7.1	8.2	8.8	10.8	-6.9	-9.8	16.6	1.9
Pakistan	0.9	18.5	7.4	2.0	2.1	-3.8	-5.6	-5.4	-2.3	1.5	1.4
Sri Lanka	0.3	38.3	0.8	3.0	7.0	2.5	10.4	12.4	-2.6	14.8	-10.7
Tajikistan	0.4	39.6	...	...	-6.3	-56.4	36.9	-29.1	19.8	55.4	-6.0
Turkmenistan	0.8	70.0	...	...	-1.9	-21.2	-31.8	8.1	11.4	20.0	19.3
Uzbekistan	2.3	47.8	...	...	-9.0	22.6	-8.4	-9.7	-13.3	-6.2	49.3
South-Eastern Asia	*11.0*	*35.7*	*10.4*	*6.8*	*7.7*	*4.9*	*3.9*	*-15.1*	*-6.4*	*21.5*	*-4.3*
Brunei Darussalam	0.1	38.6	7.6	7.9	-0.7	19.0	3.0	2.0	-3.1	-1.4	6.9
Cambodia	0.0	8.1	-7.3	-1.1	11.7	-4.7	6.8	7.5	17.6	17.5	12.6
Indonesia	2.7	23.7	17.8	3.7	4.9	6.9	14.7	-5.3	-40.7	21.1	8.1
Lao People's Democratic Republic	0.0	39.6	0.3	25.5	6.4	17.6	8.8	20.7	7.3	14.0	10.6
Malaysia	3.1	72.4	12.0	9.2	11.6	4.9	5.8	-18.8	10.6	24.4	-8.6
Myanmar	0.1	3.6	0.0	-5.1	6.7	-7.4	2.6	5.4	-10.9	0.1	12.6
Philippines	1.4	33.3	7.2	5.0	6.8	16.7	13.5	-14.7	-2.8	4.0	-0.8
Thailand	3.5	41.6	7.1	9.2	6.1	-0.6	-11.3	-21.6	10.5	27.3	-8.3
Western Asia	*16.7*	*32.4*	*13.2*	*0.8*	*5.5*	*9.5*	*8.3*	*4.8*	*-0.7*	*14.2*	*-0.6*
Armenia	0.7	46.3	...	...	-13.1	-0.6	11.6	-4.9	-1.9	7.2	2.1
Azerbaijan	0.8	39.2	...	...	11.9	37.9	18.1	15.4	-0.4	17.3	48.0
Bahrain	0.4	90.3	11.8	0.1	1.7	2.5	1.4	2.5	-4.9	7.0	2.0
Cyprus	0.3	57.0	6.5	7.1	1.8	6.7	-0.5	7.8	-1.9	10.2	4.2
Georgia	1.0	45.7	...	...	-12.3	27.0	40.6	-8.1	6.1	6.6	2.2
Iraq	0.7	17.8	18.0	-4.1	-12.4	220.6	120.0	25.8	21.0	20.1	25.4
Israel	1.9	34.7	5.6	3.3	9.2	7.3	4.0	1.7	16.1	11.4	-4.9
Jordan	0.4	92.7	16.2	2.1	2.6	9.3	-5.3	-7.1	2.3	5.0	5.3
Kuwait	1.0	57.8	18.4	1.0	1.2	10.9	-2.0	17.3	-9.8	24.1	5.9
Lebanon	0.3	90.8	4.7	-3.6	-1.2	-4.9	-8.9	-10.7	-1.3	-1.1	2.9
Oman	0.3	27.6	13.6	-1.2	7.2	10.0	13.0	13.6	-13.8	5.5	12.8
Qatar	0.2	32.1	14.0	-2.1	1.2	-0.6	-0.9	-2.6	-24.2	51.2	-0.9
Saudi Arabia	4.0	39.4	15.4	-1.7	-3.5	-11.1	0.3	4.0	-13.3	12.1	-0.7
Syrian Arab Republic	0.4	28.0	10.3	1.0	1.1	-4.1	-1.6	-6.3	11.5	-2.4	11.3
Turkey	2.6	17.6	3.1	12.6	10.8	20.5	22.4	2.3	-3.7	25.4	-24.8
United Arab Emirates	1.4	40.8	34.0	1.5	9.8	8.9	3.6	1.8	3.5	1.7	1.7
Yemen	0.3	19.5	...	...	5.1	1.9	1.4	17.2	3.8	2.1	6.0
Yemen Arab Republic (Former)	...	...	20.3	-2.1	...	...	...	...	...	...	...
Yemen Democratic (Former)	...	...	6.1	2.5	...	...	...	...	...	...	...
EUROPE	**50.2**	**27.0**	**5.2**	**4.1**	**6.0**	**5.0**	**9.8**	**9.9**	**6.4**	**11.6**	**1.8**
Eastern Europe	*7.7*	*22.8*	*7.1*	*4.8*	*11.5*	*16.1*	*12.2*	*9.3*	*-2.7*	*18.7*	*6.9*
Belarus	1.3	43.6	...	...	-10.2	10.8	26.5	-1.9	-0.2	13.4	12.4
Bulgaria	0.3	37.5	7.1	3.6	0.4	-1.9	10.9	12.1	9.3	18.6	13.0
Czech Republic	0.7	42.6	...	0.8	9.2	13.4	8.1	6.6	5.4	17.0	13.6
Hungary [3]	0.4	25.7	6.5	1.4	9.2	6.2	24.6	22.8	13.3	19.4	6.1
Poland	0.6	21.5	6.7	0.2	13.2	28.0	21.4	18.5	1.0	15.6	-0.1
Republic of Moldova	0.4	51.0	...	...	-8.9	2.5	2.3	-9.8	-12.2	19.9	2.6
Romania	0.5	26.2	8.3	-0.5	4.1	23.3	13.2	-3.6	-28.8	37.9	9.8
Slovakia	0.2	34.2	...	0.7	7.6	19.8	13.8	16.9	-6.3	10.2	11.7
Ukraine	3.2	28.7	...	...	-12.2	15.8	-4.0	2.0	-10.7	23.0	0.0
Northern Europe	*22.6*	*29.0*	*4.0*	*4.4*	*5.8*	*8.4*	*11.2*	*10.9*	*6.5*	*12.1*	*1.9*
Denmark	1.8	30.8	3.3	3.3	4.8	3.5	10.0	8.9	5.5	11.3	1.9
Estonia	0.3	49.9	...	...	2.9	7.5	29.7	12.6	-5.8	28.9	0.5
Finland	1.5	24.2	4.1	4.9	3.4	5.9	11.2	7.9	3.5	16.9	-0.2
Iceland	0.1	33.1	6.9	2.3	5.0	16.7	8.5	23.4	4.2	8.0	-9.0
Ireland	1.1	52.4	7.8	4.1	12.0	12.5	16.8	25.8	12.0	21.2	6.1
Latvia	0.4	49.0	...	...	-6.1	28.5	6.8	19.0	-5.2	4.9	12.6
Lithuania	0.5	60.6	...	...	-1.3	24.4	22.8	4.5	-10.3	4.5	18.6

Table 5.E. Average Rates of Growth of Gross Domestic Product by Expenditure - Imports of Goods and Services

Major area, region and country	Base year weights as percentage of total for world or region in 1990	Base year share as percentage of total GDP in 1990	Average rates of growth			Annual rate of change (percentage)					
			1970-1979	1980-1989	1990-1999	1996	1997	1998	1999	2000	2001
Norway	1.8	33.9	3.0	2.5	4.8	8.8	12.4	8.5	-1.8	2.7	0.9
Sweden	3.1	28.4	2.6	3.7	4.5	3.0	12.5	11.3	4.9	11.5	-3.5
United Kingdom	11.9	26.6	4.5	5.1	5.4	9.6	9.7	9.6	8.7	11.7	2.3
Southern Europe	*18.9*	*22.5*	*5.3*	*5.7*	*7.0*	*4.0*	*12.1*	*10.5*	*7.6*	*9.7*	*1.3*
Albania	0.0	23.2	6.2	2.9	-0.5	2.0	-6.1	9.4	12.1	2.0	3.3
Andorra	0.0	19.7	12.4	12.5	14.3	13.3	18.6	18.6	17.9	14.7	8.3
Bosnia and Herzegovina	0.3	56.3	...	...	6.8	48.4	30.0	20.0	19.3	10.7	7.4
Croatia	0.9	81.1	...	...	-5.7	6.8	25.1	-4.9	-3.5	3.7	9.4
Greece	1.1	27.9	7.8	5.1	6.0	7.0	14.2	9.2	3.8	14.5	-3.4
Holy See	0.0	19.7	5.5	5.3	5.1	-0.4	10.3	8.9	5.4	9.5	0.2
Italy	9.8	19.7	4.5	5.0	5.0	-0.3	10.1	8.9	5.3	9.4	0.2
Malta	0.1	98.9	4.0	4.0	5.1	-6.4	-1.5	2.5	10.1	10.5	0.3
Portugal	1.3	39.5	4.4	6.4	8.2	4.9	10.0	14.2	8.5	5.4	0.3
San Marino	0.0	19.7	8.0	0.8	29.5	-8.1	1064.1	-8.1	7.0	20.0	-0.9
Serbia and Montenegro	0.2	13.5	...	...	-0.7	152.5	3.1	22.6	-28.3	11.1	-7.5
Slovenia	0.6	78.5	...	...	2.1	2.1	11.9	10.4	8.2	6.1	2.1
Spain	4.5	19.7	6.7	8.1	9.0	8.0	13.2	13.2	12.7	10.6	3.5
TFYR Macedonia	0.1	35.9	...	...	3.1	-8.6	26.4	7.4	0.1	24.0	-16.0
Yugoslavia (Former)	...	...	7.8	2.5	...	...	...	...	...	...	...
Western Europe	*50.9*	*29.9*	*5.6*	*3.5*	*5.3*	*3.0*	*8.0*	*9.3*	*6.9*	*11.4*	*1.4*
Austria	2.8	38.4	7.2	3.4	5.8	4.9	12.0	5.7	9.0	11.6	5.9
Belgium	6.1	68.9	6.0	3.3	4.2	2.5	5.1	7.5	4.1	8.4	0.8
France	12.2	22.2	6.0	3.9	4.8	1.6	6.9	11.6	6.2	14.6	1.3
Germany	18.9	25.2	5.7	3.2	6.0	3.1	8.3	9.1	8.5	10.5	1.0
Liechtenstein	0.0	35.7	6.1	5.2	4.1	3.6	8.7	10.9	6.6	11.8	1.6
Luxembourg	0.5	100.3	3.5	5.0	7.6	7.6	13.9	15.3	13.3	14.1	5.4
Monaco	0.0	22.2	6.5	4.7	5.5	2.3	7.6	12.3	6.9	15.0	0.7
Netherlands	6.7	50.6	4.6	3.1	5.9	4.4	9.5	8.5	5.8	10.6	1.9
Switzerland	3.7	35.7	4.5	4.4	3.4	2.7	7.6	9.6	5.3	10.6	-0.2
OCEANIA	**1.6**	**19.6**	**3.5**	**6.1**	**6.0**	**8.9**	**8.1**	**3.7**	**11.9**	**-1.0**	**2.2**
Australia & New Zealand	*89.2*	*18.1*	*3.7*	*6.2*	*6.5*	*9.3*	*8.5*	*4.4*	*12.3*	*-1.1*	*2.3*
Australia	72.9	16.8	3.8	6.7	6.7	9.9	9.7	4.8	12.5	-1.3	2.3
New Zealand	16.3	26.8	3.1	4.2	5.5	6.5	2.6	2.0	11.4	-0.4	2.1
Melanesia	*8.9*	*84.5*	*2.8*	*5.9*	*1.1*	*4.2*	*3.3*	*-6.1*	*6.9*	*0.3*	*-0.6*
Fiji	1.3	67.2	7.7	4.3	3.5	4.9	-3.4	6.8	14.9	-1.6	-2.3
New Caledonia	5.2	147.2	6.5	12.4	0.0	0.5	5.7	-13.9	8.3	1.9	-1.0
Papua New Guinea	2.1	45.4	-0.3	0.3	2.0	10.7	3.2	0.4	1.4	0.6	1.2
Solomon Islands	0.2	56.8	17.1	3.9	-1.3	5.5	-4.1	1.7	-1.1	-14.3	-4.9
Vanuatu	0.2	77.8	7.7	2.9	3.1	-0.6	1.7	-0.4	15.0	-7.3	-0.5
Micronesia	*0.3*	*53.6*	*5.2*	*3.9*	*0.4*	*-6.0*	*-4.1*	*1.1*	*1.2*	*-0.6*	*1.0*
Kiribati	0.0	33.1	2.9	-4.9	4.2	3.0	5.7	5.0	6.2	0.2	1.8
Marshall Islands	0.1	147.2	11.6	14.2	-1.9	-15.9	-11.2	2.0	0.0	-1.1	1.8
Micronesia (Federated States of)	0.1	33.1	6.6	4.5	1.6	-1.8	-5.1	-2.1	0.9	2.1	1.5
Nauru	0.0	33.1	6.8	4.9	-5.4	-7.3	-7.3	-1.9	-1.9	-1.0	-0.8
Palau	0.0	33.1	2.9	-5.5	4.7	10.9	10.4	3.9	2.8	-3.9	-0.7
Polynesia	*1.7*	*36.1*	*1.8*	*1.8*	*1.7*	*2.2*	*0.4*	*1.9*	*2.6*	*8.3*	*3.5*
Cook Islands	0.1	80.6	0.9	-1.1	-2.5	-11.5	15.4	-8.8	5.8	9.8	3.0
French Polynesia	1.3	31.7	1.0	2.8	1.6	1.6	1.1	1.1	2.7	2.7	2.1
Samoa	0.2	65.1	5.2	-3.1	3.7	7.0	1.6	4.7	12.0	41.5	6.5
Tonga	0.1	65.1	3.5	4.0	0.4	4.3	-14.0	9.6	-17.5	3.2	13.2
Tuvalu	0.0	147.2	11.6	6.1	5.2	10.3	3.5	14.9	3.0	3.0	3.0

Notes for Table 5.E - Imports of goods and services

1/ 1992-2001

'Includes imports of goods plus net imports of services.

2/ 1974-1975

'Excludes Imports of goods.

3/ 1988-1991

'Does not include direct purchases abroad by resident households, except purchase of cars by Hungarian individuals for own use.

Table 6.A. Average Rates of Growth of Gross Domestic Product by Kind of Economic Activity - Agriculture, Hunting, Forestry and Fishing

Major area, region and country	Base year weights as percentage of total for world or region in 1990	Base year share as percentage of total GDP in 1990	Average rates of growth			Annual rate of change (percentage)					
			1970-1979	1980-1989	1990-1999	1996	1997	1998	1999	2000	2001
WORLD	**100.0**	**6.0**	**2.1**	**3.2**	**0.9**	**2.9**	**2.1**	**0.5**	**2.9**	**2.7**	**2.3**
DEVELOPED ECONOMIES	**31.6**	**2.6**	**1.7**	**1.2**	**1.1**	**4.3**	**2.1**	**1.0**	**2.8**	**2.3**	**-1.3**
DEVELOPING ECONOMIES	**43.1**	**14.7**	**2.5**	**3.2**	**3.1**	**4.9**	**1.8**	**3.7**	**1.5**	**1.6**	**3.3**
TRANSITION ECONOMIES	**25.3**	**18.6**	**2.4**	**6.1**	**-5.1**	**-5.4**	**3.1**	**-11.2**	**8.5**	**7.4**	**6.5**
AFRICA	**6.7**	**17.4**	**1.8**	**2.4**	**4.0**	**11.9**	**3.0**	**4.9**	**1.4**	**-0.9**	**6.7**
Eastern Africa	*17.9*	*28.4*	*2.0*	*1.8*	*3.8*	*7.8*	*2.6*	*2.7*	*2.9*	*0.0*	*4.7*
Burundi	0.6	51.2	1.6	2.2	-1.4	-9.8	-1.0	3.2	1.1	2.1	1.6
Comoros	0.1	41.4	2.2	3.6	0.0	2.0	-1.3	-1.3	-1.6	-3.0	-2.2
Djibouti [1]	0.0	2.6	-1.6	2.1	3.1	7.0	1.1	2.0	2.1	1.8	3.2
Eritrea	...	...	...	...	5.7	-6.6	2.4	79.9	0.2	-7.9	3.8
Ethiopia	...	...	...	...	3.3	14.7	3.4	-3.6	4.2	2.9	5.4
Ethiopia (Former)	2.5	27.9	0.9	0.6	0.4	...	...	...	...	...	...
Kenya	2.3	25.0	4.1	3.7	1.2	4.4	1.2	1.6	1.2	-2.0	1.2
Madagascar	1.1	31.8	0.4	-1.6	0.0	2.6	3.1	2.6	-11.3	0.6	2.4
Malawi	0.6	32.8	6.1	0.7	4.5	19.9	0.1	10.3	10.1	5.4	1.1
Mauritius	0.3	10.9	8.5	-1.3	-1.1	5.0	3.3	-1.9	-23.3	32.1	8.8
Mozambique	1.9	64.5	3.9	-0.3	5.6	8.9	8.7	7.3	5.7	-9.1	12.6
Reunion	0.2	3.9	2.7	1.7	3.8	3.0	3.2	3.0	3.1	3.0	3.1
Rwanda	1.2	48.3	4.3	0.8	0.9	19.9	4.1	10.4	8.6	8.8	7.7
Seychelles	0.0	4.8	1.2	-1.4	-0.4	4.6	4.4	0.0	-0.6	0.3	1.1
Somalia	0.8	70.5	1.4	4.0	-4.1	0.5	-4.2	0.3	12.0	3.0	3.0
Uganda	2.1	51.0	-0.9	2.3	3.6	0.2	1.1	7.2	3.0	9.7	4.9
United Republic Of Tanzania	2.0	49.5	1.9	3.8	4.2	2.4	2.2	4.2	4.2	-12.1	2.6
Zambia	0.7	16.7	-1.3	6.5	-0.3	-0.6	-5.1	-6.1	-5.6	-5.8	-5.7
Zimbabwe	1.4	14.8	2.5	2.6	4.0	19.8	3.2	5.1	4.3	1.6	3.4
Middle Africa	*10.2*	*20.7*	*1.4*	*1.9*	*1.4*	*1.1*	*5.4*	*2.5*	*6.2*	*0.4*	*8.9*
Angola	2.0	17.9	0.2	2.0	-0.5	1.9	5.6	6.3	1.3	9.1	18.2
Cameroon [2]	2.7	17.7	4.9	1.3	5.7	-0.8	8.1	-1.9	26.1	1.6	5.5
Central African Republic	0.6	42.9	2.0	2.4	3.6	-1.4	4.5	5.4	18.3	3.3	0.1
Chad	0.7	39.4	-1.2	2.7	4.8	2.8	7.3	10.8	-5.2	-2.7	7.7
Congo	0.4	14.3	3.0	6.1	-3.5	4.9	0.6	-3.2	-13.6	-31.6	21.4
Democratic Republic of the Congo	3.2	31.2	1.6	1.6	-5.2	-0.9	-3.1	0.0	-10.4	-4.3	-4.4
Equatorial Guinea	0.1	51.7	0.9	2.5	17.3	44.9	68.8	18.7	47.2	16.9	53.4
Gabon	0.5	8.0	-5.7	1.3	0.3	6.0	4.6	3.2	-32.6	-18.7	19.4
Sao Tome and Principe	0.0	28.2	8.4	-2.6	4.0	6.6	2.1	4.4	3.2	3.8	3.5
Northern Africa	*40.0*	*15.8*	*2.8*	*3.0*	*5.6*	*18.7*	*2.5*	*7.2*	*-1.0*	*-4.5*	*7.9*
Algeria	7.6	11.3	2.4	5.2	2.1	21.3	-13.5	11.4	0.0	-22.0	13.2
Egypt	12.5	16.2	4.6	4.1	3.6	2.0	3.6	3.5	3.4	3.7	3.6
Libyan Arab Jamahiriya	2.2	7.2	4.0	3.8	12.1	1.1	6.6	0.6	-2.9	1.7	2.7
Morocco	5.0	17.7	1.1	4.9	-1.3	78.0	-26.5	27.9	-16.7	-14.7	27.3
Sudan	10.6	29.1	1.8	0.4	10.0	24.8	15.2	7.1	-1.8	-2.7	8.6
Tunisia	2.1	15.7	5.3	1.0	6.1	29.5	3.0	-1.0	11.0	-1.0	-1.5
Southern Africa	*5.8*	*4.5*	*3.9*	*3.2*	*-0.4*	*22.2*	*0.1*	*-5.3*	*4.8*	*6.6*	*-3.4*
Botswana	0.2	4.7	6.7	2.1	-0.2	6.6	-7.5	5.9	-7.6	-8.8	4.8
Lesotho	0.1	19.5	5.3	-0.7	1.1	17.7	0.6	3.1	4.4	2.8	2.8
Namibia	0.3	10.6	10.0	-0.8	4.7	9.1	-6.5	6.1	6.2	8.2	-10.4
South Africa	5.1	4.2	3.5	3.6	-0.8	24.0	0.8	-6.8	5.1	7.3	-3.1
Swaziland	0.1	10.6	2.3	3.0	0.4	21.5	-1.3	1.9	8.2	-4.1	-8.5
Western Africa	*26.1*	*32.9*	*0.2*	*1.8*	*3.0*	*4.3*	*3.9*	*4.5*	*3.2*	*3.8*	*7.0*
Benin	0.8	40.0	3.6	5.8	5.3	4.8	3.6	3.8	11.3	6.4	3.1
Burkina Faso	1.3	43.4	4.4	2.7	3.0	4.9	-4.4	-4.2	13.6	1.8	15.0
Cape Verde	0.0	14.4	1.2	4.0	2.4	38.4	-5.1	2.7	11.7	3.6	21.4
Cote d'Ivoire	3.8	29.5	4.9	0.1	2.1	4.5	4.0	8.8	-8.9	6.0	22.3
Gambia	0.1	22.5	2.3	2.8	7.3	1.0	3.2	1.2	95.8	9.0	7.7
Ghana	3.0	44.8	1.1	0.8	3.1	5.2	3.8	2.6	6.9	2.1	4.0
Guinea	0.0	20.2	2.0	2.4	3.1	5.4	6.8	5.4	3.7	6.0	3.0
Guinea-Bissau	0.1	44.6	0.3	2.3	2.8	5.2	14.9	-20.3	8.1	4.7	8.5
Liberia	0.2	54.3	3.1	-5.4	1.0	30.8	69.7	31.3	19.8	21.9	5.5
Mali	1.2	45.8	-0.1	2.3	3.1	3.6	7.9	5.9	-7.4	-7.3	15.5
Mauritania	0.3	27.2	-3.0	0.5	4.4	0.2	5.0	6.4	9.1	1.5	5.6
Niger	1.1	41.6	4.6	0.4	2.4	0.2	2.6	21.1	-5.0	-8.4	-6.7
Nigeria	11.4	32.4	-2.7	3.2	3.5	4.1	4.2	4.0	5.2	5.2	3.1

Table 6.A. Average Rates of Growth of Gross Domestic Product by Kind of Economic Activity - Agriculture, Hunting, Forestry and Fishing

Major area, region and country	Base year weights as percentage of total for world or region in 1990	Base year share as percentage of total GDP in 1990	Average rates of growth 1970-1979	1980-1989	1990-1999	Annual rate of change (percentage) 1996	1997	1998	1999	2000	2001
Senegal	1.2	19.9	1.6	-0.1	1.8	5.8	-1.7	-3.5	5.7	10.7	7.6
Sierra Leone	0.3	36.9	2.6	3.6	-2.7	1.6	7.2	-8.9	-3.9	7.7	8.2
Togo	0.5	28.9	-0.9	-0.2	-0.2	3.1	4.5	-2.8	5.3	-4.6	5.5
AMERICAS	**15.9**	**2.9**	**3.1**	**1.5**	**2.7**	**4.1**	**5.1**	**2.0**	**5.1**	**5.2**	**0.0**
NORTHERN AMERICA	**9.2**	**2.0**	**2.9**	**1.0**	**3.0**	**5.3**	**8.5**	**1.8**	**5.5**	**7.4**	**-2.0**
Bermuda	0.0	0.8	3.7	4.5	1.7	-1.9	9.5	0.0	4.3	0.0	0.0
Canada	7.1	2.7	4.6	2.0	1.1	0.1	-3.4	6.2	6.5	-1.0	-7.3
United States	50.5	1.9	2.7	0.9	3.3	6.0	10.1	1.3	5.4	8.4	-1.4
LATIN AMERICA AND THE CARIBBEAN	**6.8**	**8.0**	**3.3**	**2.2**	**2.4**	**2.7**	**0.7**	**2.2**	**4.4**	**2.0**	**3.0**
Caribbean	*2.7*	*6.6*	*2.5*	*0.8*	*-1.4*	*7.2*	*-0.8*	*-3.1*	*9.7*	*3.0*	*1.0*
Anguilla	0.0	4.5	3.8	7.0	-0.3	0.5	5.1	7.2	-11.4	-7.7	11.7
Antigua and Barbuda	0.0	4.1	-1.8	-1.1	1.8	-2.0	4.8	4.2	3.3	3.3	0.9
Aruba	0.0	0.6	6.3	7.0	1.9	1.4	-4.6	-2.5	2.3	14.7	7.5
Bahamas [3]	0.0	2.3	3.0	3.0	3.0	2.9	15.3	6.9	9.4	8.4	7.9
Barbados	0.0	4.6	1.1	-2.6	-0.3	18.9	-1.6	-12.9	7.4	6.9	-9.7
British Virgin Islands	0.0	3.3	1.5	2.7	-2.8	14.3	0.0	0.0	0.0	0.0	0.0
Cayman Islands	0.0	0.3	-5.8	-0.5	-0.9	3.6	-2.8	-0.3	0.1	0.1	0.1
Cuba	1.0	11.4	3.4	0.0	-5.2	17.5	-0.2	-5.2	10.3	11.6	-1.7
Dominica	0.0	21.5	-2.6	2.1	-0.8	5.5	-1.5	-2.0	-2.1	-1.1	-11.4
Dominican Republic	0.5	12.3	3.3	1.7	1.7	1.6	3.3	1.1	6.7	5.0	5.1
Grenada	0.0	13.2	1.8	-0.8	-4.2	-12.4	-2.7	4.6	10.1	2.2	0.2
Guadeloupe	0.1	6.7	1.0	3.2	0.3	4.3	9.2	4.1	5.9	5.9	5.9
Haiti	0.4	34.9	1.6	1.2	-2.9	-0.4	-1.9	2.1	2.5	-3.6	0.6
Jamaica	0.1	6.8	1.5	-0.7	3.2	3.2	-14.3	-0.1	1.7	-11.6	0.4
Martinique	0.1	5.6	1.5	2.1	0.6	1.6	1.6	4.1	2.5	2.5	2.5
Montserrat	0.0	2.2	6.8	-3.6	-16.0	-33.7	-81.3	-33.3	7.6	46.5	-17.3
Netherlands Antilles	0.0	0.7	3.3	1.1	0.7	-15.3	0.4	-4.9	-4.8	-5.2	-3.1
Puerto Rico	0.2	1.4	1.8	1.6	1.6	20.9	-6.5	-24.0	50.7	-9.6	1.2
Saint Kitts and Nevis	0.0	5.4	1.6	-2.3	-0.2	15.8	13.7	-8.9	-9.8	-10.9	12.3
Saint Lucia	0.0	12.4	6.0	5.0	-2.0	0.8	-17.9	3.9	14.8	14.0	-24.4
Saint Vincent and the Grenadines	0.0	17.9	2.9	6.4	-1.8	-3.7	-15.2	7.5	-4.2	7.2	-6.8
Trinidad and Tobago	0.1	2.5	-1.2	0.1	2.7	3.2	4.0	-16.9	18.2	0.4	-7.0
Central America	*11.2*	*8.3*	*3.1*	*1.3*	*2.3*	*3.5*	*0.8*	*3.0*	*1.9*	*1.3*	*1.7*
Belize	0.0	18.2	3.6	2.4	6.8	6.6	13.0	-1.8	11.7	4.4	8.1
Costa Rica	0.4	11.3	2.9	2.8	4.2	1.8	1.5	8.2	4.5	0.7	0.7
El Salvador	0.4	17.1	3.9	-1.9	2.3	1.3	0.4	-0.7	7.7	-3.1	-2.1
Guatemala	0.9	25.9	5.0	1.0	2.9	2.5	2.8	3.2	2.1	2.6	1.2
Honduras	0.3	20.0	2.8	2.8	1.5	2.5	4.2	-1.9	-8.5	9.8	-0.1
Mexico	8.6	7.2	3.0	1.4	2.0	3.8	0.2	3.0	1.5	0.6	1.9
Nicaragua	0.3	29.7	0.0	2.4	4.4	7.1	8.3	3.5	7.5	12.7	3.7
Panama	0.2	9.5	2.0	2.3	2.2	1.1	0.0	6.3	2.1	1.6	0.8
South America	*28.5*	*8.1*	*3.5*	*2.7*	*2.7*	*2.0*	*0.7*	*2.2*	*5.0*	*2.2*	*3.6*
Argentina	5.3	8.1	2.9	-0.1	3.8	-1.2	0.5	8.7	2.5	-1.8	1.0
Bolivia	0.3	15.4	4.5	1.4	3.1	6.7	4.5	-4.4	2.5	3.6	1.2
Brazil	13.4	6.7	4.2	3.8	2.3	3.1	-0.8	1.3	8.0	3.0	5.1
Chile	1.0	6.7	2.1	5.5	4.9	2.8	3.4	2.3	0.0	6.7	6.5
Colombia	3.8	17.6	4.6	2.6	1.5	-1.2	0.7	0.0	0.0	5.0	0.1
Ecuador	1.0	20.1	2.8	4.1	4.8	7.6	10.0	-3.0	9.1	-0.1	0.7
French Guiana	0.1	10.0	5.7	9.7	-0.6	1.6	1.3	0.3	1.1	1.1	1.1
Guyana	0.1	38.1	0.9	-1.0	6.3	5.1	4.0	-6.6	15.8	-9.0	3.6
Paraguay	0.7	27.8	6.5	4.6	2.4	1.4	5.2	0.2	3.2	-4.4	10.5
Peru	1.2	8.4	0.1	2.2	4.0	4.5	5.0	0.7	12.6	6.4	6.5
Suriname	0.1	9.9	17.8	0.6	-0.8	1.3	-2.6	-6.4	4.0	6.6	10.8
Uruguay	0.4	11.3	-1.0	1.7	2.3	9.6	-6.1	6.5	-8.7	-3.0	-5.1
Venezuela	1.2	5.4	3.1	2.4	0.7	2.0	2.4	0.6	-2.1	2.4	2.6
ASIA	**39.7**	**9.7**	**2.0**	**3.2**	**3.1**	**2.9**	**1.4**	**2.6**	**1.0**	**2.1**	**2.4**
Eastern Asia	*39.1*	*5.4*	*1.8*	*3.0*	*1.7*	*3.9*	*0.8*	*0.4*	*1.1*	*2.1*	*1.9*
China	19.3	27.4	2.4	5.3	4.4	5.1	3.5	3.5	2.8	2.4	2.6
Democratic People's Rep. of Korea	0.7	21.8	11.9	8.1	-3.2	-3.6	-6.3	-1.1	6.2	1.3	3.7
Hong Kong SAR of China [4]	0.0	0.2	8.8	7.2	3.8	4.3	5.1	-5.0	3.4	10.2	-2.6

Table 6.A. Average Rates of Growth of Gross Domestic Product by Kind of Economic Activity - Agriculture, Hunting, Forestry and Fishing

Major area, region and country	Base year weights as percentage of total for world or region in 1990	Base year share as percentage of total GDP in 1990	Average rates of growth 1970-1979	1980-1989	1990-1999	Annual rate of change (percentage) 1996	1997	1998	1999	2000	2001
Japan	13.8	2.5	0.5	0.7	-2.8	2.4	-6.2	-3.1	-5.6	1.6	0.4
Mongolia	0.1	15.6	5.7	14.9	1.6	4.4	4.3	7.0	4.2	-14.4	-16.0
Republic of Korea	3.9	8.5	4.0	1.7	1.4	3.3	4.6	-6.6	5.4	2.0	1.9
South Central Asia	*36.8*	*26.2*	*1.8*	*3.9*	*4.7*	*3.9*	*2.7*	*3.9*	*1.3*	*0.6*	*4.3*
Afghanistan	0.5	51.9	4.2	-2.6	-0.9	6.6	13.3	5.2	-12.4	-43.7	0.0
Bangladesh	1.7	29.7	-0.3	2.4	3.1	6.0	3.2	4.7	7.4	3.1	2.8
Bhutan	0.0	42.0	6.4	6.7	3.4	6.4	4.1	2.8	5.4	5.1	6.7
India	16.8	28.2	0.3	4.4	2.9	9.6	-2.4	6.2	1.3	-0.2	5.7
Iran (Islamic Republic of)	6.1	17.5	8.1	4.0	3.2	0.0	9.0	6.4	-9.6	2.8	4.7
Kazakhstan	4.5	34.1	...	...	-7.2	-5.0	-0.9	-19.3	21.2	-3.2	17.1
Kyrgyzstan	0.8	32.9	...	...	0.4	15.2	12.3	2.9	8.2	2.6	7.3
Maldives	0.0	16.6	6.8	6.9	0.1	1.9	1.9	-5.1	2.9	-1.5	7.0
Nepal	0.3	48.8	0.8	3.5	2.5	4.4	4.1	1.0	2.7	7.1	4.0
Pakistan	2.0	22.8	2.9	4.0	4.4	0.1	4.5	1.9	6.1	-2.6	1.4
Sri Lanka [5]	0.3	22.9	2.8	1.3	2.9	-4.1	3.1	2.4	5.9	2.2	-3.8
Tajikistan	0.6	30.1	...	...	-17.1	-16.3	-16.6	-17.4	-30.7	22.6	10.2
Turkmenistan	0.2	10.9	...	...	6.3	-16.7	41.1	31.9	19.7	19.9	19.1
Uzbekistan	3.0	33.4	...	...	-2.2	-18.9	32.6	-1.0	13.1	8.7	-17.2
South-Eastern Asia	*11.8*	*18.0*	*3.7*	*3.1*	*2.4*	*3.9*	*1.7*	*-1.1*	*4.6*	*4.5*	*0.6*
Brunei Darussalam	0.0	2.4	4.8	3.6	2.5	5.1	5.5	3.4	3.4	1.8	2.3
Cambodia	0.2	50.9	-7.3	-0.3	3.4	2.3	5.5	3.0	0.0	-0.3	3.9
Indonesia	4.1	19.4	3.7	3.7	2.4	3.1	1.0	-1.3	2.2	1.7	0.6
Lao People's Democratic Republic	0.1	60.7	0.1	5.8	5.0	2.8	7.0	3.1	8.2	4.9	3.8
Malaysia	1.2	15.2	7.7	3.9	0.1	4.5	0.7	-2.8	0.5	2.0	1.8
Myanmar	2.0	57.3	4.3	2.1	4.7	5.0	3.7	2.8	11.5	10.9	4.8
Philippines	1.8	21.9	4.0	1.5	1.4	3.8	3.1	-6.4	6.5	3.4	3.7
Singapore	0.0	0.2	1.9	-5.6	6.9	9.2	14.3	-2.8	5.9	10.4	-1.5
Thailand	2.0	12.5	4.2	4.3	1.6	4.1	-0.9	-1.5	2.0	4.9	-10.1
Vietnam	0.5	38.7	-0.1	4.2	4.1	4.4	4.3	3.5	5.2	4.0	4.6
Western Asia	*12.3*	*12.7*	*1.7*	*2.8*	*3.9*	*-4.2*	*-1.3*	*10.5*	*-4.2*	*4.5*	*0.4*
Armenia	0.4	15.9	...	...	0.1	2.0	-4.5	12.8	1.4	-1.0	23.2
Azerbaijan	1.1	26.5	...	...	-5.8	3.0	-6.9	6.2	11.4	11.0	9.9
Bahrain	0.0	0.8	11.2	-1.0	4.0	12.9	-7.5	-0.7	2.7	6.0	-2.5
Cyprus	0.1	6.9	-2.4	3.0	-0.3	-5.9	-7.7	7.2	11.0	-9.1	7.4
Georgia	1.2	30.1	...	...	-12.4	-11.8	-3.5	-5.4	-4.5	-16.6	6.6
Iraq [6]	1.4	19.8	1.7	3.7	4.9	-26.9	-4.0	20.4	-7.3	8.2	2.7
Israel	0.3	2.9	4.0	-2.2	-1.6	9.1	0.2	9.6	-3.0	6.5	4.5
Jordan	0.1	7.1	4.1	9.0	1.5	3.5	-8.5	13.1	-5.2	5.8	4.5
Kuwait	0.0	0.9	0.0	16.4	-1.1	0.7	13.8	-4.3	8.9	-26.5	-2.8
Lebanon	0.0	8.8	-1.6	-6.7	9.1	2.5	-0.5	2.1	-2.0	-1.3	-0.3
Oman	0.1	2.6	4.5	9.0	4.8	-0.6	9.3	-0.6	6.8	-5.3	-19.6
Qatar	0.0	0.8	12.4	1.9	0.7	-7.3	-2.6	-14.0	16.2	1.9	-0.7
Saudi Arabia	1.2	6.4	-4.7	14.8	0.3	-13.8	3.0	1.0	2.3	3.9	0.8
Syrian Arab Republic	0.7	28.3	7.5	1.5	6.9	14.6	-2.9	22.3	-15.1	9.2	7.5
Turkey	4.8	17.5	1.7	0.6	1.5	4.4	-2.0	8.4	-5.0	3.9	-6.1
United Arab Emirates	0.1	1.6	28.4	10.7	9.4	11.8	8.8	5.6	1.0	4.9	1.9
Yemen	0.6	24.9	...	...	4.6	1.9	8.8	13.7	0.2	3.7	2.0
Yemen Arab Republic (Former)	...	...	2.9	2.8	...	...	...	...	...	...	...
Yemen Democratic (Former)	...	...	-4.3	6.4	...	...	...	...	...	...	...
EUROPE	**36.5**	**5.6**	**1.9**	**4.1**	**-2.9**	**-0.1**	**1.3**	**-4.7**	**4.7**	**3.2**	**2.0**
Eastern Europe	*51.5*	*17.1*	*2.3*	*6.3*	*-7.7*	*-5.8*	*1.6*	*-13.3*	*7.3*	*8.5*	*7.9*
Belarus	3.0	22.9	...	...	-4.6	1.5	-5.6	-1.0	-7.6	9.2	1.4
Bulgaria	0.7	17.7	7.1	-0.8	2.7	-9.4	35.3	1.2	5.5	-10.3	0.5
Czech Republic	0.5	7.7	...	0.1	5.0	6.8	-2.5	10.3	15.3	-1.4	-0.9
Czechoslovakia (Former)	...	...	-0.4	...	...	...	...	...	...	...	...
Hungary [7]	0.8	11.4	4.9	0.1	-10.4	4.1	-0.5	-1.5	0.9	-7.9	5.6
Poland	1.0	8.9	0.5	0.3	0.4	2.5	1.0	5.7	-1.6	-6.9	-7.9
Republic of Moldova	1.3	34.6	...	...	-11.3	-12.3	15.0	-6.2	-4.1	2.3	7.4
Romania	1.7	21.8	5.8	-0.5	-0.6	-2.4	4.1	-20.1	-12.4	-27.4	25.1
Russian Federation	29.8	15.5	...	...	-5.4	-6.1	1.9	-18.3	16.3	12.0	10.2
Slovakia	0.3	8.2	...	1.7	-6.6	-2.1	9.7	5.4	0.3	-2.0	10.2
Ukraine	12.3	24.6	...	...	-7.1	-9.4	-1.0	-11.1	-4.0	12.3	6.1
USSR (Former)	...	...	2.2	6.9	...	...	...	...	...	...	...
Northern Europe	*11.3*	*3.3*	*1.9*	*2.0*	*1.1*	*-0.5*	*2.0*	*-1.4*	*0.2*	*2.1*	*-4.6*
Denmark	1.0	3.8	3.5	3.8	2.3	2.5	2.2	4.0	0.1	0.8	1.3
Estonia	0.3	14.3	...	...	-4.8	-0.5	6.4	-0.6	-3.4	-2.8	4.0
Finland	1.5	5.5	3.8	0.1	0.3	-2.0	13.1	-7.9	0.8	13.0	-4.9

Table 6.A. Average Rates of Growth of Gross Domestic Product by Kind of Economic Activity - Agriculture, Hunting, Forestry and Fishing

Major area, region and country	Base year weights as percentage of total for world or region in 1990	Base year share as percentage of total GDP in 1990	Average rates of growth			Annual rate of change (percentage)					
			1970-1979	1980-1989	1990-1999	1996	1997	1998	1999	2000	2001
Iceland	0.1	10.3	5.7	2.6	-1.3	4.0	-1.7	-5.8	-1.1	-2.9	-1.7
Ireland	0.8	8.2	4.0	-1.1	-3.2	1.0	-10.2	-5.2	-10.0	3.4	-1.5
Latvia	0.8	21.1	...	...	-7.8	-7.1	6.6	-3.5	-3.5	11.4	5.4
Lithuania	1.1	26.7	...	...	-14.3	14.6	8.6	-2.6	-12.3	4.9	-4.9
Norway	0.7	3.1	0.4	1.0	2.3	-2.6	1.5	2.3	-0.7	1.3	-2.0
Sweden	1.5	3.1	-0.8	2.1	-1.1	-0.8	1.6	-5.3	2.2	3.0	-0.8
United Kingdom	3.4	1.7	1.6	3.5	0.3	-0.9	-0.9	1.7	3.2	-3.2	-11.6
Southern Europe	*17.9*	*4.8*	*1.3*	*1.0*	*2.3*	*6.5*	*1.6*	*-0.4*	*4.0*	*-0.5*	*-1.6*
Albania	0.2	40.2	7.2	1.2	2.8	3.0	1.0	5.0	3.7	4.5	4.1
Andorra	0.0	4.7	7.9	6.9	3.9	23.3	7.5	3.7	-0.7	6.0	4.1
Bosnia and Herzegovina	0.6	24.8	...	...	4.6	25.4	14.7	-24.9	106.7	10.7	7.4
Croatia	0.5	9.7	...	...	-1.8	1.1	2.3	5.6	-2.6	1.2	0.7
Greece	1.6	9.8	1.5	1.7	0.3	-3.3	0.4	2.3	6.8	-5.4	-3.0
Holy See	0.0	3.2	1.2	0.3	1.8	1.9	1.3	1.2	5.9	-2.8	-1.0
Italy	7.1	3.2	0.3	0.0	1.7	1.9	1.1	1.2	5.8	-2.9	-1.0
Malta	0.0	3.1	4.3	3.4	0.4	9.6	4.0	-3.3	-6.8	-4.1	6.1
Portugal	1.1	7.6	2.3	0.7	0.4	6.1	-8.1	-3.4	7.2	-4.4	-1.5
San Marino	0.0	3.2	0.6	-3.1	0.1	0.6	-1.6	2.8	6.7	-3.6	0.4
Serbia and Montenegro	1.1	18.1	...	...	-0.8	1.2	6.5	-3.0	-6.8	10.8	-7.4
Slovenia	0.2	5.0	...	...	-1.0	1.1	-2.9	3.1	-2.1	-1.0	-2.1
Spain	5.3	5.2	2.6	2.4	1.5	17.6	2.6	-0.6	-5.0	1.6	-3.1
TFYR Macedonia	0.1	7.5	...	...	0.7	-2.1	-0.4	3.0	0.7	-5.7	1.3
Yugoslavia (Former)	...	...	2.0	0.6	...	...	...	...	...	...	...
Western Europe	*19.4*	*2.6*	*1.4*	*1.6*	*2.1*	*3.8*	*0.1*	*3.4*	*4.0*	*-0.4*	*-0.8*
Austria	1.1	3.3	1.8	1.6	4.1	5.8	-2.6	7.7	3.3	-1.6	-0.7
Belgium	0.9	2.3	0.5	2.6	2.7	-2.4	3.6	4.9	6.7	-1.2	-4.0
France	8.3	3.4	1.3	1.0	2.1	5.1	1.7	1.7	3.7	-0.8	-0.6
Germany	5.2	1.6	1.1	1.8	1.7	6.6	-0.3	2.3	3.4	0.1	1.1
Liechtenstein	0.0	3.0	1.7	0.8	0.2	1.2	2.8	3.8	2.2	1.6	0.8
Luxembourg	0.0	1.8	0.5	0.5	-1.8	-1.7	-3.5	-12.6	26.5	-4.4	-9.6
Monaco	0.0	3.4	1.7	2.6	2.5	5.8	2.4	2.4	3.6	-13.3	4.2
Netherlands	2.4	4.1	4.1	4.1	3.2	-2.0	-5.3	9.3	6.4	0.5	-3.4
Switzerland	1.4	3.0	0.2	0.0	-0.5	0.3	1.7	2.6	0.9	0.7	-0.6
OCEANIA	**1.2**	**4.3**	**2.6**	**2.0**	**2.9**	**7.9**	**-0.9**	**1.1**	**6.9**	**-2.3**	**8.9**
Australia & New Zealand	*87.4*	*3.9*	*2.8*	*2.2*	*3.2*	*8.1*	*-0.5*	*2.8*	*7.1*	*-2.8*	*10.3*
Australia	69.5	3.5	3.0	1.9	3.0	8.2	-0.9	4.8	6.9	-4.1	12.4
New Zealand	17.9	6.5	1.7	3.6	3.8	7.7	0.7	-4.4	7.6	2.2	2.8
Melanesia	*10.8*	*22.7*	*2.0*	*1.2*	*1.3*	*8.0*	*-3.0*	*-10.3*	*6.4*	*1.3*	*-0.8*
Fiji	1.7	19.6	3.2	2.5	0.0	1.8	-13.0	-7.2	16.1	-1.2	-2.4
New Caledonia	2.5	15.6	1.7	3.2	-2.2	5.2	-11.2	-4.0	11.7	-0.7	-1.3
Papua New Guinea	6.0	28.8	1.6	-0.3	3.3	11.0	2.0	-14.0	4.3	2.8	1.2
Solomon Islands	0.5	36.6	5.0	1.5	3.6	3.5	-1.0	-2.2	-7.5	-1.7	-14.6
Vanuatu	0.2	20.7	7.7	1.1	2.1	4.5	3.3	9.1	-9.3	2.5	-14.9
Micronesia	*0.4*	*14.5*	*5.5*	*1.2*	*-2.1*	*-5.7*	*-18.3*	*10.7*	*1.6*	*-7.3*	*1.1*
Kiribati	0.0	18.6	2.9	-6.7	-0.5	-14.6	6.0	8.8	7.9	2.5	1.8
Marshall Islands	0.1	13.5	6.6	6.1	-0.5	-20.9	-9.0	-1.2	2.1	-4.3	2.2
Micronesia (Federated States of)	0.2	18.6	6.6	2.6	-1.8	2.4	-22.7	14.5	-2.2	-9.4	1.5
Nauru	0.1	18.6	6.8	3.1	-8.5	-3.4	-24.5	14.8	-4.9	-12.2	-0.8
Palau	0.0	3.8	2.9	-5.5	5.2	-25.3	-15.4	2.3	39.4	-4.6	-1.6
Polynesia	*1.4*	*6.6*	*1.6*	*2.9*	*1.3*	*0.2*	*0.8*	*0.0*	*-0.7*	*4.7*	*1.4*
Cook Islands	0.1	21.2	1.0	0.3	-2.5	4.3	12.2	-18.1	-27.5	32.4	12.7
French Polynesia	0.8	4.5	1.8	4.3	1.9	1.6	1.1	1.1	2.7	2.7	2.1
Samoa	0.2	17.4	3.1	0.4	0.7	3.2	-6.6	3.4	-3.5	0.3	-4.6
Tonga	0.2	29.9	-0.3	2.4	0.6	-8.2	3.8	-0.1	-3.1	10.8	1.3
Tuvalu	0.0	23.7	6.6	9.5	4.1	-11.1	2.3	1.2	24.3	3.0	3.0

Notes for Table 6.A - Agriculture, hunting, forestry, fishing

1/ 1991-1998
Includes livestock.

2/ 1990-1998
Includes livestock.

3/ 1989-1995
Does not include Hunting and Forestry.

4/ 2000-2001
Refers to Agriculture and fishing only.

5/ 1970-1975
Estimates on processing of tea and rubber are included in the agricultural sector.

6/ 1970-1991
Agricultural services and related activities such as cotton ginning and pressing are included in "Manufacturing".

7/ 1988-1991
Includes veterinary services and excludes operation of irrigation systems (part of Electricity, gas and water).

Table 6.B. Average Rates of Growth of Gross Domestic Product by Kind of Economic Activity - Mining, Manufacturing and Utilities

Major area, region and country	Base year weights as percentage of total for world or region in 1990	Base year share as percentage of total GDP in 1990	Average rates of growth			Annual rate of change (percentage)					
			1970-1979	1980-1989	1990-1999	1996	1997	1998	1999	2000	2001
WORLD	**100.0**	**26.4**	**3.9**	**2.3**	**3.0**	**2.9**	**4.2**	**1.3**	**3.4**	**5.6**	**-0.2**
DEVELOPED ECONOMIES	**69.8**	**24.9**	**3.2**	**2.2**	**1.8**	**1.8**	**3.5**	**1.3**	**2.6**	**4.3**	**-2.7**
DEVELOPING ECONOMIES	**19.3**	**29.0**	**6.4**	**3.0**	**5.9**	**7.0**	**6.5**	**1.9**	**5.0**	**7.9**	**2.5**
TRANSITION ECONOMIES	**10.9**	**35.3**	**7.9**	**1.0**	**-6.2**	**-0.6**	**2.1**	**-1.5**	**5.7**	**10.2**	**17.6**
AFRICA	**2.5**	**28.3**	**4.7**	**1.9**	**1.7**	**3.1**	**3.6**	**2.4**	**6.3**	**8.3**	**1.6**
Eastern Africa	*6.4*	*16.5*	*2.6*	*2.8*	*2.2*	*6.8*	*5.5*	*4.0*	*3.1*	*-1.7*	*3.6*
Burundi	0.1	17.2	5.8	6.5	-0.8	-7.6	1.0	5.0	3.0	4.0	3.5
Comoros	0.0	5.1	4.7	6.9	1.7	3.6	0.6	0.4	3.7	-2.6	-2.5
Djibouti	0.0	9.4	3.5	-0.4	-1.7	-3.8	-0.8	-12.0	2.6	4.8	7.0
Eritrea	...	...	...	...	5.3	11.3	12.3	-5.1	-0.4	-7.7	3.7
Ethiopia	...	...	...	...	11.9	5.4	7.0	10.5	11.7	3.7	8.7
Ethiopia (Former)	0.5	8.7	3.4	4.1	-8.7	...	...	...	...	...	...
Kenya	0.7	11.6	9.9	4.2	2.6	3.6	2.0	1.7	1.2	-1.4	0.9
Madagascar	0.3	14.0	3.8	5.6	-0.3	3.9	3.6	3.0	-6.2	9.0	0.3
Malawi	0.2	20.0	8.3	3.3	2.4	-4.9	1.5	2.9	4.6	-0.2	-11.7
Mauritius	0.4	24.8	8.4	7.9	5.6	6.7	6.3	6.5	1.7	10.8	5.7
Mozambique	0.3	17.1	3.9	-0.3	8.3	17.4	31.8	28.6	24.1	14.9	24.4
Reunion	0.5	13.4	3.9	5.0	4.3	3.8	3.8	3.6	3.7	3.7	3.7
Rwanda	0.3	18.8	4.9	2.4	-3.4	15.0	20.3	6.1	-3.7	-5.2	7.0
Seychelles	0.0	11.5	15.4	5.6	12.7	20.0	23.8	15.9	5.0	-1.3	-25.7
Somalia	0.0	2.5	3.6	-0.6	2.3	9.7	9.6	9.1	13.8	3.0	3.0
Uganda	0.2	6.4	-10.3	4.1	12.7	15.7	16.9	11.7	9.8	1.1	10.0
United Republic Of Tanzania	0.3	10.0	4.1	-1.5	3.4	4.5	1.7	2.9	2.9	6.0	1.4
Zambia	1.0	38.1	0.0	-0.2	-1.8	4.1	5.5	-2.0	2.1	0.5	1.6
Zimbabwe	1.6	26.9	2.3	3.8	0.7	10.1	-0.6	-1.8	-3.7	-23.6	-6.5
Middle Africa	*9.4*	*31.2*	*1.6*	*5.5*	*1.2*	*5.4*	*2.6*	*3.6*	*6.5*	*8.1*	*1.5*
Angola	2.6	37.8	1.9	4.9	3.1	9.9	7.8	8.8	4.9	2.6	2.7
Cameroon	2.6	27.4	4.2	9.7	0.0	3.1	-3.7	-4.8	53.8	1.6	5.5
Central African Republic	0.1	10.6	2.7	1.1	3.1	0.8	6.7	7.3	-5.8	6.2	4.7
Chad	0.2	18.1	-2.7	6.4	0.6	0.5	10.8	8.8	-4.0	-1.7	12.0
Congo	0.7	39.1	1.8	10.5	6.0	5.2	-0.3	-0.4	50.4	24.8	-2.0
Democratic Republic of the Congo	1.6	25.5	0.1	2.3	-6.5	-3.2	-4.9	-1.8	-10.4	-4.3	-4.4
Equatorial Guinea	0.0	4.6	4.1	-0.3	22.9	45.7	71.7	23.0	40.9	16.9	53.4
Gabon	1.6	44.0	0.6	2.2	2.8	6.2	4.7	6.5	-34.3	26.8	-4.3
Sao Tome and Principe	0.0	8.5	2.2	-2.0	-3.4	1.5	1.2	-2.2	-34.5	-1.5	4.5
Northern Africa	*43.8*	*28.1*	*5.5*	*2.1*	*2.3*	*2.1*	*3.6*	*4.9*	*11.6*	*13.6*	*1.9*
Algeria	14.7	35.5	5.0	3.0	-0.5	-3.8	3.1	4.7	18.8	34.5	-0.1
Egypt	12.9	27.1	4.7	8.6	4.8	4.6	3.2	7.4	6.1	3.3	3.8
Libyan Arab Jamahiriya	6.8	35.8	6.9	-6.0	-2.5	2.9	1.4	0.1	-0.9	0.1	3.1
Morocco	4.7	27.1	5.4	2.6	3.8	4.7	5.3	2.0	2.3	1.8	5.3
Sudan	2.7	11.8	1.5	3.8	8.4	4.6	6.3	5.0	50.6	23.6	-3.3
Tunisia	2.1	25.7	7.5	4.9	2.7	3.4	5.9	4.9	4.9	4.5	5.3
Southern Africa	*27.0*	*33.8*	*3.1*	*1.6*	*0.5*	*1.9*	*3.0*	*-0.7*	*-0.2*	*3.1*	*2.8*
Botswana	1.2	51.6	36.4	15.5	2.6	4.7	5.4	9.1	-1.1	11.0	16.8
Lesotho	0.1	13.2	6.8	10.7	8.3	13.9	28.2	-11.9	7.9	2.3	6.1
Namibia	0.5	32.1	0.7	2.5	2.4	-7.8	9.4	3.9	2.7	2.2	1.0
South Africa	25.0	33.4	3.0	1.2	0.3	1.9	2.6	-1.3	-0.2	2.7	1.9
Swaziland	0.2	32.7	8.9	13.1	4.1	1.3	5.9	2.6	0.7	0.2	0.8
Western Africa	*13.5*	*27.5*	*8.5*	*-0.4*	*2.3*	*5.3*	*4.2*	*-0.9*	*3.1*	*4.4*	*-2.7*
Benin	0.1	5.2	-0.7	-0.5	13.5	5.3	4.9	4.8	122.8	9.6	9.7
Burkina Faso	0.3	17.0	4.0	4.5	3.9	11.8	14.9	9.6	-9.9	-0.2	2.3
Cape Verde	0.0	8.2	1.8	7.6	3.5	25.8	-22.8	32.5	-19.9	33.1	11.8
Cote d'Ivoire	1.8	22.1	7.8	4.9	4.5	8.6	19.4	-1.8	14.5	-6.4	-13.6
Gambia	0.0	6.7	1.5	9.6	4.1	5.2	4.8	4.6	15.8	2.1	8.2
Ghana	0.6	14.8	-3.0	1.3	4.9	4.2	4.8	3.6	5.8	3.2	2.1
Guinea	0.4	20.9	2.8	2.5	3.9	4.8	2.6	3.9	3.7	5.0	3.0
Guinea-Bissau	0.0	7.9	2.8	-1.2	-0.8	4.3	15.4	-34.8	2.0	5.1	5.4
Liberia	0.0	13.4	3.1	-4.4	-18.5	-60.9	805.6	9.2	22.5	17.0	9.0
Mali	0.2	12.9	4.5	3.0	6.8	4.1	5.7	5.2	36.1	33.5	17.5
Mauritania	0.1	18.0	-2.2	4.5	6.4	-0.5	3.2	0.6	0.4	5.8	3.5
Niger	0.3	16.3	4.6	0.2	1.3	6.7	3.2	2.9	1.8	1.5	1.7
Nigeria	8.8	40.4	10.6	-1.9	1.1	4.8	1.1	-2.9	-1.8	6.3	-3.7

Table 6.B. Average Rates of Growth of Gross Domestic Product by Kind of Economic Activity - Mining, Manufacturing and Utilities

Major area, region and country	Base year weights as percentage of total for world or region in 1990	Base year share as percentage of total GDP in 1990	Average rates of growth 1970-1979	1980-1989	1990-1999	Annual rate of change (percentage) 1996	1997	1998	1999	2000	2001
Senegal	0.6	15.6	59.3	3.8	3.0	3.9	1.5	6.8	4.1	5.2	10.3
Sierra Leone	0.1	14.2	-4.0	-1.7	2.0	5.3	-20.5	17.9	11.6	7.6	8.3
Togo	0.2	19.8	0.9	0.7	2.1	0.8	-5.2	3.4	-3.2	8.1	-1.7
AMERICAS	**29.5**	**23.8**	**3.5**	**1.9**	**2.6**	**2.4**	**4.7**	**2.7**	**3.5**	**3.9**	**-4.8**
NORTHERN AMERICA	**24.0**	**22.9**	**3.0**	**1.9**	**2.8**	**2.0**	**4.3**	**3.1**	**4.7**	**3.8**	**-5.6**
Bermuda	0.0	5.8	3.7	0.9	1.0	-0.7	1.5	2.9	4.9	0.7	-2.0
Canada	7.4	23.1	4.0	2.1	2.4	1.2	5.0	3.4	5.0	5.6	-3.3
United States	74.0	22.9	2.9	1.9	2.8	2.0	4.2	3.0	4.6	3.6	-5.9
LATIN AMERICA AND THE CARIBBEAN	**5.5**	**28.6**	**5.8**	**1.5**	**2.1**	**4.5**	**6.3**	**1.2**	**-1.3**	**4.2**	**-1.1**
Caribbean	*1.5*	*28.8*	*5.5*	*2.9*	*2.4*	*2.5*	*9.7*	*2.4*	*1.4*	*5.9*	*2.1*
Anguilla	0.0	2.7	3.8	5.7	8.7	-4.2	16.7	10.0	25.7	6.7	1.0
Antigua and Barbuda	0.0	9.9	-1.2	9.6	2.2	8.4	5.9	4.2	7.7	6.3	4.2
Aruba	0.0	8.0	12.3	13.1	8.7	0.4	12.6	9.1	13.2	-1.0	12.4
Bahamas [1]	0.0	5.3	-2.4	0.6	1.5	0.8	13.2	5.2	8.0	7.4	7.1
Barbados	0.0	10.1	6.3	1.1	1.0	0.6	3.3	6.3	0.7	-0.7	-5.2
British Virgin Islands	0.0	6.5	4.5	12.9	5.6	8.7	28.0	9.4	-5.7	10.0	10.1
Cayman Islands	0.0	4.9	7.2	8.9	-0.3	3.6	-2.8	-0.3	0.1	0.1	0.1
Cuba	0.3	26.8	4.1	5.6	-0.5	7.8	7.9	3.0	6.3	5.1	0.8
Dominica	0.0	9.0	-2.7	8.5	3.3	5.8	4.2	12.4	-8.8	5.8	-7.9
Dominican Republic	0.1	22.5	8.0	3.0	3.8	9.9	7.4	5.1	6.2	9.2	-0.3
Grenada	0.0	6.9	0.9	9.1	3.0	3.5	8.4	7.9	11.2	10.9	-0.6
Guadeloupe	0.0	6.3	5.0	0.2	5.3	4.3	9.2	4.1	5.9	5.9	5.9
Haiti	0.0	16.3	7.0	-1.1	-7.6	3.9	0.5	1.6	1.6	-0.4	-4.7
Jamaica	0.1	29.9	-0.2	1.3	0.7	1.2	0.4	-0.4	-0.3	-34.4	1.0
Martinique	0.0	10.1	3.9	8.0	1.6	1.6	1.6	4.1	2.5	2.5	2.5
Montserrat	0.0	4.3	1.5	1.6	-14.9	10.5	-37.6	-73.6	25.8	3.6	3.5
Netherlands Antilles	0.0	9.7	3.3	0.0	1.8	2.4	-4.7	-4.4	-4.2	-4.6	-2.5
Puerto Rico	0.8	42.2	7.2	3.1	3.4	0.4	12.3	1.5	-1.7	8.8	2.9
Saint Kitts and Nevis	0.0	12.2	6.6	3.0	2.9	5.0	11.2	0.4	5.5	12.5	-7.4
Saint Lucia	0.0	9.7	2.4	8.2	0.2	-3.9	2.9	-0.9	-0.6	4.1	-1.5
Saint Vincent and the Grenadines	0.0	11.6	4.7	6.3	1.8	4.1	1.3	0.0	3.9	-2.5	3.8
Trinidad and Tobago	0.1	35.9	4.0	-2.5	2.4	0.9	4.6	6.2	11.4	6.3	2.9
Central America	*3.6*	*22.1*	*7.1*	*2.3*	*4.3*	*9.4*	*9.0*	*6.7*	*4.6*	*5.8*	*-3.1*
Belize	0.0	15.6	5.7	3.1	3.6	1.4	2.8	-1.5	0.9	21.5	11.9
Costa Rica	0.1	23.0	8.1	2.4	7.0	0.7	7.4	11.1	22.5	-2.0	-7.0
El Salvador	0.1	23.3	4.7	-1.2	4.9	2.1	7.9	6.6	3.6	3.8	4.3
Guatemala	0.1	17.8	6.7	0.7	4.0	3.0	5.4	5.0	4.1	4.8	1.3
Honduras	0.0	18.9	7.4	2.8	3.9	6.3	6.2	3.7	2.7	5.6	3.2
Mexico	3.3	22.4	7.3	2.5	4.2	10.2	9.2	6.7	4.1	6.3	-3.3
Nicaragua	0.0	19.4	2.1	-4.4	2.1	3.6	4.9	4.5	4.8	0.8	2.6
Panama	0.0	13.5	4.6	1.8	4.5	4.2	5.1	1.4	0.5	0.6	-3.6
South America	*13.5*	*31.1*	*5.6*	*1.2*	*1.4*	*3.5*	*5.2*	*-0.5*	*-3.4*	*3.5*	*-0.9*
Argentina	2.5	31.6	2.5	-1.5	3.5	6.7	9.1	1.9	-6.7	-1.3	-5.5
Bolivia	0.1	28.8	4.9	-1.4	4.0	2.4	3.6	3.5	0.5	3.7	1.5
Brazil	7.6	30.9	9.3	2.1	-0.2	2.6	3.5	-2.2	-2.1	5.5	0.0
Chile	0.6	31.5	1.5	3.3	5.2	5.2	6.7	1.1	2.1	5.5	1.7
Colombia	0.7	26.7	6.0	4.4	1.9	0.7	1.1	3.0	-2.1	3.4	-0.7
Ecuador	0.2	23.9	31.1	2.2	2.4	0.0	1.3	1.7	-6.1	-2.9	5.4
French Guiana	0.0	8.2	1.2	17.9	7.4	1.6	7.4	2.8	3.9	3.9	3.9
Guyana	0.0	13.4	1.1	-6.3	5.5	7.4	6.5	-4.6	6.3	-7.3	1.9
Paraguay	0.1	20.1	8.6	3.9	3.1	0.4	0.7	1.2	4.2	3.2	0.7
Peru	0.4	21.5	4.4	-1.0	3.3	2.6	6.7	-0.7	2.8	5.4	2.6
Suriname	0.0	20.6	10.6	-2.3	0.2	7.5	5.6	2.3	-3.1	-1.5	8.7
Uruguay [2]	0.1	28.7	3.4	-0.3	0.4	4.3	6.0	3.6	-6.5	-0.9	-4.7
Venezuela	1.2	45.7	-0.5	0.3	3.4	2.4	7.4	-0.8	-7.7	3.4	0.6
ASIA	**27.1**	**29.3**	**5.7**	**4.3**	**4.3**	**6.6**	**5.0**	**-1.0**	**4.6**	**8.3**	**2.7**
Eastern Asia	*73.1*	*30.4*	*5.4*	*5.5*	*3.9*	*6.6*	*5.4*	*-1.0*	*5.2*	*8.4*	*0.5*
China	8.7	37.4	8.6	10.6	12.9	12.1	10.5	8.9	8.1	9.6	8.8
Democratic People's Rep. of Korea	0.4	37.6	11.9	8.1	-3.2	-3.6	-6.3	-1.1	6.2	1.3	3.7
Hong Kong SAR of China	0.9	19.2	8.8	7.2	3.8	4.3	5.1	-5.0	3.4	10.2	-2.3
Japan	54.6	29.3	4.5	4.4	0.7	4.6	3.0	-5.0	1.6	6.7	-4.0

Table 6.B. Average Rates of Growth of Gross Domestic Product by Kind of Economic Activity - Mining, Manufacturing and Utilities

Major area, region and country	Base year weights as percentage of total for world or region in 1990	Base year share as percentage of total GDP in 1990	Average rates of growth			Annual rate of change (percentage)					
			1970-1979	1980-1989	1990-1999	1996	1997	1998	1999	2000	2001
Macao SAR of China	0.0	10.3	16.9	16.8	8.2	3.0	4.0	4.5	-2.3	1.5	-1.0
Mongolia	0.1	27.9	5.7	3.9	-2.1	-7.6	-4.2	4.4	1.3	2.6	12.7
Republic of Korea	4.9	31.7	16.6	10.0	7.6	7.0	6.8	-7.1	20.1	15.6	2.3
South Central Asia	*10.2*	*21.9*	*1.4*	*4.3*	*6.7*	*6.4*	*2.4*	*2.9*	*3.7*	*7.2*	*4.4*
Afghanistan	0.1	26.5	6.2	-0.2	-8.3	6.6	13.3	5.2	-12.4	-43.7	0.0
Bangladesh	0.3	15.0	-3.3	3.5	6.7	4.7	7.9	3.3	5.2	6.9	5.3
Bhutan	0.0	16.6	6.4	22.3	7.5	7.9	1.5	3.8	7.0	-3.5	28.2
India	3.9	19.8	4.6	7.3	5.9	8.2	3.0	3.2	4.2	6.2	2.9
Iran (Islamic Republic of) [3]	2.6	22.3	-0.9	0.4	5.4	7.1	3.5	2.0	3.6	7.9	3.4
Kazakhstan	1.0	23.4	...	...	-5.1	1.4	5.1	4.7	1.7	13.7	12.4
Kyrgyzstan	0.2	29.2	...	...	-9.9	3.4	37.1	5.1	-4.5	5.8	5.4
Maldives	0.0	11.5	15.3	13.5	7.5	5.9	20.8	1.3	8.8	5.8	7.6
Nepal	0.0	6.7	2.3	7.5	9.7	10.0	6.6	1.3	5.7	18.2	4.5
Pakistan	0.6	19.2	5.7	8.5	4.5	-0.6	7.0	6.6	0.7	3.7	3.1
Sri Lanka	0.1	20.0	5.2	4.7	7.5	6.5	8.7	5.7	4.9	8.9	-3.5
Tajikistan	0.2	34.2	...	...	-15.7	-34.4	-10.9	1.8	-3.9	10.4	8.6
Turkmenistan	0.5	75.9	...	...	-12.3	8.9	-45.8	-8.9	23.3	42.6	21.4
Uzbekistan	0.7	22.7	...	...	-5.6	6.2	-7.9	-0.1	0.1	0.1	18.1
South-Eastern Asia	*6.4*	*29.6*	*8.7*	*5.9*	*6.7*	*9.0*	*4.8*	*-6.9*	*7.1*	*9.2*	*0.8*
Brunei Darussalam	0.1	50.5	9.4	-6.0	0.2	0.9	1.6	-1.4	0.6	3.5	1.1
Cambodia	0.0	9.5	-7.3	-0.7	10.1	15.7	34.0	14.8	8.8	42.9	16.9
Indonesia	2.3	33.5	10.0	7.2	6.5	10.2	4.7	-8.7	2.6	5.9	3.2
Lao People's Democratic Republic	0.0	11.5	0.2	1.4	13.0	18.4	8.7	13.7	9.2	10.9	9.3
Malaysia	1.0	38.3	9.7	7.5	8.4	14.2	7.2	-9.0	10.1	15.5	-3.7
Myanmar [4]	0.1	8.7	3.5	1.7	7.7	5.9	8.5	6.7	17.7	23.1	4.8
Philippines	0.8	28.4	6.5	1.5	2.4	5.6	4.2	-0.5	1.4	5.6	2.3
Singapore	0.7	30.5	10.9	6.9	6.1	3.2	4.8	-0.2	12.9	14.4	-10.7
Thailand	1.3	25.1	10.9	9.1	7.9	7.0	2.5	-10.1	11.3	6.3	4.9
Vietnam	0.1	18.8	-0.1	4.0	11.2	13.9	13.1	11.3	9.3	10.8	10.1
Western Asia	*10.3*	*32.0*	*8.6*	*-3.2*	*3.8*	*4.9*	*5.1*	*0.7*	*-1.3*	*8.0*	*22.8*
Armenia	0.3	31.8	...	...	-7.5	1.2	1.4	-2.0	5.3	6.4	0.9
Azerbaijan	0.3	24.6	...	...	-12.4	-12.3	-3.5	-1.3	0.7	399.4	615.3
Bahrain	0.1	34.0	11.7	-5.7	6.0	2.7	2.5	7.7	8.7	7.4	4.5
Cyprus	0.1	16.4	4.7	5.2	1.2	-0.3	0.5	2.8	1.4	3.9	-1.2
Georgia	0.3	24.1	...	...	-13.6	131.9	-1.3	-3.6	5.9	0.9	0.9
Iraq [5]	0.6	24.2	11.5	-3.2	-28.4	-37.5	41.0	27.3	32.5	39.5	-13.1
Israel	0.7	19.6	2.8	4.6	5.1	3.9	5.6	4.8	0.7	11.5	-5.7
Jordan	0.1	25.1	5.2	6.8	3.8	-4.9	9.9	6.9	1.6	2.5	3.4
Kuwait	0.6	50.3	-1.8	-3.7	1.4	0.4	0.0	2.2	-8.0	-33.8	-3.4
Lebanon	0.0	17.9	0.1	-6.7	6.2	10.4	-2.6	5.2	0.9	0.8	2.0
Oman	0.4	51.8	1.6	9.0	4.0	3.6	3.2	0.5	0.7	9.5	8.8
Qatar	0.2	52.4	5.1	-0.3	7.3	3.1	43.2	17.1	7.0	16.5	8.1
Saudi Arabia	2.8	44.2	10.6	-9.9	3.9	-0.8	0.1	3.1	-5.3	6.5	-0.1
Syrian Arab Republic	0.2	20.4	7.2	9.8	10.9	25.4	17.4	4.2	-1.7	-7.8	-23.1
Turkey	2.3	25.5	6.8	5.9	4.5	7.1	10.4	2.0	-5.0	6.0	-7.5
United Arab Emirates	1.1	55.3	37.1	-1.7	3.7	13.0	-1.3	-18.6	15.6	7.1	7.4
Yemen	0.2	22.3	...	...	9.0	8.6	5.0	2.9	5.4	6.8	2.3
Yemen Arab Republic (Former)	...	...	13.1	20.9	...	...	...	...	...	...	...
Yemen Democratic (Former)	...	...	-2.0	0.9	...	...	...	...	...	...	...
EUROPE	**39.7**	**27.0**	**3.2**	**1.4**	**2.4**	**0.0**	**3.1**	**2.2**	**1.9**	**4.4**	**1.1**
Eastern Europe	*23.2*	*36.9*	*8.2*	*2.7*	*13.5*	*-1.7*	*2.0*	*-2.6*	*7.1*	*8.3*	*4.5*
Belarus	1.1	39.7	...	...	-0.7	3.6	17.1	10.5	8.1	7.9	6.4
Bulgaria	0.3	38.6	7.1	6.1	-6.1	-9.4	-10.3	5.1	-8.3	12.5	4.7
Czech Republic	0.5	34.5	...	2.6	-2.1	16.1	-0.2	-8.7	-2.0	9.3	0.7
Hungary	0.4	25.4	5.5	0.1	-1.7	3.2	11.4	8.3	7.2	9.6	-1.3
Poland	1.0	42.3	7.9	0.0	0.6	7.6	10.4	4.5	3.1	6.5	-0.7
Republic of Moldova	0.2	29.1	...	...	-12.4	-0.3	-14.9	-17.2	-7.1	18.3	4.6
Romania	0.6	40.5	11.2	-1.5	-6.6	-1.5	-9.5	-10.1	-15.8	0.6	5.2
Russian Federation	14.9	37.0	...	...	-7.0	-4.1	1.4	-5.4	10.4	9.7	4.9
Slovakia	0.3	39.5	...	-0.6	-3.8	5.0	-5.5	3.2	5.1	-5.5	3.6
Ukraine	3.8	35.9	...	...	-11.8	-4.5	-3.3	-0.8	6.2	4.2	10.0
Northern Europe	*17.5*	*24.4*	*2.3*	*2.0*	*2.3*	*1.9*	*3.9*	*2.6*	*2.5*	*4.5*	*-0.5*
Denmark	1.0	18.3	2.7	1.5	1.4	-1.6	7.1	0.1	-0.3	5.3	1.4
Estonia	0.2	40.9	...	...	-2.3	2.9	13.6	3.4	-2.3	13.6	7.0
Finland	1.3	22.6	3.9	4.0	3.6	3.3	8.7	6.7	5.3	11.0	0.0
Iceland	0.0	17.9	8.1	1.9	2.2	6.6	4.5	6.4	5.3	4.9	3.6
Ireland	0.5	27.0	6.0	3.3	8.8	4.5	15.8	14.1	12.9	8.9	6.2

Table 6.B. Average Rates of Growth of Gross Domestic Product by Kind of Economic Activity - Mining, Manufacturing and Utilities

Major area, region and country	Base year weights as percentage of total for world or region in 1990	Base year share as percentage of total GDP in 1990	Average rates of growth 1970-1979	1980-1989	1990-1999	Annual rate of change (percentage) 1996	1997	1998	1999	2000	2001
Latvia	0.3	35.1	...	...	-9.4	2.5	12.4	3.5	-5.6	4.4	8.8
Lithuania	0.2	20.6	...	...	-3.6	3.1	6.5	7.3	-9.5	6.3	16.9
Norway	1.3	27.2	4.2	2.4	3.4	4.8	5.1	-2.3	-0.4	2.7	-0.2
Sweden	2.2	21.4	1.6	2.3	3.9	2.4	6.8	6.8	8.1	9.7	-0.2
United Kingdom	10.5	25.4	1.9	1.6	1.0	1.3	1.0	1.0	0.8	1.7	-2.1
Southern Europe	*19.1*	*24.6*	*4.9*	*1.4*	*1.5*	*0.4*	*3.6*	*3.0*	*1.2*	*3.2*	*1.1*
Albania	0.0	37.2	8.3	3.5	-10.3	13.7	-5.7	4.1	6.4	5.0	5.7
Andorra	0.0	20.8	8.6	8.2	7.0	7.0	10.4	9.7	7.7	8.7	5.8
Bosnia and Herzegovina	0.1	22.2	...	...	7.4	51.3	32.0	27.0	11.6	10.7	7.4
Croatia	0.3	26.5	...	...	-6.2	3.5	6.7	5.8	2.7	3.3	5.3
Greece	0.6	18.3	7.1	1.0	0.4	2.7	-2.8	5.8	1.8	4.1	3.5
Holy See	0.0	25.0	5.5	1.3	1.3	-1.4	2.7	1.8	0.5	2.8	0.6
Italy	11.5	25.0	4.6	0.9	1.2	-1.4	2.6	1.8	0.4	2.7	0.5
Malta	0.0	34.3	14.0	3.2	2.8	0.7	3.7	7.8	2.5	5.8	-2.9
Portugal	0.7	22.5	5.1	3.4	2.4	7.2	5.4	2.8	1.2	2.0	2.0
San Marino	0.0	25.0	4.6	0.5	0.9	-2.6	0.5	7.2	6.3	2.2	0.7
Serbia and Montenegro	0.4	30.9	...	...	-10.7	9.1	15.4	2.2	-35.8	0.8	-2.9
Slovenia	0.2	33.4	...	...	-0.5	1.5	6.2	4.1	2.7	7.8	4.1
Spain	5.1	24.1	5.1	2.0	2.1	2.0	5.4	4.7	3.7	4.0	1.4
TFYR Macedonia	0.1	36.5	...	...	-5.6	4.8	3.5	2.8	-2.1	3.4	-3.2
Yugoslavia (Former)	...	...	6.0	4.6	...	...	...	...	...	...	...
Western Europe	*40.2*	*25.5*	*2.5*	*1.1*	*1.0*	*-0.5*	*2.7*	*3.1*	*0.4*	*3.8*	*0.9*
Austria	1.6	23.9	3.6	2.0	2.6	1.8	4.4	4.5	3.2	5.5	1.4
Belgium	1.9	23.5	4.5	2.6	1.9	3.5	6.7	1.3	1.7	4.6	0.2
France	10.7	21.2	3.3	0.8	2.0	0.3	3.2	5.2	3.0	3.9	1.8
Germany	20.5	29.5	1.9	1.1	0.1	-2.2	2.3	2.0	-1.8	3.8	0.4
Liechtenstein	0.0	26.1	2.4	1.6	1.1	1.2	2.8	3.8	2.2	1.6	0.8
Luxembourg	0.1	21.9	1.5	2.9	1.3	3.8	4.5	0.7	7.5	4.9	2.4
Monaco	0.0	21.2	4.3	1.8	2.6	1.0	3.9	5.9	2.8	-2.7	3.4
Netherlands	2.7	22.4	3.8	1.2	2.0	2.4	0.3	2.3	1.4	3.9	1.2
Switzerland	2.5	26.1	0.9	0.8	0.3	0.3	1.7	2.6	0.9	0.7	-0.6
OCEANIA	**1.2**	**20.6**	**2.5**	**2.6**	**2.1**	**1.7**	**2.3**	**0.9**	**2.6**	**3.6**	**1.3**
Australia & New Zealand	*97.5*	*20.7*	*2.6*	*2.6*	*2.0*	*1.7*	*2.8*	*0.8*	*2.4*	*3.8*	*1.4*
Australia	84.8	20.6	2.7	2.8	2.0	1.6	3.3	1.3	2.3	4.0	1.6
New Zealand	12.7	21.9	2.0	1.4	1.4	2.0	-0.6	-2.8	3.2	2.4	-0.1
Melanesia	*2.0*	*20.5*	*0.7*	*-0.8*	*6.6*	*3.1*	*-11.2*	*4.8*	*7.8*	*-1.0*	*-3.1*
Fiji	0.2	12.0	4.0	0.7	4.0	4.3	-0.4	4.2	9.7	-5.9	2.0
New Caledonia	0.7	19.5	1.7	7.0	1.4	-1.1	7.5	-16.4	10.5	1.9	-1.2
Papua New Guinea	1.1	26.2	0.2	-3.4	9.0	4.0	-17.0	11.8	7.2	-1.2	-4.0
Solomon Islands	0.0	4.1	6.7	3.1	6.0	3.5	-1.0	-2.2	-7.5	-1.7	-14.6
Vanuatu	0.0	7.5	7.7	6.8	3.8	6.1	-0.8	9.6	3.3	0.2	0.1
Micronesia	*0.0*	*3.2*	*4.5*	*0.0*	*5.2*	*-14.2*	*6.5*	*15.6*	*14.8*	*-13.0*	*1.3*
Kiribati	0.0	4.0	2.9	-6.2	8.6	4.9	20.5	26.7	-26.4	-45.4	1.8
Marshall Islands	0.0	1.1	6.6	6.1	14.0	-22.2	2.5	-20.1	10.0	-3.6	-0.7
Micronesia (Federated States of)	0.0	4.0	6.6	3.9	0.6	-12.3	4.2	-23.2	29.6	-15.6	1.5
Nauru	0.0	4.0	6.8	4.4	-6.3	-17.2	1.8	-23.0	26.0	-18.2	-0.8
Palau	0.0	2.5	2.9	-5.5	11.2	-22.0	6.1	268.6	30.9	-2.0	2.2
Polynesia	*0.4*	*9.8*	*4.4*	*5.7*	*2.9*	*2.1*	*0.6*	*-0.1*	*2.8*	*3.2*	*3.4*
Cook Islands	0.0	6.0	-6.4	2.5	4.0	-10.1	5.4	-3.4	14.4	-2.3	7.1
French Polynesia	0.4	9.1	5.1	7.3	3.7	1.6	1.1	1.1	2.7	2.7	2.1
Samoa	0.1	22.6	3.1	0.4	-2.1	5.1	-3.1	-10.8	0.6	7.4	14.1
Tonga	0.0	6.8	8.9	3.7	1.9	7.7	-5.3	7.2	14.0	7.5	2.6
Tuvalu	0.0	5.0	6.6	13.8	7.0	29.6	3.3	19.1	-7.0	3.0	3.0

Notes for Table 6.B - Mining, manufacturing and utilities

1/ 1989-1995
Does not include gas.

2/ 1970-1986
Electricity, gas and water supply includes sewage services.

3/ 1970-1992
Includes oil production.

4/ 1980-1998
Gas and water are included in "Other activities".

5/ 1970-1991
Gas distribution is included in "Wholesale and retail trade, restaurants and hotels".

Table 6.C. Average Rates of Growth of Gross Domestic Product by Kind of Economic Activity - Manufacturing

Major area, region and country	Base year weights as percentage of total for world or region in 1990	Base year share as percentage of total GDP in 1990	Average rates of growth			Annual rate of change (percentage)					
			1970-1979	1980-1989	1990-1999	1996	1997	1998	1999	2000	2001
WORLD	**100.0**	**21.8**	**3.7**	**2.5**	**2.6**	**2.2**	**4.5**	**0.7**	**3.2**	**5.9**	**-1.1**
DEVELOPED ECONOMIES	**72.7**	**20.9**	**3.1**	**2.2**	**1.9**	**1.6**	**4.3**	**1.4**	**2.6**	**5.0**	**-2.9**
DEVELOPING ECONOMIES	**14.5**	**19.6**	**7.0**	**4.0**	**4.1**	**5.9**	**6.1**	**-1.1**	**4.6**	**8.0**	**-0.5**
TRANSITION ECONOMIES	**12.8**	**34.4**	**8.0**	**1.1**	**-6.4**	**-0.8**	**2.7**	**-3.5**	**6.2**	**10.5**	**18.6**
AFRICA	**1.5**	**14.1**	**5.4**	**3.8**	**1.7**	**1.8**	**4.9**	**2.4**	**6.1**	**4.0**	**2.9**
Eastern Africa	*10.0*	*13.9*	*3.5*	*3.7*	*2.3*	*8.2*	*5.9*	*3.4*	*2.4*	*-2.7*	*4.0*
Burundi	0.3	16.4	5.8	6.5	-1.0	-8.1	1.0	5.0	3.0	4.0	3.5
Comoros	0.0	4.2	4.1	6.5	2.2	4.5	1.2	1.1	8.3	-2.5	-2.5
Djibouti	0.0	3.1	6.0	0.3	-1.1	-3.7	6.2	-1.9	14.8	5.4	7.7
Eritrea	...	...	...	...	5.1	11.7	12.1	-6.0	-0.6	-7.6	3.6
Ethiopia	...	...	...	...	12.1	5.4	7.0	10.5	11.7	3.7	8.7
Ethiopia (Former)	0.8	7.5	3.5	3.9	-10.9	...	...	...	...	...	...
Kenya	1.2	10.1	10.6	4.8	2.6	3.8	1.8	1.5	1.0	-1.5	0.7
Madagascar	0.5	11.8	3.6	5.6	-0.8	3.7	3.1	2.4	-6.5	8.9	0.4
Malawi	0.4	18.6	8.0	3.1	1.6	-5.6	1.0	1.5	2.5	-3.0	-14.2
Mauritius	0.8	23.4	8.3	8.0	5.3	6.6	6.0	6.1	0.9	9.4	5.0
Mozambique	0.5	14.4	3.9	-0.3	6.1	18.9	31.8	14.4	14.7	20.3	27.2
Rwanda	0.6	17.6	5.2	3.2	-3.3	15.6	19.4	4.1	-3.4	-5.3	7.2
Seychelles [1]	0.1	10.1	19.6	6.3	10.2	15.0	28.2	17.0	5.3	-4.1	-14.4
Somalia	0.0	2.0	3.0	-0.3	2.0	9.0	8.6	8.8	18.0	3.0	3.0
Uganda	0.3	5.5	-11.5	4.5	12.7	14.7	16.3	12.8	10.3	-0.5	10.3
United Republic Of Tanzania [2]	0.4	8.1	4.5	-1.6	2.8	4.7	1.5	3.1	3.1	-6.8	1.7
Zambia	1.6	29.2	1.8	3.3	2.2	5.5	7.3	3.0	5.2	4.1	4.6
Zimbabwe	2.4	20.5	3.5	4.2	0.8	14.7	-0.8	-3.4	-4.6	-27.2	-8.1
Middle Africa	*5.7*	*9.4*	*3.6*	*3.8*	*1.3*	*2.1*	*2.3*	*0.7*	*24.6*	*5.0*	*5.3*
Angola	0.7	5.0	2.1	-2.7	-1.7	1.8	5.2	8.2	7.6	8.5	10.4
Cameroon	3.6	18.6	4.4	7.9	1.9	2.6	1.3	-0.6	35.1	1.6	5.5
Central African Republic	0.1	7.4	8.0	1.9	2.9	1.1	7.0	7.6	-9.0	6.0	4.8
Chad	0.3	16.7	-2.8	6.2	0.6	1.0	11.3	9.3	-5.1	-1.8	11.8
Congo	0.3	8.4	0.8	7.0	5.4	4.6	-1.6	-2.1	52.4	24.8	-2.0
Democratic Republic of the Congo	0.2	1.4	-1.2	-0.2	-6.9	-3.6	-5.2	-2.2	-10.4	-4.3	-4.4
Equatorial Guinea	0.0	1.3	2.0	-4.6	18.4	45.0	69.3	20.0	47.9	16.9	53.4
Gabon	0.5	6.1	10.9	-3.7	-1.6	-1.0	2.3	-6.9	-8.7	22.9	-2.7
Sao Tome and Principe	0.0	4.9	3.1	-2.7	-4.5	1.1	1.1	-10.8	-34.6	-1.4	4.4
Northern Africa	*41.0*	*12.9*	*6.6*	*6.3*	*2.5*	*0.1*	*5.7*	*6.3*	*8.7*	*5.1*	*2.9*
Algeria	9.3	11.0	0.7	5.3	-9.4	-0.7	-3.0	0.4	-5.3	-16.6	2.0
Egypt [3]	15.3	15.8	5.3	8.7	5.5	0.0	7.8	9.7	7.9	4.5	4.0
Libyan Arab Jamahiriya	3.0	7.9	13.5	9.9	3.5	-1.5	8.2	-1.6	3.7	2.2	2.5
Morocco	6.5	18.4	5.3	3.6	3.4	2.9	3.4	2.1	2.7	3.5	4.2
Sudan	4.1	9.0	2.8	4.2	7.5	4.1	6.3	5.0	37.6	21.6	-2.6
Tunisia	2.8	16.9	12.0	7.2	4.3	2.7	7.5	4.3	5.6	6.6	6.9
Southern Africa	*33.7*	*20.8*	*4.9*	*1.5*	*0.2*	*1.3*	*2.9*	*-1.7*	*-0.3*	*5.0*	*3.0*
Botswana	0.2	5.0	14.3	13.3	4.3	7.8	3.6	5.4	5.7	3.5	1.6
Lesotho [4]	0.1	11.4	5.4	14.3	5.8	14.1	4.9	-3.4	-0.4	4.4	7.8
Namibia	0.4	12.5	15.0	13.8	3.2	-16.2	18.0	8.9	-3.7	3.6	6.0
South Africa	32.6	21.5	4.9	1.3	0.0	1.4	2.7	-1.9	-0.3	5.1	2.9
Swaziland	0.3	28.7	10.2	15.3	4.3	2.3	5.6	1.6	1.2	1.5	0.9
Western Africa	*9.6*	*9.7*	*7.2*	*3.6*	*2.6*	*4.8*	*8.5*	*-0.9*	*9.9*	*1.9*	*0.7*
Benin	0.1	4.5	-7.7	-2.3	15.6	5.4	5.2	5.0	123.0	9.1	8.9
Burkina Faso	0.6	15.0	3.7	4.2	3.7	5.8	16.3	9.6	-10.2	-1.5	1.8
Cape Verde	0.0	7.5	1.1	7.5	2.9	30.2	-25.8	37.1	-24.1	37.7	14.5
Cote d'Ivoire	3.2	19.7	6.3	6.8	3.6	7.1	20.4	-4.5	15.6	-5.2	-12.5
Gambia	0.0	5.7	0.8	9.9	2.8	4.0	4.2	4.0	10.0	1.6	8.4
Ghana	0.8	8.9	-1.9	0.2	3.7	3.5	4.2	2.1	10.0	3.8	3.7
Guinea	0.1	3.8	2.8	3.3	2.0	6.6	8.6	0.1	3.7	5.0	3.0
Guinea-Bissau	0.0	6.8	2.8	-1.3	-0.9	4.4	15.3	-34.8	2.0	5.1	5.4
Liberia	0.1	11.4	3.1	-4.2	-11.7	-61.8	1023.1	5.5	21.4	15.0	14.4
Mali [5]	0.3	7.8	4.2	6.1	6.1	3.9	8.4	6.2	24.9	33.6	17.5
Mauritania	0.1	6.1	3.8	4.5	8.1	4.4	6.5	5.3	12.2	0.2	6.4
Niger	0.3	8.9	4.6	0.5	-0.6	4.4	4.6	3.7	4.5	3.2	3.8
Nigeria	2.8	6.5	12.4	2.4	-0.4	2.4	0.9	-5.4	2.1	4.9	9.1
Senegal	1.0	13.1	...	4.2	3.0	3.6	0.5	7.2	4.3	5.2	10.6
Sierra Leone	0.1	7.0	3.3	-3.9	2.2	5.2	-44.5	17.9	11.7	7.6	8.3
Togo	0.1	6.9	0.1	0.9	-0.8	2.6	-18.6	3.6	-3.4	8.1	-1.7

Table 6.C. Average Rates of Growth of Gross Domestic Product by Kind of Economic Activity - Manufacturing

Major area, region and country	Base year weights as percentage of total for world or region in 1990	Base year share as percentage of total GDP in 1990	Average rates of growth			Annual rate of change (percentage)					
			1970-1979	1980-1989	1990-1999	1996	1997	1998	1999	2000	2001
AMERICAS	**28.6**	**18.7**	**3.4**	**1.7**	**2.8**	**2.7**	**5.7**	**3.5**	**3.7**	**4.7**	**-5.2**
NORTHERN AMERICA	**23.2**	**17.9**	**2.7**	**1.9**	**3.1**	**2.3**	**5.5**	**4.2**	**5.0**	**4.8**	**-5.9**
Bermuda	0.0	2.9	3.7	-0.3	0.1	-4.0	1.6	1.5	7.6	0.0	-5.6
Canada	6.6	16.0	4.5	2.2	2.6	1.1	6.6	4.9	7.0	5.4	-4.5
United States	74.4	18.1	2.6	1.9	3.1	2.4	5.4	4.1	4.8	4.7	-6.0
LATIN AMERICA AND THE CARIBBEAN	**5.4**	**23.1**	**6.4**	**1.2**	**1.5**	**4.2**	**6.4**	**0.5**	**-1.9**	**4.2**	**-1.7**
Caribbean	*1.5*	*25.8*	*6.1*	*3.2*	*2.4*	*2.6*	*10.6*	*2.2*	*1.5*	*8.4*	*2.3*
Anguilla	0.0	0.6	3.8	4.6	11.1	3.2	3.1	9.7	59.9	3.4	-17.7
Antigua and Barbuda	0.0	3.3	-3.3	6.1	0.2	4.0	6.0	5.5	4.5	3.0	3.0
Aruba	0.0	1.3	12.4	13.2	15.4	3.1	4.7	19.0	9.7	0.6	12.9
Bahamas	0.0	2.6	-3.9	-2.8	-3.1	-3.7	7.9	0.0	2.4	1.5	1.0
Barbados	0.0	6.9	6.1	-0.3	-0.1	-1.2	3.5	3.4	-2.2	-1.1	-8.0
British Virgin Islands	0.0	2.8	5.7	11.5	11.3	13.3	35.3	13.0	-7.7	12.2	12.2
Cayman Islands	0.0	1.5	9.2	6.7	-0.9	3.6	-2.8	-0.3	0.1	0.1	0.1
Cuba	0.3	23.6	4.1	5.3	-0.6	7.9	8.3	3.3	7.1	4.3	0.5
Dominica	0.0	5.9	-2.3	8.8	1.7	6.0	2.5	16.8	-17.3	8.5	-14.8
Dominican Republic [6]	0.1	20.0	7.0	3.3	3.9	10.4	7.5	5.7	6.4	9.0	-1.3
Grenada	0.0	4.2	1.2	11.2	1.6	5.4	3.0	12.7	11.2	11.7	-6.4
Haiti	0.0	15.1	7.7	-0.8	-8.2	2.5	0.6	1.9	1.2	-0.2	0.2
Jamaica	0.1	18.9	-1.1	1.5	-1.6	-2.9	-2.6	-4.6	-1.4	-21.7	0.8
Montserrat	0.0	2.1	1.6	0.7	-21.4	50.0	-45.2	-84.9	10.6	0.0	0.0
Netherlands Antilles	0.0	6.6	3.3	-1.7	0.1	4.3	-13.6	-5.7	-5.6	-6.0	-3.9
Puerto Rico	0.9	39.2	8.4	3.2	3.4	0.7	12.5	1.3	-1.4	10.6	3.3
Saint Kitts and Nevis	0.0	10.8	6.7	2.6	2.4	5.2	11.2	-0.6	7.0	11.5	-8.8
Saint Lucia	0.0	6.9	0.8	8.7	-1.7	-6.8	-0.3	-2.1	-2.7	3.0	-4.2
Saint Vincent and the Grenadines	0.0	7.3	4.0	5.7	-0.9	4.7	0.0	-6.7	0.0	-9.5	-2.6
Trinidad and Tobago	0.0	13.4	1.7	-1.1	6.9	3.6	13.3	12.9	20.0	13.7	3.9
Central America	*3.9*	*18.8*	*6.9*	*1.9*	*4.5*	*9.8*	*9.6*	*7.3*	*4.7*	*6.2*	*-3.7*
Belize	0.0	13.1	5.4	2.7	3.5	0.8	2.5	-3.2	5.0	21.4	13.2
Costa Rica	0.1	20.4	8.2	2.0	7.2	0.5	7.7	11.4	24.7	-2.9	-8.4
El Salvador	0.1	21.7	4.6	-1.3	5.1	1.7	8.0	6.6	3.7	4.1	4.2
Guatemala	0.1	15.1	6.3	0.2	2.8	1.9	2.6	3.6	2.5	1.9	1.4
Honduras	0.0	14.5	7.6	2.4	3.5	4.6	6.1	3.4	2.6	4.9	5.2
Mexico	3.6	19.0	7.1	2.2	4.4	10.8	9.9	7.4	4.2	6.9	-3.9
Nicaragua	0.0	17.6	2.1	-4.1	1.2	2.4	3.8	2.1	3.7	2.8	2.6
Panama	0.0	9.5	3.4	0.0	4.4	-1.3	6.4	3.9	-7.5	-5.3	-5.7
South America	*13.5*	*24.5*	*6.3*	*0.8*	*0.4*	*2.8*	*5.0*	*-1.8*	*-4.6*	*2.9*	*-1.4*
Argentina	2.7	26.8	2.2	-2.0	2.8	7.3	10.2	1.7	-8.6	-3.5	-7.9
Bolivia	0.1	17.0	5.8	-1.7	4.1	4.8	2.0	2.5	2.9	3.2	-0.3
Brazil	8.4	26.8	9.5	1.7	-0.7	2.1	3.2	-3.4	-2.6	5.4	0.6
Chile	0.4	17.0	0.6	3.1	4.0	3.2	4.7	-2.3	-1.3	4.0	-0.3
Colombia	0.6	17.3	6.5	2.6	0.5	-1.8	0.4	-0.3	-8.4	9.7	-0.7
Ecuador [7]	0.1	10.3	10.2	0.7	-0.1	-2.8	8.5	8.3	-23.5	-32.4	20.8
Guyana [8]	0.0	4.6	7.4	-4.9	4.4	3.9	2.3	-8.7	15.5	-13.9	2.5
Paraguay	0.1	17.3	7.8	3.2	0.9	-1.9	-0.3	1.0	0.0	1.0	1.3
Peru	0.3	15.3	3.0	-0.7	2.5	1.5	5.3	-3.2	-0.5	6.7	0.9
Suriname	0.0	11.7	13.4	-4.2	-3.3	8.5	2.8	-3.1	-7.1	9.6	4.2
Uruguay	0.2	26.3	3.4	-0.6	-0.6	4.1	5.7	1.8	-7.9	-2.1	-6.2
Venezuela [9]	0.7	20.5	5.5	1.5	1.3	-3.0	5.1	-3.9	-6.4	2.1	-0.4
ASIA	**25.4**	**23.8**	**5.4**	**5.2**	**2.5**	**5.5**	**4.2**	**-4.9**	**4.3**	**9.0**	**0.4**
Eastern Asia	77.0	26.8	5.2	5.1	1.4	4.5	3.9	-5.4	4.2	8.4	-4.0
Democratic People's Rep. of Korea	0.3	24.3	11.9	8.1	-3.2	-3.6	-6.3	-1.1	6.2	1.3	3.7
Hong Kong SAR of China	1.0	16.7	8.8	7.2	3.8	4.3	5.1	-5.0	3.4	10.2	-5.1
Japan	65.4	26.5	4.5	4.5	0.4	4.2	3.4	-5.9	1.7	7.2	-4.9
Macao SAR of China	0.0	8.3	16.9	16.8	7.2	0.3	3.9	2.5	-2.9	5.8	-3.5
Mongolia	0.0	12.4	5.7	3.9	-5.4	-19.4	-18.1	3.7	-2.8	-3.3	20.0
Republic of Korea	5.9	28.8	17.6	10.2	7.6	6.8	6.6	-7.4	21.0	15.9	2.1
South Central Asia	*10.2*	*16.7*	*4.8*	*6.3*	*7.2*	*8.1*	*2.7*	*-2.3*	*5.0*	*7.6*	*5.9*
Bangladesh	0.3	12.9	-3.4	2.6	6.5	5.1	8.5	3.2	4.8	6.7	5.0
Bhutan	0.0	8.0	6.4	12.2	9.1	7.8	0.3	2.1	3.7	-5.2	29.1
India	4.0	15.4	4.5	6.9	5.9	9.7	1.5	2.7	4.2	6.7	2.8

Table 6.C. Average Rates of Growth of Gross Domestic Product by Kind of Economic Activity - Manufacturing

Major area, region and country	Base year weights as percentage of total for world or region in 1990	Base year share as percentage of total GDP in 1990	Average rates of growth			Annual rate of change (percentage)					
			1970-1979	1980-1989	1990-1999	1996	1997	1998	1999	2000	2001
Iran (Islamic Republic of)	1.6	10.4	10.8	5.1	7.3	13.1	11.1	1.2	8.8	8.2	10.0
Kazakhstan [10]	1.4	23.4	...	...	-16.2	1.4	5.1	-66.2	2.0	14.0	13.7
Kyrgyzstan	0.3	29.2	...	...	-9.9	3.4	37.1	5.1	-4.5	5.8	5.4
Maldives	0.0	8.6	14.8	14.8	6.8	-0.4	20.2	0.2	7.8	4.2	5.1
Nepal [11]	0.0	5.8	2.0	7.3	10.0	9.0	7.1	1.7	5.7	11.1	3.5
Pakistan	0.6	15.6	5.3	8.2	3.8	-0.1	6.9	4.1	1.5	7.6	4.4
Sri Lanka [12]	0.1	16.6	5.0	3.8	7.9	7.0	9.6	6.0	4.5	9.0	-3.4
Tajikistan	0.3	34.2	...	...	-15.7	-34.4	-10.9	1.8	-3.9	10.4	8.6
Turkmenistan	0.7	75.9	...	...	-12.3	8.9	-45.8	-8.9	23.3	42.6	21.4
Uzbekistan [13]	0.9	22.7	...	...	-5.6	6.2	-7.9	-0.1	0.1	0.1	18.1
South-Eastern Asia	*6.2*	*21.6*	*9.2*	*7.3*	*7.0*	*9.6*	*5.1*	*-8.9*	*8.4*	*10.0*	*0.4*
Brunei Darussalam	0.0	9.0	11.5	-4.2	5.3	...	...	...	...	...	...
Cambodia	0.0	7.4	-7.3	2.2	10.3	17.1	36.3	15.4	9.0	44.6	17.3
Indonesia	1.9	20.7	13.8	13.2	7.4	11.6	5.3	-11.4	3.9	6.1	4.3
Lao People's Democratic Republic	0.0	9.9	0.0	3.7	12.9	18.1	9.3	9.6	7.1	7.2	11.5
Malaysia	0.9	24.2	12.7	8.7	9.7	18.2	10.1	-13.4	11.7	19.1	-6.2
Myanmar	0.1	7.8	3.1	1.4	6.2	4.6	5.0	6.7	14.5	23.4	4.8
Philippines	0.9	24.8	6.3	1.0	2.3	5.6	4.2	-1.1	1.6	5.6	2.9
Singapore [14]	0.9	28.6	11.0	6.9	6.0	2.9	4.3	-0.6	13.6	15.2	-11.7
Thailand	1.5	21.5	10.9	8.6	7.9	6.8	1.6	-11.2	12.3	6.0	5.0
Vietnam	0.1	12.3	-0.1	3.2	9.4	13.6	12.8	10.2	8.0	13.2	10.6
Western Asia	*6.5*	*15.4*	*6.5*	*4.5*	*6.1*	*6.8*	*8.7*	*2.3*	*-1.1*	*17.6*	*37.6*
Armenia [15]	0.4	31.8	...	...	-7.5	1.2	1.4	-2.0	5.3	6.4	0.9
Azerbaijan [16]	0.4	24.6	...	...	-12.4	-12.3	-3.5	-1.3	0.7	399.4	615.3
Bahrain	0.0	12.0	5.3	8.8	7.0	-2.5	2.4	2.0	6.3	2.5	2.6
Cyprus	0.1	14.2	5.8	4.8	1.0	-1.5	0.4	1.2	0.4	3.0	-2.6
Georgia [17]	0.4	24.1	...	...	-13.6	131.9	-1.3	-3.6	5.9	0.9	0.9
Iraq [18]	0.3	8.8	13.4	2.5	-16.7	-41.7	37.0	23.7	29.8	42.6	-17.7
Israel [19]	0.8	17.8	...	...	3.3	3.8	5.6	4.7	0.5	12.0	-6.3
Jordan	0.1	16.1	3.7	4.5	5.3	-7.9	10.8	8.7	1.3	1.8	2.5
Kuwait	0.2	11.6	9.5	1.2	0.9	-3.7	0.7	4.2	0.5	129.5	-7.6
Lebanon	0.0	12.6	-2.0	-6.7	2.7	-2.1	-8.4	-0.9	-0.3	0.7	0.5
Oman	0.0	2.9	2.0	24.4	5.7	-5.4	1.8	-1.7	1.0	40.2	62.7
Qatar	0.1	12.9	17.5	7.4	2.2	2.5	35.4	8.0	1.6	13.7	5.7
Saudi Arabia	0.7	8.1	3.8	0.7	5.3	10.6	4.6	2.3	4.3	4.8	3.5
Syrian Arab Republic	0.1	5.5	4.0	5.5	10.9	46.1	26.2	1.6	9.4	-8.8	...
Turkey	2.7	22.0	6.7	5.9	4.7	7.1	11.4	2.0	-5.0	6.0	-7.5
United Arab Emirates	0.2	7.4	41.7	12.8	5.0	9.5	11.6	-1.9	0.9	7.3	3.1
Yemen	0.1	8.0	...	...	2.6	0.6	1.1	3.8	0.7	6.1	5.0
Yemen Arab Republic (Former)	...	...	12.7	13.7	...	...	...	...	...	...	...
Yemen Democratic (Former)	...	...	-0.9	0.9	...	...	...	...	...	...	...
EUROPE	**43.5**	**24.1**	**3.2**	**1.5**	**2.5**	**-0.5**	**3.8**	**2.3**	**1.9**	**4.9**	**1.2**
Eastern Europe	*25.1*	*35.8*	*8.3*	*2.4*	*15.9*	*-1.8*	*2.8*	*-2.4*	*7.6*	*8.4*	*4.7*
Belarus	1.2	39.7	...	...	-0.7	3.6	17.1	10.5	8.1	7.9	6.4
Bulgaria	0.3	31.4	7.1	6.1	-6.7	-9.4	-16.8	3.2	-5.9	10.9	5.6
Czech Republic [20]	0.4	24.6	...	2.6	-0.6	13.6	6.2	-8.5	-2.1	8.0	1.8
Hungary [21]	0.3	19.1	5.5	0.7	-1.1	3.2	11.4	8.3	7.2	9.6	-0.5
Poland	0.9	32.4	7.9	0.0	2.3	8.8	14.4	7.5	4.0	7.3	-0.8
Romania	0.7	36.7	11.0	-1.5	-7.8	3.0	-5.0	-15.3	-17.0	0.6	5.2
Russian Federation [22]	16.8	37.0	...	...	-7.0	-4.1	1.4	-5.4	10.4	9.7	4.9
Slovakia	0.2	24.7	...	-0.6	-1.5	2.2	-2.5	5.2	2.9	-2.0	10.2
Ukraine	4.2	35.9	...	...	-11.8	-4.5	-3.3	-0.8	6.2	4.2	10.0
Northern Europe	*16.1*	*19.8*	*2.1*	*1.8*	*2.4*	*1.6*	*4.2*	*3.4*	*3.0*	*5.2*	*-0.4*
Denmark	1.0	15.6	2.6	1.2	0.9	-4.3	8.0	0.4	-0.5	6.7	2.6
Estonia	0.2	37.0	...	...	-1.3	2.6	16.9	6.3	-1.0	15.8	7.9
Finland	1.3	20.3	3.9	3.9	3.7	2.8	9.4	7.8	5.4	12.4	-0.5
Iceland	0.0	14.4	8.0	1.1	2.1	8.5	4.2	6.4	5.3	4.9	3.6
Ireland	0.6	25.3	6.1	3.1	8.9	5.1	16.1	16.4	13.7	8.7	6.1
Latvia	0.3	33.2	...	...	-10.1	4.1	17.1	4.0	-5.9	6.8	9.4
Lithuania [23]	0.2	20.6	...	...	-5.2	2.8	8.1	6.2	-8.7	8.8	16.5
Norway	0.6	11.6	1.7	-0.3	1.1	1.1	5.1	-2.3	-0.4	2.7	-0.2
Sweden	2.1	18.3	1.3	2.1	4.5	3.4	7.4	8.0	9.0	10.8	-0.2
United Kingdom	9.7	20.9	1.9	1.6	1.0	1.3	1.0	1.0	0.8	1.7	-2.1
Southern Europe	*18.7*	*21.6*	*5.1*	*1.5*	*1.4*	*0.0*	*4.1*	*3.1*	*0.7*	*3.5*	*1.0*
Andorra	0.0	18.1	8.2	8.5	7.0	6.4	11.1	9.9	7.5	8.7	5.8
Bosnia and Herzegovina	0.1	21.4	...	...	7.3	50.0	32.0	27.5	11.6	10.7	7.4
Greece	0.6	14.9	6.8	0.5	-0.2	3.9	-3.7	5.3	-0.1	3.6	3.8

Table 6.C. Average Rates of Growth of Gross Domestic Product by Kind of Economic Activity - Manufacturing

Major area, region and country	Base year weights as percentage of total for world or region in 1990	Base year share as percentage of total GDP in 1990	Average rates of growth			Annual rate of change (percentage)					
			1970-1979	1980-1989	1990-1999	1996	1997	1998	1999	2000	2001
Holy See	0.0	22.5	5.9	1.4	1.3	-1.7	3.3	1.8	-0.1	3.2	0.7
Italy	11.7	22.5	5.0	1.0	1.2	-1.7	3.2	1.8	-0.2	3.1	0.7
Malta	0.0	23.9	17.0	1.6	2.8	1.8	-0.7	5.3	4.0	14.3	-6.4
Portugal	0.6	19.1	5.1	3.4	1.9	8.1	5.9	2.3	0.7	2.0	2.0
San Marino	0.0	22.5	4.8	0.2	0.7	-2.7	0.4	7.2	6.2	2.1	0.6
Serbia and Montenegro	0.4	27.5	...	...	-12.8	7.0	9.1	3.8	-43.8	9.2	-6.7
Slovenia	0.2	29.9	...	...	-0.5	1.6	6.6	4.6	3.1	8.6	4.4
Spain	4.9	20.4	5.1	2.0	2.2	1.4	6.1	5.1	3.8	3.8	0.9
TFYR Macedonia [24]	0.1	34.0	...	...	-6.1	5.1	3.2	3.3	-2.3	3.3	-3.2
Yugoslavia (Former)	...	...	6.2	5.2	...	...	...	...	...	...	...
Western Europe	*40.2*	*22.6*	*2.5*	*1.3*	*1.0*	*-1.2*	*3.7*	*3.0*	*0.3*	*4.2*	*0.9*
Austria	1.6	20.6	3.6	2.2	2.7	1.6	4.3	4.8	3.1	6.5	1.2
Belgium	1.9	20.8	3.7	2.7	1.7	2.5	6.8	2.2	0.7	4.0	0.3
France	10.7	18.8	3.5	1.4	2.0	0.0	4.4	4.5	3.0	4.2	1.8
Germany	20.8	26.5	1.9	1.1	0.1	-2.9	3.4	2.1	-2.1	4.3	0.6
Liechtenstein	0.0	24.2	2.3	1.5	1.1	1.2	2.8	3.8	2.2	1.6	0.8
Luxembourg	0.1	20.1	1.4	3.2	1.1	3.8	5.5	0.8	7.6	6.1	2.4
Monaco	0.0	18.8	4.1	1.4	2.6	0.6	5.1	5.2	2.8	-1.3	3.4
Netherlands	2.4	17.7	3.9	1.8	2.3	0.6	2.5	3.0	2.4	5.0	0.2
Switzerland	2.6	24.2	0.8	0.8	0.4	0.3	1.7	2.6	0.9	0.7	-0.6
OCEANIA	**1.0**	**12.9**	**2.0**	**1.6**	**1.4**	**2.1**	**2.6**	**1.0**	**1.6**	**2.6**	**2.7**
Australia & New Zealand	*98.4*	*13.1*	*2.0*	*1.6*	*1.4*	*2.0*	*2.6*	*1.0*	*1.6*	*2.6*	*2.7*
Australia	82.4	12.5	2.0	1.7	1.4	2.0	3.3	2.0	1.0	2.7	3.0
New Zealand	16.1	17.4	1.9	1.0	1.3	1.6	-0.7	-3.8	4.7	2.0	1.1
Melanesia	*1.0*	*6.3*	*6.9*	*0.6*	*3.5*	*10.7*	*4.0*	*2.1*	*3.5*	*1.6*	*1.6*
Fiji	0.3	10.6	4.8	0.6	3.9	3.4	-0.8	4.8	9.6	-6.2	1.8
New Caledonia	0.1	1.0	1.7	8.3	6.3	-10.6	19.0	-24.5	11.7	5.1	-2.2
Papua New Guinea	0.6	8.8	7.9	0.3	3.2	15.5	5.1	2.8	1.3	4.5	2.0
Solomon Islands	0.0	2.9	8.1	2.4	5.5	3.5	-1.0	-2.2	-7.5	-1.7	-14.6
Vanuatu	0.0	5.5	7.7	7.1	3.2	8.0	-1.0	10.7	3.2	-2.8	-1.0
Micronesia	*0.0*	*1.2*	*4.1*	*0.2*	*8.4*	*-18.9*	*15.2*	*8.9*	*4.1*	*-25.2*	*0.4*
Kiribati	0.0	1.2	2.9	-3.2	17.2	0.0	24.8	51.2	-42.1	-56.9	1.8
Marshall Islands	0.0	0.9	6.6	6.1	5.5	-49.5	0.1	-5.9	11.0	0.1	-3.4
Micronesia (Federated States of)	0.0	1.2	6.6	6.0	10.5	-13.0	4.7	-11.9	40.6	-36.9	1.5
Nauru	0.0	1.2	6.8	6.5	2.9	-17.9	2.3	-11.6	36.7	-38.8	-0.8
Palau	0.0	1.2	2.9	-5.5	6.4	17.1	48.5	21.7	0.5	-2.2	1.6
Polynesia	*0.6*	*8.0*	*5.0*	*5.4*	*2.3*	*2.2*	*0.2*	*-0.4*	*2.7*	*3.1*	*3.3*
French Polynesia [25]	0.5	7.3	5.8	6.9	3.2	1.6	1.1	1.1	2.7	2.7	2.1
Samoa	0.1	19.9	3.1	0.4	-2.6	4.8	-6.1	-12.6	1.3	7.3	13.4
Tonga	0.0	5.1	9.7	3.8	0.5	11.9	0.3	11.4	16.4	0.7	2.0
Tuvalu	0.0	2.8	6.6	14.5	0.4	-4.7	25.4	20.6	-11.5	3.0	3.0

Notes for Table 6.C - Manufacturing

1/ 1987-1999
Includes mining and handicrafts.

2/ 1970-1994
Includes handicrafts.

3/ 1996-2001
Includes non-petroleum mining activities.

4/ 1991-1992
Includes handicrafts.

5/ 1987-1992
Includes handicrafts.

6/ 1970-1991
Includes handicrafts and repair services.

7/ 1970-1986
Does not include petroleum refining.

8/ 1987-2001
Includes Electricity, gas and water supply.

9/ 1984-2001
Includes petroleum refining.

10/ 1991-1997
Includes Mining and quarrying, and Electricity, gas and water supply.

11/ 1985-1998
Includes cottage industries.

12/ 1970-1975
Estimates on processing of tea and rubber are included in the agricultural sector.

13/ 1993-1997
Includes Mining and utilities.

14/ 1989-2001
Includes Agriculture, hunting, forestry, fishing, and Mining and quarrying.

15/ 1991-2001
Includes Mining and utilities.

16/ 1993-2001
Includes Mining and utilities.

17/ 1980-2001
Includes Mining and utilities.

18/ 1976-1991
Includes Agricultural services and related activities such as cotton ginning and pressing.

19/ 1970-1989

"Manufacturing" not available separatly only in "Mining, manufacturing and utilities".

20/ 1989-1990

Includes Mining and utilities.

21/ 1988-1991

Includes Gas.

22/ 1990-2001

Includes Mining and quarrying, and Electricity, gas and water supply.

23/ 1994

Includes Mining and quarrying.

24/ 1991-1997

Includes Mining and utilities.

25/ 1970-1979

Includes manufacturing of energy-generating products.

Table 6.D. Average Rates of Growth of Gross Domestic Product by Kind of Economic Activity - Construction

Major area, region and country	Base year weights as percentage of total for world or region in 1990	Base year share as percentage of total GDP in 1990	Average rates of growth 1970-1979	1980-1989	1990-1999	Annual rate of change (percentage) 1996	1997	1998	1999	2000	2001
WORLD	**100.0**	**6.3**	**3.0**	**1.9**	**0.1**	**1.8**	**1.4**	**1.4**	**1.5**	**1.8**	**0.3**
DEVELOPED ECONOMIES	**72.7**	**6.1**	**1.7**	**1.6**	**0.1**	**1.2**	**0.5**	**2.2**	**2.5**	**1.0**	**-0.7**
DEVELOPING ECONOMIES	**16.0**	**5.7**	**7.5**	**1.9**	**4.6**	**5.0**	**4.5**	**-1.2**	**-1.3**	**2.9**	**1.9**
TRANSITION ECONOMIES	**11.3**	**8.7**	**6.1**	**4.1**	**-10.3**	**-6.1**	**0.6**	**1.9**	**1.5**	**7.8**	**8.0**
AFRICA	**1.9**	**5.1**	**3.9**	**0.1**	**0.3**	**3.2**	**4.1**	**3.5**	**0.5**	**3.1**	**3.7**
Eastern Africa	*8.9*	*4.1*	*1.6*	*2.0*	*5.0*	*10.4*	*10.1*	*8.9*	*7.0*	*-2.7*	*4.9*
Burundi	0.1	3.4	11.3	2.8	1.3	-6.2	3.1	7.1	5.1	6.1	5.6
Comoros	0.0	3.2	8.3	-4.0	5.7	0.8	-2.1	-1.6	136.0	-3.3	-2.1
Djibouti	0.2	9.6	0.0	1.9	-5.9	-12.4	26.9	8.5	-2.3	3.0	4.1
Eritrea	...	...	...	...	16.3	71.8	22.1	-1.5	1.8	-8.7	4.3
Ethiopia	...	...	...	...	11.0	5.4	7.0	10.5	11.7	3.7	8.7
Ethiopia (Former)	0.7	2.5	-0.1	2.8	-15.3	...	...	...	...	...	...
Kenya	1.5	4.8	3.6	2.0	0.4	2.6	2.0	0.5	1.0	-1.0	0.0
Madagascar	0.2	1.5	0.3	6.9	2.6	5.7	3.5	2.7	37.1	4.8	31.9
Malawi	0.1	2.2	11.3	-0.5	5.1	19.3	9.9	4.8	15.1	-1.9	-6.9
Mauritius	0.5	5.6	7.7	2.7	5.6	4.8	-0.9	6.0	8.5	7.5	1.5
Mozambique	0.8	7.7	3.9	-0.3	11.3	24.0	18.1	26.2	3.4	4.7	9.7
Reunion	1.1	5.7	6.8	3.7	3.8	3.3	3.4	3.3	3.4	3.4	3.4
Rwanda	0.7	7.5	9.3	8.9	1.9	36.0	16.0	17.4	23.8	16.1	7.6
Seychelles	0.1	4.8	5.0	-5.5	10.8	14.3	11.7	12.9	5.5	8.6	31.3
Somalia	0.1	3.6	0.0	1.2	0.8	6.9	6.9	3.8	16.8	3.0	3.0
Uganda	0.7	4.7	0.0	4.7	10.1	11.4	9.4	6.1	6.9	9.4	4.0
United Republic Of Tanzania	0.7	4.7	1.0	0.8	16.5	13.2	13.8	11.4	11.4	-46.0	1.5
Zambia	0.5	3.2	-3.8	-2.5	-2.9	-12.4	33.8	-4.0	14.9	5.4	10.2
Zimbabwe	0.9	2.9	-2.6	1.0	1.3	12.0	16.6	6.0	-0.7	-5.2	-2.4
Middle Africa	*6.7*	*4.0*	*6.6*	*-2.8*	*-4.0*	*7.9*	*-6.5*	*2.1*	*-1.2*	*6.5*	*4.1*
Angola	1.1	2.9	10.1	-4.3	0.4	2.3	4.4	8.5	5.9	7.4	6.9
Cameroon	2.5	4.6	10.0	-3.6	-9.3	27.7	-30.2	-0.6	6.0	1.6	5.5
Central African Republic	0.1	2.7	3.0	2.9	7.4	1.4	7.3	7.9	32.6	7.0	4.3
Chad	0.1	1.8	-2.8	20.8	0.0	0.0	0.0	0.0	8.3	0.0	7.7
Congo	0.1	1.4	6.5	-13.8	2.8	9.7	0.9	-0.1	158.1	23.9	-1.7
Democratic Republic of the Congo	1.9	5.6	-1.8	2.2	-5.6	-1.4	-2.9	-0.8	-10.4	-4.3	-4.4
Equatorial Guinea	0.0	3.7	3.6	6.9	23.3	44.6	71.1	21.4	42.2	16.9	53.4
Gabon	0.8	3.7	10.3	-3.1	-3.9	3.0	3.4	-1.2	-40.4	24.6	-3.4
Sao Tome and Principe	0.0	6.8	3.5	-2.8	6.2	5.0	4.8	-12.1	49.2	2.0	2.7
Northern Africa	*62.0*	*7.1*	*10.1*	*1.2*	*0.7*	*3.2*	*4.9*	*3.0*	*2.5*	*3.7*	*3.2*
Algeria	23.8	10.3	8.1	2.1	-1.0	-2.8	4.3	4.1	-7.5	-13.7	2.0
Egypt	12.6	4.7	16.5	3.2	4.5	0.1	11.2	4.0	2.0	2.1	2.1
Libyan Arab Jamahiriya	12.9	12.2	14.3	-2.0	-4.0	32.0	-4.1	-5.9	9.0	33.2	9.0
Morocco	5.1	5.3	7.7	0.0	1.4	5.9	7.0	4.1	4.9	7.1	5.8
Sudan	5.7	4.5	5.1	2.7	3.2	1.6	-0.5	5.0	30.2	20.0	-2.0
Tunisia	1.9	4.1	4.8	1.8	5.5	2.8	6.8	7.1	5.5	10.1	7.1
Southern Africa	*14.0*	*3.1*	*2.0*	*-0.2*	*-0.5*	*2.1*	*3.4*	*2.6*	*-2.3*	*2.7*	*4.1*
Botswana	0.9	7.0	11.2	7.6	5.0	3.3	5.5	4.3	11.5	2.5	1.7
Lesotho	0.3	14.3	9.6	9.0	3.5	4.8	4.1	-11.9	-7.6	9.7	0.7
Namibia	0.2	2.3	11.5	-4.1	4.1	15.6	-11.8	15.3	-13.9	-5.5	51.5
South Africa	12.5	3.0	1.9	-0.3	-0.5	2.0	3.4	2.6	-2.4	2.7	4.0
Swaziland	0.1	2.5	17.0	-5.3	11.9	5.3	10.0	13.6	12.0	9.5	15.2
Western Africa	*8.4*	*3.1*	*5.8*	*-1.1*	*5.4*	*7.3*	*7.0*	*9.2*	*12.2*	*7.2*	*1.9*
Benin	0.4	6.0	6.3	0.5	6.7	6.4	5.8	5.6	-46.4	7.1	6.7
Burkina Faso	0.5	5.1	-0.9	18.8	0.3	83.5	1.0	7.6	5.8	2.2	1.0
Cape Verde	0.1	11.9	-1.9	7.5	3.2	3.2	-2.7	9.5	6.3	12.2	-26.7
Cote d'Ivoire	0.8	1.8	11.1	-2.6	8.0	22.3	6.1	-0.8	29.8	6.4	-25.7
Gambia	0.1	4.5	5.3	0.7	6.4	6.1	7.3	7.0	31.9	3.7	7.3
Ghana	1.4	6.2	-0.9	-1.4	6.3	6.1	7.8	5.1	2.0	5.1	4.8
Guinea	0.9	9.0	2.8	3.8	4.4	4.8	13.4	6.6	3.7	5.0	3.0
Guinea-Bissau	0.1	10.0	2.8	-2.7	-1.3	2.7	47.7	-54.8	3.6	15.8	7.8
Liberia	0.0	3.3	3.1	-2.5	-16.2	-61.1	442.9	28.9	22.4	5.0	4.8
Mali	0.4	4.0	3.7	-3.8	10.5	4.8	0.5	1.9	151.9	33.2	17.7
Mauritania	0.2	5.2	1.4	6.1	0.7	-1.0	4.9	-0.1	2.5	4.7	4.0
Niger	0.4	4.6	4.6	0.5	-6.9	5.6	5.3	2.9	5.6	6.7	6.2
Nigeria	2.0	1.7	9.9	-5.5	6.1	-5.5	8.6	27.0	9.9	4.1	9.1

Table 6.D. Average Rates of Growth of Gross Domestic Product by Kind of Economic Activity - Construction

Major area, region and country	Base year weights as percentage of total for world or region in 1990	Base year share as percentage of total GDP in 1990	Average rates of growth 1970-1979	1980-1989	1990-1999	Annual rate of change (percentage) 1996	1997	1998	1999	2000	2001
Senegal	0.7	3.1	...	3.6	9.0	8.8	15.2	12.7	15.8	4.5	7.7
Sierra Leone	0.0	1.9	3.7	1.3	6.1	-3.2	95.6	19.3	11.0	7.9	8.1
Togo	0.2	3.6	8.7	3.8	-5.3	5.1	-57.8	5.9	-4.4	8.7	-2.0
AMERICAS	**24.3**	**4.6**	**3.2**	**1.4**	**1.7**	**5.3**	**4.2**	**6.3**	**3.5**	**2.5**	**-1.3**
NORTHERN AMERICA	**19.9**	**4.5**	**2.5**	**1.3**	**1.9**	**5.4**	**2.9**	**7.0**	**5.4**	**2.9**	**-1.0**
Bermuda	0.0	7.4	3.7	3.5	-1.8	12.7	2.5	-20.4	37.2	-0.6	9.7
Canada	10.6	6.4	3.3	2.8	-0.3	3.6	5.6	3.1	4.9	4.2	3.8
United States	71.5	4.3	2.4	1.1	2.2	5.6	2.6	7.5	5.4	2.7	-1.6
LATIN AMERICA AND THE CARIBBEAN	**4.3**	**5.4**	**6.9**	**1.8**	**1.0**	**5.1**	**9.5**	**3.4**	**-4.0**	**0.8**	**-2.7**
Caribbean	*1.4*	*5.5*	*0.8*	*2.7*	*2.3*	*8.3*	*10.9*	*9.7*	*7.5*	*6.9*	*4.3*
Anguilla	0.0	16.7	3.8	8.4	3.8	15.3	4.0	8.0	21.2	-6.4	-17.9
Antigua and Barbuda	0.0	11.6	1.5	11.2	3.4	12.0	8.0	10.0	8.0	6.5	4.0
Aruba	0.0	7.0	8.2	9.0	4.5	10.2	32.9	7.3	-25.1	8.6	10.6
Bahamas	0.0	3.9	3.0	3.0	-8.6	-9.5	1.4	-6.0	-3.7	-4.6	-5.1
Barbados	0.0	5.6	1.0	2.4	0.6	0.0	14.6	16.4	10.9	0.0	-2.8
British Virgin Islands	0.0	5.8	-8.0	9.6	7.5	-16.1	11.5	34.5	7.7	17.3	17.3
Cayman Islands	0.0	9.5	10.1	7.4	-0.4	3.6	-2.8	-0.3	0.1	0.1	0.1
Cuba	0.4	7.3	10.1	7.5	-7.3	30.7	3.2	5.7	7.5	9.7	3.6
Dominica	0.0	6.2	0.3	4.4	3.4	-3.0	-1.7	-4.1	3.8	2.0	-4.6
Dominican Republic	0.2	6.6	10.8	6.6	6.5	6.7	17.1	19.6	17.7	5.2	0.9
Grenada	0.0	8.2	2.4	7.3	1.3	2.3	5.7	17.6	15.5	14.6	-13.9
Guadeloupe	0.1	7.4	8.7	6.1	2.6	4.3	9.2	4.1	5.9	5.9	5.9
Haiti	0.0	5.8	13.7	1.4	6.2	17.3	11.3	8.1	4.6	8.0	0.9
Jamaica	0.1	10.8	-6.9	1.9	-1.4	-5.2	-3.7	-5.9	-1.4	15.9	5.0
Martinique	0.0	4.8	1.4	9.2	2.7	1.6	1.6	4.1	2.5	2.5	2.5
Montserrat	0.0	30.3	3.1	13.9	-6.9	1.2	72.6	33.5	-13.5	-35.8	-7.7
Netherlands Antilles	0.0	6.7	3.3	-1.0	1.3	5.8	2.1	0.6	0.8	0.4	2.6
Puerto Rico [1]	0.2	2.3	-10.5	2.8	7.1	15.2	15.3	10.1	8.7	8.0	9.0
Saint Kitts and Nevis	0.0	12.0	-0.8	11.5	5.5	5.0	6.0	7.0	12.9	28.8	4.9
Saint Lucia	0.0	5.4	3.0	9.6	0.4	-4.0	0.4	3.4	0.5	-1.0	-5.0
Saint Vincent and the Grenadines	0.0	7.9	0.4	5.5	4.9	-7.4	16.0	13.8	-4.5	-12.7	5.5
Trinidad and Tobago	0.1	9.2	14.3	-7.5	6.5	3.5	18.2	15.2	6.0	5.4	5.4
Central America	*3.0*	*3.5*	*6.6*	*-0.4*	*3.5*	*7.7*	*8.8*	*4.9*	*5.4*	*4.4*	*-4.2*
Belize	0.0	6.6	7.1	7.2	2.6	-0.9	-5.7	-1.7	18.1	25.8	21.9
Costa Rica	0.1	4.3	11.5	-1.7	2.9	-17.9	6.1	17.4	-1.6	4.4	11.4
El Salvador	0.1	3.5	9.4	-2.1	3.8	2.7	6.2	8.5	-1.8	-3.4	10.0
Guatemala	0.0	2.0	14.3	-2.5	5.1	2.9	9.7	9.8	7.8	-18.3	-38.0
Honduras	0.0	4.6	5.4	3.1	0.9	-11.4	-3.0	5.3	10.5	4.2	-7.1
Mexico	2.7	3.6	6.4	-0.2	3.2	9.8	9.3	4.2	5.0	5.1	-4.5
Nicaragua	0.0	2.9	-9.9	9.4	7.8	18.2	10.0	10.4	47.2	10.4	5.2
Panama	0.0	1.1	4.6	-13.6	21.5	-4.1	5.5	6.7	16.0	2.5	-9.7
South America	*13.5*	*6.1*	*7.7*	*2.2*	*0.4*	*4.3*	*9.5*	*2.6*	*-7.0*	*-0.6*	*-3.2*
Argentina	1.8	4.4	2.8	-4.9	4.9	8.4	16.6	8.7	-7.9	-9.3	-11.6
Bolivia	0.0	3.1	4.9	-6.8	5.9	9.0	4.9	35.9	-16.9	-11.4	-7.7
Brazil	9.0	7.1	13.2	6.2	-1.5	5.2	7.6	1.5	-3.8	3.0	-2.6
Chile	0.7	7.4	-3.3	5.5	5.8	8.6	6.3	1.9	-10.0	0.2	3.8
Colombia	0.7	4.7	4.2	5.0	-3.2	-12.9	2.2	-7.2	-27.0	-2.8	3.2
Ecuador	0.1	2.0	6.3	-0.9	-3.9	1.3	2.7	-0.2	-24.9	18.3	4.0
French Guiana	0.0	12.7	1.6	7.0	1.9	1.6	0.9	1.6	1.4	1.4	1.4
Guyana [2]	0.0	4.0	0.6	-0.9	5.8	14.0	13.1	4.7	-10.0	6.6	2.0
Paraguay	0.1	5.5	19.6	3.2	2.5	3.4	0.6	1.0	2.5	2.0	-22.7
Peru	0.4	3.9	3.5	0.3	7.6	-2.3	14.9	0.6	-10.5	-4.2	-4.8
Suriname	0.0	6.1	28.1	-4.2	-2.9	7.2	-20.6	16.4	-14.6	-11.9	4.5
Uruguay	0.1	3.4	9.0	-5.0	5.2	-1.6	2.4	9.8	8.9	-11.1	-11.2
Venezuela	0.6	4.5	11.8	-9.7	3.4	1.1	17.2	-0.3	-16.5	-2.7	13.5
ASIA	**32.3**	**8.3**	**5.4**	**2.2**	**1.8**	**2.2**	**0.8**	**-2.9**	**-1.1**	**0.5**	**0.1**
Eastern Asia	*77.8*	*9.1*	*3.9*	*3.3*	*1.1*	*1.1*	*-0.2*	*-2.0*	*-1.6*	*-0.8*	*-1.5*
China	3.9	4.7	4.4	11.2	9.9	8.5	2.6	9.0	4.3	9.6	6.9
Democratic People's Rep. of Korea	0.2	6.3	11.9	8.1	-3.2	-3.6	-6.3	-1.1	6.2	1.3	3.7
Hong Kong SAR of China	0.8	5.1	8.8	7.2	3.8	4.3	5.1	-5.0	3.4	10.2	-2.8
Japan	64.9	9.8	3.4	2.6	-0.5	-0.7	-1.2	-2.5	-1.4	-2.4	-3.8

Table 6.D. Average Rates of Growth of Gross Domestic Product by Kind of Economic Activity - Construction

Major area, region and country	Base year weights as percentage of total for world or region in 1990	Base year share as percentage of total GDP in 1990	Average rates of growth 1970-1979	1980-1989	1990-1999	Annual rate of change (percentage) 1996	1997	1998	1999	2000	2001
Macao SAR of China	0.0	5.8	16.9	17.1	1.0	-26.3	-1.0	-23.2	-6.1	-29.5	29.8
Mongolia	0.0	3.1	5.7	5.3	-9.9	2.6	-2.7	-1.1	1.6	-14.6	12.4
Republic of Korea	6.2	11.4	12.0	7.5	4.8	6.9	1.4	-8.6	-9.1	-3.1	5.6
South Central Asia	*10.3*	*6.2*	*5.4*	*0.0*	*6.0*	*6.3*	*3.3*	*3.7*	*7.8*	*6.0*	*10.3*
Afghanistan	0.1	6.5	15.8	-0.7	-2.2	6.6	13.3	5.2	-12.4	-43.7	0.0
Bangladesh	0.4	5.7	-7.5	7.9	7.8	8.6	9.5	8.9	8.5	8.6	7.9
Bhutan	0.0	8.0	6.4	3.0	11.2	0.0	9.9	20.6	22.0	18.8	3.1
India	3.5	5.0	2.0	5.0	5.6	2.1	10.2	6.2	8.1	6.8	3.6
Iran (Islamic Republic of)	2.2	5.3	9.1	-5.6	2.8	12.5	-6.1	-4.2	13.5	6.5	12.4
Kazakhstan	1.9	12.1	...	...	-15.9	-21.8	8.0	15.0	8.0	14.0	27.4
Kyrgyzstan	0.2	7.7	...	...	-16.2	0.0	-17.0	-27.7	-2.0	29.7	3.9
Maldives	0.0	3.2	31.7	8.5	8.3	-6.1	35.1	11.0	4.3	-23.8	11.3
Nepal	0.1	8.6	2.0	9.3	4.4	6.6	6.1	-0.9	2.7	17.8	0.0
Pakistan	0.4	3.7	7.4	4.6	2.5	1.1	1.3	-4.9	5.2	-0.4	0.9
Sri Lanka	0.1	6.6	2.7	4.7	5.7	4.1	6.5	6.9	6.8	6.8	1.2
Tajikistan	0.3	11.0	...	...	-23.3	14.8	9.8	46.1	-17.6	19.5	4.4
Turkmenistan	0.1	4.8	...	...	6.0	90.2	-3.0	21.1	-2.3	3.7	16.8
Uzbekistan	1.1	10.6	...	...	-5.5	18.8	-7.3	7.9	-6.4	-5.9	64.5
South-Eastern Asia	*4.0*	*5.2*	*10.4*	*4.0*	*5.2*	*13.1*	*2.1*	*-24.3*	*-3.8*	*1.2*	*0.8*
Brunei Darussalam	0.0	4.3	11.1	4.1	4.9	8.1	8.9	2.0	6.6	-3.5	-2.4
Cambodia	0.0	2.4	-7.3	-3.3	10.3	-0.5	-5.2	-14.7	30.6	7.1	9.4
Indonesia	1.4	5.6	16.4	6.2	5.4	12.8	7.4	-36.4	-1.9	5.5	4.0
Lao People's Democratic Republic	0.0	2.9	-0.2	6.8	6.3	12.3	5.0	-14.1	-0.6	-9.2	13.0
Malaysia	0.4	3.9	11.2	3.1	8.2	16.2	10.6	-24.0	-4.4	1.0	2.3
Myanmar	0.1	1.8	6.9	3.9	16.0	24.6	9.8	6.5	4.4	11.9	4.8
Philippines	0.6	6.0	14.4	-2.9	2.5	10.9	16.2	-9.6	-1.6	1.4	-3.6
Singapore	0.4	5.4	5.4	4.4	11.3	23.2	16.3	2.8	-8.8	-1.7	-2.1
Thailand	1.1	6.0	5.1	9.2	-1.3	7.0	-25.6	-38.3	-6.8	-9.4	-3.0
Vietnam	0.1	3.8	-0.1	3.7	9.9	16.1	11.3	-0.5	2.4	7.5	4.9
Western Asia	*7.9*	*6.9*	*16.0*	*-4.1*	*1.5*	*-1.3*	*6.3*	*2.0*	*-5.9*	*4.4*	*-1.1*
Armenia	0.6	17.9	...	...	-19.3	25.4	3.9	10.7	7.7	28.9	3.2
Azerbaijan	0.4	8.1	...	...	5.2	110.0	66.1	52.1	4.7	2.6	5.9
Bahrain	0.1	5.8	23.2	-2.5	0.2	-14.6	-6.2	1.0	16.9	1.4	2.1
Cyprus	0.1	9.5	3.0	-0.1	1.9	-0.2	-3.9	-0.3	-0.7	-2.2	2.0
Georgia	0.4	8.7	...	...	-18.5	25.7	56.3	35.1	-17.3	2.0	5.1
Iraq	0.6	7.3	28.1	-4.4	-28.1	-62.0	71.2	26.7	-13.6	107.6	28.3
Israel	0.6	5.0	2.4	0.0	7.0	11.1	1.6	-6.2	-8.4	-3.7	-9.3
Jordan	0.0	4.0	12.3	-1.4	2.4	-3.7	-12.8	-19.1	-16.2	8.5	7.9
Kuwait	0.1	1.8	17.2	-8.0	2.8	-4.5	-2.9	-1.8	0.6	43.3	-2.1
Lebanon	0.0	3.3	-4.5	-6.7	8.2	-27.8	-8.1	-18.8	-11.5	-2.3	4.7
Oman	0.1	2.3	4.8	-0.6	3.7	-9.2	48.1	4.2	-28.0	3.6	14.8
Qatar	0.1	4.2	10.2	0.3	8.6	42.5	45.4	-24.4	-12.7	-13.1	-3.4
Saudi Arabia	2.0	8.7	22.2	-4.7	-2.0	-23.3	-0.1	2.0	-2.4	5.9	0.4
Syrian Arab Republic	0.1	3.8	17.1	-5.8	5.8	9.8	5.2	0.5	-5.1	1.9	1.3
Turkey	2.1	6.3	1.8	6.7	0.4	5.9	4.6	0.7	-12.5	4.4	-5.9
United Arab Emirates	0.6	7.9	49.6	-0.4	4.2	5.7	6.7	2.5	2.3	2.8	2.4
Yemen	0.1	2.7	...	...	1.8	28.2	28.4	1.4	0.7	8.2	21.3
Yemen Arab Republic (Former)	...	...	16.5	-3.1	...	...	...	...	...	...	...
Yemen Democratic (Former)	...	...	31.6	3.8	...	...	...	...	...	...	...
EUROPE	**40.1**	**6.5**	**1.7**	**2.1**	**-2.4**	**-1.5**	**-0.8**	**1.0**	**2.2**	**3.2**	**1.1**
Eastern Europe	*22.6*	*8.6*	*6.1*	*4.4*	*-13.6*	*-10.6*	*-2.4*	*-2.6*	*3.3*	*9.6*	*4.4*
Belarus	0.9	7.9	...	...	-8.5	-7.6	21.4	13.8	-2.4	-2.1	-5.2
Bulgaria	0.2	5.2	7.1	6.1	-4.1	-9.4	-21.4	32.4	2.9	1.4	1.5
Czech Republic	0.6	10.2	...	0.6	-7.4	-18.1	-8.3	-19.2	-2.0	-6.3	-12.5
Czechoslovakia (Former)	...	...	4.7	...	...	...	...	...	...	...	...
Hungary	0.3	5.5	1.7	0.1	-2.9	-7.2	8.2	5.8	4.3	6.9	3.1
Poland	1.0	9.7	5.7	-3.1	3.5	2.8	13.6	9.3	3.5	-0.7	-7.0
Republic of Moldova	0.2	6.5	...	...	-19.2	7.5	-15.9	-14.8	4.1	-30.4	24.5
Romania	0.4	5.4	7.7	0.4	-2.3	2.1	-18.1	-10.3	-5.3	6.0	-0.1
Russian Federation	15.0	8.9	...	...	-12.1	-15.6	-6.4	-6.5	6.1	15.9	9.9
Slovakia	0.4	13.4	...	0.2	-9.3	51.6	-1.5	-15.6	-29.9	2.7	-1.5
USSR (Former)	...	...	6.3	5.0	...	...	...	...	...	...	...
Northern Europe	*18.3*	*6.1*	*0.0*	*2.8*	*0.1*	*3.2*	*3.0*	*3.2*	*0.9*	*2.9*	*2.7*
Denmark	1.0	4.5	-2.3	1.3	-0.5	5.3	-4.1	10.1	-1.3	5.6	-3.8
Estonia	0.1	7.1	...	...	0.5	6.7	15.7	19.7	-8.7	6.7	5.5
Finland	1.8	7.4	1.0	3.5	-2.8	12.3	13.8	5.5	-1.8	0.8	-3.1
Iceland	0.1	7.5	1.5	3.1	1.8	7.1	11.3	12.0	6.5	15.0	3.8

Table 6.D. Average Rates of Growth of Gross Domestic Product by Kind of Economic Activity - Construction

Major area, region and country	Base year weights as percentage of total for world or region in 1990	Base year share as percentage of total GDP in 1990	Average rates of growth 1970-1979	Average rates of growth 1980-1989	Average rates of growth 1990-1999	Annual rate of change (percentage) 1996	1997	1998	1999	2000	2001
Ireland	0.4	4.8	6.4	-3.8	10.1	10.5	12.4	22.2	18.7	22.1	6.5
Latvia	0.3	9.4	...	...	-17.1	5.3	8.2	17.0	8.1	8.2	6.1
Lithuania	0.3	9.8	...	...	-8.9	3.4	6.6	17.0	-12.2	-19.1	7.1
Norway	0.9	4.3	2.8	2.3	-0.3	0.5	8.1	3.5	-7.1	1.2	1.2
Sweden	2.6	6.0	0.8	2.2	-1.4	-0.4	-4.5	-0.1	3.2	1.3	3.7
United Kingdom	10.7	6.2	-0.5	3.4	0.0	2.7	2.9	1.2	0.8	1.8	3.6
Southern Europe	*21.3*	*6.6*	*0.5*	*1.4*	*1.0*	*2.2*	*0.7*	*3.5*	*3.9*	*4.2*	*5.0*
Albania	0.0	6.6	7.0	2.7	6.3	18.5	-6.4	21.0	15.0	18.0	16.5
Andorra	0.0	9.2	5.4	7.9	6.0	3.4	7.1	12.2	13.6	11.0	10.2
Bosnia and Herzegovina	0.1	3.1	...	...	12.0	113.7	79.9	25.1	-14.3	10.7	7.4
Croatia	0.2	5.4	...	...	-2.4	18.8	13.0	0.5	-10.1	-7.1	2.4
Greece	1.1	7.4	3.2	-1.3	1.0	1.0	2.5	10.6	5.2	5.3	10.0
Holy See	0.0	5.8	0.9	1.4	0.1	4.0	-1.7	-0.1	1.2	2.4	4.5
Italy	11.2	5.8	0.1	1.0	0.0	4.1	-1.8	-0.2	1.1	2.3	4.4
Portugal	0.7	5.5	3.4	3.7	2.7	3.3	8.0	5.4	2.9	4.9	2.9
San Marino	0.0	5.8	0.9	0.3	0.4	2.0	-2.1	2.9	8.7	3.2	4.1
Serbia and Montenegro	0.3	6.3	...	...	-13.7	-3.4	-0.1	-5.5	-28.5	-0.6	-2.2
Slovenia	0.1	4.3	...	...	2.4	13.2	7.7	4.6	15.8	2.8	-3.5
Spain	7.5	8.5	0.2	2.6	2.0	-1.4	2.2	7.2	8.6	6.4	5.4
TFYR Macedonia	0.1	7.1	...	...	-9.5	-58.7	0.2	2.9	12.2	-3.0	-0.1
Yugoslavia (Former)	...	...	5.3	-3.7	...	...	...	...	...	...	...
Western Europe	*37.8*	*5.7*	*0.7*	*0.4*	*0.2*	*-3.2*	*-2.9*	*-0.7*	*1.5*	*1.3*	*-2.8*
Austria	1.8	6.5	3.3	-0.3	3.8	3.0	0.0	3.9	1.3	1.2	-4.8
Belgium	1.7	5.1	2.3	-0.7	1.1	-2.7	3.7	-2.2	2.5	8.7	0.1
France	11.3	5.4	0.4	0.7	-1.9	-4.5	-10.4	-0.4	2.2	6.8	0.7
Germany	16.6	5.7	0.8	-0.3	0.6	-4.0	-1.5	-2.7	0.5	-2.7	-6.5
Liechtenstein	0.0	8.3	3.0	6.4	2.5	1.2	2.8	3.8	2.2	1.6	0.8
Luxembourg	0.1	6.7	2.1	3.4	3.5	0.0	5.8	8.8	2.9	7.6	6.3
Monaco	0.0	5.4	1.2	2.0	-1.2	-3.9	-9.8	0.3	3.7	13.5	5.3
Netherlands	2.8	5.6	-1.3	0.2	0.5	-1.8	3.3	3.2	5.4	3.5	2.2
Switzerland	3.3	8.3	1.5	5.6	1.8	0.3	1.7	2.6	0.9	0.7	-0.6
OCEANIA	**1.5**	**5.8**	**1.2**	**2.9**	**2.7**	**3.7**	**9.1**	**7.5**	**6.1**	**-14.9**	**10.6**
Australia & New Zealand	*97.5*	*5.8*	*1.5*	*2.9*	*2.8*	*3.3*	*9.5*	*7.6*	*6.3*	*-15.2*	*10.9*
Australia	89.3	6.1	1.8	3.0	2.9	2.5	10.1	8.8	5.7	-15.6	11.7
New Zealand	8.2	3.9	-0.8	1.9	1.3	11.9	3.8	-6.1	13.8	-9.6	2.0
Melanesia	*1.4*	*4.1*	*-10.3*	*0.8*	*1.6*	*37.0*	*-6.2*	*3.5*	*-6.8*	*-6.8*	*-4.7*
Fiji	0.3	4.0	7.5	-3.9	4.9	-5.4	7.3	14.5	5.5	-11.4	2.9
New Caledonia	0.4	3.0	1.7	3.5	-2.7	-4.5	39.0	16.2	-23.7	4.4	2.1
Papua New Guinea	0.8	4.9	-15.3	1.0	2.4	71.4	-17.3	-3.1	-4.7	-9.8	-9.3
Solomon Islands	0.0	3.2	9.4	6.2	2.8	3.5	-1.0	-2.2	-7.5	-1.7	-14.6
Vanuatu	0.0	4.8	7.7	7.0	-4.1	-28.0	-9.9	-2.1	11.7	34.6	-3.8
Micronesia	*0.1*	*5.9*	*4.3*	*0.3*	*2.5*	*-10.8*	*12.2*	*32.8*	*-0.7*	*-17.9*	*0.3*
Kiribati	0.0	3.6	2.9	-4.7	8.9	34.7	50.3	57.4	-42.0	-46.0	1.8
Marshall Islands	0.0	11.4	6.6	6.1	-2.5	-43.5	-9.4	43.8	-0.6	9.2	-5.5
Micronesia (Federated States of)	0.0	3.6	6.6	4.2	5.4	-7.1	22.2	35.6	44.6	-38.3	1.5
Nauru	0.0	3.6	6.8	4.7	-1.8	-12.3	19.4	35.9	40.6	-40.2	-0.8
Palau	0.0	7.9	2.9	-5.5	3.8	12.8	9.1	17.9	-15.6	-0.4	3.5
Polynesia	*1.0*	*6.1*	*10.1*	*1.3*	*1.7*	*2.4*	*0.8*	*1.1*	*2.7*	*3.8*	*2.4*
Cook Islands	0.0	1.7	-1.5	-2.8	3.6	9.6	8.7	18.7	-6.8	27.6	-10.4
French Polynesia	0.9	6.2	11.6	1.3	1.7	1.6	1.1	1.1	2.7	2.7	2.1
Samoa	0.1	7.4	3.1	0.4	-0.5	3.1	6.8	-4.8	3.5	21.3	4.2
Tonga	0.0	4.9	2.6	6.7	4.6	7.9	-17.2	5.9	10.5	-1.7	9.0
Tuvalu	0.0	8.5	6.6	5.6	0.7	154.5	0.1	30.2	-21.0	3.0	3.0

Notes for Table 6.D - Construction

1/ 1970-2000

Refers to contract construction only.

2/ 1970-2001

Includes engineering and sewage services.

Table 6.E. Average Rates of Growth of Gross Domestic Product by Kind of Economic Activity - Wholesale and Retail Trade, Restaurants and Hotels

Major area, region and country	Base year weights as percentage of total for world or region in 1990	Base year share as percentage of total GDP in 1990	Average rates of growth			Annual rate of change (percentage)					
			1970-1979	1980-1989	1990-1999	1996	1997	1998	1999	2000	2001
WORLD	**100.0**	**13.9**	**3.9**	**3.4**	**3.1**	**4.5**	**5.3**	**4.1**	**3.1**	**4.5**	**3.2**
DEVELOPED ECONOMIES	**78.7**	**14.8**	**3.2**	**3.5**	**3.5**	**4.2**	**5.1**	**4.9**	**3.1**	**4.1**	**2.1**
DEVELOPING ECONOMIES	**17.7**	**14.0**	**5.9**	**3.3**	**4.4**	**5.5**	**5.7**	**1.1**	**3.2**	**5.7**	**7.1**
TRANSITION ECONOMIES	**3.6**	**6.1**	**8.6**	**3.6**	**-0.3**	**5.3**	**7.2**	**1.4**	**1.9**	**9.3**	**6.4**
AFRICA	**2.4**	**14.3**	**4.1**	**3.3**	**3.6**	**4.7**	**2.5**	**3.3**	**6.6**	**-0.2**	**5.1**
Eastern Africa	*9.1*	*11.9*	*3.0*	*2.8*	*3.1*	*6.5*	*4.5*	*3.1*	*2.8*	*0.9*	*4.9*
Burundi	0.1	4.8	1.9	7.2	-1.8	-8.0	1.0	5.3	3.1	4.2	3.7
Comoros	0.1	25.1	7.1	4.1	-1.5	0.5	-2.3	-2.5	-7.1	-1.3	8.4
Djibouti	0.1	15.6	-1.8	0.4	-0.5	2.5	4.9	4.0	-1.6	0.6	4.1
Eritrea	...	...	...	...	0.4	11.8	5.5	-16.4	-0.6	-7.5	3.6
Ethiopia	...	...	...	...	8.8	7.0	7.1	19.4	8.0	10.2	11.2
Ethiopia (Former) [1]	0.7	6.5	1.8	2.9	-6.8	...	...	...	...	...	...
Kenya [2]	1.1	9.7	1.9	4.1	3.6	8.2	3.9	2.9	1.4	1.1	1.2
Madagascar	0.4	10.2	2.8	0.6	2.2	4.0	3.8	3.4	5.6	4.8	31.9
Malawi	0.4	15.4	7.4	0.6	4.3	13.4	17.2	-6.0	10.2	-0.2	-1.9
Mauritius	0.5	15.0	8.3	5.7	6.1	8.2	6.5	5.0	4.8	6.2	2.5
Mozambique	0.1	2.9	3.9	-0.3	2.1	-0.4	9.2	11.4	2.6	2.6	6.2
Reunion	1.4	19.9	8.8	2.6	3.5	2.9	3.1	3.0	3.0	3.0	3.0
Rwanda	0.3	11.2	10.3	0.7	-2.9	-21.7	24.6	6.6	-0.2	-3.2	5.0
Seychelles	0.1	27.0	7.5	3.8	-17.2	-12.1	-14.9	-22.9	12.0	4.6	476.1
Somalia	0.1	9.2	5.7	-2.3	-4.8	7.4	7.1	3.6	-35.7	3.0	3.0
Uganda	0.6	12.6	-5.1	3.3	8.5	5.1	4.3	8.6	4.7	6.4	7.1
United Republic Of Tanzania	0.7	14.0	1.2	2.4	2.8	4.0	2.0	3.9	3.9	-9.9	3.1
Zambia	0.6	11.3	5.2	5.5	0.1	34.3	2.4	-2.6	-0.1	-1.3	-0.7
Zimbabwe	1.8	15.2	1.9	2.8	4.0	6.8	2.3	0.9	2.0	-3.0	-0.5
Middle Africa	*8.7*	*14.6*	*0.3*	*1.5*	*1.4*	*2.3*	*2.6*	*2.9*	*9.7*	*-3.5*	*5.1*
Angola [3]	1.5	10.7	0.6	1.1	0.0	2.9	5.6	6.1	4.1	4.0	5.3
Cameroon	2.8	15.0	0.7	0.1	4.0	2.4	1.9	2.1	23.1	1.6	5.5
Central African Republic	0.4	23.5	-0.4	-0.1	-2.6	-3.7	2.4	3.4	-23.8	-4.1	-4.1
Chad [4]	0.4	21.3	-0.1	5.1	2.6	1.9	4.9	2.9	1.7	1.7	10.4
Congo	0.5	13.4	4.4	2.7	-3.4	7.6	4.9	8.2	-48.1	-14.7	13.2
Democratic Rep. of the Congo [5]	2.2	17.8	0.7	2.0	-5.6	-1.9	-3.8	0.1	-10.4	-4.3	-4.4
Equatorial Guinea	0.0	7.4	4.1	2.3	24.1	46.0	71.8	21.4	41.1	16.9	53.4
Gabon	0.9	12.4	-4.2	5.5	6.8	5.1	4.3	0.3	48.1	-22.0	3.7
Sao Tome and Principe	0.0	10.8	8.4	-0.1	7.2	1.2	0.7	-27.1	156.5	-2.2	4.9
Northern Africa	*48.0*	*15.6*	*6.9*	*4.4*	*5.4*	*4.1*	*3.1*	*5.2*	*11.3*	*-1.3*	*3.3*
Algeria	10.6	12.9	6.7	3.6	2.2	6.8	2.6	4.4	-2.2	-15.2	2.3
Egypt [6]	18.5	19.7	8.4	6.8	3.4	-13.3	3.7	6.6	10.0	0.7	1.5
Libyan Arab Jamahiriya	3.2	8.5	14.7	-1.6	10.3	0.7	3.8	0.9	-5.1	1.6	2.9
Morocco [7]	4.5	13.1	5.2	4.1	8.1	84.5	-0.8	5.8	1.7	2.8	3.2
Sudan	8.9	19.9	3.2	3.7	8.9	6.9	4.6	5.0	40.8	1.6	6.2
Tunisia [8]	2.4	14.5	12.5	3.9	5.7	2.1	5.5	6.8	7.3	4.4	4.0
Southern Africa	*19.9*	*12.6*	*3.0*	*3.1*	*1.2*	*3.9*	*1.0*	*-0.8*	*0.6*	*4.4*	*3.6*
Botswana [9]	0.3	6.9	21.0	0.4	10.8	9.8	13.9	4.7	5.6	6.2	7.0
Lesotho	0.1	7.5	4.9	4.6	5.3	9.9	7.8	-5.1	-2.5	-2.0	1.2
Namibia	0.2	6.9	13.9	-1.3	4.9	6.6	8.9	7.9	0.6	5.7	3.7
South Africa	19.2	13.0	2.7	3.2	0.9	3.7	0.4	-1.1	0.3	4.3	3.4
Swaziland	0.1	8.0	3.2	4.4	5.0	4.1	8.7	8.0	8.1	5.6	4.1
Western Africa	*14.4*	*14.8*	*3.0*	*1.7*	*1.6*	*7.9*	*0.8*	*1.8*	*-4.2*	*-0.3*	*15.6*
Benin [10]	0.4	17.7	4.4	6.7	3.3	3.7	2.5	2.4	3.0	4.7	5.5
Burkina Faso	0.1	1.7	4.0	-14.2	31.1	261.1	-2.1	3.7	8.7	12.8	4.1
Cape Verde	0.1	21.2	-2.0	4.3	3.0	-0.8	10.0	7.6	8.7	5.9	-10.5
Cote d'Ivoire [11]	2.7	17.2	3.9	4.1	-0.3	4.0	-2.5	6.2	1.6	-4.5	20.3
Gambia	0.2	39.8	13.4	2.3	-3.4	5.1	4.2	3.0	-44.6	-9.3	31.5
Ghana	0.2	2.8	-1.0	3.5	8.0	8.3	9.4	7.0	5.6	4.0	5.1
Guinea	1.0	26.7	2.8	2.8	3.5	4.8	-1.3	2.6	3.7	5.0	3.0
Guinea-Bissau	0.1	25.7	11.7	5.8	-2.7	3.5	7.8	-50.3	5.5	6.8	8.5
Liberia	0.0	6.6	3.1	-0.9	-14.9	-61.5	400.0	30.7	52.0	14.8	15.2
Mali	0.5	14.1	6.7	1.8	7.7	4.7	6.1	4.9	-0.6	6.9	-9.4
Mauritania	0.2	12.5	7.7	4.4	3.9	3.3	3.5	2.5	4.8	3.6	4.6
Niger	0.5	14.1	4.6	0.8	4.7	6.2	2.1	5.8	5.1	6.4	5.7
Nigeria [12]	6.0	14.0	2.9	3.6	-0.2	2.4	2.0	-2.1	-14.6	-5.3	32.1

Table 6.E. Average Rates of Growth of Gross Domestic Product by Kind of Economic Activity - Wholesale and Retail Trade, Restaurants and Hotels

Major area, region and country	Base year weights as percentage of total for world or region in 1990	Base year share as percentage of total GDP in 1990	Average rates of growth 1970-1979	Average rates of growth 1980-1989	Average rates of growth 1990-1999	Annual rate of change (percentage) 1996	1997	1998	1999	2000	2001
Senegal	1.8	24.0	1.5	-4.7	2.9	8.5	7.4	7.9	4.1	2.1	5.6
Sierra Leone	0.2	24.7	1.3	6.9	-6.7	-2.1	-25.4	0.8	-9.8	-22.0	-4.7
Togo	0.5	21.9	5.5	0.7	-2.7	4.0	-31.1	-4.8	5.1	3.3	3.4
AMERICAS	**39.3**	**16.7**	**3.8**	**3.6**	**4.2**	**6.8**	**7.8**	**8.2**	**5.1**	**6.3**	**1.7**
NORTHERN AMERICA	**33.9**	**17.0**	**3.5**	**4.3**	**4.4**	**7.3**	**7.9**	**9.1**	**6.0**	**6.5**	**2.1**
Bermuda	0.0	19.0	3.7	-0.2	0.5	2.2	0.4	-0.2	-0.4	-3.9	-4.5
Canada	6.3	13.7	5.1	3.6	2.5	2.3	4.0	7.3	5.8	5.3	2.9
United States	79.8	17.4	3.4	4.4	4.6	7.7	8.1	9.2	6.0	6.5	2.0
LATIN AMERICA AND THE CARIBBEAN	**5.4**	**15.0**	**4.9**	**0.2**	**2.3**	**3.9**	**7.2**	**1.9**	**-1.0**	**5.1**	**-0.8**
Caribbean	*1.4*	*19.6*	*4.7*	*2.4*	*2.1*	*6.7*	*4.8*	*6.7*	*4.3*	*4.4*	*3.1*
Anguilla	0.0	33.0	3.8	10.5	4.1	-4.8	13.5	3.1	5.8	-4.4	6.1
Antigua and Barbuda	0.0	22.8	2.3	6.9	3.0	4.5	5.0	0.4	3.4	1.3	-2.8
Aruba	0.0	27.2	9.5	10.3	4.8	6.1	-0.6	11.0	2.5	8.6	11.0
Bahamas	0.1	30.8	3.0	3.0	0.7	0.4	12.5	4.3	6.8	5.8	5.2
Barbados	0.0	27.0	7.9	2.4	0.4	2.4	2.7	5.9	1.8	5.7	-4.0
British Virgin Islands	0.0	26.2	14.3	4.1	7.9	12.7	14.5	7.7	4.6	8.9	8.9
Cayman Islands	0.0	24.1	6.5	8.7	0.4	3.6	-2.8	-0.3	0.1	0.1	0.1
Cuba [13]	0.4	24.7	9.6	0.9	-4.2	8.9	-2.3	-2.7	9.1	5.4	2.7
Dominica	0.0	10.8	-4.7	8.6	4.6	2.6	2.4	1.4	2.8	1.2	-3.2
Dominican Republic [14]	0.1	17.5	7.4	4.4	7.5	10.0	12.2	8.6	9.0	10.8	-1.3
Grenada	0.0	15.2	1.5	4.8	2.9	6.4	0.3	6.6	8.4	4.4	-1.6
Guadeloupe	0.0	18.1	6.3	1.8	1.8	4.3	9.2	4.1	5.9	5.9	5.9
Haiti	0.0	16.9	5.7	0.0	-3.4	0.5	0.8	3.0	2.2	4.7	0.6
Jamaica	0.1	19.4	-3.4	1.5	2.2	1.9	1.2	-1.3	-1.0	-8.9	0.0
Martinique	0.1	18.5	5.2	5.6	1.1	1.6	1.6	4.1	2.5	2.5	2.5
Montserrat	0.0	10.2	2.3	2.3	-14.4	-33.3	-48.5	-30.3	-3.0	-13.1	-1.9
Netherlands Antilles	0.0	28.1	3.3	3.4	-0.7	-0.4	-3.8	-4.1	-3.9	-4.3	-2.2
Puerto Rico	0.4	16.0	2.2	3.8	4.6	7.7	5.8	12.6	1.5	2.3	5.4
Saint Kitts and Nevis	0.0	18.3	4.5	11.2	3.6	6.9	5.5	2.9	-0.9	-8.3	2.0
Saint Lucia	0.0	22.1	5.8	4.6	2.9	3.6	6.7	3.4	7.7	8.0	-12.8
Saint Vincent and the Grenadines	0.0	11.6	0.9	6.5	7.5	1.1	7.7	8.2	8.5	7.8	2.4
Trinidad and Tobago	0.1	15.4	3.5	-2.3	3.6	11.8	5.7	9.7	8.1	10.5	6.0
Central America	*5.2*	*22.2*	*6.1*	*1.1*	*3.2*	*4.4*	*10.1*	*5.6*	*3.0*	*11.4*	*-1.0*
Belize	0.0	15.7	2.6	3.4	4.4	-1.8	8.1	6.6	3.0	18.8	10.9
Costa Rica	0.1	17.8	5.5	0.9	5.2	-0.6	6.1	8.5	2.4	1.5	2.1
El Salvador [15]	0.1	18.1	3.3	-4.3	5.5	0.4	2.9	4.0	2.0	3.3	1.6
Guatemala	0.1	24.1	5.3	-0.3	4.0	2.7	3.8	4.5	3.2	4.2	1.5
Honduras	0.0	10.3	6.9	-0.9	2.9	4.5	3.5	3.1	0.7	4.0	3.4
Mexico	4.8	22.6	6.3	1.3	3.1	4.8	10.7	5.6	3.1	12.4	-1.3
Nicaragua [16]	0.0	25.5	-2.7	4.9	0.2	5.1	5.3	4.9	5.6	3.9	3.4
Panama	0.1	16.7	4.6	-0.7	6.2	-1.0	8.9	2.2	-2.9	1.6	-1.8
South America	*7.2*	*11.7*	*4.3*	*-0.6*	*1.8*	*3.1*	*5.9*	*-1.1*	*-4.6*	*0.7*	*-1.4*
Argentina	1.8	15.6	2.6	-1.5	4.5	7.9	10.9	3.4	-6.9	-2.4	-7.8
Bolivia	0.0	12.1	3.5	1.8	3.5	5.1	4.1	2.0	0.8	3.9	-0.9
Brazil	3.1	8.8	4.9	-0.6	0.0	1.8	3.0	-4.7	-0.6	0.5	0.7
Chile	0.3	12.2	2.4	3.1	7.2	9.5	7.6	3.5	-5.0	3.0	3.0
Colombia	0.4	11.4	6.1	2.4	0.1	-0.3	1.8	-1.5	-15.7	10.5	1.9
Ecuador	0.1	16.0	8.8	1.5	1.6	5.2	4.4	1.1	-11.3	3.8	4.3
French Guiana	0.0	13.4	20.6	9.0	3.1	1.6	-0.3	-0.2	0.4	0.4	0.4
Guyana [17]	0.0	5.8	1.8	-3.3	3.8	5.1	5.6	5.3	-8.0	5.2	0.5
Paraguay [18]	0.1	29.0	8.8	3.5	0.3	-1.1	0.1	-4.2	-9.2	-4.9	2.4
Peru	0.5	18.9	4.2	-0.7	2.8	1.4	7.5	-2.7	-1.2	4.6	0.1
Suriname	0.0	18.1	23.1	-5.0	-0.5	-6.0	11.4	2.1	-5.6	-8.8	-12.2
Uruguay	0.1	12.8	2.8	0.3	5.2	6.0	8.8	2.4	-3.4	-5.3	-3.3
Venezuela	0.7	17.6	4.7	-2.0	-0.7	-7.2	4.1	-3.0	-9.6	4.0	3.4
ASIA	**22.8**	**13.0**	**3.9**	**5.2**	**4.7**	**4.9**	**4.3**	**-1.4**	**-0.2**	**3.0**	**6.9**
Eastern Asia	*70.2*	*12.9*	*2.5*	*5.7*	*4.3*	*4.3*	*3.6*	*-2.4*	*-1.4*	*1.4*	*2.7*
China	4.1	7.7	6.0	12.8	6.1	5.4	8.5	7.7	7.2	7.8	7.5
Democratic People's Rep. of Korea	0.2	9.1	13.9	7.6	-2.7	-3.6	-6.3	-1.1	6.2	1.3	3.7
Hong Kong SAR of China	2.5	24.2	8.8	7.2	3.8	4.3	5.1	-5.0	3.4	10.2	0.0
Japan	55.5	13.2	1.7	4.8	3.8	3.7	2.9	-3.1	-4.4	-1.2	2.7

Table 6.E. Average Rates of Growth of Gross Domestic Product by Kind of Economic Activity - Wholesale and Retail Trade, Restaurants and Hotels

Major area, region and country	Base year weights as percentage of total for world or region in 1990	Base year share as percentage of total GDP in 1990	Average rates of growth			Annual rate of change (percentage)					
			1970-1979	1980-1989	1990-1999	1996	1997	1998	1999	2000	2001
Macao SAR of China	0.0	9.3	16.9	16.9	6.7	18.3	-17.0	-10.9	-5.9	13.2	-6.7
Mongolia	0.1	17.6	5.7	0.8	-1.9	2.6	23.2	-8.1	1.3	25.7	8.0
Republic of Korea	4.7	13.4	8.7	8.4	5.7	7.1	4.0	-10.9	14.1	9.8	4.0
South Central Asia	*12.6*	*11.9*	*7.3*	*4.0*	*6.3*	*7.7*	*6.5*	*6.1*	*4.4*	*5.8*	*33.3*
Afghanistan	0.1	9.1	3.4	-0.2	0.3	6.6	13.3	5.2	-12.4	-43.7	0.0
Bangladesh	0.5	12.5	6.4	3.1	5.4	5.5	6.0	6.5	7.3	6.5	5.7
Bhutan	0.0	6.5	6.4	2.4	5.6	14.0	7.4	3.2	3.1	5.6	17.9
India	4.9	11.1	4.1	6.1	7.6	7.7	7.6	7.6	7.3	3.8	62.2
Iran (Islamic Republic of)	4.5	17.5	11.0	1.7	3.4	7.6	5.0	5.2	0.5	8.1	6.7
Kazakhstan	0.8	8.1	...	...	-2.6	10.7	3.0	2.0	1.9	5.2	13.5
Kyrgyzstan	0.1	4.0	...	...	-8.7	2.3	7.7	9.5	3.9	11.4	7.0
Maldives	0.0	20.4	11.5	17.4	13.5	9.7	7.9	-5.9	6.0	5.3	4.9
Nepal	0.0	10.2	3.3	3.4	5.6	4.2	3.7	5.6	2.5	14.5	2.8
Pakistan [19]	1.0	14.9	5.5	7.1	3.3	0.7	-1.1	3.0	1.9	5.2	2.2
Sri Lanka	0.2	15.4	5.8	6.8	5.8	5.4	6.1	5.2	2.9	6.9	-4.2
Tajikistan	0.1	8.2	...	...	-5.9	112.4	46.4	13.6	-33.9	68.2	-4.7
Turkmenistan	0.0	2.1	...	...	3.5	-19.1	4.6	11.2	19.3	-3.3	20.8
Uzbekistan	0.3	3.8	...	...	9.3	36.7	26.3	4.4	11.8	14.5	8.8
South-Eastern Asia	*8.6*	*17.4*	*6.4*	*5.5*	*5.1*	*5.9*	*3.7*	*-9.4*	*3.3*	*6.9*	*4.6*
Brunei Darussalam	0.1	12.6	26.0	1.3	0.6	5.2	6.1	2.1	1.9	-2.0	2.1
Cambodia	0.0	13.7	-7.3	-2.0	2.4	-0.6	-0.1	-2.8	6.0	2.7	3.2
Indonesia [20]	2.7	17.0	7.9	6.8	4.8	8.2	5.8	-18.2	-0.1	5.6	5.1
Lao People's Democratic Republic	0.0	6.8	68.5	39.8	9.3	11.2	10.8	9.8	7.2	5.4	8.1
Malaysia	0.8	13.6	10.7	5.1	9.3	7.9	8.0	-3.4	3.1	4.8	3.0
Myanmar [21]	0.6	22.7	3.1	0.3	5.0	4.9	5.0	5.2	9.5	14.1	4.8
Philippines [22]	1.0	15.8	6.4	3.3	3.6	5.5	4.0	2.5	4.9	4.9	5.3
Singapore	1.0	18.8	7.4	6.2	7.6	6.1	6.4	-4.7	6.6	14.3	-2.8
Thailand	2.3	19.4	6.2	7.5	3.0	1.8	-3.5	-12.5	3.6	4.3	9.8
Vietnam	0.2	17.2	-0.1	5.7	6.5	9.8	6.9	4.4	2.1	6.0	4.0
Western Asia	*8.7*	*11.9*	*8.6*	*3.4*	*4.2*	*5.6*	*7.4*	*5.2*	*-0.5*	*7.5*	*-0.5*
Armenia	0.1	4.0	...	...	-3.2	11.5	4.9	6.7	11.2	8.9	10.8
Azerbaijan	0.1	2.4	...	...	18.6	39.8	27.4	22.5	23.3	0.5	11.2
Bahrain	0.1	11.2	13.1	1.7	6.3	4.1	3.4	7.4	-4.7	3.2	1.9
Cyprus	0.2	21.4	5.4	9.5	4.7	-0.1	3.1	6.5	4.2	7.0	4.0
Georgia	0.2	6.0	...	...	-1.7	-68.1	41.1	38.0	12.3	9.7	8.6
Iraq [23]	0.8	14.8	15.8	2.1	-1.4	160.3	1.3	15.9	-4.0	9.9	20.4
Israel	0.7	8.9	6.7	2.5	4.9	5.5	1.7	4.0	4.1	7.5	-2.0
Jordan	0.0	8.5	3.6	-2.9	7.8	5.5	5.2	-11.7	-2.1	2.8	3.5
Kuwait	0.2	7.6	11.7	0.5	-2.4	-3.2	0.0	5.9	2.0	32.7	1.0
Lebanon	0.1	28.4	-2.3	-6.7	4.3	-4.1	-5.6	-3.3	-1.3	3.0	3.8
Oman	0.2	11.0	6.8	8.5	6.1	5.4	6.4	10.1	-8.1	6.3	9.7
Qatar	0.1	5.5	14.8	-1.1	4.5	2.3	5.6	11.6	3.4	-1.1	12.8
Saudi Arabia	1.0	7.0	10.0	1.8	1.8	-13.2	7.2	11.3	8.5	4.8	3.9
Syrian Arab Republic	0.4	22.7	9.9	1.4	3.1	-4.4	-5.1	0.9	1.4	-7.9	7.9
Turkey	4.0	19.1	7.1	5.9	4.9	8.9	11.1	2.7	-4.9	9.5	-7.7
United Arab Emirates	0.4	9.0	42.3	2.1	6.1	11.7	4.8	4.9	3.2	3.6	2.3
Yemen	0.2	8.9	...	...	1.6	7.7	6.3	7.7	-1.0	8.6	27.0
Yemen Arab Republic (Former)	...	...	10.5	4.7	...	...	...	...	...	...	...
Yemen Democratic (Former)	...	...	-2.1	1.8	...	...	...	...	...	...	...
EUROPE	**34.0**	**12.2**	**4.2**	**2.4**	**0.6**	**1.1**	**3.0**	**3.4**	**2.4**	**3.7**	**2.1**
Eastern Europe	*7.8*	*5.6*	*8.6*	*3.7*	*-10.4*	*3.1*	*5.2*	*-0.5*	*1.5*	*9.0*	*6.1*
Belarus	0.2	3.5	...	...	-1.0	21.2	18.4	26.2	8.2	9.6	19.5
Bulgaria	0.1	5.3	7.1	6.1	-6.5	-9.4	-25.3	0.2	9.8	8.7	9.8
Czech Republic	0.4	11.5	...	1.1	3.5	0.1	4.2	9.9	0.2	1.2	6.9
Czechoslovakia (Former)	...	...	6.7	...	...	...	...	...	...	...	...
Hungary	0.4	11.7	5.3	-0.1	0.2	1.0	7.6	4.5	2.7	2.1	11.2
Poland	0.7	13.4	8.0	1.2	5.5	6.5	8.1	5.4	7.9	3.7	4.6
Republic of Moldova	0.1	5.0	...	...	-6.2	3.6	-12.5	16.6	43.5	-23.6	1.5
Romania	0.2	6.2	7.9	5.8	6.9	26.8	-8.2	6.7	8.8	4.6	1.3
Russian Federation	4.7	5.2	...	...	-1.9	1.7	5.4	-5.5	-2.4	13.1	5.9
Slovakia	0.1	4.3	...	3.8	15.0	-2.5	27.6	3.8	3.5	6.6	1.9
Ukraine	1.0	4.2	...	...	-9.9	-3.1	0.0	1.4	9.2	9.7	7.3
USSR (Former)	...	...	8.9	3.9	...	...	...	...	...	...	...
Northern Europe	*19.4*	*12.2*	*2.2*	*2.6*	*3.0*	*4.8*	*4.2*	*5.3*	*4.3*	*4.8*	*3.2*
Denmark	1.6	12.7	1.8	0.0	3.0	7.5	-0.6	4.2	3.6	1.8	1.2
Estonia	0.1	8.0	...	...	-1.6	8.6	3.5	6.4	1.2	7.4	6.7
Finland	1.5	11.7	2.5	4.3	0.0	3.4	5.4	7.9	4.0	3.7	2.7

Table 6.E. Average Rates of Growth of Gross Domestic Product by Kind of Economic Activity - Wholesale and Retail Trade, Restaurants and Hotels

Major area, region and country	Base year weights as percentage of total for world or region in 1990	Base year share as percentage of total GDP in 1990	Average rates of growth			Annual rate of change (percentage)					
			1970-1979	1980-1989	1990-1999	1996	1997	1998	1999	2000	2001
Iceland	0.1	12.5	4.5	3.4	3.8	7.3	6.9	10.9	8.1	8.8	-0.8
Ireland	0.6	13.6	6.1	1.6	5.5	17.8	8.7	8.5	5.9	13.1	8.6
Latvia	0.1	6.6	...	...	1.5	1.2	12.8	18.8	10.2	9.2	10.8
Lithuania	0.2	9.2	...	...	2.9	2.2	8.9	7.3	-3.2	9.7	5.2
Norway	1.3	11.7	4.1	1.6	3.9	8.2	5.6	5.7	2.8	2.7	1.6
Sweden	2.5	10.8	2.0	2.5	2.6	2.5	1.5	6.7	6.4	2.5	1.0
United Kingdom	11.6	12.7	1.9	2.9	2.9	4.0	4.7	4.6	4.2	5.4	3.8
Southern Europe	*28.4*	*16.5*	*4.5*	*1.9*	*2.1*	*1.4*	*3.2*	*3.2*	*1.3*	*4.0*	*2.0*
Albania	0.0	12.7	9.3	2.7	3.6	20.1	-25.0	10.0	12.0	10.0	11.0
Andorra	0.0	18.1	9.0	7.4	7.1	5.6	8.5	9.4	9.7	8.8	8.1
Bosnia and Herzegovina	0.3	23.3	...	...	6.5	50.0	21.8	5.9	36.2	10.7	7.4
Croatia	0.4	16.2	...	...	-2.5	16.7	14.6	-0.5	-8.9	6.9	9.1
Greece	1.4	17.9	5.7	2.0	2.0	5.3	8.1	3.6	2.3	4.9	7.7
Holy See	0.0	16.1	5.2	2.5	1.7	0.3	2.2	2.9	-0.4	4.8	1.9
Italy	16.5	16.1	4.3	2.1	1.6	0.3	2.1	2.9	-0.5	4.7	1.9
Malta	0.0	12.8	10.6	2.9	2.1	-0.3	-0.8	-1.4	0.0	3.2	3.4
Portugal	1.1	17.1	3.9	1.1	2.3	2.2	5.4	4.1	2.8	3.2	1.9
San Marino	0.0	16.1	5.1	2.6	2.1	-0.2	0.4	6.9	7.9	3.2	3.2
Serbia and Montenegro	0.4	13.0	...	...	-10.8	7.6	9.5	6.6	-50.6	23.4	-12.0
Slovenia	0.2	12.4	...	...	1.8	3.2	3.0	2.4	5.7	3.9	2.6
Spain	8.1	17.2	4.6	1.9	2.1	0.7	3.6	3.6	4.9	1.9	0.8
TFYR Macedonia	0.0	8.0	...	...	6.2	144.0	-2.0	3.4	7.1	27.9	-12.3
Yugoslavia (Former)	...	...	8.2	-4.6	...	...	...	...	...	...	...
Western Europe	*44.3*	*12.7*	*3.3*	*2.1*	*1.9*	*-1.0*	*2.0*	*3.1*	*2.3*	*2.2*	*1.0*
Austria	2.5	16.7	4.8	2.3	2.3	1.6	1.9	4.2	3.1	3.9	1.1
Belgium	2.4	13.1	2.2	0.2	0.3	-4.5	1.6	-0.6	-1.2	-2.7	2.8
France	14.3	12.7	4.2	2.5	1.4	-3.1	3.7	4.4	2.9	3.5	2.4
Germany	17.0	11.0	3.1	1.8	2.2	-0.6	-0.4	1.6	1.2	1.1	0.1
Liechtenstein	0.0	19.2	2.2	4.1	1.3	1.2	2.8	3.8	2.2	1.6	0.8
Luxembourg	0.2	15.7	6.0	3.6	2.8	0.1	11.5	4.1	6.0	8.3	6.9
Monaco	0.0	12.7	4.8	2.5	1.8	-2.4	4.4	5.1	2.8	5.0	3.0
Netherlands	4.0	14.5	3.8	2.2	3.8	3.6	7.5	6.7	6.3	4.4	0.0
Switzerland	4.1	19.2	0.7	3.3	0.6	0.3	1.7	2.6	0.9	0.7	-0.6
OCEANIA	**1.5**	**13.1**	**1.9**	**2.4**	**3.2**	**4.4**	**4.2**	**4.4**	**5.1**	**1.2**	**4.2**
Australia & New Zealand	*96.1*	*13.0*	*1.9*	*2.4*	*3.3*	*4.6*	*4.2*	*4.6*	*5.1*	*1.3*	*4.4*
Australia	81.9	12.6	1.9	2.7	3.4	5.3	4.5	5.1	4.7	1.0	4.4
New Zealand	14.2	15.6	1.5	0.8	2.5	0.5	2.1	1.5	7.9	3.3	3.8
Melanesia	2.2	14.0	3.8	1.8	2.5	-2.5	8.4	-3.2	8.1	-3.8	-0.2
Fiji	*0.5*	*19.7*	*5.8*	*2.4*	*4.9*	*3.3*	*2.6*	*6.2*	*9.9*	*3.6*	*6.4*
New Caledonia	0.9	16.8	1.7	3.5	-1.1	-19.3	18.6	-13.6	10.6	0.1	-2.8
Papua New Guinea [24]	0.6	9.5	4.1	-0.1	3.6	7.5	8.3	-2.3	7.8	-13.3	-3.8
Solomon Islands	0.0	7.1	7.9	3.0	6.7	3.5	-1.0	-2.2	-7.5	-1.7	-14.6
Vanuatu	0.1	27.0	7.7	1.5	5.3	3.9	-3.0	0.9	-2.0	1.5	3.7
Micronesia	*0.2*	*23.2*	*4.1*	*0.2*	*0.7*	*-4.9*	*4.1*	*0.6*	*1.6*	*-0.4*	*0.5*
Kiribati	0.0	20.1	2.9	-3.3	3.1	12.0	3.7	5.6	5.2	-0.6	1.8
Marshall Islands	0.0	22.6	6.6	6.1	-3.0	-9.6	-12.9	4.4	0.1	-4.5	2.9
Micronesia (Federated States of)	0.1	20.1	6.6	6.2	-0.2	-21.5	4.3	0.9	3.4	7.7	1.5
Nauru	0.0	20.1	6.8	6.6	-7.0	-25.9	1.9	1.1	0.6	4.4	-0.8
Palau	0.1	32.4	2.9	-5.5	4.2	14.4	10.0	-1.5	0.3	-5.2	-1.1
Polynesia	*1.5*	*22.3*	*4.9*	*4.8*	*3.3*	*1.9*	*1.2*	*1.3*	*2.8*	*3.3*	*2.2*
Cook Islands	0.0	23.9	-4.2	0.1	5.7	2.2	4.8	0.9	9.4	10.6	-0.9
French Polynesia	1.4	23.3	5.5	5.2	3.4	1.6	1.1	1.1	2.7	2.7	2.1
Samoa	0.1	13.5	3.1	0.4	1.7	14.7	7.1	6.6	7.2	8.8	8.7
Tonga	0.0	12.1	6.5	5.0	0.9	-4.2	-5.5	2.3	-6.0	17.9	-3.6
Tuvalu	0.0	18.0	6.6	-13.0	13.4	28.2	-13.5	10.2	15.8	3.0	3.0

Notes for Table 6.E - Wholesale and retail trade, restaurants and hotels

1/ 1970-1992
Restaurants and hotels are included in "Other activities".

2/ 1970-1972
Restaurants and hotels are included in "Other activities".

3/ 1985-1990
Restaurants and hotels are included in "Other activities".

4/ 1987-1992
Includes "Transport, storage and communication" and "Other activities".

5/ 1970-1977
Restaurants and hotels are included in "Other activities".

6/ 1986-1995
Includes Finance and insurance.

7/ 1996-2001
Includes Financial intermediation; real estate, renting and business actvities.

8/ 1970-2001
Restaurants and hotels are included in "Other activities".

9/ 1974-1975
Import duties is included in "Wholesale and retail trade, restaurants and hotels".

10/ 1982-1989
Restaurants and hotels are included in Education; health and social work; other community, social and personal services.

11/ 1975-1979
Item "Wholesale and retail trade, restaurants and hotels " includes the profit or loss of the Marketing Board.

12/ 1987-1994
Includes import duties.

13/ 1985-1986
Includes import duties.

14/ 1970-1991
Restaurants and hotels are included in "Other activities".

15/ 1970-2001
Restaurants and hotels are included in "Other activities".

16/ 1970-1978
Restaurants and hotels are included in "Other activities".

17/ 1970-2001
Restaurants and hotels are included in "Other activities".

18/ 1970-1996
Includes Financal intermediation, except insurance and pension funding. Restaurants and hotels are included in "Other activities".

19/ 1970-1995
Restaurants and hotels are included in "Other activities".

20/ 1970-2001
Restaurants and hotels are included in "Other activities".

21/ 1970-1998
Restaurants and hotels are included in "Other activities".

22/ 1983-1991
Restaurants and hotels are included in "Other activities".

23/ 1970-1991
Includes Distribution of gas.

24/ 1987-1999
Restaurants and hotels are included in "Other activities".

Table 6.F. Average Rates of Growth of Gross Domestic Product by Kind of Economic Activity - Transport, Storage and Communication

Major area, region and country	Base year weights as percentage of total for world or region in 1990	Base year share as percentage of total GDP in 1990	Average rates of growth 1970-1979	Average rates of growth 1980-1989	Average rates of growth 1990-1999	Annual rate of change (percentage) 1996	1997	1998	1999	2000	2001
WORLD	**100.0**	**6.7**	**4.5**	**3.6**	**4.2**	**4.5**	**4.8**	**4.2**	**5.9**	**7.1**	**1.9**
DEVELOPED ECONOMIES	**72.3**	**6.5**	**3.6**	**3.6**	**3.8**	**4.1**	**4.0**	**4.3**	**5.5**	**6.8**	**3.2**
DEVELOPING ECONOMIES	**17.8**	**6.7**	**8.6**	**3.9**	**6.5**	**7.2**	**8.2**	**4.5**	**7.0**	**8.7**	**5.0**
TRANSITION ECONOMIES	**9.9**	**8.1**	**5.6**	**3.0**	**-6.3**	**-2.6**	**1.0**	**-0.3**	**7.5**	**5.2**	**5.4**
AFRICA	**2.3**	**6.7**	**6.9**	**2.8**	**4.8**	**6.6**	**7.0**	**6.8**	**9.0**	**3.0**	**4.0**
Eastern Africa	*9.8*	*6.0*	*1.9*	*4.2*	*4.1*	*7.8*	*5.2*	*6.5*	*5.7*	*2.3*	*7.8*
Burundi	0.1	3.0	10.8	5.8	1.9	-8.5	0.3	4.4	2.4	3.4	2.9
Comoros	0.0	4.2	1.7	6.4	0.4	1.6	-1.4	-1.4	0.2	-0.8	8.1
Djibouti	0.2	14.8	0.7	2.6	7.3	-2.5	2.2	12.2	12.8	0.0	3.1
Eritrea	...	...	...	...	-1.6	2.9	0.5	-7.6	-0.6	-7.5	3.6
Ethiopia	...	...	...	...	8.4	7.0	7.1	19.4	8.0	10.2	11.2
Ethiopia (Former)	1.1	4.9	4.5	5.8	-4.5	...	...	...	...	...	...
Kenya	1.5	6.1	4.2	5.5	2.5	4.2	1.7	1.3	1.3	1.9	3.2
Madagascar	1.5	17.2	3.0	3.9	1.5	3.8	3.5	3.1	10.0	4.2	32.3
Malawi	0.2	4.2	7.2	0.4	3.0	7.6	9.5	1.1	10.8	-4.1	4.3
Mauritius	0.7	9.1	8.1	5.0	7.2	7.0	9.0	11.7	7.4	11.4	9.5
Mozambique	0.4	5.6	3.9	-0.3	5.7	10.1	17.3	4.8	9.0	1.2	21.6
Reunion	0.6	3.9	6.5	5.6	3.1	2.8	3.1	3.2	3.1	3.2	3.1
Rwanda	0.3	4.7	10.8	18.1	0.0	18.8	26.7	27.3	30.1	11.9	8.1
Seychelles	0.1	12.0	11.4	1.1	19.4	-3.0	20.7	31.3	-1.5	-0.9	-36.1
Somalia	0.2	6.6	0.8	3.5	-2.1	12.5	-4.7	7.1	-34.1	3.0	3.0
Uganda	0.4	3.7	-11.5	2.6	9.2	9.6	11.6	7.0	9.0	4.7	9.9
United Republic Of Tanzania	0.6	5.4	3.6	1.3	3.9	5.4	4.4	5.6	5.6	-18.0	2.5
Zambia	0.6	4.9	2.6	2.9	0.4	6.0	0.6	8.3	4.4	6.4	5.4
Zimbabwe	1.4	5.5	-1.2	4.1	7.0	19.8	0.9	0.8	4.7	-1.2	2.1
Middle Africa	*4.9*	*3.8*	*2.4*	*1.9*	*2.0*	*26.2*	*34.6*	*25.8*	*-45.0*	*-5.1*	*6.7*
Angola	0.9	3.2	-0.8	-1.1	1.6	3.1	6.1	8.6	5.3	2.5	4.9
Cameroon	1.6	4.0	4.7	1.0	4.4	59.9	62.6	40.5	-67.0	1.6	5.5
Central African Republic	0.2	4.7	0.4	0.2	-1.3	-3.4	2.6	3.8	-15.1	-3.7	-4.3
Chad [1]	0.2	4.0	-1.7	5.0	3.4	4.0	11.5	3.4	-3.3	0.0	17.2
Congo	0.7	9.4	3.9	4.1	-2.8	6.0	0.5	-3.3	3.0	-15.6	13.8
Democratic Rep. of the Congo	0.2	0.8	-1.7	2.7	-4.9	-0.7	-2.8	0.4	-10.4	-4.3	-4.4
Equatorial Guinea	0.0	2.1	4.0	-5.6	25.0	41.4	68.3	18.4	48.8	16.9	53.4
Gabon	1.0	6.5	5.9	5.2	2.0	0.9	3.1	-4.1	17.4	-22.7	4.2
Sao Tome and Principe	0.0	5.4	8.6	0.1	-3.5	-1.4	-1.9	-71.5	175.6	-5.6	6.8
Northern Africa	*51.5*	*7.8*	*9.7*	*3.0*	*5.6*	*5.6*	*5.0*	*4.4*	*20.6*	*3.0*	*3.7*
Algeria	8.6	4.9	11.4	3.6	3.0	6.8	2.6	4.4	4.8	-8.4	2.3
Egypt	19.8	9.8	17.5	10.7	3.5	6.2	3.4	5.3	4.3	7.1	1.2
Libyan Arab Jamahiriya	5.2	6.5	12.7	0.8	8.6	4.8	10.9	0.9	2.3	1.5	3.3
Morocco	4.5	6.2	7.3	4.1	5.7	2.8	2.4	8.7	8.1	9.4	1.0
Sudan	10.9	11.4	7.0	-3.2	8.6	4.1	5.3	2.6	85.0	1.8	6.1
Tunisia	2.4	6.8	7.6	4.3	6.5	11.1	11.1	7.7	9.2	7.6	13.2
Southern Africa	*24.4*	*7.2*	*5.7*	*2.1*	*4.5*	*5.9*	*7.6*	*6.4*	*7.3*	*4.9*	*3.9*
Botswana	0.3	2.7	14.9	15.9	11.6	0.4	4.3	9.1	16.3	2.6	5.1
Lesotho	0.1	3.7	1.6	5.1	6.5	3.4	12.3	-4.4	5.3	4.3	3.5
Namibia	0.3	4.7	12.4	0.0	5.2	5.1	7.6	-10.4	12.3	5.8	6.2
South Africa	23.7	7.4	5.6	2.1	4.4	6.1	7.6	6.7	7.1	4.9	3.9
Swaziland	0.1	5.2	9.5	3.0	4.0	-6.0	1.3	-1.3	5.1	7.3	3.4
Western Africa	*9.3*	*4.5*	*6.8*	*2.7*	*3.1*	*3.7*	*3.5*	*8.7*	*-1.9*	*1.7*	*1.2*
Benin	0.5	9.3	6.4	-0.2	3.9	5.6	4.3	4.2	-65.0	4.1	6.1
Burkina Faso	0.4	4.4	5.5	-2.0	3.6	-6.3	8.2	4.1	8.7	14.2	2.8
Cape Verde	0.1	15.1	2.4	7.2	9.7	-0.8	10.0	7.6	8.7	5.9	15.8
Cote d'Ivoire	2.5	7.3	9.2	2.0	2.4	3.0	0.0	16.7	0.4	-1.8	-6.2
Gambia	0.1	10.7	7.4	9.9	6.8	10.2	8.3	8.0	-4.1	-10.8	34.5
Ghana	0.3	1.8	3.4	5.5	6.8	5.0	7.9	5.5	5.3	6.0	5.5
Guinea	0.5	6.0	2.8	2.6	5.2	6.4	-1.1	3.8	3.7	5.0	3.0
Guinea-Bissau	0.0	3.7	11.7	5.6	-0.6	4.5	-17.5	-22.0	7.6	3.4	7.8
Liberia	0.1	10.0	3.1	1.3	-16.7	-61.3	379.2	29.6	26.8	4.8	0.0
Mali	0.3	4.7	6.6	7.1	6.1	3.0	0.5	2.2	57.7	6.6	-9.2
Mauritania	0.3	9.5	5.9	-0.1	8.2	12.4	19.0	7.4	5.6	3.2	4.8
Niger	0.3	3.8	4.6	0.2	4.6	4.7	4.5	3.5	2.1	3.3	2.7
Nigeria	1.9	2.1	8.4	-1.6	1.9	1.8	6.8	8.2	-12.4	-6.5	-0.1

Table 6.F. Average Rates of Growth of Gross Domestic Product by Kind of Economic Activity - Transport, Storage and Communication

Major area, region and country	Base year weights as percentage of total for world or region in 1990	Base year share as percentage of total GDP in 1990	Average rates of growth			Annual rate of change (percentage)					
			1970-1979	1980-1989	1990-1999	1996	1997	1998	1999	2000	2001
Senegal	1.6	10.1	...	-1.2	5.0	6.3	11.8	7.5	6.7	8.0	6.4
Sierra Leone	0.2	10.7	4.5	-1.8	-13.8	-2.8	-46.6	1.5	-10.1	-21.9	-4.8
Togo	0.3	5.6	1.0	1.9	-2.8	6.1	-49.1	-2.3	3.7	4.0	3.0
AMERICAS	**31.2**	**6.4**	**4.8**	**3.4**	**4.6**	**6.0**	**3.6**	**4.5**	**6.1**	**8.2**	**2.3**
NORTHERN AMERICA	**26.6**	**6.4**	**4.2**	**3.6**	**4.6**	**6.0**	**2.8**	**4.5**	**6.4**	**8.3**	**2.1**
Bermuda	0.0	6.5	3.7	0.5	2.5	1.3	2.6	1.0	-1.5	4.0	4.8
Canada	8.2	6.7	5.7	3.4	3.5	2.5	6.0	2.7	8.1	8.0	3.1
United States	77.0	6.4	4.0	3.6	4.7	6.3	2.5	4.7	6.2	8.3	2.0
LATIN AMERICA AND THE CARIBBEAN	**4.6**	**6.1**	**8.5**	**2.3**	**4.5**	**6.5**	**7.6**	**4.6**	**4.7**	**7.8**	**3.5**
Caribbean	*1.2*	*6.6*	*4.7*	*4.2*	*3.8*	*7.8*	*6.3*	*3.6*	*4.3*	*5.4*	*5.2*
Anguilla	0.0	10.3	3.8	6.5	8.7	3.8	22.9	4.0	11.9	5.6	5.0
Antigua and Barbuda	0.0	14.9	3.2	7.2	5.4	6.9	9.2	5.0	10.5	-1.1	1.7
Aruba	0.0	8.3	11.1	11.8	6.7	-4.3	9.1	-0.4	11.8	9.0	10.4
Bahamas	0.1	10.4	3.0	3.0	-2.2	-2.7	9.1	1.1	3.5	2.6	2.0
Barbados	0.0	7.1	3.1	3.6	1.4	2.7	2.8	2.7	3.9	1.3	1.2
British Virgin Islands	0.0	11.9	7.4	10.0	5.4	11.1	0.0	14.0	14.0	9.1	9.1
Cayman Islands	0.0	10.7	18.0	12.6	0.5	3.6	-2.8	-0.3	0.1	0.1	0.1
Cuba	0.3	6.2	4.4	5.4	-3.9	8.7	3.9	1.2	6.6	9.1	3.9
Dominica	0.0	13.3	-0.1	12.4	6.5	4.4	6.0	7.3	7.3	-3.3	-7.1
Dominican Republic	0.1	7.8	7.7	4.0	10.3	13.8	13.5	13.6	10.4	13.5	10.5
Grenada	0.0	11.1	1.2	6.4	2.4	2.6	5.1	11.5	2.0	7.1	0.1
Guadeloupe	0.0	5.8	9.3	5.4	4.2	4.3	9.2	4.1	5.9	5.9	5.9
Haiti	0.0	2.1	8.4	-1.2	-0.5	3.2	1.0	1.0	5.1	9.0	3.5
Jamaica	0.1	7.9	1.9	3.7	6.7	9.3	6.0	5.8	8.5	-41.7	9.8
Martinique	0.0	6.0	7.5	9.6	2.7	1.6	1.6	4.1	2.5	2.5	2.5
Montserrat	0.0	10.2	3.5	6.3	-4.2	-14.5	-33.4	-14.9	-11.0	16.2	-18.3
Netherlands Antilles	0.0	10.6	3.3	-5.8	1.2	-17.6	2.9	-3.7	-3.6	-4.0	-1.9
Puerto Rico	0.4	5.4	5.2	4.4	5.6	11.3	4.9	0.0	-1.1	11.0	3.2
Saint Kitts and Nevis	0.0	12.6	-0.8	11.4	7.0	7.8	4.8	1.1	6.8	3.2	4.1
Saint Lucia	0.0	14.2	6.0	9.8	3.7	4.2	0.6	3.4	7.5	4.1	2.1
Saint Vincent and the Grenadines	0.0	17.4	2.1	7.3	5.8	5.6	7.9	7.3	9.1	5.6	-5.3
Trinidad and Tobago	0.1	8.1	3.7	5.5	3.4	4.4	4.7	0.6	5.0	8.3	4.9
Central America	*5.2*	*8.3*	*10.7*	*2.7*	*5.2*	*7.5*	*9.6*	*6.8*	*7.8*	*9.5*	*3.1*
Belize	0.0	9.1	7.8	11.7	6.2	4.4	-3.3	2.8	7.3	2.6	5.0
Costa Rica	0.1	7.3	11.2	4.5	7.7	4.8	9.9	8.1	6.9	10.2	8.7
El Salvador	0.1	7.3	5.6	-1.0	6.2	1.9	7.7	4.2	9.5	6.1	2.9
Guatemala	0.1	8.0	8.2	2.5	6.0	3.6	5.9	7.6	6.8	7.5	6.4
Honduras	0.0	5.6	4.1	5.0	3.2	4.4	4.4	2.7	1.7	5.0	4.2
Mexico	4.6	8.3	11.1	2.7	5.2	8.0	9.9	6.7	7.8	9.6	2.8
Nicaragua	0.0	4.0	-0.8	-3.1	2.1	4.7	5.3	4.7	5.6	3.8	3.5
Panama	0.2	15.9	10.9	4.4	4.9	2.5	5.7	10.9	10.5	10.0	4.6
South America	*8.4*	*5.2*	*8.0*	*1.8*	*4.2*	*5.8*	*6.8*	*3.5*	*2.9*	*7.1*	*3.6*
Argentina	1.6	5.2	2.0	1.3	6.2	6.9	11.2	8.9	-1.3	1.7	-4.6
Bolivia	0.1	9.3	11.3	3.4	5.5	6.9	9.2	7.1	-0.8	2.1	1.9
Brazil	4.3	4.7	12.4	1.7	3.0	5.5	4.3	0.9	6.3	10.5	6.4
Chile	0.4	6.1	3.1	4.6	8.7	10.2	10.9	6.6	0.6	8.0	5.9
Colombia	0.7	6.6	7.8	2.7	3.6	3.8	5.8	2.5	-1.9	2.2	3.4
Ecuador	0.2	8.2	10.6	4.7	4.5	3.2	8.2	9.4	-0.3	7.7	1.7
French Guiana	0.0	7.6	16.7	12.8	2.1	1.6	-0.9	-1.5	-0.3	-0.3	-0.3
Guyana	0.0	6.7	3.2	1.0	4.7	10.9	8.9	-3.1	2.1	7.1	5.4
Paraguay	0.0	3.9	9.6	4.4	3.4	2.0	4.2	3.0	2.6	10.9	8.6
Peru	0.5	7.7	6.2	0.8	3.3	5.6	5.6	-1.0	2.2	4.2	1.8
Suriname	0.0	5.7	13.8	-0.8	5.9	11.0	6.6	5.8	1.8	25.5	26.4
Uruguay	0.1	6.5	2.7	2.2	8.4	6.9	7.1	3.3	4.8	1.5	0.4
Venezuela	0.5	4.6	7.3	0.7	2.8	1.7	9.0	5.9	1.6	8.1	8.8
ASIA	**25.0**	**6.8**	**4.5**	**5.1**	**5.4**	**4.4**	**6.8**	**3.3**	**3.2**	**6.7**	**-2.0**
Eastern Asia	*68.4*	*6.6*	*2.8*	*5.6*	*4.7*	*3.4*	*6.4*	*3.4*	*2.4*	*5.3*	*4.6*
China	6.3	6.3	7.0	9.8	10.6	11.4	10.8	10.6	9.3	7.8	8.6
Democratic People's Rep. of Korea	0.3	7.0	13.1	10.2	-2.9	-3.6	-6.3	-1.1	6.2	1.3	3.7
Hong Kong SAR of China	1.8	9.0	8.8	7.2	3.8	4.3	5.1	-5.0	3.4	10.2	3.6
Japan	52.8	6.6	1.7	4.8	3.1	1.0	4.7	2.4	-1.7	2.2	2.7

Table 6.F. Average Rates of Growth of Gross Domestic Product by Kind of Economic Activity - Transport, Storage and Communication

Major area, region and country	Base year weights as percentage of total for world or region in 1990	Base year share as percentage of total GDP in 1990	Average rates of growth			Annual rate of change (percentage)					
			1970-1979	1980-1989	1990-1999	1996	1997	1998	1999	2000	2001
Macao SAR of China	0.0	3.2	16.9	16.9	15.3	29.1	44.0	-4.2	0.7	8.6	-6.2
Mongolia	0.1	16.9	5.7	6.2	-5.3	10.1	5.8	6.9	6.1	25.2	11.8
Republic of Korea	4.4	6.7	14.4	7.4	8.9	10.6	13.4	-0.8	14.5	17.9	10.5
South Central Asia	*13.5*	*6.7*	*9.6*	*2.2*	*9.7*	*10.1*	*6.0*	*6.5*	*7.8*	*8.8*	*-33.8*
Afghanistan	0.1	4.1	8.6	-1.2	-7.7	6.6	13.3	5.2	-12.4	-43.7	0.0
Bangladesh	0.8	9.2	3.3	4.9	4.7	5.5	5.7	5.9	6.1	7.9	6.0
Bhutan	0.0	7.0	6.4	13.1	10.7	10.6	14.0	13.3	12.0	2.0	-10.0
India	4.6	5.4	6.1	7.1	7.4	8.2	7.9	8.0	8.3	8.2	...
Iran (Islamic Republic of)	3.8	7.6	14.4	-3.0	12.3	16.4	3.8	6.5	9.8	8.9	7.0
Kazakhstan	1.8	9.4	...	...	-8.6	1.5	3.3	-0.9	-0.5	18.8	9.5
Kyrgyzstan	0.2	5.6	...	...	-11.3	9.8	4.6	-1.8	3.1	5.7	-1.8
Maldives	0.0	11.0	13.8	15.6	11.3	21.4	15.6	8.3	12.0	8.1	11.9
Nepal	0.1	5.5	3.3	3.0	8.6	5.5	7.7	5.9	8.0	-4.8	6.1
Pakistan	0.9	7.6	6.5	6.1	5.1	3.8	7.2	5.1	3.6	5.0	0.1
Sri Lanka	0.2	9.9	4.6	4.8	4.9	5.8	6.4	4.7	5.1	4.9	3.2
Tajikistan	0.2	6.8	...	...	-23.4	-26.2	76.9	50.6	-53.1	113.0	-13.0
Turkmenistan	0.1	3.5	...	...	7.9	26.1	60.5	-20.7	42.3	-11.3	26.1
Uzbekistan	0.8	5.9	...	...	-0.1	-6.0	2.3	8.0	-4.1	23.6	4.7
South-Eastern Asia	*6.3*	*6.7*	*9.6*	*7.6*	*6.9*	*9.2*	*7.4*	*-4.9*	*4.5*	*9.3*	*5.4*
Brunei Darussalam	0.0	4.3	15.6	11.8	4.6	10.0	9.4	3.3	6.3	0.9	2.7
Cambodia	0.0	6.8	-7.3	-0.3	5.2	7.1	-12.6	-0.8	14.6	8.2	8.3
Indonesia	1.9	6.3	14.5	7.6	4.7	8.7	7.0	-15.1	-0.8	9.4	7.5
Lao People's Democratic Republic	0.0	5.2	0.3	1.9	5.1	10.1	10.3	6.5	5.8	9.0	8.6
Malaysia	0.7	5.9	12.6	8.7	9.2	7.4	11.8	-0.3	4.3	11.0	7.5
Myanmar	0.1	2.7	2.1	4.1	9.6	9.7	10.8	8.7	11.7	22.9	4.8
Philippines	0.6	4.9	7.4	4.5	4.4	7.4	8.2	6.5	5.3	10.4	8.8
Singapore	1.3	12.8	14.9	9.4	8.5	8.2	8.8	6.4	7.5	8.5	2.7
Thailand	1.6	7.1	6.6	8.2	7.7	11.7	4.7	-9.1	6.1	7.8	3.6
Vietnam	0.1	3.5	-0.1	4.2	6.7	7.4	8.9	3.9	6.3	7.4	6.9
Western Asia	*11.9*	*8.6*	*8.0*	*3.9*	*3.8*	*-0.4*	*10.2*	*4.5*	*0.7*	*10.6*	*1.0*
Armenia	0.3	7.0	...	...	-3.9	17.4	9.1	1.4	1.7	0.4	9.1
Azerbaijan	0.5	8.1	...	...	-16.4	-13.0	3.0	15.4	9.8	16.1	15.3
Bahrain	0.1	6.7	22.1	0.4	4.2	2.2	1.5	5.8	8.3	6.1	4.8
Cyprus	0.1	9.0	7.0	8.4	3.6	4.5	5.8	9.0	10.1	13.4	10.0
Georgia	0.4	7.4	...	...	-5.6	61.2	-2.2	-1.4	17.0	22.7	0.9
Iraq	0.9	9.0	19.0	-0.7	6.2	-16.9	68.3	7.2	5.1	20.5	9.3
Israel	1.3	8.7	2.7	5.7	2.5	8.0	5.3	6.3	3.5	6.7	-0.1
Jordan	0.1	13.9	6.5	5.4	4.4	8.9	1.6	18.8	5.8	1.3	2.7
Kuwait	0.2	3.7	9.3	4.8	4.3	12.4	6.2	12.0	12.3	55.5	-1.1
Lebanon	0.0	3.8	-1.9	-13.2	0.5	-12.6	1.2	-1.6	-3.3	5.0	10.8
Oman	0.1	4.5	16.9	11.2	10.5	7.0	13.4	16.1	4.6	3.0	18.8
Qatar	0.0	2.5	14.9	1.8	9.8	5.1	11.7	14.7	6.0	12.4	9.6
Saudi Arabia	1.7	6.3	4.7	1.8	-2.0	-32.4	5.3	4.0	2.6	4.0	8.3
Syrian Arab Republic	0.4	9.5	7.5	5.0	8.0	7.2	10.6	-0.5	8.6	5.4	4.7
Turkey	4.7	11.8	9.4	4.2	4.5	7.6	7.2	2.7	-4.9	9.5	-7.7
United Arab Emirates	0.4	4.7	31.1	3.6	6.2	4.5	2.8	4.9	4.6	4.0	6.2
Yemen	0.5	13.9	...	...	-4.1	-14.0	18.3	6.3	2.0	1.0	51.2
Yemen Arab Republic (Former)	...	...	9.6	8.4	...	...	...	...	...	...	...
Yemen Democratic (Former)	...	...	9.1	0.3	...	...	...	...	...	...	...
EUROPE	**39.6**	**6.8**	**4.1**	**3.1**	**2.9**	**2.7**	**4.3**	**4.3**	**7.8**	**6.9**	**4.3**
Eastern Europe	*20.6*	*8.3*	*5.5*	*3.2*	*-3.5*	*-4.9*	*-0.7*	*-2.0*	*9.6*	*3.5*	*4.9*
Belarus	0.7	6.5	...	...	-6.7	-2.0	6.7	2.7	2.2	2.2	2.3
Bulgaria	0.1	4.0	7.1	6.1	-2.5	-9.4	15.6	-2.4	11.2	9.6	9.8
Czech Republic	0.2	3.5	...	-0.9	2.2	-1.5	5.7	4.2	1.6	8.2	15.1
Czechoslovakia (Former)	...	...	4.7	...	...	...	...	...	...	...	...
Hungary	0.4	6.3	5.3	2.3	-2.0	1.0	7.6	4.5	2.7	2.1	3.6
Poland	0.5	5.1	8.2	2.4	-1.8	5.4	5.6	6.3	8.8	5.2	-0.8
Republic of Moldova	0.2	6.6	...	...	-18.4	7.0	4.8	-8.3	-2.7	21.4	9.1
Romania	0.4	5.8	12.4	0.5	4.5	-0.9	3.0	-7.0	59.8	-25.6	17.4
Russian Federation	15.0	9.3	...	...	-7.2	-4.7	-1.9	-3.1	9.1	6.1	3.3
Slovakia	0.2	5.9	...	-2.1	3.1	5.1	6.0	-4.6	9.4	2.2	13.5
Ukraine	3.0	7.2	...	...	-15.5	-19.0	-7.5	0.8	-7.1	2.6	10.8
USSR (Former)	...	...	5.2	3.2	...	...	...	...	...	...	...
Northern Europe	*21.8*	*7.6*	*2.5*	*3.1*	*3.7*	*4.9*	*5.4*	*4.3*	*5.1*	*5.2*	*3.1*
Denmark	1.5	6.9	1.3	2.4	3.6	6.7	2.5	-3.4	17.2	6.6	0.7
Estonia	0.1	6.4	...	...	-0.6	8.3	17.8	9.7	5.3	7.4	6.8
Finland	1.8	8.0	3.3	3.8	3.9	5.8	7.5	8.2	4.7	7.2	0.9

Table 6.F. Average Rates of Growth of Gross Domestic Product by Kind of Economic Activity - Transport, Storage and Communication

Major area, region and country	Base year weights as percentage of total for world or region in 1990	Base year share as percentage of total GDP in 1990	Average rates of growth			Annual rate of change (percentage)					
			1970-1979	1980-1989	1990-1999	1996	1997	1998	1999	2000	2001
Iceland	0.1	7.1	5.8	3.1	5.6	14.7	5.8	10.9	8.1	8.8	-0.8
Ireland	0.4	5.1	4.8	2.0	6.5	10.8	7.7	13.8	5.6	0.9	17.0
Latvia	0.3	10.4	...	...	-2.2	13.6	7.4	-2.8	0.2	7.0	9.5
Lithuania	0.3	7.8	...	...	-2.4	7.0	9.6	-0.3	6.5	8.1	1.1
Norway	1.9	10.0	4.6	3.2	5.8	6.9	6.9	5.7	2.8	2.7	1.6
Sweden	3.1	7.7	4.4	3.8	3.4	3.4	6.1	2.3	5.3	5.0	1.0
United Kingdom	12.3	7.5	1.9	2.9	2.9	4.0	4.7	4.6	4.2	5.4	3.8
Southern Europe	*21.1*	*6.8*	*5.5*	*3.3*	*2.8*	*2.1*	*4.2*	*3.6*	*3.9*	*6.0*	*6.3*
Albania [2]	0.0	3.3	7.2	4.1	-1.2	-0.9	-20.6	20.0	14.9	15.0	14.9
Andorra	0.0	8.0	13.0	8.0	9.0	9.1	10.8	8.3	9.7	8.8	8.1
Bosnia and Herzegovina	0.1	6.1	...	...	8.5	59.3	32.3	63.8	-10.0	10.8	7.4
Croatia	0.3	7.6	...	...	-3.9	7.0	3.5	4.3	-5.1	4.5	6.8
Greece	1.0	6.8	7.5	3.9	4.0	-5.6	8.4	4.1	11.9	22.7	9.0
Holy See	0.0	6.7	6.9	4.2	2.8	1.4	3.0	2.2	3.7	4.3	5.5
Italy	12.2	6.7	5.9	3.8	2.7	1.4	2.9	2.2	3.6	4.1	5.5
Malta	0.0	5.1	16.0	5.4	6.5	2.0	-0.9	7.5	11.0	-1.9	9.4
Portugal	0.7	5.9	4.6	4.7	4.1	0.9	2.7	9.2	4.6	3.2	1.9
San Marino	0.0	6.7	5.5	2.3	2.6	0.0	0.5	10.6	6.6	1.6	1.0
Serbia and Montenegro	0.3	6.5	...	...	-13.4	12.0	6.3	3.4	-9.4	-17.9	8.5
Slovenia	0.2	7.8	...	...	0.1	2.6	4.2	5.2	3.2	4.7	4.5
Spain	6.1	7.2	4.6	1.9	2.6	4.0	5.8	4.1	3.9	7.4	7.6
TFYR Macedonia	0.0	6.4	...	...	-1.3	0.4	3.3	6.9	13.7	0.8	-2.0
Yugoslavia (Former)	...	...	7.4	4.0	...	...	...	...	...	...	...
Western Europe	*36.4*	*5.8*	*3.7*	*3.0*	*4.5*	*3.8*	*4.8*	*6.1*	*11.0*	*8.9*	*4.0*
Austria	1.9	7.2	5.5	3.6	3.0	5.9	2.4	3.3	2.2	2.4	-0.9
Belgium	2.1	6.5	1.7	2.1	2.3	-1.3	-0.4	2.9	7.8	10.9	6.4
France	12.0	5.9	5.8	5.1	3.8	4.0	6.4	8.5	7.9	6.5	2.4
Germany	14.9	5.4	3.1	1.8	5.9	4.4	4.3	4.7	16.7	12.0	6.0
Liechtenstein	0.0	5.8	2.4	2.2	1.4	1.2	2.8	3.8	2.2	1.6	0.8
Luxembourg	0.1	6.7	5.9	5.0	7.5	11.1	8.4	7.5	9.8	11.9	6.9
Monaco	0.0	5.9	6.2	5.4	4.6	4.7	7.1	9.3	8.1	-10.7	3.0
Netherlands	3.2	6.5	3.8	3.1	4.8	3.7	8.6	9.4	6.8	7.7	2.3
Switzerland	2.2	5.8	0.9	1.4	0.7	0.3	1.7	2.6	0.9	0.7	-0.6
OCEANIA	**1.9**	**8.0**	**4.5**	**4.4**	**5.6**	**5.9**	**4.7**	**5.2**	**6.0**	**4.1**	**4.6**
Australia & New Zealand	*96.5*	*7.9*	*4.7*	*4.5*	*5.7*	*6.1*	*4.7*	*5.5*	*5.8*	*4.3*	*4.7*
Australia	84.5	7.9	5.1	4.6	5.5	6.3	4.8	5.6	5.1	3.5	4.4
New Zealand	12.0	8.0	2.1	3.8	6.9	4.7	3.6	5.0	10.4	9.4	6.5
Melanesia	2.6	9.9	1.7	1.4	3.6	-0.5	9.4	-7.9	12.5	-7.8	-0.7
Fiji	*0.6*	*12.9*	*10.6*	*6.5*	*6.5*	*6.1*	*1.6*	*5.8*	*15.8*	*-10.9*	*6.7*
New Caledonia	1.2	13.8	1.7	1.4	1.0	-7.9	15.7	-23.0	21.2	-1.8	-1.6
Papua New Guinea	0.7	6.1	-0.6	-1.6	4.7	4.5	6.2	0.5	1.9	-13.3	-7.4
Solomon Islands	0.0	3.9	12.8	7.1	4.3	3.5	-1.0	-2.2	-7.5	-1.7	-14.6
Vanuatu	0.1	11.4	7.7	3.7	4.8	-1.1	6.9	-0.8	0.7	3.6	4.8
Micronesia	*0.2*	*11.9*	*4.6*	*1.1*	*0.3*	*-9.9*	*7.6*	*-3.2*	*3.5*	*-1.7*	*0.3*
Kiribati	0.0	16.5	2.9	-4.5	3.0	10.9	10.7	0.8	-9.8	1.9	1.8
Marshall Islands	0.0	1.3	6.6	6.1	15.6	-3.7	-0.7	-30.1	8.1	-8.9	21.3
Micronesia (Federated States of)	0.1	16.5	6.6	4.9	1.1	-10.4	1.8	-10.2	4.2	-3.0	1.5
Nauru	0.0	16.5	6.8	5.3	-5.8	-15.4	-0.6	-9.9	1.3	-5.9	-0.8
Palau	0.0	8.0	2.9	-5.5	5.6	-15.0	26.8	5.5	13.9	-1.3	2.5
Polynesia	*0.8*	*6.8*	*2.2*	*6.0*	*3.2*	*2.7*	*1.5*	*1.5*	*5.1*	*3.7*	*2.5*
Cook Islands	0.0	9.2	-3.0	5.3	8.3	-0.7	3.7	-10.9	64.6	6.7	-14.0
French Polynesia	0.7	6.5	2.0	6.8	3.1	1.6	1.1	1.1	2.7	2.7	2.1
Samoa	0.1	10.5	3.1	0.4	2.1	14.6	4.0	11.4	6.3	10.9	12.4
Tonga	0.0	7.9	12.1	7.6	2.8	5.9	0.8	2.9	11.7	4.4	4.7
Tuvalu	0.0	0.9	6.6	1.3	6.2	32.4	19.8	-17.1	11.0	3.0	3.0

Notes for Table 6.F - Transport, storage and communication

1/ 1987-1992
Included in "Wholesale and retail trade, restaurants and hotels".

2/ 1970-2001
Includes "Other activities".

Table 6.G. Average Rates of Growth of Gross Domestic Product by Kind of Economic Activity - Other Activities

Major area, region and country	Base year weights as percentage of total for world or region in 1990	Base year share as percentage of total GDP in 1990	Average rates of growth			Annual rate of change (percentage)					
			1970-1979	1980-1989	1990-1999	1996	1997	1998	1999	2000	2001
WORLD	**100.0**	**39.1**	**4.3**	**3.2**	**10.4**	**4.2**	**11.9**	**72.0**	**7.9**	**4.8**	**-10.2**
DEVELOPED ECONOMIES	**83.5**	**43.9**	**4.0**	**3.0**	**2.6**	**2.9**	**3.2**	**3.5**	**3.0**	**3.6**	**2.5**
DEVELOPING ECONOMIES	**12.7**	**28.1**	**6.4**	**4.7**	**4.5**	**4.7**	**5.2**	**2.7**	**3.9**	**4.1**	**3.1**
TRANSITION ECONOMIES	**3.8**	**18.4**	**9.9**	**1.7**	**46.7**	**33.1**	**185.9**	**583.9**	**13.3**	**5.9**	**-23.1**
AFRICA	**1.3**	**22.6**	**4.4**	**4.0**	**2.9**	**4.4**	**3.0**	**5.2**	**5.2**	**1.9**	**1.5**
Eastern Africa	*11.2*	*23.2*	*5.3*	*4.4*	*2.5*	*3.8*	*4.0*	*4.1*	*-0.4*	*10.5*	*5.0*
Burundi	0.2	18.1	5.5	5.5	2.4	-7.0	2.0	5.9	3.9	4.9	4.4
Comoros	0.0	22.8	3.8	4.5	-1.2	1.6	-1.4	-1.4	-5.6	-0.8	8.1
Djibouti	0.1	34.3	5.4	1.9	0.7	-3.8	-0.7	-3.1	-1.9	-0.3	1.4
Eritrea	...	...	...	...	5.4	-9.8	7.2	12.6	3.2	-9.3	4.6
Ethiopia	...	...	...	...	8.4	7.0	7.1	19.4	8.0	10.2	11.2
Ethiopia (Former) [1]	1.2	17.5	6.0	4.0	2.5	...	...	...	...	...	...
Kenya [2]	2.2	31.2	7.1	5.9	2.7	4.5	3.1	2.2	1.6	0.9	1.1
Madagascar	0.7	25.3	1.9	3.4	0.6	4.0	3.7	3.3	-10.0	4.3	32.2
Malawi	0.4	25.4	9.5	4.5	3.6	6.7	10.2	-0.1	1.2	2.2	0.9
Mauritius [3]	0.5	24.9	8.1	3.7	6.0	5.1	5.7	5.9	6.7	7.8	6.3
Mozambique	0.1	2.3	3.9	-0.3	1.5	2.7	10.3	1.1	1.5	11.3	11.1
Reunion	2.2	49.9	6.2	4.1	3.1	2.8	3.0	3.1	3.0	3.0	3.0
Rwanda [4]	0.4	18.9	4.5	7.0	3.1	15.9	24.0	3.3	5.1	5.0	3.4
Seychelles	0.1	25.0	7.1	1.1	1.9	-0.8	7.1	-17.3	15.4	0.2	38.0
Somalia	0.1	9.2	8.2	-0.4	-3.3	12.2	-4.5	2.7	-33.3	3.0	3.0
Uganda	0.5	15.5	2.4	2.7	6.7	6.3	6.8	5.8	5.5	7.0	7.0
United Republic Of Tanzania	0.3	9.8	8.3	2.4	3.2	4.2	3.1	4.3	4.3	151.3	5.1
Zambia	0.4	12.1	5.0	2.7	1.1	-4.0	0.3	-1.2	-0.4	-0.7	-0.6
Zimbabwe	2.0	26.6	3.2	5.3	0.5	3.3	0.6	3.7	-14.5	19.6	0.7
Middle Africa	*9.4*	*24.8*	*2.0*	*2.0*	*-1.4*	*1.1*	*3.8*	*1.6*	*0.1*	*-4.4*	*6.4*
Angola [5]	2.3	26.9	-0.2	3.9	-1.0	2.7	5.3	6.4	-7.4	1.4	1.1
Cameroon	3.4	28.5	5.4	4.2	-3.7	0.0	4.8	0.5	-17.5	1.6	5.5
Central African Republic	0.2	16.2	1.3	-1.9	-2.9	-5.3	1.0	2.5	-18.6	-4.4	-4.0
Chad [6]	0.2	18.4	-0.6	7.8	0.4	7.0	-3.0	-3.3	12.3	2.1	5.2
Congo	0.5	22.4	5.2	4.4	-4.1	6.0	-1.3	1.8	-29.8	-15.5	13.7
Democratic Rep. of the Congo [7]	1.5	19.4	0.0	-1.6	-7.2	-4.2	-6.2	-2.1	-10.4	-4.3	-4.4
Equatorial Guinea	0.0	27.0	3.7	1.6	27.9	45.1	71.1	21.9	41.7	16.9	53.4
Gabon	1.1	25.3	2.5	-1.9	4.7	-1.3	2.3	-6.1	78.7	-22.8	4.3
Sao Tome and Principe	0.0	40.1	6.4	-1.8	0.3	3.0	2.5	9.3	-20.9	-0.2	3.8
Northern Africa	*40.5*	*20.8*	*5.4*	*4.8*	*3.3*	*6.2*	*3.0*	*5.2*	*1.8*	*-0.5*	*4.0*
Algeria	10.3	20.0	7.6	2.7	1.9	-0.1	3.6	10.0	-2.5	-15.8	2.3
Egypt [8]	9.0	10.2	4.7	7.0	6.4	39.0	4.4	4.2	5.6	4.4	4.6
Libyan Arab Jamahiriya	7.0	29.7	11.4	3.0	2.8	3.8	-2.8	2.1	3.7	4.6	2.6
Morocco [9]	5.5	25.5	6.9	12.6	-0.7	-31.4	2.3	3.7	3.4	2.8	4.6
Sudan	5.4	19.2	-0.3	3.2	2.9	4.3	5.3	3.8	-4.1	2.0	6.0
Tunisia [10]	2.6	25.0	2.0	4.5	5.1	5.3	5.4	5.1	5.4	6.7	4.7
Southern Africa	*29.5*	*29.6*	*3.8*	*3.5*	*2.4*	*4.2*	*2.5*	*2.7*	*3.8*	*3.0*	*2.1*
Botswana	0.7	22.9	17.2	13.8	7.7	6.9	5.3	8.5	7.4	5.2	4.6
Lesotho	0.2	32.7	8.5	6.9	-0.2	3.6	3.4	4.3	3.0	5.6	2.3
Namibia [11]	0.6	32.6	10.7	4.5	4.2	4.6	2.3	2.8	3.2	2.6	2.4
South Africa	27.9	29.8	3.6	3.3	2.2	4.1	2.4	2.5	3.7	2.9	2.0
Swaziland	0.2	23.3	7.1	7.1	4.2	3.0	2.4	1.8	3.5	4.2	2.1
Western Africa	*9.3*	*15.2*	*4.3*	*4.1*	*5.6*	*0.8*	*3.0*	*15.8*	*29.3*	*3.0*	*-11.3*
Benin [12]	0.3	22.0	0.0	1.5	2.5	5.4	5.0	4.9	508.5	3.8	5.0
Burkina Faso	0.4	17.8	6.2	6.4	6.7	3.2	1.9	0.9	16.6	11.7	3.3
Cape Verde	0.1	22.6	1.7	7.3	6.2	-0.8	10.0	7.6	8.7	5.9	13.9
Cote d'Ivoire	2.1	21.6	7.7	4.9	5.9	6.6	4.2	7.5	9.8	-1.7	-38.7
Gambia	0.0	17.4	3.5	3.4	-1.2	6.5	6.3	4.1	-34.7	77.5	-32.6
Ghana	0.7	14.3	5.2	4.5	5.3	2.7	7.3	4.6	9.4	5.7	4.9
Guinea	0.3	13.0	2.8	3.0	6.3	1.8	5.1	3.7	3.7	5.0	3.0
Guinea-Bissau	0.0	7.8	11.7	4.9	-1.1	4.3	-2.0	10.8	-31.3	28.8	5.0
Liberia	0.0	14.0	3.0	-7.8	-15.3	-60.2	387.9	29.8	45.5	22.4	-0.3
Mali	0.3	14.5	5.8	5.4	3.0	4.6	2.6	3.0	21.2	6.6	-9.2
Mauritania	0.2	20.4	10.8	0.1	3.4	5.2	5.1	4.8	4.9	3.5	4.6
Niger	0.5	22.1	4.6	0.4	3.6	2.6	2.4	2.2	1.3	1.6	1.5
Nigeria	2.6	9.5	13.7	6.7	10.7	-7.4	0.1	45.9	20.3	2.6	-17.9

Table 6.G. Average Rates of Growth of Gross Domestic Product by Kind of Economic Activity - Other Activities

Major area, region and country	Base year weights as percentage of total for world or region in 1990	Base year share as percentage of total GDP in 1990	Average rates of growth			Annual rate of change (percentage)					
			1970-1979	1980-1989	1990-1999	1996	1997	1998	1999	2000	2001
Senegal	1.3	27.3	3.8	11.8	3.0	1.3	5.6	7.2	3.4	3.6	3.3
Sierra Leone	0.1	10.5	5.0	4.3	-8.8	1.2	-62.7	1.5	-10.1	-21.9	-4.8
Togo	0.3	24.3	3.5	0.5	2.5	5.4	-0.8	-0.9	3.0	4.4	2.8
AMERICAS	**37.8**	**45.0**	**4.0**	**3.0**	**2.6**	**2.6**	**4.2**	**4.1**	**3.4**	**4.0**	**2.2**
NORTHERN AMERICA	**32.7**	**46.2**	**3.8**	**2.8**	**2.6**	**2.5**	**4.4**	**4.4**	**3.7**	**4.2**	**2.3**
Bermuda	0.0	56.6	3.7	2.0	3.3	3.8	4.5	6.9	2.0	3.7	1.9
Canada	7.1	41.6	4.0	2.8	2.6	0.8	3.8	3.4	4.7	3.8	3.4
United States	79.6	46.6	3.8	2.8	2.6	2.7	4.4	4.5	3.6	4.3	2.3
LATIN AMERICA AND THE CARIBBEAN	**5.0**	**38.8**	**5.9**	**4.4**	**2.8**	**2.7**	**3.5**	**2.5**	**1.9**	**2.4**	**1.4**
Caribbean	*0.8*	*31.8*	*4.7*	*4.3*	*3.1*	*4.9*	*2.5*	*2.8*	*5.8*	*1.7*	*4.7*
Anguilla	0.0	25.1	3.8	8.3	5.7	18.2	-0.8	3.6	7.1	13.3	6.4
Antigua and Barbuda	0.0	36.7	0.6	4.8	4.5	7.1	9.4	8.9	1.8	2.7	2.3
Aruba	0.0	42.2	9.5	10.6	8.0	7.8	4.9	4.6	9.4	6.1	12.4
Bahamas	0.0	30.0	0.4	1.5	1.3	0.4	12.5	4.3	6.8	5.9	5.3
Barbados	0.0	31.7	7.3	1.9	0.3	1.1	1.9	2.2	2.5	1.1	0.7
British Virgin Islands	0.0	37.9	2.5	8.2	7.4	12.0	7.1	11.9	11.9	10.4	10.5
Cayman Islands [13]	0.0	49.0	10.7	9.6	1.2	3.6	-2.8	-0.3	0.1	0.1	0.1
Cuba	0.1	23.6	5.8	7.5	0.2	2.4	0.8	3.3	2.9	3.7	7.1
Dominica	0.0	28.4	0.5	2.6	3.0	0.4	0.1	6.0	2.8	2.4	3.2
Dominican Republic [14]	0.1	25.8	7.6	4.9	3.4	6.5	3.1	3.7	3.4	3.4	3.7
Grenada	0.0	26.7	1.6	4.3	0.2	7.3	6.7	4.0	6.2	4.9	13.4
Guadeloupe	0.0	54.6	6.1	1.8	2.2	4.3	9.2	4.1	5.9	5.9	5.9
Haiti	0.0	33.7	6.5	3.2	2.5	1.4	0.5	2.3	0.8	-56.7	-1.8
Jamaica	0.0	31.7	2.8	2.5	3.0	-1.7	-8.1	-0.8	7.0	-9.2	-3.9
Martinique	0.1	52.5	5.6	4.0	1.6	1.6	1.6	4.1	2.5	2.5	2.5
Montserrat	0.0	34.9	3.9	3.6	-6.9	-29.0	-16.4	-10.8	-13.1	10.4	2.8
Netherlands Antilles	0.0	50.1	1.9	2.4	2.2	6.2	0.6	-0.2	0.0	-0.5	1.7
Puerto Rico	0.3	33.5	3.9	5.2	4.8	7.6	4.0	2.6	8.4	4.6	5.3
Saint Kitts and Nevis	0.0	28.1	5.5	5.0	4.5	5.2	6.6	1.0	2.9	6.7	1.0
Saint Lucia	0.0	26.3	6.4	5.6	1.6	2.8	2.9	4.5	1.6	3.1	0.5
Saint Vincent and the Grenadines	0.0	23.4	5.3	2.6	3.9	2.6	4.5	3.0	5.9	0.6	3.9
Trinidad and Tobago	0.0	26.2	7.4	-1.4	1.0	3.0	-4.4	1.9	3.8	4.6	6.2
Central America	*2.5*	*28.5*	*5.5*	*2.5*	*2.8*	*1.1*	*3.5*	*3.7*	*2.9*	*3.8*	*2.2*
Belize	0.0	28.3	3.5	3.3	1.3	2.0	-0.2	3.1	1.6	26.4	18.3
Costa Rica	0.1	29.4	5.2	2.4	3.7	1.7	3.6	4.6	5.1	5.1	4.5
El Salvador [15]	0.0	30.5	6.7	1.1	2.9	2.3	4.0	2.7	2.1	2.0	0.0
Guatemala	0.1	22.3	5.4	2.5	4.5	3.5	4.5	5.2	4.8	4.1	4.6
Honduras	0.0	29.7	8.6	3.5	3.1	2.7	6.7	5.5	0.1	5.2	6.8
Mexico	2.2	28.4	5.5	2.6	2.7	0.8	3.5	3.6	2.8	3.9	2.1
Nicaragua [16]	0.0	19.5	-0.6	-4.1	1.8	0.5	-0.1	2.4	2.7	2.6	2.8
Panama	0.1	43.2	6.3	2.5	4.7	6.0	3.1	5.3	6.3	1.8	0.8
South America	*10.0*	*43.4*	*6.1*	*4.9*	*2.8*	*2.9*	*3.5*	*2.2*	*1.3*	*2.0*	*0.9*
Argentina	1.5	36.2	2.9	0.8	6.0	4.2	5.7	4.0	0.7	1.9	-2.4
Bolivia	0.0	24.7	5.8	-1.6	5.0	5.2	8.4	7.8	8.0	0.1	1.7
Brazil	6.9	52.8	8.5	7.2	1.7	1.9	2.4	1.7	2.0	2.2	1.9
Chile	0.3	30.3	3.3	3.0	4.8	5.4	5.4	4.0	1.1	3.3	2.5
Colombia	0.4	28.9	5.9	3.7	5.7	10.5	6.1	0.3	-0.7	0.0	0.9
Ecuador	0.1	20.6	8.2	2.6	1.1	3.9	2.5	-0.1	-10.7	4.3	7.2
French Guiana	0.0	47.0	8.0	7.4	5.7	1.6	5.2	3.7	3.5	3.5	3.5
Guyana [17]	0.0	20.1	4.6	-0.3	1.8	4.6	3.8	1.5	0.8	4.3	-0.8
Paraguay [18]	0.0	13.7	8.4	3.5	3.6	5.4	4.2	0.7	3.8	3.2	0.1
Peru	0.3	30.0	4.0	1.0	1.6	3.5	5.2	0.4	1.7	1.5	1.2
Suriname	0.0	37.4	17.6	2.7	-0.3	3.2	2.2	4.9	-2.9	0.5	1.8
Uruguay	0.1	43.5	1.5	1.8	2.4	3.7	5.2	4.9	3.3	1.1	0.0
Venezuela	0.3	22.6	7.9	1.9	1.4	-2.4	1.1	1.2	-1.4	2.2	2.1
ASIA	**22.8**	**36.3**	**6.0**	**3.8**	**23.4**	**9.2**	**36.6**	**219.7**	**11.3**	**5.5**	**-18.2**
Eastern Asia	*81.6*	*42.0*	*5.6*	*3.9*	*5.7*	*4.4*	*3.1*	*2.8*	*2.5*	*3.5*	*3.2*
China	3.3	17.7	6.0	12.6	8.5	7.9	9.1	8.3	7.5	7.8	7.7
Democratic People's Rep. of Korea	0.2	18.2	10.8	7.6	-3.5	-3.6	-6.3	-1.1	6.2	1.3	3.7
Hong Kong SAR of China	1.6	43.3	8.8	7.2	3.8	4.3	5.1	-5.0	3.4	10.2	1.3
Japan	70.6	47.0	5.4	3.1	5.4	4.0	2.3	2.9	1.9	3.0	3.0

Table 6.G. Average Rates of Growth of Gross Domestic Product by Kind of Economic Activity - Other Activities

Major area, region and country	Base year weights as percentage of total for world or region in 1990	Base year share as percentage of total GDP in 1990	Average rates of growth			Annual rate of change (percentage)					
			1970-1979	1980-1989	1990-1999	1996	1997	1998	1999	2000	2001
Macao SAR of China	0.1	64.1	16.9	16.9	7.5	-3.3	2.4	-6.5	-7.8	3.3	-0.3
Mongolia	0.0	11.7	5.7	0.4	3.5	8.0	-0.9	-1.7	2.9	3.2	3.0
Republic of Korea	3.5	27.9	5.3	7.6	6.0	5.8	4.7	-2.1	5.0	3.7	2.7
South Central Asia	*8.0*	*21.4*	*8.4*	*1.9*	*7.4*	*4.3*	*7.4*	*7.4*	*7.5*	*3.9*	*6.5*
Afghanistan	0.0	1.8	3.2	1.1	-0.8	6.6	13.3	5.2	-12.4	-43.7	0.0
Bangladesh	0.4	24.3	3.6	5.6	4.2	3.7	4.2	4.2	4.3	4.2	4.3
Bhutan	0.0	18.4	6.4	9.9	6.9	-0.3	15.1	4.7	4.1	12.3	-23.9
India	3.2	20.0	4.1	6.5	7.5	6.6	11.7	8.9	11.1	4.5	6.8
Iran (Islamic Republic of)	2.6	27.6	12.6	-2.7	5.2	2.9	6.4	2.8	3.8	1.1	2.4
Kazakhstan	0.5	14.0	...	...	2.2	-2.8	-6.9	36.5	-1.6	6.4	25.4
Kyrgyzstan	0.1	18.5	...	...	-4.1	-7.1	-5.5	1.7	4.0	1.3	0.6
Maldives	0.0	31.2	13.5	16.0	5.6	8.3	11.3	-3.9	8.2	6.9	-10.4
Nepal	0.0	16.6	3.0	4.6	6.4	6.8	4.0	5.9	10.9	-6.0	10.1
Pakistan [19]	0.5	20.7	7.0	6.3	5.0	5.6	1.2	6.3	5.9	4.4	9.0
Sri Lanka	0.1	13.0	4.0	3.4	5.0	6.8	6.1	4.1	3.0	5.1	2.9
Tajikistan	0.1	19.2	...	...	-5.6	-65.2	16.0	80.0	124.2	-9.0	28.5
Turkmenistan	0.0	5.9	...	...	8.9	-11.0	79.5	16.5	16.7	-2.2	20.1
Uzbekistan	0.6	24.6	...	...	-2.2	7.3	-2.9	2.8	4.7	18.2	7.1
South-Eastern Asia	*3.6*	*20.6*	*6.3*	*6.4*	*5.7*	*7.1*	*6.4*	*-4.8*	*1.4*	*3.8*	*9.7*
Brunei Darussalam	0.0	28.1	11.6	11.0	6.4	7.0	6.6	4.4	6.2	6.1	6.1
Cambodia	0.0	18.3	-7.3	-0.9	3.9	6.8	-1.1	4.7	5.6	7.8	0.6
Indonesia [20]	1.0	18.1	8.7	7.5	3.0	4.7	4.8	-15.3	-2.0	3.1	2.4
Lao People's Democratic Republic	0.0	12.0	0.1	12.8	3.9	5.1	1.0	-6.1	2.5	3.6	2.5
Malaysia	0.5	24.7	9.5	6.5	8.7	9.9	12.7	-0.1	5.2	3.4	6.4
Myanmar [21]	0.1	6.8	5.3	2.4	6.8	7.7	7.3	8.0	7.5	8.4	4.8
Philippines [22]	0.5	22.9	1.8	3.0	3.6	6.8	5.8	3.3	3.0	2.2	2.3
Singapore	0.7	37.2	8.6	9.1	8.0	8.9	11.2	-0.2	5.4	6.3	3.8
Thailand	0.7	16.5	7.8	6.1	5.0	6.3	-1.4	-8.0	-5.4	1.8	38.3
Vietnam	0.1	17.9	-0.1	5.8	8.0	8.0	7.0	6.0	1.6	4.8	3.3
Western Asia	*6.8*	*26.1*	*7.7*	*3.3*	*55.8*	*62.3*	*275.8*	*653.4*	*13.6*	*6.0*	*-23.6*
Armenia	0.1	15.9	...	...	0.0	-5.3	3.4	2.9	3.6	1.1	7.7
Azerbaijan	0.2	21.5	...	...	135.1	339.9	601.1	768.7	13.8	5.9	-24.0
Bahrain	0.1	50.7	13.8	8.0	3.2	6.1	4.7	0.7	2.5	7.3	2.7
Cyprus	0.1	33.0	4.5	7.1	6.7	4.1	5.5	4.8	5.0	5.4	4.1
Georgia	0.2	19.4	...	...	-8.6	299.5	19.8	7.4	-1.8	5.5	3.1
Iraq	0.6	29.6	12.5	4.3	-13.7	16.5	45.9	13.4	-3.4	49.2	24.2
Israel	1.2	44.2	7.4	4.8	6.4	3.7	-0.2	4.7	4.0	8.6	0.7
Jordan	0.1	35.9	6.0	4.5	4.4	2.5	4.3	4.2	3.8	3.2	4.1
Kuwait	0.3	36.5	7.4	-3.4	10.2	-12.5	4.5	4.4	-0.2	33.7	1.5
Lebanon	0.1	37.7	-0.5	-5.0	7.4	22.3	19.0	10.5	12.6	2.9	3.3
Oman	0.2	29.1	12.8	8.3	4.6	1.8	5.8	-0.6	3.5	4.1	6.4
Qatar	0.1	36.3	16.1	7.3	2.6	2.2	5.8	5.6	0.2	3.5	1.9
Saudi Arabia	1.4	26.7	8.8	4.7	4.5	28.5	5.1	1.0	2.7	3.4	2.2
Syrian Arab Republic	0.1	15.4	13.1	-0.8	3.9	0.5	3.9	2.5	4.2	13.6	2.0
Turkey	1.4	18.9	4.7	2.5	2.4	2.2	2.5	4.2	1.6	1.7	-1.8
United Arab Emirates	0.4	23.1	41.5	8.6	5.2	7.2	4.2	4.3	5.0	2.7	2.7
Yemen	0.2	24.6	...	...	10.6	6.1	6.9	4.3	6.4	4.9	-37.0
Yemen Arab Republic (Former)	...	...	10.0	8.5	...	...	...	...	...	...	...
Yemen Democratic (Former)	...	...	3.9	4.9	...	...	...	...	...	...	...
EUROPE	**36.5**	**36.7**	**3.9**	**3.2**	**3.1**	**2.5**	**2.3**	**2.9**	**2.5**	**3.5**	**2.4**
Eastern Europe	*8.3*	*17.9*	*10.7*	*6.1*	*20.0*	*0.3*	*-0.9*	*3.0*	*0.7*	*5.2*	*2.4*
Belarus	0.3	17.1	...	...	0.6	0.6	8.5	4.6	5.0	5.8	3.4
Bulgaria	0.2	26.3	7.1	6.1	-6.3	-9.4	-19.8	3.1	2.5	5.3	0.7
Czech Republic	0.3	26.7	...	-1.2	3.1	11.3	-4.5	2.0	1.5	1.9	4.9
Czechoslovakia (Former)	...	...	5.2	...	...	...	...	...	...	...	...
Hungary	0.2	18.4	5.1	4.5	1.5	3.0	-0.8	3.0	3.6	5.1	7.8
Poland	0.4	24.6	16.1	1.5	-0.4	3.0	0.5	2.7	1.7	2.8	2.4
Republic of Moldova	0.1	13.6		...	-6.9	10.3	-1.8	-1.0	-4.2	-8.6	12.0
Romania	0.2	14.5	6.9	2.9	4.8	9.8	-17.5	19.8	11.7	9.3	-0.4
Russian Federation	5.2	17.6	...	...	-1.2	0.6	1.3	0.2	2.7	1.1	0.6
Slovakia	0.1	20.9	...	1.0	2.3	3.0	9.3	8.1	-2.3	10.0	3.2
Ukraine	1.2	16.2	...	...	6.2	-3.1	-4.4	7.7	-5.1	14.9	5.0
Northern Europe	*20.6*	*38.8*	*3.1*	*2.7*	*2.6*	*2.8*	*3.7*	*3.9*	*3.2*	*3.5*	*3.4*
Denmark	1.8	43.9	3.8	1.7	1.7	1.4	3.1	2.9	2.1	2.9	1.8
Estonia	0.1	36.0	...	...	-2.9	2.7	7.8	3.1	1.5	3.4	3.3
Finland	1.5	35.1	4.0	3.9	1.3	3.9	3.4	2.5	4.2	4.1	1.3
Iceland	0.1	32.7	5.8	5.0	2.8	3.3	5.1	3.8	5.2	5.1	2.2

Table 6.G. Average Rates of Growth of Gross Domestic Product by Kind of Economic Activity - Other Activities

Major area, region and country	Base year weights as percentage of total for world or region in 1990	Base year share as percentage of total GDP in 1990	Average rates of growth			Annual rate of change (percentage)					
			1970-1979	1980-1989	1990-1999	1996	1997	1998	1999	2000	2001
Ireland	0.5	31.0	7.1	4.6	7.5	8.2	9.8	9.2	9.5	9.6	8.2
Latvia	0.1	13.9	...	...	3.0	2.5	5.6	2.9	6.4	6.0	6.3
Lithuania	0.2	27.1	...	...	-5.5	2.4	5.0	3.8	4.5	1.2	2.2
Norway	1.3	36.1	3.1	2.8	2.1	2.1	3.0	3.3	5.2	2.6	3.6
Sweden	3.1	40.9	3.0	2.2	1.2	0.6	1.8	0.9	3.6	2.7	1.8
United Kingdom	12.0	39.6	2.8	2.7	2.8	3.3	4.0	4.7	2.6	3.4	3.9
Southern Europe	*22.3*	*38.9*	*4.2*	*3.4*	*2.1*	*2.3*	*2.5*	*2.6*	*2.0*	*3.7*	*3.0*
Andorra	0.0	35.0	9.7	7.8	6.9	5.7	7.7	7.6	7.5	8.7	8.3
Bosnia and Herzegovina	0.0	11.5	...	...	14.0	208.1	39.8	36.7	-17.5	10.7	7.4
Croatia	0.2	26.6	...	...	5.0	2.0	4.0	3.2	3.2	1.1	2.0
Greece	0.9	35.1	5.5	2.6	2.5	2.3	3.1	2.7	2.0	2.9	2.6
Holy See	0.0	38.8	4.7	3.6	1.6	2.5	2.0	1.6	1.9	3.1	2.2
Italy	13.2	38.8	3.8	3.2	1.5	2.5	1.8	1.6	1.8	3.0	2.2
Malta	0.0	33.2	9.4	4.8	7.2	11.0	4.7	5.5	1.9	3.3	7.1
Portugal	0.7	34.1	7.6	4.2	4.3	1.5	4.8	5.8	6.2	5.2	4.3
San Marino	0.0	38.8	4.6	4.6	3.8	4.2	3.0	6.6	10.3	4.2	3.0
Serbia and Montenegro	0.2	25.2	...	...	-9.4	6.8	12.0	7.3	-35.8	19.6	-10.7
Slovenia	0.1	27.5	...	...	3.5	5.0	4.0	3.4	4.8	4.2	3.8
Spain	6.7	43.0	4.5	4.0	2.2	0.8	2.8	3.4	2.9	4.6	4.7
TFYR Macedonia	0.0	24.6	...	...	2.0	-0.6	1.4	1.6	1.3	2.5	-2.8
Yugoslavia (Former)	...	...	7.6	0.9	...	...	...	...	...	...	...
Western Europe	*48.9*	*42.1*	*3.9*	*3.2*	*2.6*	*2.8*	*2.1*	*2.7*	*2.6*	*3.1*	*1.6*
Austria	1.8	36.3	3.6	3.0	2.4	0.9	0.5	3.8	1.1	4.8	1.5
Belgium	2.6	43.0	5.0	4.1	2.7	2.0	3.0	2.8	3.1	2.3	1.0
France	16.8	44.8	4.1	3.3	1.5	2.3	1.0	1.9	2.4	3.3	1.9
Germany	21.0	41.0	4.5	3.1	3.5	3.5	2.5	3.0	2.9	3.3	1.8
Liechtenstein	0.0	39.8	2.1	2.1	3.2	1.2	2.8	3.8	2.2	1.6	0.8
Luxembourg	0.1	43.5	8.9	5.3	6.8	2.6	8.2	7.0	2.8	5.0	2.7
Monaco	0.0	44.8	4.7	4.5	2.2	3.0	1.7	2.6	3.4	9.8	2.4
Netherlands	3.7	41.0	3.1	3.9	2.8	3.8	4.2	3.3	3.8	2.4	1.9
Switzerland	2.8	39.8	0.5	1.4	2.4	0.3	1.7	2.6	0.9	0.7	-0.6
OCEANIA	**1.7**	**40.8**	**3.8**	**4.1**	**3.4**	**4.1**	**3.7**	**5.4**	**4.0**	**3.7**	**4.0**
Australia & New Zealand	*97.5*	*41.1*	*3.8*	*4.2*	*3.4*	*4.1*	*3.8*	*5.7*	*4.0*	*3.8*	*4.1*
Australia	85.7	41.1	4.1	4.4	3.5	4.1	4.0	6.2	4.2	3.9	4.0
New Zealand	11.9	40.6	2.2	2.4	2.3	4.0	2.3	2.2	2.3	2.9	4.9
Melanesia	*1.3*	*26.7*	*2.3*	*2.3*	*2.8*	*4.6*	*3.1*	*-11.6*	*9.3*	*1.5*	*0.3*
Fiji	0.2	27.6	8.2	0.6	2.7	1.6	-3.4	0.5	8.8	-2.5	0.8
New Caledonia	0.5	31.3	1.7	6.7	3.7	9.5	4.7	-15.5	4.1	5.0	-0.2
Papua New Guinea [23]	0.5	22.5	0.6	0.3	2.1	0.8	4.4	-13.3	17.5	-0.2	1.6
Solomon Islands	0.0	29.3	8.2	2.0	2.6	3.5	-1.0	-2.2	-7.5	-1.7	-14.6
Vanuatu	0.0	28.6	7.7	3.2	3.8	4.2	5.5	-1.0	-2.2	5.2	2.3
Micronesia	*0.1*	*41.0*	*4.4*	*0.9*	*2.8*	*5.3*	*-0.9*	*-3.0*	*-1.8*	*5.4*	*0.5*
Kiribati	0.0	37.3	2.9	-3.6	6.8	7.6	2.7	5.0	4.0	9.1	1.8
Marshall Islands	0.0	50.1	6.6	6.1	-1.1	-15.1	-10.1	5.5	0.0	-3.0	1.9
Micronesia (Federated States of)	0.0	37.3	6.6	5.4	4.3	7.4	-3.4	-7.7	-4.6	13.7	1.5
Nauru	0.0	37.3	6.8	5.8	-2.8	1.4	-5.6	-7.4	-7.2	10.2	-0.8
Palau	0.0	43.7	2.9	-5.5	4.4	20.3	9.8	-1.4	0.7	-4.1	-2.0
Polynesia	*1.0*	*45.4*	*5.1*	*5.0*	*3.2*	*1.8*	*1.0*	*1.3*	*2.7*	*2.7*	*2.5*
Cook Islands	0.0	40.7	-6.1	4.9	-0.6	-2.4	-17.8	-1.3	0.3	2.5	12.5
French Polynesia	0.9	47.5	5.7	5.3	3.3	1.6	1.1	1.1	2.7	2.7	2.1
Samoa	0.0	29.1	3.1	0.4	1.3	7.3	5.5	7.1	4.1	5.3	6.5
Tonga [24]	0.0	24.5	5.3	6.7	3.2	5.6	4.5	2.4	6.4	0.9	6.3
Tuvalu	0.0	36.4	6.6	-7.5	6.5	-3.0	-0.1	29.5	0.2	3.0	3.0

Notes for Table 6.G - Other activities

1/ 1970-1992
Includes Hotels and restaurants.

2/ 1970-1972
Includes Hotels and restaurants.

3/ 1987
FISIM is netted out of Financial intermediation, real estate, renting and business activities.

4/ 1976-1986
FISIM is netted out of Financial intermediation, real estate, renting and business activities.

5/ 1985-1990
Includes Hotels and restaurants.

6/ 1987-1992
Included in "Wholesale and retail trade, restaurants and hotels".

7/ 1970-1977
Includes Hotels and restaurants.

8/ 1986-1995
Finance and insurance included in "Wholesale and retail trade, restaurants and hotels".

9/ 1996-2001
Financial intermediation; real estate, renting and business actvities are included in "Wholesale and retail trade, restaurants and hotels".

10/ 1970-2001
Includes Hotels and restaurants.

11/ 1980-1989
FISIM is netted out of Financial intermediation, real estate, renting and business activities.

12/ 1982-1989
Restaurants and hotels are included in Education; health and social work; other community, social and personal services.

13/ 1972-1991
Excludes banks and insurance companies registered in Cayman Islands but with no physical presence in the Islands.

14/ 1970-1991
Includes Hotels and restaurants.

15/ 1970-2001
Includes Hotels and restaurants.

16/ 1970-1978
Includes Hotels and restaurants.

17/ 1970-2001
Includes Hotels and restaurants.

18/ 1970-1996

Financal intermediation, except insurance and pension funding are included in "Wholesale and retail trade, restaurants and hotels". Includes Hotels and restaurants.

19/ 1970-1995

Includes Hotels and restaurants.

20/ 1970-2001

Includes Hotels and restaurants.

21/ 1970-1979

Includes Hotels and restaurants.

1980-1998

Includes Gas and water, Restaurant and hotels.

22/ 1983-1991

Includes Hotels and restaurants.

23/ 1987-1999

Includes Hotels and restaurants.

24/ 1994-2000

Includes ownership of dwellings.

D. Implicit Price Deflators of Gross Domestic Product: Individual Countries or Areas (Index Numbers 1990 = 100)

Description of Analysis In Table 7

A. Price development expressed in terms of indices of implicit price deflators of gross domestic product

In this final section of the publication, an attempt is made to present a disaggregation of economic development by analyzing the movements of prices and exchange rates in relation to overall economic growth. The period coverage includes the years 1970, 1975, 1980, 1985, and 1990 through 2001.

In Table 7, GDP indices based on current prices expressed in US dollars and national currencies are shown in columns 1 and 2. The annual changes of GDP in volume terms are reflected in column 3, where the indices are based on the movement of GDP at constant prices. Column 4 presents indices of price changes of GDP expressed in US dollars and column 5 includes indices of price changes of GDP in national currency. The price indices in columns 4 and 5 are obtained by dividing, respectively, the indices of GDP at current prices alternatively expressed in US dollars and national currencies shown in columns 1 and 2, by the volume indices presented in column 3. Column 6 provides an implied development in exchange rates derived either by dividing the GDP deflators in national currency (col. 5) by the GDP deflators converted in United States dollar listed in column 4, or by dividing the GDP indices expressed in national currencies by the United States dollar indices listed in column 2 and 1, respectively.

Although column 6 of the table reflects an implied movement of domestic exchange rates vis-à-vis the US dollar from the base year 1990, it does not illustrate the extent to which these changes have affected economic growth. For this effect, it is necessary to relate exchange rate movements in column 6 with price changes in columns 4 and 5 in order to determine whether adjustments in exchange rates have been sufficient to reflect inflationary pressures in the economy.

The data as presented in the table reflect situations in four groups of countries. In the first group, the movement of exchange rates as calculated in column 6 is exactly the same as the movement of domestic prices reflected in the price indices presented in column 5. For these countries, there is no movement over time of the price index in terms of US dollars that is presented in column 4. Thus, the price index in the latter column is always close to 100 for those countries. In this case the growth of GDP in US dollars is not affected by domestic price changes as all domestic price changes have been eliminated through the movement of the exchange rate.

A second group of countries are those having fixed exchange rates. There is no movement of the exchange rates in column 6 i.e., the index always remains 100. In this case all domestic inflation is reflected in the growth of GDP in US dollar terms.

In a third group of countries, the exchange rate index in column 6 is not fixed but lags behind the movement of domestic prices as reflected in the price indices presented in column 5. For this group of countries, the price index in terms of US dollars as presented in column 4 is higher than 100 and the countries' domestic inflation thus affects the growth of GDP in US dollars, though not to the extent that this was the case for countries with a fixed exchange rate. Only some of the domestic inflation is eliminated from the growth of GDP in US dollars through the movement of the exchange rates.

There is a fourth group of countries where the exchange rates overreact to the movements of prices in the domestic economy. For these countries, the index of exchange rates in column 6 is much higher than the price index in terms of national currency in column 5. This case implies that the price index in terms of US dollars as shown in column 4 is lower than 100 and this has the effect that the growth of GDP in terms of US dollars is lower when compared in terms of national currency.

Again, a note of caution is advised when using the price index information presented in the table. For one, the deflators shown may not be fully comparable between countries because a wide variety of methods had been applied to obtain the data on price movements. To cite an example, for some countries, explicit price indices were used directly in the calculations while for other countries implicit price indices were derived by dividing volume indices into indices of current price development of GDP. Likewise, even as the index numbers are shown for a common base year 1990 = 100, GDP data at constant prices used in the calculations actually have been compiled according to different original weight base periods.

Please be noted that the "-" symbol has been employed due to the very small magnitude of the data.

Table 7. Implicit Price Deflators of Gross Domestic Product in US Dollars and in National Currency

(Index numbers 1990 = 100)

Region, country or area and currency unit	Year	GDP in Current Prices		GDP at Constant Prices	GDP Implicit Price Deflators		Exchange Rates
		National Currency (1)	US Dollars (2)	(3)	National Currency (4)	US Dollars (5)	(6)
AFRICA							
Algeria	1970	4.6	8.3	43.9	10.5	19.0	55.3
	1975	11.1	25.2	55.6	20.0	45.3	44.2
	1980	29.3	68.4	77.1	38.0	88.8	42.8
	1985	52.6	93.7	99.4	52.9	94.3	56.1
	1990	100.0	100.0	100.0	100.0	100.0	100.0
	1991	155.5	75.4	98.8	157.4	76.3	206.3
	1992	193.9	79.5	100.2	193.5	79.4	243.7
	1993	214.6	82.3	98.2	218.5	83.9	260.4
	1994	268.3	68.6	97.0	276.6	70.7	391.2
	1995	361.7	68.0	101.2	357.4	67.2	531.8
	1996	463.6	75.8	104.2	444.9	72.8	611.1
	1997	501.5	77.8	106.2	472.2	73.3	644.2
	1998	506.9	77.3	111.2	455.7	69.5	655.7
	1999	585.9	78.8	115.2	508.5	68.4	743.4
	2000	739.3	88.0	117.2	630.7	75.1	839.8
	2001	764.0	88.6	122.2	625.0	72.5	862.1
Angola	1970	26.6	27.8	75.2	35.4	37.0	95.7
	1975	26.0	30.4	84.6	30.7	36.0	85.3
	1980	52.3	52.3	78.6	66.5	66.5	100.0
	1985	66.6	66.6	85.8	77.5	77.5	100.0
	1990	100.0	100.0	100.0	100.0	100.0	100.0
	1991	217.9	118.3	100.3	217.2	117.9	184.2
	1992	471.8	56.1	94.5	499.4	59.4	840.7
	1993	4 565.3	51.3	71.1	6 418.9	72.2	8 890.4
	1994	78 443.5	39.4	72.9	107 637.4	54.1	198 960.1
	1995	4 499 955.8	49.0	80.7	5 577 609.6	60.7	9 188 813.2
	1996	232 560 274.0	54.3	89.8	258 844 611.1	60.5	427 842 332.4
	1997	568 831 168.8	74.3	96.7	588 019 995.6	76.8	765 651 035.9
	1998	829 870 129.9	63.2	102.1	813 059 111.3	61.9	1 313 504 218.6
	1999	5 575 000 000.0	59.8	104.8	5 319 753 079.5	57.0	9 332 900 139.5
	2000	29 761 688 311.7	88.7	108.6	27 412 758 075.3	81.7	33 552 947 460.6
	2001	63 997 077 922.1	86.8	114.2	56 027 342 529.2	76.0	73 720 187 538.4
Benin	1970	13.9	13.6	56.4	24.6	24.1	102.1
	1975	22.5	28.6	68.3	33.0	41.9	78.8
	1980	48.9	63.0	72.6	67.3	86.8	77.5
	1985	93.5	56.7	94.3	99.2	60.1	165.1
	1990	100.0	100.0	100.0	100.0	100.0	100.0
	1991	106.6	102.9	104.8	101.7	98.2	103.6
	1992	113.4	116.6	109.2	103.8	106.8	97.2
	1993	118.7	114.2	112.7	105.4	101.3	104.0
	1994	165.5	81.1	116.3	142.3	69.8	203.9
	1995	199.7	108.9	123.6	161.5	88.1	183.3
	1996	224.9	119.7	129.8	173.2	92.2	187.9
	1997	248.8	116.1	135.0	184.3	86.0	214.3
	1998	270.9	125.0	140.4	192.9	89.0	216.7
	1999	280.3	127.9	147.4	196.3	86.8	226.2
	2000	319.6	122.2	155.9	205.0	78.4	261.5
	2001	346.1	128.5	163.7	211.4	78.5	269.3
Botswana	1970	1.1	2.8	7.9	13.5	35.1	38.5
	1975	4.0	10.1	19.7	20.4	51.3	39.8
	1980	12.7	30.4	33.6	37.8	90.5	41.8
	1985	32.8	32.0	53.8	60.9	59.6	102.2
	1990	100.0	100.0	100.0	100.0	100.0	100.0
	1991	115.5	106.3	108.7	106.3	97.8	108.7
	1992	127.9	112.7	115.5	110.7	97.6	113.4
	1993	139.2	106.9	115.3	120.8	92.7	130.3
	1994	168.5	116.8	119.9	140.5	97.4	144.3
	1995	187.2	125.6	123.8	151.2	101.5	149.0
	1996	216.8	121.3	130.6	165.9	92.9	178.6
	1997	270.8	138.0	138.0	196.3	100.0	196.3
	1998	307.7	135.5	149.1	206.4	90.9	227.1
	1999	328.5	132.2	155.3	211.6	85.1	248.6
	2000	387.1	141.2	167.8	230.7	84.1	274.3
	2001	448.0	142.7	183.2	244.6	77.9	314.0
Burkina Faso	1970	14.1	13.8	48.7	29.0	28.4	102.1
	1975	21.6	27.5	60.8	35.6	45.2	78.8
	1980	46.4	59.8	75.4	61.5	79.3	77.6
	1985	80.0	48.5	87.7	91.2	55.3	164.9
	1990	100.0	100.0	100.0	100.0	100.0	100.0
	1991	104.3	100.6	109.5	95.2	91.9	103.6
	1992	104.4	107.4	109.9	95.0	97.7	97.2
	1993	106.9	102.8	115.5	92.6	89.0	104.0
	1994	124.7	61.1	120.1	103.9	50.9	204.1
	1995	142.1	77.5	127.2	111.7	61.0	183.1

Table 7. Implicit Price Deflators of Gross Domestic Product in US Dollars and in National Currency

(Index numbers 1990 = 100)

Region, country or area and currency unit	Year	GDP in Current Prices: National Currency (1)	GDP in Current Prices: US Dollars (2)	GDP at Constant Prices (3)	GDP Implicit Price Deflators: National Currency (4)	GDP Implicit Price Deflators: US Dollars (5)	Exchange Rates (6)
	1996	155.6	82.8	135.5	114.9	61.1	188.1
	1997	174.5	81.4	143.2	121.8	56.8	214.4
	1998	190.1	87.7	151.1	125.8	58.1	216.5
	1999	195.0	86.2	160.8	121.3	53.6	226.3
	2000	200.5	76.7	164.6	121.8	46.6	261.4
	2001	219.3	81.4	174.1	125.9	46.8	269.0
Burundi	1970	10.9	21.4	50.2	21.8	42.6	51.2
	1975	16.6	36.1	51.8	32.1	69.7	46.1
	1980	43.5	82.8	65.3	66.7	126.9	52.6
	1985	71.9	102.0	82.9	86.7	123.0	70.5
	1990	100.0	100.0	100.0	100.0	100.0	100.0
	1991	107.8	101.7	105.3	102.3	96.5	106.0
	1992	115.1	94.6	107.3	107.3	88.2	121.7
	1993	120.4	84.9	99.7	120.7	85.1	141.8
	1994	137.3	93.1	96.7	142.0	96.3	147.5
	1995	127.1	87.1	89.8	141.4	97.0	145.8
	1996	135.0	76.3	82.1	164.3	93.0	176.7
	1997	174.3	84.7	82.4	211.6	102.8	205.8
	1998	203.5	77.8	86.2	236.2	90.3	261.6
	1999	231.6	70.4	85.3	271.5	82.5	329.1
	2000	260.2	61.8	84.5	307.9	73.2	420.6
	2001	279.0	57.5	87.2	319.8	66.0	484.5
Cameroon	1970	9.4	9.2	46.6	20.1	19.7	102.0
	1975	19.2	24.4	55.2	34.8	44.2	78.7
	1980	52.5	67.6	83.6	62.8	80.9	77.6
	1985	119.9	72.7	119.1	100.7	61.0	165.1
	1990	100.0	100.0	100.0	100.0	100.0	100.0
	1991	95.7	92.3	96.2	99.4	95.9	103.6
	1992	94.5	97.2	93.3	101.2	104.1	97.2
	1993	89.2	85.7	91.9	97.0	93.3	104.0
	1994	96.4	47.3	88.9	108.4	53.1	204.1
	1995	114.6	62.5	91.7	125.0	68.2	183.3
	1996	123.0	65.5	96.3	127.8	68.0	187.9
	1997	137.8	64.3	101.2	136.3	63.6	214.3
	1998	147.4	68.0	106.2	138.8	64.1	216.5
	1999	154.2	68.2	110.7	139.3	61.6	226.1
	2000	169.5	64.8	116.5	145.4	55.6	261.5
	2001	168.8	62.7	121.9	138.5	51.4	269.5
Cape Verde	1970	8.5	20.8	55.7	15.3	37.4	40.9
	1975	13.9	38.2	51.9	26.9	73.7	36.5
	1980	26.5	46.2	60.0	44.2	77.0	57.4
	1985	58.5	44.7	82.6	70.8	54.1	130.9
	1990	100.0	100.0	100.0	100.0	100.0	100.0
	1991	106.3	104.2	101.4	104.8	102.8	101.9
	1992	113.0	116.4	104.5	108.2	111.4	97.1
	1993	134.8	117.4	112.1	120.2	104.7	114.8
	1994	155.3	132.8	119.9	129.5	110.7	117.0
	1995	174.8	159.3	128.9	135.6	123.6	109.7
	1996	192.3	163.0	134.0	143.4	121.6	117.9
	1997	218.6	164.3	141.3	154.7	116.3	133.0
	1998	245.1	174.8	151.7	161.5	115.2	140.2
	1999	280.0	190.9	164.8	169.9	115.9	146.6
	2000	299.9	181.3	176.0	170.4	103.0	165.4
	2001	319.8	181.8	181.3	176.4	100.3	175.9
Central African Republic	1970	11.7	11.5	79.3	14.8	14.5	102.1
	1975	24.5	31.1	77.9	31.5	40.0	78.8
	1980	42.4	54.7	91.2	46.5	59.9	77.6
	1985	95.7	58.0	98.1	97.5	59.1	165.0
	1990	100.0	100.0	100.0	100.0	100.0	100.0
	1991	102.6	99.0	99.4	103.1	99.5	103.6
	1992	100.4	103.3	93.1	107.9	111.0	97.2
	1993	97.3	93.6	93.4	104.2	100.2	104.0
	1994	125.3	61.4	97.9	127.9	62.7	204.0
	1995	150.6	82.2	103.8	145.1	79.1	183.4
	1996	144.9	77.1	100.5	144.2	76.7	188.0
	1997	153.6	71.7	106.2	144.6	67.5	214.2
	1998	163.7	75.5	111.4	146.9	67.8	216.7
	1999	172.3	76.2	115.4	149.3	66.0	226.2
	2000	183.0	70.0	117.5	155.8	59.6	261.4
	2001	189.8	70.5	117.5	161.5	60.0	269.2
Chad	1970	27.3	26.7	74.6	36.5	35.8	102.0
	1975	44.7	56.8	89.8	49.8	63.3	78.7
	1980	46.3	59.6	60.1	76.9	99.1	77.6
	1985	98.4	59.6	92.0	106.9	64.8	165.0

Table 7. Implicit Price Deflators of Gross Domestic Product in US Dollars and in National Currency

(Index numbers 1990 = 100)

Region, country or area and currency unit	Year	GDP in Current Prices: National Currency (1)	GDP in Current Prices: US Dollars (2)	GDP at Constant Prices (3)	GDP Implicit Price Deflators: National Currency (4)	GDP Implicit Price Deflators: US Dollars (5)	Exchange Rates (6)
	1990	100.0	100.0	100.0	100.0	100.0	100.0
	1991	111.9	108.0	108.5	103.1	99.5	103.6
	1992	105.2	108.2	117.2	89.8	92.3	97.3
	1993	98.3	94.5	115.2	85.4	82.1	104.0
	1994	156.3	76.6	121.7	128.5	63.0	204.0
	1995	171.8	93.7	123.2	139.4	76.1	183.2
	1996	194.0	103.3	125.3	154.9	82.4	188.0
	1997	214.5	100.1	132.8	161.5	75.4	214.2
	1998	239.6	110.6	139.8	171.4	79.1	216.7
	1999	218.3	96.5	139.6	156.4	69.1	226.3
	2000	221.4	84.7	139.1	159.2	60.9	261.4
	2001	259.6	96.4	151.3	171.6	63.7	269.4
Comoros	1970	8.0	7.8	48.7	16.4	16.0	102.5
	1975	18.8	23.9	61.1	30.8	39.2	78.6
	1980	42.1	54.2	77.2	54.5	70.2	77.6
	1985	75.9	46.0	94.6	80.3	48.7	164.9
	1990	100.0	100.0	100.0	100.0	100.0	100.0
	1991	102.3	98.7	101.8	100.5	97.0	103.6
	1992	103.5	106.5	100.0	103.5	106.5	97.2
	1993	109.6	105.4	101.8	107.7	103.6	104.0
	1994	113.6	74.3	99.5	114.2	74.7	152.9
	1995	118.0	85.8	97.3	121.3	88.3	137.4
	1996	120.2	85.3	98.9	121.6	86.3	140.9
	1997	124.4	77.4	97.8	127.2	79.1	160.8
	1998	128.2	78.9	96.7	132.5	81.5	162.6
	1999	138.2	81.5	98.6	140.3	82.7	169.6
	2000	145.0	73.9	97.4	148.8	75.9	196.0
	2001	162.7	80.6	99.3	163.8	81.1	202.0
Congo	1970	9.5	9.3	36.2	26.3	25.8	101.9
	1975	19.2	24.4	47.4	40.5	51.5	78.6
	1980	47.3	60.9	61.2	77.3	99.6	77.6
	1985	127.4	77.2	102.6	124.2	75.3	164.9
	1990	100.0	100.0	100.0	100.0	100.0	100.0
	1991	100.9	97.4	102.4	98.5	95.1	103.6
	1992	101.9	104.8	104.1	97.9	100.7	97.2
	1993	99.8	95.9	103.1	96.8	93.0	104.1
	1994	128.9	63.2	97.5	132.2	64.8	204.0
	1995	138.6	75.6	99.6	139.2	75.9	183.4
	1996	170.6	90.8	103.9	164.2	87.4	187.9
	1997	177.9	83.0	103.4	172.1	80.3	214.3
	1998	150.9	69.7	107.3	140.7	64.9	216.8
	1999	179.2	79.2	103.8	172.6	76.3	226.2
	2000	280.1	107.1	112.2	249.8	95.5	261.6
	2001	265.3	98.6	115.4	229.9	85.4	269.2
Cote d'Ivoire	1970	12.8	12.6	42.8	30.0	29.4	102.0
	1975	25.8	32.7	58.3	44.2	56.1	78.8
	1980	66.4	85.6	71.6	92.7	119.4	77.6
	1985	96.8	58.7	86.9	111.4	67.5	165.0
	1990	100.0	100.0	100.0	100.0	100.0	100.0
	1991	100.5	97.0	100.1	100.4	96.9	103.6
	1992	98.4	101.2	99.4	98.9	101.8	97.2
	1993	97.5	93.8	99.0	98.5	94.7	104.0
	1994	142.6	69.9	101.2	140.9	69.1	203.9
	1995	171.2	93.4	108.3	158.1	86.2	183.4
	1996	191.8	102.1	115.6	165.9	88.3	187.9
	1997	211.3	98.6	122.2	173.0	80.7	214.4
	1998	230.3	106.3	128.4	179.3	82.8	216.5
	1999	238.9	105.6	130.9	182.4	80.7	226.0
	2000	234.9	89.8	127.4	184.3	70.5	261.4
	2001	237.7	88.3	126.3	188.2	69.9	269.2
Democratic Republic of the Congo	1970	-	20.0	87.9	-	22.8	-
	1975	-	41.0	98.8	-	41.5	-
	1980	0.6	157.4	91.6	0.7	171.8	0.4
	1985	5.3	77.0	100.3	5.3	76.7	6.9
	1990	100.0	100.0	100.0	100.0	100.0	100.0
	1991	2 108.4	97.2	91.6	2 302.8	106.2	2 168.4
	1992	78 829.8	87.7	81.9	96 193.5	107.1	89 816.5
	1993	1 201 429.2	114.4	70.9	1 694 561.8	161.4	1 049 914.4
	1994	309 696 293.0	62.1	68.2	454 408 357.4	91.1	498 801 709.5
	1995	1 768 646 717.3	60.3	68.6	2 576 918 267.1	87.9	2 931 647 630.4
	1996	12 934 345 690.0	61.7	68.0	19 016 490 081.3	90.7	20 966 361 721.4
	1997	34 854 845 913.4	63.5	64.1	54 372 066 911.8	99.1	54 865 859 648.6
	1998	44 618 133 095.1	66.5	63.1	70 734 122 752.1	105.4	67 110 173 389.1

Table 7. Implicit Price Deflators of Gross Domestic Product in US Dollars and in National Currency

(Index numbers 1990 = 100)

Region, country or area and currency unit	Year	GDP in Current Prices: National Currency (1)	GDP in Current Prices: US Dollars (2)	GDP at Constant Prices (3)	GDP Implicit Price Deflators: National Currency (4)	GDP Implicit Price Deflators: US Dollars (5)	Exchange Rates (6)
	1999	231 460 473 425.6	54.4	56.5	409 530 644 202.8	96.3	425 265 466 461.9
	2000	1 495 873 157 659.7	54.1	54.1	2 765 619 309 779.0	100.1	2 762 856 453 325.7
	2001	6 950 066 994 193.8	48.4	51.7	13 440 911 709 833.5	93.6	14 359 948 407 941.8
Djibouti	1970	18.8	15.6	70.1	26.9	22.3	120.6
	1975	37.1	37.1	86.7	42.7	42.7	100.0
	1980	74.3	74.3	84.5	87.9	87.9	100.0
	1985	76.7	76.7	82.8	92.6	92.6	100.0
	1990	100.0	100.0	100.0	100.0	100.0	100.0
	1991	102.0	102.0	96.9	105.4	105.4	100.0
	1992	105.4	105.4	102.5	102.8	102.8	100.0
	1993	105.5	105.5	107.5	98.2	98.2	100.0
	1994	111.8	111.8	104.9	106.6	106.6	100.0
	1995	111.5	111.5	110.8	100.7	100.7	100.0
	1996	108.7	108.7	105.1	103.4	103.4	100.0
	1997	107.5	107.5	110.0	97.8	97.8	100.0
	1998	108.9	108.9	109.8	99.2	99.2	100.0
	1999	117.3	117.3	112.2	104.6	104.6	100.0
	2000	121.0	121.0	113.0	107.1	107.1	100.0
	2001	125.5	125.5	115.1	109.1	109.1	100.0
Egypt	1970	2.7	9.6	33.7	8.0	28.5	28.1
	1975	4.8	18.9	43.4	11.0	43.5	25.3
	1980	15.6	34.5	57.3	27.2	60.2	45.2
	1985	37.1	82.1	81.3	45.6	100.9	45.2
	1990	100.0	100.0	100.0	100.0	100.0	100.0
	1991	123.6	61.1	100.3	123.2	60.9	202.3
	1992	142.8	66.6	100.8	141.6	66.1	214.2
	1993	158.9	73.5	106.0	150.0	69.3	216.5
	1994	185.2	84.8	110.1	168.2	77.0	218.4
	1995	208.3	95.2	115.2	180.9	82.6	219.0
	1996	241.4	110.3	121.1	199.4	91.1	218.9
	1997	260.9	119.4	125.9	207.2	94.8	218.6
	1998	279.3	127.8	133.6	209.0	95.6	218.6
	1999	308.8	141.0	140.8	219.3	100.1	219.1
	2000	325.7	145.4	145.8	223.4	99.7	224.1
	2001	346.6	135.2	150.4	230.4	89.9	256.3
Equatorial Guinea	1970	31.1	120.9	60.1	51.7	201.2	25.7
	1975	27.7	35.3	75.5	36.8	46.7	78.8
	1980	26.9	34.6	76.8	34.9	45.0	77.6
	1985	85.8	52.0	89.9	95.5	57.9	164.9
	1990	100.0	100.0	100.0	100.0	100.0	100.0
	1991	104.7	101.0	98.9	105.9	102.2	103.6
	1992	95.6	98.3	109.4	87.4	89.9	97.2
	1993	103.3	99.3	119.9	86.2	82.8	104.1
	1994	147.7	72.4	138.0	107.1	52.5	204.0
	1995	184.0	100.4	160.2	114.8	62.6	183.4
	1996	320.6	170.7	232.8	137.7	73.3	187.9
	1997	727.6	339.4	398.6	182.6	85.2	214.3
	1998	597.1	275.6	486.3	122.8	56.7	216.6
	1999	1 053.0	465.6	687.6	153.1	67.7	226.1
	2000	2 011.1	769.1	803.8	250.2	95.7	261.4
	2001	2 849.8	1 058.5	1 233.0	231.1	85.8	269.3
Eritrea	1990	100.0	100.0	100.0	100.0	100.0	100.0
	1992	71.2	52.6	57.4	124.1	91.6	135.5
	1993	118.7	49.1	55.9	212.2	87.8	241.7
	1994	161.9	61.3	61.4	263.6	99.8	264.1
	1995	205.2	69.0	63.2	324.7	109.2	297.3
	1996	232.9	75.9	67.5	345.1	112.5	306.8
	1997	255.1	78.7	72.8	350.5	108.1	324.2
	1998	281.6	81.9	75.6	372.4	108.3	343.9
	1999	299.1	78.0	76.2	392.4	102.3	383.6
	2000	290.3	73.1	70.0	414.9	104.5	397.0
	2001	334.3	81.8	72.8	459.4	112.4	408.7
Ethiopia	1990	100.0	100.0	100.0	100.0	100.0	100.0
	1992	123.6	91.3	123.6	100.0	73.9	135.3
	1993	158.5	65.6	138.4	114.6	47.4	241.8
	1994	168.4	63.8	140.6	119.8	45.4	263.9
	1995	201.4	67.7	149.2	135.0	45.4	297.4
	1996	225.5	73.5	165.1	136.6	44.5	307.0
	1997	246.4	76.0	173.6	142.0	43.8	324.2
	1998	266.8	77.6	172.7	154.5	45.0	343.3
	1999	290.9	75.8	183.6	158.5	41.3	383.8
	2000	293.9	74.0	193.5	151.9	38.3	396.6
	2001	304.2	74.4	208.7	145.7	35.7	408.1

Table 7. Implicit Price Deflators of Gross Domestic Product in US Dollars and in National Currency

(Index numbers 1990 = 100)

Region, country or area and currency unit	Year	GDP in Current Prices: National Currency (1)	GDP in Current Prices: US Dollars (2)	GDP at Constant Prices (3)	GDP Implicit Price Deflators: National Currency (4)	GDP Implicit Price Deflators: US Dollars (5)	Exchange Rates (6)
Gabon	1970	6.3	6.2	82.4	7.6	7.5	101.3
	1975	31.3	39.8	114.5	27.3	34.7	78.7
	1980	61.2	78.9	91.1	67.2	86.6	77.6
	1985	111.4	67.5	103.1	108.1	65.5	165.0
	1990	100.0	100.0	100.0	100.0	100.0	100.0
	1991	103.2	99.6	106.1	97.2	93.8	103.6
	1992	100.2	103.1	102.7	97.6	100.4	97.2
	1993	103.6	99.6	106.7	97.1	93.3	104.1
	1994	157.5	77.2	110.7	142.3	69.8	203.9
	1995	167.5	91.4	116.2	144.2	78.7	183.2
	1996	195.0	103.8	120.8	161.4	85.9	187.9
	1997	211.0	98.4	126.3	167.1	78.0	214.2
	1998	186.3	86.0	128.9	144.5	66.7	216.6
	1999	192.2	85.0	120.9	159.0	70.3	226.2
	2000	242.1	92.6	123.3	196.3	75.1	261.4
	2001	215.0	79.9	126.4	170.1	63.2	269.1
Gambia	1970	3.7	13.9	43.5	8.5	32.0	26.6
	1975	10.6	46.2	56.6	18.7	81.6	22.9
	1980	15.7	71.8	70.1	22.4	102.4	21.9
	1985	40.9	82.7	81.8	49.9	101.0	49.4
	1990	100.0	100.0	100.0	100.0	100.0	100.0
	1991	111.1	99.5	105.5	105.4	94.4	111.7
	1992	117.2	103.9	105.9	110.6	98.1	112.7
	1993	123.5	106.6	112.9	109.4	94.4	115.9
	1994	132.3	108.9	117.2	112.9	93.0	121.4
	1995	133.5	110.3	113.2	117.9	97.4	121.0
	1996	145.3	117.0	119.2	121.9	98.1	124.3
	1997	153.0	118.3	120.2	127.4	98.4	129.5
	1998	169.2	125.3	132.0	128.1	94.9	135.0
	1999	187.3	129.6	140.5	133.3	92.2	144.6
	2000	211.3	130.3	148.4	142.4	87.8	162.2
	2001	242.0	121.6	156.8	154.3	77.5	199.1
Ghana	1970	0.1	35.6	75.8	0.1	46.9	0.2
	1975	0.3	73.8	77.1	0.3	95.7	0.3
	1980	2.1	250.3	80.8	2.6	309.8	0.8
	1985	16.9	101.4	79.1	21.4	128.2	16.7
	1990	100.0	100.0	100.0	100.0	100.0	100.0
	1991	126.7	112.4	105.3	120.3	106.8	112.6
	1992	148.1	110.6	109.4	135.4	101.1	133.9
	1993	190.6	95.8	114.8	166.0	83.5	198.8
	1994	256.2	87.4	118.6	216.1	73.7	293.2
	1995	381.6	103.7	123.3	309.4	84.1	367.9
	1996	558.1	111.2	129.0	432.6	86.2	501.9
	1997	694.7	110.6	134.4	516.8	82.3	627.9
	1998	851.3	120.0	140.7	604.9	85.3	709.1
	1999	984.5	120.4	147.0	669.9	81.9	817.9
	2000	1 330.5	79.9	152.5	870.0	52.4	1 072.9
	2001	1 871.0	85.1	158.8	1 178.0	53.6	2 197.8
Guinea	1970	1.0	25.5	58.7	1.6	43.4	3.7
	1975	1.4	44.6	67.2	2.1	66.4	3.2
	1980	2.0	68.9	79.3	2.5	86.9	2.9
	1985	3.3	89.0	77.6	4.2	114.7	3.7
	1990	100.0	100.0	100.0	100.0	100.0	100.0
	1991	121.1	106.0	102.6	118.0	103.3	114.2
	1992	143.4	104.9	105.7	135.7	99.3	136.7
	1993	165.3	114.2	110.7	149.4	103.2	144.8
	1994	180.3	121.9	115.1	156.7	105.9	148.0
	1995	198.7	132.3	120.2	165.4	110.1	150.2
	1996	213.7	140.5	125.7	170.0	111.8	152.1
	1997	229.3	138.2	131.7	174.1	104.9	166.0
	1998	251.4	134.2	137.7	182.7	97.5	187.4
	1999	271.1	129.0	142.7	189.9	90.4	210.1
	2000	296.3	112.0	149.9	197.7	74.7	264.7
	2001	324.2	109.7	154.4	210.0	71.1	295.4
Guinea-Bissau	1970	0.5	40.1	55.6	0.9	72.2	1.2
	1975	0.8	70.4	64.7	1.3	108.8	1.2
	1980	1.6	101.1	61.2	2.6	165.3	1.6
	1985	7.8	106.4	82.7	9.4	128.7	7.3
	1990	100.0	100.0	100.0	100.0	100.0	100.0
	1991	167.6	100.1	103.0	162.7	97.2	167.4
	1992	302.3	95.3	105.9	285.5	90.0	317.2
	1993	463.8	100.5	108.7	426.5	92.5	461.1
	1994	571.2	96.8	116.2	491.4	83.3	589.9
	1995	867.1	104.9	121.4	714.5	86.4	827.0
	1996	1 372.0	113.7	127.4	1 076.7	89.2	1 207.1

Table 7. Implicit Price Deflators of Gross Domestic Product in US Dollars and in National Currency

(Index numbers 1990 = 100)

Region, country or area and currency unit	Year	GDP in Current Prices: National Currency (1)	GDP in Current Prices: US Dollars (2)	GDP at Constant Prices (3)	GDP Implicit Price Deflators: National Currency (4)	GDP Implicit Price Deflators: US Dollars (5)	Exchange Rates (6)
	1997	2 073.2	119.4	135.5	1 530.6	88.2	1 735.4
	1998	1 552.1	88.5	97.5	1 591.4	90.7	1 754.6
	1999	1 902.5	98.6	104.9	1 812.9	93.9	1 930.7
	2000	2 037.6	93.7	112.8	1 806.2	83.0	2 176.1
	2001	2 288.6	104.7	121.6	1 881.9	86.1	2 185.7
Kenya	1970	6.2	19.9	39.4	15.7	50.5	31.1
	1975	12.2	38.1	48.5	25.2	78.7	32.0
	1980	26.9	83.0	65.7	40.9	126.4	32.4
	1985	51.6	71.9	76.0	67.8	94.6	71.7
	1990	100.0	100.0	100.0	100.0	100.0	100.0
	1991	113.1	94.3	101.4	111.6	92.9	120.1
	1992	131.0	93.2	100.6	130.2	92.6	140.6
	1993	163.7	64.7	101.0	162.1	64.1	252.9
	1994	201.3	82.3	103.6	194.3	79.4	244.7
	1995	237.9	106.0	108.2	219.9	98.0	224.4
	1996	270.4	108.5	112.7	239.9	96.3	249.1
	1997	318.8	124.4	115.0	277.1	108.1	256.3
	1998	354.0	134.4	116.9	302.8	114.9	263.5
	1999	379.5	123.7	118.4	320.5	104.4	307.0
	2000	407.1	122.5	118.2	344.4	103.6	332.4
	2001	457.9	133.5	119.5	383.1	111.7	343.0
Lesotho	1970	3.3	11.8	31.6	10.3	37.3	27.6
	1975	6.9	24.1	40.2	17.1	59.9	28.5
	1980	18.5	61.4	64.3	28.7	95.4	30.1
	1985	35.5	41.2	69.1	51.4	59.7	86.1
	1990	100.0	100.0	100.0	100.0	100.0	100.0
	1991	118.4	110.9	103.8	114.0	106.8	106.7
	1992	146.5	132.9	108.8	134.6	122.1	110.2
	1993	166.5	131.9	112.6	147.9	117.1	126.3
	1994	185.4	135.1	116.5	159.2	116.0	137.2
	1995	211.5	150.9	121.6	174.0	124.1	140.2
	1996	253.4	152.5	133.7	189.6	114.1	166.2
	1997	295.1	165.7	144.5	204.1	114.6	178.1
	1998	307.6	144.0	137.8	223.2	104.5	213.6
	1999	347.9	147.3	138.1	251.8	106.6	236.2
	2000	374.2	139.5	140.2	267.0	99.5	268.3
	2001	405.0	121.7	144.9	279.4	84.0	332.6
Liberia	1970	72.1	72.1	248.9	29.0	29.0	100.0
	1975	141.6	141.6	279.7	50.6	50.6	100.0
	1980	212.9	212.9	307.2	69.3	69.3	100.0
	1985	245.1	245.1	282.6	86.7	86.7	100.0
	1990	100.0	100.0	100.0	100.0	100.0	100.0
	1991	90.5	90.5	85.8	105.5	105.5	100.0
	1992	58.1	58.1	55.7	104.4	104.4	100.0
	1993	41.7	41.7	37.3	111.8	111.8	100.0
	1994	34.4	34.4	29.2	117.8	117.8	100.0
	1995	35.1	35.1	28.0	125.5	125.5	100.0
	1996	41.5	41.5	31.3	132.3	132.3	100.0
	1997	75.2	75.2	63.2	119.1	119.1	100.0
	1998	93.5	93.5	81.9	114.2	114.2	100.0
	1999	114.9	114.9	100.7	114.2	114.2	100.0
	2000	136.7	136.7	121.2	112.9	112.9	100.0
	2001	136.0	136.0	127.6	106.6	106.6	100.0
Libyan Arab Jamahiriya	1970	17.8	14.1	57.7	30.8	24.5	125.7
	1975	47.2	45.1	77.3	61.0	58.4	104.5
	1980	132.0	126.3	117.2	112.7	107.8	104.5
	1985	103.3	98.8	97.7	105.8	101.2	104.5
	1990	100.0	100.0	100.0	100.0	100.0	100.0
	1991	109.9	110.9	104.7	105.0	105.9	99.2
	1992	113.9	113.3	100.3	113.5	112.9	100.5
	1993	116.5	108.1	88.7	131.4	121.9	107.8
	1994	124.4	109.8	86.6	143.8	126.9	113.3
	1995	133.3	109.0	87.4	152.6	124.8	122.3
	1996	152.1	119.1	90.8	167.5	131.1	127.8
	1997	176.6	131.1	92.0	192.0	142.5	134.7
	1998	159.1	114.4	92.4	172.2	123.9	139.0
	1999	176.5	100.1	92.5	190.8	108.2	176.3
	2000	217.2	120.7	95.5	227.5	126.4	180.0
	2001	217.0	102.9	98.6	220.0	104.4	210.7
Madagascar	1970	5.4	29.2	84.6	6.4	34.5	18.6
	1975	8.6	59.9	87.4	9.8	68.5	14.3
	1980	15.0	106.0	93.4	16.0	113.5	14.1
	1985	33.8	76.1	87.3	38.7	87.2	44.4
	1990	100.0	100.0	100.0	100.0	100.0	100.0

Table 7. Implicit Price Deflators of Gross Domestic Product in US Dollars and in National Currency

(Index numbers 1990 = 100)

Region, country or area and currency unit	Year	GDP in Current Prices		GDP at Constant Prices	GDP Implicit Price Deflators		Exchange Rates
		National Currency (1)	US Dollars (2)	(3)	National Currency (4)	US Dollars (5)	(6)
	1991	106.6	86.8	93.7	113.8	92.6	122.9
	1992	121.4	97.3	94.8	128.0	102.6	124.8
	1993	140.0	109.3	96.8	144.6	112.9	128.1
	1994	198.1	96.5	96.7	204.8	99.8	205.2
	1995	292.5	102.4	98.4	297.3	104.1	285.6
	1996	351.9	129.5	100.5	350.1	128.8	271.8
	1997	392.3	115.1	104.2	376.4	110.5	340.6
	1998	442.4	121.5	108.3	408.5	112.2	364.1
	1999	508.1	120.8	113.4	448.0	106.5	420.7
	2000	570.3	125.9	118.8	479.9	105.9	453.2
	2001	654.1	148.3	126.0	519.3	117.8	440.8
Malawi	1970	5.6	18.3	36.6	15.2	49.9	30.5
	1975	11.1	35.0	56.2	19.7	62.2	31.7
	1980	21.0	70.6	76.3	27.6	92.6	29.8
	1985	40.3	64.0	86.4	46.7	74.1	63.0
	1990	100.0	100.0	100.0	100.0	100.0	100.0
	1991	118.7	115.5	107.2	110.7	107.8	102.7
	1992	137.0	103.8	97.6	140.3	106.3	132.0
	1993	184.1	114.1	107.1	171.9	106.6	161.3
	1994	214.9	67.1	123.9	173.5	54.2	320.1
	1995	447.0	79.8	129.6	345.0	61.6	560.1
	1996	739.4	131.8	126.4	585.0	104.3	560.9
	1997	891.6	148.0	134.9	661.1	109.7	602.6
	1998	1 135.7	99.7	136.9	829.7	72.9	1 138.1
	1999	1 653.3	102.3	141.1	1 171.5	72.5	1 615.9
	2000	2 170.7	99.5	145.8	1 489.0	68.2	2 183.3
	2001	2 963.9	112.0	143.6	2 064.0	78.0	2 646.2
Mali	1970	11.2	5.5	57.3	19.5	9.6	203.1
	1975	19.0	24.1	64.6	29.3	37.3	78.6
	1980	44.0	56.7	81.8	53.8	69.3	77.6
	1985	76.1	46.1	82.6	92.2	55.9	164.9
	1990	100.0	100.0	100.0	100.0	100.0	100.0
	1991	101.2	97.7	99.8	101.4	97.8	103.7
	1992	107.9	111.0	109.5	98.6	101.4	97.2
	1993	107.3	103.2	104.9	102.3	98.4	104.0
	1994	147.3	72.2	109.1	135.0	66.2	203.9
	1995	168.7	92.0	115.7	145.9	79.6	183.3
	1996	199.8	106.3	127.3	156.9	83.5	187.9
	1997	208.2	97.1	135.9	153.1	71.4	214.4
	1998	233.1	107.6	144.0	161.8	74.7	216.6
	1999	244.5	108.1	153.9	158.9	70.3	226.0
	2000	265.1	101.4	159.5	166.2	63.5	261.7
	2001	263.2	97.7	161.8	162.6	60.4	269.2
Mauritania	1970	13.8	20.0	67.1	20.5	29.7	69.0
	1975	25.0	46.8	80.3	31.2	58.3	53.5
	1980	46.2	81.2	87.4	52.9	92.8	57.0
	1985	64.0	66.9	87.0	73.5	76.8	95.7
	1990	100.0	100.0	100.0	100.0	100.0	100.0
	1991	109.0	107.2	102.9	105.9	104.2	101.6
	1992	117.3	108.6	105.2	111.5	103.3	107.9
	1993	139.1	92.8	114.3	121.7	81.2	149.9
	1994	150.8	98.3	119.8	125.9	82.1	153.3
	1995	166.8	103.6	126.6	131.7	81.8	161.0
	1996	180.1	105.8	130.0	138.5	81.3	170.4
	1997	197.5	104.8	136.6	144.6	76.8	188.3
	1998	225.0	96.2	141.6	158.9	68.0	233.7
	1999	245.3	94.4	147.4	166.4	64.0	260.0
	2000	261.1	88.1	154.8	168.7	56.9	296.5
	2001	298.3	94.1	161.9	184.3	58.1	317.2
Mauritius	1970	2.8	7.4	30.2	9.2	24.5	37.6
	1975	8.9	21.9	49.9	17.8	43.9	40.5
	1980	22.9	44.3	55.1	41.6	80.4	51.7
	1985	43.7	42.1	69.1	63.3	60.9	103.9
	1990	100.0	100.0	100.0	100.0	100.0	100.0
	1991	112.8	107.1	104.1	108.3	102.9	105.2
	1992	130.6	124.8	110.6	118.1	112.8	104.7
	1993	149.9	126.2	116.2	129.0	108.7	118.7
	1994	166.5	137.8	121.1	137.5	113.8	120.8
	1995	182.7	156.2	126.4	144.5	123.6	116.9
	1996	205.6	170.3	133.5	154.1	127.6	120.8
	1997	229.1	161.7	141.1	162.3	114.5	141.7
	1998	258.9	160.4	149.6	173.0	107.2	161.4
	1999	279.3	164.9	154.0	181.4	107.1	169.4
	2000	310.8	176.0	168.1	184.9	104.7	176.6
	2001	342.8	174.9	177.3	193.4	98.7	195.9

Table 7. Implicit Price Deflators of Gross Domestic Product in US Dollars and in National Currency

(Index numbers 1990 = 100)

Region, country or area and currency unit	Year	GDP in Current Prices		GDP at Constant Prices	GDP Implicit Price Deflators		Exchange Rates
		National Currency (1)	US Dollars (2)	(3)	National Currency (4)	US Dollars (5)	(6)
Morocco	1970	9.4	15.3	41.1	22.9	37.3	61.4
	1975	17.1	34.8	52.2	32.7	66.6	49.1
	1980	34.8	72.9	68.6	50.8	106.3	47.8
	1985	60.8	49.8	80.6	75.5	61.8	122.2
	1990	100.0	100.0	100.0	100.0	100.0	100.0
	1991	113.9	107.8	106.9	106.5	100.8	105.7
	1992	114.1	110.2	102.6	111.2	107.3	103.6
	1993	117.1	103.8	101.6	115.2	102.2	112.7
	1994	131.2	117.5	112.1	117.0	104.8	111.6
	1995	132.3	127.7	104.7	126.4	121.9	103.7
	1996	150.0	141.9	117.5	127.6	120.7	105.7
	1997	149.6	129.4	114.9	130.1	112.6	115.5
	1998	161.6	138.7	123.7	130.6	112.1	116.5
	1999	162.4	136.5	123.6	131.3	110.4	118.9
	2000	166.3	129.0	124.9	133.2	103.4	128.8
	2001	179.9	131.2	132.9	135.3	98.7	137.1
Mozambique	1970	3.2	104.2	73.9	4.3	140.9	3.1
	1975	4.5	162.4	94.6	4.7	171.7	2.7
	1980	5.7	162.5	108.7	5.2	149.5	3.5
	1985	10.7	229.9	86.4	12.4	265.9	4.7
	1990	100.0	100.0	100.0	100.0	100.0	100.0
	1991	143.0	92.6	101.9	140.3	90.9	154.3
	1992	200.9	74.2	93.2	215.6	79.6	270.9
	1993	318.5	76.4	99.5	320.1	76.8	416.8
	1994	529.5	81.5	106.4	497.4	76.5	650.2
	1995	822.0	84.6	110.0	747.5	77.0	970.8
	1996	1 300.6	107.0	117.4	1 107.9	91.1	1 216.1
	1997	1 582.9	127.4	130.4	1 214.0	97.7	1 242.6
	1998	1 864.8	145.9	146.9	1 269.7	99.3	1 278.7
	1999	2 063.6	150.1	157.9	1 306.6	95.0	1 375.4
	2000	2 262.6	138.8	160.3	1 411.1	86.6	1 629.4
	2001	2 827.7	129.4	181.1	1 561.1	71.4	2 186.4
Namibia	1970	6.0	21.6	68.1	8.8	31.7	27.8
	1975	11.5	40.2	75.5	15.2	53.3	28.5
	1980	26.0	86.4	82.7	31.4	104.4	30.1
	1985	45.2	52.4	80.4	56.2	65.2	86.2
	1990	100.0	100.0	100.0	100.0	100.0	100.0
	1991	113.3	106.1	108.2	104.7	98.1	106.7
	1992	133.0	120.6	115.9	114.7	104.1	110.2
	1993	153.7	121.7	113.9	134.9	106.8	126.3
	1994	190.8	139.0	122.3	156.0	113.7	137.2
	1995	209.9	149.7	127.3	164.9	117.6	140.2
	1996	248.0	149.2	131.4	188.7	113.6	166.1
	1997	276.7	155.4	137.3	201.6	113.2	178.1
	1998	310.4	145.3	141.9	218.7	102.4	213.6
	1999	341.6	144.7	148.0	230.8	97.8	236.0
	2000	396.3	147.8	153.7	257.8	96.1	268.3
	2001	449.8	135.2	154.7	290.8	87.4	332.7
Niger	1970	16.3	15.9	63.0	25.8	25.3	102.0
	1975	26.4	33.6	64.2	41.2	52.3	78.8
	1980	78.6	101.3	98.9	79.5	102.4	77.6
	1985	94.8	57.5	86.9	109.2	66.2	165.0
	1990	100.0	100.0	100.0	100.0	100.0	100.0
	1991	98.6	95.2	101.4	97.2	93.8	103.6
	1992	96.6	99.3	102.2	94.5	97.3	97.1
	1993	94.9	91.2	103.2	91.9	88.4	104.0
	1994	115.4	56.6	105.8	109.0	53.5	203.7
	1995	122.3	66.7	107.9	113.4	61.9	183.2
	1996	151.4	80.6	112.1	135.1	71.9	187.9
	1997	158.7	74.0	114.8	138.3	64.5	214.4
	1998	179.5	82.9	126.1	142.4	65.7	216.7
	1999	182.1	80.5	124.1	146.8	64.9	226.2
	2000	187.7	71.8	123.7	151.7	58.0	261.6
	2001	205.1	76.2	131.1	156.5	58.1	269.4
Nigeria	1970	2.8	31.9	51.5	5.5	61.9	8.9
	1975	8.7	113.9	70.4	12.4	161.8	7.7
	1980	19.3	284.0	80.0	24.2	355.1	6.8
	1985	27.8	249.7	77.1	36.0	324.0	11.1
	1990	100.0	100.0	100.0	100.0	100.0	100.0
	1991	125.9	102.1	104.8	120.2	97.5	123.3
	1992	237.9	110.6	107.8	220.7	102.6	215.1
	1993	269.1	98.0	110.6	243.4	88.7	274.4
	1994	350.8	128.2	111.7	314.1	114.8	273.6
	1995	758.8	278.6	114.6	662.1	243.1	272.4

Table 7. Implicit Price Deflators of Gross Domestic Product in US Dollars and in National Currency

(Index numbers 1990 = 100)

Region, country or area and currency unit	Year	GDP in Current Prices		GDP at Constant Prices	GDP Implicit Price Deflators		Exchange Rates
		National Currency (1)	US Dollars (2)	(3)	National Currency (4)	US Dollars (5)	(6)
	1996	1 083.5	226.1	119.1	909.9	189.9	479.1
	1997	1 127.9	233.4	122.9	917.8	189.9	483.3
	1998	1 088.5	238.7	125.7	865.8	189.9	455.9
	1999	1 273.8	110.9	129.2	985.7	85.8	1 148.8
	2000	1 911.1	151.1	134.1	1 424.7	112.6	1 265.3
	2001	2 185.8	158.0	139.8	1 563.8	113.0	1 383.9
Reunion	1970	7.1	7.0	37.6	18.9	18.5	102.2
	1975	16.0	20.3	48.1	33.3	42.3	78.7
	1980	29.8	38.4	66.5	44.8	57.7	77.6
	1985	60.1	36.4	81.6	73.6	44.6	165.0
	1990	100.0	100.0	100.0	100.0	100.0	100.0
	1991	110.4	106.6	101.6	108.7	105.0	103.5
	1992	119.1	122.5	105.1	113.3	116.6	97.2
	1993	118.8	114.2	109.6	108.4	104.2	104.0
	1994	124.3	121.9	112.1	110.9	108.8	101.9
	1995	130.5	142.4	115.1	113.4	123.7	91.7
	1996	136.4	145.2	118.4	115.2	122.6	94.0
	1997	142.5	133.0	122.1	116.8	108.9	107.3
	1998	149.1	137.6	125.8	118.6	109.4	108.4
	1999	155.9	137.9	129.5	120.3	106.4	113.1
	2000	163.5	125.0	133.4	122.5	93.7	130.7
	2001	174.2	129.4	136.6	127.5	94.7	134.6
Rwanda	1970	11.2	9.2	47.0	23.8	19.6	121.4
	1975	27.4	24.3	49.0	55.9	49.7	112.5
	1980	56.0	49.8	79.4	70.5	62.7	112.4
	1985	90.0	73.4	90.3	99.7	81.3	122.6
	1990	100.0	100.0	100.0	100.0	100.0	100.0
	1991	110.4	72.8	96.3	114.6	75.6	151.6
	1992	112.6	69.8	102.8	109.6	67.9	161.4
	1993	144.7	82.8	93.9	154.1	88.2	174.7
	1994	86.9	32.6	48.1	180.8	67.9	266.3
	1995	174.4	55.0	64.2	271.8	85.6	317.5
	1996	220.9	59.5	73.7	299.7	80.7	371.4
	1997	292.1	80.0	84.3	346.5	94.9	365.1
	1998	325.2	86.0	92.0	353.3	93.4	378.3
	1999	328.3	81.2	98.0	335.0	82.9	404.1
	2000	353.3	74.9	104.1	339.2	71.9	471.8
	2001	379.6	70.8	111.0	342.0	63.8	536.1
Sao Tome and Principe	1970	7.4	37.1	64.3	11.6	57.7	20.1
	1975	10.7	59.9	78.4	13.6	76.4	17.8
	1980	19.7	81.4	116.4	17.0	69.9	24.3
	1985	28.1	90.3	106.3	26.5	85.0	31.2
	1990	100.0	100.0	100.0	100.0	100.0	100.0
	1991	139.2	98.8	101.2	137.5	97.7	140.7
	1992	176.5	78.7	101.9	173.2	77.3	224.1
	1993	248.1	82.7	103.0	240.8	80.3	299.9
	1994	439.9	86.1	105.3	417.8	81.7	511.4
	1995	783.2	79.0	107.4	729.2	73.6	990.8
	1996	1 198.8	78.0	109.0	1 099.7	71.5	1 538.0
	1997	2 424.3	76.3	110.1	2 201.9	69.3	3 177.3
	1998	3 406.1	70.9	112.9	3 018.2	62.8	4 806.1
	1999	4 049.9	81.5	115.7	3 501.1	70.5	4 966.1
	2000	4 478.8	80.5	119.1	3 759.2	67.5	5 569.2
	2001	5 115.2	82.9	123.9	4 128.2	66.9	6 170.7
Senegal	1970	15.6	15.3	62.2	25.0	24.6	101.6
	1975	26.4	33.5	69.9	37.7	47.9	78.7
	1980	40.7	52.4	73.7	55.3	71.2	77.7
	1985	74.7	45.2	85.5	87.4	52.9	165.2
	1990	100.0	100.0	100.0	100.0	100.0	100.0
	1991	100.0	96.5	99.6	100.4	96.9	103.6
	1992	102.8	105.8	101.8	101.0	103.9	97.2
	1993	99.1	95.3	99.5	99.6	95.7	104.1
	1994	130.3	63.9	102.4	127.3	62.4	204.0
	1995	144.0	78.5	107.2	134.3	73.2	183.5
	1996	153.4	81.6	112.8	135.9	72.4	187.7
	1997	164.6	76.8	119.0	138.4	64.5	214.6
	1998	177.0	81.7	125.8	140.7	64.9	216.8
	1999	188.5	83.4	132.1	142.8	63.1	226.3
	2000	200.7	76.8	139.4	144.0	55.1	261.3
	2001	217.8	80.9	147.2	148.0	55.0	269.1
Seychelles	1970	5.6	5.4	40.3	13.8	13.3	103.8
	1975	14.8	13.1	48.9	30.3	26.9	112.6
	1980	47.9	40.0	70.4	68.0	56.8	119.7
	1985	61.3	45.8	75.8	80.8	60.4	133.8

Table 7. Implicit Price Deflators of Gross Domestic Product in US Dollars and in National Currency

(Index numbers 1990 = 100)

Region, country or area and currency unit	Year	GDP in Current Prices: National Currency (1)	GDP in Current Prices: US Dollars (2)	GDP at Constant Prices (3)	GDP Implicit Price Deflators: National Currency (4)	GDP Implicit Price Deflators: US Dollars (5)	Exchange Rates (6)
	1990	100.0	100.0	100.0	100.0	100.0	100.0
	1991	100.7	101.6	102.7	98.0	98.9	99.1
	1992	112.9	117.7	109.8	102.8	107.2	95.9
	1993	124.8	128.6	119.2	104.7	107.8	97.1
	1994	125.0	132.0	116.0	107.8	113.8	94.7
	1995	123.0	137.9	115.1	106.9	119.8	89.2
	1996	127.1	136.5	120.7	105.3	113.1	93.1
	1997	143.8	152.7	134.9	106.6	113.2	94.2
	1998	162.7	165.1	144.9	112.3	113.9	98.6
	1999	169.3	169.1	147.8	114.5	114.4	100.1
	2000	174.1	162.6	149.9	116.1	108.5	107.0
	2001	173.8	158.4	151.4	114.8	104.6	109.8
Sierra Leone	1970	0.4	65.4	72.0	0.5	90.7	0.6
	1975	0.6	99.9	81.2	0.7	122.9	0.6
	1980	1.2	173.5	88.7	1.4	195.5	0.7
	1985	5.0	148.0	102.8	4.8	143.9	3.3
	1990	100.0	100.0	100.0	100.0	100.0	100.0
	1991	200.2	102.6	97.2	206.0	105.6	195.1
	1992	340.4	103.2	83.9	405.6	123.0	329.8
	1993	486.0	129.7	78.8	617.0	164.7	374.6
	1994	565.6	146.0	78.9	717.0	185.1	387.4
	1995	739.0	148.2	77.6	952.5	191.0	498.7
	1996	909.9	149.7	82.3	1 105.5	181.8	608.1
	1997	849.9	131.1	67.8	1 253.0	193.3	648.2
	1998	1 076.6	104.3	67.3	1 600.7	155.0	1 032.7
	1999	1 319.2	110.7	61.8	2 134.7	179.2	1 191.2
	2000	1 383.8	100.2	64.2	2 157.1	156.2	1 381.0
	2001	1 545.3	117.8	67.6	2 285.4	174.3	1 311.2
Somalia	1970	0.1	34.3	66.3	0.2	51.7	0.4
	1975	0.3	76.2	79.0	0.3	96.4	0.3
	1980	1.0	277.1	90.2	1.1	307.2	0.4
	1985	5.0	222.4	98.5	5.1	225.7	2.3
	1990	100.0	100.0	100.0	100.0	100.0	100.0
	1991	134.2	61.8	99.0	135.5	62.4	217.1
	1992	147.6	58.7	87.1	169.4	67.3	251.7
	1993	228.3	100.2	87.1	262.0	115.1	227.6
	1994	281.0	113.2	68.8	408.3	164.5	248.2
	1995	369.5	112.9	68.8	536.9	164.0	327.4
	1996	498.8	126.8	71.5	697.6	177.3	393.5
	1997	648.5	149.1	69.6	932.0	214.3	434.9
	1998	810.6	193.7	71.3	1 136.7	271.7	418.4
	1999	1 013.2	202.5	72.8	1 391.6	278.1	500.4
	2000	1 013.2	185.2	75.0	1 351.1	246.9	547.2
	2001	966.1	100.1	77.2	1 250.7	129.6	965.0
South Africa	1970	4.5	16.3	61.8	7.3	26.4	27.7
	1975	9.6	33.6	73.9	13.0	45.5	28.6
	1980	22.1	73.5	86.1	25.7	85.4	30.1
	1985	44.4	51.6	92.1	48.3	56.0	86.3
	1990	100.0	100.0	100.0	100.0	100.0	100.0
	1991	114.5	107.3	99.0	115.7	108.4	106.7
	1992	128.4	116.5	96.9	132.6	120.3	110.2
	1993	147.0	116.4	98.1	149.9	118.7	126.3
	1994	166.4	121.2	101.2	164.3	119.7	137.3
	1995	189.1	134.9	104.4	181.2	129.2	140.2
	1996	213.2	128.3	108.9	195.8	117.8	166.2
	1997	236.6	132.9	111.8	211.7	118.9	178.0
	1998	255.2	119.4	112.6	226.6	106.0	213.8
	1999	277.0	117.3	115.0	240.9	102.0	236.2
	2000	306.3	114.2	118.9	257.7	96.1	268.2
	2001	336.5	101.1	121.5	276.9	83.2	332.8
Sudan	1970	0.4	5.7	52.6	0.8	10.9	7.3
	1975	1.1	14.3	61.5	1.8	23.3	7.7
	1980	3.0	26.7	74.9	4.0	35.7	11.2
	1985	11.2	22.0	81.1	13.9	27.1	51.3
	1990	100.0	100.0	100.0	100.0	100.0	100.0
	1991	204.6	132.4	106.0	192.9	124.8	154.6
	1992	454.2	21.0	110.7	410.2	18.9	2 170.4
	1993	934.6	26.4	113.8	821.3	23.2	3 540.1
	1994	2 445.4	38.0	119.9	2 039.4	31.7	6 433.4
	1995	5 352.7	41.5	126.3	4 239.2	32.8	12 924.4
	1996	6 824.1	24.6	130.0	5 248.6	18.9	27 770.4
	1997	11 077.2	31.6	138.7	7 984.9	22.8	35 021.5
	1998	13 155.8	29.5	145.7	9 031.6	20.2	44 710.9

Table 7. Implicit Price Deflators of Gross Domestic Product in US Dollars and in National Currency

(Index numbers 1990 = 100)

Region, country or area and currency unit	Year	GDP in Current Prices: National Currency (1)	GDP in Current Prices: US Dollars (2)	GDP at Constant Prices (3)	GDP Implicit Price Deflators: National Currency (4)	GDP Implicit Price Deflators: US Dollars (5)	Exchange Rates (6)
	1999	16 176.4	28.8	155.7	10 388.5	18.5	56 154.1
	2000	19 615.1	34.3	166.5	11 783.7	20.6	57 202.4
	2001	20 675.6	36.0	175.3	11 795.7	20.5	57 540.0
Swaziland	1970	3.5	12.5	21.0	16.5	59.6	27.7
	1975	9.6	33.6	37.1	25.9	90.6	28.6
	1980	20.4	67.8	49.2	41.5	137.8	30.1
	1985	36.1	42.0	61.5	58.7	68.4	85.8
	1990	100.0	100.0	100.0	100.0	100.0	100.0
	1991	108.0	101.2	102.6	105.2	98.6	106.7
	1992	124.2	112.7	104.1	119.3	108.3	110.2
	1993	149.0	118.0	107.8	138.2	109.4	126.3
	1994	180.5	131.6	111.4	162.1	118.1	137.3
	1995	219.6	156.7	115.6	190.0	135.5	140.2
	1996	252.4	151.9	120.2	210.0	126.4	166.1
	1997	293.5	164.8	124.8	235.2	132.1	178.0
	1998	330.6	154.7	128.8	256.8	120.2	213.6
	1999	373.2	158.0	133.3	280.0	118.6	236.1
	2000	427.8	159.5	136.1	314.4	117.2	268.3
	2001	486.9	146.3	138.4	351.7	105.7	332.7
Togo	1970	17.1	16.8	68.9	24.9	24.4	102.0
	1975	30.0	38.1	75.8	39.6	50.3	78.7
	1980	55.9	72.0	88.7	63.0	81.1	77.7
	1985	79.1	47.9	83.0	95.2	57.7	165.0
	1990	100.0	100.0	100.0	100.0	100.0	100.0
	1991	96.9	93.6	100.9	96.1	92.7	103.7
	1992	103.7	106.7	97.2	106.7	109.8	97.2
	1993	82.4	79.2	83.9	98.3	94.5	104.0
	1994	127.5	62.5	97.5	130.7	64.1	203.9
	1995	152.6	83.2	106.1	143.8	78.4	183.4
	1996	173.5	92.4	110.3	157.3	83.7	187.9
	1997	204.4	95.3	115.1	177.6	82.8	214.5
	1998	195.3	90.1	112.6	173.5	80.1	216.6
	1999	203.5	90.0	115.8	175.7	77.7	226.1
	2000	207.2	79.2	113.6	182.3	69.7	261.5
	2001	219.4	81.5	116.8	187.8	69.8	269.1
Tunisia	1970	7.0	11.7	34.7	20.1	33.6	59.8
	1975	16.1	35.2	51.8	31.1	67.9	45.8
	1980	32.7	71.0	70.4	46.5	100.9	46.1
	1985	64.9	68.3	86.4	75.1	79.0	95.1
	1990	100.0	100.0	100.0	100.0	100.0	100.0
	1991	111.2	105.6	103.9	107.0	101.7	105.2
	1992	126.7	125.8	112.0	113.1	112.4	100.6
	1993	135.6	118.6	114.5	118.4	103.6	114.3
	1994	146.2	127.0	118.1	123.8	107.5	115.2
	1995	157.7	146.4	120.9	130.4	121.1	107.7
	1996	176.3	159.1	129.5	136.1	122.8	110.8
	1997	193.2	153.5	136.6	141.5	112.4	125.9
	1998	208.6	160.9	143.1	145.8	112.4	129.7
	1999	228.1	168.9	151.8	150.3	111.3	135.0
	2000	246.7	158.1	158.9	155.3	99.5	156.1
	2001	265.9	162.3	166.6	159.6	97.4	163.9
Uganda	1970	-	50.5	70.3	-	71.8	-
	1975	-	115.8	71.1	-	162.9	-
	1980	0.1	667.9	68.2	0.2	979.2	-
	1985	1.7	109.9	75.7	2.3	145.2	1.6
	1990	100.0	100.0	100.0	100.0	100.0	100.0
	1991	138.7	81.1	105.5	131.5	76.8	171.2
	1992	230.2	87.1	110.4	208.5	78.9	264.3
	1993	250.7	90.0	118.2	212.2	76.1	278.8
	1994	323.2	141.5	130.9	246.8	108.1	228.3
	1995	374.0	165.5	143.6	260.5	115.3	225.9
	1996	409.2	167.7	151.6	270.0	110.7	243.9
	1997	451.3	178.7	159.7	282.7	111.9	252.6
	1998	518.0	179.1	171.2	302.6	104.6	289.3
	1999	570.0	168.0	179.7	317.2	93.5	339.3
	2000	584.9	152.5	194.0	301.5	78.6	383.6
	2001	633.3	154.7	206.3	306.9	75.0	409.2
United Republic Of Tanzania	1970	1.3	35.5	54.7	2.4	64.8	3.7
	1975	2.7	71.3	68.1	4.0	104.8	3.8
	1980	5.7	136.1	78.3	7.3	173.8	4.2
	1985	15.2	169.8	82.7	18.4	205.2	9.0
	1990	100.0	100.0	100.0	100.0	100.0	100.0
	1991	127.0	113.0	105.7	120.1	106.9	112.3
	1992	173.3	113.5	109.4	158.3	103.7	152.7

Table 7. Implicit Price Deflators of Gross Domestic Product in US Dollars and in National Currency

(Index numbers 1990 = 100)

Region, country or area and currency unit	Year	GDP in Current Prices		GDP at Constant Prices	GDP Implicit Price Deflators		Exchange Rates
		National Currency (1)	US Dollars (2)	(3)	National Currency (4)	US Dollars (5)	(6)
	1993	190.7	91.8	114.0	167.3	80.5	207.8
	1994	247.5	94.7	117.4	210.7	80.7	261.1
	1995	410.2	139.2	121.6	337.3	114.5	294.6
	1996	511.7	172.1	126.7	403.7	135.8	297.3
	1997	638.8	203.5	130.9	487.8	155.4	313.9
	1998	756.7	222.1	137.5	550.4	161.5	340.8
	1999	873.6	228.8	144.8	603.3	158.0	381.8
	2000	981.3	239.1	148.5	661.0	161.1	410.3
	2001	1 111.8	247.4	157.2	707.2	157.4	449.3
Zambia	1970	1.0	40.7	82.0	1.2	49.6	2.4
	1975	1.5	70.0	93.1	1.6	75.2	2.1
	1980	3.0	113.7	91.7	3.2	124.0	2.6
	1985	7.6	73.1	95.4	7.9	76.6	10.3
	1990	100.0	100.0	100.0	100.0	100.0	100.0
	1991	189.9	89.0	99.4	191.0	89.5	213.4
	1992	461.3	81.1	101.5	454.5	79.9	568.8
	1993	1 200.2	80.3	101.3	1 185.0	79.3	1 494.3
	1994	1 814.9	82.1	92.6	1 960.5	88.7	2 210.3
	1995	2 427.9	85.1	90.4	2 684.5	94.1	2 852.8
	1996	3 239.4	81.2	96.4	3 359.9	84.3	3 985.6
	1997	4 211.3	97.0	99.6	4 228.3	97.4	4 341.2
	1998	5 102.1	83.0	97.7	5 219.9	84.9	6 148.3
	1999	6 802.8	86.3	99.9	6 808.7	86.4	7 880.4
	2000	8 827.4	85.9	103.5	8 529.7	83.1	10 264.4
	2001	10 665.1	89.5	108.8	9 798.8	82.2	11 920.7
Zimbabwe	1970	5.0	17.2	49.5	10.1	34.8	29.0
	1975	9.3	40.0	62.2	14.9	64.3	23.2
	1980	16.0	61.1	65.0	24.6	94.0	26.2
	1985	42.3	64.3	80.0	52.9	80.4	65.8
	1990	100.0	100.0	100.0	100.0	100.0	100.0
	1991	137.8	93.3	105.5	130.6	88.4	147.7
	1992	160.0	76.9	98.1	163.1	78.4	208.0
	1993	197.6	74.7	100.2	197.3	74.6	264.5
	1994	261.3	78.6	106.0	246.5	74.1	332.7
	1995	287.3	81.3	106.2	270.7	76.6	353.4
	1996	398.0	97.6	117.2	339.7	83.3	407.8
	1997	479.1	97.0	120.3	398.3	80.6	494.2
	1998	667.0	69.1	123.8	538.9	55.8	965.8
	1999	978.9	62.7	122.9	796.6	51.0	1 562.0
	2000	1 536.9	84.8	113.3	1 357.0	74.9	1 811.7
	2001	2 297.4	102.3	105.0	2 188.2	97.5	2 244.3
NORTHERN AMERICA							
Bermuda	1970	13.0	13.0	67.1	19.3	19.3	100.0
	1975	24.0	24.0	78.3	30.7	30.7	100.0
	1980	46.0	46.0	95.2	48.3	48.3	100.0
	1985	71.8	71.8	95.6	75.1	75.1	100.0
	1990	100.0	100.0	100.0	100.0	100.0	100.0
	1991	104.3	104.3	101.6	102.7	102.7	100.0
	1992	105.2	105.2	97.4	108.0	108.0	100.0
	1993	114.0	114.0	102.0	111.8	111.8	100.0
	1994	117.1	117.1	102.5	114.2	114.2	100.0
	1995	127.4	127.4	109.7	116.1	116.1	100.0
	1996	134.2	134.2	112.9	118.9	118.9	100.0
	1997	144.7	144.7	116.6	124.0	124.0	100.0
	1998	152.9	152.9	120.6	126.7	126.7	100.0
	1999	163.8	163.8	124.9	131.2	131.2	100.0
	2000	170.1	170.1	127.4	133.6	133.6	100.0
	2001	180.2	180.2	126.8	142.2	142.2	100.0
Canada	1970	13.3	14.9	50.1	26.5	29.6	89.5
	1975	25.6	29.4	63.6	40.3	46.2	87.2
	1980	46.4	46.3	76.1	61.0	60.9	100.2
	1985	71.5	61.1	86.9	82.2	70.3	116.9
	1990	100.0	100.0	100.0	100.0	100.0	100.0
	1991	100.7	102.5	97.9	102.9	104.8	98.2
	1992	102.9	99.3	98.7	104.2	100.6	103.6
	1993	106.8	96.6	101.0	105.7	95.6	110.6
	1994	113.3	96.8	105.9	107.0	91.4	117.1
	1995	119.2	101.3	108.8	109.5	93.1	117.6
	1996	123.0	105.3	110.6	111.2	95.2	116.8
	1997	129.7	109.3	115.3	112.5	94.8	118.7
	1998	134.4	105.7	120.0	112.0	88.1	127.1
	1999	144.1	113.2	126.6	113.9	89.4	127.4
	2000	156.6	123.1	132.3	118.4	93.0	127.3
	2001	160.5	120.9	134.2	119.6	90.1	132.7

Table 7. Implicit Price Deflators of Gross Domestic Product in US Dollars and in National Currency

(Index numbers 1990 = 100)

Region, country or area and currency unit	Year	GDP in Current Prices		GDP at Constant Prices	GDP Implicit Price Deflators		Exchange Rates
		National Currency (1)	US Dollars (2)	(3)	National Currency (4)	US Dollars (5)	(6)
United States	1970	17.8	17.8	53.1	33.6	33.6	100.0
	1975	28.1	28.1	60.9	46.2	46.2	100.0
	1980	48.2	48.2	73.2	65.9	65.9	100.0
	1985	72.6	72.6	85.3	85.1	85.1	100.0
	1990	100.0	100.0	100.0	100.0	100.0	100.0
	1991	103.1	103.1	99.5	103.6	103.6	100.0
	1992	108.9	108.9	102.6	106.2	106.2	100.0
	1993	114.5	114.5	105.3	108.7	108.7	100.0
	1994	121.6	121.6	109.6	111.0	111.0	100.0
	1995	127.6	127.6	112.5	113.4	113.4	100.0
	1996	134.8	134.8	116.6	115.6	115.6	100.0
	1997	143.6	143.6	121.8	117.9	117.9	100.0
	1998	151.6	151.6	127.1	119.3	119.3	100.0
	1999	160.2	160.2	132.3	121.1	121.1	100.0
	2000	169.8	169.8	137.3	123.6	123.6	100.0
	2001	174.2	174.2	137.7	126.5	126.5	100.0
LATIN AMERICA AND THE CARIBBEAN							
Anguilla	1970	3.8	5.2	29.0	13.2	17.8	74.2
	1975	7.8	9.8	33.9	23.1	28.8	80.2
	1980	16.0	16.0	42.6	37.7	37.7	100.0
	1985	35.6	35.6	50.7	70.2	70.2	100.0
	1990	100.0	100.0	100.0	100.0	100.0	100.0
	1991	102.8	102.8	81.8	125.6	125.6	100.0
	1992	111.7	111.7	88.4	126.4	126.4	100.0
	1993	121.8	121.8	95.0	128.2	128.2	100.0
	1994	136.2	136.2	101.8	133.8	133.8	100.0
	1995	137.7	137.7	97.5	141.2	141.2	100.0
	1996	145.4	145.4	100.9	144.1	144.1	100.0
	1997	163.0	163.0	110.2	147.9	147.9	100.0
	1998	173.4	173.4	115.9	149.6	149.6	100.0
	1999	192.7	192.7	126.0	153.0	153.0	100.0
	2000	198.6	198.6	125.8	157.8	157.8	100.0
	2001	202.7	202.7	127.9	158.5	158.5	100.0
Antigua and Barbuda	1970	10.8	14.6	47.4	22.8	30.8	74.0
	1975	16.8	21.0	46.3	36.3	45.2	80.3
	1980	33.0	33.0	55.4	59.5	59.5	100.0
	1985	60.0	60.0	72.2	83.1	83.1	100.0
	1990	100.0	100.0	100.0	100.0	100.0	100.0
	1991	107.9	107.9	102.7	105.0	105.0	100.0
	1992	112.0	112.0	103.6	108.1	108.1	100.0
	1993	120.6	120.6	108.9	110.8	110.8	100.0
	1994	132.1	132.1	115.6	114.3	114.3	100.0
	1995	130.4	130.4	126.1	103.5	103.5	100.0
	1996	142.8	142.8	116.5	122.5	122.5	100.0
	1997	153.5	153.5	123.0	124.8	124.8	100.0
	1998	163.8	163.8	129.1	126.9	126.9	100.0
	1999	172.1	172.1	135.4	127.0	127.0	100.0
	2000	177.8	177.8	136.5	130.2	130.2	100.0
	2001	183.0	183.0	139.6	131.1	131.1	100.0
Argentina	1970	-	22.0	86.9	-	25.3	-
	1975	-	37.1	100.0	-	37.1	-
	1980	-	146.3	111.8	-	130.9	-
	1985	-	62.4	101.2	-	61.6	-
	1990	100.0	100.0	100.0	100.0	100.0	100.0
	1991	262.5	134.2	110.5	237.5	121.5	195.5
	1992	328.8	161.8	121.9	269.8	132.8	203.2
	1993	343.1	167.5	129.5	265.0	129.3	204.9
	1994	373.5	182.3	137.1	272.5	133.0	204.9
	1995	374.4	182.6	133.2	281.2	137.1	205.1
	1996	394.9	192.6	140.5	281.0	137.1	205.0
	1997	424.9	207.3	151.9	279.7	136.4	205.1
	1998	433.7	211.6	157.8	274.9	134.1	205.0
	1999	411.4	200.7	152.4	269.9	131.7	204.9
	2000	412.4	146.3	151.2	272.7	96.7	282.0
	2001	389.9	139.8	144.6	269.7	96.7	278.9
Aruba	1970	35.4	35.4	16.0	221.8	221.8	100.0
	1975	45.9	45.9	24.7	186.1	186.1	100.0
	1980	59.5	59.5	38.1	156.2	156.2	100.0
	1985	77.1	77.1	58.8	131.1	131.1	100.0
	1990	100.0	100.0	100.0	100.0	100.0	100.0
	1991	105.3	105.3	104.0	101.3	101.3	100.0
	1992	110.9	110.9	108.2	102.6	102.6	100.0
	1993	116.9	116.9	112.5	103.9	103.9	100.0
	1994	123.1	123.1	119.2	103.2	103.2	100.0

Table 7. Implicit Price Deflators of Gross Domestic Product in US Dollars and in National Currency

(Index numbers 1990 = 100)

Region, country or area and currency unit	Year	GDP in Current Prices: National Currency (1)	GDP in Current Prices: US Dollars (2)	GDP at Constant Prices (3)	GDP Implicit Price Deflators: National Currency (4)	GDP Implicit Price Deflators: US Dollars (5)	Exchange Rates (6)
	1995	122.2	122.2	126.3	96.7	96.7	100.0
	1996	127.7	127.7	133.9	95.4	95.4	100.0
	1997	141.8	141.8	141.8	99.9	99.9	100.0
	1998	154.1	154.1	150.3	102.5	102.5	100.0
	1999	159.6	159.6	159.2	100.2	100.2	100.0
	2000	171.9	171.9	168.7	101.9	101.9	100.0
	2001	174.8	174.8	178.8	97.8	97.8	100.0
Bahamas	1970	16.5	16.4	55.8	29.5	29.5	100.0
	1975	23.7	23.7	41.8	56.8	56.8	100.0
	1980	47.2	47.2	77.4	61.0	61.0	100.0
	1985	71.3	71.3	91.2	78.1	78.1	100.0
	1990	100.0	100.0	100.0	100.0	100.0	100.0
	1991	94.8	94.8	96.8	97.9	97.9	100.0
	1992	93.8	93.8	91.2	102.8	102.8	100.0
	1993	93.7	93.7	93.1	100.6	100.6	100.0
	1994	100.2	100.2	91.3	109.8	109.8	100.0
	1995	100.7	100.7	90.3	111.5	111.5	100.0
	1996	101.5	101.5	94.1	107.9	107.9	100.0
	1997	102.3	102.3	97.2	105.2	105.2	100.0
	1998	103.1	103.1	100.1	102.9	102.9	100.0
	1999	103.9	103.9	105.4	98.5	98.5	100.0
	2000	104.7	104.7	110.2	95.0	95.0	100.0
	2001	105.5	105.5	114.6	92.0	92.0	100.0
Barbados	1970	10.8	10.8	61.2	17.6	17.6	100.0
	1975	23.6	23.4	71.2	33.2	32.9	100.9
	1980	50.3	50.3	91.1	55.2	55.2	100.0
	1985	70.1	70.1	89.3	78.4	78.4	100.0
	1990	100.0	100.0	100.0	100.0	100.0	100.0
	1991	98.7	98.7	95.8	102.9	102.9	100.0
	1992	92.3	92.3	89.0	103.7	103.7	100.0
	1993	96.2	96.2	89.8	107.1	107.1	100.0
	1994	101.3	101.3	93.8	108.0	108.0	100.0
	1995	108.8	108.8	95.9	113.4	113.4	100.0
	1996	116.1	116.1	98.3	118.1	118.1	100.0
	1997	128.3	128.3	101.0	127.0	127.0	100.0
	1998	138.0	138.0	105.2	131.1	131.1	100.0
	1999	144.3	144.3	108.3	133.3	133.3	100.0
	2000	150.7	150.7	111.6	135.0	135.0	100.0
	2001	148.0	148.0	108.6	136.3	136.3	100.0
Belize	1970	9.5	11.4	41.5	22.8	27.4	83.2
	1975	23.3	25.8	50.7	45.9	50.8	90.4
	1980	48.0	48.0	61.3	78.3	78.3	100.0
	1985	51.6	51.6	62.5	82.6	82.6	100.0
	1990	100.0	100.0	100.0	100.0	100.0	100.0
	1991	106.7	106.7	102.6	104.0	104.0	100.0
	1992	115.4	115.4	108.8	106.1	106.1	100.0
	1993	130.0	130.8	116.7	113.0	113.0	100.0
	1994	136.2	136.2	118.6	114.8	114.8	100.0
	1995	144.7	144.7	123.5	117.1	117.1	100.0
	1996	148.9	148.9	125.5	118.6	118.6	100.0
	1997	151.8	151.8	129.5	117.2	117.2	100.0
	1998	155.2	155.2	131.4	118.1	118.1	100.0
	1999	169.9	169.9	140.0	121.3	121.3	100.0
	2000	186.7	186.7	154.5	120.8	120.8	100.0
	2001	189.0	189.0	162.3	116.5	116.5	100.0
Bolivia	1970	-	20.8	67.2	-	30.9	-
	1975	-	49.3	89.0	-	55.4	-
	1980	-	103.1	98.5	-	104.7	-
	1985	18.6	133.8	89.4	20.8	149.7	13.9
	1990	100.0	100.0	100.0	100.0	100.0	100.0
	1991	123.9	109.8	105.3	117.7	104.3	112.8
	1992	142.5	115.9	107.0	133.2	108.4	122.9
	1993	158.4	117.8	111.6	142.0	105.6	134.5
	1994	179.0	122.9	116.8	153.2	105.2	145.6
	1995	208.7	138.0	122.2	170.8	112.9	151.3
	1996	243.1	152.0	127.6	190.5	119.1	159.9
	1997	269.7	162.8	133.9	201.4	121.6	165.6
	1998	303.2	174.6	140.6	215.6	124.1	173.7
	1999	311.8	170.2	141.2	220.8	120.5	183.2
	2000	334.6	171.7	144.6	231.4	118.7	194.9
	2001	340.9	163.7	146.3	233.0	111.9	208.2
Brazil	1970	-	15.3	38.1	-	40.2	-
	1975	-	46.7	62.1	-	75.2	-
	1980	-	56.1	85.8	-	65.4	-

Table 7. Implicit Price Deflators of Gross Domestic Product in US Dollars and in National Currency

(Index numbers 1990 = 100)

Region, country or area and currency unit	Year	GDP in Current Prices		GDP at Constant Prices	GDP Implicit Price Deflators		Exchange Rates
		National Currency (1)	US Dollars (2)	(3)	National Currency (4)	US Dollars (5)	(6)
	1985	-	45.3	90.5	-	50.1	-
	1990	100.0	100.0	100.0	100.0	100.0	100.0
	1991	553.9	93.0	101.3	546.8	91.8	595.6
	1992	5 889.0	89.1	100.8	5 842.6	88.4	6 609.3
	1993	129 512.1	100.0	105.7	122 490.5	94.6	129 482.6
	1994	3 208 220.0	124.6	112.0	2 865 234.5	111.3	2 574 334.7
	1995	5 936 702.2	160.7	116.7	5 087 333.6	137.7	3 694 505.2
	1996	7 155 799.2	176.8	119.8	5 973 128.2	147.6	4 046 834.8
	1997	7 999 699.6	184.3	123.7	6 466 111.6	149.0	4 339 672.2
	1998	8 398 838.0	179.7	124.0	6 773 830.5	145.0	4 671 607.2
	1999	8 946 928.6	122.4	125.0	7 159 317.9	98.0	7 305 426.4
	2000	10 117 462.0	137.3	130.6	7 747 346.2	105.1	7 371 404.6
	2001	11 025 204.3	116.1	132.6	8 317 576.3	87.6	9 494 950.1
British Virgin Islands	1970	6.6	6.6	32.3	20.5	20.5	100.0
	1975	8.9	8.9	35.3	25.2	25.2	100.0
	1980	18.1	18.1	49.1	36.9	36.9	100.0
	1985	30.0	30.0	57.2	52.5	52.5	100.0
	1990	100.0	100.0	100.0	100.0	100.0	100.0
	1991	105.4	105.4	102.0	103.3	103.3	100.0
	1992	115.2	115.2	104.6	110.1	110.1	100.0
	1993	121.7	121.7	108.3	112.4	112.4	100.0
	1994	144.1	144.1	114.5	125.9	125.9	100.0
	1995	160.1	160.1	120.2	133.2	133.2	100.0
	1996	183.8	183.8	131.7	139.5	139.5	100.0
	1997	212.9	212.9	144.5	147.3	147.3	100.0
	1998	246.6	246.6	161.1	153.1	153.1	100.0
	1999	275.3	275.3	175.7	156.6	156.6	100.0
	2000	287.4	287.4	193.5	148.6	148.6	100.0
	2001	323.1	323.1	213.0	151.7	151.7	100.0
Cayman Islands	1970	2.6	2.7	16.1	16.4	16.5	99.4
	1975	7.7	7.7	24.7	31.3	31.3	100.0
	1980	18.6	18.6	39.5	47.1	47.1	100.0
	1985	44.7	44.7	60.3	74.2	74.2	100.0
	1990	100.0	100.0	100.0	100.0	100.0	100.0
	1991	104.4	104.4	101.3	103.0	103.0	100.0
	1992	116.6	116.6	100.7	115.8	115.8	100.0
	1993	126.3	126.3	101.6	124.3	124.3	100.0
	1994	137.1	137.1	102.1	134.3	134.3	100.0
	1995	144.0	144.0	101.6	141.6	141.6	100.0
	1996	151.9	151.9	101.8	149.2	149.2	100.0
	1997	165.6	165.6	102.3	161.9	161.9	100.0
	1998	174.7	174.7	103.9	168.1	168.1	100.0
	1999	180.8	180.8	105.4	171.5	171.5	100.0
	2000	191.6	191.6	106.7	179.7	179.7	100.0
	2001	203.1	203.1	107.9	188.2	188.2	100.0
Chile	1970	-	27.7	58.3	-	47.5	-
	1975	0.4	23.0	52.1	0.7	44.2	1.6
	1980	11.3	88.0	75.0	15.0	117.3	12.8
	1985	28.7	54.4	72.2	39.7	75.3	52.7
	1990	100.0	100.0	100.0	100.0	100.0	100.0
	1991	130.9	114.3	108.0	121.2	105.8	114.6
	1992	164.2	138.1	121.2	135.5	113.9	119.0
	1993	194.4	146.7	129.7	149.9	113.1	132.5
	1994	231.4	167.9	137.1	168.8	122.5	137.8
	1995	279.9	215.1	151.7	184.5	141.8	130.1
	1996	305.8	226.1	162.9	187.7	138.8	135.2
	1997	339.9	247.1	173.7	195.7	142.3	137.5
	1998	357.6	236.9	179.3	199.5	132.1	151.0
	1999	363.8	218.0	177.5	204.9	122.8	166.9
	2000	395.8	225.4	185.3	213.6	121.6	175.7
	2001	413.0	198.3	190.5	216.7	104.1	208.2
Colombia	1970	0.7	17.9	41.8	1.6	42.8	3.7
	1975	2.0	32.5	55.1	3.6	59.0	6.1
	1980	7.8	82.9	71.5	10.9	116.0	9.4
	1985	24.6	86.6	70.0	30.7	100.4	28.3
	1990	100.0	100.0	100.0	100.0	100.0	100.0
	1991	129.1	102.4	102.0	126.5	100.4	126.0
	1992	165.7	109.6	106.1	156.1	103.3	151.1
	1993	218.0	126.9	112.2	194.3	113.1	171.8
	1994	281.6	167.4	118.0	238.7	141.9	168.2
	1995	352.1	193.8	124.1	283.7	156.1	181.7
	1996	420.0	203.5	126.7	331.6	160.7	206.3
	1997	507.5	223.4	131.0	387.5	170.6	227.1
	1998	585.8	206.3	131.7	444.7	156.6	284.0

Table 7. Implicit Price Deflators of Gross Domestic Product in US Dollars and in National Currency

(Index numbers 1990 = 100)

Region, country or area and currency unit	Year	GDP in Current Prices: National Currency (1)	GDP in Current Prices: US Dollars (2)	GDP at Constant Prices (3)	GDP Implicit Price Deflators: National Currency (4)	GDP Implicit Price Deflators: US Dollars (5)	Exchange Rates (6)
	1999	632.1	180.8	126.2	500.8	143.2	349.7
	2000	724.5	174.3	129.7	558.8	134.4	415.8
	2001	790.4	172.6	131.5	601.2	131.3	457.9
Costa Rica	1970	1.2	17.3	45.5	2.7	37.9	7.1
	1975	3.2	34.3	61.0	5.3	56.3	9.4
	1980	7.9	84.6	78.8	10.1	107.4	9.4
	1985	37.9	68.7	79.9	47.4	86.0	55.1
	1990	100.0	100.0	100.0	100.0	100.0	100.0
	1991	132.0	98.7	102.3	129.1	96.6	133.6
	1992	173.6	118.2	111.6	155.5	105.9	146.8
	1993	206.3	132.9	119.9	172.0	110.8	155.2
	1994	249.6	145.5	125.6	198.8	115.9	171.5
	1995	317.0	161.5	130.5	242.9	123.8	196.2
	1996	370.3	163.3	131.6	281.3	124.0	226.9
	1997	449.2	176.9	139.0	323.2	127.2	254.1
	1998	545.7	194.3	150.7	362.2	129.0	280.8
	1999	679.3	217.8	163.1	416.6	133.6	311.8
	2000	740.3	220.0	166.0	446.0	132.5	336.6
	2001	811.0	225.8	167.8	483.4	134.6	359.1
Cuba	1970	26.4	26.4	43.8	60.3	60.3	100.0
	1975	49.6	49.6	57.1	86.9	86.9	100.0
	1980	66.6	66.6	67.0	99.3	99.3	100.0
	1985	97.5	97.5	101.0	96.5	96.5	100.0
	1990	100.0	100.0	100.0	100.0	100.0	100.0
	1991	82.7	82.7	89.3	92.6	92.6	100.0
	1992	75.9	75.9	79.0	96.1	96.1	100.0
	1993	76.8	76.8	67.2	114.3	114.3	100.0
	1994	97.7	97.7	67.7	144.4	144.4	100.0
	1995	110.7	110.7	69.4	159.5	159.5	100.0
	1996	116.1	116.1	74.8	155.3	155.3	100.0
	1997	116.8	116.8	76.7	152.4	152.4	100.0
	1998	121.7	121.7	77.6	156.7	156.7	100.0
	1999	129.8	129.8	82.5	157.4	157.4	100.0
	2000	140.7	140.7	87.1	161.5	161.5	100.0
	2001	145.5	145.5	89.7	162.2	162.2	100.0
Dominica	1970	12.3	16.6	64.8	19.0	25.6	74.2
	1975	16.1	20.0	54.6	29.5	36.7	80.4
	1980	35.3	35.3	65.1	54.3	54.3	100.0
	1985	58.9	58.9	77.6	76.0	76.0	100.0
	1990	100.0	100.0	100.0	100.0	100.0	100.0
	1991	106.0	106.0	102.1	103.8	103.8	100.0
	1992	114.7	114.7	104.7	109.6	109.6	100.0
	1993	119.8	119.8	104.4	114.8	114.8	100.0
	1994	128.8	128.8	105.9	121.7	121.7	100.0
	1995	131.0	131.0	108.0	121.4	121.4	100.0
	1996	141.3	141.3	111.8	126.4	126.4	100.0
	1997	140.5	140.5	111.6	127.0	127.9	100.0
	1998	155.1	155.1	118.2	131.3	131.3	100.0
	1999	160.1	160.1	118.9	134.6	134.6	100.0
	2000	161.2	161.2	119.1	135.4	135.4	100.0
	2001	157.4	157.4	114.0	138.0	138.0	100.0
Dominican Republic	1970	2.3	19.5	39.6	5.8	49.3	11.8
	1975	5.5	47.3	61.0	9.1	77.6	11.7
	1980	10.2	87.1	78.7	13.0	110.7	11.7
	1985	21.5	59.0	86.6	24.9	68.1	36.6
	1990	100.0	100.0	100.0	100.0	100.0	100.0
	1991	154.3	103.6	100.8	153.1	102.8	148.9
	1992	183.5	122.4	111.0	165.2	110.3	149.8
	1993	206.3	138.7	117.3	175.9	118.3	148.7
	1994	229.9	148.9	121.9	188.6	122.2	154.3
	1995	269.1	168.7	127.5	211.1	132.4	159.4
	1996	299.1	185.1	138.0	216.7	134.1	161.6
	1997	275.8	164.8	149.3	184.7	110.4	167.3
	1998	310.6	173.4	160.4	193.7	108.1	179.2
	1999	357.3	190.0	173.2	206.3	109.7	188.1
	2000	413.0	214.5	185.9	222.2	115.4	192.5
	2001	464.1	233.4	191.8	242.0	121.7	198.8
Ecuador	1970	15.7	15.7	34.7	45.2	45.2	100.0
	1975	40.3	40.3	59.4	68.0	68.0	100.0
	1980	109.8	109.8	81.3	135.0	135.0	100.0
	1985	149.3	149.3	90.4	165.2	165.2	100.0
	1990	100.0	100.0	100.0	100.0	100.0	100.0
	1991	110.0	110.0	105.0	104.7	104.7	100.0
	1992	118.4	118.4	108.8	108.9	108.9	100.0

Table 7. Implicit Price Deflators of Gross Domestic Product in US Dollars and in National Currency

(Index numbers 1990 = 100)

Region, country or area and currency unit	Year	GDP in Current Prices: National Currency (1)	GDP in Current Prices: US Dollars (2)	GDP at Constant Prices (3)	GDP Implicit Price Deflators: National Currency (4)	GDP Implicit Price Deflators: US Dollars (5)	Exchange Rates (6)
	1993	133.9	133.9	111.0	120.6	120.6	100.0
	1994	165.1	165.1	116.2	142.1	142.1	100.0
	1995	179.5	179.5	118.2	151.9	151.9	100.0
	1996	189.1	189.1	121.1	156.2	156.2	100.0
	1997	210.1	210.1	126.0	166.8	166.8	100.0
	1998	206.7	206.7	128.6	160.7	160.7	100.0
	1999	148.2	148.2	120.5	123.0	123.0	100.0
	2000	141.7	141.7	123.9	114.3	114.3	100.0
	2001	186.9	186.9	130.2	143.5	143.5	100.0
El Salvador	1970	7.0	19.3	72.8	9.7	26.5	36.6
	1975	12.3	33.6	95.1	12.9	35.4	36.4
	1980	24.4	66.9	100.1	24.4	66.9	36.5
	1985	39.3	107.6	91.1	43.1	118.1	36.5
	1990	100.0	100.0	100.0	100.0	100.0	100.0
	1991	116.7	99.7	103.6	112.7	96.3	117.0
	1992	136.6	111.9	111.4	122.6	100.4	122.1
	1993	165.4	130.2	119.6	138.3	108.9	127.0
	1994	193.9	152.1	126.8	152.9	119.9	127.5
	1995	227.8	178.2	134.9	168.8	132.1	127.8
	1996	247.4	193.5	137.2	180.2	141.0	127.8
	1997	267.0	208.8	143.1	186.6	146.0	127.8
	1998	288.0	225.3	148.4	194.0	151.8	127.8
	1999	298.9	233.8	153.6	194.7	152.3	127.8
	2000	315.1	246.5	156.9	200.8	157.1	127.8
	2001	329.5	257.9	159.8	206.2	161.4	127.8
French Guiana	1970	4.4	4.3	14.7	29.9	29.3	102.0
	1975	8.8	11.2	31.0	28.4	36.1	78.7
	1980	18.7	24.1	40.5	46.1	59.4	77.6
	1985	48.6	29.5	61.7	78.8	47.7	165.2
	1990	100.0	100.0	100.0	100.0	100.0	100.0
	1991	113.5	109.5	111.9	101.4	97.9	103.6
	1992	122.2	125.7	120.9	101.1	104.0	97.2
	1993	122.4	117.7	117.3	104.3	100.3	104.0
	1994	126.1	123.7	124.5	101.3	99.3	102.0
	1995	128.1	139.8	126.5	101.3	110.5	91.7
	1996	131.1	139.5	128.5	102.0	108.6	93.9
	1997	134.1	125.1	130.6	102.7	95.8	107.2
	1998	137.2	126.6	132.7	103.4	95.4	108.4
	1999	140.4	124.1	134.8	104.1	92.1	113.0
	2000	143.6	109.8	137.0	104.8	80.2	130.7
	2001	146.9	109.1	139.2	105.6	78.4	134.7
Grenada	1970	11.0	14.9	68.1	16.2	21.9	74.0
	1975	19.7	24.5	73.9	26.6	33.1	80.4
	1980	37.3	37.3	76.4	40.0	40.0	100.0
	1985	57.5	57.5	96.6	59.5	59.5	100.0
	1990	100.0	100.0	100.0	100.0	100.0	100.0
	1991	104.8	104.8	102.9	101.8	101.8	100.0
	1992	106.8	106.8	104.0	102.7	102.7	100.0
	1993	108.7	108.7	102.7	105.9	105.9	100.0
	1994	113.7	113.7	106.3	107.0	107.0	100.0
	1995	119.9	119.9	109.6	109.4	109.4	100.0
	1996	128.1	128.1	112.9	113.4	113.4	100.0
	1997	136.7	136.7	117.5	116.4	116.4	100.0
	1998	148.0	148.0	126.0	117.4	117.4	100.0
	1999	164.1	164.1	135.4	121.2	121.2	100.0
	2000	178.2	178.2	144.1	123.7	123.7	100.0
	2001	188.5	188.5	149.1	126.5	126.5	100.0
Guadeloupe	1970	8.7	8.6	48.3	18.1	17.8	101.7
	1975	18.6	23.6	61.7	30.1	38.3	78.6
	1980	38.6	49.7	76.2	50.6	65.2	77.6
	1985	64.5	39.1	77.5	83.2	50.4	165.1
	1990	100.0	100.0	100.0	100.0	100.0	100.0
	1991	108.0	104.2	82.1	131.5	126.9	103.6
	1992	118.2	121.6	88.1	134.1	138.0	97.2
	1993	128.9	124.0	94.5	136.4	131.1	104.0
	1994	144.1	141.4	101.5	141.9	139.2	101.9
	1995	145.8	159.0	97.1	150.1	163.7	91.7
	1996	154.0	163.9	101.3	152.0	161.8	93.9
	1997	171.0	159.5	110.7	154.5	144.2	107.1
	1998	182.3	168.2	115.2	158.2	146.0	108.4
	1999	188.2	166.4	116.0	162.2	143.5	113.0
	2000	201.2	153.9	121.3	165.8	126.8	130.8
	2001	215.1	159.8	126.9	169.5	125.9	134.6

Table 7. Implicit Price Deflators of Gross Domestic Product in US Dollars and in National Currency

(Index numbers 1990 = 100)

Region, country or area and currency unit	Year	GDP in Current Prices		GDP at Constant Prices	GDP Implicit Price Deflators		Exchange Rates
		National Currency (1)	US Dollars (2)	(3)	National Currency (4)	US Dollars (5)	(6)
Guatemala	1970	5.5	24.9	52.9	10.5	47.1	22.3
	1975	10.6	47.7	69.4	15.3	68.7	22.3
	1980	23.0	103.0	91.7	25.0	112.4	22.2
	1985	32.6	146.1	86.6	37.6	168.7	22.3
	1990	100.0	100.0	100.0	100.0	100.0	100.0
	1991	137.8	123.0	103.7	133.0	118.6	112.1
	1992	157.3	136.5	108.7	144.8	125.6	115.3
	1993	187.2	149.0	112.9	165.8	131.9	125.7
	1994	217.6	169.7	117.5	185.2	144.4	128.3
	1995	248.1	191.6	123.3	201.3	155.4	129.5
	1996	278.2	206.3	126.9	219.2	162.5	134.9
	1997	314.5	232.6	132.4	237.6	175.7	135.2
	1998	354.2	248.5	138.7	255.3	179.1	142.5
	1999	386.4	234.7	144.1	268.2	162.9	164.6
	2000	423.9	245.0	149.2	284.1	164.2	173.0
	2001	461.0	263.1	152.7	302.0	172.4	175.2
Guyana	1970	3.4	67.6	111.5	3.1	60.6	5.1
	1975	7.6	127.3	135.0	5.6	94.3	5.9
	1980	9.6	149.3	132.0	7.3	113.0	6.5
	1985	12.5	116.6	110.1	11.4	105.9	10.8
	1990	100.0	100.0	100.0	100.0	100.0	100.0
	1991	248.7	87.9	106.0	234.6	83.0	282.7
	1992	298.3	94.4	114.3	261.1	82.6	316.1
	1993	377.4	117.7	123.7	305.2	95.2	320.6
	1994	481.4	137.6	134.1	359.1	102.6	350.0
	1995	563.5	156.9	140.9	400.0	111.4	359.1
	1996	632.2	178.1	150.8	419.3	118.1	355.0
	1997	681.0	189.1	160.2	425.1	118.0	360.3
	1998	689.4	181.1	157.5	437.9	115.0	380.8
	1999	789.4	175.3	163.5	482.9	107.3	450.0
	2000	830.0	179.9	161.3	514.6	111.5	461.5
	2001	852.5	179.9	164.4	518.6	109.4	474.0
Haiti	1970	12.7	12.7	63.1	20.1	20.1	100.0
	1975	26.1	26.1	76.1	34.3	34.3	100.0
	1980	52.9	52.9	100.4	52.7	52.7	100.0
	1985	76.9	76.9	95.7	80.3	80.3	100.0
	1990	100.0	100.0	100.0	100.0	100.0	100.0
	1991	108.6	90.0	100.3	108.3	89.7	120.7
	1992	114.9	58.6	87.0	132.0	67.4	195.8
	1993	173.4	67.6	83.2	208.4	81.3	256.3
	1994	245.0	81.5	78.8	311.1	103.4	300.9
	1995	284.2	94.0	81.9	347.0	114.8	302.3
	1996	344.0	109.5	83.8	410.3	130.7	313.9
	1997	409.0	122.8	85.4	479.2	143.9	333.0
	1998	466.0	139.0	87.8	530.7	158.3	335.2
	1999	523.6	154.6	89.5	585.2	172.7	338.9
	2000	590.4	139.4	89.7	658.3	155.5	423.3
	2001	677.2	138.6	88.2	768.3	157.2	488.7
Honduras	1970	11.0	22.7	46.5	23.7	48.7	48.7
	1975	17.9	36.9	55.7	32.2	66.2	48.6
	1980	40.9	84.2	78.7	52.0	106.9	48.6
	1985	58.1	119.4	85.7	67.7	139.3	48.6
	1990	100.0	100.0	100.0	100.0	100.0	100.0
	1991	130.1	100.6	103.3	126.0	97.5	129.2
	1992	150.0	112.2	109.1	137.5	102.8	133.8
	1993	181.0	115.0	115.9	156.2	99.3	157.3
	1994	230.2	112.6	114.3	201.3	98.5	204.4
	1995	299.2	129.9	119.0	251.4	109.1	230.4
	1996	381.0	133.8	123.3	309.1	108.6	284.6
	1997	489.1	154.7	129.4	377.9	119.5	316.2
	1998	561.8	172.6	133.2	421.9	129.6	325.5
	1999	614.9	177.9	130.7	470.6	136.2	345.5
	2000	698.1	193.5	137.2	509.0	141.0	361.0
	2001	784.7	208.5	141.3	555.4	147.6	376.3
Jamaica	1970	3.8	33.0	84.6	4.5	39.0	11.5
	1975	8.5	67.4	92.3	9.2	73.0	12.6
	1980	15.7	63.2	78.4	20.0	80.5	24.8
	1985	36.8	47.5	78.8	46.7	60.3	77.4
	1990	100.0	100.0	100.0	100.0	100.0	100.0
	1991	148.4	88.0	100.9	147.1	87.2	168.7
	1992	255.7	80.0	102.5	249.5	78.1	319.5
	1993	356.4	102.6	104.5	341.0	98.2	347.3
	1994	477.0	103.6	105.5	452.3	98.2	460.6
	1995	602.5	123.2	106.5	565.5	115.6	489.2
	1996	715.0	138.4	105.4	678.2	131.3	516.5

Table 7. Implicit Price Deflators of Gross Domestic Product in US Dollars and in National Currency

(Index numbers 1990 = 100)

Region, country or area and currency unit	Year	GDP in Current Prices: National Currency (1)	GDP in Current Prices: US Dollars (2)	GDP at Constant Prices (3)	GDP Implicit Price Deflators: National Currency (4)	GDP Implicit Price Deflators: US Dollars (5)	Exchange Rates (6)
	1997	777.1	157.7	103.6	750.1	152.2	492.8
	1998	823.5	161.9	103.3	797.6	156.8	508.7
	1999	885.7	163.0	102.8	861.6	158.5	543.6
	2000	991.4	166.8	103.5	958.1	161.2	594.4
	2001	1 078.3	168.4	105.3	1 024.4	160.0	640.3
Martinique	1970	8.3	8.1	41.5	20.0	19.6	102.0
	1975	17.4	22.1	52.5	33.1	42.1	78.6
	1980	31.6	40.7	61.9	51.0	65.7	77.6
	1985	64.6	39.2	77.1	83.8	50.8	165.0
	1990	100.0	100.0	100.0	100.0	100.0	100.0
	1991	107.6	103.8	96.0	112.0	108.1	103.6
	1992	114.4	117.6	97.6	117.2	120.5	97.3
	1993	118.8	114.3	99.2	119.8	115.2	104.0
	1994	122.8	120.4	100.8	121.8	119.5	101.9
	1995	125.0	136.4	102.5	122.0	133.1	91.7
	1996	128.8	137.1	104.1	123.6	131.6	93.9
	1997	132.2	123.4	105.8	124.9	116.6	107.1
	1998	141.0	130.1	110.2	127.9	118.1	108.3
	1999	145.5	128.7	110.9	131.2	116.0	113.1
	2000	151.6	115.9	113.3	133.8	102.3	130.8
	2001	157.9	117.3	115.7	136.5	101.4	134.6
Mexico	1970	0.1	15.1	44.1	0.2	34.2	0.6
	1975	0.2	37.3	60.6	0.3	61.6	0.5
	1980	0.6	79.0	83.6	0.8	94.5	0.8
	1985	6.8	74.9	92.0	7.4	81.4	9.1
	1990	100.0	100.0	100.0	100.0	100.0	100.0
	1991	128.5	119.7	104.2	123.3	114.8	107.4
	1992	152.3	138.4	108.0	141.0	128.1	110.1
	1993	170.0	153.5	110.1	154.4	139.4	110.8
	1994	192.2	160.2	115.0	167.2	139.3	120.0
	1995	248.6	108.9	107.9	230.5	101.0	228.2
	1996	341.8	126.5	113.4	301.3	111.5	270.2
	1997	429.6	152.6	121.1	354.7	126.0	281.5
	1998	520.6	160.3	127.2	409.2	126.0	324.8
	1999	621.7	182.9	131.8	471.6	138.7	340.0
	2000	742.4	220.8	140.6	528.1	157.1	336.2
	2001	780.3	234.9	140.2	556.6	167.6	332.1
Montserrat	1970	7.3	9.8	39.7	18.3	24.8	73.8
	1975	14.0	17.4	48.6	28.9	35.9	80.5
	1980	36.6	36.6	61.4	59.6	59.6	100.0
	1985	55.0	55.0	69.0	79.6	79.6	100.0
	1990	100.0	100.0	100.0	100.0	100.0	100.0
	1991	83.1	83.1	79.1	105.1	105.1	100.0
	1992	87.6	87.6	81.2	107.8	107.8	100.0
	1993	92.3	92.3	83.3	110.9	110.9	100.0
	1994	94.8	94.8	84.0	112.8	112.8	100.0
	1995	89.7	89.7	77.6	115.5	115.5	100.0
	1996	72.5	72.5	61.0	118.9	118.9	100.0
	1997	60.5	60.5	48.8	124.0	124.0	100.0
	1998	55.6	55.6	43.9	126.8	126.8	100.0
	1999	52.3	52.3	38.4	136.3	136.3	100.0
	2000	51.8	51.8	37.3	138.8	138.8	100.0
	2001	51.7	51.7	34.4	150.2	150.2	100.0
Netherlands Antilles	1970	15.9	15.1	71.5	22.2	21.1	105.2
	1975	25.3	25.2	76.7	33.0	32.8	100.6
	1980	47.9	47.6	99.2	48.3	48.0	100.6
	1985	60.4	60.1	94.2	64.2	63.8	100.6
	1990	100.0	100.0	100.0	100.0	100.0	100.0
	1991	104.9	104.9	101.8	103.0	103.0	100.0
	1992	109.9	109.9	105.2	104.5	104.5	100.0
	1993	117.1	117.1	110.0	106.5	106.5	100.0
	1994	125.9	125.9	116.0	108.5	108.5	100.0
	1995	129.8	129.8	116.4	111.6	111.6	100.0
	1996	135.9	135.9	117.9	115.3	115.3	100.0
	1997	139.5	139.5	117.2	119.0	119.0	100.0
	1998	134.6	134.6	114.8	117.3	117.3	100.0
	1999	133.6	133.6	112.6	118.6	118.6	100.0
	2000	137.0	137.0	110.0	124.6	124.6	100.0
	2001	140.1	140.1	110.0	127.4	127.4	100.0
Nicaragua	1970	-	23.8	109.7	-	21.7	-
	1975	-	48.8	143.8	-	33.9	-
	1980	-	67.1	114.6	-	58.5	-
	1985	-	134.1	118.3	-	113.3	-
	1990	100.0	100.0	100.0	100.0	100.0	100.0

Table 7. Implicit Price Deflators of Gross Domestic Product in US Dollars and in National Currency

(Index numbers 1990 = 100)

Region, country or area and currency unit	Year	GDP in Current Prices		GDP at Constant Prices	GDP Implicit Price Deflators		Exchange Rates
		National Currency (1)	US Dollars (2)	(3)	National Currency (4)	US Dollars (5)	(6)
	1991	2 379.7	78.5	99.8	2 384.2	78.7	3 029.5
	1992	2 954.2	83.3	100.2	2 948.5	83.1	3 548.1
	1993	3 542.5	88.8	99.8	3 549.6	89.0	3 988.3
	1994	3 945.6	82.7	103.1	3 825.8	80.2	4 770.3
	1995	4 566.1	85.3	107.6	4 244.3	79.3	5 352.2
	1996	5 340.3	89.2	112.7	4 737.7	79.1	5 989.5
	1997	6 130.3	91.4	118.5	5 174.3	77.2	6 702.5
	1998	7 211.2	96.0	123.3	5 848.9	77.9	7 508.2
	1999	8 611.6	102.8	132.4	6 504.9	77.6	8 382.6
	2000	10 169.8	113.0	139.6	7 284.0	80.9	9 003.7
	2001	11 285.0	118.9	143.9	7 842.4	82.6	9 494.4
Panama	1970	18.9	18.9	46.1	40.9	40.9	100.0
	1975	34.3	34.3	58.0	59.1	59.1	100.0
	1980	66.7	66.7	78.8	84.7	84.7	100.0
	1985	94.2	94.2	94.2	100.0	100.0	100.0
	1990	100.0	100.0	100.0	100.0	100.0	100.0
	1991	110.0	110.0	109.4	100.5	100.5	100.0
	1992	125.0	125.0	118.4	105.6	105.6	100.0
	1993	136.5	136.5	124.9	109.3	109.3	100.0
	1994	145.6	145.6	128.4	113.4	113.4	100.0
	1995	148.8	148.8	130.7	113.9	113.9	100.0
	1996	153.4	153.4	134.3	114.2	114.2	100.0
	1997	162.9	162.9	140.3	116.1	116.1	100.0
	1998	175.9	175.9	146.5	120.1	120.1	100.0
	1999	181.4	181.4	151.2	120.0	120.0	100.0
	2000	188.6	188.6	154.9	121.8	121.8	100.0
	2001	191.9	191.9	156.3	122.7	122.7	100.0
Paraguay	1970	1.2	11.3	31.8	3.6	35.5	10.1
	1975	2.9	28.7	44.9	6.5	63.9	10.2
	1980	8.7	84.5	73.8	11.7	114.4	10.2
	1985	21.5	86.3	82.6	26.1	104.5	25.0
	1990	100.0	100.0	100.0	100.0	100.0	100.0
	1991	127.9	118.7	102.5	124.8	115.8	107.8
	1992	149.4	122.4	104.3	143.2	117.4	122.0
	1993	185.2	130.6	108.6	170.5	120.2	141.8
	1994	231.1	149.2	112.0	206.3	133.2	154.9
	1995	273.4	171.3	117.2	233.2	146.1	159.6
	1996	305.9	182.9	118.7	257.6	154.0	167.3
	1997	323.3	182.6	121.8	265.4	149.9	177.1
	1998	362.0	163.3	121.3	298.4	134.6	221.7
	1999	372.9	147.0	121.9	305.9	120.6	253.6
	2000	415.8	146.7	121.5	342.3	120.7	283.6
	2001	434.3	130.1	124.8	348.1	104.3	333.7
Peru	1970	-	20.0	77.7	-	25.8	-
	1975	-	45.6	99.0	-	46.0	-
	1980	-	57.2	112.4	-	50.9	-
	1985	-	49.9	110.2	-	45.3	-
	1990	100.0	100.0	100.0	100.0	100.0	100.0
	1991	485.1	118.0	102.8	472.0	114.8	411.1
	1992	768.3	115.9	101.3	758.3	114.4	662.8
	1993	1 183.8	111.9	106.2	1 115.2	105.4	1 058.1
	1994	1 684.8	144.2	119.8	1 406.8	120.4	1 168.4
	1995	2 065.7	172.2	130.0	1 588.5	132.4	1 199.8
	1996	2 340.3	179.2	133.3	1 755.9	134.5	1 305.5
	1997	2 688.1	189.6	142.3	1 889.3	133.2	1 418.4
	1998	2 846.0	182.5	141.5	2 011.0	129.0	1 558.9
	1999	2 986.2	165.8	142.9	2 090.3	116.1	1 800.4
	2000	3 192.0	171.8	147.3	2 166.6	116.6	1 858.1
	2001	3 243.5	173.8	147.5	2 199.3	117.8	1 867.0
Puerto Rico	1970	17.5	17.5	48.2	36.3	36.3	100.0
	1975	27.8	27.8	56.3	49.3	49.3	100.0
	1980	49.4	49.4	69.6	71.0	71.0	100.0
	1985	68.0	68.0	80.3	84.7	84.7	100.0
	1990	100.0	100.0	100.0	100.0	100.0	100.0
	1991	107.3	107.3	104.6	102.6	102.6	100.0
	1992	114.4	114.4	109.4	104.5	104.5	100.0
	1993	122.9	122.9	114.0	107.8	107.8	100.0
	1994	132.1	132.1	119.2	110.8	110.8	100.0
	1995	140.4	140.4	121.9	115.2	115.2	100.0
	1996	149.2	149.2	127.9	116.7	116.7	100.0
	1997	167.5	167.5	135.0	124.1	124.1	100.0
	1998	179.1	179.1	142.2	125.9	125.9	100.0
	1999	189.1	189.1	145.7	129.8	129.8	100.0
	2000	210.3	210.3	153.8	136.7	136.7	100.0
	2001	226.9	226.9	160.6	141.2	141.2	100.0

Table 7. Implicit Price Deflators of Gross Domestic Product in US Dollars and in National Currency

(Index numbers 1990 = 100)

Region, country or area and currency unit	Year	GDP in Current Prices: National Currency (1)	GDP in Current Prices: US Dollars (2)	GDP at Constant Prices (3)	GDP Implicit Price Deflators: National Currency (4)	GDP Implicit Price Deflators: US Dollars (5)	Exchange Rates (6)
Saint Kitts and Nevis	1970	7.9	10.6	41.4	19.0	25.7	73.9
	1975	17.2	21.5	48.4	35.6	44.3	80.4
	1980	30.1	30.1	57.2	52.6	52.6	100.0
	1985	49.0	49.0	72.7	67.4	67.4	100.0
	1990	100.0	100.0	100.0	100.0	100.0	100.0
	1991	103.4	103.4	102.3	101.1	101.1	100.0
	1992	114.2	114.2	123.8	92.3	92.3	100.0
	1993	124.6	124.6	131.8	94.5	94.5	100.0
	1994	139.3	139.3	138.8	100.4	100.4	100.0
	1995	144.9	144.9	143.8	100.8	100.8	100.0
	1996	154.3	154.3	153.2	100.7	100.7	100.0
	1997	172.7	172.7	163.5	105.6	105.6	100.0
	1998	180.3	180.3	165.4	109.0	109.0	100.0
	1999	191.5	191.5	171.2	111.8	111.8	100.0
	2000	207.3	207.3	177.1	117.1	117.1	100.0
	2001	215.9	215.9	181.0	119.3	119.3	100.0
Saint Lucia	1970	7.0	9.4	32.9	21.2	28.7	73.9
	1975	11.5	14.3	41.5	27.6	34.4	80.2
	1980	27.2	27.2	51.6	52.6	52.6	100.0
	1985	39.3	39.3	67.5	58.1	58.1	100.0
	1990	100.0	100.0	100.0	100.0	100.0	100.0
	1991	107.6	107.6	100.6	107.0	107.0	100.0
	1992	119.5	119.5	107.9	110.8	110.8	100.0
	1993	119.6	119.6	108.2	110.5	110.5	100.0
	1994	124.6	124.6	109.7	113.6	113.6	100.0
	1995	133.1	133.1	110.8	120.1	120.1	100.0
	1996	137.3	137.3	114.0	120.4	120.4	100.0
	1997	139.0	139.0	113.1	122.9	122.9	100.0
	1998	150.8	150.8	118.4	127.4	127.4	100.0
	1999	164.5	164.5	122.5	134.2	134.2	100.0
	2000	170.3	170.3	123.4	138.1	138.1	100.0
	2001	176.3	176.3	124.0	142.2	142.2	100.0
Saint Vincent and the Grenadines	1970	6.9	9.3	41.5	16.6	22.5	73.8
	1975	13.3	16.6	40.2	33.1	41.2	80.3
	1980	29.9	29.9	55.6	53.7	53.7	100.0
	1985	56.9	56.9	73.2	77.8	77.8	100.0
	1990	100.0	100.0	100.0	100.0	100.0	100.0
	1991	107.1	107.1	100.2	106.9	106.9	100.0
	1992	117.8	117.8	108.1	108.9	108.9	100.0
	1993	120.4	120.4	110.1	109.3	109.3	100.0
	1994	122.6	122.6	106.8	114.8	114.8	100.0
	1995	133.1	133.1	115.9	114.9	114.9	100.0
	1996	140.6	140.6	117.2	120.0	120.0	100.0
	1997	148.2	148.2	120.7	122.8	122.8	100.0
	1998	160.4	160.4	127.8	125.5	125.5	100.0
	1999	166.4	166.4	133.0	125.0	125.0	100.0
	2000	169.2	169.2	135.0	125.3	125.3	100.0
	2001	175.7	175.7	135.2	129.9	129.9	100.0
Suriname	1970	16.8	23.1	70.7	23.7	32.7	72.5
	1975	29.4	42.7	83.6	35.1	51.1	68.7
	1980	50.1	73.0	91.3	54.9	79.9	68.7
	1985	55.1	80.2	100.6	54.8	79.7	68.8
	1990	100.0	100.0	100.0	100.0	100.0	100.0
	1991	118.3	103.4	103.4	114.4	100.0	114.4
	1992	161.2	84.8	100.7	160.1	84.2	190.1
	1993	347.0	70.5	93.4	371.6	75.5	492.2
	1994	2 025.9	39.2	96.4	2 101.3	40.7	5 162.9
	1995	7 240.1	42.5	96.8	7 478.4	43.9	17 035.1
	1996	9 589.0	62.1	98.8	9 702.0	62.8	15 449.0
	1997	10 732.5	69.5	105.4	10 186.8	66.0	15 434.5
	1998	12 843.2	83.2	108.1	11 882.3	77.0	15 431.6
	1999	23 940.2	72.3	106.6	22 448.4	67.8	33 109.7
	2000	36 978.7	72.6	105.6	35 031.4	68.8	50 917.7
	2001	57 861.8	69.0	110.7	52 261.7	62.3	83 887.2
Trinidad and Tobago	1970	7.6	16.2	76.2	10.0	21.3	46.9
	1975	24.6	48.2	87.1	28.2	55.3	51.0
	1980	69.5	123.0	127.3	54.6	96.7	56.5
	1985	83.9	145.5	112.0	74.9	129.9	57.7
	1990	100.0	100.0	100.0	100.0	100.0	100.0
	1991	104.7	104.7	102.7	102.0	102.0	100.0
	1992	107.3	107.3	101.0	106.3	106.3	100.0
	1993	113.7	90.3	99.5	114.2	90.7	125.9
	1994	136.1	97.6	103.1	132.0	94.7	139.4
	1995	147.2	105.2	107.2	137.3	98.1	140.0

Table 7. Implicit Price Deflators of Gross Domestic Product in US Dollars and in National Currency

(Index numbers 1990 = 100)

Region, country or area and currency unit	Year	GDP in Current Prices: National Currency (1)	GDP in Current Prices: US Dollars (2)	GDP at Constant Prices (3)	GDP Implicit Price Deflators: National Currency (4)	GDP Implicit Price Deflators: US Dollars (5)	Exchange Rates (6)
	1996	160.6	113.6	112.7	142.5	100.9	141.2
	1997	166.5	113.2	120.4	138.3	94.0	147.1
	1998	176.7	119.3	129.7	136.3	92.0	148.2
	1999	199.1	134.4	143.5	138.8	93.7	148.1
	2000	239.0	161.3	159.6	149.7	101.0	148.2
	2001	263.2	179.5	163.8	160.7	109.6	146.6
Uruguay	1970	-	27.5	70.9	-	38.7	-
	1975	0.1	41.4	76.6	0.1	54.0	0.2
	1980	0.9	115.2	95.5	0.9	120.7	0.7
	1985	4.9	56.6	83.3	5.9	67.9	8.7
	1990	100.0	100.0	100.0	100.0	100.0	100.0
	1991	207.2	120.1	103.2	200.8	116.4	172.5
	1992	398.1	153.9	112.6	353.7	136.7	258.7
	1993	604.3	179.3	115.5	523.2	155.2	337.1
	1994	900.9	208.9	123.9	726.9	168.5	431.4
	1995	1 252.3	230.7	122.1	1 025.4	188.9	542.8
	1996	1 671.6	245.2	128.9	1 296.6	190.2	681.7
	1997	2 094.5	259.4	135.3	1 548.3	191.8	807.2
	1998	2 394.4	267.4	141.0	1 698.7	189.7	895.5
	1999	2 423.8	164.9	137.5	1 762.2	119.9	1 469.7
	2000	2 483.9	162.6	135.6	1 832.3	119.9	1 528.2
	2001	2 526.7	157.1	131.0	1 928.5	119.9	1 608.4
Venezuela	1970	2.8	29.1	62.7	4.4	46.4	9.5
	1975	6.3	68.5	79.8	7.8	85.9	9.1
	1980	13.5	147.3	94.0	14.3	156.7	9.1
	1985	20.4	127.5	88.0	23.2	144.9	16.0
	1990	100.0	100.0	100.0	100.0	100.0	100.0
	1991	133.3	110.0	109.7	121.4	100.3	121.0
	1992	181.3	124.3	116.4	155.8	106.8	145.9
	1993	239.3	123.6	116.7	205.0	105.9	193.6
	1994	380.6	120.2	114.0	334.0	105.5	316.6
	1995	600.4	159.2	118.5	506.9	134.4	377.2
	1996	1 291.5	150.3	118.2	1 092.4	127.2	858.8
	1997	1 901.7	159.9	125.8	1 512.1	127.2	1 188.8
	1998	2 302.6	160.2	126.0	1 827.8	127.2	1 436.9
	1999	2 745.5	150.4	118.3	2 320.6	127.2	1 824.4
	2000	3 617.4	155.3	122.1	2 961.8	127.2	2 328.5
	2001	4 006.8	159.6	125.5	3 191.6	127.2	2 509.1
ASIA							
Afghanistan	1970	11.2	26.9	78.0	14.4	34.4	41.9
	1975	19.6	46.9	116.3	16.8	40.4	41.6
	1980	27.0	66.2	117.3	23.0	56.4	40.8
	1985	34.1	72.7	131.0	26.0	55.5	46.8
	1990	100.0	100.0	100.0	100.0	100.0	100.0
	1991	142.9	99.4	99.4	143.8	100.0	143.8
	1992	197.8	86.9	86.9	227.5	100.0	227.5
	1993	236.3	77.5	77.5	304.8	100.0	304.8
	1994	275.1	69.9	75.2	365.8	92.9	393.8
	1995	514.0	66.6	71.7	717.1	92.9	771.9
	1996	1 533.5	71.0	76.4	2 007.9	92.9	2 161.4
	1997	2 233.0	80.4	86.5	2 581.6	92.9	2 778.9
	1998	2 350.0	84.6	91.0	2 581.6	92.9	2 778.9
	1999	2 059.6	74.2	79.8	2 581.6	92.9	2 778.9
	2000	1 159.8	41.8	44.9	2 581.6	92.9	2 778.9
	2001	1 159.8	41.8	44.9	2 581.6	92.9	2 778.9
Armenia	1990	100.0	100.0	100.0	100.0	100.0	100.0
	1991	158.8	60.4	88.3	179.8	68.4	262.9
	1992	621.7	2.1	51.4	1 208.5	4.2	28 773.8
	1993	8 478.9	3.1	46.9	18 074.9	6.6	273 862.1
	1994	371 861.0	4.3	49.4	752 619.3	8.7	8 650 796.6
	1995	1 038 179.7	8.5	52.8	1 965 737.4	16.1	12 209 549.1
	1996	1 314 400.2	10.6	55.9	2 350 857.9	18.9	12 438 401.6
	1997	1 598 917.8	10.8	57.8	2 767 810.5	18.8	14 722 396.3
	1998	1 899 184.6	12.5	62.0	3 062 769.0	20.2	15 162 222.8
	1999	1 962 913.6	12.2	64.0	3 065 745.6	19.1	16 051 024.1
	2000	2 050 170.6	12.7	67.8	3 023 755.1	18.7	16 169 813.4
	2001	2 336 720.2	14.0	74.3	3 145 148.7	18.9	16 640 998.4
Azerbaijan	1990	100.0	100.0	100.0	100.0	100.0	100.0
	1991	182.3	69.4	99.3	183.5	69.9	262.5
	1992	1 644.0	2.0	76.9	2 139.0	2.6	82 269.2
	1993	10 715.0	7.1	59.1	18 129.2	12.1	149 828.1
	1994	127 789.0	5.4	47.5	269 103.7	11.4	2 360 558.8
	1995	727 762.6	11.0	41.9	1 737 934.0	26.2	6 633 335.9
	1996	932 005.5	14.4	42.4	2 198 109.7	34.0	6 465 028.5

Table 7. Implicit Price Deflators of Gross Domestic Product in US Dollars and in National Currency

(Index numbers 1990 = 100)

Region, country or area and currency unit	Year	GDP in Current Prices		GDP at Constant Prices	GDP Implicit Price Deflators		Exchange Rates
		National Currency (1)	US Dollars (2)	(3)	National Currency (4)	US Dollars (5)	(6)
	1997	1 077 176.0	18.0	44.9	2 401 097.8	40.1	5 987 775.1
	1998	1 173 472.0	20.2	49.3	2 378 684.1	40.9	5 815 853.5
	1999	1 287 544.3	20.8	53.0	2 430 091.5	39.3	6 183 438.9
	2000	1 609 174.6	24.0	58.9	2 733 687.8	40.7	6 716 677.6
	2001	1 796 855.4	25.7	64.7	2 777 541.1	39.7	6 996 325.2
Bahrain	1970	7.4	5.8	33.1	22.3	17.6	126.7
	1975	25.4	24.1	61.9	41.0	39.0	105.1
	1980	76.9	76.7	100.7	76.4	76.2	100.3
	1985	91.2	91.2	83.0	109.8	109.8	100.0
	1990	100.0	100.0	100.0	100.0	100.0	100.0
	1991	105.9	105.9	104.6	101.3	101.3	100.0
	1992	110.7	110.7	112.7	98.2	98.2	100.0
	1993	121.1	121.1	127.2	95.2	95.2	100.0
	1994	129.7	129.7	126.9	102.2	102.2	100.0
	1995	136.3	136.3	131.9	103.3	103.3	100.0
	1996	142.1	142.1	137.3	103.5	103.5	100.0
	1997	147.9	147.9	141.6	104.5	104.5	100.0
	1998	144.0	144.0	148.3	97.1	97.1	100.0
	1999	154.2	154.2	154.7	99.7	99.7	100.0
	2000	185.6	185.6	163.0	113.9	113.9	100.0
	2001	194.0	194.0	168.7	115.0	115.0	100.0
Bangladesh	1970	6.8	32.5	63.2	10.8	51.3	21.1
	1975	13.2	38.0	57.1	23.1	66.6	34.7
	1980	27.7	62.0	68.6	40.4	90.4	44.7
	1985	55.9	69.0	82.5	67.7	83.6	81.0
	1990	100.0	100.0	100.0	100.0	100.0	100.0
	1991	108.6	102.6	104.2	104.2	98.5	105.8
	1992	113.9	101.1	109.0	104.5	92.8	112.6
	1993	123.1	107.5	113.4	108.5	94.8	114.5
	1994	138.6	119.2	119.0	116.4	100.1	116.3
	1995	151.2	129.7	124.5	121.4	104.2	116.5
	1996	164.2	135.8	131.2	125.1	103.5	120.9
	1997	181.9	143.3	138.1	131.7	103.7	127.0
	1998	199.7	147.2	144.8	137.9	101.6	135.7
	1999	215.5	151.7	153.4	140.4	98.9	142.0
	2000	230.4	152.8	161.5	142.7	94.6	150.8
	2001	246.7	152.8	169.3	145.7	90.3	161.4
Bhutan	1970	6.9	16.2	23.9	29.0	67.7	42.8
	1975	17.5	36.5	30.7	56.8	118.7	47.9
	1980	22.0	48.9	49.2	44.7	99.4	45.0
	1985	48.0	67.9	68.3	70.3	99.5	70.7
	1990	100.0	100.0	100.0	100.0	100.0	100.0
	1991	110.4	85.0	103.5	106.7	82.1	130.0
	1992	127.5	86.1	108.2	117.9	79.6	148.1
	1993	144.3	82.9	114.7	125.8	72.2	174.2
	1994	172.3	96.2	122.1	141.2	78.8	179.2
	1995	202.0	109.0	131.1	154.0	83.1	185.3
	1996	237.0	117.1	138.0	171.7	84.8	202.5
	1997	287.3	138.5	148.4	193.6	93.3	207.5
	1998	327.9	139.1	157.9	207.6	88.1	235.6
	1999	383.8	156.0	169.6	226.3	92.0	246.0
	2000	435.4	169.6	179.3	242.9	94.6	256.8
	2001	484.2	179.6	189.9	255.0	94.6	269.6
Brunei Darussalam	1970	8.4	5.0	53.3	15.7	9.3	168.8
	1975	42.6	32.5	72.8	58.4	44.7	130.6
	1980	162.1	137.3	118.1	137.3	116.2	118.2
	1985	119.1	98.1	98.1	121.5	100.1	121.4
	1990	100.0	100.0	100.0	100.0	100.0	100.0
	1991	101.7	106.7	104.0	97.8	102.6	95.3
	1992	100.9	112.2	102.9	98.0	109.1	89.8
	1993	101.2	113.5	103.4	97.8	109.8	89.1
	1994	102.7	121.9	105.3	97.6	115.8	84.3
	1995	113.6	145.3	108.5	104.7	133.9	78.2
	1996	118.1	151.8	112.3	105.1	135.1	77.8
	1997	123.7	151.0	116.9	105.8	129.1	82.0
	1998	124.6	135.0	118.1	105.5	114.3	92.3
	1999	109.8	117.4	121.1	90.6	96.9	93.5
	2000	114.3	120.2	124.5	91.8	96.5	95.1
	2001	117.1	118.4	126.4	92.6	93.7	98.8
Cambodia	1970	1.5	154.7	219.0	0.7	70.7	1.0
	1975	1.2	127.6	149.1	0.8	85.6	0.9
	1980	1.2	121.3	104.4	1.1	116.2	0.9
	1985	2.3	140.1	91.2	2.6	153.6	1.7
	1990	100.0	100.0	100.0	100.0	100.0	100.0

Table 7. Implicit Price Deflators of Gross Domestic Product in US Dollars and in National Currency

(Index numbers 1990 = 100)

Region, country or area and currency unit	Year	GDP in Current Prices		GDP at Constant Prices	GDP Implicit Price Deflators		Exchange Rates
		National Currency (1)	US Dollars (2)	(3)	National Currency (4)	US Dollars (5)	(6)
	1991	223.2	132.8	107.6	207.4	123.4	168.1
	1992	419.0	138.4	115.1	363.8	120.2	302.7
	1993	904.4	140.7	119.9	754.5	117.4	642.7
	1994	941.3	154.7	129.1	729.3	119.9	608.3
	1995	1 120.8	191.3	136.7	819.9	139.9	586.1
	1996	1 227.9	195.7	143.0	858.7	136.9	627.2
	1997	1 351.2	191.8	149.1	906.0	128.6	704.5
	1998	1 570.3	175.4	152.3	1 030.8	115.1	895.6
	1999	1 739.4	191.1	162.8	1 068.4	117.4	910.1
	2000	1 787.0	194.6	175.3	1 019.6	111.0	918.6
	2001	1 846.9	197.3	186.4	991.0	105.8	936.7
China	1970	12.3	23.9	25.1	49.1	95.3	51.5
	1975	16.4	42.1	32.3	50.7	130.4	38.9
	1980	24.7	78.7	42.0	58.7	187.4	31.3
	1985	47.7	77.6	70.0	68.1	110.8	61.5
	1990	100.0	100.0	100.0	100.0	100.0	100.0
	1991	116.2	104.4	110.6	105.1	94.4	111.3
	1992	145.4	126.1	126.3	115.1	99.8	115.3
	1993	189.1	156.9	143.4	131.8	109.4	120.5
	1994	255.2	141.6	161.8	157.7	87.5	180.2
	1995	319.2	182.8	178.9	178.5	102.2	174.7
	1996	370.6	213.2	196.0	189.1	108.8	173.8
	1997	406.5	234.5	213.3	190.5	109.9	173.3
	1998	427.7	247.1	230.0	186.0	107.4	173.2
	1999	448.0	258.8	246.2	182.0	105.1	173.2
	2000	488.2	282.1	265.7	183.7	106.1	173.1
	2001	523.7	302.6	285.1	183.7	106.1	173.1
Cyprus	1970	9.0	9.8	38.2	23.4	25.8	90.7
	1975	10.2	12.6	31.8	31.9	39.6	80.6
	1980	29.7	38.6	54.5	54.6	70.9	77.0
	1985	57.9	43.3	71.6	80.9	60.5	133.7
	1990	100.0	100.0	100.0	100.0	100.0	100.0
	1991	104.7	103.2	100.7	103.9	102.5	101.4
	1992	121.4	123.7	110.1	110.2	112.3	98.1
	1993	128.1	118.0	110.9	115.5	106.4	108.6
	1994	142.8	132.9	117.3	121.7	113.2	107.5
	1995	156.8	158.7	124.5	125.9	127.5	98.7
	1996	162.8	159.9	126.9	128.3	126.1	101.7
	1997	171.0	152.4	130.0	131.5	117.2	112.2
	1998	183.6	162.4	136.4	134.7	119.1	113.1
	1999	196.3	165.7	142.6	137.7	116.1	118.6
	2000	214.7	158.0	149.9	143.2	105.4	135.9
	2001	229.5	163.4	155.9	147.2	104.8	140.5
Democratic People's Rep. of Korea	1970	17.3	17.0	17.3	99.8	98.4	101.4
	1975	30.4	29.9	30.4	99.8	98.4	101.4
	1980	52.3	51.6	52.4	99.8	98.4	101.4
	1985	83.7	82.6	83.9	99.8	98.4	101.4
	1990	100.0	100.0	100.0	100.0	100.0	100.0
	1991	92.2	93.1	94.9	97.2	98.1	99.1
	1992	80.2	82.9	87.6	91.5	94.6	96.7
	1993	68.0	69.9	84.5	80.4	82.7	97.2
	1994	54.6	55.9	82.8	65.9	67.5	97.6
	1995	30.6	31.2	79.4	38.6	39.3	98.2
	1996	62.4	63.0	76.5	81.6	82.4	99.0
	1997	60.9	61.4	71.7	84.9	85.7	99.1
	1998	60.6	61.1	70.9	85.5	86.3	99.1
	1999	60.6	61.2	75.3	80.5	81.3	99.0
	2000	62.6	63.1	76.3	82.0	82.8	99.0
	2001	65.0	65.6	79.1	82.2	82.9	99.2
Georgia	1990	100.0	100.0	100.0	100.0	100.0	100.0
	1991	127.9	48.7	78.9	162.2	61.7	262.9
	1992	924.1	3.2	43.5	2 126.4	7.3	29 128.8
	1993	1 843.6	10.0	30.7	5 998.9	32.5	18 458.2
	1994	120 723.9	7.3	27.5	438 352.6	26.5	1 654 160.8
	1995	246 809.2	12.6	28.3	873 651.5	44.8	1 950 115.0
	1996	257 026.4	13.6	31.4	818 181.7	43.2	1 893 939.1
	1997	309 956.6	15.9	34.7	892 366.5	45.8	1 948 398.5
	1998	336 825.9	16.1	35.7	942 615.7	45.2	2 085 433.0
	1999	378 616.8	12.5	36.8	1 029 146.9	33.9	3 035 831.6
	2000	401 971.3	13.5	37.5	1 071 950.0	36.1	2 969 390.6
	2001	442 185.1	14.2	39.3	1 126 457.4	36.2	3 111 760.8
Hong Kong SAR of China	1970	4.0	5.1	22.6	17.5	22.5	77.8
	1975	8.5	13.3	30.8	27.5	43.3	63.5
	1980	24.3	38.1	53.3	45.7	71.5	63.9

Table 7. Implicit Price Deflators of Gross Domestic Product in US Dollars and in National Currency

(Index numbers 1990 = 100)

Region, country or area and currency unit	Year	GDP in Current Prices: National Currency (1)	GDP in Current Prices: US Dollars (2)	GDP at Constant Prices (3)	GDP Implicit Price Deflators: National Currency (4)	GDP Implicit Price Deflators: US Dollars (5)	Exchange Rates (6)
	1985	46.6	46.6	69.8	66.8	66.8	100.0
	1990	100.0	100.0	100.0	100.0	100.0	100.0
	1991	114.8	115.0	105.1	109.2	109.5	99.7
	1992	133.8	134.6	111.6	119.8	120.6	99.3
	1993	154.3	155.4	118.7	130.0	130.9	99.3
	1994	174.1	175.5	125.2	139.0	140.1	99.2
	1995	185.3	186.6	130.1	142.5	143.4	99.4
	1996	204.7	206.2	135.7	150.9	152.0	99.3
	1997	227.3	228.7	142.6	159.4	160.4	99.4
	1998	216.4	217.6	135.5	159.7	160.6	99.4
	1999	210.7	211.5	140.1	150.3	151.0	99.5
	2000	217.8	217.8	154.4	141.1	141.1	100.0
	2001	216.2	216.0	155.4	139.2	139.0	100.1
India	1970	8.1	18.8	42.2	19.1	44.6	42.8
	1975	14.7	30.7	48.6	30.3	63.3	47.9
	1980	25.4	56.5	56.6	44.9	99.9	44.9
	1985	49.0	69.3	73.5	66.6	94.2	70.7
	1990	100.0	100.0	100.0	100.0	100.0	100.0
	1991	115.2	88.6	100.4	114.7	88.3	129.9
	1992	131.8	89.0	105.9	124.5	84.1	148.0
	1993	151.4	86.9	111.1	136.3	78.2	174.3
	1994	178.4	99.6	119.5	149.3	83.3	179.2
	1995	209.3	113.0	128.5	162.9	87.9	185.3
	1996	241.1	119.1	138.0	174.6	86.3	202.3
	1997	268.3	129.3	144.2	186.0	89.7	207.4
	1998	306.7	130.1	152.8	200.7	85.2	235.6
	1999	340.0	138.2	163.7	207.7	84.5	245.8
	2000	367.9	143.3	170.1	216.3	84.2	256.9
	2001	401.4	148.9	179.3	223.9	83.1	269.4
Indonesia	1970	1.5	7.8	25.2	6.1	30.9	19.7
	1975	6.0	26.6	37.2	16.1	71.6	22.5
	1980	21.6	63.3	54.4	39.6	116.4	34.0
	1985	46.0	76.3	71.6	64.3	106.7	60.3
	1990	100.0	100.0	100.0	100.0	100.0	100.0
	1991	118.5	112.0	108.9	108.8	102.8	105.8
	1992	133.9	121.6	116.8	114.7	104.1	110.2
	1993	156.4	138.1	125.3	124.8	110.2	113.2
	1994	181.3	154.6	134.7	134.6	114.8	117.2
	1995	215.5	176.6	145.8	147.9	121.2	122.0
	1996	252.6	198.7	157.2	160.7	126.4	127.1
	1997	297.7	188.5	164.6	180.9	114.6	157.9
	1998	453.3	83.4	143.0	317.0	58.3	543.7
	1999	521.5	122.4	144.1	361.9	84.9	426.3
	2000	608.0	133.0	151.2	402.2	88.0	457.0
	2001	707.1	127.0	156.2	452.8	81.3	556.9
Iran (Islamic Republic of)	1970	2.1	5.3	58.4	3.6	9.0	40.0
	1975	9.2	25.7	93.1	9.9	27.6	35.9
	1980	18.1	48.4	76.8	23.6	63.0	37.5
	1985	43.0	89.3	99.0	43.5	90.2	48.2
	1990	100.0	100.0	100.0	100.0	100.0	100.0
	1991	136.7	111.5	110.6	123.6	100.7	122.7
	1992	181.4	117.8	117.4	154.5	100.4	153.9
	1993	270.9	57.5	114.9	235.7	50.0	471.4
	1994	358.2	55.4	116.9	306.4	47.4	646.4
	1995	493.2	54.0	120.8	408.4	44.7	913.6
	1996	675.4	58.2	128.8	524.3	45.1	1 162.5
	1997	801.5	54.5	135.8	590.4	40.1	1 472.3
	1998	913.3	53.8	140.9	648.1	38.2	1 696.6
	1999	1 209.9	54.8	143.3	844.0	38.2	2 209.4
	2000	1 596.7	52.6	150.7	1 059.2	34.9	3 035.0
	2001	1 868.6	57.3	158.3	1 180.4	36.2	3 260.8
Iraq	1970	5.4	8.9	40.5	13.3	22.1	60.2
	1975	17.6	35.1	61.2	28.7	57.4	50.0
	1980	68.5	110.7	110.7	61.9	100.0	61.9
	1985	66.5	82.5	82.5	80.6	100.0	80.6
	1990	100.0	100.0	100.0	100.0	100.0	100.0
	1991	85.6	33.9	33.9	252.6	100.0	252.6
	1992	212.3	38.9	38.9	545.9	100.0	545.9
	1993	534.3	27.2	27.2	1 963.6	100.0	1 963.6
	1994	2 645.0	27.4	27.4	9 635.9	100.0	9 635.9
	1995	8 331.6	26.4	26.4	31 618.8	100.0	31 618.8
	1996	10 212.8	26.9	26.9	37 961.6	100.0	37 961.6
	1997	14 035.9	33.6	33.6	41 737.9	100.0	41 737.9
	1998	19 616.9	38.7	38.7	50 725.0	100.0	50 725.0

Table 7. Implicit Price Deflators of Gross Domestic Product in US Dollars and in National Currency

(Index numbers 1990 = 100)

Region, country or area and currency unit	Year	GDP in Current Prices		GDP at Constant Prices	GDP Implicit Price Deflators		Exchange Rates
		National Currency (1)	US Dollars (2)	(3)	National Currency (4)	US Dollars (5)	(6)
	1999	29 230.6	41.8	41.8	69 985.2	100.0	69 985.2
	2000	31 758.0	46.4	46.4	68 501.4	100.0	68 501.4
	2001	38 109.6	53.3	53.3	71 479.7	100.0	71 479.7
Israel	1970	-	10.5	42.3	-	24.8	-
	1975	-	25.1	61.1	-	41.1	-
	1980	0.1	41.1	69.7	0.1	58.9	0.2
	1985	27.4	46.8	80.9	33.9	57.9	58.5
	1990	100.0	100.0	100.0	100.0	100.0	100.0
	1991	128.7	113.8	107.3	119.9	106.1	113.0
	1992	154.6	126.8	115.3	134.1	109.9	122.0
	1993	178.4	127.1	119.7	149.1	106.2	140.4
	1994	214.0	143.3	128.4	166.7	111.6	149.4
	1995	248.2	166.2	137.2	180.9	121.1	149.4
	1996	287.8	181.8	144.1	199.7	126.2	158.2
	1997	322.5	188.5	148.5	217.2	126.9	171.2
	1998	354.0	187.8	152.8	231.6	122.9	188.4
	1999	387.2	188.6	157.0	246.5	120.1	205.2
	2000	422.0	208.7	169.6	248.9	123.1	202.2
	2001	425.9	204.2	168.1	253.4	121.5	208.6
Japan	1970	16.8	6.8	43.3	38.9	15.7	247.8
	1975	34.1	16.6	54.0	63.0	30.8	204.5
	1980	55.1	35.2	67.0	82.4	52.6	156.7
	1985	73.9	44.9	78.9	93.7	56.9	164.7
	1990	100.0	100.0	100.0	100.0	100.0	100.0
	1991	106.3	114.3	103.3	102.9	110.7	93.0
	1992	109.1	124.7	104.3	104.6	119.6	87.5
	1993	110.0	143.3	104.6	105.2	137.0	76.8
	1994	111.3	157.6	105.7	105.3	149.2	70.6
	1995	112.8	173.7	107.7	104.8	161.3	65.0
	1996	115.8	154.1	111.4	104.0	138.4	75.1
	1997	118.3	141.6	113.4	104.3	124.8	83.6
	1998	116.9	129.3	112.2	104.2	115.2	90.5
	1999	115.2	146.4	112.3	102.6	130.4	78.7
	2000	116.1	156.0	115.4	100.6	135.2	74.4
	2001	114.8	136.8	115.9	99.1	118.0	84.0
Jordan	1970	7.9	14.8	43.5	18.2	33.9	53.7
	1975	14.6	30.4	43.0	34.0	70.6	48.2
	1980	44.8	99.8	82.1	54.5	121.5	44.9
	1985	75.7	127.3	105.9	71.5	120.3	59.4
	1990	100.0	100.0	100.0	100.0	100.0	100.0
	1991	107.0	104.3	101.8	105.1	102.4	102.6
	1992	136.7	133.5	118.2	115.7	112.9	102.5
	1993	147.1	140.9	123.7	118.9	113.9	104.4
	1994	164.9	156.6	129.8	127.0	120.7	105.2
	1995	178.9	169.5	138.1	129.5	122.7	105.5
	1996	186.7	174.8	141.0	132.4	123.9	106.9
	1997	194.6	182.2	145.3	133.9	125.3	106.9
	1998	211.6	198.1	149.6	141.4	132.4	106.8
	1999	216.0	202.2	151.9	142.3	133.2	106.8
	2000	225.3	210.9	156.0	144.5	135.2	106.9
	2001	237.7	222.5	161.4	147.3	137.9	106.8
Kazakhstan	1990	100.0	100.0	100.0	100.0	100.0	100.0
	1991	179.4	68.3	88.7	202.2	77.0	262.6
	1992	2 543.7	8.8	84.0	3 028.8	10.4	29 123.1
	1993	30 732.0	16.3	76.2	40 317.1	21.4	188 397.7
	1994	442 306.5	16.6	66.6	663 912.6	24.9	2 666 315.7
	1995	1 059 305.8	23.2	61.2	1 732 072.7	37.9	4 570 112.7
	1996	1 478 728.8	29.3	61.5	2 405 842.4	47.6	5 054 290.8
	1997	1 746 527.1	30.8	62.5	2 794 042.6	49.3	5 667 429.2
	1998	1 810 367.0	30.8	61.3	2 952 264.8	50.2	5 881 005.6
	1999	2 106 157.6	23.5	63.0	3 344 329.8	37.3	8 966 031.6
	2000	2 715 557.2	25.4	69.1	3 927 126.2	36.8	10 671 538.6
	2001	3 395 194.6	30.8	78.5	4 325 982.1	39.3	11 007 588.0
Kuwait	1970	19.3	15.6	173.0	11.1	9.0	123.3
	1975	65.4	65.1	137.2	47.7	47.4	100.6
	1980	145.6	155.3	138.6	105.0	112.1	93.7
	1985	121.1	116.1	107.8	112.3	107.7	104.3
	1990	100.0	100.0	100.0	100.0	100.0	100.0
	1991	58.8	59.6	61.1	96.1	97.6	98.5
	1992	109.3	107.6	114.1	95.9	94.3	101.7
	1993	135.7	129.7	152.5	89.0	85.0	104.7
	1994	138.5	134.6	165.7	83.6	81.2	103.0
	1995	148.7	143.8	168.0	88.5	85.6	103.4
	1996	174.6	168.2	163.5	106.8	102.9	103.8

Table 7. Implicit Price Deflators of Gross Domestic Product in US Dollars and in National Currency

(Index numbers 1990 = 100)

Region, country or area and currency unit	Year	GDP in Current Prices: National Currency (1)	GDP in Current Prices: US Dollars (2)	GDP at Constant Prices (3)	GDP Implicit Price Deflators: National Currency (4)	GDP Implicit Price Deflators: US Dollars (5)	Exchange Rates (6)
	1997	170.0	161.7	165.4	102.8	97.8	105.1
	1998	143.7	136.0	170.6	84.2	79.7	105.6
	1999	166.8	158.0	162.2	102.8	97.4	105.5
	2000	206.3	194.0	145.9	141.4	133.0	106.3
	2001	188.8	177.5	144.2	130.9	123.1	106.3
Kyrgyzstan	1990	100.0	100.0	100.0	100.0	100.0	100.0
	1991	216.1	82.2	92.1	234.8	89.3	262.9
	1992	1 732.0	6.0	79.3	2 183.6	7.5	29 114.7
	1993	12 511.0	7.7	67.1	18 657.6	11.5	162 240.0
	1994	28 082.2	8.6	53.6	52 404.6	16.1	325 494.4
	1995	37 722.2	11.6	50.7	74 430.9	22.9	325 025.8
	1996	54 670.6	14.2	54.3	100 735.6	26.2	384 487.0
	1997	71 695.6	13.8	59.7	120 187.2	23.1	520 290.9
	1998	79 863.1	12.8	60.9	131 097.2	21.0	624 272.4
	1999	113 887.9	9.7	63.1	180 356.2	15.4	1 171 144.2
	2000	152 705.4	10.7	66.6	229 344.8	16.0	1 433 405.0
	2001	172 624.5	11.9	70.1	246 148.3	16.9	1 456 498.8
Lao People's Democratic Republic	1970	-	34.7	57.8	-	60.0	-
	1975	-	62.3	63.1	0.1	98.8	0.1
	1980	1.4	98.0	59.3	2.3	165.2	1.4
	1985	13.8	177.3	81.2	17.0	218.4	7.8
	1990	100.0	100.0	100.0	100.0	100.0	100.0
	1991	117.8	118.8	104.0	113.3	114.2	99.2
	1992	137.9	136.3	111.3	123.8	122.4	101.1
	1993	155.2	153.4	117.8	131.7	130.2	101.2
	1994	180.8	178.3	127.4	141.9	139.9	101.4
	1995	231.6	203.7	136.4	169.8	149.4	113.7
	1996	281.7	216.4	145.8	193.2	148.5	130.1
	1997	359.2	201.8	155.9	230.4	129.4	178.1
	1998	692.1	148.5	162.1	426.9	91.6	466.0
	1999	1 681.8	167.6	173.9	967.1	96.4	1 003.2
	2000	2 231.4	200.2	184.0	1 212.6	108.8	1 114.5
	2001	2 557.6	202.1	194.5	1 315.3	104.0	1 264.7
Lebanon	1970	0.2	52.9	243.0	0.1	21.8	0.5
	1975	0.4	115.9	260.2	0.1	44.5	0.2
	1980	0.7	144.9	225.1	0.3	64.4	0.5
	1985	1.5	65.0	136.0	1.1	47.8	2.3
	1990	100.0	100.0	100.0	100.0	100.0	100.0
	1991	197.2	147.6	138.3	142.6	106.8	133.5
	1992	478.9	194.4	144.5	331.4	134.5	246.4
	1993	671.6	268.1	154.6	434.3	173.4	250.5
	1994	767.1	317.4	167.0	459.3	190.0	241.7
	1995	909.7	390.0	177.9	511.5	219.3	233.2
	1996	1 030.8	455.9	185.0	557.2	246.5	226.0
	1997	1 125.6	508.2	191.5	587.9	265.5	221.4
	1998	1 204.4	552.2	197.2	610.7	280.0	218.1
	1999	1 295.9	597.4	205.1	631.9	291.3	216.9
	2000	1 328.3	612.5	209.2	635.0	292.8	216.9
	2001	1 388.1	640.0	215.5	644.2	297.0	216.9
Macao SAR of China	1970	4.0	5.4	23.3	17.4	23.0	75.7
	1975	9.0	14.1	33.6	26.8	42.0	63.8
	1980	20.1	31.6	48.4	41.5	65.2	63.7
	1985	41.8	42.0	67.1	62.4	62.6	99.7
	1990	100.0	100.0	100.0	100.0	100.0	100.0
	1991	115.9	116.1	103.7	111.8	112.0	99.8
	1992	151.0	151.9	117.4	128.6	129.4	99.4
	1993	172.7	173.9	123.5	139.8	140.7	99.4
	1994	191.5	193.0	128.8	148.7	149.8	99.3
	1995	211.4	212.9	133.0	158.9	160.0	99.3
	1996	211.2	212.7	132.5	159.5	160.6	99.3
	1997	213.5	214.8	132.1	161.6	162.6	99.4
	1998	198.3	199.4	126.1	157.3	158.2	99.4
	1999	187.3	188.0	122.2	153.2	153.8	99.6
	2000	190.0	190.0	127.9	148.6	148.5	100.1
	2001	190.3	190.0	130.6	145.7	145.5	100.1
Malaysia	1970	8.9	7.9	22.9	38.9	34.4	113.1
	1975	18.8	21.2	37.5	50.0	56.5	88.5
	1980	44.8	55.6	56.5	79.3	98.5	80.5
	1985	65.1	70.9	72.5	89.8	97.8	91.8
	1990	100.0	100.0	100.0	100.0	100.0	100.0
	1991	113.5	111.6	109.5	103.6	101.9	101.7
	1992	126.5	134.4	119.3	106.1	112.6	94.2
	1993	144.6	151.9	131.1	110.3	115.9	95.2
	1994	164.1	169.2	143.2	114.7	118.2	97.0

Table 7. Implicit Price Deflators of Gross Domestic Product in US Dollars and in National Currency

(Index numbers 1990 = 100)

Region, country or area and currency unit	Year	GDP in Current Prices: National Currency (1)	GDP in Current Prices: US Dollars (2)	GDP at Constant Prices (3)	GDP Implicit Price Deflators: National Currency (4)	GDP Implicit Price Deflators: US Dollars (5)	Exchange Rates (6)
	1995	186.8	201.8	157.2	118.8	128.3	92.6
	1996	213.1	229.1	173.0	123.2	132.4	93.1
	1997	236.6	227.5	185.6	127.5	122.6	104.0
	1998	237.9	163.9	172.0	138.3	95.3	145.1
	1999	252.6	179.8	182.5	138.4	98.5	140.5
	2000	287.3	204.5	197.7	145.3	103.4	140.5
	2001	281.0	200.0	198.6	141.5	100.7	140.5
Maldives	1970	3.6	7.2	10.7	33.7	67.8	49.7
	1975	7.4	12.2	18.1	40.7	67.4	60.4
	1980	17.3	21.8	33.6	51.3	64.9	79.0
	1985	28.9	38.9	60.8	47.6	64.0	74.4
	1990	100.0	100.0	100.0	100.0	100.0	100.0
	1991	121.0	112.8	107.7	112.4	104.7	107.4
	1992	145.6	131.6	114.4	127.3	115.0	110.7
	1993	170.8	148.9	121.4	140.7	122.6	114.8
	1994	200.2	165.1	129.5	154.6	127.5	121.3
	1995	228.8	185.7	138.7	165.0	133.9	123.2
	1996	263.1	213.5	150.9	174.3	141.5	123.2
	1997	292.4	237.3	167.8	174.3	141.4	123.3
	1998	308.6	250.5	164.0	188.2	152.7	123.2
	1999	324.9	263.6	176.2	184.4	149.6	123.3
	2000	341.5	277.1	184.3	185.3	150.4	123.2
	2001	346.9	270.7	188.1	184.4	143.9	128.1
Mongolia	1970	36.9	39.7	34.0	108.5	116.9	92.8
	1975	48.3	65.1	44.5	108.5	146.2	74.2
	1980	64.5	95.9	59.5	108.5	161.2	67.3
	1985	89.6	102.7	82.8	108.2	124.0	87.3
	1990	100.0	100.0	100.0	100.0	100.0	100.0
	1991	180.7	81.8	90.8	199.1	90.2	220.7
	1992	452.0	45.8	82.1	550.3	55.7	988.0
	1993	1 588.3	25.3	79.7	1 993.7	31.8	6 269.5
	1994	2 706.8	28.3	81.5	3 321.2	34.7	9 571.2
	1995	4 101.4	39.4	86.6	4 733.6	45.5	10 403.5
	1996	4 881.7	38.4	88.7	5 500.6	43.2	12 732.9
	1997	6 262.8	34.2	92.3	6 788.1	37.0	18 346.2
	1998	6 169.5	31.6	95.5	6 460.9	33.1	19 519.3
	1999	6 847.4	28.9	97.8	6 998.1	29.5	23 722.4
	2000	7 729.7	30.9	98.9	7 817.5	31.3	24 976.0
	2001	8 570.6	33.7	100.0	8 573.2	33.7	25 439.8
Myanmar	1970	8.9	15.0	58.0	15.3	25.9	59.1
	1975	15.5	19.5	66.2	23.3	29.5	79.0
	1980	25.4	31.0	88.3	28.8	35.1	82.1
	1985	36.8	35.0	111.4	33.1	31.4	105.4
	1990	100.0	100.0	100.0	100.0	100.0	100.0
	1991	122.9	99.3	99.3	123.7	100.0	123.7
	1992	164.1	108.9	108.9	150.7	100.0	150.7
	1993	237.1	115.5	115.5	205.3	100.0	205.3
	1994	311.2	124.2	124.2	250.6	100.0	250.6
	1995	398.0	132.8	132.8	299.7	100.0	299.7
	1996	521.2	141.3	141.3	368.8	100.0	368.8
	1997	730.3	149.3	149.3	489.0	100.0	489.0
	1998	1 026.7	156.7	156.7	655.1	100.0	655.1
	1999	1 063.0	165.7	165.7	641.5	100.0	641.5
	2000	1 236.5	174.8	174.8	707.5	100.0	707.5
	2001	1 490.7	183.1	183.1	813.9	100.0	813.9
Nepal	1970	9.5	27.5	51.3	18.5	53.7	34.5
	1975	16.0	42.8	56.1	28.6	76.3	37.5
	1980	22.6	55.3	63.0	35.9	87.7	40.9
	1985	45.0	72.5	80.0	56.3	90.7	62.1
	1990	100.0	100.0	100.0	100.0	100.0	100.0
	1991	116.4	91.8	106.4	109.4	86.3	126.8
	1992	144.5	99.4	110.7	130.5	89.7	145.5
	1993	165.8	100.2	115.0	144.2	87.1	165.6
	1994	192.7	114.6	124.4	154.8	92.1	168.1
	1995	211.9	120.0	128.8	164.6	93.2	176.6
	1996	240.7	124.7	135.6	177.5	91.9	193.1
	1997	271.2	137.3	142.5	190.4	96.4	197.5
	1998	290.9	129.5	145.8	199.5	88.8	224.7
	1999	330.7	142.3	151.9	217.8	93.7	232.4
	2000	365.5	151.0	161.7	226.1	93.4	242.1
	2001	394.7	154.7	169.6	232.7	91.2	255.2
Oman	1970	2.5	2.3	27.8	9.0	8.4	107.1
	1975	17.1	19.0	36.6	46.6	51.9	89.8
	1980	48.6	54.1	45.0	108.1	120.3	89.9

Table 7. Implicit Price Deflators of Gross Domestic Product in US Dollars and in National Currency

(Index numbers 1990 = 100)

Region, country or area and currency unit	Year	GDP in Current Prices: National Currency (1)	GDP in Current Prices: US Dollars (2)	GDP at Constant Prices (3)	GDP Implicit Price Deflators: National Currency (4)	GDP Implicit Price Deflators: US Dollars (5)	Exchange Rates (6)
	1985	79.9	89.0	86.8	92.1	102.5	89.9
	1990	100.0	100.0	100.0	100.0	100.0	100.0
	1991	97.1	97.1	106.0	91.5	91.5	100.0
	1992	106.6	106.6	115.1	92.6	92.6	100.0
	1993	106.9	106.9	122.1	87.6	87.6	100.0
	1994	110.5	110.5	126.8	87.2	87.2	100.0
	1995	118.1	118.1	132.9	88.9	88.9	100.0
	1996	130.7	130.7	136.8	95.6	95.6	100.0
	1997	135.5	135.5	145.2	93.3	93.3	100.0
	1998	120.5	120.5	149.2	80.8	80.8	100.0
	1999	134.5	134.5	148.8	90.3	90.4	99.9
	2000	170.0	170.0	157.0	108.3	108.3	100.0
	2001	170.7	170.7	171.6	99.5	99.5	100.0
Pakistan	1970	5.0	22.6	33.1	15.1	68.3	22.1
	1975	12.8	28.1	40.7	31.4	68.9	45.6
	1980	27.3	59.8	55.6	49.0	107.4	45.6
	1985	50.4	68.7	75.5	66.8	91.0	73.4
	1990	100.0	100.0	100.0	100.0	100.0	100.0
	1991	118.7	108.3	107.8	110.1	100.4	109.7
	1992	130.6	113.0	109.2	119.6	103.5	115.6
	1993	153.0	118.1	113.3	135.0	104.3	129.4
	1994	182.8	129.8	118.9	153.8	109.2	140.8
	1995	207.7	142.5	124.7	166.6	114.3	145.8
	1996	237.9	143.2	125.9	189.0	113.7	166.2
	1997	262.4	138.5	129.1	203.2	107.3	189.4
	1998	287.9	138.4	133.9	215.1	103.4	208.0
	1999	308.4	135.6	139.6	221.0	97.2	227.4
	2000	334.7	134.8	143.4	233.5	94.0	248.4
	2001	365.1	127.4	149.7	243.9	85.1	286.6
Philippines	1970	3.7	15.1	47.6	7.7	31.7	24.3
	1975	10.0	33.6	63.0	15.9	53.3	29.8
	1980	22.6	73.2	84.6	26.7	86.6	30.8
	1985	53.1	69.4	79.4	66.9	87.4	76.5
	1990	100.0	100.0	100.0	100.0	100.0	100.0
	1991	115.9	102.5	99.4	116.5	103.1	113.0
	1992	125.5	119.6	99.8	125.8	119.8	105.0
	1993	136.9	122.7	101.9	134.4	120.4	111.6
	1994	157.2	144.6	106.3	147.8	136.0	108.7
	1995	176.9	167.3	111.3	158.9	150.3	105.7
	1996	201.6	187.0	117.8	171.1	158.7	107.8
	1997	225.3	185.8	123.9	181.8	149.9	121.3
	1998	247.4	147.1	123.2	200.8	119.4	168.2
	1999	276.3	171.9	127.4	216.9	134.9	160.8
	2000	307.1	168.9	133.0	230.9	127.0	181.8
	2001	337.9	161.1	137.3	246.2	117.4	209.7
Qatar	1970	5.4	4.1	52.6	10.2	7.8	130.8
	1975	36.2	33.6	64.9	55.9	51.7	108.1
	1980	107.0	106.5	81.6	131.1	130.5	100.5
	1985	83.6	83.6	84.5	98.9	98.9	100.0
	1990	100.0	100.0	100.0	100.0	100.0	100.0
	1991	93.5	93.5	99.2	94.3	94.3	100.0
	1992	103.9	103.9	108.8	95.5	95.5	100.0
	1993	97.2	97.2	108.2	89.9	89.9	100.0
	1994	100.2	100.2	110.7	90.5	90.5	100.0
	1995	110.6	110.6	114.0	97.0	97.0	100.0
	1996	123.1	123.1	119.5	103.0	103.0	100.0
	1997	153.5	153.5	148.2	103.6	103.6	100.0
	1998	139.3	139.3	160.7	86.7	86.7	100.0
	1999	168.4	168.4	165.8	101.5	101.5	100.0
	2000	241.3	241.3	182.4	132.3	132.3	100.0
	2001	232.7	232.7	193.7	120.1	120.1	100.0
Republic of Korea	1970	1.5	3.5	21.3	7.1	16.3	43.6
	1975	5.7	8.4	31.2	18.3	26.8	68.3
	1980	21.1	24.6	43.6	48.4	56.4	85.8
	1985	45.5	37.0	63.6	71.5	58.2	122.9
	1990	100.0	100.0	100.0	100.0	100.0	100.0
	1991	121.1	116.9	109.2	110.9	107.0	103.6
	1992	137.4	124.6	115.2	119.3	108.2	110.3
	1993	155.2	136.9	121.5	127.7	112.6	113.4
	1994	180.9	159.3	131.5	137.5	121.2	113.4
	1995	211.0	193.7	143.2	147.3	135.2	108.9
	1996	234.1	205.9	152.9	153.1	134.7	113.7
	1997	253.5	188.6	160.6	157.9	117.5	134.4
	1998	248.5	125.5	149.8	165.9	83.8	198.0

Table 7. Implicit Price Deflators of Gross Domestic Product in US Dollars and in National Currency

(Index numbers 1990 = 100)

Region, country or area and currency unit	Year	GDP in Current Prices		GDP at Constant Prices	GDP Implicit Price Deflators		Exchange Rates
		National Currency (1)	US Dollars (2)	(3)	National Currency (4)	US Dollars (5)	(6)
	1999	270.0	160.7	166.2	162.5	96.7	168.0
	2000	291.9	182.7	181.7	160.7	100.6	159.7
	2001	308.5	169.1	187.3	164.7	90.3	182.4
Saudi Arabia	1970	5.8	4.9	58.0	10.1	8.4	120.2
	1975	42.0	44.7	100.5	41.8	44.5	93.9
	1980	125.2	141.0	147.7	84.8	95.5	88.8
	1985	80.1	82.8	89.1	89.9	93.0	96.7
	1990	100.0	100.0	100.0	100.0	100.0	100.0
	1991	112.8	112.8	109.8	102.7	102.7	100.0
	1992	117.7	117.7	112.8	104.3	104.3	100.0
	1993	113.2	113.2	112.1	101.0	101.0	100.0
	1994	114.8	114.8	112.7	101.9	101.9	100.0
	1995	122.1	122.1	113.2	107.8	107.8	100.0
	1996	150.7	150.7	114.8	131.3	131.3	100.0
	1997	157.6	157.6	117.8	133.8	133.8	100.0
	1998	139.5	139.5	121.1	115.1	115.1	100.0
	1999	154.0	154.0	120.1	128.2	128.2	100.0
	2000	180.3	180.3	126.0	143.1	143.1	100.0
	2001	178.2	178.2	127.5	139.8	139.8	100.0
Singapore	1970	8.6	5.1	20.9	40.9	24.2	169.0
	1975	19.8	15.1	32.9	60.2	46.0	130.9
	1980	37.0	31.3	49.5	74.7	63.2	118.2
	1985	57.3	47.2	66.8	85.8	70.7	121.4
	1990	100.0	100.0	100.0	100.0	100.0	100.0
	1991	111.3	116.7	107.3	103.7	108.8	95.3
	1992	117.8	131.0	111.7	105.4	117.3	89.9
	1993	137.3	154.0	125.9	109.0	122.3	89.1
	1994	157.1	186.4	140.3	112.0	132.9	84.3
	1995	173.5	221.9	151.5	114.5	146.4	78.2
	1996	188.9	242.9	163.1	115.8	148.9	77.8
	1997	206.7	252.3	177.1	116.7	142.5	81.9
	1998	202.7	219.6	176.9	114.6	124.1	92.3
	1999	206.4	220.7	189.2	109.1	116.7	93.5
	2000	235.5	247.7	208.6	112.9	118.7	95.1
	2001	226.1	228.7	204.3	110.7	111.9	98.9
Sri Lanka	1970	4.5	30.0	43.3	10.3	69.2	14.9
	1975	8.5	48.6	50.6	16.8	96.1	17.5
	1980	21.5	52.1	66.1	32.5	78.8	41.2
	1985	49.6	73.2	84.8	58.6	86.4	67.8
	1990	100.0	100.0	100.0	100.0	100.0	100.0
	1991	116.3	112.6	104.8	111.0	107.4	103.4
	1992	132.7	121.3	109.4	121.3	110.8	109.5
	1993	157.2	130.3	117.0	134.4	111.4	120.6
	1994	182.2	147.7	123.6	147.4	119.5	123.3
	1995	208.4	162.9	130.4	159.8	124.9	127.9
	1996	242.7	175.9	135.3	179.3	130.0	137.9
	1997	280.3	190.3	144.0	194.6	132.1	147.3
	1998	318.1	197.8	150.9	210.8	131.1	160.8
	1999	346.4	196.5	157.4	220.0	124.8	176.3
	2000	391.6	203.8	166.8	234.8	122.1	192.3
	2001	436.6	195.7	164.5	265.4	118.9	223.2
Syrian Arab Republic	1970	2.6	12.5	35.3	7.2	35.4	20.3
	1975	7.7	39.0	65.8	11.7	59.3	19.7
	1980	19.1	91.1	91.0	21.0	100.2	21.0
	1985	31.0	105.0	105.0	29.5	100.0	29.5
	1990	100.0	100.0	100.0	100.0	100.0	100.0
	1991	116.1	107.9	107.9	107.6	100.0	107.6
	1992	138.5	122.4	122.4	113.1	100.0	113.1
	1993	154.2	128.8	128.8	119.7	100.0	119.7
	1994	188.6	138.1	138.1	136.6	100.0	136.6
	1995	212.8	147.8	147.8	144.0	100.0	144.0
	1996	257.5	162.3	162.3	158.7	100.0	158.7
	1997	277.9	170.4	170.4	163.0	100.0	163.0
	1998	294.6	182.0	182.0	161.9	100.0	161.9
	1999	305.3	175.5	175.5	173.9	100.0	173.9
	2000	336.9	176.6	176.6	190.8	100.0	190.8
	2001	353.2	182.6	182.6	193.5	100.0	193.5
Tajikistan	1990	100.0	100.0	100.0	100.0	100.0	100.0
	1991	183.6	69.9	91.5	200.6	76.3	262.9
	1992	88.4	23.8	62.0	142.6	38.5	370.4
	1993	96.9	6.2	51.9	186.8	12.0	1 556.7
	1994	244.7	6.7	40.8	599.6	16.3	3 678.5
	1995	956.2	5.2	35.8	2 674.4	14.5	18 444.1
	1996	4 226.0	9.5	29.8	14 190.4	32.0	44 345.0

Table 7. Implicit Price Deflators of Gross Domestic Product in US Dollars and in National Currency

(Index numbers 1990 = 100)

Region, country or area and currency unit	Year	GDP in Current Prices: National Currency (1)	GDP in Current Prices: US Dollars (2)	GDP at Constant Prices (3)	GDP Implicit Price Deflators: National Currency (4)	GDP Implicit Price Deflators: US Dollars (5)	Exchange Rates (6)
	1997	7 101.4	8.4	30.3	23 446.4	27.8	84 339.6
	1998	14 043.8	12.0	31.9	44 034.0	37.8	116 492.1
	1999	18 423.3	9.9	33.1	55 705.6	30.0	185 685.3
	2000	24 750.7	7.9	35.8	69 101.6	22.2	311 268.5
	2001	34 412.3	9.7	39.5	87 183.3	24.5	355 850.2
Thailand	1970	6.8	8.4	24.4	27.8	34.2	81.3
	1975	14.0	17.5	32.1	43.6	54.7	79.7
	1980	30.3	37.9	47.0	64.6	80.7	80.0
	1985	48.4	45.6	61.2	79.0	74.4	106.2
	1990	100.0	100.0	100.0	100.0	100.0	100.0
	1991	114.8	115.1	108.6	105.7	106.0	99.7
	1992	129.6	130.6	117.4	110.5	111.3	99.3
	1993	144.9	146.4	127.0	114.1	115.3	99.0
	1994	166.2	169.1	138.5	120.0	122.1	98.3
	1995	191.7	196.8	151.2	126.7	130.1	97.4
	1996	211.1	213.2	160.2	131.8	133.1	99.0
	1997	216.7	176.8	158.0	137.2	111.9	122.6
	1998	211.8	131.0	141.4	149.8	92.7	161.6
	1999	212.1	143.5	147.6	143.7	97.2	147.8
	2000	224.6	143.2	154.5	145.4	92.7	156.9
	2001	233.5	134.5	157.3	148.5	85.5	173.7
Timor-Leste	1990	100.0	100.0	100.0	100.0	100.0	100.0
	1991	112.0	112.0	112.2	99.8	99.8	100.0
	1992	121.6	121.6	121.7	99.9	99.9	100.0
	1993	138.1	138.1	139.2	99.2	99.2	100.0
	1994	154.6	154.6	157.6	98.1	98.1	100.0
	1995	174.4	174.4	172.5	101.1	101.1	100.0
	1996	203.6	203.6	191.1	106.5	106.5	100.0
	1997	212.3	212.3	199.1	106.6	106.6	100.0
	1998	207.7	207.7	194.8	106.6	106.6	100.0
	1999	126.2	126.2	196.5	64.2	64.2	100.0
	2000	145.4	145.4	205.9	70.7	70.7	100.0
	2001	172.5	172.5	236.7	72.9	72.9	100.0
Turkey	1970	0.1	11.9	40.4	0.1	29.4	0.3
	1975	0.2	31.0	53.5	0.3	57.9	0.5
	1980	1.3	45.7	60.2	2.2	75.9	2.9
	1985	8.9	44.6	76.3	11.7	58.5	20.0
	1990	100.0	100.0	100.0	100.0	100.0	100.0
	1991	160.3	100.2	100.9	158.8	99.3	159.9
	1992	278.2	105.6	107.0	260.1	98.7	263.5
	1993	504.2	119.7	115.6	436.3	103.6	421.1
	1994	984.2	86.7	109.3	900.7	79.4	1 134.4
	1995	1 974.9	112.4	117.1	1 686.2	95.9	1 758.3
	1996	3 758.2	120.4	125.3	2 998.8	96.1	3 120.5
	1997	7 336.3	126.0	134.8	5 443.9	93.5	5 822.4
	1998	13 286.8	132.9	138.9	9 563.8	95.7	9 993.5
	1999	19 695.5	122.7	132.4	14 877.4	92.7	16 049.0
	2000	31 695.7	132.2	142.1	22 300.7	93.0	23 979.2
	2001	46 153.0	98.2	131.6	35 063.0	74.6	47 001.3
Turkmenistan	1990	100.0	100.0	100.0	100.0	100.0	100.0
	1991	193.4	73.6	95.3	203.0	77.2	263.0
	1992	10.5	36.3	81.0	13.0	44.8	29.0
	1993	131.8	50.2	82.2	160.3	61.0	262.8
	1994	1 146.5	39.8	68.0	1 686.2	58.5	2 882.4
	1995	8 579.5	51.5	63.1	13 596.7	81.6	16 662.6
	1996	101 996.8	20.9	67.3	151 492.3	31.0	488 684.8
	1997	146 168.2	23.5	59.7	245 032.3	39.4	621 909.4
	1998	184 141.3	25.1	62.6	293 989.9	40.0	734 974.8
	1999	263 894.7	33.8	72.7	363 206.8	46.5	781 089.9
	2000	337 473.7	43.2	85.4	394 962.4	50.6	780 558.1
	2001	445 565.8	57.1	103.0	432 753.6	55.4	781 143.7
United Arab Emirates	1970	2.5	2.0	5.0	51.3	39.6	129.5
	1975	31.8	29.5	46.8	68.0	63.0	107.9
	1980	88.6	87.7	97.5	90.8	89.9	101.0
	1985	80.2	80.2	89.0	90.1	90.1	100.0
	1990	100.0	100.0	100.0	100.0	100.0	100.0
	1991	100.4	100.4	100.2	100.2	100.2	100.0
	1992	103.5	103.5	103.0	100.5	100.5	100.0
	1993	104.5	104.5	102.1	102.3	102.3	100.0
	1994	111.9	111.9	104.4	107.2	107.2	100.0
	1995	125.2	125.2	111.8	112.0	112.0	100.0
	1996	140.3	140.3	123.4	113.7	113.7	100.0
	1997	144.3	144.3	125.8	114.7	114.7	100.0
	1998	135.9	135.9	117.0	116.2	116.2	100.0

Table 7. Implicit Price Deflators of Gross Domestic Product in US Dollars and in National Currency

(Index numbers 1990 = 100)

Region, country or area and currency unit	Year	GDP in Current Prices		GDP at Constant Prices	GDP Implicit Price Deflators		Exchange Rates
		National Currency (1)	US Dollars (2)	(3)	National Currency (4)	US Dollars (5)	(6)
	1999	147.4	147.3	119.9	122.9	122.9	100.0
	2000	157.9	157.8	126.4	124.9	124.9	100.0
	2001	168.9	168.9	132.7	127.3	127.3	100.0
Uzbekistan	1990	100.0	100.0	100.0	100.0	100.0	100.0
	1991	189.8	72.2	99.5	190.7	72.6	262.7
	1992	1 368.8	4.7	88.5	1 547.4	5.3	29 196.2
	1993	15 764.7	11.3	86.4	18 241.8	13.1	139 250.4
	1994	200 054.3	13.4	81.9	244 185.6	16.3	1 498 071.2
	1995	933 664.2	20.9	81.2	1 149 977.4	25.7	4 474 620.2
	1996	1 723 933.4	28.7	82.6	2 087 844.4	34.7	6 016 842.7
	1997	3 012 118.4	31.9	86.9	3 467 639.5	36.7	9 448 609.0
	1998	4 366 812.5	30.8	90.7	4 815 328.8	33.9	14 204 509.7
	1999	6 563 859.7	35.1	94.7	6 932 984.1	37.1	18 687 288.7
	2000	10 038 852.9	28.3	98.3	10 215 218.4	28.8	35 469 508.3
	2001	15 012 025.9	21.7	102.7	14 617 953.7	21.2	68 952 611.8
Vietnam	1970	-	61.6	61.9	-	99.6	-
	1975	-	62.9	56.0	-	112.3	-
	1980	-	65.7	58.4	0.1	112.6	0.1
	1985	0.3	90.5	80.8	0.4	112.0	0.4
	1990	100.0	100.0	100.0	100.0	100.0	100.0
	1991	182.8	118.1	106.0	172.5	111.4	154.8
	1992	263.5	152.5	115.1	228.8	132.4	172.8
	1993	334.3	203.7	124.4	268.7	163.7	164.1
	1994	425.5	251.6	135.4	314.3	185.8	169.2
	1995	545.6	320.4	148.3	367.8	216.0	170.3
	1996	648.4	381.0	162.2	399.8	234.9	170.2
	1997	747.5	426.6	175.4	426.2	243.2	175.2
	1998	860.5	424.3	185.5	463.8	228.7	202.8
	1999	953.3	443.2	194.4	490.4	228.0	215.1
	2000	1 058.6	484.4	207.5	510.2	233.4	218.6
	2001	1 156.3	509.0	221.7	521.5	229.6	227.1
Yemen	1990	100.0	100.0	100.0	100.0	100.0	100.0
	1991	118.2	96.4	100.3	117.8	96.1	122.6
	1992	147.8	120.6	105.2	140.4	114.6	122.5
	1993	183.4	149.6	109.5	167.5	136.7	122.5
	1994	235.8	192.4	111.9	210.7	172.0	122.5
	1995	393.2	94.4	124.0	317.1	76.1	416.7
	1996	566.6	59.0	131.3	431.5	44.9	961.0
	1997	683.9	51.8	141.9	481.8	36.5	1 320.0
	1998	653.5	47.1	148.9	438.9	31.7	1 384.5
	1999	871.5	54.8	154.4	564.4	35.5	1 589.9
	2000	1 061.7	64.3	162.3	654.1	39.6	1 651.8
	2001	1 042.3	60.6	169.8	613.8	35.7	1 719.3
EUROPE							
Albania	1970	38.5	59.7	48.3	79.8	123.7	64.5
	1975	68.2	105.6	64.8	105.2	163.0	64.5
	1980	92.4	102.2	88.5	104.4	115.5	90.4
	1985	100.3	110.9	97.9	102.4	113.3	90.4
	1990	100.0	100.0	100.0	100.0	100.0	100.0
	1991	97.6	46.5	72.0	135.5	64.6	209.8
	1992	301.5	31.1	66.8	451.2	46.6	968.2
	1993	745.5	56.6	73.2	1 018.2	77.3	1 317.2
	1994	1 096.7	89.8	79.3	1 383.2	113.2	1 221.9
	1995	1 366.8	114.2	89.9	1 521.1	127.1	1 196.8
	1996	1 671.3	123.9	98.0	1 704.9	126.4	1 348.8
	1997	2 032.5	105.7	91.1	2 229.8	116.0	1 922.2
	1998	2 739.7	140.9	98.4	2 783.8	143.1	1 945.4
	1999	3 010.8	169.4	105.6	2 852.2	160.5	1 777.1
	2000	3 207.1	172.9	113.8	2 819.4	152.0	1 854.9
	2001	3 510.6	189.5	120.0	2 924.7	157.9	1 852.2
Andorra	1970	2.1	3.1	21.4	10.0	14.6	68.5
	1975	6.4	11.3	35.9	17.7	31.5	56.2
	1980	20.8	29.6	51.1	40.7	57.9	70.3
	1985	47.9	28.7	68.3	70.0	42.0	166.7
	1990	100.0	100.0	100.0	100.0	100.0	100.0
	1991	114.7	112.5	107.2	106.9	104.9	101.9
	1992	129.8	129.2	113.7	114.1	113.6	100.4
	1993	141.4	113.3	118.5	119.3	95.5	124.9
	1994	158.4	120.5	127.8	123.9	94.3	131.4
	1995	179.5	146.7	138.0	130.0	106.3	122.3
	1996	199.7	160.7	148.3	134.6	108.3	124.3
	1997	222.6	155.0	161.6	137.7	95.9	143.6
	1998	248.8	169.8	176.4	141.0	96.2	146.6

Table 7. Implicit Price Deflators of Gross Domestic Product in US Dollars and in National Currency

(Index numbers 1990 = 100)

Region, country or area and currency unit	Year	GDP in Current Prices		GDP at Constant Prices	GDP Implicit Price Deflators		Exchange Rates
		National Currency (1)	US Dollars (2)	(3)	National Currency (4)	US Dollars (5)	(6)
	1999	278.5	181.8	192.0	145.1	94.7	153.2
	2000	313.2	176.8	208.7	150.0	84.7	177.1
	2001	349.3	191.5	224.0	155.9	85.5	182.3
Austria	1970	21.1	9.2	55.4	38.1	16.6	229.5
	1975	36.8	24.0	67.2	54.8	35.8	153.1
	1980	55.9	49.1	79.0	70.8	62.2	113.8
	1985	75.4	41.5	85.3	88.4	48.6	181.9
	1990	100.0	100.0	100.0	100.0	100.0	100.0
	1991	107.2	104.4	103.3	103.8	101.0	102.8
	1992	113.6	117.6	105.7	107.5	111.2	96.7
	1993	117.5	114.8	106.1	110.7	108.2	102.3
	1994	123.8	123.2	108.9	113.7	113.2	100.4
	1995	129.0	145.4	110.7	116.5	131.4	88.7
	1996	133.3	143.1	112.9	118.0	126.8	93.1
	1997	136.6	127.2	114.7	119.1	111.0	107.3
	1998	142.7	131.0	119.2	119.7	110.0	108.8
	1999	147.6	129.9	122.5	120.5	106.1	113.6
	2000	155.0	118.0	126.8	122.2	93.1	131.3
	2001	158.6	117.2	127.6	124.2	91.9	135.1
Belarus	1990	100.0	100.0	100.0	100.0	100.0	100.0
	1991	201.2	76.6	98.6	204.0	77.6	262.9
	1992	2 135.1	7.4	89.1	2 396.2	8.3	28 869.9
	1993	227 556.6	10.3	82.4	276 272.0	12.5	2 210 176.0
	1994	410 928.4	9.1	72.7	564 900.4	12.5	4 519 203.2
	1995	2 803 755.2	16.2	65.1	4 303 973.4	24.9	17 285 033.7
	1996	4 430 466.5	22.3	67.0	6 617 367.8	33.3	19 871 975.4
	1997	8 471 826.8	21.7	74.6	11 356 495.0	29.1	39 025 756.0
	1998	16 216 191.7	23.4	80.9	20 045 130.1	28.9	69 360 311.8
	1999	69 885 997.7	18.7	83.7	83 507 506.8	22.4	372 801 369.6
	2000	210 942 263.3	16.0	88.5	238 267 170.4	18.1	1 316 393 206.6
	2001	396 609 699.8	19.0	92.7	427 771 945.9	20.5	2 086 692 419.0
Belgium	1970	19.5	13.0	58.8	33.1	22.1	149.8
	1975	35.2	32.0	70.1	50.2	45.6	110.1
	1980	54.1	61.8	82.0	66.0	75.4	87.5
	1985	74.7	42.0	85.9	86.9	48.9	177.7
	1990	100.0	100.0	100.0	100.0	100.0	100.0
	1991	104.8	102.5	101.8	102.9	100.7	102.2
	1992	110.0	114.3	103.4	106.4	110.6	96.2
	1993	113.3	109.4	102.4	110.7	106.9	103.6
	1994	119.4	119.3	105.7	113.0	112.9	100.1
	1995	123.8	140.3	108.2	114.4	129.7	88.2
	1996	126.7	136.8	109.5	115.7	124.9	92.6
	1997	133.0	124.2	113.4	117.2	109.5	107.0
	1998	137.9	127.0	115.7	119.2	109.7	108.7
	1999	144.3	127.3	119.4	120.8	106.6	113.3
	2000	151.5	115.6	123.8	122.4	93.4	131.0
	2001	155.7	115.4	124.8	124.8	92.5	134.9
Bosnia and Herzegovina	1990	100.0	100.0	100.0	100.0	100.0	100.0
	1991	191.7	110.5	87.9	218.1	125.7	173.5
	1992	324.2	10.6	65.0	499.1	16.3	3 062.0
	1993	28 060.7	9.4	47.4	59 175.6	19.8	298 866.7
	1994	57 333.8	8.4	50.5	113 528.6	16.6	683 907.2
	1995	192 883.2	15.6	67.2	287 168.6	23.2	1 237 795.7
	1996	278 083.4	21.0	100.8	276 011.0	20.8	1 326 976.0
	1997	425 465.1	27.8	128.8	330 433.7	21.6	1 529 785.6
	1998	494 618.5	31.8	158.5	312 081.5	20.1	1 552 644.3
	1999	580 081.0	35.7	185.4	312 877.8	19.3	1 621 128.5
	2000	635 972.7	33.9	205.3	309 728.3	16.5	1 877 141.2
	2001	690 880.1	35.8	220.5	313 373.4	16.2	1 934 403.7
Bulgaria	1970	28.9	54.0	41.5	69.5	130.0	53.5
	1975	39.2	71.5	60.6	64.7	118.1	54.8
	1980	56.8	96.5	81.6	69.6	118.2	58.9
	1985	71.8	152.7	97.9	73.3	155.9	47.0
	1990	100.0	100.0	100.0	100.0	100.0	100.0
	1991	299.0	36.8	89.0	333.5	41.1	811.4
	1992	442.5	41.5	83.1	532.1	49.9	1 066.3
	1993	658.6	52.3	81.9	804.0	63.8	1 260.2
	1994	1 157.9	46.8	83.4	1 388.2	56.2	2 470.1
	1995	1 939.5	63.2	85.8	2 260.7	73.7	3 067.4
	1996	3 880.1	47.8	77.7	4 991.9	61.5	8 116.9
	1997	38 406.3	50.0	73.4	52 328.7	68.1	76 841.0
	1998	49 396.9	61.5	76.3	64 710.4	80.5	80 385.6

Table 7. Implicit Price Deflators of Gross Domestic Product in US Dollars and in National Currency

(Index numbers 1990 = 100)

Region, country or area and currency unit	Year	GDP in Current Prices: National Currency (1)	GDP in Current Prices: US Dollars (2)	GDP at Constant Prices (3)	GDP Implicit Price Deflators: National Currency (4)	GDP Implicit Price Deflators: US Dollars (5)	Exchange Rates (6)
	1999	52 413.5	62.5	78.1	67 117.5	80.0	83 896.9
	2000	58 940.1	60.8	82.3	71 613.8	73.9	96 906.4
	2001	65 252.8	65.4	85.6	76 211.5	76.4	99 753.3
Croatia	1990	100.0	100.0	100.0	100.0	100.0	100.0
	1991	157.3	90.7	78.9	199.3	114.9	173.5
	1992	964.9	41.3	69.7	1 385.0	59.3	2 335.6
	1993	13 904.9	44.0	64.1	21 700.3	68.7	31 587.0
	1994	31 173.3	58.9	67.8	45 952.2	86.8	52 940.3
	1995	35 073.8	75.9	72.5	48 394.6	104.8	46 178.1
	1996	38 495.8	80.2	76.7	50 160.5	104.5	48 000.5
	1997	44 139.3	81.9	82.0	53 852.1	99.9	53 906.0
	1998	49 056.6	87.3	84.0	58 391.7	103.9	56 199.9
	1999	50 473.8	80.3	83.3	60 624.3	96.5	62 823.1
	2000	54 373.9	74.4	85.7	63 468.1	86.8	73 119.9
	2001	58 078.1	78.8	88.9	65 315.1	88.7	73 636.0
Czech Republic	1980	73.2	92.1	87.0	84.2	105.9	79.5
	1985	83.5	87.4	92.4	90.3	94.6	95.5
	1990	100.0	100.0	100.0	100.0	100.0	100.0
	1991	120.4	73.3	88.4	136.2	82.9	164.3
	1992	134.6	85.5	87.9	153.0	97.2	157.4
	1993	162.9	100.3	88.0	185.2	114.0	162.5
	1994	188.9	117.8	89.9	210.0	131.0	160.3
	1995	220.5	149.2	95.3	231.5	156.5	147.9
	1996	250.2	165.5	99.4	251.8	166.5	151.2
	1997	268.3	151.9	98.6	272.0	154.0	176.6
	1998	293.7	163.3	97.6	301.0	167.3	179.9
	1999	303.8	157.7	98.0	309.8	160.9	192.5
	2000	317.0	147.4	101.2	313.1	145.6	215.0
	2001	347.4	163.9	104.4	332.9	157.1	211.9
Denmark	1970	14.8	12.2	70.7	20.9	17.3	120.8
	1975	27.1	29.2	76.1	35.5	38.3	92.7
	1980	46.7	51.3	85.6	54.6	60.0	91.0
	1985	76.8	44.9	93.9	81.8	47.8	171.1
	1990	100.0	100.0	100.0	100.0	100.0	100.0
	1991	103.9	100.5	101.1	102.8	99.4	103.4
	1992	107.6	110.3	101.7	105.7	108.4	97.5
	1993	109.1	104.1	101.7	107.2	102.3	104.8
	1994	117.0	113.8	107.3	109.1	106.1	102.8
	1995	122.3	135.2	110.2	111.0	122.6	90.5
	1996	128.5	137.2	113.0	113.7	121.4	93.7
	1997	135.3	126.7	116.4	116.2	108.9	106.7
	1998	140.0	129.3	119.3	117.4	108.4	108.3
	1999	146.3	129.8	122.4	119.6	106.1	112.7
	2000	155.2	118.8	125.9	123.2	94.3	130.6
	2001	160.6	119.4	127.7	125.7	93.5	134.4
Estonia	1990	100.0	100.0	100.0	100.0	100.0	100.0
	1991	207.6	79.0	92.0	225.7	85.9	262.7
	1992	1 615.7	9.2	72.5	2 227.9	12.7	17 542.5
	1993	2 736.2	13.8	66.3	4 124.0	20.8	19 826.9
	1994	3 744.1	19.2	65.0	5 757.9	29.5	19 518.3
	1995	5 126.8	29.8	68.0	7 538.7	43.8	17 211.6
	1996	6 571.7	36.4	70.7	9 292.5	51.4	18 078.8
	1997	8 028.7	38.5	78.1	10 279.4	49.3	20 850.7
	1998	9 218.7	43.6	82.0	11 236.0	53.2	21 120.3
	1999	9 568.4	43.4	81.5	11 743.9	53.3	22 033.6
	2000	10 935.9	42.9	87.1	12 557.8	49.3	25 472.2
	2001	12 106.1	45.9	91.8	13 190.5	50.0	26 381.0
Finland	1970	8.9	8.1	51.6	17.3	15.7	110.2
	1975	20.3	21.1	64.0	31.7	33.0	96.1
	1980	37.3	38.3	73.6	50.7	52.0	97.5
	1985	64.6	39.9	85.0	76.0	46.9	162.0
	1990	100.0	100.0	100.0	100.0	100.0	100.0
	1991	95.5	90.3	93.7	101.8	96.3	105.7
	1992	93.1	79.5	90.6	102.7	87.7	117.1
	1993	94.2	63.0	89.6	105.1	70.4	149.3
	1994	99.9	73.1	93.1	107.2	78.5	136.6
	1995	107.9	94.5	96.7	111.6	97.8	114.1
	1996	111.9	93.1	100.5	111.3	92.7	120.1
	1997	121.4	89.4	106.9	113.5	83.6	135.8
	1998	131.9	94.4	112.1	117.7	84.2	139.8
	1999	135.9	93.1	115.9	117.3	80.4	145.9
	2000	147.6	87.4	122.3	120.7	71.5	168.8
	2001	153.9	88.6	123.1	125.0	71.9	173.9

Table 7. Implicit Price Deflators of Gross Domestic Product in US Dollars and in National Currency

(Index numbers 1990 = 100)

Region, country or area and currency unit	Year	GDP in Current Prices		GDP at Constant Prices	GDP Implicit Price Deflators		Exchange Rates
		National Currency (1)	US Dollars (2)	(3)	National Currency (4)	US Dollars (5)	(6)
France	1970	12.3	12.1	56.6	21.8	21.4	101.9
	1975	22.8	29.0	67.1	34.0	43.2	78.7
	1980	43.5	56.1	78.3	55.6	71.6	77.7
	1985	72.1	43.7	85.2	84.6	51.3	164.9
	1990	100.0	100.0	100.0	100.0	100.0	100.0
	1991	104.0	100.3	101.0	103.0	99.4	103.6
	1992	107.6	110.7	102.5	105.0	108.0	97.2
	1993	109.1	104.9	101.6	107.4	103.3	104.0
	1994	113.3	111.1	103.7	109.2	107.1	102.0
	1995	117.1	127.7	105.4	111.1	121.2	91.7
	1996	120.1	127.8	106.6	112.7	119.9	94.0
	1997	124.0	115.6	108.6	114.1	106.5	107.1
	1998	129.4	119.4	112.3	115.2	106.3	108.4
	1999	134.3	118.7	115.9	115.8	102.4	113.1
	2000	140.7	107.6	120.3	116.9	89.4	130.8
	2001	146.2	108.6	122.8	119.0	88.4	134.6
Germany	1970	27.6	12.2	60.6	45.5	20.1	226.4
	1975	42.0	27.6	67.8	62.0	40.7	152.3
	1980	60.1	53.5	79.7	75.5	67.1	112.5
	1985	74.9	41.1	84.4	88.7	48.7	182.1
	1990	100.0	100.0	100.0	100.0	100.0	100.0
	1991	108.8	105.9	105.1	103.5	100.8	102.7
	1992	116.8	120.9	107.4	108.7	112.5	96.6
	1993	119.8	117.1	106.3	112.7	110.2	102.3
	1994	125.7	125.2	108.8	115.6	115.1	100.4
	1995	130.5	147.1	110.7	117.9	132.9	88.7
	1996	132.8	142.6	111.5	119.1	127.9	93.1
	1997	135.6	126.3	113.1	119.9	111.7	107.3
	1998	139.7	128.3	115.3	121.2	111.3	108.9
	1999	143.3	126.1	117.6	121.8	107.2	113.6
	2000	147.0	111.9	121.0	121.5	92.5	131.4
	2001	150.0	110.9	121.7	123.3	91.1	135.3
Greece	1970	2.5	13.4	59.6	4.3	22.5	19.1
	1975	5.9	29.2	76.1	7.7	38.3	20.1
	1980	15.6	58.1	93.4	16.7	62.2	26.8
	1985	42.6	48.8	94.0	45.3	51.9	87.3
	1990	100.0	100.0	100.0	100.0	100.0	100.0
	1991	123.5	107.4	103.1	119.8	104.2	115.0
	1992	142.8	118.7	103.8	137.5	114.4	120.2
	1993	160.8	111.2	102.2	157.4	108.8	144.7
	1994	182.3	119.1	104.2	175.0	114.3	153.1
	1995	204.4	139.8	106.4	192.1	131.4	146.2
	1996	224.6	147.9	108.9	206.3	135.8	151.9
	1997	248.6	144.3	112.9	220.3	127.9	172.2
	1998	270.4	145.1	116.7	231.8	124.3	186.5
	1999	288.0	149.7	120.9	238.8	123.8	192.9
	2000	311.0	134.9	125.9	247.0	107.1	230.6
	2001	334.8	139.4	131.1	255.4	106.3	240.3
Holy See	1970	4.5	8.6	49.6	9.1	17.4	52.3
	1975	10.2	18.7	62.4	16.3	29.9	54.5
	1980	27.8	38.9	76.4	36.4	50.9	71.5
	1985	59.4	37.3	83.8	70.9	44.5	159.3
	1990	100.0	100.0	100.0	100.0	100.0	100.0
	1991	109.5	105.7	101.8	107.6	103.9	103.6
	1992	115.4	112.2	102.6	112.5	109.3	102.9
	1993	118.9	90.5	101.7	116.9	89.0	131.3
	1994	125.6	93.3	103.8	121.0	89.9	134.6
	1995	135.7	99.8	106.8	127.0	93.4	136.0
	1996	144.4	112.1	107.9	133.7	103.9	128.7
	1997	151.0	106.2	110.3	136.9	96.3	142.2
	1998	158.0	109.0	112.3	140.7	97.1	144.9
	1999	163.3	107.7	114.2	143.0	94.3	151.6
	2000	171.8	98.0	117.6	146.1	83.3	175.4
	2001	179.5	99.4	119.7	149.9	83.0	180.6
Hungary	1970	16.3	17.2	56.2	29.0	30.6	94.8
	1975	23.6	33.9	76.1	31.0	44.6	69.5
	1980	35.3	68.5	89.3	39.5	76.7	51.5
	1985	50.6	63.8	97.4	51.9	65.4	79.4
	1990	100.0	100.0	100.0	100.0	100.0	100.0
	1991	110.5	93.4	88.1	125.4	106.1	118.2
	1992	130.1	104.1	85.4	152.4	121.9	125.0
	1993	156.9	107.9	84.9	184.8	127.0	145.5
	1994	193.0	116.0	87.4	220.8	132.7	166.4
	1995	246.0	123.7	88.7	277.2	139.4	198.9
	1996	302.0	125.1	89.9	335.9	139.1	241.5

Table 7. Implicit Price Deflators of Gross Domestic Product in US Dollars and in National Currency

(Index numbers 1990 = 100)

Region, country or area and currency unit	Year	GDP in Current Prices: National Currency (1)	GDP in Current Prices: US Dollars (2)	GDP at Constant Prices (3)	GDP Implicit Price Deflators: National Currency (4)	GDP Implicit Price Deflators: US Dollars (5)	Exchange Rates (6)
	1997	374.2	126.6	94.0	398.0	134.7	295.5
	1998	442.0	130.3	98.6	448.3	132.2	339.1
	1999	499.2	133.0	102.7	486.1	129.5	375.4
	2000	577.1	129.3	108.0	534.2	119.7	446.3
	2001	650.6	143.5	112.2	579.9	127.9	453.4
Iceland	1970	0.1	8.4	41.3	0.3	20.4	1.5
	1975	0.6	22.4	56.3	1.1	39.9	2.8
	1980	4.4	53.9	76.3	5.8	70.7	8.2
	1985	33.2	46.6	85.5	38.8	54.5	71.2
	1990	100.0	100.0	100.0	100.0	100.0	100.0
	1991	108.2	106.9	100.1	108.1	106.8	101.2
	1992	108.1	109.5	96.8	111.7	113.2	98.7
	1993	111.4	96.1	97.7	114.1	98.4	116.0
	1994	118.4	98.6	101.7	116.4	97.0	120.0
	1995	121.9	109.8	101.8	119.7	107.9	110.9
	1996	130.8	114.6	107.0	122.2	107.1	114.1
	1997	141.3	116.2	112.0	126.2	103.7	121.7
	1998	156.4	128.5	118.2	132.4	108.7	121.8
	1999	167.2	134.7	122.8	136.1	109.7	124.1
	2000	181.4	134.5	129.6	140.0	103.8	134.9
	2001	204.2	122.1	133.4	153.1	91.6	167.1
Ireland	1970	6.1	8.9	44.1	13.9	20.2	68.8
	1975	14.4	19.2	56.1	25.6	34.3	74.6
	1980	35.5	44.1	70.1	50.7	63.0	80.5
	1985	67.5	43.1	79.5	84.9	54.3	156.4
	1990	100.0	100.0	100.0	100.0	100.0	100.0
	1991	103.8	101.0	101.9	101.8	99.1	102.7
	1992	110.3	113.4	105.3	104.7	107.7	97.2
	1993	119.1	106.3	108.2	110.1	98.3	112.0
	1994	128.1	115.8	114.4	111.9	101.2	110.6
	1995	145.0	140.5	125.7	115.3	111.8	103.1
	1996	159.9	154.7	135.8	117.8	113.9	103.4
	1997	184.8	169.4	150.7	122.6	112.4	109.1
	1998	213.6	183.9	164.0	130.3	112.1	116.2
	1999	247.2	202.2	182.3	135.6	110.9	122.3
	2000	283.4	200.4	200.4	141.4	100.0	141.4
	2001	315.3	216.6	211.8	148.9	102.3	145.6
Italy	1970	5.1	9.8	56.1	9.1	17.4	52.3
	1975	10.6	19.4	64.8	16.3	29.9	54.5
	1980	29.1	40.7	79.9	36.4	50.9	71.5
	1985	61.6	38.7	86.9	70.9	44.5	159.3
	1990	100.0	100.0	100.0	100.0	100.0	100.0
	1991	109.1	105.3	101.4	107.6	103.9	103.6
	1992	114.9	111.7	102.2	112.5	109.3	102.9
	1993	118.4	90.1	101.3	116.9	89.0	131.3
	1994	125.2	93.0	103.5	121.0	89.9	134.6
	1995	135.3	99.5	106.5	127.0	93.4	136.0
	1996	144.0	111.8	107.7	133.7	103.9	128.7
	1997	150.4	105.8	109.9	136.9	96.3	142.2
	1998	157.3	108.5	111.8	140.7	97.1	144.9
	1999	162.5	107.1	113.6	143.0	94.3	151.6
	2000	170.7	97.3	116.9	146.1	83.3	175.4
	2001	178.4	98.8	119.0	149.9	83.0	180.6
Latvia	1990	100.0	100.0	100.0	100.0	100.0	100.0
	1991	229.5	87.4	89.6	256.2	97.5	262.8
	1992	1 608.9	7.3	58.4	2 756.9	12.5	22 055.2
	1993	2 349.5	11.6	49.7	4 729.1	23.3	20 296.6
	1994	3 271.3	19.5	50.0	6 542.3	38.9	16 818.3
	1995	3 730.6	23.5	49.6	7 521.9	47.5	15 835.6
	1996	4 496.0	27.2	51.4	8 743.4	52.9	16 528.2
	1997	5 236.2	30.0	55.7	9 395.8	53.9	17 431.9
	1998	5 753.0	32.5	58.4	9 854.2	55.6	17 723.4
	1999	6 229.5	35.5	60.0	10 375.9	59.0	17 586.3
	2000	6 964.0	38.2	64.1	10 856.3	59.6	18 215.3
	2001	7 621.1	40.4	69.1	11 033.0	58.5	18 859.8
Liechtenstein	1970	24.4	7.8	58.3	41.9	13.3	315.0
	1975	40.2	21.6	64.6	62.2	33.5	185.7
	1980	53.3	44.2	76.6	69.5	57.6	120.7
	1985	72.8	41.2	85.3	85.4	48.3	176.8
	1990	100.0	100.0	100.0	100.0	100.0	100.0
	1991	105.5	102.2	99.6	106.0	102.7	103.2
	1992	108.6	107.3	99.7	108.9	107.6	101.2
	1993	111.4	104.7	99.6	111.8	105.1	106.4
	1994	114.3	116.1	100.6	113.7	115.4	98.5

Table 7. Implicit Price Deflators of Gross Domestic Product in US Dollars and in National Currency

(Index numbers 1990 = 100)

Region, country or area and currency unit	Year	GDP in Current Prices		GDP at Constant Prices	GDP Implicit Price Deflators		Exchange Rates
		National Currency (1)	US Dollars (2)	(3)	National Currency (4)	US Dollars (5)	(6)
	1995	117.0	137.4	101.8	114.9	135.0	85.1
	1996	118.8	133.6	103.0	115.4	129.7	89.0
	1997	121.9	116.7	105.9	115.1	110.2	104.4
	1998	126.2	121.0	109.7	115.1	110.3	104.4
	1999	130.6	120.8	112.8	115.8	107.1	108.1
	2000	137.4	113.0	117.4	117.0	96.3	121.5
	2001	143.1	117.8	120.2	119.1	98.0	121.5
Lithuania	1990	100.0	100.0	100.0	100.0	100.0	100.0
	1991	309.2	117.7	94.3	327.9	124.8	262.7
	1992	2 539.7	9.5	74.3	3 419.5	12.8	26 714.8
	1993	8 642.5	13.3	62.2	13 890.3	21.3	65 212.7
	1994	12 605.7	21.1	56.1	22 452.7	37.6	59 714.6
	1995	17 973.8	29.9	58.0	30 994.4	51.6	60 066.7
	1996	23 541.3	39.2	60.7	38 768.7	64.5	60 106.5
	1997	28 590.8	47.6	65.1	43 890.3	73.1	60 041.5
	1998	32 058.2	53.4	68.5	46 819.7	78.0	60 025.3
	1999	31 808.1	53.0	65.8	48 337.8	80.5	60 047.0
	2000	33 667.1	56.1	68.3	49 294.2	82.1	60 041.7
	2001	35 763.1	59.5	72.4	49 423.3	82.3	60 052.6
Luxembourg	1970	17.1	11.4	47.8	35.7	23.9	149.4
	1975	26.9	24.4	55.1	48.8	44.3	110.2
	1980	41.2	47.1	61.7	66.8	76.4	87.4
	1985	63.6	35.8	69.8	91.2	51.3	177.8
	1990	100.0	100.0	100.0	100.0	100.0	100.0
	1991	110.6	108.3	108.6	101.8	99.6	102.2
	1992	116.8	121.4	110.6	105.6	109.8	96.2
	1993	129.0	124.6	115.3	111.9	108.1	103.5
	1994	138.7	138.5	119.7	115.9	115.8	100.1
	1995	143.9	163.2	121.4	118.6	134.4	88.2
	1996	151.7	163.8	125.4	121.0	130.5	92.7
	1997	168.7	157.6	135.9	124.2	116.0	107.1
	1998	185.3	170.6	145.2	127.6	117.4	108.7
	1999	205.6	181.4	157.9	130.2	114.9	113.3
	2000	232.2	177.2	171.9	135.1	103.1	131.0
	2001	240.6	178.3	174.0	138.2	102.5	134.8
Malta	1970	12.9	9.8	25.2	51.1	39.0	131.0
	1975	22.6	18.6	39.5	57.1	47.2	121.0
	1980	53.3	49.1	68.2	78.2	72.0	108.6
	1985	64.8	43.9	74.2	87.3	59.2	147.5
	1990	100.0	100.0	100.0	100.0	100.0	100.0
	1991	109.8	108.0	106.3	103.4	101.6	101.8
	1992	119.1	118.6	111.2	107.0	106.6	100.4
	1993	127.9	106.4	116.2	110.1	91.5	120.3
	1994	140.0	117.7	122.8	114.0	95.9	118.9
	1995	155.9	140.3	130.6	119.4	107.5	111.1
	1996	163.5	144.1	135.5	120.6	106.4	113.3
	1997	175.3	144.4	142.0	123.5	101.7	121.4
	1998	185.4	151.7	146.9	126.2	103.2	122.3
	1999	198.2	157.9	152.6	129.9	103.5	125.5
	2000	212.0	153.8	159.9	132.6	96.2	137.8
	2001	222.1	156.8	166.1	133.7	94.4	141.6
Monaco	1970	10.9	10.7	49.9	21.8	21.4	101.9
	1975	20.5	26.1	60.4	34.0	43.2	78.7
	1980	40.6	52.3	73.1	55.6	71.6	77.7
	1985	69.6	42.2	82.2	84.6	51.3	164.9
	1990	100.0	100.0	100.0	100.0	100.0	100.0
	1991	104.7	101.0	101.7	103.0	99.4	103.6
	1992	109.1	112.2	103.9	105.0	108.0	97.2
	1993	111.4	107.1	103.7	107.4	103.3	104.0
	1994	116.4	114.1	106.5	109.2	107.1	102.0
	1995	121.1	132.1	109.1	111.1	121.2	91.7
	1996	125.1	133.1	111.0	112.7	119.9	94.0
	1997	130.0	121.2	113.9	114.1	106.5	107.1
	1998	136.5	126.0	118.5	115.2	106.3	108.4
	1999	142.6	126.1	123.1	115.8	102.4	113.1
	2000	150.0	114.7	128.5	116.7	89.2	130.8
	2001	155.9	115.8	131.7	118.4	87.9	134.7
Netherlands	1970	23.7	11.9	60.0	39.5	19.9	198.5
	1975	43.1	31.0	70.3	61.3	44.1	139.0
	1980	66.0	60.4	80.1	82.4	75.5	109.1
	1985	82.2	45.1	85.3	96.4	52.8	182.6
	1990	100.0	100.0	100.0	100.0	100.0	100.0
	1991	105.4	102.7	102.5	102.8	100.2	102.6
	1992	109.7	113.6	104.2	105.2	109.0	96.5

Table 7. Implicit Price Deflators of Gross Domestic Product in US Dollars and in National Currency

(Index numbers 1990 = 100)

Region, country or area and currency unit	Year	GDP in Current Prices		GDP at Constant Prices	GDP Implicit Price Deflators		Exchange Rates
		National Currency (1)	US Dollars (2)	(3)	National Currency (4)	US Dollars (5)	(6)
	1993	112.7	110.5	105.2	107.2	105.1	102.0
	1994	118.3	118.4	107.9	109.7	109.7	100.0
	1995	124.3	140.9	111.1	111.9	126.9	88.2
	1996	129.6	139.9	114.5	113.2	122.2	92.6
	1997	137.2	128.1	118.9	115.4	107.7	107.1
	1998	145.7	133.7	124.0	117.4	107.8	108.9
	1999	153.8	135.4	129.0	119.2	105.0	113.5
	2000	165.6	126.0	133.3	124.2	94.6	131.3
	2001	176.5	130.5	135.0	130.8	96.7	135.3
Norway	1970	12.5	11.0	48.4	25.9	22.7	114.1
	1975	23.4	28.0	61.6	38.0	45.5	83.5
	1980	43.3	54.8	77.3	56.0	70.9	79.0
	1985	75.3	54.8	91.5	82.3	60.0	137.2
	1990	100.0	100.0	100.0	100.0	100.0	100.0
	1991	105.9	102.3	103.6	102.2	98.7	103.5
	1992	108.7	109.5	107.0	101.6	102.3	99.3
	1993	114.3	100.8	110.0	103.9	91.7	113.3
	1994	120.2	106.6	115.7	103.8	92.1	112.7
	1995	129.0	127.4	120.8	106.8	105.5	101.2
	1996	141.3	137.1	127.1	111.1	107.9	103.0
	1997	152.9	135.3	133.7	114.4	101.2	113.0
	1998	155.8	129.2	137.2	113.5	94.2	120.5
	1999	169.7	136.2	140.2	121.0	97.2	124.5
	2000	202.1	143.8	144.1	140.2	99.7	140.6
	2001	210.0	146.2	146.9	143.0	99.5	143.7
Poland	1970	0.1	32.9	60.8	0.2	54.0	0.4
	1975	0.2	70.5	97.0	0.3	72.6	0.4
	1980	0.4	89.6	102.9	0.4	87.0	0.5
	1985	1.7	111.1	102.0	1.7	109.0	1.6
	1990	100.0	100.0	100.0	100.0	100.0	100.0
	1991	144.4	129.7	93.0	155.3	139.5	111.3
	1992	205.2	143.0	95.3	215.2	150.0	143.5
	1993	278.0	145.8	98.9	281.2	147.5	190.6
	1994	401.8	168.0	104.1	385.9	161.3	239.2
	1995	549.9	215.4	111.4	493.8	193.5	255.2
	1996	692.2	243.9	118.1	586.3	206.6	283.8
	1997	843.1	244.2	126.1	668.4	193.6	345.2
	1998	988.0	270.1	132.2	747.1	204.2	365.9
	1999	1 097.9	262.9	137.6	797.9	191.1	417.5
	2000	1 271.4	277.9	143.1	888.6	194.2	457.6
	2001	1 337.4	310.3	144.5	925.3	214.7	431.0
Portugal	1970	2.1	10.3	45.7	4.5	22.5	20.0
	1975	4.4	24.6	56.6	7.8	43.4	18.0
	1980	14.7	41.8	72.6	20.2	57.5	35.1
	1985	41.2	34.4	75.9	54.2	45.4	119.4
	1990	100.0	100.0	100.0	100.0	100.0	100.0
	1991	114.9	113.4	104.4	110.1	108.6	101.4
	1992	129.4	136.7	105.5	122.7	129.6	94.7
	1993	136.1	120.7	103.3	131.7	116.8	112.8
	1994	147.5	126.6	104.3	141.3	121.4	116.4
	1995	159.1	150.1	108.8	146.2	137.9	106.0
	1996	169.7	156.8	112.7	150.6	139.2	108.2
	1997	183.0	148.8	117.1	156.3	127.1	123.0
	1998	198.7	157.3	122.5	162.2	128.4	126.3
	1999	212.6	161.0	127.2	167.2	126.7	132.0
	2000	227.4	149.0	131.8	172.5	113.0	152.7
	2001	242.0	154.0	134.0	180.6	114.9	157.2
Republic of Moldova	1990	100.0	100.0	100.0	100.0	100.0	100.0
	1991	204.2	77.7	97.6	209.2	79.6	262.8
	1992	1 513.8	2.4	80.5	1 880.0	3.0	62 666.7
	1993	14 362.0	2.6	57.2	25 121.9	4.6	546 128.3
	1994	37 356.5	5.8	39.5	94 592.5	14.8	639 138.5
	1995	51 101.7	7.6	38.9	131 203.7	19.4	676 307.7
	1996	61 495.3	8.9	36.7	167 750.0	24.3	690 329.2
	1997	70 322.6	10.1	37.3	188 722.0	27.2	693 830.9
	1998	71 940.9	8.9	34.8	206 578.3	25.6	806 946.5
	1999	97 173.5	6.2	33.7	288 758.2	18.3	1 577 913.7
	2000	126 337.5	6.8	34.4	367 674.9	19.7	1 866 370.1
	2001	149 994.5	7.8	36.4	411 534.6	21.3	1 932 087.3
Romania	1970	26.5	37.5	34.2	77.5	109.6	70.7
	1975	44.8	50.2	58.5	76.6	85.9	89.2
	1980	56.5	70.4	83.8	67.4	84.0	80.2
	1985	72.7	95.1	97.4	74.6	97.7	76.4
	1990	100.0	100.0	100.0	100.0	100.0	100.0

Table 7. Implicit Price Deflators of Gross Domestic Product in US Dollars and in National Currency

(Index numbers 1990 = 100)

Region, country or area and currency unit	Year	GDP in Current Prices		GDP at Constant Prices	GDP Implicit Price Deflators		Exchange Rates
		National Currency (1)	US Dollars (2)	(3)	National Currency (4)	US Dollars (5)	(6)
	1991	256.9	75.4	87.1	295.0	86.6	340.6
	1992	702.8	51.2	79.4	884.6	64.4	1 373.6
	1993	2 335.6	68.9	80.7	2 895.5	85.5	3 386.5
	1994	5 802.1	78.6	83.8	6 921.0	93.8	7 378.5
	1995	8 408.9	92.8	89.8	9 362.2	103.3	9 063.1
	1996	12 696.8	92.3	93.4	13 599.3	98.9	13 750.6
	1997	29 483.6	92.3	87.7	33 614.1	105.2	31 952.6
	1998	43 573.8	110.1	83.5	52 192.5	131.9	39 569.7
	1999	63 616.0	93.1	82.5	77 085.4	112.8	68 338.1
	2000	93 292.2	96.4	84.0	111 075.9	114.8	96 756.0
	2001	134 536.9	103.8	88.4	152 187.2	117.5	129 521.0
Russian Federation	1990	100.0	100.0	100.0	100.0	100.0	100.0
	1991	217.1	82.6	95.0	228.5	87.0	262.6
	1992	2 950.2	8.8	81.2	3 632.2	10.9	33 322.9
	1993	26.6	17.9	74.2	35.9	24.1	149.0
	1994	94.8	28.8	64.7	146.4	44.5	329.0
	1995	239.1	34.9	62.1	385.2	56.3	684.2
	1996	333.1	43.3	60.0	555.1	72.2	768.8
	1997	384.8	44.3	60.5	635.5	73.2	868.2
	1998	425.5	29.2	57.6	739.0	50.7	1 457.6
	1999	740.0	20.0	60.7	1 219.3	33.0	3 694.8
	2000	1 134.1	26.9	66.2	1 714.4	40.6	4 222.7
	2001	1 403.4	32.0	69.5	2 020.5	46.1	4 382.9
San Marino	1970	5.1	9.8	56.1	9.1	17.4	52.3
	1975	10.6	19.4	64.8	16.3	29.9	54.5
	1980	29.1	40.7	79.9	36.4	50.9	71.5
	1985	61.6	38.7	86.9	70.9	44.5	159.3
	1990	100.0	100.0	100.0	100.0	100.0	100.0
	1991	109.1	105.3	101.4	107.6	103.9	103.6
	1992	114.9	111.7	102.2	112.5	109.3	102.9
	1993	118.4	90.1	101.3	116.9	89.0	131.3
	1994	125.2	93.0	103.5	121.0	89.9	134.6
	1995	135.3	99.5	106.5	127.0	93.4	136.0
	1996	144.0	111.8	107.7	133.7	103.9	128.7
	1997	150.4	105.8	109.9	136.9	96.3	142.2
	1998	164.7	113.6	118.1	139.4	96.2	144.9
	1999	182.3	120.2	128.8	141.6	93.3	151.8
	2000	191.6	109.2	132.4	144.6	82.5	175.3
	2001	200.1	110.8	134.8	148.5	82.2	180.7
Serbia and Montenegro	1990	100.0	100.0	100.0	100.0	100.0	100.0
	1991	157.4	90.7	88.4	178.1	102.6	173.6
	1992	131.0	128.9	63.7	205.6	202.3	101.6
	1993	70.1	44.7	44.1	158.9	101.2	157.0
	1994	69.9	43.7	45.2	154.5	96.6	159.9
	1995	128.7	85.3	48.0	268.1	177.8	150.8
	1996	232.3	53.2	50.8	457.1	104.7	436.6
	1997	320.0	63.9	54.6	586.4	117.2	500.3
	1998	434.2	51.5	55.9	776.3	92.1	842.9
	1999	559.2	59.1	43.7	1 280.2	135.3	946.2
	2000	1 116.8	37.3	46.5	2 403.1	80.4	2 988.9
	2001	2 047.1	35.2	43.9	4 661.3	80.2	5 812.1
Slovakia	1980	70.4	88.6	93.8	75.1	94.4	79.6
	1985	83.5	87.4	93.3	89.4	93.6	95.5
	1990	100.0	100.0	100.0	100.0	100.0	100.0
	1991	115.0	70.0	85.5	134.6	81.9	164.3
	1992	119.5	75.9	79.8	149.7	95.1	157.4
	1993	140.5	82.0	81.3	172.7	100.8	171.3
	1994	168.0	94.1	85.6	196.3	110.0	178.5
	1995	196.6	118.8	91.1	215.8	130.4	165.5
	1996	217.2	127.2	96.4	225.3	131.9	170.8
	1997	244.9	130.8	101.8	240.4	128.4	187.2
	1998	267.8	136.4	105.9	252.9	128.9	196.2
	1999	288.8	125.3	107.3	269.2	116.8	230.5
	2000	314.1	122.5	109.6	286.4	111.7	256.4
	2001	341.9	126.9	113.3	301.9	112.1	269.3
Slovenia	1990	100.0	100.0	100.0	100.0	100.0	100.0
	1991	177.6	72.9	91.1	194.9	80.0	243.6
	1992	517.4	72.0	86.1	600.7	83.7	717.7
	1993	729.4	72.9	88.6	823.5	82.3	1 000.6
	1994	941.7	82.8	93.3	1 009.5	88.7	1 138.1
	1995	1 129.0	107.8	97.1	1 162.5	111.0	1 047.3
	1996	1 298.7	108.6	100.6	1 291.6	108.0	1 195.9
	1997	1 477.6	104.7	105.1	1 405.4	99.6	1 411.0
	1998	1 653.6	112.7	109.1	1 515.4	103.3	1 467.0

Table 7. Implicit Price Deflators of Gross Domestic Product in US Dollars and in National Currency

(Index numbers 1990 = 100)

Region, country or area and currency unit	Year	GDP in Current Prices		GDP at Constant Prices	GDP Implicit Price Deflators		Exchange Rates
		National Currency (1)	US Dollars (2)	(3)	National Currency (4)	US Dollars (5)	(6)
	1999	1 854.2	115.5	114.8	1 615.1	100.6	1 605.5
	2000	2 051.0	104.3	120.1	1 707.7	86.8	1 967.4
	2001	2 320.7	108.2	123.7	1 876.7	87.5	2 144.8
Spain	1970	5.2	7.6	52.4	10.0	14.6	68.5
	1975	12.0	21.4	67.9	17.7	31.5	56.2
	1980	30.5	43.4	74.9	40.7	57.9	70.3
	1985	56.2	33.7	80.3	70.0	42.0	166.7
	1990	100.0	100.0	100.0	100.0	100.0	100.0
	1991	109.7	107.6	102.5	106.9	104.9	101.9
	1992	118.1	117.6	103.5	114.1	113.6	100.4
	1993	122.2	97.9	102.4	119.3	95.5	124.9
	1994	130.0	98.9	104.9	123.9	94.3	131.4
	1995	140.1	114.6	107.8	130.0	106.3	122.3
	1996	148.6	119.6	110.4	134.6	108.3	124.3
	1997	158.2	110.1	114.8	137.7	95.9	143.6
	1998	169.0	115.3	119.8	141.0	96.2	146.6
	1999	180.9	118.1	124.9	144.9	94.6	153.2
	2000	195.0	110.1	130.1	149.9	84.6	177.2
	2001	208.6	114.3	133.6	156.2	85.6	182.5
Sweden	1970	12.7	14.5	66.4	19.1	21.8	87.6
	1975	22.1	31.6	75.5	29.3	41.8	70.1
	1980	38.7	54.1	80.6	47.9	67.1	71.4
	1985	63.3	43.6	88.4	71.6	49.3	145.2
	1990	100.0	100.0	100.0	100.0	100.0	100.0
	1991	106.1	103.9	98.9	107.3	105.0	102.2
	1992	105.3	107.0	97.2	108.4	110.1	98.5
	1993	106.2	80.7	95.4	111.3	84.6	131.6
	1994	113.2	86.8	99.4	113.9	87.4	130.3
	1995	121.7	101.0	103.4	117.7	97.7	120.5
	1996	124.8	110.2	104.7	119.2	105.2	113.3
	1997	129.9	100.7	107.3	121.0	93.8	129.0
	1998	135.6	101.0	111.2	122.0	90.8	134.4
	1999	142.8	102.3	116.3	122.8	88.0	139.5
	2000	150.9	97.5	121.3	124.4	80.3	154.9
	2001	155.7	89.2	122.7	126.9	72.7	174.6
Switzerland	1970	30.2	9.6	72.1	41.9	13.3	315.0
	1975	46.7	25.1	75.1	62.2	33.5	185.7
	1980	56.8	47.1	81.6	69.5	57.6	120.7
	1985	74.8	42.3	87.5	85.4	48.3	176.8
	1990	100.0	100.0	100.0	100.0	100.0	100.0
	1991	105.2	101.9	99.2	106.0	102.7	103.2
	1992	107.9	106.6	99.1	108.9	107.6	101.2
	1993	110.2	103.6	98.6	111.8	105.1	106.4
	1994	112.7	114.4	99.1	113.7	115.4	98.5
	1995	114.5	134.5	99.6	114.9	135.0	85.1
	1996	115.3	129.6	99.9	115.4	129.7	89.0
	1997	117.0	112.0	101.7	115.1	110.2	104.4
	1998	119.8	114.7	104.1	115.1	110.3	104.4
	1999	122.4	113.2	105.6	115.9	107.2	108.1
	2000	127.8	105.1	109.0	117.3	96.5	121.6
	2001	130.8	107.6	109.9	118.9	97.9	121.5
TFYR Macedonia	1990	100.0	100.0	100.0	100.0	100.0	100.0
	1991	181.5	104.6	93.8	193.5	111.5	173.5
	1992	2 326.7	51.7	87.7	2 653.9	59.0	4 498.1
	1993	11 671.8	56.8	81.1	14 388.2	70.0	20 554.6
	1994	28 883.2	75.6	79.7	36 242.3	94.8	38 230.3
	1995	33 442.7	99.9	78.8	42 436.5	126.8	33 467.3
	1996	34 808.5	98.5	79.7	43 652.3	123.6	35 317.4
	1997	36 492.8	82.6	80.9	45 115.3	102.1	44 187.4
	1998	37 645.8	78.2	83.3	45 209.7	94.0	48 095.4
	1999	38 525.2	76.6	85.5	45 061.5	89.6	50 291.9
	2000	42 778.7	73.5	89.9	47 608.4	81.8	58 201.0
	2001	43 309.7	72.0	86.3	50 207.6	83.5	60 128.9
Ukraine	1990	100.0	100.0	100.0	100.0	100.0	100.0
	1991	179.0	68.1	91.4	195.9	74.6	262.6
	1992	3 013.8	8.4	82.4	3 656.5	10.1	36 203.0
	1993	88 786.2	13.0	70.7	125 586.4	18.5	678 845.4
	1994	720 819.8	14.7	54.5	1 323 004.8	26.9	4 918 233.5
	1995	3 264 456.3	14.8	47.9	6 820 349.8	30.8	22 143 992.9
	1996	4 881 377.2	17.8	43.1	11 337 205.8	41.3	27 450 861.5
	1997	5 590 718.6	20.0	41.8	13 384 649.3	47.9	27 942 900.4
	1998	6 143 293.4	16.7	41.0	14 999 140.6	40.8	36 762 599.5

Table 7. Implicit Price Deflators of Gross Domestic Product in US Dollars and in National Currency

(Index numbers 1990 = 100)

Region, country or area and currency unit	Year	GDP in Current Prices: National Currency (1)	GDP in Current Prices: US Dollars (2)	GDP at Constant Prices (3)	GDP Implicit Price Deflators: National Currency (4)	GDP Implicit Price Deflators: US Dollars (5)	Exchange Rates (6)
	1999	7 810 898.2	12.6	40.9	19 101 397.1	30.8	62 017 523.1
	2000	10 183 832.3	12.5	43.3	23 518 921.8	28.8	81 662 922.9
	2001	12 226 946.1	15.2	47.3	25 850 520.0	32.0	80 782 875.0
United Kingdom	1970	9.2	12.5	63.4	14.6	19.7	74.1
	1975	19.0	23.6	70.4	27.0	33.6	80.4
	1980	41.4	54.2	76.8	53.9	70.5	76.5
	1985	63.7	46.0	85.0	74.9	54.2	138.2
	1990	100.0	100.0	100.0	100.0	100.0	100.0
	1991	105.2	104.5	98.6	106.6	105.9	100.7
	1992	109.6	108.3	98.8	110.9	109.6	101.2
	1993	115.3	97.4	101.3	113.8	96.1	118.4
	1994	122.3	105.4	106.0	115.3	99.4	116.0
	1995	129.0	114.7	109.1	118.3	105.1	112.6
	1996	136.8	120.2	112.0	122.2	107.3	113.9
	1997	145.5	134.2	115.8	125.7	115.9	108.5
	1998	154.2	143.8	119.2	129.4	120.7	107.2
	1999	161.9	147.6	122.1	132.6	120.9	109.7
	2000	170.5	145.3	125.8	135.5	115.5	117.3
	2001	178.2	144.5	128.5	138.7	112.4	123.4
OCEANIA							
Australia	1970	9.6	13.8	55.1	17.5	25.1	69.7
	1975	20.0	33.5	63.9	31.2	52.3	59.7
	1980	36.6	53.4	74.1	49.4	72.1	68.5
	1985	62.4	55.8	85.9	72.6	65.0	111.7
	1990	100.0	100.0	100.0	100.0	100.0	100.0
	1991	102.2	102.0	100.3	101.9	101.7	100.2
	1992	107.1	100.8	103.9	103.1	97.0	106.3
	1993	112.4	97.9	108.0	104.0	90.6	114.8
	1994	118.5	111.0	112.6	105.3	98.6	106.8
	1995	126.4	120.0	117.3	107.7	102.3	105.3
	1996	133.2	133.5	121.7	109.4	109.7	99.7
	1997	141.1	134.1	127.2	110.9	105.5	105.1
	1998	148.8	119.7	133.9	111.1	89.4	124.3
	1999	158.0	130.6	139.3	113.4	93.8	120.9
	2000	168.2	124.9	141.7	118.7	88.2	134.6
	2001	179.2	118.7	147.3	121.7	80.6	151.0
Cook Islands	1970	9.9	18.5	103.7	9.5	17.9	53.1
	1975	13.1	26.3	76.0	17.2	34.6	49.7
	1980	22.6	36.8	73.8	30.6	49.9	61.3
	1985	52.3	43.3	85.0	61.5	51.0	120.6
	1990	100.0	100.0	100.0	100.0	100.0	100.0
	1991	112.8	109.0	107.1	105.3	101.8	103.4
	1992	125.2	112.7	113.5	110.2	99.3	111.0
	1993	139.1	126.0	118.0	117.9	106.8	110.4
	1994	150.5	149.6	122.6	122.8	122.0	100.7
	1995	144.8	159.2	117.2	123.5	135.8	90.9
	1996	139.2	160.3	117.0	118.9	137.0	88.8
	1997	134.7	149.2	113.8	118.4	131.2	90.2
	1998	136.6	122.5	109.0	125.3	112.4	111.5
	1999	145.3	128.9	115.3	126.1	111.8	112.8
	2000	160.2	122.0	126.6	126.5	96.4	131.2
	2001	178.2	125.6	130.4	136.7	96.3	142.0
Fiji	1970	9.7	16.5	49.3	19.7	33.4	59.0
	1975	28.4	51.1	66.3	42.8	77.2	55.4
	1980	49.7	90.0	79.7	62.3	112.8	55.2
	1985	66.5	85.3	83.8	79.3	101.8	77.9
	1990	100.0	100.0	100.0	100.0	100.0	100.0
	1991	103.1	103.5	97.3	106.0	106.4	99.6
	1992	116.4	114.7	103.3	112.7	111.0	101.5
	1993	127.5	122.4	106.0	120.3	115.6	104.1
	1994	135.0	136.5	111.3	121.2	122.6	98.9
	1995	141.4	148.9	114.1	123.9	130.5	94.9
	1996	149.8	158.1	117.6	127.3	134.4	94.7
	1997	154.5	158.5	116.6	132.5	135.9	97.5
	1998	159.3	118.7	118.3	134.7	100.4	134.2
	1999	185.1	139.2	129.8	142.7	107.3	133.0
	2000	177.7	123.6	126.1	140.9	98.0	143.8
	2001	193.5	125.8	129.4	149.6	97.3	153.8
French Polynesia	1970	7.4	7.3	34.2	21.6	21.2	101.9
	1975	15.5	19.7	44.2	35.1	44.6	78.7
	1980	33.4	43.0	56.0	59.6	76.8	77.6
	1985	78.2	47.4	78.5	99.6	60.3	165.2
	1990	100.0	100.0	100.0	100.0	100.0	100.0
	1991	105.2	101.6	103.9	101.3	97.7	103.7
	1992	108.3	111.4	107.9	100.5	103.3	97.3

Table 7. Implicit Price Deflators of Gross Domestic Product in US Dollars and in National Currency

(Index numbers 1990 = 100)

Region, country or area and currency unit	Year	GDP in Current Prices		GDP at Constant Prices	GDP Implicit Price Deflators		Exchange Rates
		National Currency (1)	US Dollars (2)	(3)	National Currency (4)	US Dollars (5)	(6)
	1993	113.5	118.7	111.4	101.9	106.6	95.6
	1994	130.2	127.7	125.7	103.6	101.6	102.0
	1995	128.6	140.3	122.8	104.8	114.3	91.7
	1996	132.2	140.7	124.8	105.9	112.8	93.9
	1997	135.5	126.4	126.2	107.3	100.1	107.2
	1998	138.8	128.1	127.6	108.8	100.4	108.4
	1999	142.9	126.4	130.9	109.1	96.5	113.1
	2000	147.1	112.5	134.4	109.5	83.7	130.8
	2001	151.3	112.4	137.3	110.2	81.9	134.6
Kiribati	1970	35.2	50.5	124.3	28.3	40.6	69.7
	1975	115.6	193.9	252.2	45.8	76.9	59.6
	1980	67.4	98.3	87.4	77.1	112.5	68.5
	1985	83.8	74.9	92.0	91.1	81.5	111.8
	1990	100.0	100.0	100.0	100.0	100.0	100.0
	1991	119.4	119.1	106.9	111.7	111.4	100.3
	1992	126.8	119.3	105.2	120.5	113.4	106.3
	1993	133.5	116.3	107.0	124.8	108.7	114.8
	1994	149.3	139.9	115.9	128.8	120.7	106.7
	1995	170.5	161.9	122.2	139.5	132.5	105.3
	1996	174.9	175.3	125.8	139.0	139.3	99.8
	1997	182.1	173.1	133.0	136.9	130.2	105.1
	1998	201.2	161.9	139.6	144.1	116.0	124.2
	1999	220.6	182.3	148.3	148.7	122.9	121.0
	2000	214.7	159.5	148.6	144.5	107.3	134.7
	2001	212.1	140.5	151.3	140.2	92.9	150.9
Marshall Islands	1970	10.7	10.7	29.1	36.8	36.8	100.0
	1975	21.3	21.3	46.5	45.7	45.7	100.0
	1980	34.0	34.0	47.9	71.1	71.1	100.0
	1985	55.9	55.9	61.1	91.5	91.5	100.0
	1990	100.0	100.0	100.0	100.0	100.0	100.0
	1991	105.1	105.1	101.1	104.0	104.0	100.0
	1992	116.0	116.0	101.2	114.7	114.7	100.0
	1993	126.7	126.7	105.3	120.4	120.4	100.0
	1994	137.7	137.7	101.2	136.0	136.0	100.0
	1995	153.2	153.2	111.2	137.8	137.8	100.0
	1996	141.3	141.3	93.6	151.0	151.0	100.0
	1997	134.2	134.2	84.8	158.3	158.3	100.0
	1998	138.6	138.6	85.7	161.7	161.7	100.0
	1999	141.0	141.0	85.8	164.4	164.4	100.0
	2000	142.0	142.0	85.0	167.1	167.1	100.0
	2001	145.9	145.9	86.4	168.8	168.8	100.0
Micronesia (Federated States of)	1970	15.8	15.8	35.2	44.9	44.9	100.0
	1975	36.7	36.7	56.3	65.2	65.2	100.0
	1980	51.1	51.1	57.9	88.1	88.1	100.0
	1985	67.4	67.4	83.7	80.6	80.6	100.0
	1990	100.0	100.0	100.0	100.0	100.0	100.0
	1991	112.0	112.0	108.3	103.4	103.4	100.0
	1992	118.6	118.6	111.5	106.4	106.4	100.0
	1993	133.5	133.5	122.1	109.3	109.3	100.0
	1994	134.6	134.6	119.6	112.5	112.5	100.0
	1995	142.2	142.2	123.2	115.4	115.4	100.0
	1996	143.8	143.8	121.0	118.9	118.9	100.0
	1997	139.3	139.3	114.7	121.4	121.4	100.0
	1998	138.4	138.4	112.3	123.2	123.2	100.0
	1999	143.4	143.4	113.3	126.5	126.5	100.0
	2000	151.1	151.1	115.8	130.6	130.6	100.0
	2001	157.3	157.3	117.5	133.9	133.9	100.0
Nauru	1970	17.7	25.5	34.8	51.0	73.2	69.7
	1975	29.2	49.0	48.4	60.4	101.3	59.6
	1980	48.1	70.2	67.4	71.4	104.2	68.5
	1985	79.2	70.9	93.8	84.5	75.6	111.8
	1990	100.0	100.0	100.0	100.0	100.0	100.0
	1991	99.5	99.3	96.3	103.4	103.2	100.2
	1992	95.3	89.7	89.2	106.8	100.5	106.3
	1993	91.2	79.5	82.7	110.4	96.1	114.9
	1994	87.3	81.8	76.6	114.0	106.8	106.7
	1995	83.6	79.4	71.0	117.8	111.9	105.3
	1996	80.1	80.3	65.8	121.7	122.0	99.8
	1997	76.6	72.9	61.0	125.7	119.5	105.2
	1998	78.2	63.0	59.8	130.7	105.2	124.2
	1999	79.9	66.0	58.7	136.0	112.4	121.0
	2000	86.6	64.3	58.1	148.9	110.6	134.6
	2001	92.1	61.0	57.7	159.6	105.7	151.0

Table 7. Implicit Price Deflators of Gross Domestic Product in US Dollars and in National Currency

(Index numbers 1990 = 100)

Region, country or area and currency unit	Year	GDP in Current Prices: National Currency (1)	GDP in Current Prices: US Dollars (2)	GDP at Constant Prices (3)	GDP Implicit Price Deflators: National Currency (4)	GDP Implicit Price Deflators: US Dollars (5)	Exchange Rates (6)
New Caledonia	1970	15.3	15.0	58.0	26.3	25.8	101.9
	1975	25.4	32.3	68.4	37.1	47.2	78.6
	1980	36.3	46.7	67.4	53.8	69.3	77.6
	1985	55.8	33.8	66.8	83.4	50.6	164.8
	1990	100.0	100.0	100.0	100.0	100.0	100.0
	1991	108.7	104.9	103.9	104.6	101.0	103.6
	1992	112.4	115.6	105.0	107.1	110.1	97.3
	1993	116.0	121.4	105.7	109.8	114.8	95.6
	1994	122.5	120.1	108.4	113.0	110.8	102.0
	1995	131.5	143.4	114.8	114.5	124.9	91.7
	1996	134.0	142.6	115.4	116.1	123.6	93.9
	1997	134.6	125.6	117.7	114.3	106.7	107.1
	1998	146.7	135.4	114.0	128.7	118.8	108.3
	1999	170.6	150.9	115.0	148.4	131.2	113.1
	2000	173.1	132.4	117.4	147.5	112.8	130.8
	2001	184.1	136.8	116.5	158.1	117.5	134.6
New Zealand	1970	8.0	15.0	69.8	11.5	21.5	53.5
	1975	15.5	31.2	85.5	18.1	36.5	49.6
	1980	32.1	52.4	83.0	38.7	63.1	61.3
	1985	63.2	52.4	97.1	65.1	53.9	120.8
	1990	100.0	100.0	100.0	100.0	100.0	100.0
	1991	99.7	96.4	98.7	101.1	97.7	103.5
	1992	103.0	92.7	99.8	103.2	92.9	111.1
	1993	111.5	101.0	106.2	105.0	95.1	110.4
	1994	119.4	118.7	111.8	106.8	106.2	100.6
	1995	126.8	139.4	116.4	108.9	119.7	91.0
	1996	133.0	153.2	120.5	110.4	127.1	86.9
	1997	137.8	152.7	122.3	112.7	124.9	90.2
	1998	139.5	125.1	122.8	113.6	101.9	111.5
	1999	146.4	129.9	128.9	113.6	100.8	112.7
	2000	155.6	118.5	132.3	117.6	89.6	131.3
	2001	167.2	117.8	136.9	122.1	86.0	142.0
Palau	1970	14.2	14.2	126.5	11.2	11.2	100.0
	1975	46.8	46.8	256.6	18.2	18.2	100.0
	1980	23.2	23.2	88.9	26.1	26.1	100.0
	1985	50.0	50.0	75.6	66.1	66.1	100.0
	1990	100.0	100.0	100.0	100.0	100.0	100.0
	1991	111.6	111.6	103.9	107.4	107.4	100.0
	1992	125.8	125.8	105.5	119.2	119.2	100.0
	1993	135.3	135.3	107.6	125.7	125.7	100.0
	1994	138.0	138.0	105.6	130.7	130.7	100.0
	1995	155.1	155.1	113.3	136.9	136.9	100.0
	1996	166.9	166.9	125.7	132.8	132.8	100.0
	1997	183.7	183.7	138.7	132.4	132.4	100.0
	1998	225.5	225.5	144.2	156.4	156.4	100.0
	1999	212.4	212.4	148.2	143.3	143.3	100.0
	2000	240.2	240.2	142.4	172.0	172.0	100.0
	2001	285.8	285.8	141.4	202.2	202.2	100.0
Papua New Guinea	1970	22.0	23.5	77.8	28.2	30.2	93.4
	1975	37.8	47.2	89.0	42.4	53.0	80.0
	1980	60.4	85.9	87.8	68.8	97.9	70.3
	1985	78.1	74.6	93.6	83.4	79.7	104.6
	1990	100.0	100.0	100.0	100.0	100.0	100.0
	1991	117.2	117.6	109.5	107.0	107.4	99.6
	1992	134.6	133.2	122.5	109.9	108.8	101.0
	1993	155.1	151.4	144.7	107.2	104.6	102.5
	1994	171.5	161.9	153.3	111.8	105.6	105.9
	1995	187.6	140.0	148.3	126.6	94.4	134.1
	1996	219.3	158.8	159.7	137.3	99.4	138.1
	1997	225.1	149.5	153.5	146.7	97.4	150.6
	1998	250.6	115.4	160.2	156.4	72.0	217.2
	1999	279.8	104.0	158.9	176.1	65.4	269.3
	2000	307.6	105.6	156.9	196.0	67.3	291.2
	2001	321.2	90.5	154.0	208.6	58.8	354.8
Samoa	1970	9.1	29.3	79.2	11.5	37.0	31.1
	1975	18.4	67.1	92.1	20.0	72.8	27.5
	1980	30.6	76.9	107.3	28.5	71.6	39.8
	1985	58.4	60.1	105.1	55.6	57.2	97.2
	1990	100.0	100.0	100.0	100.0	100.0	100.0
	1991	103.3	99.4	97.6	105.8	101.9	103.8
	1992	87.6	82.1	95.3	91.9	86.1	106.7
	1993	92.5	83.2	97.6	94.7	85.2	111.2
	1994	107.3	97.7	94.0	114.1	104.0	109.7
	1995	106.7	99.6	100.0	106.6	99.6	107.0
	1996	119.6	112.2	107.3	111.4	104.5	106.6

Table 7. Implicit Price Deflators of Gross Domestic Product in US Dollars and in National Currency

(Index numbers 1990 = 100)

Region, country or area and currency unit	Year	GDP in Current Prices		GDP at Constant Prices	GDP Implicit Price Deflators		Exchange Rates
		National Currency (1)	US Dollars (2)	(3)	National Currency (4)	US Dollars (5)	(6)
	1997	134.6	121.5	108.5	124.0	111.9	110.8
	1998	141.8	111.1	111.1	127.6	100.0	127.6
	1999	150.4	115.3	114.0	131.9	101.1	130.5
	2000	166.7	117.2	121.9	136.8	96.1	142.4
	2001	183.3	121.7	129.9	141.1	93.7	150.6
Solomon Islands....................................	1970	5.4	15.4	40.2	13.5	38.2	35.3
	1975	9.4	31.1	47.8	19.7	65.1	30.3
	1980	22.6	69.0	75.9	29.8	90.9	32.8
	1985	45.0	76.9	81.9	54.9	93.8	58.5
	1990	100.0	100.0	100.0	100.0	100.0	100.0
	1991	113.7	105.9	106.0	107.2	99.9	107.3
	1992	145.0	125.2	119.5	121.4	104.8	115.8
	1993	171.2	135.8	124.2	137.9	109.4	126.1
	1994	199.9	153.6	135.6	147.4	113.3	130.1
	1995	236.0	175.2	144.7	163.0	121.1	134.6
	1996	273.2	193.7	149.8	182.4	129.3	141.1
	1997	288.5	196.3	146.4	197.1	134.1	147.0
	1998	327.9	172.2	148.0	221.6	116.4	190.4
	1999	349.5	182.7	146.0	239.3	125.1	191.3
	2000	327.0	162.5	125.6	260.4	129.4	201.2
	2001	335.5	164.3	119.3	281.2	137.7	204.2
Tonga..	1970	7.1	10.2	49.5	14.3	20.6	69.4
	1975	16.9	28.3	57.4	29.4	49.3	59.6
	1980	31.8	46.3	65.7	48.4	70.5	68.7
	1985	58.4	52.3	98.5	59.3	53.0	111.9
	1990	100.0	100.0	100.0	100.0	100.0	100.0
	1991	116.5	115.0	106.4	109.5	108.1	101.3
	1992	125.5	119.2	106.7	117.6	111.8	105.2
	1993	130.2	120.5	110.7	117.7	108.8	108.2
	1994	133.3	129.2	116.2	114.7	111.2	103.1
	1995	134.9	135.9	119.2	113.1	114.0	99.2
	1996	142.2	147.7	118.8	119.7	124.3	96.3
	1997	141.2	143.1	118.9	118.8	120.3	98.8
	1998	148.8	127.6	121.8	122.2	104.8	116.6
	1999	161.2	129.1	125.5	128.5	102.8	125.0
	2000	177.4	129.1	133.9	132.4	96.4	137.3
	2001	188.3	113.5	137.9	136.5	82.3	165.9
Tuvalu..	1970	7.9	11.3	56.8	13.8	19.9	69.3
	1975	13.6	22.8	90.7	15.0	25.1	59.8
	1980	32.7	47.6	93.4	35.0	51.0	68.6
	1985	41.2	36.9	73.2	56.3	50.4	111.7
	1990	100.0	100.0	100.0	100.0	100.0	100.0
	1991	106.6	106.4	103.6	102.9	102.7	100.2
	1992	119.3	112.3	106.5	112.1	105.4	106.4
	1993	115.3	100.4	110.9	104.0	90.6	114.8
	1994	127.9	119.8	122.3	104.6	98.0	106.7
	1995	129.9	123.3	116.1	111.8	106.2	105.3
	1996	139.1	139.5	128.1	108.6	108.9	99.7
	1997	152.8	145.3	132.5	115.3	109.6	105.2
	1998	180.4	145.2	152.3	118.4	95.3	124.2
	1999	187.7	155.1	156.9	119.6	98.9	120.9
	2000	203.0	150.8	161.6	125.6	93.3	134.6
	2001	219.5	145.5	166.5	131.9	87.4	150.9
Vanuatu..	1970	19.9	23.1	39.0	51.0	59.1	86.3
	1975	28.8	48.7	61.8	46.7	78.8	59.3
	1980	43.9	75.3	67.5	65.1	111.6	58.3
	1985	73.0	80.6	102.4	71.3	78.7	90.6
	1990	100.0	100.0	100.0	100.0	100.0	100.0
	1991	114.6	120.1	113.3	101.1	106.0	95.4
	1992	120.3	124.1	118.7	101.3	104.6	96.8
	1993	126.0	121.3	125.8	100.1	96.4	103.8
	1994	141.1	141.9	137.8	102.4	102.9	99.5
	1995	144.9	151.3	137.8	105.1	109.8	95.7
	1996	151.4	158.7	141.3	107.2	112.3	95.5
	1997	156.3	157.9	143.4	109.0	110.1	99.0
	1998	166.1	152.4	146.6	113.3	104.0	108.9
	1999	165.6	150.2	143.0	115.8	105.0	110.3
	2000	176.4	150.0	148.4	118.9	101.1	117.6
	2001	180.5	145.4	147.6	122.3	98.5	124.2

Table 7. Implicit Price Deflators of Gross Domestic Product in US Dollars and in National Currency

(Index numbers 1990 = 100)

Region, country or area and currency unit	Year	GDP in Current Prices: National Currency (1)	GDP in Current Prices: US Dollars (2)	GDP at Constant Prices (3)	GDP Implicit Price Deflators: National Currency (4)	GDP Implicit Price Deflators: US Dollars (5)	Exchange Rates (6)
New Caledonia	1970	15.3	15.0	58.0	26.3	25.8	101.9
	1975	25.4	32.3	68.4	37.1	47.2	78.6
	1980	36.3	46.7	67.4	53.8	69.3	77.6
	1985	55.8	33.8	66.8	83.4	50.6	164.8
	1990	100.0	100.0	100.0	100.0	100.0	100.0
	1991	108.7	104.9	103.9	104.6	101.0	103.6
	1992	112.4	115.6	105.0	107.1	110.1	97.3
	1993	116.0	121.4	105.7	109.8	114.8	95.6
	1994	122.5	120.1	108.4	113.0	110.8	102.0
	1995	131.5	143.4	114.8	114.5	124.9	91.7
	1996	134.0	142.6	115.4	116.1	123.6	93.9
	1997	134.6	125.6	117.7	114.3	106.7	107.1
	1998	146.7	135.4	114.0	128.7	118.8	108.3
	1999	170.6	150.9	115.0	148.4	131.2	113.1
	2000	173.1	132.4	117.4	147.5	112.8	130.8
	2001	184.1	136.8	116.5	158.1	117.5	134.6
New Zealand	1970	8.0	15.0	69.8	11.5	21.5	53.5
	1975	15.5	31.2	85.5	18.1	36.5	49.6
	1980	32.1	52.4	83.0	38.7	63.1	61.3
	1985	63.2	52.4	97.1	65.1	53.9	120.8
	1990	100.0	100.0	100.0	100.0	100.0	100.0
	1991	99.7	96.4	98.7	101.1	97.7	103.5
	1992	103.0	92.7	99.8	103.2	92.9	111.1
	1993	111.5	101.0	106.2	105.0	95.1	110.4
	1994	119.4	118.7	111.8	106.8	106.2	100.6
	1995	126.8	139.4	116.4	108.9	119.7	91.0
	1996	133.0	153.2	120.5	110.4	127.1	86.9
	1997	137.8	152.7	122.3	112.7	124.9	90.2
	1998	139.5	125.1	122.8	113.6	101.9	111.5
	1999	146.4	129.9	128.9	113.6	100.8	112.7
	2000	155.6	118.5	132.3	117.6	89.6	131.3
	2001	167.2	117.8	136.9	122.1	86.0	142.0
Palau	1970	14.2	14.2	126.5	11.2	11.2	100.0
	1975	46.8	46.8	256.6	18.2	18.2	100.0
	1980	23.2	23.2	88.9	26.1	26.1	100.0
	1985	50.0	50.0	75.6	66.1	66.1	100.0
	1990	100.0	100.0	100.0	100.0	100.0	100.0
	1991	111.6	111.6	103.9	107.4	107.4	100.0
	1992	125.8	125.8	105.5	119.2	119.2	100.0
	1993	135.3	135.3	107.6	125.7	125.7	100.0
	1994	138.0	138.0	105.6	130.7	130.7	100.0
	1995	155.1	155.1	113.3	136.9	136.9	100.0
	1996	166.9	166.9	125.7	132.8	132.8	100.0
	1997	183.7	183.7	138.7	132.4	132.4	100.0
	1998	225.5	225.5	144.2	156.4	156.4	100.0
	1999	212.4	212.4	148.2	143.3	143.3	100.0
	2000	246.2	246.2	142.4	172.9	172.9	100.0
	2001	285.8	285.8	141.4	202.2	202.2	100.0
Papua New Guinea	1970	22.0	23.5	77.8	28.2	30.2	93.4
	1975	37.8	47.2	89.0	42.4	53.0	80.0
	1980	60.4	85.9	87.8	68.8	97.9	70.3
	1985	78.1	74.6	93.6	83.4	79.7	104.6
	1990	100.0	100.0	100.0	100.0	100.0	100.0
	1991	117.2	117.6	109.5	107.0	107.4	99.6
	1992	134.6	133.2	122.5	109.9	108.8	101.0
	1993	155.1	151.4	144.7	107.2	104.6	102.5
	1994	171.5	161.9	153.3	111.8	105.6	105.9
	1995	187.6	140.0	148.3	126.6	94.4	134.1
	1996	219.3	158.8	159.7	137.3	99.4	138.1
	1997	225.1	149.5	153.5	146.7	97.4	150.6
	1998	250.6	115.4	160.2	156.4	72.0	217.2
	1999	279.8	104.0	158.9	176.1	65.4	269.3
	2000	307.6	105.6	156.9	196.0	67.3	291.2
	2001	321.2	90.5	154.0	208.6	58.8	354.8
Samoa	1970	9.1	29.3	79.2	11.5	37.0	31.1
	1975	18.4	67.1	92.1	20.0	72.8	27.5
	1980	30.6	76.9	107.3	28.5	71.6	39.8
	1985	58.4	60.1	105.1	55.6	57.2	97.2
	1990	100.0	100.0	100.0	100.0	100.0	100.0
	1991	103.3	99.4	97.6	105.8	101.9	103.8
	1992	87.6	82.1	95.3	91.9	86.1	106.7
	1993	92.5	83.2	97.6	94.7	85.2	111.2
	1994	107.3	97.7	94.0	114.1	104.0	109.7
	1995	106.7	99.6	100.0	106.6	99.6	107.0
	1996	119.6	112.2	107.3	111.4	104.5	106.6

Table 7. Implicit Price Deflators of Gross Domestic Product in US Dollars and in National Currency

(Index numbers 1990 = 100)

Region, country or area and currency unit	Year	GDP in Current Prices		GDP at Constant Prices	GDP Implicit Price Deflators		Exchange Rates
		National Currency (1)	US Dollars (2)	(3)	National Currency (4)	US Dollars (5)	(6)
	1997	134.6	121.5	108.5	124.0	111.9	110.8
	1998	141.8	111.1	111.1	127.6	100.0	127.6
	1999	150.4	115.3	114.0	131.9	101.1	130.5
	2000	166.7	117.2	121.9	136.8	96.1	142.4
	2001	183.3	121.7	129.9	141.1	93.7	150.6
Solomon Islands	1970	5.4	15.4	40.2	13.5	38.2	35.3
	1975	9.4	31.1	47.8	19.7	65.1	30.3
	1980	22.6	69.0	75.9	29.8	90.9	32.8
	1985	45.0	76.9	81.9	54.9	93.8	58.5
	1990	100.0	100.0	100.0	100.0	100.0	100.0
	1991	113.7	105.9	106.0	107.2	99.9	107.3
	1992	145.0	125.2	119.5	121.4	104.8	115.8
	1993	171.2	135.8	124.2	137.9	109.4	126.1
	1994	199.9	153.6	135.6	147.4	113.3	130.1
	1995	236.0	175.2	144.7	163.0	121.1	134.6
	1996	273.2	193.7	149.8	182.4	129.3	141.1
	1997	288.5	196.3	146.4	197.1	134.1	147.0
	1998	327.9	172.2	148.0	221.6	116.4	190.4
	1999	349.5	182.7	146.0	239.3	125.1	191.3
	2000	327.0	162.5	125.6	260.4	129.4	201.2
	2001	335.5	164.3	119.3	281.2	137.7	204.2
Tonga	1970	7.1	10.2	49.5	14.3	20.6	69.4
	1975	16.9	28.3	57.4	29.4	49.3	59.6
	1980	31.8	46.3	65.7	48.4	70.5	68.7
	1985	58.4	52.3	98.5	59.3	53.0	111.9
	1990	100.0	100.0	100.0	100.0	100.0	100.0
	1991	116.5	115.0	106.4	109.5	108.1	101.3
	1992	125.5	119.2	106.7	117.6	111.8	105.2
	1993	130.2	120.5	110.7	117.7	108.8	108.2
	1994	133.3	129.2	116.2	114.7	111.2	103.1
	1995	134.9	135.9	119.2	113.1	114.0	99.2
	1996	142.2	147.7	118.8	119.7	124.3	96.3
	1997	141.2	143.1	118.9	118.8	120.3	98.8
	1998	148.8	127.6	121.8	122.2	104.8	116.6
	1999	161.2	129.1	125.5	128.5	102.8	125.0
	2000	177.4	129.1	133.9	132.4	96.4	137.3
	2001	188.3	113.5	137.9	136.5	82.3	165.9
Tuvalu	1970	7.9	11.3	56.8	13.8	19.9	69.3
	1975	13.6	22.8	90.7	15.0	25.1	59.8
	1980	32.7	47.6	93.4	35.0	51.0	68.6
	1985	41.2	36.9	73.2	56.3	50.4	111.7
	1990	100.0	100.0	100.0	100.0	100.0	100.0
	1991	106.6	106.4	103.6	102.9	102.7	100.2
	1992	119.3	112.3	106.5	112.1	105.4	106.4
	1993	115.3	100.4	110.9	104.0	90.6	114.8
	1994	127.9	119.8	122.3	104.6	98.0	106.7
	1995	129.9	123.3	116.1	111.8	106.2	105.3
	1996	139.1	139.5	128.1	108.6	108.9	99.7
	1997	152.8	145.3	132.5	115.3	109.6	105.2
	1998	180.4	145.2	152.3	118.4	95.3	124.2
	1999	187.7	155.1	156.9	119.6	98.9	120.9
	2000	203.0	150.8	161.6	125.6	93.3	134.6
	2001	219.5	145.5	166.5	131.9	87.4	150.9
Vanuatu	1970	19.9	23.1	39.0	51.0	59.1	86.3
	1975	28.8	48.7	61.8	46.7	78.8	59.3
	1980	43.9	75.3	67.5	65.1	111.6	58.3
	1985	73.0	80.6	102.4	71.3	78.7	90.6
	1990	100.0	100.0	100.0	100.0	100.0	100.0
	1991	114.6	120.1	113.3	101.1	106.0	95.4
	1992	120.3	124.1	118.7	101.3	104.6	96.8
	1993	126.0	121.3	125.8	100.1	96.4	103.8
	1994	141.1	141.9	137.8	102.4	102.9	99.5
	1995	144.9	151.3	137.8	105.1	109.8	95.7
	1996	151.4	158.7	141.3	107.2	112.3	95.5
	1997	156.3	157.9	143.4	109.0	110.1	99.0
	1998	166.1	152.4	146.6	113.3	104.0	108.9
	1999	165.6	150.2	143.0	115.8	105.0	110.3
	2000	176.4	150.0	148.4	118.9	101.1	117.6
	2001	180.5	145.4	147.6	122.3	98.5	124.2

كيفية الحصول على منشورات الأمم المتحدة

يمكن الحصول على منشورات الأمم المتحدة من المكتبات ودور التوزيع في جميع أنحاء العالم . استعلم عنها من المكتبة التي تتعامل معها أو اكتب إلى : الأمم المتحدة ، قسم البيع في نيويورك أو في جنيف .

如何购取联合国出版物

联合国出版物在全世界各地的书店和经售处均有发售。请向书店询问或写信到纽约或日内瓦的联合国销售组。

HOW TO OBTAIN UNITED NATIONS PUBLICATIONS

United Nations publications may be obtained from bookstores and distributors throughout the world. Consult your bookstore or write to: United Nations, Sales Section, New York or Geneva.

COMMENT SE PROCURER LES PUBLICATIONS DES NATIONS UNIES

Les publications des Nations Unies sont en vente dans les librairies et les agences dépositaires du monde entier. Informez-vous auprès de votre libraire ou adressez-vous à : Nations Unies, Section des ventes, New York ou Genève.

КАК ПОЛУЧИТЬ ИЗДАНИЯ ОРГАНИЗАЦИИ ОБЪЕДИНЕННЫХ НАЦИЙ

Издания Организации Объединенных Наций можно купить в книжных магазинах и агентствах во всех районах мира. Наводите справки об изданиях в вашем книжном магазине или пишите по адресу: Организация Объединенных Наций, Секция по продаже изданий, Нью-Йорк или Женева.

COMO CONSEGUIR PUBLICACIONES DE LAS NACIONES UNIDAS

Las publicaciones de las Naciones Unidas están en venta en librerías y casas distribuidoras en todas partes del mundo. Consulte a su librero o diríjase a: Naciones Unidas, Sección de Ventas, Nueva York o Ginebra.

Litho in United Nations, New York
53894—November 2003—2,395
ISBN 92-1-161465-1

United Nations publication
Sales No. E.03.XVII.17
ST/ESA/STAT/SER.X/31